The Calling of the Church in Times of Polarization

Edited by Heleen Zorgdrager and Pieter Vos
This Edition Edited by Anthony Uyl$_{\text{MTS}}$

Devoted Publishing
Ingersoll, Ontario, Canada 2024

The Calling of the Church in Times of Polarization

Edited by Heleen Zorgdrager and Pieter Vos
This Edition by Anthony Uyl~MTS~

This book was originally published by Brill, Leiden/Boston.

The reformatted text of *The Calling of the Church in Times of Polarization* is all protected under Copyright ©2024 Devoted Publishing. The covers, background, layout and Devoted Publishing logo are Copyright ©2024 Devoted Publishing. This edition is published by Devoted Publishing a division of 2165467 Ontario Inc.

Note on Creative Commons 4.0 Attribution status: Although all the text in this document is from the CC-BY, the layout, formatting and note changes makes this book a copyrighted work. The original document remains in the CC-BY and can be found here:

https://doi.org/10.1163/9789004527652

For details on CC-BY go to http://creativecommons.org/licenses/by/4.0/.

Drop Cap and Table of Contents fonts are AnglicanText by Typographer Mediengestaltung and used under a Free For Commercial Use License (FFC).

ISBN: 978-1-77356-511-8

Contact Us Online:
Email: office@devotedpub.com
For more information on Biblical Demonology and issues with the occult in modern evangelicalism, check out the editors' Substack Blog *Reformed Demonology*: reformeddemonology.substack.com

The content and subject matter of this book in no way represents or reflects the opinions or beliefs of any person that owns, works for, is associated with, or is under contract with 2165467 Ontario Inc. or any of its trade name companies. These trade name companies include any that ceased operation before the publication of this book, companies operating at the time of the publication of this book, or any new trade name companies operating after the publication of this book.

This book has been publsihed solely for the purposes of academic research to further understand the defences and critiques of theological positions and/or any theological opponents.

Table of Contents

NOTES ON CONTRIBUTORS — 9

INTRODUCTION — 15
Pieter Vos
   1. Polarization: Us-Them Thinking — 18
   2. Theology and Polarization — 19
   3. Polarization in Church and Society — 25
   4. Polarization and the Reformed Tradition — 28
   5. The Calling of the Church — 30

PART 1: POLARIZATION IN CHURCH AND SOCIETY — 37

CHAPTER 1 — 39
Can Conviviality Trump Polarization? Exploring the Notion of Conviviality as Calling of the Church in Times of Polarization
Nadine Bowers Du Toit
   1. Introduction — 39
   2. Deep Cleavages — 40
   3. The South African Scenario — 41
   4. Why The Notion Of Conviviality? — 43
   5. Engaging Conviviality In Times Of Polarization — 45
   6. Conclusion — 52

CHAPTER 2 — 57
Re-Forming the Conversation as a Response to Polarization: A Case Study Exploration of the Dallas Statement
Thandi Soko-de Jong
   1. Introduction — 57
   2. The Case Study: The Statement on Social Justice and the Gospel — 63
   3. Re-Forming the Conversation: Responding to the Statement with Views from Social Justice's (Reformed) Evangelical Proponents — 71
   4. Evaluation: Imagining *Re-Forming the Conversation* as a Calling for the Church in Times of Polarization — 74
   5. Conclusion — 77
   Bibliography — 77

CHAPTER 3 — 83
Retrieving the Concept of *Unio Mystica cum Christo* and Applying it to Concepts of Sexuality in a Pluralistic Postmodern Culture
Willem van Vlastuin
   1. Introduction — 83
   2. Sexuality in a Pluralistic Postmodern Culture — 84
   3. Paul's Application of Identity in Christ — 88
   4. Retrieving Paul's Identity in Christ in the Postmodern Context — 93
   Bibliography — 100

Chapter 4 — 105
Theological Assessment of the Gender and Sexuality Debate in the Netherlands: The Case of the 'Nashville Statement'
Heleen Zorgdrager
- 1. Introduction — 105
- 2. The Case of the Nashville Statement — 108
- 3. The Global Neo-Conservative Campaign for 'Traditional Family Values' — 110
- 4. The Campaign for 'Traditional Family Values' in the Netherlands — 113
- 5. Union With Christ: Moving Beyond Identity Politics? — 118
- 6. Notions For A Theology Of Sexuality Beyond Identity Politics — 122
- 7. Conclusion — 127
- Bibliography — 128

Chapter 5 — 137
Passivity, Abuse, and Self-Sacrifice: Daoism and Feminist Christology
Jaeseung Cha
- 1. Introduction — 137
- 2. Feminism in Daoism — 139
- 3. Feminism and Christ's Sacrifice — 142
- 4. Abuse and Necessity — 146
- 5. Self-Sacrifice and Violence — 149
- 6. Revision of Atonement Theology — 151
- 7. Conclusion — 153
- Bibliography — 155

Chapter 6 — 157
"Remove the Sandals From Your Feet": Holiness in the Dutch Euthanasia Debate
Annemarieke van der Woude
- 1. Introduction — 157
- 2. Why Holiness? — 157
- 3. The Secularization of Holiness — 159
- 4. Holiness in the Bible — 160
- 5. Holiness of the Divine — 163
- 6. Holiness of the People — 164
- 7. Old Testament Anthropology — 165
- 8. Conclusion: A Cautious Commitment — 167
- Bibliography — 168

Chapter 7 — 175
Sowing Hope in a Polarized Agricultural Debate
Jan Jorrit Hasselaar, Philipp Pattberg and Peter-Ben Smit
- 1. Introduction — 175
- 2. Dutch Agriculture — 177
- 3. Wicked Problems — 178
- 4. Governance Of Wicked Problems — 181
- 5. Hope — 182

    6. Courageous Conversations — 184
    7. Food Valley Case Study — 185
    8. Ecclesial Innovation — 187
    9. Conclusion — 192
    Bibliography — 193

Part 2: Polarization and the Reformed Tradition — 197

Chapter 8 — 199
Reformed Social Theology: Contexts and Constants
David Fergusson
    1. Introduction — 199
    2. Elements of a Reformed Political Theology — 199
    3. The Vestiges of Christendom? — 205
    4. Transpositions of Reformed Social Theology — 210
    5. Conclusion — 216
    Bibliography — 216

Chapter 9 — 221
Prelude to a "Post-Xenophobic" Future: Interrogating the 1618 Baptism Debate at the Synod Of Dort
David Douglas Daniels III
    1. Introduction — 221
    2. Definition Of Xenophobia and Xenogenerosity — 222
    3. Baptism Debate at Dort in 1618 — 223
    4. Periodization: Prior to Modern Racism and Orientalism — 225
    5. Difference at the 1618 Baptism Debate at Dort — 226
    6. Religious Differences — 227
    7. Religious Rights of Strangers — 228
    8. Religious Responsibilities to Strangers — 230
    9. The Xenophobic Incorporation of the Stranger as Subordinate — 231
    10. The Xenogenerous Inclusion of the Stranger as Peer — 232
    11. The Topic of Baptism and the Global South After Dort — 233
    12. Conclusion — 235
    Bibliography — 237

Chapter 10 — 241
Protestant Schools and Hospitals in the Context of Religious Polarization in Yogyakarta
Jozef Mepibozef Nelsun Hehanussa
    1. Introduction — 241
    2. Religious Encounters in the Land of Ngayogyakarta Hadiningrat — 242
    3. Spreading Christian Faith and Polarization in the Christian Mission — 245
    4. Christian Schools and Hospital in the Context of Religious Polarization — 250
    5. Rise of Intolerance — 252
    6. Closing Remarks — 255

Bibliography — 256

Chapter 11 — 259
Election and Hope: Van Ruler and Dort
Allan J. Janssen†
  1. Introduction — 259
  2. Van Ruler on Election — 261
  3. Dort — 265
  Bibliography — 270

Chapter 12 — 273
Polarization and the Pursuit of Unanimity in the Church: Ecclesiastical Decision-Making in the Dutch Reformed Tradition
Klaas-Willem de Jong and Jan Dirk Th. Wassenaar
  1. The Introduction of the Majority Principle — 274
  2. The Majority Principle Under Pressure — 279
  3. The Majority Principle Reworded — 286
  4. Conclusions — 289
  Bibliography — 291

Part 3: The Calling of the Church — 299

Chapter 13 — 301
Fighting Against Polarization: The Indonesian Communion of Churches, Religious Plurality and Sexual Orientations in Indonesia
Emanuel Gerrit Singgih
  1. Introduction — 301
  2. The pgi and Recognition of Spiritual Groups and Adat Society — 303
  3. The pgi and the Plight of lgbt Communities — 309
  4. Closing Remarks — 315
  Bibliography — 316

Chapter 14 — 321
Developing *Koinonia* in an Age of Polarization
Elizabeth Welch
  1. Introduction — 321
  2. The Origins and Significance of *Koinonia* — *322*
  3. The Separation of Churches Historically — 324
  4. Ecumenism as a Response to Polarization — 327
  5. An Example of Dialogue: International Reformed Anglican Dialogue (irad), 2015–2020 — 330
  6. Conclusion — 336
  Bibliography — 337

Chapter 15 — 339
No Calling Without Being Called: The *Vocatio Interna* at the Heart of Sanctification
Henk van den Belt
  1. Called by God — 339
  2. Historical Summary — 340

3. Called into the Fellowship of Christ — 344
4. Called unto Liberty and Holiness — 347
5. Conclusion — 351
Bibliography — 353

CHAPTER 16 — 357
'They are *in* the World, but not *of* the World': Biblical and Contextual Reflections on Church, Alterity and Self-Otherizing
Najib George Awad
1. Introduction — 357
2. Alterity in the New Testament: When Christ's Followers Relate to the World — 358
3. Alterity and Self-Otherizing in Context: The Protestants in Greater Syria — 365
4. Concluding Remarks — 371
Bibliography — 372

CHAPTER 17 — 379
Theology of Migration in the Discourse of the World Council of Churches and the Ecumenical Council of Churches in Hungary (2015–2019)
Viktória Kóczián
1. Introduction — 379
2. The Social and Theological Teachings of the wcc on Migration — 380
3. The Approach of the ecch to Migration — 383
4. Conclusion — 396
Bibliography — 399

CHAPTER 18 — 403
Against Polarization: Forming a Sense of 'Otherness' From a Conversation Between Anthropology and Neo-Calvinism
Louise C. Prideaux
1. Introduction — 403
2. Cultural Anthropological InsightsiInto 'the Other' and 'Otherness' — 407
3. 'Otherness' in Neo-Calvinism — 410
4. Sphere Sovereignty, 'Otherness' and 'Commonness' — 414
5. Being Formed into 'Otherness' — 415
6. Conclusion — 417
Bibliography — 418

EPILOGUE — 421
Heleen Zorgdrager
1. Theology of Retrieval and of Liberation — 422
2. Classical Reformed Notions Reread and Retrieved — 423
3. Unity and Holiness — 424
4. Other Constructive Proposals — 426
5. Conclusion — 427
Bibliography — 428

NOTES ON CONTRIBUTORS

Najib George Awad
PhD, is an Arab-American (originally from Syria) theologian, religious studies scholar, author and poet. He was Professor of Christian Theology and Eastern Christian Thought and director of the PhD Program in Islamic Studies and Christian-Muslim Relations at Hartford International University, Connecticut USA. His latest monographs in English are *Orthodoxy in Arabic Terms* (2015), *Umayyad Christianity* (2018), and *After-Mission, Beyond Evangelicalism*: *The Indigenous 'Injīliyyūn' in the Arab-Muslim Context of Syria-Lebanon* (2020).

Henk van den Belt
PhD, is Professor of Systematic Theology at the Faculty of Religion and Theology, VU Amsterdam, and director of the Herman Bavinck Center for Reformed and Evangelical Theology. He has edited *Restoration through Redemption*: *John Calvin Revisited* (2013) and published on the authority of Scripture, the history of Reformed theology, neocalvinism and pneumatology. He is an ordained minister of the Protestant Church in the Netherlands, and serves at the IRTI Management Team.

Nadine Bowers Du Toit
PhD, is Associate Professor in Theology and Development (Diaconia) at the Faculty of Theology, University of Stellenbosch. Her research focuses on the intersection between religion and social justice, with a special focus on the role of faith communities in the South African context. Nadine currently serves as the vice president of the International Academy of Practical Theology.

Jaeseung Cha
PhD, is Associate Professor of Foundational and Constructive Theology at New Brunswick Theological Seminary and a General Synod professor of the Reformed Church in America. His publications include *Doctrine of the Atonement in Seven Theologians* (2014), *Why am I still a Christian* (2020), and articles and book chapters on theological methodology,

Reformed ecclesiology, Christ and Daoism, and the atonement.

David Douglas Daniels III
PhD, is the Henry Winters Luce Professor of World Christianity at McCormick Theological Seminary in Chicago, USA (1987–present) and the Professor Extraordinarius, Institute of Gender Studies, at the University of South Africa. He serves on the editorial board of the *Journal of World Christianity* (2008–present), as a member of the American Academy of Religion, and a former president of the Society for Pentecostal Studies. His current research explores the role of Ethiopic (Ge'ez) among Catholics and Protestants during the Long Reformation, 1500–1700, as well as African Christians in 16th-century Europe.

David Fergusson
PhD, is Regius Professor of Divinity at the University of Cambridge. He was the former Professor of Divinity at the University of Edinburgh (2000–2020). He is a Fellow of the Royal Society of Edinburgh and a Fellow of the British Academy. Recently he co-edited the three-volume *History of Scottish Theology* (2019).

Jan Jorrit Hasselaar
PhD, is economist and theologian. He directs the Amsterdam Centre for Religion & Sustainable Development at the Faculty of Religion and Theology, VU University. He chaired the working group on sustainability of the Dutch Council of Churches (2011–2018). He is a Research Fellow of the University of the Western Cape. His main work is on theology as a perspective on the good life based on hope in conversation with economics, religion and society at large. A recent publication is *Water in Times of Climate Change: A Values-driven Dialogue* (2021).

Jozef Mepibozef Nelsun Hehanussa
PhD, is a fulltime lecturer at the Faculty of Theology of the Universitas Kristen Duta Wacana in Yogyakarta, Indonesia. He teaches Church History, Ecumenism and Social Theology. He is an ordained minister of the Protestant Church in Western Indonesia. His publications include *Menapaki Jalan Reformasi* (*Walking the Path of Reform*, 2021) and *Kekristenan Di Asia* (*Christianity in Asia*, 2021).

Allan J. Janssen†
(1948–2020) PhD, was an affiliate professor of Theological Studies at the New Brunswick Theological Seminary and a General Synod professor of the Reformed Church in America. His publications include *Kingdom, Office, and Church: A Study of A.A. van Ruler's Doctrine of Ecclesiastical Office* (2006); *A Collegial Bishop? Classis and Presbytery*

at Issue (2010, edited with Leon van den Broeke); *Confessing the Faith Today: A Fresh Look at the Belgic Confession* (2016); *Constitutional Theology: Notes on the Book of Church Order of the Reformed Church in America* (2019); *A Collegial Bishop Revisited: Classis and Presbytery at Issue* (2021, edited with Leon van den Broeke). He served the congregations in Port Ewen, New York, The First Reformed Church of Bethlehem in Selkirk, New York, and the Community Church in Glen Rock, New Jersey (Reformed Church in America). He died from complications of the corona virus on April 3, 2020.

Klaas-Willem de Jong
PhD, LLM, is Assistant Professor of Church Polity at the Protestant Theological University, Amsterdam/Groningen and an ordained minister of the Protestant Church in the Netherlands. He published on various themes such as church history, the history of the classical Reformed liturgy in the Netherlands, church polity and the relationship between state law and ecclesial law. He is co-founder of the Society for Protestant Church Polity and the Journal *International Studies in Protestant Church Polity*.

Viktória Kóczián
MA, is a Reformed theologian currently working on her PhD dissertation at the VU Amsterdam, in the area of migration and ecclesiology with special emphasis on the theology of catholicity and unity in relation to socio-cultural identities. She obtained her master of theology at the University of Edinburgh. She is an ordained minister of the Reformed Church in Hungary.

Philipp Pattberg
PhD, is Professor of Transnational Environmental Governance and Policy, and head of the Environmental Policy Analysis department at the Institute for Environmental Studies, Faculty of Science, VU Amsterdam. He is currently the director of the inter-faculty Amsterdam Sustainability Institute and general director of the Netherlands Research School for Socio-Economic and Natural Sciences of the Environment (SENSE). He has published widely on climate change governance, in particular with regards to the effectiveness, accountability and legitimacy of non-state climate action.

Louise C. Prideaux
PhD, is a lay church leader and resident theologian in the Mission Community of Littleham-cum-Exmouth with Lympstone in Devon, UK. She published Approaching the Complex, Cultural 'Other': Towards a

Renewal of Christian Cultural Engagement in the Reformed Tradition (PhD thesis Exeter University, 2020). She also teaches music.

Emanuel Gerrit Singgih
PhD, is a minister emeritus of the Protestant Church in Western Indonesia and professor at the Theological Faculty, Duta Wacana Christian University, Yogyakarta, Indonesia. His recent books are *Menafsir LGBT dengan Alkitab* (Interpreting LGBT through the Bible, 2019); *Dari Ruang Privat ke Ruang Publik* (From Private Space to Public Space, 2020); and *Teologi Ekologi* (Ecological Theology, 2021).

Peter-Ben Smit
PhD, is Professor of Contextual Biblical Interpretation (Dom Hélder Câmara Chair) at VU Amsterdam and Professor (by special appointment) of Ancient Catholic Church Structures and the History and Doctrines of the Old Catholic Churches at Utrecht University. Recent research focuses on public theological topics such as crisis in biblical texts and their reception, resulting in the editorship of *Crisis as a Catalyst: Early Christian Texts and the Covid-19 Pandemic*, thematic issue of the *Journal for the Study of the New Testament* (43, 2021).

Thandi Soko-de Jong
MA, is a PhD candidate at the Protestant Theological University in the Netherlands. She received her research master in African Studies at the African Studies Centre, University of Leiden, and a master in Theology and Development at the University of KwaZulu-Natal, South Africa. Her research interests include Intercultural Theology and theological topics that are devoted to the perspectives of African Christian theologies.

Willem van Vlastuin
PhD, is Professor of Theology and Spirituality of Reformed Protestantism at the VU Amsterdam. He is also Dean of the seminary of the Hersteld Hervormde Kerk at this university and research associate at the University of the Free State in Bloemfontein. He is an ordained minister of the Hersteld Hervormde Kerk. His publications include *Be Renewed: A Theology of Personal Renewal* (2014) and *Catholic Today: A Reformed Conversation on Catholicity* (2020).

Pieter Vos
PhD, is Professor of Military Chaplaincy Studies and Associate Professor of Ethics at Protestant Theological University, Amsterdam/Groningen. He is director of the International Reformed Theological Institute and Editor-in-Chief of *Journal of Reformed Theology*. His publications include *The Law of God: Exploring God and Civilization* (2014, edited

with Onno Zijlstra); *Liturgy and Ethics: New Contributions from Reformed Perspectives* (2018, edited); and *Longing for the Good Life: Virtue Ethics after Protestantism* (2020).

Jan Dirk Th. Wassenaar
PhD, is an ordained minister of the Protestant Church in the Netherlands and an associated researcher at the Protestant Theological University, Amsterdam/Groningen. In 1999 he obtained his doctorate with a thesis on the Dutch theologian dr. O. Noordmans (1871–1956). He mainly publishes in the field of church history and church order.

Elizabeth Welch
PhD, is an ordained minister of the United Reformed Church in the UK. She was a former Synod Moderator and Moderator of the General Assembly, served as the Reformed Co-chair of the International Reformed-Anglican Dialogue (2015–2020), and is Chair of the Society for Ecumenical Studies, UK (2010 to present). Recently she published *The Holy Spirit and Worship: Transformation and Truth in the Theologies of John Owen and John Zizioulas* (2020).

Annemarieke van der Woude
PhD, received her doctoral degree in Old Testament Studies. She is an ordained minister in a liberal congregation and a former pastor in a nursing home. She is also a lecturer in Spiritual Care at Radboud University, Nijmegen. She contributes to the Dutch debate on euthanasia and completed life by regular publications in national newspaper *Trouw*.

Heleen Zorgdrager
PhD, is Professor of Systematic Theology and Gender Studies at the Protestant Theological University, Amsterdam, and a visiting professor of Ecumenical Theology at the Ukrainian Catholic University in Lviv, Ukraine. She publishes on postcolonial debates about sexuality, gender, religion, and 'traditional values' versus human rights, and on rethinking Protestant soteriology from the tradition of *theosis*. She is an ordained minister of the Protestant Church in the Netherlands and serves as a member of the IRTI Management Team.

INTRODUCTION
Pieter Vos

> I note the obvious differences
> Between each sort and type
> But we are more alike, my friends,
> Than we are unalike.
>
> We are more alike, my friends,
> Than we are unalike.
> MAYA ANGELOU[1]

In many societies all over the world, an increasing polarization between contrasting groups can be observed. Tendencies of polarization—forms of us-them thinking—extend from the political to the economic and from the religious to the social sphere. Fuel for polarization are prejudices about differences in ethnicity, race, religion, culture, gender, sexuality, and class. Driven by fears about losing what is regarded as valuable, one group begins to question the moral legitimacy of another group and even demonizes this group as the cause of imagined or real threats. These 'culture wars'[2] are often motivated by a longing for a strong and fixed (group) identity, which is constructed as being in contrast with the (attributed) identity of the other group. Polarization is not just diversity, disagreement or holding different views, but, as Lauren Swayne Barthold explains, "occurs when a fear born of difference transforms into 'us-versus-them' thinking." Moreover, polarization rules out any form of compromise and "shuts down the desire to communicate."[3]

On the political level, polarization becomes manifest in populist movements with the explicit aim to polarize against others and distance themselves entirely from any political establishment, as for

---

1. From the poem "Human Family," https://allpoetry.com/Human-Family.
2. The term was coined by James Davison Hunter, *Culture Wars*: *The Struggle to Define America* (New York: Basic Books, 1991).
3. Lauren Swayne Barthold, *Overcoming Polarization in the Public Sphere*: *Civic Dialogue* (London: Palgrave Macmillan, 2020), 2.

instance in new populist political parties in many European countries. In some cases, populists succeed in occupying important positions in the governments of democratic countries, as in the USA and Hungary. Often, they promote nationalism and protectionism as counterforce to a globalizing world. Different but related is the polarized discourse against newcomers of those who claim to be native to the country, for instance native inhabitants of European countries who fear the arrival of large numbers of migrants from the African continent. This discourse often suggests such migrants are associated with the worldwide danger of Muslim extremism. In other cases, religious or ethnic minorities are regarded as not belonging to the national identity and therefore marginalized and oppressed, as for instance in Indonesia. Worldwide, debates about racism are highly polarized, as recently became manifest in the Black Lives Matter movement and the opposition it received. In addition, sociologists and political scientists observe an increasing tension between high-educated people, who often live in cities and have a global orientation, on the one hand, and less-educated people, who often live in the countryside or poor neighborhoods in the cities and are locally oriented, on the other.[4]

All these processes of polarization affect the church as well. The church worldwide and locally is often deeply divided on highly contested issues, as for instance on how one views same-sex relationships, nationalism, or migrants. There is a great gulf between the so-called 'main-line' (or ecumenical) and the so-called 'evangelicals,' a gulf which can be experienced within one church community. As a result, Christians tend to define themselves in opposition to other Christians, as either orthodox or liberal, either conservative or progressive, either anti or pro same-sex relationships. The controversy regarding the Nashville Statement, with its bold, conservative claims about sexuality and gender roles and the sometimes fierce reactions it provoked from progressive Christians, demonstrates that the churches themselves are part of, and internally experiencing, polarization.

Given this increasing (or at least ongoing) polarization of various groups within societies as well as within churches, what may be the calling of the church? How can the church contribute to societies and faith communities where people of different backgrounds and convictions live together peacefully? What should be the role of the church in society?

---

4. Cf. Kristen Bialik, "Key Findings about American Life in Urban, Suburban and Rural Areas," American Pew Research 2018, https://www.pewresearch.org/fact-tank/2018/05/22/key-findings-about-american-life-in-urban-suburban-and-rural-areas/; Mark Bovens & Wille Anchrit, *Diplomademocratie: Over de spanning tussen meritocratie en democratie* (Diploma democracy: On the tension between meritocracy and democracy) (Amsterdam: Bert Bakker, 2011).

How can we cope with polarization within and between the churches and their theologians? How may the Bible and tradition shed light on these questions?

These questions have been addressed at the thirteenth biennial conference of the International Reformed Theological Institute (IRTI), which took place from July 4 till 7, 2019 at Vrije Universiteit and Protestantse Theologische Universiteit in Amsterdam, the Netherlands. This volume contains a selection of keynotes and papers presented at the conference in their elaborated and extended form and reflect the discussions and exchange that took place between the around 100 theologians that attended this conference from all over the world.

The theme touches upon the heart of what IRTI basically is and wants to be. In 1995, IRTI was founded with the aim to bridge polarities, i.e., polarities between the East and the West, the North and the South. The fall of the Iron Curtain and the end of the apartheid regime in South Africa created the *momentum* for its foundation, making it possible to bring together various Reformed theologians from Hungary, South Africa, the Netherlands, and the USA. This was followed by theologians from Asia, in particular Indonesia and South Korea, which joined the network as well. From the start, the aim has been to contribute to 'Living Reformed Theology,' which means doing theology in post-colonial, post-communist and post-apartheid contexts, i.e., going beyond polarities, in a Reformed ecumenical spirit searching for the catholicity of the church. At the same time, it must be noted that Reformed theology also has tended to increase polarization by polemizing and building the Reformed identity in strong opposition to others, rather than searching for unity and catholicity. Polarization is part of the Reformed heritage as well, and it is still present within churches that split and push theological and ethical controversies to the extreme.

The IRTI conference took place in the year of the international celebration of the 400th anniversary of the Synod of Dordrecht (1618–1619), which was held by the Dutch Reformed Church, in particular to settle a divisive controversy initiated by the rise of Arminianism. The synod typically exemplifies the ambivalence in the Reformed tradition. On the one hand, the Synod of Dort may be seen as an instance of the transnational, ecumenical character of the Reformed identity, with the participation of various international representatives. In times of tribulation, it contributed to national and social unity, certainly thanks to the privileged position of the Reformed Church in the Netherlands. On the other hand, the Synod of Dort itself contributed to polarization in how it dealt with religious and political conflict at the time and how its Canons were promoted or blamed in its aftermath. The same holds for another relevant and influential document to which the Synod of Dort agreed: the so-called Church Order of Dort (1619). For centuries this Church Order influenced to a great extent not only how the Dutch Reformed Church was organized internally, but also how the church related to society as a whole and to the government in particular. Its influence was not limited to the Netherlands. In more or less revised form, the Church Order is still used in various Reformed denominations in North America, South Africa, Indonesia, the Netherlands, Australia, and New Zealand. Interestingly, it contains regulations about the relation between church and government as well as all kinds of public affairs such as marriage, charity, education, funerals, and disciplinary jurisdiction. It allows for great difference within the church and in this respect guards against polarization. At the same time, the Order has been used as a political tool, at times making it an instrument of polarization.

1. Polarization: Us-Them Thinking

Given the polarized contexts in society and church, scholars must urgently analyze the very nature of polarization, both as a concept and as a concrete phenomenon. Originally the concept stems from the natural sciences, designating how light, radiation, or magnetism moves in different directions. Outside natural science, polarization refers to how people think, especially when two views emerge that drive people apart, like two opposing magnets.

Dutch philosopher and expert on polarization processes Bart Brandsma describes polarization primarily as a "thought construct," a cognitive frame basically built on images of opposite poles, in which always two identities are set against each other: men against women, Muslims against Western people, politicians against citizens, homosexuals against heterosexuals, black against white.[5] According to Barthold, "polarization occurs when fear of certain identity-based difference leads to avoidance, and avoidance leads to hostile stereotypes that result in 'us-versus-them' thinking."[6] As such, polarization is an activity, the activity of dividing. That is why polarization is not a valueneutral term that just describes a state of affairs. Polarization is making a sharp division, dividing a population or group into opposing fractions.

In all cases of polarization, a dynamic of us versus them is at work.[7] In polarization processes, the normal multiplicity of differences in a society

---

5. Bart Brandsma, *Polarisation: Understanding the Dynamics of Us versus Them* (Schoonrewoerd: BB in Media, 2017), 18.
6. Barthold, *Overcoming Polarization*, 3.
7. Barthold, *Overcoming Polarization*, 2; Brandsma, *Polarisation*, 13.

increasingly is aligned along a single dimension and people increasingly perceive and describe what is going on in politics and society in terms of 'us' and 'them,'[8] defining oneself in strong contrast with the other. In-group/out-group dynamics immediately come into play. The language of belonging, safety and even survival is evoked, framed in terms of 'us-versus-them.' Such language draws on deep emotional structures, in particular fear of losing protection and safety. People fall back on us-them thinking when they are afraid and when the only answer to the question 'who will protect me?' is 'my own group.'[9] This is why rational argument can be so ineffective in bringing polarized groups to common ground or peaceful coexistence.[10]

Dutch philosopher Hans Achterhuis describes the us-them dynamics as one of the main sources of violence, in particular ethnic violence and genocide, either religiously motivated or inflamed by nationalistic movements.[11] This does not mean that polarization is the same as conflict and violence. As Brandsma clarifies, there is an important difference between conflict on the one hand and polarization on the other. A conflict always features directly involved parties, who are so to say the immediately identifiable "problem owners"; "The characteristic of a conflict is that the actors have chosen a position, because they are participating, whether they want to or not."[12] This includes not only opposing parties, but also those who want to make a compromise, or those who try to sidestep. All are part of the rising tension and conflict. Polarization is fundamentally different; it "always involves a choice whether or not to assume the position of problem owner. Deciding to join in is itself a crucial choice for 'the actors.' Are we or are we not going to participate in the black-and-white thinking and to what extent?"[13]

2. THEOLOGY AND POLARIZATION

Given these preliminary characteristics of polarization, the question is how theology and theologians decide whether to join in. This is an important question, since one can easily be entrapped in the dynamics of polarization and unintendedly become the victim of polarization. One

---

8. Jennifer McCoy, Tahmina Rahman and Murat Somer, "Polarization and the Global Crisis of Democracy: Common Patterns, Dynamics, and Pernicious Consequences for Democratic Polities," *American Behavioral Scientist* 62:1 (2018), 16–42, https://doi.org/10.1177/0002764218759576.

9. Cf. Michael Ignatieff, *Etnische conflicten en het moderne geweten* (Ethnic conflicts and modern conscience) (Amsterdam: Contact, 1999), 57.

10. Barthold, Overcoming Polarization, 3.

11. Hans Achterhuis, *Met alle geweld: Een filosofische zoektocht* (With all violence: A philosophical enquiry) (Rotterdam: Lemniscaat, 2010), 311–397.

12. Brandsma, *Polarisation*, 15.

13. Brandsma, *Polarisation*, 15.

trap is that we take polarization as just a given state of affairs in which we take a position somewhere on the spectrum between two extremes, with the result that the language of polarization from the start permeates our perception and perverts our theological understanding. The risk is that speaking in terms of polarization itself evokes and strengthens the language of division and driving apart. It seduces us to reduce complex matters to a matter of mutually excluding polarities. If we adopt this language from the start, how could we ever overcome the duality of one position excluding the other? This could prevent us from the possibility of seeing it differently. Moreover, all kinds of terms have become affected by polarization, as Robin Lovin states:

> We are so polarized that any terms we might use to begin a discussion of shared goals are already the property of one side or the other. Freedom, responsibility, rights, duties, choice, and even life itself have acquired connotations that identify the politics of those who use the words. This makes it easy to tweet about what you already believe, but almost impossible to think together about what the human good is in relation to political choices that we actually face.[14]

Thus, the first theological task seems to practice a 'hermeneutics of suspicion,' in order to unmask the polarizing effects and aims in the language of polarization itself.

Importantly, the language of polarization presupposes that division is primary. This presupposition should be questioned. One of the descriptions mentioned in Merriam Webster's dictionary helps us acquire a different understanding. Polarization is described as "division into two sharply distinct opposites, especially a state in which the opinions, beliefs, or interests of a group or society *no longer range along a continuum* but become concentrated at opposing extremes."[15] This description of polarization as a concentration into opposing groups that *formerly ranged on a continuum* indicates that in polarization division is not primary, but always secondary. It is secondary to a primary status in which the continuum is original.

This means that potential solutions may be expected from rediscovering the continuum. To put it simply, when people who were formerly united are driven apart, we need to re-envision what precisely united them before they were driven apart. To speak theologically, what matters is reconciliation, in the sense of reconciling what has been divided. For what is essential is not what makes 'us' different from

---

14. Robin W. Lovin, "Reimagining Christian Realism: Church in an Amoral Time," *The Christian Century*, February 27, 2019, 26–29, 27.

15. https://www.merriam-webster.com/dictionary/polarization (accessed August 23, 2020; emphasis mine).

'them,' but rather that we are just like other people. This is described in a text by Maya Angelou, which was nicely performed by the King's Singers in the song 'We are': "We are more alike, my friends, / Than we are unalike." In a polarized world, people emphasize the differences, reducing them to polarities and using them as fuel for conflict. Starting from our basic human alikeness, we see commonality behind differences.

Here we get a glimpse of the calling of the church in times of polarization. Reconciliation is the central unifying story of the Christian faith. And the church lives from the gospel of "God reconciling the world to himself in Christ … entrusting to us the message of reconciliation" (2 Corinthians 5:19). Being part of and truthful to this story is the calling of the church. In many cases it will be an open question what this means *in concreto*. But at least we can say that it deeply changes our perception of what is at stake. Polarization is neither the first word nor necessarily the last.

Yet, overcoming polarization and reconciling what has become divided is a difficult task for several reasons. First of all, those who are in particular responsible for polarization, positioning themselves at the extremes of the spectrum, are not interested in reconciliation at all. Distinguishing between five roles in polarization processes, Brandsma describes the driving actor of polarization as "the pusher," the one who supplies fuel to polarization by continuously setting the opposite pole in an evil light. The aim is to exert maximum pressure on those in the middle, "the silent ones," to choose a party. Pushers like Donald Trump, Geert Wilders or Marine le Pen use their simple one-liners ("Mexicans are profiteers," "Refugees are testosterone bombs," or "they cannot integrate") not primarily for the sake of those who have joined them already, "the joiners," but in order to press "the silent ones" to start to think in such terms and to choose one of the poles. Because this is where ground can be gained, it is most important to the pusher to make an impact on this middle group, not necessarily to win them over for their own camp, but to force them to choose, either for or against.[16] The effect is what may be called "the disappearing center."[17] It is tempting to oppose such pushers with similar munition. However, in that case one becomes a pusher oneself. As Brandsma observes, "In the polarization between right and left, the pushers on the left (the 'cosmopolitans') are very certain of one thing. 'Right-wing voters are wrong.'"[18] Both pushers think that evil is on the other side. Moral self-righteousness drives the pushers, both on the right and on the left, and supplies

---

16. Brandsma, *Polarisation*, 26–7, 33.

17. Cf. Alan I. Abramowitz, The Disappearing Center: Engaged Citizens, Polarization, and American Democracy (New Haven: Yale University Press, 2010).

18. Brandsma, *Polarisation*, 27.

them with lots of energy. The only way is to become 'more extreme' while moderating means losing face. In any case, the pushers want to strengthen polarization:

> Anyone who does not choose black-and-white thinking is a thorn in the pusher's side. We are wrong to think that the opposite pole is the pusher's target. For pushers, the opposite pole is the subject of conversation—sometimes 'the enemy'—but their actual target is the middle group.[19]

Secondly, building bridges between the extremes that the pushers on both poles have created is difficult. It is the work of the "bridge builder," the fourth role Brandsma distinguishes. The bridge builder spots the deficiencies in the worldview of both poles and tries to do something about polarization by intervening, in particular by arranging dialogues and by producing counter-narratives, e.g., demonstrating the humanity of Muslims, the rights of foreigners or the inhuman misery of refugees. However, the bridge builder unintendedly supplies fuel to polarization, as Brandsma notes:

> On the way, the bridge builder does something that really pleases the pusher. The bridge builder supplies fuel to the polarization despite their best intentions. Organising a dialogue between the pushers, providing a podium to the opposite poles (read: confirming polarisation's right to exist) as well as producing counter-narratives is what supplies the fuel. The pushers tolerate bridge builders because they give them impetus. ... It is a major misconception of the bridge builder to think that you can build a bridge from the middle of a ravine. ... Pushers tolerate bridgebuilders, but in the meantime are seldom interested in having a real talk with their opposite pole. Geert Wilders and Marine le Pen do not want to talk with their counterparts. Jihadists are not open to talking with secular thinkers. The pushers expand their monologue.[20]

Moreover, when polarization increases, the middle zone more and more becomes a danger zone. Whereas the middle zone was tolerated in an earlier stage, a time may come when tolerance is zero. The bridge builder may become a "scapegoat," which is Brandsma's fifth role. Because bridge builders are not entirely trusted, they are easily seen as traitors.[21]

Finally, as Brandsma observes, the similarity of people is not just the basis for overcoming polarization but also its source. Referring to René Girard's theory of mimetic desire, he states that we do not have original desires, but desire what others desire. In resembling the desire of the other, the other is a model. At the same time, the other is an obstacle,

---

19. Brandsma, *Polarisation*, 33–34.
20. Brandsma, *Polarisation*, 37.
21. Brandsma, *Polarisation*, 40.

because not all can have what all desire.²²

These short observations indicate that there is no simple cure to polarization. The complex dynamics of polarization easily make one powerless. There are no simple solutions. Organizing dialogues between the opposing parties may even fuel polarization rather than contribute to depolarization. In dialogue, often the identity of the other is central, with the aim to further harmony between the opposing parties. This may be effective in a preventing stage, but counter-productive in a stage in which polarization has increased and escalated into (violent) conflict. As Brandsma demonstrates, what is needed in that stage is not trying to understand the other, but adequate skills to deal with conflict. Dialogue and reflection are not adequate during the conflict, but after escalation, when the opposing groups have become tired of conflict and violence, they can be appropriate. Religions, life views, and faith communities may contribute significantly in this final stage, the stage of reconciliation. According to Brandsma, religions and life views are not the cause of the major conflicts of our time, but rather provide sources of reflection that enable people to deal with conflicts.

> The question is not whether we can use these sources to convince each other, or even if we tell each other about them. The question is: can we use these sources to form an attitude that enables us to deal well with conflict? … Now the other's identity is not central, but instead, a fundamental recalibration of our own attitude…²³

Similarly, Barthold proposes a model of dialogue that is aimed at effecting a shift of perspective in how one thinks about the other rather than shoring up better arguments: "In dialogue there is a re-orientation toward underlying meanings and values that expose a fundamental human connection with the other; our stories about the other, about ourselves, and about the nature of our relationship begin to change."²⁴

Here, church and theology come into view. Surprisingly, following Brandsma and Barthold, the core task of church and theology in contributing to depolarization and reconciliation in society is not so much to become a bridge builder between the opposing parties, but rather to try to understand the meaning of one's own faith tradition with regard to the attitude towards life, conflicts, and how to deal well with them. Following this line of thought, one could say that the calling of the church is first of all to be the church, and to understand what it means to be the church, i.e., being a community gathered around Christ which practices a Christ-like attitude in dealing with conflict and polarization.

---

22. Brandsma, *Polarisation*, 63–64.
23. Brandsma, *Polarisation*, 79.
24. Barthold, *Overcoming Polarization*, 4.

From this follows that the primary theological task is contextual self-explanation, i.e., to explain the meaning of the Christian faith and the church in particular with regard to conflicts and processes of polarization in which the church and its members actually are involved. This task asks for theology as critical self-reflection, as recalibration of one's basic view and life attitude in light of scripture and tradition, in particular with regard to how the other is seen. Similarly, dialogue is not primarily about understanding the other, but about understanding oneself. As Barthold argues, dialogue "draws on personal experiences articulated in first-person narratives."[25] It is first and foremost about "self-change."[26] In turn, precisely this first-person approach encourages one to avoid generalizations about the other and prevents one from speaking about, much less for, the other, acknowledging the other as sharing a common humanity and in concretely experiencing the other as a 'Thou.'[27] In a second instance, such a fundamental recalibration of one's own views and attitudes from the sources and in dialogue can contribute to a new 'we,' a new understanding of the common good, not as the primary aim or as a preliminary condition, but as a by-product, so to speak, of deep, critical, and honest self-reflection. The result is the creation of a new space, a new horizon, in which not only one's own position is seen anew, but also that of the other, enabling the creation of a new, shared perspective.[28]

All this asks for both analyses of polarization and conflict in particular contexts and profound theological and ecclesiological reflection, as well as theological reflections on and evaluations of the role and meaning of the Reformed theological tradition with regard to polarization. Therefore, in this volume three subthemes in particular are addressed, which order the various contributions: (1) polarization in church and society, (2) polarization and the Reformed tradition, and (3) the calling of the church. In the first section the focus is on analyzing contemporary phenomena of polarization in church and society as well as the search for adequate ways of preventing and overcoming polarization. The second part focusses more specifically on the Reformed tradition, its social and political view and in particular the role of the Canons and Church Order of Dort. The final part of this volume is more specifically devoted to the calling of the church and how the church may contribute to depolarization and reconciliation.

---

25. Barthold, *Overcoming Polarization*, 5.
26. Barthold, *Overcoming Polarization*, 111.
27. Barthold, *Overcoming Polarization*, 91, 93–95, 112, referring to Martin Buber.
28. Barthold, *Overcoming Polarization*, 111.

3. POLARIZATION IN CHURCH AND SOCIETY

The first sub-theme addresses the phenomenon of polarization and how it appears *in concreto* in debates on racism, social justice, sexuality and gender, feminism, euthanasia, and ecology and agriculture in various contexts. Attention is paid to the specific contexts and situations in various countries such as South Africa, the USA, Malawi, the Netherlands, and South Korea. Adequate responses to polarization depend on the particular contexts and situations, socio-political conditions and also how local congregations understand themselves and their role in society. It has been part of the Reformed identity that the context of every church is acknowledged as an important factor in the way discernment takes place. What is precisely at stake in a particular situation of polarization? Given the specific contexts, what is precisely the challenge for church and theology in these situations? Do church and theology themselves play a role in processes of polarization? Which theological concepts and approaches are promising in countering polarization?

In the first chapter, "Can Conviviality Trump Polarization?" Nadine Bowers du Toit explores polarization with regard to race, class and religion, in deeply divided societies, in particular in post-apartheid South Africa. Against this background, the author introduces the notion of conviviality, i.e., the art and practice of living together. Conviviality has recently been revived within the field of diaconia as a way to think anew about what it means to live together in solidarity, and to share resources in the joint struggle for human dignity and a sustainable community. Bowers du Toit argues that conviviality is directly linked to calls for justice, dignity, and a shared understanding of the common good as a way to seek and build life-giving community in direct opposition to the fragmentation brought about through increasing polarization. This contribution explores the possibilities inherent in this notion for challenging faith communities to engage forces of polarization at the grassroots level.

In the next chapter, Thandi Soko-de Jong focusses on the question of how unprecedented exchanges of polarizing content between populations in our times should be engaged. The task is to address the factors that drive polarization, such as fear, disconnection, apathy, and hate. Soko-de Jong also examines some common pitfalls in the social engagement of Reformed faith communities, pointing to the need for more conscientious commitment to including the voices of its members that are negatively affected by fallouts of polarization conflict. Including these voices challenges the idea that the Reformed tradition speaks with universal authority while only privileging as orthodox the voices that conform to its traditional, Western roots. To elaborate on this point, the author examines the Statement on Social Justice and the Gospel (also known as the Dallas Statement), to show the need for reforming the conversation between different sides of polarizing topics such as sexuality, gender, immigration, religion, race, and so on. The growth of robust engagement can potentially enrich the fabric of Reformed Theology, enabling it to better respond to polarizing issues as they arise. For further practical illustrations, Soko-de Jong draws from research among faith communities in Southern Malawi focusing on experiences of faith, *tcheni pa kalanka* (orthodoxy) and health, a combination of topics that has its own polarizing elements.

In Chapter 3, Willem van Vlastuin addresses polarized debates on sexuality and gender in the Netherlands and in postmodern Western culture, which is very sensitive to, and polarized by, pronouncements about sexuality. Against this background, van Vlastuin explores the apostle Paul's understanding of the Christian identity in the mystical union with Christ, as detailed in the New Testament, and its implications for understanding sexuality. As marriage refers to the Christian identity in Christ as the body, determined by Christ as the head, the holiness of marriage is central in the apostle's treatment of sexual life. The author applies these Biblical investigations to the current cultural context. First, reading the Bible means that one hears the voice of the eternal Word, namely Jesus Christ, in an existential way. Second, finding one's identity in Christ means one must have a struggle with one's old identity in this world. This personal struggle is part of the suffering of the whole of creation, caused by the expectation of the breakthrough of the kingdom of God. Third, in union with Christ, sexual identity is not made absolute because the main issue is holiness. The author argues that these perspectives give direction to both heterosexuals and homosexuals, transgender people and bisexuals.

In a different approach, Heleen Zorgdrager addresses the same topic in an analysis of the dynamics of polarization around sexuality and gender in the Netherlands which became manifest in the case of the Nashville Statement, in January 2019. Zorgdrager contextualizes the debate both locally and globally, addresses the dynamics of polarization and the identity-politics involved, and seeks to find a theological way forward beyond oppositions that tend to emphasize and prioritize 'identity' in the debate. Zorgdrager demonstrates how 'Nashville' is situated within international neo-conservative campaigns for 'traditional family values' and contextualized in the Dutch political landscape, in particular in the 'culturalization' of Christian identity in the political party that openly supported the Nashville Statement, the SGP. Some contemporary orthodox Reformed theologians, critical of modern identity discourses, depart from grounding identity first and foremost 'in Christ', such as van Vlastuin in the preceding chapter. According to Zorgdrager, however, they disconnect this identity from the body's desires or even oppose them. She then suggests three possible ways to move beyond the polarized sexuality debates in church and society: to opt for the notion of sacramental character (Mark Jordan/Marco Derks) instead of identity, to embrace the concept of the broken middle (Gillian Rose), and to envision the church as a learning community on a transformative journey, dedicated to conversational openness on matters of gender and human sexuality.

In "Passivity, Abuse, and Self-Sacrifice: Daoism and Feminist Christology," Jaeseung Cha continues reflecting on gender. Cha shows how polarized debates on gender in both Western and East Asian contexts, as for instance on the ordination of women, reflect polarized debates on the theological understanding of the crucifixion of Christ, in particular between traditional atonement theology and feminist theological critiques of atonement as a glorification of suffering and martyrdom. In order to find an alternative to this polarization, the author analyzes the feminist nature of the non-dominating and non-violent sacrificial deity in Daoism. It is women, not men, who represent this passive, non-violent but also active and productive power of the Dao. This sheds light on the fact that Christianity is not the only religion to value the sacrificial aspect of the Deity, and that sacrifice may neither necessarily be violent nor submissive. This understanding is brought into a dialogue with critical feminist views on atonement as abusive and violent sacrifice and results in a proposal for a revision of classical atonement theology, thus finding a way beyond polarization in acknowledging both feminist theological criticism of oppressive aspects of atonement and the central meaning of Christ's crucifixion as sacrificial love aimed at transformative justice.

In Chapter 6, Annemarieke van der Woude relates the notion of holiness to the Dutch euthanasia debate. In the Netherlands, the number of people dying on request—both euthanasia and physician-assisted suicide are regulated in the Dutch Euthanasia Act (2002)—is increasing. What is more, the files of reported euthanasia show that the number of people dying on request without a life-threatening disease is growing as well. In the public domain, this is a highly contested issue that often leads to polarization between opposing groups. Van der Woude argues that the biblical notion of holiness can serve as a meaningful concept to go beyond polarities. In scripture, holiness is not a static attribute, but a dynamic one: nothing is holy in and of itself, but anything can *become* holy. The author proposes approaching the multi-layered issue of dying on request with the same timidity as that of Moses when he drew near to the burning bush where the Lord called him. She elaborates on the liturgical as well as on the ethical aspect of holiness and concludes that in the combination of the two the Christian faith tradition can contribute to a new understanding of the common good, in believers as well as non-believers.

In the final chapter in this first section of this book, titled "Sewing Hope in a Polarized Agricultural Debate," Jan Jorrit Hasselaar, Philipp Pattberg and PeterBen Smit focus on increasing conflicting and polarized positions in debates on agriculture in the Netherlands between farmers, consumers, supermarkets, banks and activists. This polarization in agriculture can be understood as a 'wicked problem,' which does not allow for a one-dimensional solution, but rather asks for a new perspective that stimulates cooperation and transformation of agriculture instead of conflict and polarization. To this end, the authors explore Jonathan Sacks' concept of hope, understood as a narrative of individual and societal transformation, and show that the concept of hope can be promising in relation to joint decision making in situations of increasingly polarized positions and large uncertainty. Diversity and conflicting positions are considered as a source of creativity and renewal instead of polarization. This concept of hope also provides a governance structure to develop trust, hope, and love in times of transition. The approach that is developed can be viewed as issuing from the structure of the biblical canon and the hermeneutics implied in it. Operationalized in a case study in the Food Valley region in the Netherlands, Sacks' concept of hope indeed appears to be promising.

4. POLARIZATION AND THE REFORMED TRADITION

The second sub-theme is devoted to the question of what the Reformed tradition may contribute to the understanding of and the response to polarization. The position of the church in a particular country depends on how church, state and society are related. In turn, this affects how the church may respond to processes of polarization. For instance, the role of the church and its contribution to society are dependent upon how much space the government gives to societal initiatives and associations in general and religious communities in particular. Traditionally, in Western countries there is much space for such initiatives. The separation between church and state was precisely intended to save the church from governmental interventions in religious affairs. This created many opportunities for churches to contribute to civil society. When the freedom of religion or the freedom of opinion is under pressure, this requires a different approach from the church.

How the church relates to the state and to society and what this means for its calling with regard to the various phenomena of polarization to a great extent depend on historical backgrounds and developments. In his contribution, David Fergusson outlines various traditional themes of Reformed social and political theology: politics as vocation, civil resistance, coordination of church and state, democratic tendencies, nationalist ideals, and economic concerns. While many of the Reformed churches initially followed a Christendom model of church-state partnership, this has been problematized in the modern era. An assessment of the place of these national churches is offered, followed by a consideration of ways in which the classical themes might be retrieved at a time of rising populism and polarization.

In the next chapter, David Daniels addresses the threat of xenophobia, which fractures many societies around the world, and relates it to an illuminating debate at the Synod of Dort in 1618 on baptizing children of non-Christian parents in Asia. Daniels demonstrates that this debate offers an inclusive framing of incorporating new peoples into the Christian community. Occurring prior to the rise of modern racism and orientalism, the progressive currents in the 1618 baptism debate point to a constructive manner in which difference can inform how societies think of community and peoplehood in terms other than ancestry, land, and language, supplying an alternative to the polarizing currents within today's world. As an alternative to xenophobia and its polarizing force, the author introduces Fred Moten's concept of xenogenerosity, which means generosity toward strangers.

In Chapter 10, Jozef Hehanussa addresses religious polarization in Yogyakarta. He highlights that in Yogyakarta tolerance and harmony have prevailed for centuries since the beginning of encounters between religions. Local people have welcomed new faiths, even consciously integrating spiritual practices of other religions (Hindu, Buddhism, and Islam) into their own religious practices. Therefore, syncretism could be found in each religion in the city. The situation changed when Christianity was introduced by the Dutch Reformed, who, rejecting syncretism, kept a radical distance from Javanese cultural traditions. Nowadays, tendencies of polarization have grown stronger as the influence of religious radical groups in society has also become stronger. These groups oppose the presence of other religions, especially Christianity, in the city and accuse Christian schools and hospitals of being agents of 'Christianization,' although today these organizations are primarily social in their purposes. Hehanussa shows that religious polarization in Yogyakarta has a strongly negative impact on interfaith relations, including social services to the community.

In his contribution titled "Election and Hope: Van Ruler and Dort," Allan Janssen, who passed away one year after the IRTI conference, explores how the doctrine of election found in the Canons of the Synod of Dort might provide a theological foundation for hope in the contemporary, highly polarized world. Furthermore, Janssen demonstrates how the theology of Arnold A. van Ruler, himself an advocate of Dortian theology, may assist in this effort through his doctrine of election. The author examines Van Ruler's more extensive comments on election, only recently published (in Dutch). His understanding of election as "actual," i.e., as the action of God toward the believer, an action that has its origin in the eternality of God's love, offers possibilities for the contemporary believer to engage with Dort in fresh ways.

In the final contribution to this part of the volume, Klaas-Willem de Jong and Jan Dirk Th. Wassenaar take as the starting point of their reflection on polarization and the Reformed tradition article 31 of the Church Order of Dort, which reads: "that which is decided by majority vote shall be considered settled and binding unless it is proved to conflict with the Word of God or with the articles adopted in this general synod." From the beginning of the Reformation in the Netherlands, this approach has been questioned in church and theology. In their article, an overview is offered of positions and practices in successively the period up to the Synod of Dordrecht (1618–19), the last decades of the 19th century and the second half of the 20th century. The authors conclude that decision making in the church cannot just be a case of simple majority, but should recon with the nature of the church as unity in Christ. Two extremes should be avoided. On the one hand, it should be avoided that decision makers in the church force their own way of understanding this unity in ecclesiastical practice onto others and increase polarization. On the other hand, it should be avoided that unity in Christ becomes abstract, allowing for all kinds of differences and views, so that in the end this unity becomes indifferent and has no real implications for overcoming conflict and fulfilling its call towards polarization.

5. THE CALLING OF THE CHURCH

This brings us to the question central to the final part of this volume: What is, theologically speaking, the calling of the church, given the specific challenges in particular contexts? Whereas the first sub-theme starts reflection from society and its challenges, this sub-theme addresses similar questions but starting from the church's self-understanding, i.e., from ecclesiology.

Though in the Western world religion is conceived as basically restricted to the private sphere of life where one may choose to relate to a church or other religious community, churches still play their role in the public sphere. Governments and civilians regularly ask for the support of churches because of the binding potential of religion and its contribution to civil society. However, what is the calling of the church in countries and regions where the church has a minority position and is permanently at risk of becoming the victim of societal polarization between groups of different religious backgrounds, sometimes ending up in violence? What is the calling of the church in African or Asian countries that are still deeply marked by ethnic, religious and social-economic polarizations, regularly exploding in violent conflicts?

In Chapter 13, Gerrit Singgih describes how in Indonesia violence against those who are regarded by the majority as deviating from true religious tenets has increased sharply. In particular, LGBT people and those who support them have become the target of attacks, resulting in a criminalization of these people, as exemplified in the Indonesian Constitutional Court charge of homosexual acts as criminal offenses. At the same time, the Constitutional Court has recognized local religions of Adat Society as of equal status as the official six world religions. The author shows that oppression of LGBT people in Indonesia is related to interreligious polarization, through which LGBT people have become the scapegoats. Responding to these instances of polarization, the Communion of Churches in Indonesia (PGI) both re-examined the traditional theology of mission and sent a Pastoral Statement, imploring the member churches to reconsider their negative attitude toward LGBT people. The Pastoral Statement on LGBT was rejected by the majority of the member churches. The positive impact is that the outside world, for instance Muslims who advocate acceptance of LGBT people, welcomes the PGI initiative on LGBT. In this sense, the PGI has established signs of hope for all people of Indonesia, thus strengthening the calling of the church to contribute to overcoming polarization.

Elizabeth Welch addresses the issue of polarization in terms of the separation and division of churches in the 2nd millennium and offers an understanding of *koinonia* as central to the calling of the church on its way to address polarization both in the church and the world. A brief history is given of different separations of the churches, followed by a look at twentieth-century ecumenical developments, from the 1920 World Mission Conference in Edinburg, via the Second Vatican Council, to the World Council of Churches' work in the area of *koinonia*, and international dialogues that have taken up this theme. *Koinonia* is seen as God's gift and calling, arising out of the *koinonia* found in the Trinity, which draws people to the gift of the fullness of God's inclusive love and calls people to live in relationship with one another, despite divisions, differences and diversities. Welch examines International Reformed Anglican dialogue as a particular example of two traditions of the church looking at their separate lives and seeing the way in which they can come closer together by embracing more fully the gift of God's *koinonia*.

In "No Calling without Being Called: The *Vocatio Interna* at the Heart of Sanctification," Henk van den Belt argues that the Reformed understanding of the inward work of the Holy Spirit is helpful for understanding the calling of the church with regard to polarization. There is no Christianity without conflict, because all Christians are called into the kingdom of God. Still, they are called to strive for peace. After a short historical survey on the background of the use of *vocatio*, this chapter dwells on the two sides of the church's calling. The church is called out of the world and to liberty and holiness. The Reformed emphasis on the work of the Spirit, however, shows that the most essential borderline is not the one between the church and the world, but between the Spirit and the flesh. This emphasis also sheds light on the nature of sanctification as a call to freedom and holiness and away from passivity and pride.

The question of how the church perceives its own alterity in relation to its existence and mission in the world is taken up critically by Najib Awad. He unearths the self-otherizing tendency in a perception of alterity that can make the church one of the causes of polarization in the world, rather than a victim of it. Reading Christ's prayer in John 17 on 'being in the world, but not of the world' from a Levinasian perspective of alterity, Awad argues that this sheds critical light on Jesus followers' perception of alterity. It means that Christians, like all other humans, makes them be who they are vis-à-vis their relation to others, not only by virtue of their faith convictions. Rather than separating the disciples from the world, Jesus is afraid that his disciples' relation to him would create in them a sense of alterity that will turn them eventually into a 'separate anti-society' entity. Next, the author sheds light on a contextual, down-to-earth example of a Protestantism in one part of the world, namely Protestants in Greater Syria, whose self-otherizing perception of alterity alienates them from the world of the Orient. By placing themselves in this state of 'foreignness' (Julia Kristeva) they willingly or unwillingly contribute to furthering rather than overcoming polarization. This example shows that today's Christianity might be responsible for forms of polarization in the world due to how it perceives its own alterity.

In Chapter 17, Viktória Kóczián takes the response of the Churches in Hungary to migrants as the starting point. First, she shows how the World Council of Churches (WCC), being actively involved in fighting for the rights of refugees and migrants, has reacted to major events in the so-called 'migrant crisis' since 2015 and has voiced its opinion in different statements and speeches. Kóczián examines the theology behind these reactions and how it deals with issues of national identity and self-understanding of the member churches. Next, Kóczián focusses on the Ecumenical Council of Churches in Hungary (ECCH), which shares member churches with the WCC, but has not been committed to the defense of migrants in the same way as the WCC. The Hungarian example shows how an ecumenical organization performs its tasks in a divided society, as a communion of churches polarized in themselves while aiming at unity. However, WCC concerns such as supporting and welcoming refugees in the destination countries, integrating them in societies, hospitality and fighting against racism are less prominent in the Hungarian discourse. Rather, in this discourse the limitation of incoming migrants is defended as a theologically valid solution to fears and concerns in society. The contrast between the two ecumenical organizations raises the question as to what ecumenical theology has to offer and what the unity of Christians can mean against the backdrop of the migration crisis in Europe. Kóczián suggests that in order to take another step towards unity, the churches must acknowledge underlying fears about losing identities in the host countries on the one hand, and make practices of dialogue and ecumenical common services in contexts of migration fruitful to overcoming such fears on the other hand.

In the final chapter, Louise Prideaux argues that a pursuit of Christ-centered 'otherness' presents an answer to the question how the church may respond to polarization in society. 'Otherness' is a popular theme in contemporary cultural anthropology, particularly in considering the meaning of culture, the implications of binding cultural communities to repeated patterns of past behavior, and the awareness that every person brings their own partiality to every social relationship. From the insights of Louise Lawrence, Mario Aguilar, Joel Robbins, and Will Rollason it becomes clear that the prioritization of 'the other' in cultural engagement is paramount. Robbins acknowledges that the idea of 'otherness' is borrowed from theology. Taking up this observation, Prideaux interestingly shows that a theological 'otherness' is present in the theology of the neo-Calvinist Abraham Kuyper. Through a recontextualization of sphere sovereignty into this idea of 'otherness' that is informed by Kuyper's commitment to freedom of conscience and his concern for the poor, 'the other' becomes both a theological and a social priority. Prideaux finds an extension of Kuyper's theology in the idea of 'commonness,' which provides a necessary counterpart for 'otherness' in cultural engagement, that preserves inclusivity and visible unity at the same time as the distinctiveness of the cultural 'other.' In addition, Herman Bavinck's exhortation to confess Christ in all areas of life gives the idea of 'otherness' its distinctly Christian character. As the church is formed into this sense of 'otherness', Prideaux concludes, it will be better equipped to respond to polarization in society through all its encounters with the cultural 'other.'

In an epilogue, Heleen Zorgdrager makes concluding observations and reflections on the theme of polarization and the calling of the church. She points out similarities and differences in theological approaches between the authors, how these are derived from Reformed, ecumenical and other theological and non-theological sources, and what the authors offer constructively to understanding the calling of the church in times of polarization.

BIBLIOGRAPHY

Abramowitz, Alan I. *The Disappearing Center*: *Engaged Citizens, Polarization, and American Democracy*. New Haven: Yale University Press, 2010.

Achterhuis, Hans. *Met alle geweld*: *Een filosofische zoektocht* (With all violence: A philosophical enquiry). Rotterdam: Lemniscaat, 2010.

Barthold, Lauren Swayne. *Overcoming Polarization in the Public Sphere*: *Civic Dialogue*. London: Palgrave Macmillan, 2020.

Bialik, Kirsten. "Key Findings about American Life in Urban, Suburban and Rural Areas." *American Pew Research*. (2018). https://www.pewresearch.org/fact-tank/2018/05/22/key-findings-about-american-life-in-urban-suburban-and-rural-areas/.

Bovens, Mark and Wille Anchrit. *Diplomademocratie*: *Over de spanning tussen meritocratie en democratie* (Diploma democracy: On the tension between meritocracy and democracy). Amsterdam: Bert Bakker, 2011.

Brandsma, Bart. *Polarisation*: *Understanding the Dynamics of Us versus Them*. Schoonrewoerd: BB in Media, 2017.

Hunter, James Davison. *Culture Wars*: *The Struggle to Define America*. New York: Basic Books, 1991.

Ignatieff, Michael. *Etnische conflicten en het moderne geweten* (Ethnic conflicts and modern conscience). Amsterdam: Contact, 1999.

Lovin, Robin W. "Reimagining Christian Realism: Church in an Amoral Time." *The Christian Century* (2019): 26–9.

McCoy, Jennifer, Tahmina Rahman and Murat Somar. "Polarization and the Global Crisis of Democracy: Common Patterns, Dynamics, and Pernicious Consequences for Democratic Polities." *American Behavioral Scientist* 62 no. 1 (2018): 16–42. https://doi.org/10.1177/0002764218759576.

Part 1: Polarization in Church and Society

Chapter 1
Can Conviviality Trump Polarization?
Exploring the Notion of Conviviality as Calling of the Church in Times of Polarization
Nadine Bowers Du Toit

1. Introduction

The title is, of course, meant to bring to mind one of the most polarizing global political figures of our generation in a play on the word 'trump.'[1] In many ways Donald Trump has become the poster child for populist leaders everywhere as we see a rise in neoliberal capitalist, fascist-like politics across the globe. Discourse, often fueled by and connected to the religious and fundamentalist right and which excludes the most vulnerable in society such as migrants, people of color, women, and indigenous peoples and ignores the looming climate crisis in favor of extractive neoliberal capitalist motives. Trump's uncritical support by individuals such as Franklin Graham and James Dobson[2]—American fundamentalists with widespread evangelical support—and also Brazilian president Bolsanaro's support by Brazilian Pentecostals—is particularly worrying as we seek to discern the calling of the church in times of polarization.[3] At the grassroots level we see the outworking of empire as the increasing marginalization of the most vulnerable and widening divisions between race, culture and religion.

In this article, I firstly seek to explore some of the thinking around the notion of polarization—also with regard to the manner in which media

---

1. This article was originally presented as a keynote lecture at the International Reformed Theological Institute held at Vrije Universiteit and Protestant Theological University, 4–7 July 2019.

2. John Fea, "How Evangelical Leaders Surrounded Clinton During Last Presidential Impeachment Process," https://www.washingtonpost.com/religion/2019/09/27/how-evangelical-leaders-surrounded-clinton-during-last-presidential-impeachment-process/ (accessed March 8, 2020).

3. Amy Smith and Ryan Lloyd, "Top Pentecostal Leaders Supported the Far Right in Brazil's Presidential Campaign," https://www.vox.com/mischiefs-of-faction/2018/10/8/17950304/pentecostals-bolsonaro-brazil (accessed May 4, 2020).

heightens fissures with regard to race, class and religion, followed with a distinctly South African perspective on our current political polarization. I then present the notion of conviviality as a possible antidote to engaging faithfully at grassroots within what seems like an increasingly VUCA (Volatile, Uncertain, Complex, and Ambiguous) world and bring this into conversation with stories from grassroots (again with a largely South African flavor) and with other theological conversation partners in seeking to discern the church's role in polarizing times.

2. DEEP CLEAVAGES

According to De Klerk

> deeply divided societies are societies with deep ethnic, linguistic, regional, religious, or other emotional and polarizing cleavages. Citizens of deeply divided societies are segregated along polarizing lines which reduce interaction between different groups in society… and could result in different segments of society living in parallel spheres, where people are unable to think outside their own group, which could result in alienation and distrust.[4]

Indeed, the volatility, uncertainty, complexity, and ambiguity of a VUCA world often fosters fear on the most primal level and results in individuals and groups aligning themselves with ideological, political or religious positions that most closely affirm their own in order to protect themselves against 'othered' ways of being in the world and thus assume what could be termed a false sense of safety.

Polarization is most commonly discussed in the broad political sense as "the extent to which partisans view each other as a disliked group."[5] However, in this paper we will take a broader perspective. This of course implies that there are in and out groups, dependent on which side of the fence you are sitting and also apparently on who you are listening to, too. Studies with regard to the influence of media argue that "rather than being motivated to avoid dissonance, people prefer likeminded information as a strategy to process information with less cognitive effort."[6] Studies regarding implicit bias found for example that biases occur even among those who profess to be impartial, such as

---

4. Leo De Klerk, *Political Polarisation in post-Apartheid South Africa: A Case Study on Institutional Design, Race and Politics in South Africa from 1994–2016* (Master Thesis: University of Utrecht, 2016), 12.

5. Shanto Iyengar, Gaurev Sood and Yphtach Lelkes, "Affect, Not Ideology: A Social Identity Perspective on Polarization," *Public Opinion Quarterly* 76:3 (2012), 405–431.

6. Yonghuan Kim, "Does Disagreement Mitigate Polarisation? How Selective Exposure and Disagreements Affect Political Polarisation," *Journalism and Mass Communication Quarterly* 92:4 (2015), 915–937, 917.

judges (or academics?) and that while "these biases do not necessarily correspond with our professed beliefs and views, they generally favor our own group and affect our actual behavior."[7] Furthermore, "because likeminded information is considered more credible and convincing compared with dissonant information, people prefer likeminded news and information."[8] The latter is not helped by social media such as Facebook, whose algorithms pick up your most likeminded information which in turn links to websites and adverts, which only seek to reinforce your views. This is worrying if one considers that scholars show that "selective exposure to similar points of view and avoidance of challenging information will likely hurt democracy."[9] Mutz argues that, therefore:

> Citizens need a range of common experiences to develop a broader understanding of others, and sharing common experiences with different others may lead to social consensus. By contrast if people are not exposed to others opinions, they are less likely to be aware of others legitimate rationales and even their own rationales. In addition, if people expose themselves only to similar points of view and ignore contrasting perspectives, they are less likely to be tolerant of challenging viewpoints.[10]

It is this point that is picked up on later as we explore the notion of conviviality and its possible relevance to 'trumping' polarization.

3. THE SOUTH AFRICAN SCENARIO

In South Africa, we have seen a fragmentation of the dream of the rainbow nation. A nation, which has overcome the horrors of colonialism and Apartheid to achieve the dream of a bloodless transition to a democratic dispensation termed 'post-Apartheid.' To many—particularly people of color in South Africa—the rainbow has faded and dark clouds have gathered in its wake. These clouds are the lingering inequality and poverty still plaguing many South Africans 25 years later as the nation was recently identified once again as the most unequal country in the world by a World Bank Report—with race skewed inequality still a key feature.[11] Despite the fact that white people on average still earn up to

---

7. Ken Wykstra, *The Myth of Equality: Uncovering the Roots of Injustice and Privilege* (Illinois: Intervarsity, 2017), 143.
8. Wykstra, *The Myth of Equality*, 143.
9. Kim, "Does Disagreement Mitigate Polarisation," 916.
10. Kim, "Does Disagreement Mitigate Polarisation," 917.
11. Nico Gouws, "SA Most Unequal Country in World: Poverty Shows Apartheid's Enduring Legacy," https://www.timeslive.co.za/news/south-africa/2018-04-04-poverty-shows-how-apartheid-legacy-endures-in-south-africa (accessed May, 3 2019); Tiaan Meiring, Catherine Kannemeyer and Elanri Potgieter, *The Gap between Rich and Poor: South African Society's Biggest Divide Depends on Where You Think You Fit In* (SALDRU:

four times more than black people and the majority of the poor in South Africa are black, the past few years have witnessed the re-emergence of the white right—possibly best represented by Afrikaans country singer Steve Hofmeyr—who claim that white people are persecuted and even experience genocide as evidenced by the murder on farms. While farm murders are horrific, they can by no means be termed 'white genocide' at this point, when compared to the high rates of murder with regards to all population groups.[12] The recent elections held in May 2019 further indicate a worrying trend as the Freedom Front Plus (a decidedly rightist party) achieved a drastic increase in votes—largely supposedly garnered from the more centrist Democratic Alliance party. These trends point to rising racial tensions in light also of the Black Land First movement's explicit emphasis that it was not interested in white members or voters and their leader's worrying outburst that white people will be killed for their land—a position which only fuels the white genocide narrative.[13] What lies at the heart of the continuing and now deepening cleavages of polarization between race groups? According to the Institute for Justice and Reconciliation's 2014 Barometer:

> Apartheid regulated and enforced the psychological segregation of South Africa's constitutive population groups. Apart from the economic dispossession that coincided with forced removals and the enforcement of pass laws to police geographic segregation, the imposition of these laws also had a profound effect on the psyche of all south Africans, instilling a "toxic understanding" of intergroup relations.[14]

South Africa is a notoriously religious nation with over 80% expressing affiliation to Christianity,[15] yet it remains unclear how religion (as it well does in countries such as the US or Brazil) plays any clear role in party political polarization. While the so-called Christian party, the ACDP,[16]

Working Paper Series Number 220, 2018), 5.

12. Nechama Brodie, "Are White Afrikaners Really Being Killed Like Flies?" https://africacheck.org/reports/are-white-afrikaners-really-being-killed-like-flies/ (accessed May 2, 2019).

13. Azzarah Karrim, "Mngxitama's Comments Inciting People to Take Up Arms and Start Killing People Says Afriforums Roets," https://www.news24.com/SouthAfrica/News/mngxitamas-comments-inciting-people-to-take-up-arms-and-start-killing-people-says-afriforums-roets-20191113 (accessed May 2, 2019).

14. *National Action Plan to Combat Racism, Racial Discrimination, Xenophobia and Related Intolerance* (2016–2021) (Draft for public consultation: South African Government, 2016), 23, https://www.gov.za/sites/default/files/gcis_document/201903/national-action-plan.pdf.

15. Jakobus Schoeman, "South African Religious Demography: The 2013 General Household Survey," *HTS Teologiese Studies/Theological Studies* 73 (2017), a3837, https://doi.org/10.4102/hts.v73i2.3837.

16. African Christian Democratic Party.

saw a slight increase in votes in the recent elections, its focus on the type of individualized moral single voter issues such as abortion, the death penalty and gay marriage appear to only appeal to a small minority of self-professed Christians if they only achieved 0.84% of the votes and over 80% of the population self-identify as Christians.[17] Christians are, therefore, just as likely (or more accurately more likely if one inspects voting statistics) to vote for any of the political parties on offer. What is interesting to note is that in the South African governments National Action Plan to Combat Racism—nowhere are religious groups listed as a key actor in combating and eliminating racism, racial discrimination, xenophobia and related intolerance.[18] Civil society is indeed listed, but no reference is made to religion. This is perhaps not surprising in a secularized Western Europe, but for South Africans who still have vivid memories of the church's double legacy in both supporting and opposing Apartheid, religion can and must be public—for better or for worse.

4. WHY THE NOTION OF CONVIVIALITY?

In terms of this discourse, why is the notion of conviviality introduced within the context of rising polarization? It is important to note that I work in the field of Theology and Development, or more commonly known as Diaconia within the European context, and within our field this notion has become a helpful heuristic tool. I, therefore, also draw extensively in this piece on the work of Tony Addy, an experienced ecumenical diaconic academic and practitioner, within the context of the Lutheran World Federation and the Eastern European educational institution, Interdiac. The term conviviality of course relates to the term 'con-vivere,' which asks "how can we live together?" and in times of polarization this is certainly a question that centers our discourse and practice.[19] It is important to note that in the expansion of this term, three roots of this term have been identified.

Its most immediate roots lie within the context of Spanish history and the word 'Convivencia,' in reference to a time when Muslims, Jews and Catholics resided in relative peace on the Iberian Peninsula and the "study of Convivencia has been given impetus by the need to

---

17. Digital Editors, "South African Election Results," https://www.thesouthafrican.com/news/2019-south-africa-election-results-national-provincial-all-votes/ (accessed June 1, 2019). Cf. Sheldon Morais, "What the Numbers Tell Us About the General Elections," https:// www.news24.com/elections/news/2019-vs-2014-what-the-numbers-tell-us-about-the-general-elections-20190512 (accessed June 1, 2019).

18. *National Action Plan*, 38–44.

19. Tony Addy and Ulla Sirto, "Conviviality as a Vision and Approah for a Diaconal Society," In *International Handbook on Ecumencial Diakonia*, eds. Godwin Ampony, Martin Buscher, Beate Hoffmann, Felicite Ngnintedem, Dennis Solon and Dietrich Werner (Oxford: Regnum, 2021), 401.

understand how different religious, ethnic and cultural groups come to live peaceably together."[20]

Secondly, the term has most popularly been used by Ivan Illich in his book *Tools for Conviviality*. A Croatian-Austrian with both Jewish and Catholic parents, Illich (a priest) trained those from the "global north going to work in Latin America to work with sensitivity and not to impose their values." His use of the word means "the autonomous and creative relationship between people, people and their environment and with technology. He considered conviviality to be freedom realized in personal independence and as such, an intrinsic ethical value."[21] In this way notions of power and culture and the way they intersect within the global system are explored.

The third way in which it is rooted, refers to the use of the word as "the sociable pleasure of people coming together and enjoying conversation and discussion in a relaxed manner, not under any constraints sharing a meal. Conviviality, therefore, relates to friendly dealings and also to relationships unconstrained by organizations or technology."[22] Often in today's context this can be most clearly reflected in the simple sharing of food and drink and it should be pointed out that within diaconal "and other engagement with refugees as well as with marginalized groups, the joint preparation and sharing of food is very often a feature."[23] It also has links to the Eucharistic meal which will later be explored. Addy also notes, in line with Paul Gilroy's work, that "conviviality could also

---

20. Addy and Siirto, "Conviviality as a Vision and Approach for a Diaconal Society," 401. Some scholars have labelled this a somewhat mythical notion in terms of the realities of Spain at the time and claim that the way in which this is often cited is romanticized. It can nevertheless still be used as a way into discussing inter-religious engagement (cf. Aomar Boum, "The Performance of Convivencia: Communities of Tolerance and the Reification of Toleration," Religion Compass 6:3 (2012), 174–184, 10.1111/j.1749-8171.2012.00342.x).

21. Tony Addy, *Seeking Conviviality… The Art and Practice of Living Together: A New Core Concept for Diaconia* (Český Těšín: Interdiac, 2017), 7, 8. Cf. Ivan Illich, *Tools for Conviviality* (London: Marion Boyars, 2009), ch. 2, https://www.panarchy.org/illich/conviviality.html. According Illich: "A convivial society would be the result of social arrangements that guarantee for each member the most ample and free access to the tools of the community and limit this freedom only in favour of another member's equal freedom. At present people tend to relinquish the task of envisaging the future to a professional élite. They transfer power to politicians who promise to build up the machinery to deliver this future. They accept a growing range of power levels in society when inequality is needed to maintain high outputs. Political institutions themselves become draft mechanisms to press people into complicity with output goals. What is right comes to be subordinated to what is good for institutions. Justice is debased to mean the equal distribution of institutional wares" (https://www.panarchy.org/illich/conviviality.html).

22. Addy, *Seeking Conviviality*, 4.

23. Addy, *Seeking Conviviality*, 4.

be used as a way to describe everyday life in multicultural and diverse areas," where boundaries of race, class and culture are crossed every day in a manner which may not go very deep, but through which common humanity is shared.[24]

5. Engaging Conviviality In Times Of Polarization

In light of what has been discussed, I would like to suggest three possible ways in which this notion could be engaged to assist us to discern the calling of the church in times of polarization and attempt to bring it into conversation with theological reflection and praxis.

5.1 Conviviality as Challenge to Boundary Making

One of the ways in which polarization occurs is through boundary making and marking. This process of exclusion works according to Volf through

> cutting the bonds that connect, taking oneself out of the pattern of interdependence and placing oneself in a position of sovereign independence. The other then emerges either as an enemy that must be pushed away from the self and driven out of its space or as a nonentity—a superfluous being—that can be disregarded and abandoned.[25]

In other words, those who are not likeminded and do not share our views are avoided. This form of boundary making elevates us and dehumanizes the other in such a way that those who do not share our political views, social identities or religious identity (or other identity markers) are 'othered.' Convivial thinking requires, however, that we work for peace and reconciliation, but that this work recognizes the need to acknowledge and value diverse ways of thinking and being in an effort to restore trust and conviviality.[26] In this way seeking conviviality is not merely seeking tolerance of the other—it is also a "step towards resolving intolerance through dialogue and practice."[27] It is possibly even an acknowledgement and identification of the implicit bias that drives 'othering' as starting point. This is hard work and will require courageous, faithful Christ followers who faithfully continue to push

---

24. Addy and Siirto, "Conviviality as a Vision and Approach for Diaconal Work in Society," 401.

25. Miroslav Volf, *Exclusion and Embrace: A Theological Exploration of Identity, Otherness and Reconciliation* (Nashville: Abingdon, 1996), 67.

26. Tony Addy, "Seeking Conviviality—A New Core Concept for the Diaconal Church," in *The Diaconal Church*, eds. Stephanie Dietrich, Kari Karsrud Korslien, Kjell Nordstokke and Knud Jørgensen (Oxford: Regnum Books, 2019), 5.

27. Addy, "Seeking Conviviality," 5.

in and engage tough issues around race, class, religion and gender for example in the face of fear driven needs to feel safe.[28]

In what was termed by many as a polarizing engagement during the #Feesmustfall student protests at our university[29] (and in the context of our own faculty of theology), is for me an excellent example of what seeking conviviality through dialogue could start as. In a tense, yet open, dialogue with students at our faculty around transformation a student called Jeffery Ngobeni burst out in anger: "we loved white people, but they didn't love us back."[30] I remember the moment like it was yesterday and while many white people in the room only heard anger—I heard pain, I heard rejection, I heard socio-economic suffering...The core of his pain was at the core of human experience—our need to be loved. He wasn't asking for the soft version of love. The kind of love offered by our Truth and Reconciliation Commission's reconciliatory apologies, where white people were called on to apologize for the sins of Apartheid, but not challenged to address the socio-economic injustices that were its fruits. He was getting to the heart of neighborly love in South Africa. He was challenging us: what does it really mean to love our neighbor in a context of inequality where most black people are poor and most white people are middle class to rich? What will it cost? That is at the heart of restorative justice in South Africa. In this case, love for the so called 'other' may look like confrontational, polarizing dialogue but really it is the most radical form of working our way towards neighborliness of the kind that cannot push the other aside—it is a call for neighborly interdependence, which takes the first steps towards conviviality as life together. Looking back on this encounter, it becomes clear to me that this seemingly polarizing confrontation crossed boundaries and challenged us to become the robust faculty we are today—as we learn from each other how to become better neighbors, who cross from tolerance to embrace.[31]

Addy notes that unlike the term *koinonia*, which has a possibly closed connotation as it most popularly refers to fellowship within

---

28. Cf. Emmanuel Levinas, *Emmanuel Levinas: Basic Philosophical Writings*, eds. Adriaan Peperzak, Simon Critchley and Robert Bernasconi (Indiana: Bloomington, 1996), 52–54.

29. These protests took place at institutions of higher learning across South Africa between 2015–2017 and were a call for greater access to higher education, decolonized curricula and transformation.

30. The student provided permission for me to use his name and recount this story—my version of the retelling was also discussed with him. It is important to note that he not only gave permission, he asked that I use his name.

31. See also Robert Vosloo, "Traumatic Memory, Representation and Forgiveness: Some Remarks in Conversation with Antjie Krog's Country of My Skull," *In die Skriflig* 46 (2015), 1–7, 3.

the body of believers, the notion of conviviality asks for more porous boundaries that extends to common action with others in society in order to work for the common good.[32] In a recent Masters class with ordained ministers from several denominations, it became clear that one of the reasons why they struggled to engage the issues of community, was that they centered their thinking in terms of church, rather than Kingdom. Some, despite years of theological education and ministry recognized with great dismay that they had in fact equated the Kingdom with the church. The community was seen as "out there" and the church was centered—a problematic ecclesiology which failed to recognize that the Kingdom invites all towards the restorative action of *shalom* and that the church is the open armed servant of the Kingdom in this response to the world.

5.2 Conviviality as Invitation to Reciprocity and Power Sharing

What has become clear in the relationships between powerful populist presidents, such as Trump, Bolsonaro and even South Africa's own corrupt former President Zuma and church leaders, is that their alignment with the fundamentalist church is rooted in power. Both parties seek power—religious entities seek the influence that political ties bring and political entities seek the legitimacy that religious affiliation often provides. Empire demands religious justification and uses god-talk to "call up a conjured reality of evil on the other side."[33] In fact, a few short years ago, Rev Franklin Graham (son of Billy Graham) called for a day of prayer for Trump describing it as a type of "spiritual warfare," necessary because Trump's many accomplishments "make him very unpopular with the Devil and the kingdom of darkness."[34] In this case the enemy is all those that oppose Trump, and Boesak notes that

> since the enemy is not humans, but 'evil,' any and all means are justified; there is no possibility for error on the side of those who represent goodness. This theological stance harbors within itself another ideological trait: it closes itself off from all self-criticism or correction. It ascribes to itself an attribute only ascribable to God: that of sinlessness.[35]

---

32. Addy, "Seeking Conviviality," 1.
33. Alan Boesak, "Theological Reflections of Empire," in *Globalisation: The Political of Empire, Justice and the Life of Faith*, eds. Alan Boesak and Len Hansen (Stellenbosch: Sun Media, 2009), 60.
34. Micheal Gerson, "Franklin Graham Has Played His Ultimate Trump Card," https://www.washingtonpost.com/opinions/franklin-graham-has-played-his-ultimate-trump-card/2019/06/03/22a50b18-862b-11e9-98c1-e945ae5db8fb_story.html?noredirect=on &utm_term=.a5e427af6892 (accessed May 2, 2019).
35. Boesak, *Theological Reflections*, 60.

We are called to resist these forces of empire that often seek to marginalize the poorest and most vulnerable and claims to be all powerful "based on a false premise that it can save the world through the creation of wealth and prosperity, claiming sovereignty over life and demanding total allegiance, which amounts to idolatry. Like Moloch it demands 'an endless flow of sacrifices from the poor and creation.'"[36]

The diaconal praxis of conviviality provides one such way in which we can resist at grassroots as it recognizes the interconnectedness of justice and dignity for all, based upon the understanding that Jesus was in the midst of those who were suffering from injustice and marginalization and indeed challenged the powers that be even unto death. It is also a praxis that upends the way in which power is usually practiced amongst the "least of these."[37] More often than not, in working with marginalized groups such as migrants, asylum seekers, the unemployed, vulnerable women and children and other oppressed groups, there is the tendency to respond with charitable action of the kind that "projectizes" their marginalization and poverty—leading us to once again separate them from ourselves and make them objects of charity dependent on our power to give.[38]

In reflecting on the concept of conviviality from a theological perspective we must therefore "move firmly away from the concept of working for other people, or the church for others, but rather with other people "– the church with others."[39] Addy further emphasizes that we need to

> move away from simply well-meaning actions for other needy people towards sharing life, based on empathy, reciprocity and presence... seeking conviviality implies that openness to the 'other' is a condition for our faithful Christian living as persons or as congregations. The people of God are those who can work with the marginalized other without wanting to dominate.[40]

This action works against the second aspect of exclusion as identified by Volf: "Second, exclusion can entail erasure of separation, not recognizing the other as someone who in his or her otherness belongs to the pattern

---

36. Boesak, *Theological Reflections*, 60. See also Accra Document (paragraph 10).

37. Addy, *Seeking Conviviality*, 20.

38. Nadine Bowers Du Toit, "The Elephant in the Room: The Need to Re-Discover the Intersection between Poverty, Powerlessness and Power in 'Theology and Development' Praxis," *HTS Teologiese Studies/Theological Studies* 72 (2016), 1–9 a3459, http://dx.doi.org/10.4102/hts.v72i4.3459.

39. Addy, "Seeking Conviviality—A New Core Concept for the Diaconal Church," 19.

40. Addy, "Seeking Conviviality—A New Core Concept for the Diaconal Church," 19.

of interdependence. The other then emerges as an inferior being who must either be assimilated by being made like the self or subjugated to the self."[41]

It recognizes that "we too are needy, with self-sufficiency giving away to solidarity... we are all beggars."[42] This relates to the call for interdependence within the notion of conviviality as conceptualized by Illich and also links to the African notion of Ubuntu—"I am because we are," *muntu ngumuntu ngabantu*. My humanity is tied to yours and, therefore, exclusion and inequality is not an option. The oppression of Empire through assimilation and subjugation of those deemed inferior by the system cannot stand where my humanity is bound to the so called other. My wealth and prosperity and that of the earth is bound up in relation to you—and we are called to work together for the good life. Conviviality also calls for interdependent solidarity in standing against the forces of Empire to "stand where God stands" (Belhar Confession, Article 4) "namely against injustice and with the wronged; that in following Christ the church must witness against all the powerful and privileged who selfishly seek their own interests and thus control and harm others."[43] Simangaliso Khumalo points out that part of practicing Ubuntu is that "we take sides with those that are in need, we support strangers by sharing our humanity with them and thus restoring their own humanity in the process."[44] In diaconal praxis that acknowledges the need for a pilgrimage of justice and peace, convivial diaconal praxis also seeks to confront the economic and political power structures that produce injustice. Seeking conviviality, therefore, not only offers an alternative vision for society and informs practice, but also offers a kind of prophetic critique of "present structures which obstruct convivial life together."[45] Such critique in certain instances could be viewed as polarizing and risky, but confronting power for the sake of the other makes moral demands.

5.3 CONVIVIALITY AS LIFE TOGETHER

As I wrote this article, our Muslim community was celebrating Eid and I reflected on the notion of hospitality through what we in the Cape

---

41. Volf, *Exclusion and Embrace*, 67.

42. Erik Herrmann, "Compassion, Mercy, and Diakonia," *Concordia Journal* 37 (2001), 270–2, 272.

43. *Confession of Belhar*, 1986, https://kerkargief.co.za/doks/bely/CF_Belhar.pdf.

44. Simangaliso Khumalo, "Ubuntu as an Asset for the Church in the Context of Migration and Interculturality," in *Pluralisation and Social Change: Dynamics of Lived Religion in South Africa and in Germany*, eds. Lars Charbonnier, Johan Cilliers, Mattias Moder, Cas Wepener and Birgit Weyel (Berlin: De Gruyter, 2018), 157–172, 161.

45. Tony Addy, "Populism, Sustainability and Economics," paper presented at CEC Peace Conference, Paris September 2019.

call the 'Boeka table.' This is a long table often set on the streets of communities and where everyone in the community is invited to break the fast with the Muslim community during the month of Ramadan. An act, which in one community riddled by gangsterism and poverty, was said to bring a cease fire of warring gangs.[46] Conviviality as "the sociable pleasure of people coming together and enjoying conversation and discussion in a relaxed manner, not under any constraints sharing a meal. Conviviality, therefore, relates to friendly dealings and also to relationships unconstrained by organizations or technology."[47] In sharing meals and life together, there is also an element of the potential for life giving fun—of sharing cultures through the adventure of food and drink. A foretaste of the feast table set for all. I was particularly encouraged by a young Dutch Reformed Church (DRC)[48] Minister in the central city and a minister of the oldest DRC church in South Africa—still for many a symbol of the way in which state and church oppressed people of color—has met for meals and meetings with the Muslim community (most of whose ancestors were the oppressed slaves and victims of Apartheid supported by this denomination) in the wake of the New Zealand and Sri Lankan terrorist attacks[49] in 2019, to build community. His clear commitment to Christ and openness to fellow citizens is to be admired. While some in the denomination felt that he was syncretic and have even instituted church polity complaints against him, these convivial actions by Muslims and Christians in the city go a long way towards promoting *shalom* in our city.[50]

The notion of hospitality is closely tied to that of conviviality, but Addy notes that while "a hospitable attitude may be a precursor to conviviality … it still implies that the one offering hospitality defines the terms of the relationship. If one is a guest one is expected to leave and if one stays and becomes a member of the community, hospitality in its original meaning ends!"[51] Addy is, here, possibly referring to the kinds of hospitality that "keep people needy strangers while fostering an illusion of relationship and connection. It both disempowers and

---

46. Dan Meyer, "Gangs Down Weapons as Thousands Gather to Break Fast in Manenberg," https://www.timeslive.co.za/news/south-africa/2019-05-27-gangs-down-weapons-as-thousands-gather-to-break-fast-in-manenberg/ (accessed May 23, 2019).

47. Addy, *Seeking Conviviality*, 4.

48. This denomination is renowned for its support of the Apartheid state during that era.

49. The Sri Lankan attacks on Christian churches were perpetrated by an extremist Muslim group, while the New Zealand attacks were on a mosque, initiated by a white supremacist.

50. This has been documented on the minister's own Facebook page and in the South African Afrikaans press.

51. Addy, *Seeking Conviviality*, 19.

domesticates guests while it reinforces the hosts power, control and sense of generosity."[52] Conviviality as life together invites the kind of hospitality that recognises these power dimensions: "if we are hospitable, we can welcome the stranger and maybe learn something, it may change us or not. If we work for conviviality, we do not reckon with the 'other' leaving and therefore we have to live together."[53]

An initiative in my home city of Cape Town, one of the initiatives that stands out as a local congregation's engagement in crossing boundaries of power, race and class in a convivial manner has been the St Peters Community Supper. St Peters is an Episcopal Church situated near the inner city, which hosts what they call a community supper each week, which brings together church members and street people from the surrounding areas for a meal of equals. Each week between 80–120 people come together to eat a meal.[54] A recent PhD by an Anglican priest on the supper argues that during colonial times and Apartheid "we had no shared rights and no shared human identity" and that "ethnocentrism, or our status as oppressor or oppressed precluded a shared human identity," but that "these former categories are being erased, or certainly blurred at the Supper as people share a meal."[55] He notes that while this is not instantaneous, one of the values of the meal is openly stated as 'we work at equalizing power'—this is not a charitable meal for the homeless, but rather a meal of equals where they "become neighbors and friends by hearing each other's stories" and sharing the love of Jesus.[56] Respondent P11 says, "what I appreciate mostly of the community dinners that for the hour that I am here then I am human... there are people who are interested in me" [P11:2].[57] He also notes in his study the need for privileged white people to stop "claiming an 'innocence' and an unawareness of what happens when white people position themselves in a space"—in drawing on Boesak's earlier work over 40 years ago—he calls on them to make a "deliberate effort is to be made to eschew innocence and give power away."[58] To be in terms of Philippians 2—kenotic/ self-emptying. Living together, often requires

---

52. Catherine Pohl, *Making Room: Recovering Hospitality as Christian Tradition* (Grand Rapids: Eerdmans, 1999), 120.

53. Addy, "Seeking Conviviality—A New Core Concept for the Diaconal Church," 6.

54. Benjamin Aldous, *Towards an Assessment of Fresh Expressions of Church in ACSA (The Anglican Church of Southern Africa) through an Ethnographic Study of the Community Supper at St Peters Church in Mowbray, Cape Town* (PhD in Practical Theology, University of Stellenbosch, 2018), 102.

55. Aldous, *Fresh Expressions of Church*, 161.
56. Aldous, *Fresh Expressions of Church*, 162.
57. Aldous, *Fresh Expressions of Church*, 162.
58. Aldous, *Fresh Expressions of Church*, 165.

that we empty ourselves of our prejudices and blind spots and expose ourselves to others worlds and ways of being and doing in the world. For South Africans (and perhaps in many other contexts) at least, this is one of the first steps towards less toxic intergroup relations.

In concluding this article, it is fitting to end with the Eucharist, because what greater symbol remains as challenge to life together? Addy notes that:

> In the Eucharist we express gratitude for the food and drink we have to share—and implicitly for the work of those who produced it. But we share equally, which is a powerful symbol contrary to the usual pattern of sharing resources in everyday life. It is not surprising that the Eucharist is the central act of the Christian liturgy, because it makes visible our conviviality with each other and with God in Christ. We recognize that God is present in the world and active with all people and we are invited through the Eucharist to share the liturgy after the liturgy in which we re-enact the symbolism concretely in compassion for the other.[59]

In polarizing times, we are challenged to share the liturgy after the liturgy— to share the grace we have received in concrete and sacrificial ways. I wonder, coming from a country where Sunday is the most segregated time of the week,[60] how our understandings of Eucharist can draw us into convivial sharing of life together across lines of class and culture?

6. CONCLUSION

The title of this paper considers the question of whether conviviality can indeed 'trump' polarization. The answer to this question is not simple or unnuanced, more especially in light of some of the 'deep cleavages' identified in society, but it is hoped that an interpretation of conviviality which challenges exclusion, invites reciprocity and power sharing and seeks the notion of 'life together' could go some way towards engaging these divisions. Perhaps because I am a Pentecostal, I would like to end this article by arguing that living in conviviality requires the creativity and empowerment of the Spirit. To live 'con-vivier' is not easy—it requires courage to acknowledge our own perspectives as limited, to

---

59. Addy, *Seeking Conviviality*, 20.
60. This was famously quoted by Martin Luther King jnr. with reference to America during the civil rights era. Cf. Eddie van der Borght, "Sunday Morning—The Most Segregated Hour: On Racial Reconciliation as Unfinished Business for Theology in South Africa and Beyond. Inaugural Lecture Delivered upon Accepting the Position of VU University Amsterdam Desmond Tutu Chair Holder in the Areas of Youth, Sports and Reconciliation, at the Faculty of Theology of VU University Amsterdam on 7 October 2009," https://research.vu.nl/ws/portalfiles/portal/2632701/Oratie+Borght.pdf (accessed March 8, 2020).

engage power and to seek the shalom of our world. The challenges of an increasingly VUCA world, in which we see the rise of populism, fear of the 'other,' growing climate change due to extractive capitalism and pressing marginalization of the most vulnerable in our society as markers of a polarizing global world perhaps calls to mind the chaos at creation. We as the church will need the power and creativity of the Spirit to hover over us as we seek the fullness of God's shalom in polarizing times.

BIBLIOGRAPHY

Addy, Tony. *Seeking Conviviality... The Art and Practice of Living Together: A New Core Concept for Diaconia*. Český Těšín: Interdiac, 2017.

Addy, Tony and Sirto, Ulla. "Conviviality as a Vision and Approach for a Diaconal Society," In *International Handbook on Ecumencial Diakonia*, eds. Godwin Ampony, Martin Buscher, Beate Hoffmann, Felicite Ngnintedem, Dennis Solon and Dietrich Werner, 399–411. Oxford: Regnum, 2021.

Addy, Tony. "Seeking Conviviality—A New Core Concept for the Diaconal Church." In *The Diaconal Church*, eds. Stephanie Dietrich, Kari Karsrud Korslien, Kjell Nordstokke and Knud Jørgensen, 158–170. Oxford: Regnum Books, 2019.

Addy, Tony. "Populism, Sustainability and Economics." paper presented at CEC Peace Conference, Paris September 2019.

Aldous, Benjamin. *Towards an Assessment of Fresh Expressions of Church in ACSA (The Anglican Church of Southern Africa) through an Ethnographic Study of the Community Supper at St Peters Church in Mowbray, Cape Town*. PhD diss., University of Stellenbosch, 2018.

Boesak, Alan. "Theological Reflections of Empire." In *Globalisation: The Political of Empire, Justice and the Life of Faith*, eds. Alan Boesak and Len Hansen, 59–72. Stellenbosch: Sun Media, 2009.

Borght, Eddie van der. "Sunday Morning—The Most Segregated Hour: On Racial Reconciliation as Unfinished Business for Theology in South Africa and Beyond. Inaugural Lecture Delivered upon Accepting the Position of VU University Amsterdam Desmond Tutu Chair Holder in the Areas of Youth, Sports and Reconciliation, at the Faculty of Theology of VU University Amsterdam on 7 October 2009." Accessed March 8, 2020. https://research.vu.nl/ws/portalfiles/portal/2632701/Oratie+Borght.pdf

Bowers Du Toit, Nadine. "The Elephant in the Room: The Need to Re-Discover the Intersection between Poverty, Powerlessness and Power in 'Theology and Development' Praxis," *HTS Teologiese Studies/Theological Studies* 72 (2016), 1–9, http://dx.doi.org/10.4102/hts.v72i4.3459.

Boum, Aomar. "The Performance of Convivencia: Communities of Tolerance and the Reification of Toleration." *Religion Compass* 6:3 (2012): 174–184.

Brodie, Nechama. "Are White Afrikaners Really Being Killed Like Flies?" Accessed May 2, 2019. https://africacheck.org/reports/are-white-afrikaners-really-being-killed-like-flies/.

Fea, John. "How Evangelical Leaders Surrounded Clinton During Last Presidential Impeachment Process." Accessed March 8, 2020. https://www.washingtonpost.com/religion/2019/09/27/how-evangelical-leaders-surrounded-clinton-during-last-presidential-impeachment-process/.

Gerson, Micheal. "Franklin Graham Has Played His Ultimate Trump Card." Accessed May 2, 2019. https://www.washingtonpost.com/opinions/franklin-graham-has-played-his-ultimate-trump-card/2019/06/03/22a50b18-862b-11e9-98c1-e945ae5db8fb_story.html?noredirect=on&utm_term=.a5e427af6892.

Gouws, Nico. "SA Most Unequal Country in World: Poverty Shows Apartheid's Enduring Legacy." Accessed May 3, 2019. https://www.timeslive.co.za/news/south-africa/2018-04-04-poverty-shows-how-apartheid-legacy-endures-in-south-africa.

Herrmann, Erik. "Compassion, Mercy, and Diakonia." *Concordia Journal* 37 (2001): 270–2.

Illich, Ivan. *Tools for Conviviality*. London: Marion Boyars, 2009.

Iyengar, Shanto, Gaurev Sood and Yphtach Lelkes. "Affect, Not Ideology: A Social Identity Perspective on Polarization." *Public Opinion Quarterly* 76:3 (2012): 405–431.

Karrim, Azzarah. "Mngxitama's Comments Inciting People to Take Up Arms and Start Killing People Says Afriforums Roets." Accessed May 2, 2019. https://www.news24.com/SouthAfrica/News/mngxitamas-comments-inciting-people-to-take-up-arms-and-start-killing-people-says-afriforums-roets-20191113.

Khumalo, Simangaliso. "Ubuntu as an Asset for the Church in the Context of Migration and Interculturality." In *Pluralisation and Social Change: Dynamics of Lived Religion in South Africa and in Germany*, eds. Lars Charbonnier, Johan Cilliers, Mattias Moder, Cas Wepener and Birgit Weyel, 157–172. Berlin: De Gruyter, 2018.

Kim, Yonghuan. "Does Disagreement Mitigate Polarisation? How Selective Exposure and Disagreements Affect Political Polarisation." *Journalism and Mass Communication Quarterly* 92:4 (2015), 915–937.

Klerk, Leo de. *Political Polarisation in post-Apartheid South Africa: A Case Study on Institutional Design, Race and Politics in South Africa from 1994–2016*. (Master Thesis: University of Utrecht, 2016).

Levinas, Emmanuel. *Emmanuel Levinas: Basic Philosophical Writings*, eds. Adriaan Peperzak, Simon Critchley and Robert Bernasconi. Indiana: Bloomington, 1996.

Meiring, Tiaan, Catherine Kannemeyer and Elanri Potgieter. *The Gap between Rich and Poor: South African Society's Biggest Divide Depends on Where You Think You Fit In*. SALDRU: Working Paper Series Number 220 (2018).

Meyer, Dan. "Gangs Down Weapons as Thousands Gather to Break Fast in Manenberg." Accessed May 23, 2019. https://www.timeslive.co.za/news/south-africa/2019-05-27-gangs-down-weapons-as-thousands-gather-to-break-fast-in-manenberg/.

Morais, Sheldon. "What the Numbers Tell Us About the General Elections." Accessed June 1, 2019. https://www.news24.com/elections/news/2019-vs-2014-what-the-numbers-tell-us-about-the-general-elections-20190512.

National Action Plan to Combat Racism, Racial Discrimination, Xenophobia and Related Intolerance (2016-2021) (Draft for public consultation: South African Government, 2016), 23, https://www.gov.za/sites/default/files/gcis_document/201903/national-action-plan.pdf

Pohl, Catherine. *Making Room*: *Recovering Hospitality as Christian Tradition*. Grand Rapids: Eerdmans, 1999.

Schoeman, Jakobus. "South African Religious Demography: The 2013 General Household Survey." HTS *Teologiese Studies/Theological Studies* 73.2 (2017). https://doi.org/10.4102/hts.v73i2.3837.

Smith, Amy, Ryan Lloyd. "Top Pentecostal Leaders Supported the Far Right in Brazil's Presidential Campaign." Accessed May 4, 2020. https://www.vox.com/mischiefs-of-faction/2018/10/8/17950304/pentecostals-bolsonaro-brazil.

Volf, Miroslav. *Exclusion and Embrace*: *A Theological Exploration of Identity, Otherness and Reconciliation*. Nashville: Abingdon, 1996.

Vosloo, Robert. "Traumatic Memory, Representation and Forgiveness: Some Remarks in Conversation with Antjie Krog's Country of My Skull." In *In die Skriflig* 46 (2015): 1–7.

Wykstra, Ken. *The Myth of Equality*: *Uncovering the Roots of Injustice and Privilege*. Illinois: Intervarsity, 2017.

Digital Editors, "South African Election Results," https://www.thesouthafrican.com/news/2019-south-africa-election-results-national-provincial-all-votes/.

CHAPTER 2
RE-FORMING THE CONVERSATION AS A RESPONSE TO POLARIZATION: A CASE STUDY EXPLORATION OF THE DALLAS STATEMENT
Thandi Soko-de Jong

> Love those you disagree with.
> Wish them the very things you wish for yourself,
> Wish them the fullness of life.
>   ANON.

1. INTRODUCTION

Polarization is not new. It manifests itself in society in different ways over time and space. In recent years, the socially connective power of the internet has facilitated unprecedented exchanges between people. But with no mechanism to moderate these exchanges, some have used digital media[1] as a platform to further intensify polarization with devastating consequences. Most terrorists, for example, now rely on social media to recruit new members, disseminate their ideologies and broadcast their crimes.[2] Considering this changing landscape of polarization; this chapter aims to respond to the question this book seeks to address: *What is the church's role in these times of polarization*? It does so by, firstly, narrowing the question down to the context of our shared Reformed tradition and examining how some among us have used digital media to fuel polarization today. Secondly, it shows that divisive online activity can reflect our fragmented Reformed

---

1. "Digital media refers to audio, video, and image content that has been encoded. Encoding content involves converting audio and video input into digital media formats. Typically, this includes social networking sites, website advertisements, blogs, vlogs, and podcasts." Megha Shah, "Traditional Media vs. New Media: Which is Beneficial," *Tech Funnel*, https://www.techfunnel.com/martech/traditional-media-vs-new-media-beneficial/.

2. See, for example, Gabriel Weimann, *New Terrorism and New Media* (Washington: Commons Lab of the Woodrow Wilson International Center for Scholars, 2014), http://www.wilsoncenter.org/publication/newterrorism-and-new-media.

communities. Thirdly, at the conclusion of the chapter I will suggest that we "re-form" the status quo by more intentionally moving away from polarized exchanges to a more inclusive exchange of knowledge, ideas and experiences that reflect the rich diversity of our Reformed Christian family.

In what follows, I will focus on a distinct strand of Reformed expression, the Reformed Evangelical tradition. This paper applies the term "Reformed Evangelical" to describe denominations and congregations that combine Evangelical doctrines such as baptism by immersion[3] and personal salvation; with the five points of Calvinism,[4] also known as TULIP.[5] I have some affiliation with this tradition as I was a member of a Southern Baptist Convention missionary-founded church when I lived in my home country, Malawi. With that in mind, I will present a case study that shows how Reformed tradition can be a catalyst for polarization because of its tendency to privilege the voices of the powerful over marginalized voices. This will be followed by a discussion that recommends *re-forming* dialogue as a possible contribution to defusing polarization. Particularly between voices whose knowledge, ideas and life experiences are markedly different.

The paper will discuss as a case study the *Statement on Social Justice and the Gospel* (also known as the Dallas Statement). The Statement was published in the United States of America in 2018. It is a unique document that, on the one hand, reflects the fact that Reformed and (for example) Evangelical-theology does have common ground. On the other hand, it shows that faith communities can build their identity based on their strong opposition to others, rather than searching for unity and catholicity.[6] The latter is a factor that can contribute to polarization by emphasizing an opposition between a faith community's values and those of groups it perceives as dangerous and a threat to its survival.[7]

Before delving into discussing the theory of polarization in detail, let us first note its definition here briefly. Polarization occurs when two (or more) groups of people are driven apart by opposing views, beliefs, ideologies, fears, etcetera. According to Pieter Vos, this is "often

---

3. See for example the congregation under discussion in this paper, Grace Community Church's explanation: Grace Community Church, "Frequently Asked Questions about Baptism," https://www.gracechurch.org/membership/posts/859 (accessed February 12, 2019).

4. See for example: Grace Community Church, "What we Teach,", https://www.gracechurch.org/about/distinctives/what-we-teach (accessed February 12, 2019).

5. TULIP typically refers to: total depravity (based on Genesis 3), unconditional election (predestination), limited atonement (not all will be saved), irresistible grace, and perseverance of the saints (sanctification).

6. Pieter Vos, "Introduction," 3.

7. Vos, "Introduction," 4–5.

motivated by a longing for a strong and fixed (group) identity, which is constructed as being in contrast with the (attributed) identity of the other group."[8] We see this among Christian communities in the tendency to define ourselves in opposition to other Christians.[9] Examples include the opposition between orthodox/liberal, the so-called mainline/evangelical, and conservative/progressive etcetera binaries. Against this background, this chapter aims to call attention to the dynamics that exploit such oppositions and fuel polarization and to suggest that the worldwide church's calling in times of polarization includes addressing those dynamics head-on in order to better promote unity and catholicity. Thus, we now turn our discussion to the dynamics that undergird polarization as described by Bart Brandsma.

1.1 BART BRANDSMA'S THEORY OF POLARIZATION

Brandsma describes polarization as a social process that begins simply with a thought construct of "us" and "them." It is then shaped by five agents: the "pushers," the "joiners/recruits," the "silent," the "bridge builders," and the "scapegoats."[10] Pushers, according to Brandsma, are public influencers whose purpose is to affirm a group's position on an issue by making opposing groups appear suspicious or dangerous. He adds that pushers solidify their influence by amassing "joiners/recruits." Recruits are members of the public that have been successfully persuaded into believing that the only viable option for supporting their cause and ensuring its success is to join a pusher's political and/or ideological platform. The "silent," on the other hand, are the "unrecruited" members of society whose position ranges from indifference, neutrality to nuanced thinking about the issues that the "pushers" have framed into a "black-and-white" narrative.[11] The "bridge builders" are those who, with usually the best intentions, try to promote dialogue, understanding, and harmony between opposing "pushers" (and their "recruits"). Unfortunately, this approach may only serve to further establish the two groups as polar opposites. The "bridge builder" may even be suspected of having a hidden agenda or perhaps taking sides. Finally, the "scapegoats" are the target or perceived threat that the pushers identify as dangerous to their cause. The "scapegoat" is usually from the "silent" or "bridge builder" groups.

In light of how these five play a role in how polarization operates

---

8. Vos, "Introduction," 1.
9. Vos, "Introduction," 7–9.
10. Bart Brandsma, *Polarisatie: Inzicht in de Dynamiek van Wij-Zij Denken*. Schoonrewoerd: BB in Media, 2016, translated as *Polarisation: Understanding the Dynamics of Us versus Them*. See also: https://www.polarisatie.nl.
11. Brandsma, *Polarisation*, inside of front cover.

in society, Brandsma highlights the problematic role of traditional media.[12] He points out that the media has played a significant role in the growing public profiles of pushers. He argues that it is the regular and prominent presence of polarization pushers in news cycles that has further cemented their success in digital media. Therefore, he argues that traditional media must take the responsibility of defusing polarization by widening coverage to include equally the overlooked perspectives from members of the public that have not yet been recruited into one camp or the other. He explains that traditional media can potentially re-introduce much-needed nuance to "hot button" issues and lead to more constructive public engagement that defuses polarization early. In my view, this approach is a helpful step, however, it does not leave room to consider that it may not be in the interest of traditional media to defuse polarization entirely, so long as the adage that "bad news sells better than good news"[13] remains in force. However, it is in the direct interest of the church, defined as all followers of Christ, to defuse polarization because as part of our "call to be witnesses to Christ by demonstrating his love and concern for the world"[14] and not willing participants in the status quo of divisiveness that sows hatred, fear and violence. Therefore, this is an important conversation for the church to have as a stakeholder in society alongside the media and all who are making efforts to address polarization in various contexts around the world.

Taking this a step further, the task of the church and theology is to consciously avoid being limited to the role of the "bridge builder." Rather, as argued previously by Vos,[15] the core task includes practicing critical self-reflection in light of scripture and tradition in order to seek to understand the meaning of the Christian faith and the church with regard to conflicts and processes of polarization. Therefore, the task of the church and theology is to seek to understand one's own faith tradition (and its implications) with regard to attitudes towards life, conflicts, and how to deal well with them. Thus, in a context of polarization, this approach can contribute to a better praxis of *being* church. In other words, the church's calling is to actively pursue and apply what it means to be a community of believers in a context of polarization by "being a

---

12. "Traditional media refers to mediums that are part of our culture for over half a century. These forms include television, radio, print advertisements, and billboards." Shah, "Traditional Media vs. New Media."

13. Maria Arango-Kure, Marcel Garz and Armin Rott, "Bad News Sells: The Demand for News Magazines and the Tone of Their Covers." *Journal of Media Economics* 27:4 (2014), 199–214, https://doi.org/10.1080/08997764.2014.963230.

14. "Missio Dei and the Mission of the Church," *Wycliffe Global Alliance*, https://www.wycliffe.net/more-about-what-we-do/papers-and-articles/missio-dei-and-the-mission-of-the-church.

15. Vos, "Introduction," 10.

community gathered around Christ which practices a Christ-like attitude in dealing with conflict and polarization."[16] With this in mind, let us now apply Brandsma's theory to our case study.

1.2 BRANDSMA'S THEORY AND THE CALLING OF THE CHURCH IN TIMES OF POLARIZATION

Brandsma's theory of the dynamics of polarization is useful for examining the case study in the sections that follow. It guides how we can identify polarized dynamics. Needless to say, the intention is not to attack the Dallas Statement's signers. Rather, this exploration aims to show how churches and theologies contribute to polarization. Thus, for the case study, it is important to note that the signers of the Statement are located in a political/ideological environment where some of the main "pushers" that influence public discourse on polarizing issues are arguably right-wing and left-wing pundits. These include politicians, academics, news corporations and social media influencers divided primarily along the *Republican* (political right) versus *Democrat* (political left) dichotomy.[17] Regarding our case study that takes place in the context of US Reformed Evangelicalism, right and left-wing ideologies impact it in different ways. Moreover, the case study is impacted by the global phenomenon of the so-called "culture wars,"[18] that pit conservative values against liberal values and thus limit dialogue between the two sides.[19] One of the outcomes of culture wars is the tendency to politicize academic/scientific enterprise to benefit either of the two sides.[20]

Relating this dichotomy back to the US Reformed Evangelical context of our case study, we see that some communities that find themselves divided on these grounds seem to respond to polarization by paying close attention to some fundamental, theological principles. Among these is the Reformed principle[21] of *sola scriptura* (scripture alone).[22] Thus, some who make this option apply *sola scriptura* to (most) matters

---

16. Vos, "Introduction," 10.

17. See Matthew Levendusky, *The Partisan Sort: How Liberals Became Democrats and Conservatives Became Republicans* (Chicago: University of Chicago Press, 2009).

18. See Yvonna S. Lincoln and Gaile S. Cannella, "Qualitative Research, Power, and the Radical Right," *Qualitative Inquiry* 10:2 (2004), 175–201, https://doi.org/10.1177/1077800403262373.

19. Lincoln and Cannella, "Qualitative Research, Power, and the Radical Right."

20. See for example Daniel K. Williams, *God's Own Party: The Making of the Christian Right* (New York: Oxford University Press, 2012), 12–13.

21. Najeeb G. Awad, "Should We Dispense with *Sola Scriptura*? Scripture, Tradition and Postmodern Theology," Dialog 47:1 (2008), 64–79. https://doi.org/10.1111/j.1540-6385.2008.00368.x.

22. See also Anna Case-Winters, "Sola Scriptura: Then and Now," *Reformed World* 66:1 (2016), 2–23, http://wcrc.ch/wp-content/uploads/2016/11/ReformedWorld66-1.pdf.

of doctrine that are found in the realm of public debate, including those that relate to social justice issues. This position differs, for instance, from that taken by those whose hermeneutics focus primarily on Jesus and his teachings/interpretation of the scriptures. An example is liberation theology which focuses on the liberatory aspects of Jesus' ministry in relation to social justice.[23] Another example of a differing position to note is that of those who stress the role of the Spirit in their hermeneutics. Within the Reformed tradition, an example is the work of some feminist Reformed theologians who take this position.[24] In the case of the USA, not surprisingly, conversations between these theological positions (and more) prove difficult and often reflect elements of partisan gridlock[25] in their wider context. Before exploring this further in the case study, let us briefly look at how the paper envisions engaging the two sides, along the lines of this paper's headline: *re-forming the conversation as a calling for the church in times of polarization*.

1.3 RE-FORMING THE CONVERSATION: A PALAVER HUT MODEL

An image that comes to mind for *re-forming* our conversation is the concept of the *palaver hut*. The palaver hut is a West African meeting place where people go in to deliberate (palaver) while facing each other in a circle (and not across a table) with the aim of emerging from the hut after having reached an amicable resolution. The goal is to find a way forward on an issue without having to agree on every point or being seen to have won/lost ground.[26] This is an important point for reflection in our engagement on polarizing issues, that moving forward often requires that we engage with each other without the need to force our opinions and win theological legitimacy but rather to move forward in fulfilling our calling to be witnesses to Christ's love and concern for the world as expressed in the diversity of our shared Reformed tradition. Additionally, this model also precludes the power play of a host/guest situation. When both parties enter into "palaver," this potentially guards against privileging either (a) a powerful hosting party, who may feel more entitled to setting and controlling the agenda, or (b) a powerful guest who

---

23. See Emily Swan and Ken Wilson, *Solus Jesus: A Theology of Resistance* (Canton: Front Edge Publishing, 2018).

24. Johanna W.H. van Wijk-Bos, *Reformed and Feminist: A Challenge to the Church* (Louisville: Westminster/John Knox Press, 1991), 32.

25. On the partisan gridlock in US politics, see, for example, Kenneth S. Lowande and Sidney M. Milkis, "'We Can't Wait': Barack Obama, Partisan Polarization and the Administrative Presidency," *The Forum* 12:1 (2014), 3–27, doi:10.1515/for-2014-0022.

26. Jan Paulsson, *The Idea of Arbitration*, Clarendon Law Series (Oxford: Oxford University Press, 2013), 7.

may want to manipulate the outcome. I suggest that the symbolism of the palaver hut has the potential to discourage either party from taking advantage of the other.

2. The Case Study: The Statement on Social Justice and the Gospel

2.1 Introduction

To start with, let me point out that it is not this chapter's intention to argue for social justice. Rather, by presenting the case study on the polarizing *Statement on Social Justice and the Gospel*, I hope to show the urgent need for re-forming how we engage across divided communities in Reformed tradition. Secondly, in discussing the case study, I will not rely on specific (Reformed) theologies but will draw from broad themes familiar to the Reformed tradition, such as *orthodoxy*, *justice*, *love* and *compassion*. Thirdly, for a definition of the term "social justice," I base my interpretation on its historic development beginning in the early 19th century "during the Industrial Revolution and subsequent civil revolutions throughout Europe,"

> Which aimed to create more egalitarian societies and remedy capitalistic exploitation of human labor. Because of the stark stratifications between wealthy and the poor during this time, early social justice advocates focused primarily on capital, property, and the distribution of wealth. By the mid20th century, social justice had expanded from being primarily concerned with economics to include other spheres of social life [such as] the environment, race, gender, and other causes and manifestations of inequality.[27]

From my own Malawian context, I have experienced social justice as the belief that closing the gap between the powerful and the marginalized, and taking care of the environment are important parts of practicing faith and conforming to the philosophy of *umunthu*.[28] *Umunthu*, known elsewhere on the African continent as *ubuntu*[29] is a philosophy that informs traditional belief systems that, at their best, encourage a relational and

---

[27]. Pachamama, "What is Social Justice," https://www.pachamama.org/social-justice/what-is-social-justice (accessed April 16, 2019).

[28]. See for example Kundai Chirindo, "Bantu Sociolinguistics in Wangari Maathai's Peacebuilding Rhetoric," *Women's Studies in Communication* 39:4 (2016), 442–459.

[29]. Loosely translated, Ubuntu philosophy is practiced by in most parts of the African continent. It is "at the base of the African philosophy of life and belief systems in which the peoples' daily-lived experiences are reflected." It is used by many "on a daily basis to settle disputes and conflicts at different levels on the continent and is therefore central to the idea of reconciliation" (Dani W. Nabudere, *Ubuntu Philosophy: Memory and Reconciliation* (Austin: Texas Scholar Works, 2005), 1).

inclusive society. Thus, in many cases, the successes of political and cultural leaders are measured by how many citizens they have pulled out of poverty; how much they have improved access to quality health care and other basic services, and their contribution to sustainable agricultural livelihoods.[30] We now turn to the case study to consider these interpretations.

2.2 The History and Formation of the Document

The *Statement on Social Justice and the Gospel* was first drafted in Dallas, Texas, in June 2018 and published online in September 2018. The Statement is also known as the *Dallas Statement*[31] and will here onwards be referred to simply as the Statement. It has an official list of "initial signers," made up of the allmale leaders[32] who contributed to its first drafts and there are now just over 11,000 signatures[33] with a mix of individuals and churches signing. The Statement and its effects are not only interesting for case study purposes, but it is also interesting in the wider discussion about polarization due to the growing influence of the US Evangelical community in general regarding socio-political issues in the US and around the world.

Among the initial signers, the most influential is John MacArthur and thus the Statement is often attributed to him. John Fullerton MacArthur Jr. is an American pastor and writer born in 1939. He has been the lead pastor-teacher of the large, non-denominational congregation, Grace Community Church in Sun Valley, California, since 1969.[34] MacArthur is relatively well-known for his political influence.[35] MacArthur is also known academically as the president of The Master's University in

---

30. Steve de Gruchy, "An Olive Agenda: First thoughts on a metaphorical theology of development," Johannesburg Anglican Eco-Spiritual Initiative 2010, http://jaei.org.za/wp-content/uploads/2017/10/De-Gruchy-An-Olive-Agenda.pdf (accessed March 12, 2019).

31. Southern Baptist Convention Voices (SBCVoices), "Why I Cannot and Will Not Sign the 'Social Justice and the Gospel Statement' (by Ryan Burton King)," https://sbcvoices.com/why-i-cannot-and-will-not-sign-the-social-justice-and-the-gospel-statement-by-ryan-burton-king/ (accessed March 12, 2019).

32. John MacArthur, Voddie Baucham, Phil Johnson, James White, Tom Ascol, Josh Buice, Justin Peters, Tom Buck, Jeremy Vuolo, Darrell Harrison, Michael O'Fallon, Anthony Mathenia, Craig Mitchell. See The Statement on Social Justice and the Gospel, "Initial Signers," https://statementonsocialjustice.com/ (accessed March 12, 2019).

33. As of April 30, 2019.

34. Grace Community Church, "John MacArthur," https://www.gracechurch.org/Leader/MacArthur/John (accessed February 12, 2019).

35. See for example Mark Wingfield, "MacArthur says Trump called to Support his Defiance of COVID Orders." *Baptist News Global*, https://baptistnews.com/article/macarthur-says-trump-called-to-support-his-defiance-of-covid-orders/#.X42RP9Azbcc (accessed February 12, 2019).

Santa Clarita, California,[36] and the founder of The Master's Seminary in Los Angeles.[37] As a writer, his publications include the MacArthur Study Bible, and as a broadcaster, he owns the internationally syndicated Christian teaching radio program Grace to You.[38]

In terms of its purpose, the Statement was written in the wake of four major occurrences on the US Reformed and/or Evangelical landscape,[39] namely:

a. the election of a proponent of social justice, James David (J. D.) Greear[40] as president of the Southern Baptist Convention on June 13, 2018;
b. an open letter by Beth Moore (evangelist, author and Bible teacher) calling for reformation in light of misogyny against female leadership in the Church on May 3, 2018;[41]
c. the Revoice Conference in St. Louis, which highlighted LGBTQI+ Christians (June 27–29, 2018);[42]
d. the MLK50 Conference, the commemoration of 50 years since the assassination of Martin Luther King, in Memphis, which held forums on race relations and the church, continuing talks that had been taking place online in the form of Evangelicals advocating for racial reconciliation (April 3–4, 2018).[43]

Thus, it becomes clear that the specific concern of the Statement is to challenge advocacy for social justice as gender, racial and sexuality

---

36. "TMU President Dr. John MacArthur," https://www.masters.edu/about/president (accessed March 12, 2019).

37. "John MacArthur," https://www.tms.edu/bio/johnmacarthur/ (accessed March 12, 2019).

38. Grace to You, Broadcasts, https://www.gty.org/broadcasts/radio (accessed March 12, 2019).

39. Heather Clark, "Not 'a Central Part' of the Mission? Why Statement on 'Social Justice' Is Stirring Debate Over Church's Role in Justice, Mercy," *Christian News Network* 2018, https://christiannews.net/2018/09/26/a-central-part-of-the-mission-statement-opposing-socialjustice-stirs-debate-over-role-of-the-church-in-social-issues/ (accessed March 12, 2019).

40. See, for example, J.D. Greear, "Social Justice (A Gospel Issue?), Christians in the Twoparty System, & A Powerful Senate Speech on Sexual Assault," https://jdgreear.com/blog/social-justice-gospel-issue-christians-two-party-system-powerful-senate-speech-sexual-assault/ (accessed March 12, 2019).

41. Beth Moore, "A Letter to My Brothers," https://blog.lproof.org/2018/05/a-letter-to-my-brothers.html (accessed March 12, 2019).

42. "General Sessions," https://revoice.us/events/revoice18/ (accessed March 12, 2019).

43. The Gospel Coalition, "MLK50: Gospel Reflection from the Mountain Top," https://www.thegospelcoalition.org/conference/mlk50/ (accessed March 12, 2019).

equality in the Reformed Evangelical landscape. Thus, the authors state that "the rapidity with which these deadly ideas have spread from the culture at large into churches and Christian organizations—including some that are Evangelical and Reformed—necessitates the issuing of this statement now." This is elaborated further as follows:

> Specifically, we are deeply concerned that values borrowed from secular culture are currently undermining Scripture in the areas of race and ethnicity, manhood and womanhood, and human sexuality. The Bible's teaching on each of these subjects is being challenged under the broad and somewhat nebulous rubric of concern for "social justice." If the doctrines of God's Word are not uncompromisingly reasserted and defended at these points, there is every reason to anticipate that these dangerous ideas and corrupted moral values will spread their influence into other realms of biblical doctrines and principles ...[44]

Gender, race and sexuality are already deeply polarized issues in today's world. Some pushers of polarization have established their platforms for or against these issues and in light of that, the Statement's style of prescribing their position of orthodoxy on these complex topics can be seen to be supportive of typical polarizing discourse whereby the "us" believes they are right and the "them" are wrong. Let us further explore the document, paying attention to how it is structured.

2.3 STRUCTURE

The Statement is in a confessional style of "We affirm" and "We deny"[45] statements on the following fourteen articles: *Scripture, Imago Dei, Justice, God's Law, Sin, Gospel, Salvation, The Church, Heresy, Sexuality and Marriage, Complementarianism, Race/Ethnicity, Culture and Racism*. The format for each is a heading directly followed by what the drafters affirm, followed by what they deny, and finally a list of supporting Bible texts. There is also a resources section and an appendix which provides additional information and answers questions relating to the articles.

2.4 CONTENT

The fourteen articles complement each other in arguing that it is only the preaching of the Gospel which is central to the role of the church. All social justice issues are secondary, and involvement in them depends on convictions at the congregational level or, indeed, at the personal level. To this end, all the articles are summed up in *Article I: Scripture* which

---

44. The Statement on Social Justice and the Gospel, "For the Sake of Christ and His Church," https://statementonsocialjustice.com (accessed March 20, 2019).

45. This format is similar to another Evangelical statement, the "Nashville Statement," https:// cbmw.org/nashville-statement/ (accessed March 20, 2019).

affirms that "the Bible is God's Word, breathed out by him. It is inerrant, infallible, and the final authority for determining what is true (what we must believe) and what is right (how we must live). All truth claims and ethical standards must be tested by God's final Word, which is Scripture alone." And denies that "Christian belief, character, or conduct can be dictated by any other authority, and that the postmodern ideologies derived from intersectionality, radical feminism, and critical race theory are consistent with biblical teaching." The rest of the articles affirm and elaborate on this doctrinal position. Already, the *Article I: Scripture* separates social justice from righteousness. This is in contrast with the position of others in the Reformed community. For example, the ACCRA Confession[46] or the association of the World Communion of Reformed Churches (WCRC) with the Joint Declaration on the Doctrine of Justification which affirms the interrelatedness of justice and justification by arguing:

> That both of these meanings are conveyed with the same word reflects the fact that they are profoundly related. The one who is justified by faith is called to act in a righteous way. As a consequence, the doctrine of justification cannot be seen in the abstract, divorced from the reality of injustice, oppression and violence in today's world.[47]

Furthermore, the Statement seems to fall short of making its arguments clear. For instance, it is vague about delivering its argument because of its haziness in defining any of the terms it refers to as "secular" or "social justice." Perhaps this is the Statement authors' way of arguing their points without recognizably acknowledging academic research they disagree with. Thus, it often makes broad statements; for example, the entire *Article III: Justice* does not define justice, it only states that:

> WE AFFIRM that since he is holy, righteous, and just, God requires those who bear his image to live justly in the world. This includes showing appropriate respect to every person and giving to each one what he or she is due. We affirm that societies must establish laws to correct injustices that have been imposed through cultural prejudice.
>
> WE DENY that true justice can be culturally defined or that standards of justice that are merely socially constructed can be imposed with the same authority as those that are derived from Scripture. We further deny that Christians can live justly in the world under any principles other than

---

46. World Alliance of Reformed Churches, "The Accra Confession Covenanting for Justice in the Economy and the Earth," https://www.presbyterianmission.org/wp-content/uploads/accra-confession1.pdf (accessed March 20, 2019).

47. World Communion of Reformed Churches, "Association of the World Communion of Reformed Churches with the Joint Declaration on the Doctrine of Justification," http:// wcrc.ch/wp-content/uploads/2017/10/WCRC-Association-to-JDDJ-EN.pdf (accessed March 20, 2019).

the biblical standard of righteousness. Relativism, socially constructed standards of truth or morality, and notions of virtue and vice that are constantly in flux cannot result in authentic justice.[48]

Tom Ascol, one of the Statement's contributors, responded to concerns about the Statement's tendency to use vague language by explaining that "the group wanted to also leave room for conscience and interpretation because various churches will do things differently and "would view cultural engagement in significantly different ways."[49] Thus, the reader is left to reach their own conclusions on what "intersectionality," "radical feminism," and "critical race theory" represent.

This type of approach is in contrast with statements like the Belhar Confession, a 1982 theological statement against apartheid by the Dutch Reformed Mission Church in South Africa, which did not shy away from demystifying terms, stating, for instance, that: *"the church as the possession of God must stand where the Lord stands, namely against injustice and with the wronged; that in following Christ the church must witness against all the powerful and privileged who selfishly seek their own interests and thus control and harm others."*[50] It is not a surprise then that with its clear definitions the Belhar Confession's impact was far-reaching in contributing to the fall of apartheid, in contrast to the Dutch Reformed Church in South Africa (NGK),[51] which was "tightly insulated within its own hermeneutic circle"[52] based on the fundamental principles of racial *volkstheologie*. Contrasting the Belhar Confession's approach with that of the Statement it seems that, similar to the NGK, the Statement is simply conforming to the rhetoric of polarization "pushers" (as described by Brandsma) that use abstract language to maintain a particular status quo. In this case, the status quo is the rejection of the push to eradicate sexism, homophobia and racism in church and society. Having outlined the content, let us briefly consider the divided reception

---

48. The Statement on Social Justice and the Gospel, "Introduction," 2019.

49. With the relative newness of the Statement and limited academic publications that respond to it, the paper has relied heavily on the 21-page, in-depth news piece published by Christian News Network titled "Not 'A Central Part' of the Mission? Why Statement on ''Social Justice' is Stirring Debate over Church's Role in Justice, Mercy" in which some of the writers of the statement were invited to respond to questions; and readers active in missions and outreach gave their opinions and/or posed questions. See Steve de Gruchy, "An Olive Agenda."

50. The Dutch Reformed Mission Church (DRMC), "The Belhar Confession," https://www.rca.org/belhar-confession (accessed May 1, 2019).

51. Nederduitse Gereformeerde Kerken.

52. Dunbar T. Moodie, "Confessing Remorse about the Evils of Apartheid: The Dutch Reformed Church in the Nineteen-Eighties," paper presented at the WITS Institute for Social and Economic Research (WISER) conference, Witwatersrand, October 29, 2018, https://wiser.wits.ac.za/system/files/seminar/Moodie2018.pdf (accessed May 1, 2019).

of the Statement from MacArthur's supporters before bringing these into dialogue with some key perspectives on gender, race and sexuality from Reformed and Evangelical proponents of social justice.

2.5 (Divided) Reception From Among MacArthur's Supporters

Among those, who align themselves with the Statement's conservative interpretation of Reformed Evangelicalism, are US missionaries abroad and activists, particularly anti-abortion and racial equality activists. They were quick to point out that the Statement risks being interpreted as against all forms of social justice–including what is referred to as mercy missions but also advocacy against abortion policy.[53] Mercy missions are charity interventions,[54] in which many missionaries abroad have made social justice approaches central to their mission of spreading the Gospel in order to holistically tackle the root causes of challenges they seek to address. In some cases, this involves outright political advocacy as part of their carrying out of the Great Commission (Matt. 28: 18–20)[55] in solidarity with oppressed or marginalized groups that stand to lose, for example, land, livelihoods and access to resources. But these are scenarios at the individual level. In his article, "The Reformed Identity and Mission from the Margins," Roderick Hewitt describes experiences at the macro level as the "arrested missional development" borne out of the tendency to have an "uncritical alliance with neoliberalism and neo-conservative socio-economic, political and theological discourses."[56]

Similarly, anti-abortion and racial equality activists opposed the Statement's negative view of social justice as a whole, appealing to the influence in their faith tradition of the likes of William Wilberforce and Charles Spurgeon (anti-slavery activists)[57] and the social reform activism

---

53. Trevor Johnson, https://christiannews.net/2018/09/26/a-central-part-of-the-mission-statement-opposing-social-justice-stirs-debate-over-role-of-the-church-in-social-issues / (accessed May 1, 2019).

54. Merriam Webster Dictionary.

55. Trevor Johnson, https://christiannews.net/2018/09/26/a-central-part-of-the-mission-statement-opposing-social-justice-stirs-debate-over-role-of-the-church-in-social-issues / (accessed May 1, 2019).

56. Roderick Hewitt, "The Reformed Identity and Mission from the Margins," *Stellenbosch Theological Journal* 3:2 (2017), 99–122, 99.

57. Spurgeon is quoted as saying: "I have been amused with what Wilberforce said the day after they passed the Act of Emancipation. He merrily said to a friend when it was all done, 'Is there not something else we can abolish?' That was said playfully, but it shows the spirit of the church of God. She lives in conflict and victory; her mission is to destroy everything that is bad in the land." Charles Spurgeon, "The Best War Cry," Sermon delivered on March 4th, 1883, https://www.spurgeongems.org/vols28-30/chs1709.pdf (accessed May 1, 2019).

of William Carey in India,[58] arguing that these leaders were exemplary in not separating the Gospel from their social activism. Their nuanced concerns seem to find common ground with proponents of social justice, particularly in drawing attention to the fact that the Gospel is not detached from the suffering in society. However, like the Statement, they too seem to draw the line when it comes to acknowledging the voice of Reformed Evangelical women, people of color and LGBTQI+[59] persons on these issues. For instance, in the extensive investigation by the Christian News Network into responses to the Statement from this faith community published in September 2018, the examples of social justice that are highlighted are male, European and heterosexual.[60] As such, they do not refer to figures like Martin Luther King, a Black Baptist leader (regarding anti-racism) or, in the case of abortion, the reflections of Rachel Held Evans, a woman whose views on the topic are rooted in the Evangelical tradition.[61] Rather, on this point, they seem to share the Statement's denial of social justice's challenge to the gender, sexuality and racial status quo they accept, as implied by Baptist missionary Trevor Johnson's[62] reduction of social justice to charitable works as follows:

> Christians are to always be striving for justice ... it's just that "modern 'social justice' is not the same as true biblical justice ... the Church has always worked for justice and missionaries have always defended the rights of the poor and needy. Let's defend the gospel, yes, but let's remember that this gospel leads to action![63]

---

58. Brian K. Pennington, *Was Hinduism Invented? Britons, Indians, and the Colonial Construction of Religion* (Oxford: Oxford University Press, 2005), 42.

59. This initialism is an umbrella term for people who identify as Lesbian, Gay, Bisexual, Trans (transgender, trans woman, trans man), Queer, Intersex and all other sexualities that are not cisgender and heterosexual.

60. Namely William Carey, Charles Spurgeon, R.C. Sproul, William Wilberforce, https://christiannews.net/2018/09/26/a-central-part-of-the-mission-statement-opposing-socialjustice-stirs-debate-over-role-of-the-church-in-social-issues/ (accessed May 1, 2019).

61. Her pragmatism is not limited to the progressive/conservative binary, she tackles a wide range of moral and social justice topics that span the spectrum of progressive and conservative discourse(s). See, for example, her response to John Piper on patriarchy, Rachel Held Evans, "Patriarchy Doesn't 'Protect' Women: A Response to John Piper," https://rachelheldevans.com/blog/why-progressive-christians-should-care-about-abortion-gosnell (accessed May 1, 2019).

62. US Baptist missionary in Indonesia with Heartcry Missionary Society. His biography is available on http://www.heartcrymissionary.com/trevor-johnson (accessed May 1, 2019).

63. Phil Johnson, https://christiannews.net/2018/09/26/a-central-part-of-the-mission-statement-opposing-social-justice-stirs-debate-over-role-of-the-church-in-social-issues/ (accessed May 1, 2019).

In the interest of applying the suggestion of re-forming the conversation and Brandsma's theory of presenting diverse views as an important part of defusing polarization, I will next attempt to bring the Statement's message into conversation with feminist, LGBTQIA+ and people of color who are Reformed and/ or Evangelical leaders. In keeping with the Statement's use of the internet (a typical way of discussing polarizing issues in our times as mentioned earlier), I have selected online reflections by the ministers Rasool Berry and Emily Swan, and the late writer and speaker, Rachel Held Evans. I will start with an open letter to the Statement by Rasool Berry.[64]

3. RE-FORMING THE CONVERSATION: RESPONDING TO THE STATEMENT WITH VIEWS FROM SOCIAL JUSTICE'S (REFORMED) EVANGELICAL PROPONENTS

3.1 RASOOL BERRY

Rasool Berry is an African American Baptist teaching pastor from Brooklyn's Bridge Church with a background in Africana Studies and Sociology. His academic background seems to fit well into the "secular knowledge" camp the Statement distances itself from. He summarizes his outlook on social justice by introducing his name, Rasool, which means 'messenger' in Arabic which he relates to his passion for "communicating, especially about the Message that God is pursuing reconciliation, peace and redemption in the world through us."[65] In light of this, his open letter is a rebuttal of the Statement's description of social justice given through the lens of his own social location as an African American Baptist leader with deep knowledge and experience in the fields of sociology,[66] African American social justice issues and the role of African American Christian communities in the Civil Rights movements of the twentieth century.[67] His contribution is important because it

---

64. Rasool Berry, "An Open Letter to John MacArthur About Social Justice," https://rberryblog.wordpress.com/2018/09/07/an-open-letter-to-john-macarthur-about-social-justice/ (accessed May 1, 2019).

65. Bridge Church New York City, "Leadership," https://bridgechurchnyc.com/leadership/ (accessed May 1, 2019).

66. Berry, "Open Letter."

67. Rachel Held Evans tweeted: "Seeing lots of white Evangelicals writing (critically or skeptically) about "social justice" without even acknowledging, much less drawing from, the deep well of African American theology/biblical studies on this matter and how it has fueled Civil Rights movements past & present" (@rachelheldevans, August 18, 2018).

provides a perspective missing particularly from the Statement's discussion of race. The following is an excerpt from his open letter that captures his main arguments:

> Dear John ... recently you took aim at what you believe is the most dangerous heresy you've ever faced: the growing Christian advocacy for "social justice." I read your string of posts making the case that the Church is being lured away from the Gospel message and down a road that leads to destruction with great interest and greater disappointment. As an African American pastor who has studied and experienced this issue personally, I believe your post, and the *Statement on Social Justice* launched in tandem with it, are the actual dangers to the Church at this moment. I have taken the time to respond with as much detail as I can because I, too, love the universal Church, and I also believe in this particular moment she is in danger of falling away from a clear understanding of the Gospel in the United States. We need to talk more and do more about social justice–not less.
>
> To demonstrate your historic concern and the shared convictions between you and "black leaders," you invoked your ministry partnership[68] with a leader I respect deeply, Dr. John Perkins. You described experiencing discrimination first-hand and your awareness of the injustices in our nation. You also acknowledged that the gospel of Jesus Christ is the solution to resolve "ethnic animus." What is unclear is how you think we are to apply the gospel to the social injustices you personally witness. We know your friend's view through his own writing on the subject. *Justice is any act of reconciliation that restores any part of God's creation back to its original intent, purpose or image. When I think about justice that way, it doesn't surprise me at all that God loves it. It includes both the acts of social justice and the restorative justice found on the cross.*[69]

At the core of Berry's criticism is that MacArthur has stated before that he has personally witnessed social injustice during his partnership with African American leaders. However, the Statement is unclear about how we are to apply the gospel to the social injustices he has witnessed. Berry offers his suggestion by invoking Perkin's view that the gospel of Jesus Christ includes both the acts of social justice and restorative justice.

3.2 RACHEL HELD EVANS

Rachel Held Evans, born in 1982, renowned speaker, New York Times bestselling author, and social media influencer,[70] was, until her untimely death in early 2019, very vocal on social justice issues and Evangelicalism. Her background in conservative, non-denominational Evangeli-

---

68. John MacArthur, "Social Injustice and the Gospel," https://www.gty.org/library/blog/B180813 (accessed May 1, 2019).

69. John M. Perkins, *Dream with Me*: *Race, Love, and the Struggle We Must Win* (Grand Rapids: Baker Publishing Group, 2017).

70. Rachel Held Evans, https://rachelheldevans.com/about/.

cal tradition informed her position that I find relevant to this discussion, particularly in how she weaves together the fundamentals of Evangelical faith with a feminist rationale for social justice engagement. One example is her proposal for a more holistic approach to the abortion debate between pro-choice versus pro-life positions:

> It seems to me that Christians who are more conservative and Christians who are more liberal, Christians who are politically prolife and Christians who are politically pro-choice, should be able to come together on this and advocate for life in a way that takes seriously the complexities involved and that honors both women and their unborn children. In other words, instead of focusing all of our efforts on making "supply" [abortion] illegal, perhaps we should work on decreasing demand. And instead of pretending like this is just an issue of women's rights, perhaps we should acknowledge the very real and very troubling moral questions surrounding a voluntarily terminated pregnancy.[71]

In sum, her views on social justice and feminism hold that, although Christianity isn't simply a social justice movement, its responsibility is not an either/or choice between the Gospel message and social engagement. Rather it includes both.[72]

3.3 EMILY SWAN

Lastly, Emily Swan is an Evangelical queer writer and co-pastor at Blue Ocean Church in Ann Arbor, Michigan. Her academic background is multi-disciplinary. Apart from studying Mandarin and Amdo Tibetan languages at the university level, she also studied history and theology. Swan is a co-author (with co-pastor Ken Wilson) of the book *Solus Jesus: A Theology of Resistance*.[73] Her and Wilson's perspective, as given in this book, is relevant because it challenges a Reformed doctrine many take for granted. They argue that five hundred years ago, the Protestant Reformation claimed the Bible as the authoritative guide for Christian living and proclaimed, "*Sola Scriptura*! Only Scripture"! However, they point out that as the church continues to grow in its contextual relevance, the church is shifting back to where it should be: in Jesus, thus, *Solus Jesus*! This is based on John 1: 14, "The Word became flesh and made his dwelling among us. We have seen his glory, the glory of the one and only Son, who came from the Father, full of grace and truth"

---

71. Rachel Held Evans "Why Progressive Christians Should Care About Abortion," https://rachelheldevans.com/blog/why-progressive-christians-should-care-about-abortion gosnell (accessed May 1, 2019).

72. See Rachel Held Evans, *A Year of Biblical Womanhood* (Nashville: Thomas Nelson Publishers, 2012).

73. Emily Swan and Ken Wilson, *Solus Jesus: A Theology of Resistance* (Canton: Front Edge Publishing, 2018).

(NIV).

This position seems to affirm Karl Barth's position on Jesus Christ as the living Word to whom the words of the Bible witnesses.[74] Considering this, they sum up their contribution to the discussion of social justice and the gospel as follows:

> Our task—whether facing issues of LGBTQ+ inclusion, or care for this beautiful, fragile earth, or systemic racism or militarism—is not simply to marshal biblical texts to 'prove' this or that position. Rather, our task is to position ourselves as humble and curious followers of Jesus and to discern the way, the truth, and the life in him.[75]

Their approach does not offer a concrete answer to polarized issues that influence church and society. However, their choice to assume a humble and curious position in response to such issues helps them to avoid being "pushers" of polarization.

4. EVALUATION: IMAGINING *RE-FORMING THE CONVERSATION* AS A CALLING FOR THE CHURCH IN TIMES OF POLARIZATION

Having brought the preceding three perspectives into conversation with the Statement on Social Justice and the Gospel, let us finally and briefly imagine how the suggestion of re-forming the conversation in our tradition that was introduced above can be applied to what has emerged from this case study so far. To achieve this, I will draw a few key insights from my ongoing empirical research conducted in Malawi, which includes a focus on belief and social engagement.[76]

4.1 TCHENI PA KALANKA

Two interview respondents from my ongoing study in Malawi related how their social justice activism and their Reformed theological orientation are not mutually exclusive. Rather, they find ways to integrate both as much as possible without distorting either of them. A typical contextual model for this approach is the *tcheni pa kalanka* ethos. Although this ethos is formally held by only the Nkhoma Synod of the Church of Central Africa Presbyterian (CCAP, Malawi), its interpretation is emulat-

---

74. See Karl Barth, *Church Dogmatics I/1 The Doctrine of the Word of God*, Part 1. Translated by G.W. Bromiley (Edinburgh: T&T Clark, 2004). Also Karl Barth, *Dogmatics in Outline*, transl. by G.T. Thomson (New York: Harper & Row Publishers, 2004), 66.

75. Swan and Wilson, *Solus Jesus*, xv.

76. Thandi Soko-de Jong, "Jesus as Healer Beliefs: From Experiences of Treatable but Incurable Health Conditions" (forthcoming).

ed by many across the Malawian Reformed landscape including the two respondents/informants.

Transliterated, *tcheni pa kalanka* means, "the bicycle chain must remain on the sprocket"[77] and it means that: just as a properly working bicycle's chain must remain fixed in place while it moves forward, so should a Synod maintain strong roots in the Word of God.[78] In other words, it must, for example, engage in social praxis with the knowledge that Reformed theology has the capacity to be transformative, liberating and life-giving. In practice, this means a Synod should be willing to contribute to the conversation with transformative and liberating hermeneutics as a counterargument to the position of those who argue that scripture has nothing to do with social justice (such as the Statement). By doing so, they can potentially dissuade the latter from affirming elements of a status quo that affirms destructive, life-denying injustices. Applying the *tcheni pa kalanka* ethos must always seek to embrace dialogue using the *palaver hut* model. Particularly concerning polarized issues, taking on either the offensive or defensive position inhibits an honest, power symmetric dialogue. Rather, effort should go into each side testing their position against the scrutiny of the opposing view with the hope that each party gains a more informed understanding of the issue concerned and then, ideally, finds common ground on how to address it.[79]

How this ethos can be applied will differ from context to context. However, when applied to the informants' comments above, the ethos can describe their openness to take on board new ideas, methods and expertise that they do not have themselves without compromising their doctrinal beliefs. More importantly, it is an openness to engage with others with a twofold intention: to build more positive and prophetic social relevance and to deepen faith through critical self-reflection. As Hewitt warns: "The death of the reformed identity is therefore assured when it ends up with unquestioning certitude about issues of life and faith without being open to honest and critical engagement of the text and context."[80] One of the informants, a Presbyterian minister[81] (not from the CCAP), explained that he is both a minister and the director of the development office of a non-profit organization. In integrating his

---

77. Chatha Msangaambe, "Laity Empowerment with Regard to the Missional Task of the CCAP in Malawi," (Doctoral thesis, University of Stellenbosch, 2011), 107.

78. Phoebe F. Chifungo, "Women in the CCAP Nkhoma Synod: A Practical Theological Study of their Leadership Roles" (PhD diss., University of Stellenbosch, 2014), 2.

79. Hewitt, "Reformed Identity and Mission from Margins," 122.

80. Hewitt, "Reformed Identity and Mission from Margins," 122.

81. Name withheld. Interview I conducted in Blantyre, Malawi, February 8, 2018.

pastoral and development vocation, he follows the example of Jesus' holistic ministry as described in Luke 4: 18–19 which says, "I have been anointed to preach the good news, to heal the broken-hearted to give sight to the blind." He explains that:

> In as much as we are preaching from the pulpit, there are also practical issues that need to be addressed in our communities. I have developed the constitution for the development arm of the non-governmental organization I work for so that we can take on the issues of economy, health and other social issues as one way of equipping the church, especially my church, to empower our communities.

And on the partnership between the church and relevant experts, he noted:

> A partnership can be in different areas of expertise and from different perspectives such as formal partnerships with experts in the health sector. Also, why not have an expert speak during a church function? For instance, why not have someone who is knowledgeable about a topic pertinent to the community come in and speak to us? For example, there are many congregants who do not have access to information about diseases like cancer or mental illness and it becomes a problem as they try to manage them.

In sum, he highlights that, in order to serve communities holistically, the church must be open to receiving input from professionals with relevant knowledge on issues it seeks to address. This contrasts with the Statement that undermines bodies of knowledge which it deems secular. John MacArthur believes, for example, that:

> … by definition psychology the study of the soul is a secular, godless, unbiblical approach to analyzing humanity [and] designing solutions to their problems. But the truth is, man in his fallen condition cannot really make a completely clear and accurate assessment of the human condition.

In my view, this approach is harmful because it ignores practical, tested solutions that are in many cases beneficial to human beings. Rather, *tcheni pa kalanka*, in its openness to incorporating the efforts of other professions, seems to be a more helpful ethos for faith communities because it pursues solutions to people's real-life problems without having to compromise on matters of orthodoxy.[82] Affirming this, a Baptist exec-

---

82. For an affirmation of this approach, see for example: World Council of Churches, "Together Towards Life: Mission and Evangelism in Changing Landscapes," Geneva, September 5, 2012, https://www.oikoumene.org/en/resources/documents/commissions/mission-and-evangelism/together-towards-life-mission-and-evangelism-in-changing-landscapes, 19–21 (accessed May 1, 2019).

utive in a world mission organization[83] concluded that:

> In an ideal situation, the church should be able to seamlessly complement the efforts of professionals in different disciplines. Their training has value. Our clergy and the laity should be able to walk alongside professionals because their input can positively transform our communities at so many levels.

5. Conclusion

Using the case study of the Reformed Evangelical *Statement on Social Justice and the Gospel*, this chapter has suggested that one of the callings for the church in these times of polarization is to *re-form* our conversation. After all, Reformed theological identity is rooted in the task of taking the task of listening and reflecting seriously.[84] Thus, this paper has suggested how (a) the concept of the Palaver Hut, (b) the *tcheni pa kalanka* ethos, and (c) the contributions of knowledge, ideas and experience from those that are marginalized in discussions can be tools that potentially *re-form* how we converse, what we converse about and why we should be open to conversation. We can all benefit from understanding the perspective of an opposing view, even when we do not agree with it. In this regard, examples like Rachel Evans' rhetoric on abortion offer "better"/re-forming dialogue by challenging us to ask and address deeper questions about root causes of issues we find contentious; and thereby our actions will (hopefully) better reflect the love and wisdom of God and biblical standards of righteousness and social justice statements. This can and will ultimately defuse polarization in our spheres of influence as Christians, whose divine imperative it is to love, according to 1 John 4:7–8, "Dear friends, let us love one another, for love comes from God. Everyone who loves has been born of God and knows God."[85]

Bibliography

Arango-Kure, Maria, Marcel Garz and Armin Rott. "Bad News Sells: The Demand for News Magazines and the Tone of Their Covers." *Journal of Media Economics* 27:4 (2014):199–214. https://doi.org/10.1080/08997764.2014.963230.

Awad, Najeeb G. "Should We Dispense with Sola Scriptura? Scripture, Tradition and Postmodern Theology," *Dialog* 47:1 (2008):64–79. https://doi.org/10.1111/j.1540-6385.2008.00368.x.

---

83. Name withheld. Interview I conducted in Blantyre, Malawi, August 23, 2018.
84. Hewitt, "Reformed Identity and Mission from Margins," 122.
85. NIV.

Barth, Karl. *Church Dogmatics I/1 The Doctrine of the Word of God, Part 1*. Translated by G.W. Bromiley. Edinburgh: T&T Clark, 2004.

Barth, Karl. *Dogmatics in Outline*, transl. by G.T. Thomson. New York: Harper & Row Publishers, 2004.

Berry, Rasool. "An Open Letter to John MacArthur About Social Justice." Accessed May 1, 2019. https://rberryblog.wordpress.com/2018/09/07/an-open-letter-to-john-macarthur-about-social-justice/

Brandsma, Bart. *Polarisatie: Inzicht in de Dynamiek van Wij-Zij Denken*. Schoonrewoerd: BB in Media, 2016.

Bridge Church New York City. "Leadership." Accessed May 1, 2019. https://bridge churchnyc.com/leadership/.

Case-Winters, Anna. "Sola Scriptura: Then and Now," *Reformed World* 66:1 (2016):2–23. http://wcrc.ch/wp-content/uploads/2016/11/ReformedWorld66-1.pdf.

Chifungo, Phoebe F. "Women in the CCAP Nkhoma Synod: A Practical Theological Study of their Leadership Roles." PhD diss., University of Stellenbosch, 2014.

Chirindo, Kundai. "Bantu Sociolinguistics in Wangari Maathai's Peacebuilding Rhetoric." *Women's Studies in Communication* 39:4 (2016):442–459.

Clark, Heather. "Not 'a Central Part' of the Mission? Why Statement on 'Social Justice' Is Stirring Debate Over Church's Role in Justice, Mercy." *Christian News Network* 2018. Accessed March 12, 2019. https://christiannews.net/2018/09/26/a-central-part-of-the-mission-statement-opposing-social-justice-stirs-debate-over-role-of-the-church-in-social-issues/.

Grace Community Church's explanation: Grace Community Church. "Frequently Asked Questions about Baptism." Accessed February 12, 2019. https://www.gracechurch.org/membership/posts/859.

Grace Community Church. "What we Teach." Accessed February 12, 2019. https://www.gracechurch.org/about/distinctives/what-we-teach.

Grace Community Church. "John MacArthur." Accessed February 21, 2019. https://www.gracechurch.org/Leader/MacArthur/John.

Greear, J.D. "Social Justice (A Gospel Issue?), Christians in the Two-party System, & A Powerful Senate Speech on Sexual Assault." Accessed March 12, 2019. https://jdgreear.com/blog/social-justice-gospel-issue-christians-two-party-system-powerful-senate-speech-sexual-assault/.

Gruchy, Steve de. "An Olive Agenda: First thoughts on a metaphorical theology of development." *Johannesburg Anglican Eco-Spiritual Initiative* 2010. Accessed March 12, 2019. http://jaei.org.za/wp-content/uploads/2017/10/De-Gruchy-An-Olive-Agenda.pdf.

Held Evans, Rachel. *A Year of Biblical Womanhood*. Nashville: Thomas Nelson Publishers, 2012.

Held Evans, Rachel. "Patriarchy Doesn't 'Protect' Women: A Response to John Piper." Accessed May 1, 2019. https://rachelheldevans.com/blog/why-progressive-christians-should-care-about-abortion-gosnell.

Held Evans, Rachel. "Why Progressive Christians Should Care About Abortion." Accessed May 1, 2019. https://rachelheldevans.com/blog/why-progressive-christians-should-care-about-abortion-gosnell.

Hewitt, Roderick. "The Reformed Identity and Mission from the Margins." *Stellenbosch Theological Journal* 3:2 (2017):99–122.

Levendusky, Matthew. *The Partisan Sort: How Liberals Became Democrats and Conservatives Became Republicans*. Chicago: University of Chicago Press, 2009.

Lincoln, Yvonna S. and Gaile S. Cannella. "Qualitative Research, Power, and the Radical Right," *Qualitative Inquiry* 10:2 (2004):175–201. https://doi.org/10.1177/1077800403262373.

Lowande, Kenneth S. and Sidney M. Milkis. "'We Can't Wait': Barack Obama, Partisan Polarization and the Administrative Presidency." *The Forum* 12:1 (2014):3–27.

MacArthur, John. "Social Injustice and the Gospel." Accessed May 1, 2019. https://www.gty.org/library/blog/B180813.

Moodie, Dunbar T. "Confessing Remorse about the Evils of Apartheid: The Dutch Reformed Church in the Nineteen-Eighties." paper presented at the WITS Institute for Social and Economic Research (WISER) conference, Witwatersrand, October 29, 2018. Accessed May 1, 2019. https://wiser.wits.ac.za/system/files/seminar/Moodie2018.pdf

Moore, Beth. "A Letter to My Brothers." Accessed March 12, 2019. https://blog.lproof.org/2018/05/a-letter-to-my-brothers.html.

Msangaambe, Chatha. "Laity Empowerment with Regard to the Missional Task of the CCAP in Malawi." Doctoral thesis, University of Stellenbosch, 2011.

Nabudere, Dani W. *Ubuntu Philosophy*: *Memory and Reconciliation*. Austin: Texas Scholar Works, 2005.

Pachamama. "What is Social Justice." Accessed April 16, 2019. https://www.pachamama.org/social-justice/what-is-social-justice.

Paulsson, Jan. *The Idea of Arbitration*. Clarendon Law Series. Oxford: Oxford University Press, 2013.

Pennington, Brian K. *Was Hinduism Invented*? *Britons, Indians, and the Colonial Construction of Religion*. Oxford: Oxford University Press, 2005.

Perkins, John M. *Dream with Me*: *Race, Love, and the Struggle We Must Win*. Grand Rapids: Baker Publishing Group, 2017.

Shah, Megha. "Traditional Media vs. New Media: Which is Beneficial," *Tech Funnel*. https://www.techfunnel.com/martech/traditional-media-vs-new-media-beneficial/.

Southern Baptist Convention Voices (SBCVoices). "Why I Cannot and Will Not Sign the 'Social Justice and the Gospel Statement' (by Ryan Burton King)." Accessed March 12, 2019. https://sbcvoices.com/why-i-cannot-and-will-not-sign-the-social-justice-and-the-gospel-statement-by-ryan-burton-king/

Soko-de Jong, Thandi. "Jesus as Healer Beliefs: From Experiences of Treatable but Incurable Health Conditions." (forthcoming).

Spurgeon, Charles. "The Best War Cry." Sermon delivered on March 4th, 1883. Accessed May 1, 2019. https://www.spurgeongems.org/vols28-30/chs1709.pdf.

Swan, Emily and Ken Wilson. *Solus Jesus*: *A Theology of Resistance*. Canton: Front Edge Publishing, 2018.

The Dutch Reformed Mission Church (DRMC). "The Belhar Confession." Accessed May 1, 2019. https://www.rca.org/belhar-confession.

The Gospel Coalition. "MLK50: Gospel Reflection from the Mountain Top." Accessed March 12, 2019. https://www.thegospelcoalition.org/conference/mlk50/.

The Statement on Social Justice and the Gospel. "For the Sake of Christ and His Church." Accessed March 20, 2019. https://statementonsocialjustice.com.

Weimann, Gabriel. *New Terrorism and New Media*. Washington: Commons Lab of the Woodrow Wilson International Center for Scholars, 2014. http://www.wilsoncenter.org/publication/newterrorism-and-new-media.

Wijk-Bos, Johanna W.H., van. *Reformed and Feminist*: *A Challenge to the Church*. Louisville: Westminster/John Knox Press, 1991.

Wingfield, Mark. "MacArthur says Trump called to Support his Defiance of COVID Orders." *Baptist News Global*. Accessed February 12, 2019. https://baptistnews.com/article/macarthur-says-trump-called-to-support-his-defiance-of-covid-orders/#.X42RP9Azbcc

Williams. Daniel K. *God's Own Party*: *The Making of the Christian Right*. New York: Oxford University Press, 2012.

World Alliance of Reformed Churches. "The Accra Confession Covenanting for Justice in the Economy and the Earth." Accessed March 20, 2019. https://www.presbyterianmission.org/wp-content/uploads/accra-confession1.pdf.

World Council of Churches, "Together Towards Life: Mission and Evangelism in Changing Landscapes." Geneva, September 5, 2012. Accessed May 1, 2019. https://www.oikoumene.org/en/resources/documents/commissions/mission-and-evangelism/together-towards-life-mission-and-evangelism-in-changing-landscapes.

World Communion of Reformed Churches. "Association of the World Communion of Reformed Churches with the Joint Declaration on the Doctrine of Justification." Accessed March 20, 2019. http://wcrc.ch/wp-content/uploads/2017/10/WCRC-Association-to-JDDJ-EN.pdf.

CHAPTER 3
Retrieving the Concept of *Unio Mystica cum Christo* and Applying it to Concepts of Sexuality in a Pluralistic Postmodern Culture
Willem van Vlastuin

1. Introduction

Media attention on the untimely publication of the Dutch translation of the 'Nashville-Statement' revealed how sensitive Western culture is to pronouncements about sexuality, and how much it is polarized by them. Thoughts about sexuality do not only touch upon contemporary lifestyles, worldviews and fundamental needs, but also upon our deepest existential identity. This development coheres with changes to our authentic self. For this reason, only a few things touch and divide people, churches and societies more deeply than these issues. We see that sexual issues, much like issues about race, ethnicity, class and religion, polarize churches and societies, and thus people react by excluding identities and groups.

In this chapter, it is the existential implications related to our identity which are of most interest. Because the New Testament offers us an application of the identity in Christ to sexual life in a pre-modern context in which sexuality was also very important, perhaps the retrieval of these understandings can be made fruitful in our postmodern context. The relevance of retrieving these old interpretations of sexual life is of primary importance for the church, which may be able to act as a countermovement in contemporary society.

In this contribution, I start by investigating sexual life in our present-day culture. Next, I investigate how Paul applied finding one's identity in Christ to sexual life in the New Testament. These two investigations lead to a retrieval of Paul's application to the current cultural context.

2. SEXUALITY IN A PLURALISTIC POSTMODERN CULTURE

The history of the development of our culture is characterized by its turn towards the human subject.[1] While the pre-modern phase of our culture could be characterized by a super-personal order in which the human subject had its place, in modernity there came a clear shift. The names of Rene Descartes (1596– 1650) and Immanuel Kant (1724–1894) are significant here. Descartes broke with Aristotle's thinking about substances and put the relationship between the knowing subject and known object central.[2] Immanuel Kant continued this approach, turning more to interpreting the human subject.[3]

With this turn to the human subject came the objectification of the human being in which the human mind was understood as the result of causal processes. Some years ago, Dick Swaab published a bestseller entitled *We Are Our Brains*.[4] The suggestion made by this title is that human beings can be reduced to the summation of their brain cells. When the human cells die, the human existence ends.[5] The touching book *Homo Deus* by Yuval Noah Harari confirmed this impression, saying human thought could be reduced to mini-electric streams and that Artificial Intelligence surpassed human intelligence.[6] Words such as physicalization, mechanization, quantification and objectification were used to characterize this development.[7]

In the 1960s there were several revolts by students in the Western

---

1. Charles Taylor, *A Secular Age* (Cambridge: Harvard University Press, 2007), 146. See also his *Sources of the Self: The Making of the Modern Identity* (Cambridge: Harvard University Press, 1989), 129–136.

2. For Descartes' *ego cogito, ergo sum*, see his *Principia Philosophiae* ... (Amsterdam: Elsevier, 1677), 2.

3. For Kant's turn to the subject, compare Cornelis van der Kooi, *As in a Mirror: John Calvin and Karl Barth on Knowing God. A Diptych* (Leiden: Brill, 2005), 225–248.

4. Dick F. Swaab, *We Are Our Brains: A Neurobiography of the Brain, from the Womb to Alzheimer's*, transl. J. Hedley-Prôle (New York: Spiegel & Grau, 2014), original: Wij zijn ons brein: Van baarmoeder tot Alzheimer (Amsterdam: Contact, 2010).

5. Therefore, Bertrand Russel concluded that human life is meaningless in his *Why I Am not a Christian* which is typified by New York Public Library as one of the most influential books of the 20ᵉ century.

6. Yuval Noah Harari, *Homo Deus: A Brief History of Tomorrow* (London: Penguin Random House, 2016). According to the great physicist Stephen Hawking the primitive forms of Artificial Intelligence has been useful for humanity, but "the development of full artificial intelligence could spell the end of human race," https://www.bbc.com/news/technology-30290540 (accessed October 1, 2020).

7. Hans W. de Knijff wrote about a 'catastrophic' situation, *Tegenwoordigheid van geest als Europese uitdaging: Over secularisatie, wetenschap en christelijk geloof* (Presence of mind as a European challenge: On secularization, science and Christian faith) (Zoetermeer: Boekencentrum, 2013), 13, 15.

world.⁸ Afterwards it was concluded that these revolts were not incidental, but heralded in a new era—postmodernism. This does not mean that we abruptly went from one phase to another phase in culture. We still acknowledge the enormous value of empirical research which is characteristic of modernity.

Nevertheless, something has changed, even in science. Philosophers of science acknowledge that science is not neutral, but works within paradigms of unproven presuppositions.⁹ These presuppositions are not only academic, but also moral, political, economic and cultural. This implies that strict rationalism is decreasing and that there is a new sense that there is more than what can simply be measured. In this context, spirituality, religion and meaning receive new attention and become more relevant.

While the search for objective truth drove modernity, in our postmodern culture we are unhappy with absolute claims of truth. We shudder, in particular, when we hear moral claims made on religious grounds. Meanwhile we concentrate on the small stories of the individual human being. We speak of a re-appreciation of the individual subject.¹⁰ Perhaps we can say that the emotions and the interpretations of the individual subject are a new form of truth. We have to take each other's feelings completely seriously. In short, the shift to the human subject in postmodernity has come to a preliminary completion.¹¹

These cultural developments interacted with our understanding of sexuality. Until the mid-nineteenth century, people spoke about homosexual behavior and Sigmund Freud (1856–1939) categorized people for the first time according to their sexual orientation.¹² In the course of this century, people began to speak of homosexuality in medical and psychological terms. Carl Westphal, in 1870, was the first psychiatrist to use the word 'nature' to describe a homosexual orientation.¹³ The use of this concept soon became normal, so that

---

8. Geert Buelens, *De jaren zestig: Een cultuurgeschiedenis* (The sixties: A cultural history) (Amsterdam: Ambo, 2018).

9. Thomas S. Kuhn, *The Structure of Scientific Revolutions* (Chicago: Chicago University Press, 2012, originally published 1962).

10. Compare for the theological consequences John Webster, "The Human Person," in *The Cambridge Companion to Postmodern Theology*, ed. Kevin J. Vanhoozer (Cambridge: Cambridge University Press 2003), 219–234.

11. Brad S. Gregory speaks about 'hyperpluralism,' *The Unintended Reformation: How a Religious Revolution Secularized Society* (Cambridge: Cambridge University Press, 2012), 369. Every individual "must be the sovereign of his or her own Cartesianized universe, determining his or her own truth, making his or her own meanings, and following his or her own desires" (385).

12. Christopher Yuan, *Holy Sexuality and the Gospel: Sex, Desire, and Relationships Shaped by God's Grand Story* (New York: Penguin, 2018), 10.

13. Compare Michel Foucault, *The History of Sexuality*, 3 volumes (New York:

homosexuality became identified as a person's identity.

While the climax of the persecution of homosexuals in the bloody twentieth century was an expression of modernity that could not tolerate exceptions,[14] postmodernity led to a new interpretation of homosexuality linked to the cultural shift. Living well is no longer about living according to external moral norms and values, but about living according to our authentic selves.[15]

The need to be oneself expresses itself in the exercise of our sexuality, because our sexuality is a core aspect of our personality.[16] While the premodern human being was primarily religious and wanted to know the meaning of life, in postmodernity the religious regime has been exchanged for the sexual regime. Sexuality coheres with the meaning of life; we are our sexuality and sexuality is a determining factor of our identity.[17]

These developments led to a revolution in sexual morality.[18] Alfred Kinsey (1894–1956) can be seen as the father of sexology and, as a couple, Simone de Beauvoir and Jean Paul Sartre were role models for free love. Herbert Marcuse promoted the motto: 'Make love, not war.' When the pill was introduced in the 1960s, developments quickly followed: sexuality was separated from reproduction, the laws in the Netherlands changed, adultery was no longer a crime, and pornography and prostitution became accepted in law.

Although the emancipation of homosexuals started from the beginning of the twentieth century in the church,[19] in society the

---

Bloomsbury, 1986–1992), Vol. I, 43.

14. See also Foucault, *History of Sexuality*, Vol. I, 17–23, 33; Graham Robb, *Strangers: Homosexual Love in the Nineteenth Century* (New York: Norton, 2005), 30.

15. Charles Taylor, *The Ethics of Authenticity* (Cambridge: Harvard University Press, 1991), 29.

16. Marco Derks describes how the call to be yourself is intertwined with the call for sexual freedom in our culture, *Constructions of Homosexuality and Christian Religion in Contemporary Public Discourse in the Netherlands* (Doctoral thesis Utrecht University, 2019), 80–85.

17. The autobiographical notions of Christopher Yuan confirm this, *Holy Sexuality and the Gospel*, 8–9.

18. According to Hans Boutelier, *Het seculiere experiment: Hoe we van God los gingen samenleven* (The secular experiment: How we lived together apart from God) (Amsterdam: Boom, 2015), 108–109. Marc Cortez gave an overview of this development in the third chapter of his *Theological Anthropology: A Guide for the Perplexed* (London: T&T Clark, 2010), 41–67, especially 47–57.

19. David Bos describes the developments in evangelical, orthodox-reformed and pietistic reformed Christians in the Netherlands, "Homo-af: De opkomst van de ex-homoseksueel in Nederland" (Gay-off: The rise of the ex-gay in the Netherlands), in *Genot en gebod: Huwelijk en seksualiteit in protestants Nederland vanaf 1800*, eds. David J. Bos en John Exalto (Utrecht: KokBoekencentrum, 2019), 128–155.

breakthrough occurred in the 1960s.[20] On April 4, 2001, the Netherlands became the first country to legalize same-sex marriage.[21] Several countries followed suit and it has become the Netherland's 'best moral export product.'[22]

At the same time, it appears that the postmodern approach to sexuality involves polarization because thinkers and opinion leaders among religious movements and conservative thinkers distance themselves from, and oppose, this approach. One of the adversaries of the postmodern approach toward sexuality is Gabrielle Kuby,[23] a Roman-Catholic activist who frames the developments concerning sexuality and gender as an ideology[24] and suggests there is a conspiracy; her approach is also interpreted as anti-gender ideology. Her message is that the Western world uses the concept of emancipation to deny biological diversity between man and woman, to destroy the family and to reject sexual norms.

Apart from this ideological polarization, most homosexual people are not driven by such visions; they simply want to have a peaceful life and live according to their sexual identity. Their longings cannot be identified with our pornographic culture. At the same time, there are also people with a homosexual orientation who prefer to be heterosexual. It can be difficult for these people to maintain themselves in a culture in which sexuality has become characteristic of our identity, as they may feel pressure to 'come out' and be themselves.

---

20. David J. Bos, "'Equal Rites before the Law': Religious Celebrations of Same-Sex Relationships in the Netherlands, 1960's–1990's" (accessed October 1, 2020).

21. Boris Dittrich, *Een blauwe stoel in paars*: *Verhalen uit de Tweede Kamer* (A blue chair in purple: Stories from the Dutch parliament) (Amsterdam: Van Gennep, 2001), 73.

22. Derks refers to several thinkers and organisations who interpret gay marriage in this sense, *Constructions of Homosexuality and Christian Religion*, 19, 34–36, 95–97, 112, 150.

23. Gabrielle Kuby, *The Global Sexual Revolution*: *Destruction of Freedom in the Name of Freedom* (Kettering: Angelico Press, 2015).

24. "An ideology is a collection of normative beliefs and values that an individual or group holds for other than purely epistemic reasons. In other words, these rely on basic assumptions about reality that may or may not have any factual basis. The term is especially used to describe systems of ideas and ideals which form the basis of economic or political theories and resultant policies. In these there are tenuous causal links between policies and outcomes owing to the large numbers of variables available, so that many key assumptions have to be made. In political science, the term is used in a descriptive sense to refer to political belief systems" (Wikipedia, accessed June 7, 2019).

3. Paul's Application of Identity in Christ

Over the last years, perhaps decades, in New Testament research, in systematic theology and in the historical-theological study of Calvinism, the concepts of mystical union and participation have been analyzed from several perspectives and with several applications.[25] Paul's expression of being 'in' Christ is at the root of this research. According to his interpretation, the believer does not only believe in Christ and is saved by Him, but is saved in a unity of life with Christ which is expressed in baptism.

Several metaphors in the New Testament explain this mystical union with Christ; one of the leading ones is the union between husband and wife.[26] John uses the metaphor of the branches that are united with the vine, take succor from the vine and bear its fruit.[27] The strongest metaphor used is that of the union between head and body.[28] These metaphors imply that we cannot think of believers in isolation from Christ or vice versa. Branches without a vine and bodies without a head cannot exist. In the early church, this unity was expressed in the theologoumenon of *totus Christus* which stated that Christ was only complete in his body.[29]

---

25. For the biblical reflection on this theme, see Michael J. Thate, Kevin J. Vanhoozer, Constantine R. Campbell (eds), '*In Christ' in Paul* (Tübingen: Mohr Siebeck, 2014); for the systematic reflection, see Hans Burger, *Being in Christ: A Biblical and Systematic Investigation in a Reformed Perspective* (Eugene: Wipf & Stock, 2008). This theme provoked particular interest in reformed theology, John V. Fesko, *Beyond Calvin: Union with Christ and Justification in Early Modern Reformed Theology (1517–1700)* (Göttingen: Vandenhoeck & Ruprecht, 2012), 53–75; Julie Canlis, *Calvin's Ladder: A Spiritual Theology of Ascent and Ascension* (Grand Rapids: Eerdmans, 2010); J. Todd Billings, "United to God through Christ: Assessing Calvin on the Question of Deification," *Harvard Theological Journal* 98:3 (2005), 315–334; J. Todd Billings, *Calvin, Participation, and the Gift: The Activity of Believers in Union with Christ* (Oxford: Oxford University Press, 2008).

26. Eph. 5:22–32.

27. John 15:1–8.

28. Rom. 12:4–5; 1 Cor. 12:12–31; Eph. 4:15–16.

29. On John 5:20–23 Augustine wrote: "Let us rejoice, then, and give thanks that we are made not only Christians, but Christ," *Homilies on the Gospel of John*, NPNF1, 7:140. In the same volume we find these words: "To that flesh the Church is joined, and so there is made the whole Christ, Head and body" (462). Believers are not only Christians, but Christ. So can Christ speak through the head or through the members, *Enarrationes in Psalmos* 140, 3. In this way, the talk of the church is the talk of Christ and vice versa, *Enarrationes in Psalmos* 30.2, 4. Also Calvin could say that Christ is not complete without believers, Comm. Eph. 1:23, https://www.ccel.org/ccel/calvin/calcom41.iv.ii.v.html (accessed June 12, 2019). This interpretation of the church means that the church is not only the work of God as creation is, but is also the body of Christ, see Robert W. Jenson, *Systematic Theology*, 2 Vols (Oxford: Oxford University Press, 1997–1999), Vol. 2, 167.

In Pauline writings, we find implications of this mystical union. The mystical union with Christ is such a reality that believers are created in Christ,[30] die with Christ,[31] are crucified with Christ,[32] buried with Christ,[33] baptized into Christ,[34] raised with Christ,[35] ascended into heaven,[36] were justified in Christ,[37] glorified in Christ[38] and are sanctified in Christ.[39] This means that, in the Christ-position, the old reality has already disappeared and the new age has become a reality.[40] It also implies that union with Christ is a pneumatological reality that affects the thinking, longing, willing and the direction of love in believers.[41] Believers are daily renewed after the image of Christ.[42] Another implication is that the Christian's citizenship is primarily in heaven.[43]

One might ask whether we can speak of a Pauline concept, because the word 'concept' can give the impression that it relates to a theoretical interpretation. However, this approach misses the existential depth of the mystical union, because this union is not about an interpretation, but concerns the existential identity of the believer. For this contribution, it is important to understand the position 'in' Christ as the identity of a Christian.[44]

It is necessary to understand the existential consequence of the Christian faith. The Christian is not a 'normal' human being with a few morals and habits added on. He or she does not have a partial acceptance of Christian views; being a Christian is much more radical

---

30. Eph. 2:10.
31. Rom. 6:6.
32. Gal. 2:20.
33. Col. 2:12.
34. Rom. 6:3.
35. Rom. 6:5, Eph. 2:4, Col. 3:1. In John 5:24 we also find the comparable reality that the Christian shares the eternal life of Christ.
36. Eph. 2:6.
37. Rom. 3:24.
38. Rom. 8:30.
39. 1 Cor. 1:2.
40. 2 Cor. 5:17.
41. Gal. 5:22.
42. 2 Cor. 4:16.
43. Phil. 3:20. A striking example of a creative application of the spiritual union with Christ can be found in the Heidelberg Catechism. While the tradition before the Heidelberg Catechism acknowledged the threefold office of Christ (*munus triplex*), the Heidelberg Catechism includes the consequence and applied the offices to the Christian as well. The argument is that the Christian is 'a member of Christ by faith' and thus 'a partaker of his anointing', compare Willem van Vlastuin, "The Promise of Unio Mystica," in Arnold Huijgen (ed.), *The Spirituality of the Heidelberg Catechism: Papers of the International Conference on the Heidelberg Catechism Held in Apeldoorn* 2013 (Göttingen: Vandenhoeck & Ruprecht, 2015), 168–185, here 174–176.
44. Compare Gal. 2:19–20 and Phil. 1:21.

and existential.[45] This means that the Christian does not give Christ a particular place in his life, but just the opposite: the life of the Christian is incorporated in Christ's being and body.

Because this incorporation into Christ's reality involves the personal identity of a Christian, it touches all aspects and dimensions of life. From this point of view, the apostle develops a radical understanding of the Christian life. Being baptized in Christ implies that the believer's identity is neither Jewish nor Greek, neither bonded nor free, neither male nor female.[46] These 'natural' identities are not completely denied, but they are not essential or decisive in Christ's body. This is also true for sinful 'nature'. While Paul acknowledges the power of sin in his body,[47] he identifies believers as Christians and not as sinners.[48]

Belonging to Christ's body in a spiritual sense has huge implications for the physical body. Because the believer understands his life not as his own life, he cannot use his body according to his own wishes. We can say that a Christian has no hands, because his hands are Christ's. His ears, his tongue, his complete life is Christ's body. The believer, therefore, does not reason from his own interests in his civil life, but interprets his interests in the perspective of Christ's kingdom. Augustine's expression—that the old man uses God to enjoy the earth, while the new man uses the earth to enjoy God—is telling in this regard.[49]

The basis for this attitude is the deep conviction that Christ paid a huge ransom for the body of the believer and the believer expects his body to be glorified with the risen Christ.[50] For this reason, S. Lorenzen concluded that the resurrection of the body of the believer is implied in the image of God.[51] Only if God's grace is fulfilled in the body, is the adoption fulfilled.[52] At the same time, we can say that the beginnings of this fulfilment are already present. By the power of the Spirit, believers are already drawn into this eschatological future, so that they, by the Spirit as the first fruit of the eschaton, begin to live after the order of Christ's new world. This order of Christ's new world is expressed in the

---

45. Paul writes that he denies everything except Christ for Christ and his sake, Phil. 3:7–8.

46. Gal. 3:27–28. It is remarkable that Jesus teaches us to hate our parents, children, spouses and our lives compared to Christ, Luke 14:26, see also Matt. 10:37.

47. Rom. 7:14–25; Gal. 5:17; 1 Tim. 1:15.

48. Col. 1:2. Compare Willem van Vlastuin, *Be Renewed: A Theology of Personal Renewal* (Göttingen: Vandenhoeck & Ruprecht, 2014), 175–177.

49. *De Civitate* 15.7.

50. 1 Cor. 15:42–49.

51. Stefanie Lorenzen, *Das Paulinische Eikon-Konzept: Semantische Analyse zur Sapientia Salomonis zu Philo und den Paulusbriefen* (Tübingen: Mohr Siebeck, 2008), 157–159. See also 195–198, 205, 262.

52. Rom. 8:23.

fruit of the Spirit,[53] while the exhortations in Paul's oeuvre explain that this new order coheres with God's concrete commandments.[54]

In this context, it is interesting to see how this applies to sexuality. Paul's friend Luke refers to Jesus' explanation of the resurrection in which marriage will be absent.[55] It can be argued that this approach was related to the concept of marriage as an image of the unity between Christ and his church.[56] Because of the 'marriage' with Christ, Christians look forward to the complete union with their spiritual bridegroom. One could expect this eschatological understanding of marriage to lead to a relativization of marriage and, in a certain sense, we see this relativism in the Paulinian letter to Ephesus.[57] Paul understands the relationship of marriage as a mirror of the relationship between Christ and the church. Christians should not absolutize marriage, because it is not our brides or grooms who are all, it is Christ. Paul confirms this conviction with his own single life and persuades the congregation that a single life is good and, in a certain sense, preferable.[58]

This interpretation of marriage does not imply, however, a complete relativization of marriage or a disinterestedness in sexual life. Quite the opposite. Because marriage is a mirror of Christ and his church, Paul exhorts men to love their wives as Christ loves his church and sacrificed himself for the church.[59] He can also write that husbands and wives are equal in their sexual lives and that the wife has *exousia* (power) over the body of her husband.[60]

1 Peter 3:1–7 offers us some remarkable interpretations.[61] While the first impression about this text is that women and wives occupy a secondary position compared to men, careful exegesis teaches us that the gospel—unlike the former social order—accepts that a wife may

---

53. Gal. 5:24.
54. Rom. 8:3–4, 13.
55. Luke 20:34–36.
56. See Richard B. Hays, *The Moral Vision of the New Testament: A Contemporary Introduction to New Testament Ethics* (Edinburgh: T&T Clark, 1997), 364, 366. Although there is no view of marriage as an image of the unity between Christ and his church in Luke, there is no reason to presuppose a great difference in the understanding of marriage in Luke and Paul, partly because they were friends and worked together. Above all, we see that both Luke and Paul relativize marriage.
57. Eph. 5:32.
58. 1 Cor. 7:25–40.
59. Eph. 5:25.
60. 1 Cor. 7:3–5. Compare Matthew Rueger, *Sexual Morality in a Christless World* (Saint Louis: Concordia Publishing House, 2016), 64–66.
61. Compare Arnold Huijgen, *Lezen en laten lezen: Gelovig omgaan met de Bijbel* (To read and to let read: Treating the Bible with faith) (Utrecht: Kokboekencentrum Uitgevers, 2019), 204–215.

confess another religion than her husband.⁶² That the wife was addressed explicitly, that her beauty was inward and that she was called upon not to be afraid was also revolutionary. In fact, this passage in the New Testament respects women. In this context, it is understandable that the gospel was attractive to women, because they had fewer rights in the society of that time.⁶³

But Paul was also at odds with the culture of that time because of his belief that sexual intercourse should only take place within the marriage of a husband and wife. In the Greek-Roman culture of the New Testament, sexuality was expressed in several forms;⁶⁴ Julius Caesar was every woman's man and every man's woman, a sort of bisexual, and Emperor Nero had a same-sex marriage.⁶⁵ Pederasty was a well-known practice at the time and understood to be the highest form of love.⁶⁶ Women were valued less than slaves; they were only necessary for having children and could be discarded on grounds of infertility. Notwithstanding this clash with the environmental culture,⁶⁷ Paul pleaded his 'new' interpretation of sexual life with apostolic authority.

Apparently, Paul's message had positive effects. When writing to the church of Corinth, he referred to people who had had a sexual life of the sort that was conventional at the time, but who had then denied that way of living.⁶⁸ In Paul's letters to the churches, we see the importance of the Christian interpretation of sexual life. He writes about this theme with absolute earnestness. Fornicators, idolaters, adulterers or abusers will not inherit the kingdom of God.⁶⁹ Christians have to mortify fornication, uncleanness, inordinate affection, evil concupiscence and covetousness.⁷⁰ These texts in the Paulinian writings make it very clear that the Christian's identity in Christ has huge consequences for their

---

62. Karen H. Jobes, *1 Peter* (Grand Rapids: Baker, 2005), 202–204.
63. Compare Rueger, *Sexual Morality*, 76.
64. Compare Thomas K. Hubbard (ed.), *Homosexuality in Greece and Rome: A Sourcebook of Basic Documents* (London: University of California Press, 2003); Rueger, *Sexual Morality*, 12–22, 40–41, 66–68. In an interview with John L. Allen jr. in 2004 Tom Wright acknowledged that in Paul's times all types of sexual behavior were exhibited, "Interview with Anglican Bishop N.T. Wright of Durham, England," http://www.nationalcatholicreporter.org/word/wright.htm (accessed October 4, 2019).
65. Dio Cassius, *Roman History* (Cambridge: Harvard University Press, 1927), Vol. 8, 159.
66. See also Craig A. Williams, *Roman Homosexuality* (New York: Oxford University Press, 1999).
67. The Christian denial to partake in public offerings to idols or the emperor was experienced as anti-human, as atheism and as a threat to public order, Rueger, *Sexual Morality*, 41, 83.
68. 1 Cor. 6:9–11.
69. 1 Cor. 6:9. Compare 1 Timothy 1:10.
70. Col. 3:5.

sexual life, because Christ's identity does not cohere with extra-marital relationships. This implies that the Christian has not only to deny the scheme of this world,[71] but his own longings and attitudes as well.[72]

We can conclude that finding one's identity in Christ is essential to Paul's understanding of the Christian identity. This identity in Christ has important consequences for understanding sexuality. Because marriage refers to our identity in Christ as the body, which is determined by Christ as the head, the holiness of marriage is central in the apostle's treatment of sexual life.[73]

4. Retrieving Paul's Identity in Christ in the Postmodern Context

After investigating the turn to the human subject in postmodernity and the interpretation of our identity in Christ in Paul's writings, a consideration of how Paul's approach can be applied in the present context of the church now follows.

4.1 Understanding Scripture as '*Viva Vox*'

First, Christians have many tensions when treating sexuality in a postmodern context. They also interact with several different attitudes, ranging from the most liberal to the most conservative. Orthodox Christians in the Roman-Catholic Church and in the Reformed tradition agree about the unique place that marriage between husband and wife has, but they differ in their attitudes to same-sex marriage. Some Christians even understand the present conflict as an ideological war; the Nashville Statement is a good example of this. Other Christians reject 'Nashville' because of its impersonal attitude and its modern approach,[74] but are convinced that the Christian faith does not accept same-sex relationships and argue that gays should be celibate. This position is very similar to the understanding that celibacy can be compensated by having an asexual friendship. In the Netherlands 'Heart of Homo's' gives

---

71. Rom. 12:2.

72. Eph. 4:22, 5:3–4; Col. 3:5, 8–9. Matt. 16:24 explains that followers of Jesus have to deny themselves.

73. Queer theologians argue that the image of Christ's body in 1 Cor. 12 might be a more inspiring image for sexual equality and justice than the marriage of Christ's body with Christ as head. In this essay about the mystical union with Christ, we see that Paul used the image of the head and the body as a metaphor for the mystical union and its sexual implications.

74. Jan Mudde, "Bijbel, exegese en homosexualiteit" (Bible, exegesis and homosexuality), in *Homoseksualiteit en de kerk* (Homosexuality and the church), eds. Maarten van Loon, Henk Medema and Jan Mudde (Amsterdam: Buijten & Schipperheijn, 2019), 22–32, here 24–25.

voice to this interpretation.[75] There are also Christians who use the tolerance shown to divorce in the Old Testament to accept (or tolerate) some same-sex marriages.[76] In the Protestant Church in the Netherlands, same-sex marriage is accepted but the church underlines its difference from the traditional heterosexual marriage.[77] Other Christians argue for a new hermeneutics, one in which a marriage of love and faithfulness between husband and wife is reinterpreted as a relationship of love and faithfulness between two people, citing the fact that gay relationships were unknown during the time of the New Testament.[78]

What these different interpretations of scripture all have in common is their concern about the understanding and application of scripture as a normative holy book. This approach to scripture belongs to the great Christian tradition and is expressed in detail in the protestant *sola scriptura*. Acknowledging this authority of scripture, we see that the Heidelberg Catechism interprets scripture as an existential interaction with Christ.[79] Billings refers to this approach to scripture as a 'Trinitarian Hermeneutic.'[80]

This approach implies—first—a high regard for the Bible, because the external Word relates us to the eternal Word and the real knowledge of scripture is the real spiritual knowledge of Christ. Second, this approach implies a certain functionalizing of scripture, because scripture is not an end in itself. Scripture is, as it were, the clothing of Christ, but the clothing is not the person himself. Third, this approach implies that pastors are not preaching scripture if they make an accurate exegesis without preaching Christ.[81]

In this contribution I want to join this 'Trinitarian Hermeneutic' of

---

75. https://hartvanhomos.nl/vriendschap (accessed June 17, 2019).

76. For the unfamiliarity of the current gay in the early church, compare Gerard den Hertog, "Hoe verwijst Jezus naar het 'in den beginne'?" (How does Jesus refer to 'in the beginning'?), in *Homoseksualiteit en de kerk*, 58–68. Paul Avis calls same-sex marriage "the lesser of two evils, the greater evil being enforced celibacy and accompanying loneliness," *Eros and the Sacred* (New York: Morehouse, 1989), 147.

77. Church order of Protestant Church in the Netherlands, ordinantie 5.4, https://www.protestantsekerk.nl/thema/kerkorde (accessed June 17, 2019).

78. Compare Wim Dekker, "Aanvaarding: Tot hoever gaat dat?" (Acceptance: How far does that go?), in *Homoseksualiteit en de kerk*, 69–78, 77–78.

79. Compare Willem van Vlastuin, "Heidelberg's Relevance for a Postmodern Age: The Doctrine of Scripture in the Heidelberg Catechism Revisited," *International Journal of Systematic Theology* 17:1 (2015), 26–45.

80. J. Todd Billings, *The Word of God for the People of God: An Entryway to the Theological Interpretation of Scripture* (Grand Rapids: Eerdmans, 2010), 86.

81. Edward Farley, "Toward a New Paradigm in Preaching," in *Preaching as a Theological Task: World, Gospel, Scripture*, eds. Thomas G. Long and Edward Farley (Louisville: Westminster John Knox Press, 1996), 165–175. Compare Fred B. Craddock, *Preaching* (Nashville: Abingdon Press, 1985), 28; Thomas G. Long, *Preaching and the Literary Forms of the Bible* (Philadelphia: Fortress Press, 1989), 126.

scripture. This does not mean that I wish to deny the normative and informational dimension of scripture, but I read the Bible primarily as God's voice, the viva vox. In this approach the Bible is not 'read' by us, but 'heard' by us. Listening to God's voice in scripture emphasizes God's act of speaking rather than our act of reading. In a certain sense, we do not read the Bible, but we are read from the Bible.[82] This also implies that we listen more with our heart than we do with our head. In this approach, the effect of scripture on us is primarily relational rather than informational.

This existential approach to scripture transcends and breaks through the subject-object divorce of modernity, because Christ as the speaking Subject is decisive. The starting point is not the individual subject, but the heavenly Subject Christ. In the heart of the reading of scripture, we hear the heart of Christ at the deepest level of our hearts. We cannot organize this existential intercourse with Christ, only experience our dependence upon the Holy Spirit.

4.2 Understanding Our Identity in Christ

This insight leads to a second consideration. While our postmodern culture takes us in a hyper-individualistic direction using our own individualistic identity is a starting point,[83] being interpreted by Christ's voice in scripture takes us in an opposite direction. Instead of our own identity being our starting point, Christ is our identity and the starting point of interpretation. We do not interpret Christ through our own individual or postmodern interpretative framework, but Christ interprets our identity. Perhaps we can speak here of being 'overpowered' by the Holy Spirit.

This is a paradoxical reality. We have to deny ourselves and our own identity.[84] In this sense the gospel does not confirm our existence, our sexual identity, but confronts us with the reality of the old eon which has to be forsaken. For our flesh, this is a hard job and seems to go against our wellbeing. The opposite is also true. Losing ourselves to Christ means that we get ourselves, and our identities in Christ, back. Christians experience this change as a gain. We are crucified to the world and the world is crucified to us, because the crucified Christ is

---

82. Compare Huijgen, *Lezen en laten lezen*.

83. René van Woudenberg problematized the concept of identity and argued that our identity remains the same through time no matter how great the changes in our character and attitudes may be, "Veelheid van Identiteiten, Fundamentele Identiteit en Dualisme" (Multitude of Identities, Fundamental Identity and Dualism), *Algemeen Nederlands Tijdschrift voor Wijsbegeerte* 110:3 (2018), 315–333.

84. Matt. 16:24. Megan K. DeFranza also acknowledges that in Christ all our identities are put to death. In her approach this implies breaking through the binary gender order, *Sex Difference in Christian Theology: Male, Female, and Intersex in the Image of God* (Grand Rapids: Eerdmans, 2015).

our life[85] in whom we experience the fulfilment of the deepest longings.[86] In this sense our identity in Christ coheres with the love for ourselves.[87]

The confrontational power of the existential meeting with the living Christ through his Word involves everybody in the congregation. Even Paul himself, who was already a Christian and had been an apostle for many years, experienced this. Being confronted with God's law, he estimated himself in terms of the flesh.[88] He made a similar judgment when writing to his spiritual son Timothy, describing himself as the greatest of sinners.[89]

This confrontational interpretation of the gospel is the deepest way of understanding the gospel. The riches in Christ imply the bankruptcy of this old eon and belonging to this old eon puts us against Christ and his gospel.[90] Participation in the old eon of the present world also implies that we have lost all hope of an eschatological future.[91] But there's also a paradox here. Everyone who denies this judgment will be judged, while accepting this judgment frees us from it and allows us to participate in Christ's liberty. We are saved from being—as Luther called it—*incurvatus in se* (closed up in ourselves)[92] and so we can flourish in a real relationship with Christ, the triune God, and our neighbors.

The denial of our present identity also involves our sexual identity. While our culture encourages us to understand ourselves as lesbians, homosexuals, bisexuals, transgender people, or heterosexuals, in the realm of God's kingdom this identity is (relatively) denied in order to interpret ourselves as being in Christ.[93] Our sexuality is no longer *who* we are, but *how* we are.[94] Understanding ourselves through Christ's identification with us means we understand the meaning of our lives, the history of this world, the essence of our sufferings and our deepest identity. What seems a loss appears to be a profit.

It is helpful to consider which aspects of this eschatological framework of interpreting ourselves differ from a protological framework of interpretation; a framework of interpretation that people can use to deny the classification of Christians along gender- and sexual

---

85. Gal. 6:14.
86. We find a classic interpretation of this mystery in Augustine: "Restless is our heart until it comes to rest in thee," *Confessiones* 1.1.
87. Matt. 22:34–40.
88. Rom. 7:14.
89. 1 Tim. 1:15.
90. John 15:18–25.
91. 1 John 2:17.
92. Compare Luther, WA 56:304.
93. For this approach see also Derks, *Constructions of Homosexuality*, 76, 86, 89–90, 92; Hays, *Moral Vision*, 390–391.
94. Compare Yuan, *Holy Sexuality*, 41.

identity categories, because human beings cannot be reduced to their sexual identity. The abolition of this classification is also helpful for a number of gay people who do not feel comfortable and do not experience themselves as being in these categories.[95] This struggle with identity makes it difficult for some homosexuals to accept themselves.

The difference between the protological and the eschatological viewpoints is the radicalism of the eschatological approach. In the protological approach our identity remains, although the burden of the struggling members of the church is somewhat relieved by the interpretation that our identity is more than our sexuality. But the protological approach will always remind us that our identities are not fully what they should be unless a solution to these burning existential issues is found. In the eschatological approach, however, our old identity, including all its defects, is crucified with Christ and undergoes a radical renewal in Christ.

Heterosexuals and homosexuals, transgender people and bisexuals are equal in their struggle with this self-denial, because the powers of the old eon that do not accept this self-denial are still present within us. The struggle with this self-denial offers an interpretative framework which we can use to account for sin and falling, for being unhappy, and for having negative emotions. We are not living in paradise yet, but are still part of the old reality. With all creation we suffer, we are in travail and we expect the revelation of God's children in his kingdom.[96]

4.3 UNDERSTANDING OUR SEXUAL IDENTITY

What do the foregoing considerations imply for our sexuality? Thinking from our identity in Christ relativises our old identities. Our work, our study, our sport, our gender, our sexual orientation, our relationships and our sinful character can all be part of our self-identity. In union with Christ, these identities are no longer decisive for our self-understanding. This new self-understanding coheres with the transformation according to the image of God's Son.[97]

This also appears in the notion that, in God's eschatological kingdom, marriage was fulfilled in the union and communion with Christ. This approach is nuanced. First, we do not speak about the abolishment of marriage but about its fulfilment. From the perspective in Christ, we are

---

95. According to Joseph N. Nicolosi, *Reparative Therapy of Male Homosexuality: A New Clinical Approach* (New Jersey: Jason Aronson, 1997), 13; *Diagnostic and Statistical Manual of Mental Disorders* (Washington: American Psychiatric Association, 2000), 582. Derks pleads for other reasons for a deconstruction of identity politics, *Constructions of Homosexuality*, 93.

96. Rom. 8:22–23.

97. 2 Cor. 3:18, 4:4.

not primarily husband and wife, but brother and sister.[98] Second, this approach implies that reproduction does not belong to the eschaton.[99] In the third place, the eschaton reveals a reality in which our human need for intimacy finds its primary fulfilment in the relationship with Christ and also within his body.[100] It seems that this relationship in the eschaton is more than the marriage in the proton. Therefore, from our point of view, we cannot speak about sexuality in the eschaton.[101] The need and the practice of intimacy can be acknowledged, sexual differentiation as male and female will continue, but sexual intercourse according to our experience cannot be expected in the eschaton.

Because we understand the church as the first beginning of the eschatological kingdom of God, sexual orientations are not decisive. I think this understanding of our identity in Christ relieves us from the need to have our own identity performed in this life. This does not deny sexuality in this life, or the difficult struggles of believers in the congregation, but sexuality is not made absolute, and our understanding of self is not determined by our sexual identity. This can function as a starting point to reflect upon the meaning of our lives.

Understanding that the church is also the temple of the Holy Spirit leads to yet another consideration. Living in union with Christ does not only have an eschatological dimension, it has a pneumatological dimension too. In Christ's body we experience the first fruit of the Spirit, which implies that we are renewed day by day until we inherit eternal youth. For this reason, thinking in terms of fixed positions is not supported by the Bible. This has huge implications for our sexuality. Without suggesting that sexual identities have to be changed and can 'easily' be changed, we cannot deny the effect of the spiritual union with Christ on sexual desires and on our character.[102]

---

98. Mark 3:31–35.

99. Compare Robert Song, *Covenant and Calling: Towards a Theology of Same-Sex Relationships* (London: SCM Press, 2014), Chapter 3.

100. This order is motivated by Mark 12:30–31, loving God is the first commandment and loving our neighbor the second. Here I differ from Derks, who seems to deny that the relationship with Christ can be primary, *Constructions of Homosexuality*, 88.

101. Gijsbert van den Brink and Kees van der Kooi write that we remain sexual beings in the eschaton, *Christian Dogmatics: An Introduction* (Grand Rapids: Eerdmans, 2017), 286.

102. Derks proposes the concept of 'sacramental characters' instead of 'being in Christ,' *Constructions of Homosexuality*, 89–114. I agree with him to reject the sociological and individualistic interpretation of 'being in Christ', but implying the pneumatological dimension in this concept includes also the transformation of the character, the sensitiveness for the corporative dimension of Christ's body and the unity of the external and internal aspects. Furthermore, the sacrament of baptism expresses the relationship with Christ. Therefore, the concept of 'sacramental characters' has no advantage over 'being in Christ', but the latter has a richer meaning.

Consciousness of the indwelling of the Holy Spirit leads us to a new understanding of our bodies; our bodies are redeemed by Christ and ultimately his. This teaches us to ask for his guidance in how we use our bodies and to be dependent upon him for our acts. This reality brings us to the preliminary question: are we willing to live God's will without conditions? In our hearts is the tendency to design our own plan, reason about the worth of our plan, and ask God's blessing for it. Union with Christ leads to the opposite attitude. To use a metaphor: we sign a blank sheet of paper which God uses to fill in the plan of our lives.

This leads to the insight that the first issue for believers is not their opinion about sexuality ethics, but is the question: do we accept Christ as our Lord, even if he asks us to live a lifestyle which goes against our own desires?[103] Our sexual behaviors, erotic desires, romantic feelings, sentimental relationships, and even all our platonic friendships must conform to Jesus Christ's plan and nothing else.[104] The primary issue concerning sexuality is about holiness. Do we want to live a holy life? Do we accept the strictness of our Lord who had compassion for the weak and the sinners and, at the same time, was very strict about our sexual lust?[105] This question faces heterosexuals and homosexuals, transgender people and bisexuals alike. Heterosexuals in a faithful heterosexual marriage can live in a selfish way, using their wives to satisfy their own lust. Heterosexuals can idolize heterosexual marriage.[106] To put it in an ultimately existential way: heterosexuality will not bring us to heaven, only faith in Christ can do this. Or to put it another way: both homosexuals and heterosexuals have to fight against their own selfish lust if they want to enter God's kingdom.

Heterosexuals and homosexuals experience temptations to behave in an unclean way and have their own struggles with sin. Even Jesus was tempted to sin; temptations in and of themselves are not sinful. The narrative of the gospels clarify that Jesus was tempted in every respect.[107] Thus, Jesus was victorious against every temptation. The comfort for believers is not only that they are not tempted more than their will to resist[108] but, above all, that heterosexuals and homosexuals can test Christ's triumph,[109] because they are united with Christ and share in his victory through the Spirit.

---

103. Compare Matt. 8:18–22.
104. I took this sentence from Yuan, *Holy Sexuality*, 195.
105. For Jesus' warm-heartedness, compare Luke 15:1, for his strictness see Matt. 5:28, for the combination see John 8:1–11.
106. Tim Keller, *Counterfeit Gods: The Empty Promises of Money, Sex, and Power, and the Only Hope that Matters* (New York: Penguin, 2016), xix.
107. Matt. 4:1–11. Compare also Heb. 4:15.
108. 1 Cor. 10:13.
109. Rom. 8:37.

These considerations put the church in a very special position in the world today. Only the church has the paradigm which enables another framework that we can use to interpret the identity of each other in the Christian congregation. We do not learn this from our culture; our culture will learn this from the church, and in the church we learn this from the gospel that is beyond our culture.[110] We will need much practice in the church to understand each other as brothers and sisters primarily and essentially in this eschatological perspective. In this way, the church does not understand itself as a mediator in a polarized society, but practices its eschatological shalom in its early beginnings and lives in the hope of complete wholeness in Christ.

BIBLIOGRAPHY

Augustine. *Homilies on the Gospel of John*, NPNF1, 7:140. Accessed June 12, 2019. https://www.ccel.org/ccel/calvin/calcom41.iv.ii.v.html.

Billings, J. Todd. *The Word of God for the People of God: An Entryway to the Theological Interpretation of Scripture*. Grand Rapids: Eerdmans, 2010.

Billings, J. Todd. *Calvin, Participation, and the Gift: The Activity of Believers in Union with Christ*. Oxford: Oxford University Press, 2008.

Billings, J. Todd. "United to God through Christ: Assessing Calvin on the Question of Deification." *Harvard Theological Journal* 98:3 (2005):315–334.

Bos, David. "'Equal Rites before the Law': Religious Celebrations of Same-Sex Relationships in the Netherlands, 1960's–1990's". *Theology & Sexuality* 23.3:188–208.

Bos, David. "Homo-af: De opkomst van de ex-homoseksueel in Nederland." (Gay-off: The rise of the ex-gay in the Netherlands) In *Genot en gebod: Huwelijk en seksualiteit in protestants Nederland vanaf 1800*, eds. David J. Bos en John Exalto: 128–155. Utrecht: KokBoekencentrum, 2019.

Boutelier, Hans. *Het seculiere experiment: Hoe we van God los gingen samenleven* (The secular experiment: How we lived together apart from God). Amsterdam: Boom, 2015.

---

110. Compare 1 Cor. 2:9.

Brink, Gijsbert van den, Kees van der Kooi. *Christian Dogmatics: An Introduction*. Grand Rapids: Eerdmans, 2017.

Buelens, Geert. *De jaren zestig: Een cultuurgeschiedenis*. Amsterdam: Ambo, 2018.

Burger, Hans. *Being in Christ: A Biblical and Systematic Investigation in a Reformed Perspective*. Eugene: Wipf & Stock, 2008.

Canlis, Julie. *Calvin's Ladder: A Spiritual Theology of Ascent and Ascension*. Grand Rapids: Eerdmans, 2010.

Cassius, Dio. *Roman History*. Cambridge: Harvard University Press, 1927.

Cortez, Marc. *Theological Anthropology: A Guide for the Perplexed*. London: T&T Clark, 2010.

Craddock, Fred B. *Preaching*. Nashville: Abingdon Press, 1985.

DeFranza, Megan K. *Sex Difference in Christian Theology: Male, Female, and Intersex in the Image of God*. Grand Rapids: Eerdmans, 2015.

Dekker, Wim. "Aanvaarding: Tot hoever gaat dat?" (Acceptance: How far does that go?) In *Homoseksualiteit en de kerk*, eds. Maarten van Loon, Henk Medema and Jan Mudde, 22–32. Amsterdam: Buijten & Schipperheijn, 2019.

Derks, Marco. *Constructions of Homosexuality and Christian Religion in Contemporary Public Discourse in the Netherlands*. Doctoral thesis Utrecht University, 2019.

Descartes, *Principia Philosopiae…* Amsterdam: Elsevier, 1677.

Dittrich, Boris. *Een blauwe stoel in paars: Verhalen uit de Tweede Kamer* (A blue chair in purple: Stories from the Dutch parliament). Amsterdam: Van Gennep, 2001.

Farley, Edward. "Toward a New Paradigm in Preaching." In *Preaching as a Theological Task: World, Gospel, Scripture*, eds. Thomas G. Long and Edward Farley, 165–175. Louisville: Westminster John Knox Press, 1996.

Fesko, John V. *Beyond Calvin: Union with Christ and Justification in Early Modern Reformed Theology (1517–1700)*. Göttingen: Vandenhoeck & Ruprecht, 2012.

Foucault, Michel. *The History of Sexuality*, 3 volumes. New York: Bloomsbury. 1986– 1992. Vol. I.

Gregory, Brad S. *The Unintended Reformation: How a Religious Revolution Secularized Society*. Cambridge: Cambridge University Press, 2012.

Harari, Yuval Noah. *Homo Deus: A Brief History of Tomorrow*. London: Penguin Random House, 2016.

Hays, Richard B. *The Moral Vision of the New Testament: A Contemporary Introduction to New Testament Ethics*. Edinburgh: T&T Clark, 1997.

Hertog, Gerard den. "Hoe verwijst Jezus naar het 'in den beginne'?" In *Homoseksualiteit en de kerk*, eds. Maarten van Loon, Henk Medema and Jan Mudde, 22–32. Amsterdam: Buijten & Schipperheijn, 2019.

Hubbard, Thomas K. *Homosexuality in Greece and Rome: A Sourcebook of Basic Documents*. London: University of California Press, 2003.

Arnold Huijgen, *Lezen en laten lezen: Gelovig omgaan met de Bijbel* (To read and to let read: Treating the Bible with faith). Utrecht: Kokboekencentrum Uitgevers, 2019.

Jenson, Robert W. *Systematic Theology, 2 Vols*. Oxford: Oxford University Press, 1997–99.

Jobes, Karen H. *1 Peter*. Grand Rapids: Baker, 2005.

Keller, Tim. *Counterfeit Gods: The Empty Promises of Money, Sex, and Power, and the Only Hope that Matters*. New York: Penguin, 2016.

Knijff, Hans W. de. *Tegenwoordigheid van geest als Europese uitdaging: Over secularisatie, wetenschap en christelijk geloof*. Zoetermeer: Boekencentrum, 2013.

Kooi, Cornelis van der. *As in a Mirror: John Calvin and Karl Barth on Knowing God*. A Diptych. Leiden: Brill, 2005.

Kuby, Gabrielle. *The Global Sexual Revolution: Destruction of Freedom in the Name of Freedom*. Kettering: Angelico Press, 2015.

Kuhn, Thomas S. *The Structure of Scientific Revolutions*. Chicago: Chicago University Press, 2012.

Lorenzen, Stefanie. *Das Paulinische Eikon-Konzept*: *Semantische Analyse zur Sapientia Salomonis zu Philo und den Paulusbriefen*. Tübingen: Mohr Siebeck, 2008.

Long, Thomas G. *Preaching and the Literary Forms of the Bible*. Philadelphia: Fortress Press, 1989.

Mudde, J. "Bijbel, exegese en homosexualiteit" (Bible, exegesis and homosexuality). In *Homoseksualiteit en de kerk* (Homosexuality and the church), eds. Maarten van Loon, Henk Medema and Jan Mudde, 22–32. Amsterdam: Buijten & Schipperheijn, 2019.

Nicolosi, Joseph N. *Reparative Therapy of Male Homosexuality*: *A New Clinical Approach*. New Jersey: Jason Aronson, 1997.

Nicolosi, Joseph N. *Diagnostic and Statistical Manual of Mental Disorders*. Washington: American Psychiatric Association, 2000.

Robb, Graham. *Strangers*: *Homosexual Love in the Nineteenth Century*. New York: Norton, 2005.

Rueger, Matthew. *Sexual Morality in a Christless World*. Saint Louis: Concordia Publishing House, 2016.

Swaab, Dick F. *We Are Our Brains*: *A Neurobiography of the Brain, from the Womb to Alzheimer's* transl. J. Hedley-Prôle. New York: Spiegel & Grau, 2014.

Song, Robert. *Covenant and Calling*: *Towards a Theology of Same-Sex Relationships*. London: SCM Press, 2014.

Taylor, Charles. *A Secular Age*. Cambridge: Harvard University Press, 2007.

Taylor, Charles. *The Ethics of Authenticity*. Cambridge: Harvard University Press, 1991.

Taylor, Charles. *Sources of the Self*: *The Making of the Modern Identity*. Cambridge: Harvard University Press, 1989.

Thate, Michael J. Kevin J. Vanhoozer, Constantine R. Campbell (eds). '*In Christ*' *in Paul*. Tübingen: Mohr Siebeck, 2014.

Vlastuin, Willem van. "The Promise of *Unio Mystica*." In *The Spirituality of the Heidelberg Catechism*: *Papers of the International Conference on the Heidelberg Catechism Held in Apeldoorn 2013*. Arnold Huijgen (ed.), 168–185. Göttingen: Vandenhoeck & Ruprecht, 2015.

Vlastuin, Willem van. "Heidelberg's Relevance for a Postmodern Age: The Doctrine of Scripture in the Heidelberg Catechism Revisited." In *International Journal of Systematic Theology* 17:1 (2015): 26–45.

Vlastuin, Willem van. *Be Renewed*: *A Theology of Personal Renewal*. Göttingen: Vandenhoeck & Ruprecht, 2014.

Webster, J. "The Human Person." In *The Cambridge Companion to Postmodern Theology*, eds. Kevin J. Vanhoozer, 219–234. Cambridge: Cambridge University Press 2003.

Williams, Craig A. *Roman Homosexuality*. New York: Oxford University Press, 1999.

Woudenberg, René van. "Veelheid van Identiteiten, Fundamentele Identiteit en Dualisme." (Multitude of Identities, Fundamental Identity and Dualism). In *Algemeen Nederlands Tijdschrift voor Wijsbegeerte* 110:3 (2018): 315–333.

Yuan, Christopher. *Holy Sexuality and the Gospel*: *Sex, Desire, and Relationships Shaped by God's Grand Story*. New York: Penguin, 2018.

CHAPTER 4
THEOLOGICAL ASSESSMENT OF THE GENDER AND SEXUALITY DEBATE IN THE NETHERLANDS: THE CASE OF THE 'NASHVILLE STATEMENT'
Heleen Zorgdrager

1. INTRODUCTION

It is striking that in contemporary Europe there are more tensions about religion than there have been since the early twentieth century. Tensions today are not about the political power of church and religion in relation to the state, as they used to be in the past; tensions today are about sharing or not sharing a common set of values, norms, and practices.[1] A cultural gap has arisen between conservative religious communities and secular society, and *within* the religious sphere between more conservative and more liberal-minded communities and believers. The term 'culture wars' is often applied to these conflicts and polarization on issues such as abortion, homosexuality, same-sex marriage, women's rights, reproductive rights, and family.[2] The broader categories of gender and sexuality are involved in all these controversial issues. Also, current debates on nationalism and ethnicity, the demand for a 'strong' nation, and the need to protect the nation against 'a flux of immigrants' are often intertwined with themes related to gender and sexuality, as we shall see below.

One might wonder why gender and sexuality have become so forefront in today's political and religious debates. From the more general viewpoint of cultural anthropology, issues of marriage, gender,

---

1. Olivier Roy and the Robert Schuman Centre for Advanced Studies, *Rethinking the Place of Religion in European Secularized Societies: The Need for More Open Societies.* Conclusions of the Research Project Religio West (European University Institute, March 2016), 4, https://cadmus.eui.eu/handle/1814/40305 (accessed April 15, 2021).

2. The term 'culture war' to characterize today's political battle on conservative and progressive values was introduced by James Davison Hunter, *Culture Wars: The Struggle to Define America* (New York: Basic Books, 1991).

and procreation are at the core of the conception of what a society is.[3] They are fundamentally related to the construction and consolidation of cultural and social order. Religion plays a role in this.[4] It is a two-way traffic: religion is a social and symbolic structure which affects gender and sexuality, and religion is affected by social systems of gender and sexuality.[5] This elucidates why religion, gender, and sexuality are intrinsically related in their social manifestation, but does not yet explain why today's religious-political debates tend to focus on diverging opinions, values, norms, and practices concerning gender and sexual diversity.

A widely supported explanation, building on Michel Foucault's theory exposed in *The History of Sexuality*,[6] is that people's identities in modern times have become increasingly tied to their sexuality. We may assume that gender and sexual relations have always been fundamental to human beings' experience of themselves, each other, and the environment. However, in modernity, since the early nineteenth century, the emerging medical discourse on sexuality taught to frame these experiences in a very specific way. Sexuality became a key attribute of the person, a central mark of his or her identity. In late-modern culture, with the dominant paradigm of identity being that of 'romantic expressivism' (Charles Taylor), individuals learned to express their authentic selves in terms of their sexual identity in order to realize their full humanity.[7] The 1960s revolution of authenticity centered around sexual values, morals, and practices. In the Netherlands, acceptance of sexual diversity (usually labelled as 'homosexuality') became a major identity marker of secularist groups and advocates. Whilst the phenomenon of sexual diversity gained public importance, religion increasingly was considered to be a private matter, and became contested in its public and most characteristic manifestation.[8] This 'opposing pairing' of religion and

---

3. Roy, *Rethinking the Place of Religion*, 3.

4. Anna Stewart and Simon Coleman, "Contributions from Anthropology," in *The Oxford Handbook of Theology, Sexuality, and Gender*, ed. Adrian Thatcher (Oxford: Oxford University Press, 2015), 105–119.

5. Marta Trzebiatowska, "Contributions from Sociology," in *The Oxford Handbook of Theology, Sexuality, and Gender*, 120–136, 121. As anthropologists Talal Assad (1983) and Sabah Mahmood (2005) have pointed out, religion is not to be found only in systems of meaning, but is always articulated in the entanglement of actors in more material and mundane networks of family, economy, and politics.

6. Michel Foucault, *The History of Sexuality Volume 1*: *An Introduction* (London: Allen Lane, 1979); *The History of Sexuality Volume 2*: *The Use of Pleasure* (London: Penguin Books, 1992); *The History of Sexuality Volume 3*: *The Care of the Self* (London: Penguin Books, 1990).

7. Charles Taylor, *Sources of the Self: The Making of the Modern Identity* (Cambridge: Cambridge University Press, 1989).

8. Linda Martín Alcoff and John D. Caputo (eds), *Feminism, Sexuality and the*

sexual diversity is manifested in the current culture wars. Positions with regard to sexual diversity have become emblems of fiery cultural battles to mark boundaries of religious and secular identities.

In this essay, I take as a case study the turmoil in society, politics, and churches around the so-called Nashville Statement.[9] The Nashville Statement, that is presented by its authors as "a joint statement on biblical sexuality," was imported in the Netherlands in January 2019.[10] The publication of the Nashville Statement manifested and fueled the polarization on gender and sexuality in the Netherlands, although there were unintended positive side effects as well. I will seek to analyze the dynamics of polarization in the case of the Nashville Statement, and ask the question: how shall we theologically address these dynamics of polarization and the identity-politics involved, and what could be a theological way forward beyond oppositions that tend to emphasize and prioritize 'identity' in the debate?

Polarization refers to the splitting of society into two distinct groups that are at different ends of a spectrum. Dutch philosopher Bart Brandsma describes the dynamics of polarization as a social process that begins with a thought construct of 'us' and 'them,' which is then fueled by 'pushers.'[11] The best way to give rise to polarization is to engage in talks about identity. Pushers of the conflict make judgmental comments on the other, in order to make the opposite pole suspect. A strategy to defuse polarization requires intervention at an early stage. Efforts should be made to strengthen the middle group, the potential 'bridgebuilders,' and to remain nuanced by hearing stories from a diversity of perspectives.

Return of Religion (Bloomington and Indianapolis: Indiana University Press, 2011); David Bos and Marco Derks, "Inleiding: God, seks en politiek. Themanummer over een spannende driehoeksverhouding" (Introduction: God, sex, and politics. Special issue on an exciting triangle), *Religie en Samenleving* 11:2 (2016), 97–100; Marco Derks, *Constructions of Homosexuality and Christian Religion in Contemporary Public Discourses in the Netherlands. Quaestiones Infinitae*, vol. 123 (Doctoral thesis Utrecht University, 2019); Marco Derks and Mariecke van den Berg (eds), *Public Discourses about Homosexuality and Religion in Europe and beyond* (London: Palgrave Macmillan, 2020).

9. Council on Biblical Manhood and Womanhood, "Nashville Statement," 2017, https://cbmw.org/nashville-statement/ (accessed April 15, 2021).

10. Werkgroep Nashville-verklaring, "Nashville-verklaring. Een gezamenlijke verklaring over Bijbelse seksualiteit," 2019, https://nashvilleverklaring.nl (accessed April 15, 2021).

11. Bart Brandsma, *Polarisation: Understanding the Dynamics of Us versus Them* (Schoonrewoerd: BB in media, 2017); see also John Paul Lederach, *The Moral Imagination: The Art and Soul of Building Peace* (Oxford: Oxford University Press, 2010).

2. The Case of the Nashville Statement

The Nashville Statement originates from the Southern Baptist Convention 2017 in the USA. It was promoted by the Council on Biblical Manhood and Womanhood, established in 1987 by Wayne Grudem.[12] On the initiative of seven Dutch Protestant pastors, the Nashville Statement was translated and imported into the Netherlands. The Nashville Statement is a typical product from a complex American context that combines evangelicalism and fundamentalism, a certain Victorian sexual repression and strong undercurrents of sexism and misogyny. The translated Statement and its signatures were prematurely leaked to the Dutch press.[13] The manifest was signed by over two hundred pastors, mainly from the Restored Reformed Church (Hersteld Hervormde Kerk), the Reformed Congregations (Gereformeerde Gemeenten), the Reformed League (Gereformeerde Bond, conservative wing in the Protestant Church of the Netherlands), the Christian Reformed Church (Christelijk-Gereformeerde Kerk), and some Evangelical and Baptist churches. Furthermore, it was signed by two lecturers of theology at the Seminary of the Restored Reformed Church at the VU University Amsterdam, whilst also a prominent Christian-conservative member of parliament, Kees van der Staaij, party leader of the SGP, supported the Statement.[14]

The Nashville Statement is drafted in the literary genre of a confession of faith, with affirmations and denials. It affirms the created, unchangeable nature of manhood and womanhood. It condemns same-sex relations, transgender sex-reassignment surgery, the use of gender-terminology and feminist aspirations. The extensive yet little specific enumeration of references to Biblical texts are not part of the original text but were later added. In the USA, the publication reinforced polarized positions. While Owen Strachan, Baptist theologian and former president of the Council on Biblical Manhood and Womanhood,

---

12. Wayne Grudem is Professor of Theology and Biblical Studies at Phoenix Seminary, Phoenix, Arizona; with John Piper he edited the influential book Recovering Biblical Manhood and Womanhood: A Response to Evangelical Feminism (first edition 1991, second edition Wheaton: Crossway, 2006).

13. Because the Dutch version of the Nashville Statement was leaked prematurely, some signatories withdraw their support or said that they, while supporting the content, never intended to sign. The initiators soon removed the list from their website. The website Geenstijl, however, kept and published a copy of it: https://www.geenstijl.nl/5145658/zo-en-nu-mogen-de-jankers-weer-whatallahboutisms-huilen/ (accessed April 15, 2021).

14. After publication, Van der Staaij declared that he was not intending to sign the Nashville Statement, but that he gave in an initial stage his support to translation into Dutch, because the Statement contained "the Biblical notions on marriage, family, and sexuality," https://nos.nl/artikel/2266443-van-der-staaij-blijft-staan-voor-bijbelse-noties-in-anti-lhbti-pamflet.html; https://www.nporadio1.nl/achtergrond/13964-van-der-staaij-handtekening-nashville-was-geen-bewuste-actie (accessed April 15, 2021).

praised the Nashville Statement as "a moment of remarkable unanimity of the spirit,"[15] queer Lutheran pastor Nadia Bolz-Weber scorned the manifest as "a document that doubles down on conservative Christian views on sexuality and gender"[16] and causes tremendous harm to people. Together with her parishioners of the House for All Sinners & Saints in Denver, she responded to it with the parodying Denver Statement, a line-by-line rewriting of the Nashville Statement affirming the goodness of all sexual and gendered beings.[17]

The impact in the Netherlands, however, was in comparison much greater and affected more levels of society. For Dutch society, such a public manifestation of fundamentalist beliefs on gender and sexuality was new. Although there was some support for the Nashville Statement, it was much more criticized by religious leaders for its lack of pastoral concern towards LGBT people. Human rights organizations and non-religious politicians condemned its discriminatory contents. The Minister of Education, Culture, and Science, Ingrid van Engelshoven, spoke out against the Statement, as did the mayor of Amsterdam, Femke Halsema. The COC, advocacy organization for LGBT in the Netherlands, made an official complaint at the Office of the Prosecutor, who in March 2020 finally concluded that publication of the Nashville Statement was not liable to punishment. Many public buildings, including churches and universities, flew the rainbow flag as a sign of solidarity with LGBT people. These symbolic performances demonstrated how much moral positions on sexuality and gender have become *shibbolets* of the right faith, whether it be religious or secular.

Also in conservative Reformed church communities, many were unhappy or at least had mixed feelings about the Nashville Statement. Perhaps they could agree with its theological line of thinking, but the manner of articulation and the complete lack of pastoral concern were not appreciated. The fear was that such a manifest would only polarize instead of serving a more trustful and honest conversation on the delicate issues of gender and sexuality.[18] As a positive side effect, Christian media

---

15. Colin Smothers, "Owen Strachan: The Nashville Statement 'is a moment of remarkable unanimity of spirit," website *Council on Biblical Manhood and Womanhood*, September 1, 2017, https://cbmw.org/2017/09/01/owen-strachan-the-nashville-statement-is-a-moment-of-remarkable-unanimity-of-spirit/ (accessed April 15, 2021).

16. Nadia Bolz-Weber, *Shameless: A Sexual Revolution* (London: Canterbury Press Norwich, 2019), 81–82.

17. The integral text of the Denver Statement is included in Bolz-Weber, Shameless, 94–97. A theological critique of the Nashville Statement also by Megan K. DeFranza, "Good News for Gender Minorities," in *Understanding Transgender Identities: Four Views*, eds. James K. Beilby and Paul Rhodes Eddy (Grand Rapids: Baker Academics, 2019), 147–178.

18. See, for instance, the professors of the (Christian-Reformed) Theological

began to give the floor to LGBT people in traditional church communities, to hear their highly personal stories about how they negotiated their sexual orientation or gender identity with their Christian faith. In terms of the polarization model of Brands, these newspapers and broadcasting channels were playing the role of 'bridge builders.' Hearing and reading these stories of LGBT persons made many conservative Christians in the Netherlands more careful and reluctant to harsh condemnation of non-normative sexual and gender identities on biblical grounds, exactly the opposite of what 'Nashville' had intended. *Nolens volens* it became a measure for a beginning acceptance of homosexuality in conservative Protestant environments.[19]

3. THE GLOBAL NEO-CONSERVATIVE CAMPAIGN FOR 'TRADITIONAL FAMILY VALUES'

'Nashville' has an interesting contradictory character. It is a public witness on sexuality and gender; however, it doesn't address the wider society but very articulated "Christians who are faithful to the Bible."[20] It is a testimony first of all for the in-group. Why then go so public with it?

To unravel this complexity, I will describe the historic emergence of the neo-conservative 'traditional (family) values' discourse as a new and in fact very modern public ideology, which at the same time provided churches with a discourse to demarcate their identity against that of secular society. For the specifics of the Dutch situation, it will be illuminating to analyze the role of parliamentarian Kees van der Staaij who signed the Nashville Statement. Supported by a constituency of conservative Reformed Christians, he plays his part in intensifying identity politics in regard to gender and sexuality, which may lead to further societal polarization.

Today's 'culture wars' on (supposed) secular or religious values with regard to gender and sexuality trace back to the 1960s. A first indication was the encyclical letter *Humanae Vitae* of Pope Paul VI in

---

University Apeldoorn, Arnold Huijgen and Maarten Kater, "Na bezinning door kerken pas visie op genderideologie" (Only after reflection by churches a view on gender ideology), *Reformatorisch Dagblad*, December 28, 2018, revised January 17, 2019.

19. Matthijs D. Appelman and Ruard R. Ganzevoort, "Refo houdt zich steeds intensiever bezig met onderwerp homoseksualiteit" (Reformed are getting busy more and more with the topic of homosexuality), Reformatorisch Dagblad, December 16, 2019, https://www.rd.nl/opinie/refo-houdt-zich-steeds-intensiever-bezig-met-onderwerp-homoseksualiteit-1.1617912 (accessed April 15, 2021).

20. See the Preamble of the Nashville Statement.

1968.²¹ Only a few years after the modernizing attempt of the Second Vatican Council under the spiritual leadership of his predecessor John Paul XXIII, the new pope issued this document which put sexual morals at the core of the preoccupations of the Catholic Church. Both in Europe and the USA, contraception and abortion became the central issues of an ongoing assault by conservative and fundamentalist churches on secular modernity, later culminating in the battle against same-sex marriage. The debate on the nature of gender, family, and reproduction goes to the core of the conception of what a society is or should be. Whereas since the 1960s civil society in many parts of the world put gender and sexuality norms into question, the Vatican has focused more and more on themes of gender, family, and reproduction. At the earliest since the UN International Conference on Population and Development in Cairo in 1994, and the World Conference on Women in Beijing in 1995, the Vatican started to develop a counter-strategy against 'gender ideology' as they labelled the enemy image.²² A recent document of the Congregation on Catholic Education defies gender ideology as "an ideology that is given the general name of 'gender theory', which denies the difference and reciprocity in nature of a man and a woman and envisages a society without sexual differences, thereby eliminating the anthropological basis of the family."²³

In the USA, white Evangelicals went ahead of the political-religious campaign for 'traditional family values.' In the 1970s and 1980s they used this rallying cry as they worked to stem the tide of social and political change caused by women's liberation, the civil rights movement, the sexual revolution, and the rise of global economy.²⁴ The opposition

---

21. Encyclical Letter *Humanae Vitae*, http://www.vatican.va/content/paul-vi/en/encyclicals/documents/hf_p-vi_enc_25071968_humanae-vitae.html (accessed April 15, 2021); Roy, Rethinking the Place of Religion, 4; Maria Behrensen, Marianne Heimbach-Steins and Linda E. Hennig, "Einleitung," in *Gender—Nation—Religion: Ein internationaler Vergleich von Akteursstrategien und Diskursverflechtungen*, eds. Maria Behrensen a.o. (Frankfurt/ New York: Campus Verlag, 2019), 7–24, 14–15.; Andreas Püttmann, "Geschlechterordnung und Familismus als Policy-Angebote des Rechtspopulismus und Autoritarismus für das katholische Milieu," in *Gender—Nation—Religion*, 51–80.

22. Behrensen a.o., "Einleitung," 12.

23. Document of the Congregation on Catholic Education, *Male and Female He Created Them: Towards a Path of Dialogue on the Question of Gender Theory in Education* (Vatican City, 2019), par. 2, http://www.vatican.va/roman_curia/congregations/ccatheduc/documents/rc_con_ccatheduc_doc_20190202_maschio-e-femmina_en.pdf (accessed April 15, 2021).

24. Seth Dowland, *Family Values and the Rise of the Christian Right* (Philadelphia: University of Pennsylvania Press, 2015), 11–12; Silas Morgan, "American Masculinity, Feminism, and the Politics of Fatherhood," in Gender-Nation-Religion, ed. Behrensen a.o., 101–123, 106.

against reproductive rights of women, same-sex relations, sexual education programs, and social government programs such as health care, poverty assistance, and public housing were all seen as damaging to the American family. The campaign for the 'traditional American family' was motivated on social, political and theological grounds. The family was viewed as the foundation of God's moral vision for a society built on and organized around biblical principles.[25] Two primary beliefs are at the core of the 'traditional values' narrative[26]:

1. The belief that manhood and womanhood are a natural given, part of the created order.
2. The belief that lines of authority matter and must be observed in order for society to function well. The 'traditional family' becomes the model for all structures of authority in society and nation. Traditional values are always patriarchal values. Theologically, it is anchored in a 'headship theology' that argues on the basis of key texts such as Gen. 2–3, 1 Cor. 11: 1–16 an Eph. 5: 22–33 that manhood and womanhood are complementary in the sense of a hierarchical role-order of leading and serving, and that the father/husband is assigned to be the head of the family in accordance to God's order for humanity.[27] Masculinity and fatherhood receive primary theological significance, to undergird and legitimate their sociopolitical power and privilege.

So, from different confessional strains and political contexts, the religious neo-conservative movement for 'traditional family values' arose. It has gone global since, working through transnational pro-family organizations such as the Federation of Catholic Family Associations in Europe (FACFE)[28] and the International Organization for the Family (IOF)[29] with its influential annual World Congress of Families.[30] Strong and unlikely political alliances are built between the Vatican, American Evangelicals, the Russian Orthodox Church, African Indigenous Churches, and Islamic leaders to pursue a 'traditional values' and 'anti-genderist'[31]

---

25. Morgan, "American Masculinity," 106–107.
26. Dowland, *Family Values*, 11.
27. Morgan, "American Masculinities," 112–113; a clear example of 'headship theology' is the collection of essays edited by Wayne Grudem and John Piper, *Recovering Biblical Manhood and Womanhood: A Response to Evangelical Feminism*, see note 12.
28. https://www.fafce.org (accessed April 15, 2021).
29. https://www.profam.org (accessed April 15, 2021).
30. About the XIII World Congress of Families in Verona, 2019, see https://wcfverona.org (accessed April 15, 2021).
31. Roman Kuhar and David Paternotte (eds), *Anti-Gender Campaigns in Europe: Mobilizing against Equality* (Washington: Rowman and Littlefield, 2017);

agenda in the domain of global politics and human rights.

Increasingly, they and their spokespersons, with a prominent role for the Catholic German sociologist Gabriela Kuby, find themselves in discursive and activist intertwinement with populist and far right organizations, parties and groups.[32]

4. THE CAMPAIGN FOR 'TRADITIONAL FAMILY VALUES' IN THE NETHERLANDS

Turning to the Netherlands, we can situate the 'Nashville' campaign within this wider neo-conservative religious movement. The seven pastors, who took the initiative, were inspired by the narrative of 'traditional family values' that anchors in a 'headship theology.' They applied similar strategies of polarization, like creating an enemy image (e.g., 'gender ideology' or 'gender delusion'),[33] and making the opponent suspicious by feeding conspiracy theories (e.g., 'the influential homo-lobby').[34] In the dynamics of polarization also groups on the other side started creating enemy images, like 'hate-christians' ('haatgristenen').[35]

At the same time, we cannot draw a straight line from the North-

---

Sonja A. Strube, Rita Perintvalvi, Rafaela Hemet, Miriam Metze and Cicek Sahbaz (eds), *Anti-Genderismus in Europa: Allianzen von Rechtspopulismus und religiösem Fundamentalismus. Mobilisierung—Vernetzung—Transformation* (Bielefeld: Transcript Verlag, 2020), Open Access: https://www.transcript-verlag.de/pdfgen/html2pdf/create.php (accessed April 15, 2021).

32. Gabriela Kuby's book *The Global Sexual Revolution: The Destruction of Freedom in the Name of Freedom* (New York: LifeSite/Angelico Press, 2015; originally published in German in 2012) became a bestseller and was actively promoted both by Roman-Catholic bishops and new right/far right groups in Germany and elsewhere, see Sonja Angelika Strube, "Rechtspopulismus und konfessionelle Anti-Gender-Bewegung: Milieu-übergreifende Allianzen und rhetorische Strategien im deutschen Sprachraum," in *Gender—Nation—Religion*, ed. Behrensen a.o., 25–49, 29. Kuby accepted the invitation to speak at the Kremlin-backed event "Large Family and the Future of Humanity," an alternative conference that was organized instead of the planned World Congress of Family in Moscow, which faced cancellations because of Russia's annexation of Crimea. Püttmann, "Geschlechterordnung und Familismus," 61–63.

33. "Nashville initiator: De kerken zwegen bij nazi-ideologie, bij gender-ideologie gebeurt dat weer" (Nashville initiator: The churches were silent on Nazi ideology, with gender ideology it happens again), interview with Piet de Vries, lecturer at the Restored Reformed Seminary at VU University, *Algemeen Dagblad*, February 1, 2020, https://www.ad.nl/binnenland/nashville-initiator-kerken-zwegen-bij-nazi-ideologie-bij-gender-ideologie-gebeurt-dat-weer~ac8ec6b3/ (accessed April 15, 2021).

34. "'The day after': ds. M. Klaassen blikt terug op Nashville" ('The day after': Rev. M. Klaassen looks back on Nashville), *Reformatorisch Dagblad*, January 15, 2019, https://cip.nl/71497-the-days-after-ds-m-klaassen-blikt-terug-op-nashville-ophef (accessed April 15, 2021).

35. The term 'haat-gristenen' is an invention by the website Geenstijl, https://www.geenstijl.nl (accessed April 15, 2021).

American neo-conservative religious movement to the Netherlands. Therefore, given the context, the Dutch neo-conservative movement had a too specific genesis, as Merijn Oudenampsen demonstrates in his illuminating study on the conservative revolution in the Netherlands.[36] We need to describe this process briefly, in order to understand the newness and impact of the 'Nashville' phenomenon in the Dutch context, and how it marks a new stage in the public debate on sexuality and gender.

The conservative backlash, already going on since the 1970s in the USA, reached the Netherlands only in the 1990s and the first decennium of the new century. Conservative-liberal politicians such as Frits Bolkestein, Pim Fortuyn, Geert Wilders, and Ayaan Hirsi Ali introduced the ideas of new-right Anglo-American thinkers (Bernard Lewis, Samuel Huntington, Daniel Bell, Roger Scruton, John Gray, Francis Fukuyama) in the Dutch political context.[37] For this introduction, a complex process of translation was required. This had to do with the particularity of the Dutch situation. The progressive values of the 1960s protest-movement (gender equality, reproductive rights, LGBT rights, individual freedom, and tolerance) had found a self-evident place in the Dutch society. Oudenampsen, following historian James Kennedy, points to the Dutch political culture with its typical accommodating attitude.[38] Ideologies and conflicts around ideologies are relatively absent. If there is a dominant political ideology, it is 'organicism,' understood as a doctrine that tends to conceive Dutch society as a differentiated, historically developing and organic entity. There is a stress on the inevitability of sociopolitical adaptations over time. From this accommodating attitude it can be explained that political elites in the Netherlands did not resist the progressive 1960s movement, like they did in the USA, but chose 'to go with the flow' and to incorporate certain elements in their own agenda. Neoconservative politicians in the Netherlands knew they would only be successful in creating sufficient support if they embraced the discourse of emancipation. They did it in a paradoxical way: on the one hand they presented themselves as defenders of 'Western' progressive values, such as women's emancipation and sexual diversity, against the Islam; on the other hand, they pointed to the progressive 'baby-boomers' as the main

---

36. Merijn Oudenampsen, *De conservatieve revolutie: Een ideeëngeschiedenis van de Fortuyn-opstand* (The Conservative Revolution: A History of Ideas of the Fortuyn Rebellion) (Amsterdam: Merijn Oudenampsen en Nijmegen: Uitgeverij Vantilt, 2018). Based on his doctoral thesis *The Conservative Embrace of Values* (University of Amsterdam, 2018).

37. Oudenampsen, *De conservatieve revolutie*, 111–124.

38. Oudenampsen, *De conservatieve revolutie*, 10–15, 318–319; James Kennedy, "New Babylon and the Politics of Modernity," *Sociologische gids* 44:5–6 (1997), 361–374.

culprits of all kinds of problems, from the failed integration of migrants to the erosion of national identity.

Angela McRobbie speaks in this regard about a 'complex conservative backlash' in Western-Europe and the UK, manifesting a less traditional conservative-Christian character than in the USA.[39] She adopts the term 'conservative backlash' from Susan Faludi, as the 'coordinated conservative reaction to fight the achievements of feminism.'[40] She adds the adjective 'complex' because the conservative counter-movement in Western Europe does not straight-away oppose feminism or sexual diversity, but creates a new synthesis in which moderate forms of emancipation are incorporated. It does so in such a way that the larger agenda of feminism can be effectively put away as outdated and superfluous. McRobbie calls this complex backlash *postfeminism*. The emancipation of women and gays has been completed, according to the new right. The only challenge that remains is to defend those achievements against the threat of Islamization.

How shall we situate the politics of the SGP, as an important backbone of the 'Nashville' campaign, within this larger picture of neo-conservatism in the Netherlands? Conservative Reformed people in the Netherlands have their own political party, the SGP (Staatkundig Gereformeerde Partij).[41] Since 1918, it is the political body of the 'bevindelijk gereformeerden,' a conservative movement within Dutch Calvinism, that emphasizes the necessity and experience of being born again in order to be saved, together with a literalist view of the Bible. Geographically these believers can be located on the Dutch Biblebelt. The movement embraces a strict conservative lifestyle and strongly opposes secularism. In the elections of 2017, the SGP retained its three seats in the Parliament (out of 150). Most signatories of the Nashville Statement belong to the constituency of the SGP, while the Evangelicals and Baptist who signed it may feel more at home in the other small Christian party, the ChristenUnie. The ChristenUnie however, immediately distanced itself publicly from 'Nashville.'[42]

---

39. Angela McRobbie, "Post-feminism and popular culture," Feminist Media Studies 4:3 (1991), 255–264. See Oudenampsen, *De conservatieve revolutie*, 198–202.

40. Susan Faludi, *Backlash: The Undeclared War Against Women* (New York: Vintage, 1991).

41. Half of the membership is member of the 'Gereformeerde Gemeenten,' a quarter is member of another 'bevindelijk gereformeerde' church, and a quarter is a member of the 'Gereformeerde Bond' in the Protestant Church and the 'Hersteld Hervormde Kerk.'

42. The leader of the Christen Unie, Gert-Jan Segers, declared on January 7, 2019: "I have not signed the Nashville Statement because I'm afraid that it doesn't serve the conversation about homosexuality. The conversation about this topic is important, affects people, and should therefore—whatever your conviction is—be conducted in full respect and openness." https://www.christenunie.nl/blog/2019/01/07/Nashville

The SGP opts for a more aggressive strategy, most likely because it finds itself in different waters. Right-wing populism sails alongside. The anti-Islam position of SGP, its attachment to law-and-order and the nation, and its outspoken nativism—being the belief that the territory of the nation should be primarily reserved to descendants of the own people—, brings the party close to the ideas of right populist parties. On the other hand, however, its theocratic principle—the belief that the nation is under God's absolute sovereignty—is fairly incompatible with populism.[43] Notwithstanding this fact, many of the voters of the SGP feel attracted to the firm speeches and standpoints of rightwing populist leaders such as Geert Wilders (Party for Freedom, PVV) and Thierry Baudet (Forum for Democracy, FvD). Popular among nationalist populists is the expression of the 'Judeo-Christian culture' as the dominant culture ('Leitkultur') for the nation. In particular the young generation of SGP-voters seems to embrace this 'culturalization' of Christianity, as the belief that the Dutch cultural identity bears the stamp of Christianity.[44] Under this influence, a shift is taking place in the ideology of SGP, from confessional arguments to cultural arguments, e.g., when it comes to rejection of the place of Islam in society. Ernst van den Hemel points to the risk that this tendency of embracing religion for its cultural value may in the end place the party for difficult dilemma's.[45] How to navigate between, on the one hand, what populist leaders praise as achievements of Dutch culture with its 'Judeo-Christian roots,' and what, on the other hand, is really far removed from the Reformed conservative beliefs, namely full gender equality and the acceptance of sexual and gender diversity? It leads the SGP into a splits position between culturalization and confessional identity. Party leader Kees van der Staaij is aware of the problems and risks. Therefore he insists on a

---

(accessed April 15, 2021).

43. See Simon Otjes and André Krouwel, "De SGP-kiezer: Wel radicaal en rechts maar niet radicaalrechts populistisch?" (The SGP voter: Radical and right-wing but not radical rightwing populist?), in *Theocratie en populisme: Staatkundig gereformeerden en de stem van het volk* (Theocracy and populism: Political reformed and the voice of the people), ed. Koos-jan de Jager (Apeldoorn: Labarum Academic, 2020), 179–201.

44. Ernst van den Hemel, "Korte rokjes tegen de Islam? De SGP en het boemerangeffect van geculturaliseerd christendom" (Short skirts against Islam? The SGP and the boomerang effect of culturalized Christianity), in *Theocratie en populisme*, 149–178. The notion 'Judeo-Christian culture' is a modern invention, in right-wing populism used to exclude those who are deemed not to subscribe to Western values, and applied particularly to Muslims, see Philip C. Almond, "Is there really such a thing as 'Judeo-Christian Tradition'?" website *ABC Religion and Ethics*, February 14, 2019, https://www.abc.net.au/religion/is-there-really-a-judeo-christian-tradition/10810554 (accessed April 15, 2021).

45. Van den Hemel, "Korte rokjes," 214–219.

sharp demarcation between Christian values and secular values.⁴⁶ His service record on extra-parliamentarian actions on issues of marriage, family, and reproduction attests to this.⁴⁷ In this context of contestation, I understand Van der Staaij's support for the Nashville Statement also as a deliberate performative act, prompted by the need to publicly establish and affirm a distinct identity marker of 'Christian values,' in a time where the nativist and culturalizing tendencies in his own party are blurring the boundaries with secular culture.

However, we could ask: doesn't Van der Staaij himself fall into the trap of a culturalization of religion? In supporting this import product from the Christian right in the USA, he in fact embraces a highly cultural discourse of 'Christian identity' marked by moral positions on gender and sexuality. Defense of 'traditional values' is undertaken from a perceived 'Christian identity' which presents itself more as a cultural marker than as a religious marker.⁴⁸ This is really not far away from how the radical-right adhere to the 'Judeo-Christian' tradition with its assumed stabilizing values of family, the hierarchical gender order, pro-life policies, the idea of ethnic purity, and the nation. The nation is threatened and weakened, and must defend itself against the invasion of Islam. In particular Baudet from the Forum for Democracy actively adopts elements of traditional values rhetoric. Van der Staay's campaign for Christian family values does not so much distinguish him from secular right parties, but brings him closer to these groups.

Sander Rietveld, who investigated the entanglement of the radical-right and orthodox Christianity in the Netherlands, points to an additional reason why Christian conservatives tend to support right-wing populism.⁴⁹ It is the experience of loss and a certain sense of victimhood among orthodox Reformed Christians. They have become a minority in a deeply secularized society. They realize that it is impossible to impose their sacred values on the rest; what remains of the theocratic ideal of a Christian nation ruled by God's authority is a kind of second-best option: to ally with the 'cultural Christians' of the right populist parties in order

---

46. Van den Hemel, "Korte rokjes," 225.

47. Van der Staaij joined the *March for Life* in 2011. In 2015, he launched a large-scale campaign against adultery, agitated by billboards of the dating site Second Love along the highway. He placed billboards with the text "Adultery. The family game with only losers." Two years later, on Valentine's Day, he placed a full-page message of love in major Dutch newspapers, under the headline "Choose One Another," in which he called for fidelity in love relationships. See De Jager (ed.), *Theocratie en populisme*, 204, 132–233.

48. Roy, *Rethinking the Place of Religion*, 3.

49. Sander Rietveld, *Nieuwe kruisvaarders: De Heilige Alliantie tussen orthodoxe christenen en radicaal-rechtse populisten* (New Crusaders: The Holy Alliance between orthodox Christians and radical-right populists), (Amsterdam: Prometheus, 2021).

to at least bring a Christian glow over the society.

Furthermore, there is also the internal threat. Defense against the secular society and against more liberal parts of Christianity is required to hold back the growing plurality and fragmentation in the own faith community when it comes to moral attitudes and practices with regard to sexuality and gender. Orthodox Reformed churches in the Netherlands, and many Evangelical churches as well, are facing the empirical reality of shifting sexual and gender mores within their communities, in particular among the young generations (e.g., having sex before marriage, use of contraceptives, political agency of women, and so on).[50] Above all, unity must be preserved. The manifest of 'Nashville' marks a watershed. With some exaggeration we can say that sexual ethics, over against dogmatic faith issues, have become the emblem of ecclesiastical and political-religious cohesion.

5. Union With Christ: Moving Beyond Identity Politics?

We see the weaknesses and traps of identity discourses, on different levels. Posing Christian identity and values *against* secular identity and values in the realm of sexuality can make one fall into the trap of culturalization of religion. Posing liberal sexual identity, as the freedom to celebrate sexual diversity, *against* conservative religion can make one fall into the trap of absolutizing sexuality as the way to human fulfilment.[51] Such 'common enemy' identity politics reinforces the polarization.[52]

Theologians have started working on methods and approaches to move beyond identity politics in matters of gender and sexuality. As queer theologian Marco Derks rightfully states: the emphasis on the concept of identity can be found both in secular and theological pro-LGBT discourse and in conservative Christian discourse.[53] In the dominant script of

---

50. Ad de Bruijne, "Culture Wars About Sexuality: A Theological Proposal for Dialogue," in *Public Discourses About Homosexuality and Religion in Europe and Beyond*, 105–124, 109–110.

51. Cf. Mark Jordan: "Outside Christian churches, rightly ordered sexuality promises present salvation. Inside many churches, right words about sexuality now determine your eternal salvation." In Mark Jordan, "The Return of Religion during the Reign of Sexuality," in *Feminism, Sexuality and the Return of Religion*, eds. Linda Martín Alcoff and John D. Caputo (Bloomington and Indianapolis: Indiana University Press, 2011), 39–54, 41.

52. Francis Fukuyama, *Identity: The Demand for Dignity and the Politics of Resentment* (New York: Farrar, Straus and Giroux, 2018); Kwame Anthony Appiahs, *The Lies That Bind: Rethinking Identity* (New York: Liveright, 2018); Amartya Sen, *Identity and Violence: The Illusion of Destiny* (New York: W.W. Norton Company, 2007); Mark Lilla, *The Once and Future Liberal: After Identity Politics* (New York: Harper, 2017).

53. Derks, *Constructions of Homosexuality*, 80.

LGBT discourse, sexual identity is viewed as a core aspect of a person's identity that needs to be discovered, developed, cultivated and profiled. The freedom of 'being yourself' is understood as a moral and, by many Christian gays, also a religious calling. In this, they affirm the modernist view of sexuality as a key characteristic of a person's identity. Christian ethicist Ad de Bruijne has underlined that this late modern discourse on sexual identity resonates with the Christian doctrine of creation and can be viewed as its desacralized result: "Sexuality too has become valued as just a phenomenon within God's good creation."[54]

Turning to today's conservative Christian narrative—be it the Nashville Statement or the above quoted recent Vatican document—, we notice that it is not that all different from the 'being yourself' homosexuality script, since it also relies on the modern concept of sexuality as the core of a person's identity. The difference is that Christian conservatives bind the sexual identity of the person to his/her biological sex, consider genitals to be leading for the process of self-expression, and prioritize procreative sex above non-procreative sex.

A naturalist interpretation of the creation narratives Gen 1 and 2 is leading here, yet Elizabeth Stuart also points to a soteriological undercurrent in this view of sexuality. Stuart analyzes how in twentieth-century theology maleness and femaleness have become theological categories and how sexuality has become caught up in the drama of salvation. Theologies of marriage and sexuality from Karl Barth to Hans Urs von Balthasar express that human beings only become truly human when men and women are in relationship to each other. In this view, heterosexuality is propelled to the heart of the Christian project.[55]

Recently, an alternative discourse has been developed. For some Dutch orthodox Protestant theologians, among them also who identify as gay, grounding sexual ethics in the doctrine of creation in this static form does not satisfy anymore. They propose an approach that focuses on 'identity in Christ.' The argument goes that our identity lies primarily in Christ, not in sexual feelings or experiences. Biblical scholar Wolter Rose argues, that for a Christian a homosexual identity is always subordinated to a religious identity 'in Christ.' He writes, that "choosing a gay script means organizing all aspects of who you are around your homosexual orientation. You are primarily gay."[56] Instead, he emphasizes that our

---

54. De Bruijne, "Culture Wars About Sexuality," 112.

55. Cf. Elizabeth Stuart, "The Theological Study of Sexuality," in *The Oxford Handbook of Theology, Sexuality, and Gender*, 18–31, 21.

56. Wolter Rose, "We hebben elkaar wat te vertellen" (We have something to tell each other), in *Open en kwetsbaar: Christelijk debat over homoseksualiteit* (Open and vulnerable: Christian debate on homosexuality), ed. Ad de Bruijne (Barneveld: De Vuurbaak, 2012), 115–122, 118.

primary identity is 'in Christ.' To live according to the 'being in Christ' script does not mean that one's homosexual orientation is not important anymore.[57] Yet, it is relativized and subordinated as a secondary identity. Rose prefers to speak of a 'together with Christ' script (cf. Rom 8:17), and of love of or friendship with Christ.[58] In practice, for Rose, it leads to the choice of celibacy, while keeping open one self to committed friendship relations.

Positive aspects of the identity 'in Christ' or 'with Christ' approaches are that they break away from the naturalistic reasoning of creation-based theologies of sexuality. This alternative discourse has a decisive eschatological orientation, "it has not yet been revealed what we will be" (1 John 3: 2), and even corresponds to some extent with the queer approach. The queer approach aims to liberate erotic desires from normative sexual identities and a binary gender system.[59] Christian identity, as constituted in baptism, is profoundly eschatological, relativizes all other identities, and deprives the categories of sexuality and gender from their ultimate meaning. It may free us to the 'affections of the flesh' and to co-creating in and with the divine Spirit new forms of community and relationship, beyond what historic Christianity has deemed 'decent.'[60] However, this is not the direction which Rose and fellow-thinkers take. Limiting the choice of life-style to either heterosexual marriage or celibacy (with a gnostic-like contempt of the desires of the flesh) is far away from the queer perspective of doing justice to a multiplicity of sexual and gendered desires.

It should make us cautious how the 'identity in Christ' or 'unio mystica cum Christo' script has quickly gained ground in evangelical and orthodox Protestant theologies of sexuality in the USA, from where it influences European theology. A prominent propagandist and inspirator for the 'union with Christ' script is the much sought-after speaker Rosaria Butterfield,[61] who used to identify as a lesbian activist, converted to Christianity, became a member of the Reformed Presbyterian Church, decided "to submit all sexual desires to Christ"

---

57. Rose, "We hebben elkaar wat te vertellen," 120.
58. Rose, "We hebben elkaar wat te vertellen," 117.
59. Stuart, "The Theological Study of Sexuality," 24–27; Linn Marie Tondstad, *Queer Theology* (Eugene: Cascade Books, 2018).
60. See the works on theology of the flesh by Marcella Althaus-Reid, Mayra Rivera, Gerard Loughlin, Graham Ward, Mark Jordan and others.
61. Rosaria Champagne Butterfield, *The Secret Thoughts of an Unlikely Convert: An English Professor's Journey into the Christian Faith* (Pittsburgh: Crown and Covenant Publications, 2012); *Openness Unhindered: Further Thoughts of an Unlikely Convert on Sexual Identity and Union with Christ* (Pittsburgh: Crown and Covenant Publications, 2015); "Sexual Identity and Union with Christ," lecture at Geneva College, April 21, 2016, https://www.youtube.com/watch?v=oEsj9Hh59uw (accessed April 15, 2021).

and now is in a heterosexual marriage and mother of a teenager son. In her view, being in 'union with Christ' competes fundamentally with a sexual identity as gay or lesbian. "There is no middle ground" between 'union with Christ' and 'homosexual desires.' The latter are 'fallen desires' because they do not respect the 'nature of the garden' (of Eden). Sexual identity is a false secular concept, according to Butterfield. Any compromise here would be equal to 'surrender.' Only in biblical marriage based on ontological and essential maleness and femaleness can human sexuality glorify God.

Butterfield's theology shows unequivocally how a 'union with Christ' script can go together with full condemnation of non-heterosexual orientations and desires. From this background, it is no surprise that Butterfield signed the Nashville Statement and affirms it as a matter of *status confessionis*: "By God through the merit and power of Jesus Christ, here I stand."[62]

The 'unio mystica cum Christo' script thus can go in various directions when it comes to ethical implications for a person's lifestyle. For Butterfield, being 'in Christ' and being 'homosexual' or living same sex desires are mutually excluding. For Rose, being 'with Christ' and being in relationship with someone from the same sex can go together as long as the friendship remains platonic. For Wim van Vlastuin (see his contribution in this volume),[63] having our identity in Christ relativizes all other identities and relieves us from the need to have our own identity performed in this life. Potentially, this may be a critical notion. However, he simultaneously argues that in apostle Paul's view there is an indissoluble relation between the holiness of marriage, exclusively understood as between a husband and a wife, and 'identity in Christ.'[64] Because of this privileging of heterosexuality in van Vlastuin's reasoning here and elsewhere,[65] there remains no proper place for

---

62. Rosaria Butterfield, "Why I Signed the Nashville Statement," website *Council on Biblical Manhood and Womanhood*, August 31, 2017, https://cbmw.org/2017/08/31/rosaria-butterfield-why-i-signed-the-nashville-statement/ (accessed April 15, 2021).

63. Wim van Vlastuin, "Retrieving the Concept of *Unio Mystica cum Christo* for the Application to Sexuality in a Pluralistic Postmodern Culture," 68–88.

64. "Because marriage refers to our identity in Christ as the body that is determined by Christ as the head, the holiness of marriage is central in the apostle's treatment of sexual life," Van Vlastuin, "Retrieving the Concept," 78.

65. In a lecture at a study day of the platform Bijbels Beraad M/V (Biblical Council on Manhood/ Womanhood), which is the continuation of the Nashville-group in the Netherlands, Van Vlastuin emphasized that the Bible begins with the order of (heterosexual) marriage and ends with the wedding of the Lamb. Therefore, he stated, heterosexual marriage is inextricably related to Christology. Lecture "Wat is waarheid?" (What is Truth?), website *Bijbels Beraad M/V*, September 2020, https://www.bijbelsberaadmv.nl/2021/02/15/luister-lezing-prof-dr-van-vlastuin-tijdens-besloten-studiedag/ (accessed April 15, 2021).

equally acknowledging same-sex sexualities as desires that may be lived out. Referring to the pneumatological dimension of being in Christ, he points to "huge implications for our sexuality."[66] Here in Reformed theology, he writes, we enter the field of sanctification, of the Spirit's transformation of human life. How will it look like? The next sentence reveals the author's unsuccessfully hidden 'erotic injustice'[67] towards same-sex sexualities: "Without suggesting that sexual identities have to be changed and can 'easily' be changed, we cannot deny the effect of the spiritual union with Christ on sexual desires and on our character." Although he hastens to explain that this transformative effect will apply equally to heterosexuals and homosexuals, it becomes clear that the impact for the latter is far more drastic: it shall lead to a denial of the full realization of their sexualities.

The three interpretations of Butterfield, Rose, and van Vlastuin have in common that they all construct an identity 'in Christ' that is disconnected from the body's desires or even opposed to them.[68] The risk is evident. If this *theological* notion of identity 'in Christ' conflates with the *sociological* notion of Christian identity, we see how such theological discourse may fuel a Christian identity politics, of which 'Nashville' was a sad low.[69]

6. NOTIONS FOR A THEOLOGY OF SEXUALITY BEYOND IDENTITY POLITICS

In this final section, I want to explore three possible approaches that may lead beyond the polarization of sexual identity politics. First, I affiliate with the proposal of Mark Jordan,[70] Andy Buechel,[71] and Marco Derks[72] to speak of 'sacramental characters' instead of 'sexual identities' and 'identity in Christ.' Second, I believe that the notion of the 'broken middle' of philosopher Gillian Rose offers creative space to dwell in, and protects against premature theological 'healing' in unfruitful identity positions. And third, I would like to derive from these theoretical concepts some core spiritual values for a conversational, non-violent attitude in

---

66. Van Vlastuin, "Retrieving the Concept," 83.
67. From the essay of Gayle Rubin, "Thinking Sex: Notes for a Radical Theory of the Politics of Sexuality," in *Pleasure and Danger*, ed. Carole Vance (Routledge and Paul Kegan, 1984); reprinted in *The Lesbian and Gay Studies Reader*, eds. Henry Abelove, Michele Aina Barale and David M. Halperin (New York: Routledge, 1994).
68. Compare Derks, *Constructions of Homosexuality*, 92.
69. Compare Derks, *Constructions of Homosexuality*, 93.
70. Jordan, "The Return of Religion," 52–54.
71. Andy Buechel, *That We Might Become God: The Queerness of Creedal Christianity* (Eugene: Cascade Books, 2015).
72. Derks, *Constructions of Homosexuality*, 77–94.

matters of divergent theological views and beliefs on sexuality.

6.1 Gesturing Towards a Sacramental Character

Derks suggests to work towards "a better *theological* understanding" of the meaning of 'identity in Christ.'[73] Therefore, we should better avoid the term 'identity' and follow the queer approach of Jordan and Buechel to speak of a 'sacramental character' that is inaugurated by baptism. A sacramental character, according to the *Catechism of the Catholic Church*, is an indelible spiritual 'seal' or 'mark' by which the baptized person is configured to Christ.[74] This classic theological concept is retrieved by Jordan when he radicalizes the queer approach. Sacramental characters are not 'identities': "Absent a legal code..."[75] Christian sexual ethics has to derive its principles from mimetic, unstable characters rather than regulations. These characters are imitated from biblical narratives and the rich lives of saints, beyond good and bad; they are performed and mediated through rites and liturgies. It renders them a complex temporality that cannot be captured by any identity. For Jordan, there is not a single 'Christian identity,' but a multiplicity of sacramental characters. He sees them close to drag or camp. He claims that Christianity remains "a repository of archaic, transgressive characters of desire and gender."[76] They challenge and resist the modern regime of sexuality, which is a regime of identities, and make an openness to the unspeakable erotic.

I am sympathetic with this approach. In a creative and integrative way, it avoids the pitfalls of adopting identity politics in a Christian jacket, be it of the conservative or progressive kind. I would like to bring together the concept of 'sacramental character' with the 'new asceticism' approach to sexuality as proposed by Sarah Coakley.[77] She

---

73. Derks, *Constructions of Homosexuality*, 89.

74. *Catechism of the Catholic Church*, 1993, par. 1121: "The three sacraments of Baptism, Confirmation, and Holy Orders confer, in addition to grace, a sacramental character or 'seal' by which the Christian shares in Christ's priesthood and is made a member of the Church according to different states and functions. This configuration to Christ and to the Church, brought about by the Spirit, is indelible, it remains forever in the Christian as a positive disposition for grace, a promise and guarantee of divine protection, and as a vocation to divine worship and to the service of the Church. Therefore these sacraments can never be repeated." https://www.vatican.va/archive/ENG0015/_INDEX (accessed April 15, 2021).

75. Jordan, "The Return of Religion," 52.

76. From Derks, *Constructions of Homosexuality*, 91, reference to Mark Jordan, *Recruiting Young Love*: *How Christians Talk about Homosexuality* (Chicago and London: The University of Chicago Press, 2011).

77. Sarah Coakley, *God, Sexuality and the Self*: *An 'Essay on the Trinity'* (Cambridge: Cambridge University Press, 2013); The New Asceticism: Sexuality, Gender and the Quest for God (London: Bloomsbury, 2015).

also strives to move theologically beyond the polarized identity-positions in the sexuality and gender debates. For Coakley, sexuality is deeply connected to spiritual reality, such as the contemplative love for God or even God's own innertrinitarian desires. She wants to address the issues of sexuality and gender more profoundly than in the current debates. Her approach is one of re-enchantment of sexuality and of liberating gender and sexual identities from false desires to dominate and control, by contemplatively drawing these realities in the light of God as source and purpose of human desires. The 'new asceticism' she proposes aims at intensification, transformation, and purification of desire, not at extinction of it, and without privileging heterosexual desires. Authentic eros is rooted in God. Trinitarian desire energizes reality. Our erotic desire will reflect and embody God's desire, by not wanting to possess, own or control someone, nor simply to create pleasures for ourselves, but by wanting our bodies and their activities to bring joy to someone other than ourselves. Rowan Williams calls this 'the body's grace,' since desiring and being desired by another person helps us to understand what it is to desire and be desired by God.[78]

6.2 ATTENDING TO THE BROKEN MIDDLE

As another helpful notion, I consider Gillian Rose's socio-philosophical concept of the 'broken middle.' Gillian Rose, née Stone (1947–1995), was a philosopher, social theorist, and Jewish convert to Christian religion. In her highly original work she offers a language for the co-belonging of religion and politics, and the secular and the sacred. She developed a novel account to faith, inspired by her reading of Hegel and Kierkegaard, and the Jewish emphasis on observation of the law. She opted for a secular faith, as a mode of social practice. Faith is a practice: it is the practice of continuing to grapple with the world, realizing that the world is, and always will be, uncertain. Yet, in every moment, we are called to act. In her memoir *Love's Work* (1995) she impressively testifies to it in a personal voice.

I believe that Gillian Rose's idea of 'attending to the broken middle' can be made fertile in our theological search to move beyond the polarizing dynamics of the sexuality debate. She develops the notion of the broken middle in the context of understanding the strained relationship between Judaism and Christianity, and between theology and philosophy. It is a concept with several layers. Important in the background is her re-interpretation of Hegel. She reads Hegel's philosophy not as about synthetizing oppositions but rather about dwelling in the contradictions.

---

78. Rowan Williams, "The Body's Grace," in *Theology and Sexuality: Classic and Contemporary Readings*, ed. Eugene F. Rogers (Oxford: Blackwell, 2002), 309–321.

On the one hand, the 'broken middle' expresses the epistemological condition, how thinking the absolute is rooted in the actuality of experience, in the risk of asserting oneself in the 'broken middle' and at the same time having an awareness of it that actually manifests: thinking the absolute is experienced both as dichotomy and as beyond dichotomy. On the other hand, the 'broken middle' can be read as a twentieth-century version of Kierkegaard's 'suspense of the ethical.'[79] It refers us to the utterly mundane, everyday experience of living amidst social realities of ambiguity and contradiction, in which we have to act as if there is no law. There is a law, yet acting as a free person never depends on law only.

In this actual life, we experience a tension between, as Gillian Rose puts it metaphorically, the city of New Jerusalem and the city of Old Athens.[80] The one refers to a love-based community ideal, the second to a law-based ideal. In none of these cities the human being lives. She inhibits a third city, that of ordinary life. There in the 'broken middle' between love and law, between the aspirations of love and posited social norms, the human being negotiates life. This condition raises anxiety. Anxiety belongs to true freedom. A faithful person, and we may look at Abraham, experiences anxiety. She realizes that all actions are continually implicated in violence and yet she perseveres in acting, in putting herself at risk in any given social or political act, in the commitment "to stay in the fray, in the revel of ideas and risk" that is living.[81] Faith is needed when the law is suspended. Faith is needed all of the time because navigating social norms with excellence always involves anxiety. Failure is inextricably part of this faithful work of love.

Gillian Rose criticizes most political theologies, because they run into the void and try to mend the broken middle. They provide holistic solutions, and want to drive us closer to a world of 'holy middles' by replacing Old Athens by New Jerusalem.[82] But the broken middle cannot be mended and should not be evaded. Sacralization is a way of evading. Instead, theology needs to attend to the broken middle, dwell in its ambiguity and contradictions, take the risk of negotiating difference or

---

79. Part One of Gillian Rose, *The Broken Middle* (Hoboken: John Wiley and Sons, 1992), 3–114; Gregory David Parry, *The 'Void' in Simone Weil and the 'Broken Middle' in Gillian Rose: The Genesis of the Search for Salvation* (Doctoral thesis Durham University, 2006), 249–258, http://etheses.dur.ac.uk/1300/ (accessed April 15, 2021).

80. Rose, *The Broken Middle*, 277–295; see Parry, *The 'Void'*, 259–289; Anna Rowlands in a lecture about Gillian Rose on YouTube, *St. Johns Timeline*, 4 July, 2018. https://www.youtube.com/watch?v=8h9cXMnORFw (accessed April 15, 2021).

81. Gillian Rose, *Love's Work* (London: Chatto and Windus Limited, 1995), 135.

82. Rose, *The Broken Middle*, 272–282; Parry, *The 'void'*, 261. Rose criticizes for instance John Milbank's political theology, for it mends the middle with holiness without examination of its brokenness.

otherness in any given order.[83]

What could the notion of 'attending to the broken middle' possibly contribute to a theology of sexuality that resists polarizing tendencies? A theology of the broken middle is first and foremost aware of complexities and contradictions of the lived life. These complexities are most intimately experienced in our sexual desires and relationships, in a mixture of pleasure and pain, surrender and withdrawal, hope and disappointment, violence and tenderness, power and love, might and grace. A theology of the broken middle is an existential theology. It does neither dogmatically hold to concepts, nor to biblical 'truths' on sexuality and gender, but attends to living persons who freely yet anxiously are navigating their lives between love and social norms. A theology of the broken middle acknowledges that social norms are not rigid and static. In moments of crisis, social norms are suspended. Examples of such moments of suspension, besides Abrahams' sacrifice, are for Gillian Rose crises of illness, bereavement, separation from a loved one, or natural disasters.[84] We can add: also moments in which our experienced sexualities and genders make us extremely vulnerable to ourselves and to the social world we live in, and make us honestly question the moral and religious norms we live by. Faithful living then means whole-heartedly participating, indeed as a sacramental character, in the practice of testing norms against reality, always willing to revise the concepts, energized by a greater love and acceptance.

For a Christian faith community, that centers its faith on the crucified and risen Christ, attending to the broken middle should almost be a naturally given.[85] A church pre-eminently would be able to accept the paradox of the broken middle as a creative paradigm for building community through an open conversation, without suppressing any internal theological conflict. Attending to the broken middle holds difference and reconciliation together. It can never go with identity politics which in fact evades the broken middle.

---

83. Parry, *The 'void'*, 259.

84. Gillian Rose, *Love's Work*, 98. See also Vincent Lloyd, "The Secular Faith of Gillian Rose," *Journal of Religious Ethics* 36:4 (2008), 683–705.

85. This idea is elaborated by Anderson H. M. Jeremiah, "Dalit Christians in India: Reflections from the 'Broken Middle,'" *Studies in World Christianity* 17:3 (2011), 258–274.

7. Conclusion

As Andrew Shranks notes:

> Thus the church of the broken middle would be one that was essentially dedicated to conversational openness of every kind. Its worship would be a celebration of conversational openness, as the will of God; its whole prayer life would be a cultivation of the virtues that make for good conversation.[86]

I envision the church of the broken middle as a church where conversation is rooted in the transformative love of God that works from below, from the broken and wounded middle. The conversation seeks to engage people of good will everywhere in a transformative journey grounded in love, which is the foundation of justice and peace. It offers companionship to those who join the pilgrimage by celebrating the gifts of every individual, visiting the wounds, and transforming the injustices.[87] Honoring the worth and dignity of every person is a hallmark of the church's conversations. In these conversations, personal stories in their very concreteness and endless ambiguity are carefully listened to and begin to defuse tensions and conflicts that were perpetuated by ideological contestation.

My analysis of the polarized debate on the Nashville Statement in the Netherlands has shown that framing the contesting positions in terms of 'identity' will not advance the conversation. The inclination of conservative Reformed groups, both in politics and in the church, to respond to secularizing threats by increasingly marking their Christian identity with clear-cut and unnegotiable views of gender and sexuality, may seem to be a full religious response but actually brings them close to a present-day form of cultural Christianity, in fact a form of civil religion. This civil religion is based on the defense of 'traditional (family) values'. Relatively late it has also gained a foothold in the Netherlands. In the discourse of right-wing populist parties, the concept of a 'Judeo-Christian civilization' is strategically adopted and interwoven with a nationalist, authoritarian, and ethnocentric narrative, in which anti-genderism and anti-LGBTI rhetoric play a key role as mobilizing tools. At first sight, the move by some theologians towards a higher 'identity in

---

86. Andrew Shranks, *Against Innocence: Gillian Rose's Reception and Gift of Faith* (London: SCM Press, 2008), 162.

87. These are the dimensions of the Pilgrimage of Justice and Peace process to which the World Council of Churches invites its member churches and all people of good will. See WCC Central Committee, *An Invitation to the Pilgrimage of Justice and Peace*, July 8, 2014, Geneva. https://www.oikoumene.org/en/resources/documents/central-committee/geneva-2014/an-invitation-to-the-pilgrimage-of-justice-and-peace (accessed April 15, 2021).

Christ' brings in a potentially critical notion. However, in the elaboration heterosexuality functions as an implicit theological norm and the critical potential gets lost. My proposal is to open up and advance the debate by theologically opting for the notions of 'sacramental character' and 'new asceticism'—without assuming any heterosexual privilege—, and to embrace the concept of the broken middle.

A church attending to the broken middle gracefully offers space to all kinds of sacramental characters, grateful and proud of their bodies and human needs such as love and sexuality, celebrating the gifts of creation, giving thanks to the Creator and Redeemer of all, and worshipping in a freedom that is beyond words. Between the city of Old Athens and the city of New Jerusalem, the church of Jesus Christ may live and breathe as a learning community on a transformative journey, dwelling with forbearance and hope in the broken middle. It may provide a place where people feel safe to share about their gendered experiences and human sexuality in the earthly brokenness of glory and shame, of fleshly vulnerability and divine exaltation, of feeling safe and being at risk. "To live, to love, is to be failed, to forgive, to have failed, to be forgiven, for ever and ever."[88]

BIBLIOGRAPHY

Alcoff, Linda Martín and John D. Caputo. Eds. *Feminism, Sexuality and the Return of Religion*. Bloomington and Indianapolis: Indiana University Press, 2011.

Almond, Philip C. "Is there really such a thing as 'Judeo-Christian Tradition'?" Website ABC *Religion and Ethics*, February 14, 2019. Accessed April 15, 2021. https://www.abc.net.au/religion/is-there-really-a-judeo-christian-tradition/10810554.

Appelman, Matthijs D. and Ruard R. Ganzevoort. "Refo houdt zich steeds intensiever bezig met onderwerp homoseksualiteit" (Reformed are getting busy more and more with the topic of homosexuality). *Reformatorisch Dagblad*, December 16, 2019. Ccessed April15, 2021. https://www.rd.nl/opinie/refo-houdt-zich-steeds-intensiever-bezig-met-onderwerp-homoseksualiteit-1.1617912.

Appiah, Kwame Anthony. *The Lies That Bind: Rethinking Identity*. New York: Liveright, 2018.

---

88. Gillian Rose, *Love's Work*, 98.

Behrensen, Maria; Marianne Heimbach-Steins and Linda E. Hennig. "Einleitung." In *Gender—Nation—Religion: Ein internationaler Vergleich von Akteursstrategien und Diskursverflechtungen*. Eds. Maria Behrensen a.o., 7–24. Frankfurt/New York: Campus Verlag, 2019.

Bolz-Weber, Nadia. *Shameless: A Sexual Revolution*. London: Canterbury Press Norwich, 2019.

Bos, David and Marco Derks. "Inleiding: God, seks en politiek. Themanummer over een spannende driehoeksverhouding" (Introduction: God, sex, and politics. Special issue on an exciting triangle). *Religie en Samenleving* 11:2 (2016): 97–100.

Brandsma, Bart. *Polarisation: Understanding the Dynamics of Us versus Them*. Schoonrewoerd: BB in media, 2017.

Bruijne, Ad de. "Culture Wars About Sexuality: A Theological Proposal for Dialogue." In *Public Discourses about Homosexuality and Religion in Europe and beyond*, eds. Marco Derks and Mariecke van den Berg, 105–124. London: Palgrave Macmillan, 2020.

Buechel, Andy. *That We Might Become God: The Queerness of Creedal Christianity*. Eugene: Cascade Books, 2015.

Butterfield, Rosaria Champagne. *The Secret Thoughts of an Unlikely Convert: An English Professor's Journey into the Christian Faith*. Pittsburgh: Crown and Covenant Publications, 2012.

Butterfield, Rosaria Champagne. *Openness Unhindered: Further Thoughts of an Unlikely Convert on Sexual Identity and Union with Christ*. Pittsburgh: Crown and Covenant Publications, 2015.

Butterfield, Rosaria Champagne. "Sexual Identity and Union with Christ." Lecture at Geneva College, April 21, 2016. Accessed April 15, 2021. https://www.youtube.com/watch?v=oEsj9Hh59uw.

Butterfield, Rosaria. "Why I Signed the Nashville Statement." Website *Council on Biblical Manhood and Womanhood*, August 31, 2017. Accessed April 15, 2021. https://cbmw.org/2017/08/31/rosaria-butterfield-why-i-signed-the-nashville-statement/.

Catechism of the Catholic Church, 1993. Accessed April 15, 2021. https://www.vatican.va/archive/ENG0015/_INDEX.HTM.

Coakley, Sarah. *God, Sexuality and the Self: An 'Essay on the Trinity'*. Cambridge: Cambridge University Press, 2013.

Coakley, Sarah. *The New Asceticism: Sexuality, Gender and the Quest for God*. London: Bloomsbury, 2015.

Congregation on Catholic Education. *Male and Female He Created Them: Towards a Path of Dialogue on the Question of Gender Theory in Education*. Vatican City, 2019. Accessed April 15. 2021). http://www.vatican.va/roman_curia/congregations/ccatheduc/documents/rc_con_ccatheduc_doc_20190202_maschio-e-femmina_en.pdf.

Council on Biblical Manhood and Womanhood. "Nashville Statement." 2017. Accessed April 15, 2021. https://cbmw.org/nashville-statement/.

DeFranza, Megan K. "Good News for Gender Minorities." In *Understanding Transgender Identities: Four Views*, eds. James K. Beilby and Paul Rhodes Eddy, 147–178. Grand Rapids: Baker Academics, 2019.

Derks, Marco. *Constructions of Homosexuality and Christian Religion in Contemporary Public Discourses in the Netherlands*. Quaestiones Infinitae, vol. 123. Doctoral thesis Utrecht University, 2019.

Derks, Marco and Mariecke van den Berg. Eds. *Public Discourses about Homosexuality and Religion in Europe and beyond*. London: Palgrave Macmillan, 2020.

Dowland, Seth. *Family Values and the Rise of the Christian Right*. Philadelphia: University of Pennsylvania Press, 2015.

Faludi, Susan. *Backlash: The Undeclared War Against Women*. New York: Vintage, 1991.

Foucault, Michel. *The History of Sexuality Volume 1: An Introduction*. London: Allen Lane, 1979.

Foucault, Michel. *The History of Sexuality Volume 2: The Use of Pleasure*. London: Penguin Books, 1992.

Foucault, Michel. *The History of Sexuality Volume 3: The Care of the Self*. London: Penguin Books, 1990.

Fukuyama, Francis. *Identity: The Demand for Dignity and the Politics of Resentment*. New York: Farrar, Straus and Giroux, 2018.

Grudem, Wayne and John Piper. Eds. *Recovering Biblical Manhood and Womanhood: A Response to Evangelical Feminism*. Second edition. Wheaton: Crossway, 2006.

Hemel, Ernst van den. "Korte rokjes tegen de Islam? De SGP en het boemerangeffect van geculturaliseerd christendom" (Short skirts against Islam? The SGP and the boomerang effect of culturalized Christianity). In *Theocratie en populisme: Staatkundig gereformeerden en de stem van het volk* (Theocracy and populism: Political reformed and the voice of the people), ed. Koos-jan de Jager, 149–178. Apeldoorn: Labarum Academic, 2020.

Huijgen, Arnold and Maarten Kater. "Na bezinning door kerken pas visie op genderideologie" (Only after reflection by churches a view on gender ideology). *Reformatorisch Dagblad*, December 28, 2018, revised January 17, 2019.

Humanae Vitae. Accessed April 15, 2021. http://www.vatican.va/content/paul-vi/en/encyclicals/documents/hf_p-vi_enc_25071968_humanae-vitae.html.

Hunter, James Davison. *Culture Wars: The Struggle to Define America*. New York: Basic Books, 1991.

Jeremiah, Anderson H. M. "Dalit Christians in India: Reflections from the 'Broken Middle.'" *Studies in World Christianity* 17:3 (2011): 258–274.

Jordan, Mark. *Recruiting Young Love: How Christians Talk about Homosexuality*. Chicago and London: The University of Chicago Press, 2011.

Jordan, Mark. "The Return of Religion during the Reign of Sexuality." In *Feminism, Sexuality and the Return of Religion*, eds. Linda Martín Alcoff and John D. Caputo, 39–54. Bloomington and Indianapolis: Indiana University Press, 2011.

Kennedy, James. "New Babylon and the Politics of Modernity." *Sociologische gids* 44:5–6 (1997): 361–374.

Kuby, Gabriela. *The Global Sexual Revolution: The Destruction of Freedom in the Name of Freedom*. New York: LifeSite/Angelico Press, 2015.

Kuhar, Roman and David Paternotte. Eds. *Anti-Gender Campaigns in Europe*: *Mobilizing against Equality*. Washington: Rowman and Littlefield, 2017.

Lederach, John Paul. *The Moral Imagination*: *The Art and Soul of Building Peace*. Oxford: Oxford University Press, 2010.

Lilla, Mark. *The Once and Future Liberal*: *After Identity Politics*. New York: Harper, 2017.

Lloyd, Vincent. "The Secular Faith of Gillian Rose." *Journal of Religious Ethics* 36:4 (2008): 683–705.

McRobbie, Angela. "Post-feminism and popular culture." *Feminist Media Studies* 4:3 (1991): 255–264.

Morgan, Silas. "American Masculinity, Feminism, and the Politics of Fatherhood." In *Gender—Nation—Religion*: *Ein internationaler Vergleich von Akteursstrategien und Diskursverflechtungen*. Eds. Maria Behrensen a.o., 101–123. Frankfurt/New York: Campus Verlag, 2019.

"Nashville initiator: De kerken zwegen bij nazi-ideologie, bij gender-ideologie gebeurt dat weer" (Nashville initiator: The churches were silent on Nazi ideology, with gender ideology it happens again). *Algemeen Dagblad*, February 1, 2020. Accessed April 15, 2021. https://www.ad.nl/binnenland/nashville-initiator-kerken-zwegen-bij-nazi-ideologie-bij-gender-ideologie-gebeurt-dat-weer~ac8ec6b3/.

Otjes, Simon and André Krouwel. "De SGP-kiezer: Wel radicaal en rechts maar niet radicaalrechts populistisch?" (The SGP voter: Radical and right-wing but not radical right-wing populist?). In *Theocratie en populisme*: *Staatkundig gereformeerden en de stem van het volk* (Theocracy and populism: Political reformed and the voice of the people), ed. Koos-jan de Jager, 179–201. Apeldoorn: Labarum Academic, 2020.

Oudenampsen, Merijn. *De conservatieve revolutie*: *Een ideeëngeschiedenis van de Fortuyn-opstand* (The Conservative Revolution: A History of Ideas of the Fortuyn Rebellion). Amsterdam: Merijn Oudenampsen en Nijmegen: Uitgeverij Vantilt, 2018.

Oudenampsen, Merijn. *The Conservative Embrace of Values*. Doctoral thesis. University of Amsterdam, 2018.

Parry, Gregory David. *The 'Void' in Simone Weil and the 'Broken Middle' in Gillian Rose: The Genesis of the Search for Salvation*. Doctoral thesis Durham University, 2006. Accessed April 15, 2021. http://etheses.dur.ac.uk/1300/.

Püttmann, Andreas. "Geschlechterordnung und Familismus als Policy-Angebote des Rechtspopulismus und Autoritarismus für das katholische Milieu." In *Gender—Nation—Religion: Ein internationaler Vergleich von Akteursstrategien und Diskursverflechtungen*. Eds. Maria Behrensen a.o., 51–80. Frankfurt/New York: Campus Verlag, 2019.

Rietveld, Sander. *Nieuwe kruisvaarders: De Heilige Alliantie tussen orthodoxe christenen en radicaal-rechtse populisten* (New Crusaders: The Holy Alliance between orthodox Christians and radical-right populists). Amsterdam: Prometheus, 2021.

Rose, Gillian. *Love's Work*. London: Chatto and Windus Limited, 1995.

Rose, Gillian. *The Broken Middle*. Hoboken: John Wiley and Sons, 1992.

Rose, Wolter. "We hebben elkaar wat te vertellen" (We have something to tell each other). In *Open en kwetsbaar: Christelijk debat over homoseksualiteit* (Open and vulnerable: Christian debate on homosexuality), ed. Ad de Bruijne, 115–122. Barneveld: De Vuurbaak, 2012.

Roy, Olivier and the Robert Schuman Centre for Advanced Studies. *Rethinking the Place of Religion in European Secularized Societies: The Need for More Open Societies*. Conclusions of the Research Project Religio West. European University Institute, March 2016. Accessed April 15, 2021. https://cadmus.eui.eu/handle/1814/40305.

Rubin, Gayle. "Thinking Sex: Notes for a Radical Theory of the Politics of Sexuality." In *Pleasure and Danger*, ed. Carole Vance. Routledge and Paul Kegan, 1984. Reprinted in *The Lesbian and Gay Studies Reader*, eds. Henry Abelove, Michele Aina Barale and David M. Halperin. New York: Routledge, 1994.

Sen, Amartya. *Identity and Violence: The Illusion of Destiny*. New York: W.W. Norton Company, 2007.

Shranks, Andrew. *Against Innocence: Gillian Rose's Reception and Gift of Faith*. London: SCM Press, 2008.

Smothers, Colin. "Owen Strachan: The Nashville Statement 'is a moment of remarkable unanimity of spirit," website *Council on Biblical Manhood and Womanhood*. September 1, 2017. Accessed April 15, 2021. https://cbmw.org/2017/09/01/owen-strachan-the-nashville-statement-is-a-moment-of-remarkable-unanimity-of-spirit/.

Stewart, Anna and Simon Coleman. "Contributions from Anthropology." In *The Oxford Handbook of Theology, Sexuality, and Gender*, ed. Adrian Thatcher, 105–119. Oxford: Oxford University Press, 2015.

Strube, Sonja A.; Rita Perintvalvi; Rafaela Hemet; Miriam Metze and Cicek Sahbaz. Eds. *Anti-Genderismus in Europa: Allianzen von Rechtspopulismus und religiösem Fundamentalismus. Mobilisierung—Vernetzung—Transformation*. Bielefeld: Transcript Verlag, 2020. Open Access: https://www.transcript-verlag.de/pdfgen/html2pdf/create.php.

Strube, Sonja Angelika. "Rechtspopulismus und konfessionelle Anti-Gender-Bewegung: Milieu-übergreifende Allianzen und rhetorische Strategien im deutschen Sprachraum." In *Gender—Nation—Religion: Ein internationaler Vergleich von Akteursstrategien und Diskursverflechtungen*. Eds. Maria Behrensen a.o., 25–49. Frankfurt/ New York: Campus Verlag, 2019.

Stuart, Elizabeth. "The Theological Study of Sexuality." In *The Oxford Handbook of Theology, Sexuality, and Gender*, ed. Adrian Thatcher, 18–31. Oxford: Oxford University Press, 2015.

Taylor, Charles. *Sources of the Self: The Making of the Modern Identity*. Cambridge: Cambridge University Press, 1989.

"'The day after': ds. M. Klaassen blikt terug op Nashville" ('The day after': Rev. M. Klaassen looks back on Nashville). *Reformatorisch Dagblad*, January 15, 2019. Accessed April 15, 2021. https://cip.nl/71497-the-days-after-ds-m-klaassen-blikt-terug-op-nashville-ophef.

Tondstad, Linn Marie. *Queer Theology*. Eugene: Cascade Books, 2018.

Trzebiatowska, Marta. "Contributions from Sociology." In *The Oxford Handbook of Theology, Sexuality, and Gender*, ed. Adrian Thatcher, 120–136. Oxford: Oxford University Press, 2015.

Vlastuin, Wim van. "Wat is waarheid?" (What is Truth?). Website *Bijbels Beraad M/V*, September 2020. Accessed April 15, 2021. https://www.bijbelsberaadmv.nl/2021/02/15/luister-lezing-prof-dr-van-vlastuin-tijdens-besloten-studiedag/.

Werkgroep Nashville-verklaring. "Nashville-verklaring. Een gezamenlijke verklaring over Bijbelse seksualiteit." 2019. Accessed April 15, 2021. https://nashvilleverklaring.nl.

Williams, Rowan. "The Body's Grace." In *Theology and Sexuality: Classic and Contemporary Readings*, ed. Eugene F. Rogers, 309–321. Oxford: Blackwell, 2002.

WCC Central Committee. *An Invitation to the Pilgrimage of Justice and Peace*, July 8, 2014, Geneva. Accessed April 15, 2021. https://www.oikoumene.org/en/resources/documents/central-committee/geneva-2014/an-invitation-to-the-pilgrimage-of-justice-and-peace.

CHAPTER 5
PASSIVITY, ABUSE, AND SELF-SACRIFICE: DAOISM AND FEMINIST CHRISTOLOGY
Jaeseung Cha

1. INTRODUCTION

Throughout its short history, Korean Christianity has seen a critical division between women and men. While some leaders view the polarization of women and men in Korea as a hidden legacy that fosters unintended divisions, others argue that it is still an intentional and lasting reality in Korea. The two phenomena of polarization, intentional and hidden, are by no means new here in the United States. For example, the Reformed Church of America has been ordaining women for decades. The intension to overcome the polarization was clearly pronounced, but some classes are still secretly and unofficially reluctant to have women ministers. The polarization between women and men is also theologically critical. It has influenced the discussion of Christ's crucifixion as we can see, especially by feminist theologians, in harsh critiques of atonement theology and their ecclesial implications and social practices. This chapter will explore the Daoist view of woman and Western feminist theology of the atonement in order to advocate an alternative to polarization.

Many assume that the gender issue in the church is rooted in Confucian culture, where there is substantial discrimination against women in terms of the five principles of Confucian ethics.[1] Nei Ze (內則) of Liji (禮記), one of the five Confucian scriptures, describes in various ways how to distinguish between women and men in their lifestyle and virtues: "The men should not speak of what belongs to the

---

1. "There should be affection between father and son; righteousness between sovereign and minister; difference between husband and wife; order between old and young; and fidelity between friends (父子有親君臣有義夫婦有別長幼有序朋友有信)," Mengzi, *Teng Wen Gong I*. Difference (別) is often interpreted as mutual respect between husband and wife in their respective roles, but it has impacted Asian society not only as a functional difference, but also as a substantial limitation of women in relation to men.

inside (of the house), nor the women of what belongs to the outside;" "On the road, a man should take the right side, and a woman the left;" and "At the age of seven, boys and girls must not occupy the same mat nor sit together."[2]

Not many people (including Asians) are, however, aware of an aspect of the philosophical tradition of Daoism, in which a profound clue about feminism can be found. In Daoism, the female is the divine being of creation,[3] and the revealed name of the Dao, the deity of Daoism, (which is apophatic in nature) is Mother.[4] Furthermore, in Daoist political principles, the female is considered superior to the male.[5] One may doubt if talk of the female and "Mother" signifies a genuine ontological superiority of female over male, or if they simply represent the Dao's nature metaphorically—with the feebleness and passivity of women and children,[6] along with the sacrifice of empty vessels,[7] symbolizing the harmony and production of nature and human beings. What is clear, however, is that in Daoism passivity is viewed not only as passive stillness but also as an active power to produce and embrace all things, and it is women, not men, who represent this nature of the Dao. The Dao produces but does not possess; it advances but does not dominate.[8] Thus, in Daoism, genuine power is viewed as the Dao's "non-dominating/non-violent sacrificial" power, which is found in women, rather than the dominating violent power of men. Does this non-dominating feminine promote the passivity of women, or might it suggest a new perspective for Christian feminism?

One modern critique of Christianity is that the tradition values a passive endurance of pain and suffering and even glorifies violent abuse because of the patriarchal power structure of God's demand of Christ's sacrifice on the cross. Joanne Carlson Brown and Rebecca Parker are among those who radically relate the cross to violence and sexism. In their view, since the central image of the cross communicates the message that suffering is redemptive, self-sacrifice not only becomes a virtue, but is the definition of a faithful identity, and thus the cross glorifies suffering. Even liberation theology, with atonement at its center, is seen to encourage martyrdom and victimization. The critical problem these authors find is that the cross promotes and perpetuates abuse and

---

2. "男不言內 女不言外," "道路 男子由右 女子由左," and "七年男女不同席."
3. "谷神不死 是謂玄牝 玄牝之門 是謂天地根," *Dao De Jing* 6.
4. "無名天地之始 有名萬物之母," *Dao De Jing* 1.
5. "牝常以靜勝牡," *Dao De Jing* 61.
6. "知其雄 守其雌 為天下谿 為天下谿 常德不離 復歸於嬰兒," *Dao De Jing* 28.
7. "道沖而用之或不盈," *Dao De Jing* 4.
8. "生而不有… 長而不宰," *Dao De Jing* 51.

violence, especially the abuse of women in the church. Through the cross, divine child abuse is paraded as salvific, the child who suffers without raising his voice is lauded as the hope of the world, and the theology of original sin and Christ's suffering in bearing sin on the cross perpetuates women's role as suffering servant. We now have a serious challenge: If Christ's sacrifice is the very root of sexism, do we have to do away with the atonement?

We confront polarized gender issues in Western and East Asian contexts, whether hidden or intentional, and highly polarized theological debates on the atonement with traditional theology pitted against feminist theology. This chapter will contribute to a deeper analysis of various important concepts of the atonement theology, through which we may be able to find a way to embrace both the ever-increasing value of feminist theology and the central message of Christianity in Christ's crucifixion. We will first explore the nature of feminism in Daoism in order to show how the non-violent passivity and embrace of women reveals the sacrificial deity in Daoism. This may shed light on the fact that Christianity is not the only religion to value the sacrificial aspect of the Deity, and that sacrifice may not necessarily be violent. Next, since this non-violent, passive and embracing sacrifice could also be the source of the submissiveness of women in Asia, this chapter will analyze Brown and Parker's view of Western feminism, focusing on their criticisms of the traditional and contemporary theology of the atonement and its relevance for feminism. The chapter will then move on to a critical dialogue with feminist views on (1) abuse and necessity, and (2) self-sacrifice and violence. Lastly, pointing out the complexity of the interwoven issues between the cross, atonement theology, and its implications and application, a revision of atonement theology is suggested that reflects a twofold aspect of the four acts of Christ.

2. FEMINISM IN DAOISM

Although Daoism, with its multifaced tradition, has related to women in various ways and its relationship in doing so is often ambiguous, it has commonly held that esoteric knowledge and secret powers are closely linked with the feminine.[9] This is distinctive in the early scripture, *Dao De Jing*. One of the most intriguing parts of the *Dao De Jing* is chapter sixty-one, where we can clearly see the superiority of woman to man in relation to a political principle:

> A great state [country] should flow downward. This is the [political] principle of intersection, and this is the nature of female. The female

---

9. Catherine Despeux and Livia Kohn, *Women in Daoism* (Cambridge: Three Pines Press, 2003), 1.

always overcomes the male by her stillness. She lowers herself in her stillness. Thus, if the great state condescends to the small states, it gains them; if the small states condescend to the great state, they can gain it.¹⁰

The female here is analogous to the great state, winning males through her stillness and humility. The idea that "she lowers herself in her stillness," however, seems to be problematic for Western feminism. Does this indicate submissiveness and passivity of women in Daoism? Or is it closer to the nature of the Dao?

The sacrificial stillness of Daoism must not be interpreted through the Western dualistic criterion of doing and non-doing, because on the one hand it is linked to *wuwei* (無爲, non-action), which in its receptivity leads to the Dao, while on the other hand it actively creates all, as we can see in the concept of "produces but does not possess (生而不有)": "A holy one manages affairs without doing anything (*wuwei*, 無爲), and conveys his instructions without the use of speech. All things spring up in themselves but the holy one does not ignore [anything]; the holy one produces but does not possess."¹¹ Thus, the stillness in which the female always wins is not so much unconsciously forcing the nature of women to submit themselves to men, but is the essence of the very Dao, the Deity of Daoism, who sacrificially creates all, surpassing the boundary between non-doing and doing.

Furthermore, this non-possessive nature of the Dao not only produces all, but also cares for all. Interestingly, the concept of "produces but does not possess" occurs in two other chapters in relation to the work of nourishing: "The Dao produces [all things] and nourishes them; it produces them and does not possess."¹² Chapter fifty-one unfolds this twofold aspect of the Dao:

> The Dao produces and nourishes [all things]. They receive their forms according to the nature of each and are completed according to the circumstances of their condition. Therefore, all things without exception honor the Dao, and exalt its outflowing operation. This honoring of the Dao and exalting of its operation is not the result of any ordination, but always a spontaneous tribute. Thus, the Dao produces [all things], nourishes them, brings them to their full growth, nurses them, completes them, matures them, maintains them, and overspreads them. It produces but does not possess them; it acts but does not expect; *it advances but does not dominate*. This is called its mysterious virtue (emphasis mine).¹³

10. "大國者下流 天下之交 天下之牝 牝常以靜勝牡 以靜爲下 故大國以下小國 則取小國 小國以下大國 則取大國."
11. "聖人處無爲之事 行不言之教 萬物作焉而不辭 生而不有," *Dao De Jing* 2.
12. "生之 畜之 生而不有," *Dao De Jing* 10.
13. "道生之 德畜之 物形之 勢成之 是以萬物莫不尊道而貴德 道之尊 德之貴 夫莫之命常自然 故道生之 德畜之 長之育之 亭之毒之 養之覆之 生而不有 爲而不恃 長而不宰 是謂玄德," *Dao De Jing* 51.

The Dao creates, nourishes, grows, matures, maintains, and overspreads all things. The deity in Daoism is both the creator and the sustainer of creation. Yet the way the Dao engages in the cosmos and with human beings is striking: it is a gentle and sacrificial caring, not a dominating and forcing power.

We must comprehend the Daoist feminine in the context of the Daoist simultaneity of passivity and activity, or the Daoist passivity of non-violent sacrifice. The female in Daoism is the mysterious Creator who is called the "mysterious woman" (玄牝), and who is also the gate and the root of heaven and earth,[14] just as an empty space can embrace others, and a deep valley gives water of life to nature. As the Dao is mysterious and dark,[15] but lives in even the smallest,[16] so the mystery of creation and nature is not known to us, but is revealed as Mother:

> There was something in chaos and complete before Heaven and Earth were born. It is silent, formless, independent, and unchanging, reaching everywhere but in no danger. It may be regarded as the Mother of all things. I do not know its name, and the word I can say is the Dao. Making an effort further to give it a name, I call it the Great.[17]

Mu (母), Mother, is the only being or existence to portray the Dao, while the deity is formless, unknown, unchanging, and omnipresent. Two points are worth noting here: (1) the Mother is the revealed name of the Dao and (2) *greatness* has a female nature, not male strength. The Mother is the revelation of the Dao in the very first chapter of *Dao De Jing*: Having no name is the origin of all things, but having their names is the Mother.[18]

This great Mother is contrasted with all other people in various ways:

> While the multitude of the ordinary people look satisfied and pleased as if enjoying a great banquet and as if ascending a tower, I alone seem to be frugal and still ... Secular people seem to be bright and discerning but I alone dark, dull, and confused ... I alone am different from all others, but I value the nursing mother.[19]

The essential contrast here is between the active, flourishing, bright, and extending ordinary people and the author, who is in darkness, dullness,

---

14. "是謂玄牝 玄牝之門 是謂天地根," *Dao De Jing* 6.
15. "玄之又玄," *Dao De Jing* 1.
16. "同其塵," *Dao De Jing* 4, 56.
17. "有物混成 先天地生 寂兮寥兮 獨立不改 周行而不殆 可以為天下母 吾不知其名字之曰道 強為之名曰大," *Dao De Jing* 25.
18. "無名天地之始 有名萬物之母."
19. "衆人熙熙 如享太牢 如春登臺 我獨怕兮其未兆.... 俗人昭昭 我獨若昏 俗人察察我獨悶悶.... 我獨異於人 而貴食母," *Dao De Jing* 20.

and confusion, and who does not value anything but the nursing mother. The reason that the author respects the mother is because the Dao, like the mother, embraces and cares for all, not forcing or manipulating them: "The Great Dao extends everywhere ... clothes and feeds all, but does not act as master."[20]

The fact that respect for the caring role of a mother can be found in any culture may cause us to think that feminism would be peripheral in Daoism. It should be noted, however, that "having space for all as an empty vessel"[21] and "being foreign to self"[22] are the actual contents of the Daoistic non-violent sacrifice. In this Daoistic context, women in their creating, embracing, and caring power are viewed as superior to men, who are attracted by dominating and forcing power. In light of the concepts of Daoist act and sacrifice, the feminine in Daoism must be understood in terms of the twofold nature of the Dao: (1) passive sacrifice, represented visually so we can grasp it in the images of the valley, the empty vessel, and women and (2) active creation and care for all things, not by forcing and dominating, but by embracing them. What is at stake here is that the two dimensions in Daoism are simultaneous and interconnected: Precisely because of its passive and non-violent sacrifice, the Dao creates and cares for all things, or, as the Dao actively creates and cares for all, it does not forcefully dominate, but passively sacrifices itself for all. Nonviolent sacrifice is the very nature of the Dao's creation and caring and is most manifestly represented by the feminine. Can this non-violent sacrifice provide a clue to the issues of Western feminism?

3. Feminism and Christ's Sacrifice

The view that Christ's sacrifice on the cross is harmful to women is dominant among many feminist theologians. Joanne Carlson Brown and Rebecca Parker seek the abrogation of the atonement, as follows:

> We must do away with the atonement, this idea of a blood sin upon the whole human race which can be washed away only by the blood of the lamb. This bloodthirsty God is the God of the patriarchy who at the moment controls the whole Christian tradition. This raises the key question for oppressed people seeking liberation within this tradition: If we throw out the atonement is Christianity left?[23]

---

20. "大道汎兮... 衣養萬物而不為主," *Dao De Jing*, 34.
21. "The Dao is an empty vessel. However often we use it, it cannot be used up, 道沖而用之或不盈," *Dao De Jing* 4.
22. The holy one treats self as if it were foreign to self, and yet that person is preserved, 外其身而身存," *Dao De Jing* 7.
23. Joanne Carlson Brown and Rebecca Parker, "For God So Loved the World?" In *Violence against Women and Children: A Christian Theological Sourcebook*, eds. Carol

Because of this bloody, violent, and abusive atonement, they define Christianity as having an abusive theology that glorifies suffering.[24] Their criticism includes both traditional and contemporary views of the atonement. Unfortunately, their understanding of traditional atonement theology is based solely on Gustaf Aulén's three models from *Christus Victor: A Historical Study of the Three Main Types of the Idea of Atonement*, which are the victory model, the objective/Anselmian model, and the subjective/Aberlardian model. They interpret the victory model as a journey of suffering toward victory and comment critically that "suffering is a prelude to triumph and is in itself an illusion" and that "Jesus' death becomes a paradigm for a stage in a psychological process to be patiently endured."[25] They point out the problem with the mechanism of the model of salvation—which is not salvation *from* pain but *through* pain—is that believers are persuaded to endure suffering as a prelude to new life.[26] They then conclude that victimization never leads to triumph and that the victory theory of the atonement defames all those who suffer and trivializes tragedy.[27] Although we must remember that the church has often emphasized victory *through* pain and forcefully applied it to women, it is unclear from scripture if Christ's victory is depicted as one *from* pain or *through* pain. Several biblical texts highlight *victory* over death and evil, rather than its process.[28]

Brown and Parker also criticize Anselm's theology of satisfaction: "[Anselm's] view of justice is not that wrong should be righted but that wrongs should be punished."[29] The idea that justice is established through adequate punishment is at the heart of their criticism.[30] This is despite the fact that the idea of the God-man's satisfaction for God's honor and for what it ought to be is stronger than the idea of punishment in Anselm's atonement theology. After interpreting Anselm's atonement theology as a portrayal of a tyrant God,[31] Brown and Parker abruptly conclude the section by attempting to link Christ's blood, menstrual blood, circumcision blood, and women's experience as follows: In the biblical tradition menstrual blood is a sign of ritual uncleanness; circumcision, often interpreted as men's menstruation, implies men's power; and the image of Jesus's blood carries an implicit, silent devaluation of women.[32]

J. Adams and Marie M. Fortune (New York: Continuum, 1995), 36–59, 56.
    24. Brown and Parker, "For God So Loved the World?" 56.
    25. Brown and Parker, "For God So Loved the World?" 39–40.
    26. Brown and Parker, "For God So Loved the World?" 40.
    27. Brown and Parker, "For God So Loved the World?" 40.
    28. 1 Cor. 15: 25–26, 55; Col. 2: 13–15.
    29. Brown and Parker, "For God So Loved the World?" 41.
    30. Brown and Parker, "For God So Loved the World?" 41.
    31. Brown and Parker, "For God So Loved the World?" 41.
    32. Brown and Parker, "For God So Loved the World?" 43–44.

Certainly we must acknowledge that blood in scripture could be used in various ways to devalue women. Yet, Brown and Parker's interpretation of Anselm's atonement theology is problematic, since Anselm does not come close to any sort of ritual atonement theology—the words "blood" and "sacrifice" occur only once in his *Cur Deus Homo*.[33] Furthermore, it is not easy to follow the logic that links Christ's blood on the cross to a contrast in scripture between the blood of women's menstruation and that of men's circumcision.

The moral example theory of the atonement in which Christ's willingness to die is set up as an example for us to follow is also problematic for Brown and Parker. They hold that, in theory, Christ's victimization should suffice for our moral edification, but in reality, races, classes, and women have been victimized, while at the same time their victimization has been heralded as a persuasive reason for inherently sinful men to become more righteous.[34] Their criticism unveils the logical problem of the moral example theory: Christ's death as a moral value must have a prior value to that of morality, for example, sacrifice, because death as such cannot be a moral value. The hidden connection between moral example and sacrifice could cause the problem of victimization. It is, however, to be noted that the moral example theory emphasizes love as a moral value rather than victimization and that Brown and Parker's criticism is not as much about atonement theology as about its application.

Now, we must pay more attention to Brown and Parker's analysis of three contemporary trends in theology: (1) the Suffering God, (2) the Necessity of Suffering, and (3) the Negativity of Suffering. The authors appreciate the value of a Suffering God theology, because of its shared aspect, in that God suffers with us and the cross creates relationship and community where relationship has been lost.[35] They also consider the active aspect of suffering by quoting Moltmann, who wrote: "Jesus did not suffer passively from the world in which he lived, but incited it against himself by his message and the life he lived."[36] They go on to make a distinction between an "acceptance of suffering" and a "commitment to life," as follows:

> Was God not with us in our suffering before the death of Jesus? Did the death really initiate something that did not exist before? It is true that ...

---

33. "For it is a strange thing if God so delights in, or requires, the blood of the innocent, that he neither chooses, nor is able, to spare the guilty without the sacrifice of the innocent" (*CDH* I.10).

34. Brown and Parker, "For God So Loved the World?" 44.

35. Brown and Parker, "For God So Loved the World?" 48–49.

36. Jürgen Moltmann, The Crucified God (New York: Harper & Row, 1974), 51, quoted by Brown and Parker, "For God So Loved the World?" 49.

fullness of life involved feeling the pain of the world. But it is not true that being open to all of life is the equivalent of choosing to suffer. Nor is it right to see the death of Jesus as a symbol for the life-giving power of receptivity to reality. It is not acceptance of suffering that gives life; it is commitment to life that gives life. The question ... is not, Am I willing to suffer? but Do I desire fully to live? This distinction is subtle and, to some, specious but in the end it makes a great difference in how people interpret and respond to suffering. If you believe that acceptance of suffering gives life, then your resources for confronting perpetrators of violence and abuse will be numbered.[37]

What is the difference between acceptance of suffering and commitment to life here? It seems that Brown and Parker put both "choosing suffering" and "receptivity to reality" in the same category as "acceptance of suffering," in opposition to "commitment to life." Certainly, we should not choose or accept suffering simply for the sake of suffering. Yet, what if we are already living under critical suffering and pain—and of course we are—and how can we simply commit to "life" only, without encountering suffering? Is "encountering suffering" a type of "accepting" or "choosing"? These questions lead us to the second trend Brown and Parker discuss, the necessity of suffering. Is Christ's suffering caused by human reality or by divine necessity?

Returning to biblical themes of hope, some contemporary liberation theologians deal with the concept of the necessity of suffering, interpreting the crucifixion of Jesus as a sign that before the dawn of a new age, a period of struggle, violence, sacrifice, and pain will inevitably occur.[38] The authors quote Martin Luther King Jr.'s claim that suffering can be a most creative and powerful social force[39] and that the only violence the Gospel allows is violence to oneself.[40] Yet Brown and Parker point out the problem with a martyrdom theology is that when the perpetrators of violence seek to silence the faithful with threats, the faithful believe that they are in a situation of blessedness.[41] Since this clouds the reality that the perpetrators resist change by using violence, we must not mythologize violence as part of a divinely ordained process of transformation.[42] Although I agree with them that suffering should

---

37. Brown and Parker, "For God So Loved the World?" 49.
38. Brown and Parker, "For God So Loved the World?" 50.
39. Martin Luther King Jr. quoted in *A Testament of Hope*, ed. James Washington (New York: Harper & Row, 1986), 47, Brown and Parker, "For God So Loved the World?" 51.
40. Martin Luther King Jr. quoted in *The Church is All of You*, ed. James Brockman (Minneapolis: Winston Press, 1984), 94, Brown and Parker, "For God So Loved the World?" 51.
41. Brown and Parker, "For God So Loved the World?" 51.
42. Brown and Parker, "For God So Loved the World?" 52.

not be romanticized and that King's view of non-violence can promote the passivity of the oppressed, I still question the nature of the suffering in the martyrdom theology discussed above. Is the "inevitability of suffering" mostly related to a human reality, or does it happen because God ordains the process by necessity?

The third trend, according to Brown and Parker, is perhaps the most radical, in that it rejects the concept that human suffering can have positive or redemptive aspects.[43] The focal theme can be understood with the concepts of "a Racist God" or "a Sadistic God," both of which reject the suffering servant motif.[44] William Jones, for example, argues that all suffering is negative, based on the fact that even after the event of the cross, the oppression and suffering continue, and that as the oppressors justify their position, the oppressed are persuaded to endure.[45] Jones suggests a humanocentric theism in which God acts a persuader rather than a coercer, and in which human activity is decisive for salvation and liberation.[46] In labeling all suffering as negative, Jones suggests that our traditional faith is part of what oppresses us. According to Brown and Parker, Jones does not go far enough, in that he fails to raise the question of a sadist God: Why was the crucifixion necessary? Did God demand it and sacralize the suffering of Jesus?[47] They then conclude that we must do away with the atonement, because the Christian God is bloodthirsty and patriarchal if God is indeed the God of the cross.

Certainly, suffering must not be justified. We constantly kill Christ if we wrongly interpret his death to justify our own violence and abuse. Women's experience is one of the most valuable reflections on Christ's crucifixion. Yet, the problems in Brown and Parker's argument related to their theology of atonement are not trivial. In what follows, I will discuss the issues raised above before briefly suggesting my own theology of the atonement as a clue to how we might revisit the reality and meaning of Christ's crucifixion.

4. ABUSE AND NECESSITY

The critical challenge of feminism for abuse is relevant (1) for seeing the cross between Jesus's Godward action and God's action in Christ on behalf of humans, (2) for understanding Christ's own will, and (3) for defining necessity. Apparently, these three matters are interrelated. If we see the cross only through the framework of Christ's Godward action,

---

43. Brown and Parker, "For God So Loved the World?" 52.
44. Brown and Parker, "For God So Loved the World?" 54–55.
45. Brown and Parker, "For God So Loved the World?" 54.
46. Brown and Parker, "For God So Loved the World?" 54–55.
47. Brown and Parker, "For God So Loved the World?" 55.

there is no way to avoid the problem of divine abuse.[48] God is the violent and sadistic God who demands the blood of God's own *monogenes*. Various concepts in the theological tradition, such as "appeasement," "propitiation," "satisfaction," and even "obedience," can promote this image of God if we limit them to "Christ's action toward God" only. Yet it is hard to believe that there has been anyone in theological history who has not included the aspect of "God's work for human beings" in their atonement theology. The challenge from feminism is, of course, more critical. Even in this aspect of "God's action in Christ toward humans," it is possible to perceive the same problem of violence and abuse, if God demanded the blood of Jesus "without Jesus' voluntary will" and "by necessity."

Yet, in reply, Jesus' action on the cross is twofold. On the one hand, Jesus obeys God, as we find in his prayer at Gethsemane: "Abba, Father, for you all things are possible; remove this cup from me; yet, not what I want, but what you want."[49] God appears to be the primary subject who activates the Son's crucifixion. This can be seen in Romans 3:25 as well: "Whom God set forth as a propitiation by His blood, through faith, to demonstrate His righteousness, because in His forbearance God had passed over the sins that were previously committed." God is the one who sets forth Christ's bloody death as a propitiation. At the same time, it must be noted that Jesus' prayer of obedience at Gethsemane is made in the context of a great sense of intimacy with his Father, Abba, and this obedience with intimacy presupposes a personal relationship with God, rather than a coerced and impersonal order. The personal relationship of the Trinity—handing all over to the Son,[50] the Father's love of the Son because of the Son's voluntary sacrifice,[51] and love by mutual glorifying and indwelling[52]—is far more dynamic than a coerced obedience. Moreover, the aspect of "the cross as Christ's own voluntary action" must not be ignored, as Christ himself declares, "The Son of Man came not to be served but to serve, and to give his life a ransom for many,"[53] and, "No one takes it from Me, but I lay it down of Myself. I have power to lay it down, and I have power to take it again. This command I have

---

48. "As long as the death of Jesus is aimed God-ward, one cannot avoid the implication that death is the means through which God enables reconciliation, and thus God uses or sanctions a violent death," (J. Denny Weaver, "The Nonviolent Atonement: Human Violence, Discipleship and God," in *Stricken by God: Nonviolent Identification and the Victory of Christ*, eds. Brad Jersak and Michael Hardin [Grand Rapids: Eerdmans, 2007], 316–55, 342).

49. Mk. 14: 36.
50. Lk. 10: 21–22.
51. Jn. 10: 17.
52. Jn. 17: 4–5; 17: 21–26.
53. Mk. 10: 45.

received from My Father."⁵⁴ Thus, the relationship between God and Christ on the cross is personal and multi-dimensional.

Another issue related to abuse concerns whether God demands Christ's death by divine necessity. I have already raised the question of the difference between reality and necessity, and so the undergirding issue here is how to understand the human situation and the action of the personal God. What is the primary cause of the necessity of Christ's crucifixion between God and humans? This question is crucially relevant to the feminist view of sin.⁵⁵ Joy Ann McDougall argues that Kathryn Tanner's concept of sin as a "refusal" or "blockage" of "God's gift-giving" responds well to feminist critiques of the root paradigm of sin as pride.⁵⁶ Without ignoring the critical point that humankind is wholly trapped in the bondage of sin, McDougall avoids the forensic framework of sin in two ways: (1) there is no legal court established to decide humanity's case and (2) the radically transcendent and beneficent God keeps showering good gifts on creation so as to heal human beings, so that they may receive and share God's blessings.⁵⁷ There is no sense of necessity, either in God or in humans, for a legal decision of death or punishment, if sin is not a forensic crime, but a blindness to God's gift. All we need to do, in her view, is open our eyes and, thus Christ's death on the cross becomes superfluous.

What these theologians do not fully discuss in their arguments, however, is the profundity of the divine relationship with humans and the crucial nature of the human condition. Nicholas Wolterstorff defines justice, not in terms of Aristotle's view that justice consists in a person's receiving what is due to him or her, but from the biblical writers' perspective, who assert that God loves justice, not as retributive punishment, but as a social action for the oppressed.⁵⁸ God punishes wrong-doers, even with various types of death, not for the sake of "justice as such" but to transform them and lead them to God: "My child, do not despise the LORD's discipline or be weary of his reproof, for the LORD reproves the one he loves, as a father the son in whom he delights."⁵⁹ God is not a human being, but the Holy One, coming not

---

54. Jn. 10: 18.

55. Linda Peacore asserts that the failure of feminist theology to adequately deal with the subject of women's sin leads to flaws in feminist atonement theology (Linda D. Peacore, *The Role of Women's Experience in Feminist Theologies of Atonement* [Eugene: Pickwick, 2010], 162).

56. Joy Ann McDougall, "Sin—No More? A Feminist Re-Visioning of a Christian Theology of Sin," *Anglican Theological Review* 88:2 (2006), 232–233.

57. McDougall, "Sin—No More?" 233–234.

58. Nicholas Wolterstorff, "Justice as a Condition of Authentic Liturgy," *Theology Today* 48:1 (1991), 6–21, 8.

59. Prov. 3: 11–12.

in wrath not because God does not heal evil-doers, but because God loves and leads them to Godself with bands of a transformative cord.[60] "Love only by a constant blessing of gifts," as implied in McDougal's view, is a human illusion and is itself abusive because it could constantly spoil wrong-doers. Goodness and mercy follow us by way of the path of righteousness.[61] Justice is not negated, but embraced by God, neither for the sake of justice itself nor by following an impersonal legal system, but from the love of the personal God who interacts with and restores sinners, victims, and oppressors. Thus, the divine justice and punishment of the personal God is not *retributive* but *transformative and restorative*. This is a substantial difference between Christianity and Daoism, for in the latter there is no personal interaction of the Dao for building up justice.

The human condition is much more acute than a legal status. We are broken in our relationship with others, abandoned by and abandoning ourselves, our neighbors, and our social and political systems, killed by and killing others, and living in violence, suffering and pain, absurdity, meaninglessness, and nothingness. The "necessity" of the cross lies neither in God's demand nor in a forensic system, but in the miserable human beings whom Christ has come to serve,[62] and who Christ leads to the house of God with great compassion and love.[63] If humans are violent and Christ's death is not the necessary violence of a chosen death, but a voluntary sacrifice for the sake of transforming violent humans, finding the root of human violence in the cross is itself violent and the cross is indeed made a scapegoat by such thinking.

5. SELF-SACRIFICE AND VIOLENCE

Another issue raised by feminists is whether Christ's death as self-sacrifice glorifies suffering, which then promotes human violence, including patriarchal oppression. Some are so critical of the cross as the root source of human oppression and violence that they seek to do away with Christianity and find liberation in Eastern religions.[64] What a challenge!

---

60. Hos. 11: 3–9.
61. Ps. 23: 3, 6.
62. Mk. 10: 45.
63. Jn. 10: 7–16.
64. "It is fascinating to note that Gross (a Jew who has converted to Buddhism) believes that there are motifs present in Eastern religion which are very different from those found within monotheism. They may be much more acceptable to feminists ..." (Daphne Hampson, *After Christianity* [Valley Forge: Trinity Press International, 1996], 126), "Many, though, dive into Buddha's deep waters to learn how to peacefully and without harm confront racism and other systems of oppression and to heal the devastating impact that racism, classism, sexism, and heterosexism can have on the psyches of black women, children, and men. While no community is perfect, it is the case that many

Christ's death is radically violent, as reflected in atonement language, with words such as "blood," "wrath," "sacrifice," "propitiation and expiation," "retribution," and most critically, "crucifixion." The traumatic impact of language must not be ignored. Yet the feminists' critique concerns more than the psychological impact of atonement theology, because it touches on the actual content: Is Christ' sacrifice on the cross Christ's choice, and does it thus promote and glorify suffering?[65] What is the nature of Christ's suffering on the cross?

No one would seek to suffer for the sake of suffering, except perhaps masochists. This implies that suffering is multi-layered, and is connected to other values. Our daily life explains this. We voluntarily sacrifice ourselves, our time, energy, and desire for the sake of achieving our goals. For instance, we must take great pains for several years practicing the violin to reach a certain level of musical accomplishment. We also sacrifice ourselves in order to build and recover various relationships and make a better community. "Not entirely sticking to ourselves" is the first step when engaging in any type of relationship with others. We *sacrifice* a certain part of ourselves and make space for others or put ourselves in the position of others. Even in a baseball game, a sacrificial bunt, which is a batter's act of deliberately bunting the ball in a manner that allows a runner on base to advance causes the sacrificing player to suffer by going out. More importantly, we greatly respect soldiers and firefighters, who sacrifice their lives for our country. Death matters here, and they risk and sacrifice their lives to the extent of death. Is their death violent? William C. Placher, dealing with the feminist critique, writes as follows:

> God bears the burdens of others in ways that transcend our powers, and I have already admitted that in Christ's being at once innocent and the bearer of our sin there is mystery beyond explaining. Still, we experience analogies to such vicarious burden bearing, and it seems odd to react in moral horror to the theological claim when we find its human analogies so generally natural and admirable.[66]

If we experience a variety of vicarious burden bearings, why should God not bear human limitations? It seems illogical to interpret Christ's sacrifice as the root cause of human oppression and a "glorification of suffering" when we praise and "glorify" those who sacrifice their lives for

---

black women are exploring Buddhism even while engaging an everyday translation of lived Christian liberation theology into Buddhist tongue" (Melanie L. Harris, "Buddhist Resources for Womanist Reflection," *Buddhist-Christian Studies* 34 [2014], 107–114, 110–111).

65. Brown and Parker, "For God So Loved the World?" 49.

66. William C. Placher, "Christ Takes our Place: Rethinking Atonement," *Interpretation* 53:1 (1999), 5–20, 17.

the sake of others.

We thus need further clarification of the idea that sacrifice is violent. Following feminist views, "a coerced suffering and sacrifice" must be violent and, thus, passively enduring a coerced suffering promotes violence. Such suffering could be either individual or collective/systematic, conscious or unconscious. "Self" in this type of self-sacrifice turns out to be a "sacrificing self, forced by others or systems," which suggests violence. There are two dimensions to the question of coercion in feminist critiques: (1) Is Christ's self-sacrifice a type of "sacrificing self, coerced by others"? and (2) Are women coerced to follow Christ's self-sacrifice? The former is closer to a theology of the cross while the latter to its implication and application.

One of the great contributions of feminist theology is to expose the critical reality that the church and theology have promoted the oppression of women, by emphasizing the "voluntary" sacrifice of Christ on the cross. Previously, the non-voluntary nature of the Son's death by necessity was the major issue for feminists because of the implications of child abuse. Now, "voluntariness" has become problematic, because the "self" in Christ's "self-sacrifice" is understood by feminists as a deceptive and manipulated voluntariness: Women delude themselves that they are following Christ's self-sacrifice actively but, *de facto*, are forced to do so by social and ecclesial individuals and systems. What is of significance is a strange combination of passivity and activity. Christ's self-sacrifice promotes women's self-sacrifice, which is active in the sense of self-doing, but passive if women are coerced to follow Christ's model and if the content of the self-sacrifice ends up as "sacrificing self for the sake of sacrifice." When this happens, as feminists point out, the very activeness of the self in self-sacrifice is nothing but self-abnegation and self-destruction. Does Christ's self-sacrifice on the cross have the nature of self-abnegation? Or is it that the church has misused the cross to justify its oppression of women in church and society? Considering the complex way that the cross, the theology of the cross, and its implication and application are all interwoven, we need to revisit the theology of the atonement, which is the source of the issue of how to live out Christ's sacrifice in our daily lives.

6. REVISION OF ATONEMENT THEOLOGY

Many theologians attempt to reshape their theology of the atonement by making a shift from negative connotations of punishment and sacrifice to positive ones, such as love and gifts. Non-violent atonement views have become a dominating trend in atonement theologies. We may also learn from the gentle, embracing, and non-violent way of sacrifice of the

Dao in Daoism.

Yet the bare reality of Christ's crucifixion is that it is a harsh type of violent death. If it is a gift, we must explain in what way a gift can be given via this violent death. Treasuring a constructive value of the cross without grounding it in the destructive reality of death would be a naïve and superficial interpretation of the cross. In response, biblical authors witness two dimensions of Christ's sacrifice: (1) it is passive, destructive, and retrospective on the one hand, and (2) it is active, constructive, and prospective on the other. Christ on the cross becomes sin, gives himself as ransom for many, cleanses and purifies sins, destroys evil, and dies for all that all may die in him.[67] The world is under the power of sin, death and injustice, and Christ's death is the death of sin, death and injustice, retrospectively for the past and present reality of the world, because he takes away the sin of the world.[68] Yet his death is not only the passive destruction of death and sin, but is also the active construction of the life and gifts of God. Because of Christ's death, we live in Christ as new humans, with reconciliation, peace, liberation, life, and love. God in Christ reconciles us and the world to Godself, by making peace through his blood.[69] He gives us life from death, redemption from the curse of the law, as well as freedom, and liberation from sin.[70] He saves creation from decay and shows the divine love within the Trinity and sacrificial love for all.[71] These two aspects are not separated, but are interwoven with each other. Without the destructive aspect, there would be no way to explain why liberation, freedom, and love can be achieved by way of death, because "death as such" cannot have any values of freedom and love. Without the constructive aspect, Christ's sacrifice would remain retributive justice or sacrificial victimhood, and lose its transformative value for a new humanity. The mystery of the cross lies in this paradoxical simultaneity of the two: between punishment and forgiveness; between passively sharing our sorrow and pains and actively bearing our limitations and drawing all to Godself; and between passively dying in a violent crucifixion by the world and actively reconciling that violent world to God by divinely embracing peace and love.

What happens on the cross is the comprehensive act of God in Christ: exposing, sharing, bearing, and drawing. Christ's death holistically exposes the violent world—Roman political power, the Jewish religious conspiracy, the intensified violence of social gatherings, and betrayal by ambitious followers. Christ shares himself, his body and blood,

---

67. 2 Cor. 5: 21; Mk. 10: 45; 1 Jn. 1: 7–9; Heb. 1: 3; Col. 2: 14; 2 Cor. 5: 24.
68. Jn. 1: 29.
69. Eph. 2: 15; 2 Cor. 5: 18–20; Col. 1: 20.
70. Jn. 3: 16; Rom. 11: 15; Gal. 3: 13; 4: 5; Jn. 8: 36; Gal. 2: 4; 5: 1, 13; Rom. 8: 2.
71. Rom. 8: 21; Jn. 10: 17; Rom. 5: 8; Gal. 2: 20; 1 Jn. 3: 16.

with us,⁷² shares human suffering and abandonment,⁷³ bears sins, diseases and pains,⁷⁴ and draws all people to God, reconciling them to Godself and each other.⁷⁵ Rather than working for a legal solution, this comprehensive work of Christ on the cross is the way a loving and compassionate God deals with the critical human condition. Our atonement theology, therefore, must not be overwhelmed by a single layer of interpretation, but instead needs to embrace the holistic and comprehensive reality of the cross, as the two aspects and the four acts suggest. Exposing, sharing, bearing, and drawing are not at all close to "glorifying suffering." It is through the profound compassion of God that God suffers on the cross and bears human sufferings. This also suggests that we must expose the injustice of the world and fight against it by sharing and bearing the suffering of others in solidarity with all humans. In this sense, the fourfold act of Christ is the most powerful and intensive resistance to violence and abuse. On this foundation, we can further rebuild the traditional concepts of punishment, substitution, sacrifice, victory, and satisfaction with more nuanced notions, not of retributive but of transformative justice, divine sharing and bearing of human sins and death instead of substituting them, non-coercive, life-giving sacrifice to serve and embrace others rather than coerced, bloody victimization, victory as an active fight *against* injustice and oppression and *for* reconciliation and peace of the world, and encountering critical human reality and committing to abundant life.

7. CONCLUSION

Polarization between women and men is one of the most critical issues both in the Western and non-Western world, whether that polarization is intentional or hidden. It is more crucial in the theological discussion of the atonement, as we can see in the feminist theologians' critical analyses of it. Daoism is the oldest philosophy and religion of feminism: Female represents the Dao which sacrificially creates and nourishes all, but never dominates. This non-violent sacrifice challenges Christian faith and the theology of Christ's crucifixion in which feminists find the root cause of abuse and violence against women. The non-violent sacrifice of Daoist feminism implies two things: (1) not all sacrifice is violent and (2) the embrace and care of the feminine in non-violent sacrifice can promote passive endurance of suffering.⁷⁶

---

72. Mk. 14: 22–24.
73. Mk. 15: 34.
74. 1 Pet. 2: 24; Isa. 53: 4.
75. Jn. 12:32; Eph. 2: 14–22.
76. Chen Gu Ying enumerates seven drawbacks to Daoism, two of which are related to passivity: i.e., that submission of oneself to nature may weaken human will,

Brown and Parker argue that the Christian God is abusive and violent because God demands the necessary bloody death of the Son, who passively accepts it (as abuse) on the one hand, and who sacrifices himself on the other, which could promote Christian violence against and oppression of women. Three issues they see as crucial are that (1) God demands the Son's death by necessity, (2) Christ passively accepts this and (3) he sacrifices himself by coercion. Their criticism includes not only the stark reality of the cross—a violent death—but also atonement theology, its psychological implications, and its ecclesial and social application. Narrowing down to the atonement theology, my dialogue with feminist criticism can be summarized in three points. First, the relationship of the personal God with the Son is much more dynamic and intimate than they suggest, and Christ willingly accepts his death. Second, the necessity of Christ's sacrifice lies neither in God nor in a legal system, but in the reality of human beings and the world. We neither passively accept suffering nor actively choose to suffer, but encounter pain and suffering in our daily lives—Christ was crucified not out of necessity but because of reality—and thus God wants to transform, restore, and heal us rather than execute justice for justice's sake. Third, Christ's sacrifice of self is not a self-abnegation but a divine self-sacrifice for others. Indeed, self-sacrifice for others can be found in human affairs, such as in sports and in the actions of soldiers and firefighters whom we glorify. These three points are grounded in the comprehensive biblical witness of Christ's crucifixion, which can reshape our notions of passivity, activity, violence and non-violence in the fourfold act of Christ: (1) passivity— Christ accepts suffering and pain as he exposes the violent world and shares its pains, (2) activity— his death is a fight against injustice and a building of reconciliation, as Christ draws all to himself, (3) violence—the world violently crucifies him on the cross, and (4) non-violence—Christ embraces and bears the violent world and sinful human beings.

Does the Daoist sacrifice of non-violence provide us with a better format for feminism than the radical death of Christ on the cross? Lessons we learn from a comparison between Daoist feminism and Christian theology of the atonement are not trivial. The *personal God* in Christ radically and sacrificially engages in the suffering of human beings and the injustice of the world, whereas the sacrifice of the impersonal Dao is close to *our* perception of human reality: The empty space of a container and the weakness of women and children

---

reason, and feeling, which are distinct from nature, and that the stillness that comes from following nature may give us a mental peace but may harm human creativity (Gu Ying Chen (陳鼓應), *A New Perspective of Lao-Zhuang* (老莊新論), trans. Jin Sik Choi (Seoul, Sonamu, 1997), 78–79.

produce and nourish creation. On the one hand, church and society must remember that the radical sacrifice of Christ can be easily twisted into the practice of imperialistic and sexist oppression. A non-violent embrace and a gentle space for others in Daoism could offer a profound lesson for radical Christianity, especially at the level of theological implication and ecclesial application. It teaches us all not to promote any type of coerced endurance of suffering and reveals the deceptive activeness of self-destruction. On the other hand, we must not forget that the radical sacrifice of Christ is the very heart of the Gospel: God is not idly remote from our pain and suffering, but is critically present in us by exposing the violence of the world, sharing and bearing our suffering and pains, and actively and compassionately transforming and leading us to Godself. The divine, personal, and costly love and justice is the substantial uniqueness of Christianity that cannot be found in Daoism.

BIBLIOGRAPHY

Brockman, James. Ed. *The Church is All of You*. Minneapolis: Winston Press, 1984.

Brown, Joanne Carlson and Rebecca Parker. "For God So Loved the World?" In *Violence against Women and Children: A Christian Theological Sourcebook*, eds. Carol J. Adams and Marie M. Fortune, 36–59. New York: Continuum, 1995.

Chen, Gu Ying. *A New Perspective of Lao-Zhuang*, trans. Jin Sik Choi. Seoul: Sonamu, 1997.

Despeux, Catherine and Livia Kohn. *Women in Daoism*. Cambridge: Three Pines Press, 2003.

Hampson, Daphne. *After Christianity*. Valley Forge: Trinity Press International, 1996.

Harris, Melanie L. "Buddhist Resources for Womanist Reflection." *Buddhist-Christian Studies* 34 (2014): 107–114.

McDougall, Joy Ann. "Sin—No More? A Feminist Re-Visioning of a Christian Theology of Sin." *Anglican Theological Review* 88:2 (2006): 232–233.

Moltmann, Jürgen. *The Crucified God*. New York: Harper & Row, 1974.

Peacore, Linda D. *The Role of Women's Experience in Feminist Theologies of Atonement*. Eugene: Pickwick, 2010.

Placher, William C. "Christ Takes our Place: Rethinking Atonement." *Interpretation* 53:1 (1999):5–20.

Washington, James. Ed. *A Testament of Hope*. New York: Harper & Row, 1986.

Weaver, J. Denny. "The Nonviolent Atonement: Human Violence, Discipleship and God." In *Stricken by God: Nonviolent Identification and the Victory of Christ*, eds. Brad Jersak and Michael Hardin, 316–55. Grand Rapids: Eerdmans, 2007.

Wolterstorff, Nicholas. "Justice as a Condition of Authentic Liturgy." *Theology Today* 48:1 (1991): 6–21.

CHAPTER 6
"REMOVE THE SANDALS FROM YOUR FEET": HOLINESS IN THE DUTCH EUTHANASIA DEBATE
Annemarieke van der Woude

1. INTRODUCTION

> Earth's crammed with heaven,
> And every common bush afire with God;
> But only he who sees, takes off his shoes—
> The rest sit round it, and pluck blackberries.[1]

These verses from Elizabeth Barrett Browning immediately show the precariousness of my endeavor. I want to introduce the biblical notion of holiness into the Dutch euthanasia debate. However, the poet formulates in an accurate and humorous way that it is easy to violate what is holy: "only he who sees, takes off his shoes—The rest sit round it, and pluck blackberries." To regard something as holy, sensitivity is needed, but not everybody shows sensitivity. What might be perceived as unassailable—holy—is vulnerable at the same time. It can easily be neglected and overlooked.

2. WHY HOLINESS?

It is far from obvious to reflect on holiness in relation to euthanasia. Would not suffering serve as a more adequate concept in relation to dying on request?[2] One could argue that we, people living in an affluent so-

---

1. A few verses from the poem "Aurora Leigh" from Elizabeth Barrett Browning ("Seventh Book"). It was first published in 1857. Taken from Elizabeth Barrett Browning, *Aurora Leigh and Other Poems. Introduced by Cora Kaplan* (London: The Women's Press, 1978), 304.

2. See for the Dutch discussion, e.g., Gijsbert van den Brink, "Lijden in de Bijbel: Een verkenning" (Suffering in the Bible: An exploration), *Lijden en volhouden*, Lindeboomreeks 19, eds. Theo Boer and Dick Mul (Amsterdam: Buijten & Schipperheijn Motief, 2016), 19–35; J. Belder and A.A. Teeuw, *Mijn leven voltooid*? (My life completed?), Artios-reeks, (Heerenveen: Groen, 2018), esp. 105–107. See also *12 artikelen over voltooid leven* (Twelve articles on 'completed life'), Geloven op goede

ciety in the first quarter of the twenty-first century, have lost the ability to endure suffering. It is stated that requests for euthanasia would possibly diminish, would we be more able to bear pain and dependency. In addition, from a religious perspective one could bring forward that, in God's creation, suffering is not the final and last word.

The main reason why I will not explore suffering is the following: People who lobby for self-determination in end-of-life issues do not consider suffering as a potential source of meaning but, instead, as a fundamental reason for their wish to die at a moment chosen by themselves. The introduction of the notion of suffering into the Dutch debate on euthanasia would end the conversation even before it has started. Instead of overcoming polarization, this concept would only supply fuel to us versus them thinking.

Another contribution from scripture to the debate on euthanasia would seem to be the commandment: "You shall not murder" (Ex. 20:13).[3] Does this commandment not formulate in plain language that, from a biblical perspective, it is forbidden to terminate someone's life? In fact, this is a hermeneutical question. Does the sixth commandment refer to euthanasia? I do not think so. The Ten Commandments offer guiding principles for living together as a community in which you honor God and honor other persons. The prohibition to kill a person in a violent and unjust way is at stake here, not the issue of dying on request.

In order to explain why I choose holiness as my topic, I need to spend a few words on the Dutch situation. Regarding end-of-life decisions the Netherlands are totally unique. Since 2002, the Dutch Euthanasia Act regulates both euthanasia and physician-assisted suicide.

Ever since, the number of people dying on request is growing. In 2019, it concerned more than 6,300 men and women.[4] The files of reported euthanasia also show that, in addition to the number of terminally ill people, the number of people without a life-threatening disease is growing as well. These patients are categorized under three headings: suffering from dementia, from a psychiatric disorder and from multiple afflictions related to old age.

The debate on euthanasia in the Netherlands has become highly polarized.[5] For those at the one end of the spectrum, consideration with

---

gronden, eds. Henk Post and Bert van Veluw (Utrecht: KokBoekencentrum, 2020).

3. Quotations from scripture are taken from the *New Revised Standard Version*.

4. See the annual report of the Dutch regional euthanasia review committees: Regionale Toetsingscommissies Euthanasie, *Jaarverslag 2019 Regionale Toetsingscommissies Euthanasie* (Annual report 2019 Regional Euthanasia Review Committees) (Den Haag: Xerox/OBT, 2020).

5. Pauline S.C. Kouwenhoven, Ghislaine J.M.W. van Thiel, Agnes van der Heide, Judith A.C. Rietjens and Johannes J.M. van Delden, "Developments in Euthanasia Practice in the Netherlands: Balancing Professional Responsibility and the Patient's

every human being's vulnerability is an important value. This position can be observed both within and without the confines of church communities. Within a faith community, this notion is often translated as every human being is a creature made by God. Those who adhere to vulnerability as an essential characteristic of human existence, are inclined to make a caricature of their opponents in the debate on euthanasia, by using the 'slippery slope' argument: If we allow euthanasia for the terminally ill now, termination of life will eventually become an easy and cheap solution to shortages in the care for the elderly.

For those at the other end of the spectrum, autonomy is an important value. They, in turn, tend to demonize their opponents, by stating that, if these would get their way, others would determine for you when your life is compatible with human dignity; they also tend to evoke the spectre of being forced to wile away your life as a zombie in a nursing home.

In this tumultuous and often emotional debate, I am looking for a biblical notion that can serve as a bridge between these two extremes. It is my intention to lend the bible—more specifically: the Old Testament—relevance in actual dilemmas, even though these dilemmas did not exist in biblical times.[6] I hold, that 'holiness' serves as a good candidate, because it does not point to a characteristic of a person or an object, but to a dynamic force.

3. THE SECULARIZATION OF HOLINESS

"Das Heilige ist in aller Munde," holiness is on everyone's tongue, as Jochen Schmidt states.[7] Holiness has migrated from the religious realm

Autonomy," *European Journal of General Practice* 25:1 (2019), 44–48. Cf. Lynn A. Jansen, Steven Wall and Franklin G. Miller, "Drawing the Line on Physician-Assisted Death," *Journal of Medical Ethics* 45:1 (2019), 190–197. The authors propose to restrict physician-assisted death (PAD) to terminally ill people. On the experiences of Dutch pastors in questions regarding end-of-life issues, see Theo Boer, Ronald Bolwijn, Maaike Graafland, Wim Graafland and Annemarieke van der Woude, "Pastores in de PKN en hun ervaringen met euthanasie" (Pastors in the Dutch Protestant Church and their experiences with euthanasia), *Kerk en Theologie* 70:2 (2019), 151–172.

6. On the complexity of using biblical notions in matters of ethics, see Christian Frevel, "Orientierung! Grundfragen einer Ethik des Alten Testaments," *Mehr als Zehn Worte? Zur Bedeutung des Alten Testaments in ethischen Fragen*, Quaestiones Disputatae 273, ed. Christian Frevel (Freiburg: Herder, 2015), 9–57.

7. Jochen Schmidt, "Kultur der Heiligkeit: Über theologische Rede vom Unverfügbaren in einem säkularen Zeitalter," *Zeitschrift für Theologie und Kirche* 113 (2016), 279–90, 279. See also Jochen Schmidt, "Erzählte Heiligkeit: Über Unverfügbarkeit und Menschenwürde," *Zeitschrift für Evangelische Ethik* 61 (2017), 120–124. Cf. Hans Joas, *Die Macht des Heiligen: Eine Alternative zur Geschichte der Entzauberung* (Berlin: Suhrkamp Verlag, 2017). In his philosophical anthropology, Joas states that holiness has not disappeared in modern societies, but instead that the perspectives on what is seen as holy have been multiplied. See also, e.g., *Everyday Life and the Sacred: Re/Configuring Gender Studies in Religion, Studies in Theology*

into everyday life practice. Schmidt searches for ways to connect a secularized notion of holiness with a Christian one. He takes the concept 'unavailability' ("Unverfügbarkeit") as his point of departure. Not everything that is unavailable necessarily approaches holiness. Schmidt mentions the future as an example. It is not at our disposal, but neither does it carry with it the notion of holiness. The latter only happens when vis-a-vis the person or thing which has been set apart—the first part of Schmidt's definition, a neutral attitude is impossible—the second part of his definition.

An example of an experience which, on the continuum of being unavailable, is closer to holiness, is looking at a work of art. The effect a painting has, is beyond the control of the artist. A work of art emanates something to which the onlooker responds with attentive observation. In a museum, one does not move around in the way one does in a supermarket. It may not be obvious to attribute works of art a holy status, but it can not be denied that art evokes something which requires a fitting reaction.

Schmidt would state, that that which has been set apart, makes an appeal. This appeal can be heard by anyone, but in the Christian tradition, it will be interpreted as an appeal from God, according to Schmidt.

4. HOLINESS IN THE BIBLE

In the biblical tradition, nothing is holy in and of itself, but anything can *become* holy. What does this mean for the concepts of life and death: are they holy?

According to biblical standards, being alive points to being in connection, as Christian Frevel states.[8] In particular, this means being in connection with God: "Therefore my heart is glad, and my soul rejoices; my body also rests secure. For you don't give me up to Sheol, or let your faithful one see the Pit. You show me the path of life. In your presence there is fullness of joy; in your right hand are pleasures forevermore" (Ps. 16:9–11).[9]

---

and Religion 23, eds. Angela Berlis, Anne-Marie Korte and Kune Biezeveld (Leiden & Boston: Brill, 2017); Lynda Sexson, *Ordinarily Sacred* (Charlottesville: The University of Virginia Press, 1992); Gordon Lynch, *The Sacred in the Modern World: A Cultural Sociological Approach* (Oxford: Oxford University Press, 2012); Philip Sheldrake, *Spaces for the Sacred: Place, Memory and Identity*, The Hulsean Lectures 2000 (London: SCM Press, 2001).

8. Christian Frevel, "Anthropologie," *Handbuch theologischer Grundbegriffe zum Alten und Neuen Testament*, eds. Angelika Berlejung and Christian Frevel (Darmstadt: Wissenschaftliche Buchgesellschaft, 2012³), 1–7, 2: "Leben ist für den Menschen im AT immer ein In-BeziehungStehen."

9. Cf. Kathrin Liess, *Der Weg des Lebens: Psalm 16 und das Lebens- und Todesverständnis der Individualpsalmen*, Forschungen zum Alten Testament 2.5

Does this mean that life is itself holy? Not *a priori*. In the way we treat living creatures, we could honor their holy status, but this is not self-evident. In the Western part of the world we violate the existence of plants, animals and human beings in all possible ways. It is the negative side of our high standard of living. But there is also a positive side. When someone suffers from a severe disease, we are grateful that we have instruments and medicines to interfere. So, I argue that showing respect for the untouchable status of life does not include that it is prohibited, in all circumstances, to try to influence the course of events.[10]

In the biblical tradition, life as such is not holy and the same holds true for death. In the Old Testament, death can exert its influence, even when a person has not died yet. Like 'life,' 'death' is defined in relation to the community. It signifies the experience of being cut off from the community, even though one is fully alive.[11] Remember Job: after having lost his loved ones and all his possessions, he curses the day of his birth: "Let the day perish in which I was born, and the night that said, 'A man-child is conceived.' Why did I not die at birth, come forth from the womb and expire?" (Job 3:3; 11).

Also in the book of Psalms we find texts that describe death as the loss of connection with people and with God. In Psalm 88 for instance, the psalmist experiences his painful condition simultaneously with his inability to be in contact with the Divine: "I am counted among those who go down to the Pit; I am like those who have no help, like those forsaken among the dead, like the slain that lie in the grave, like those whom you remember no more, for they are cut off from your hand. Do you work wonders for the dead? Do the shades rise up to praise you? Are your wonders known in the darkness, or your saving help in the land of forgetfulness?" (Ps. 88:4–5; 10; 12).[12]

(Tübingen: Mohr Siebeck, 2004).

10. Cf. Franz-Josef Bormann, "Ist die Vorstellung eines 'natürlichen Todes' noch zeitgemäß? Moraltheologische Überlegungen zu einem umstrittenen Begriff," *Sterben: Dimensionen eines anthropologischen Grundphänomens*, eds. Franz-Josef Bormann and Gian Domenico Borasio (Berlin & Boston: De Gruyter, 2012), 325–350.

11. Cf. Els van Wijngaarden, *Ready to Give up on Life: A Study into the Lived Experience of Older People who Consider their Lives to Be Completed and no Longer Worth Living* (Amersfoort: Wilco, 2016). In her thesis Van Wijngaarden describes the experiences of Dutch elderly people with a so-called 'completed life' as an incapability of making connection: with themselves, with their proxies and with society. Cf. also Nienke P.M. Fortuin, *The Search for Meaning in Later Life: An Empirical Exploration of Religion and Death*, Death Studies: Nijmegen Studies in Thanatology 6 (Zürich: Lit Verlag, 2020). In her thesis Fortuin distinguishes three master narratives of ageing: 'ageing as decline,' 'active ageing' and 'ageing as inner growth.'

12. Other examples are Ps.6; 22; 49; 73. See also Walter Groß, "Zum alttestamentlichjüdischen Verständnis von Sterben und Tod," Sterben, Bormann and Borasio, 465–480. Cf. *Tod und Jenseits im alten Israel und in seiner Umwelt*:

In scripture, holiness entails that something or somebody is taken from everyday life and is set apart, for a specific task or destiny. The core of priestly theology—a literary tradition in the Old Testament in which holiness is a central concept—can be formulated as setting apart in order to experience proximity. In the Bible, this means proximity of the Divine, and can be attained in two ways: liturgy and ethics.[13]

The liturgical aspect of holiness is concerned with the rites. It can involve a designated space, such as the temple; persons who are set apart, like the priests and Levites who serve as singer, sentinel or overseer in the Jerusalem temple. It can involve sacred times, such as the Sabbath, or feasts like Pesach. But objects also can be holy, such as ointment with which liturgical utensils, or people that enter into a ministry, are anointed.

Holiness is an active force that is transferable. Interaction with holy things was enwrapped in rules. Fear of desecration and defilement was everywhere around. Leviticus contains many of these regulations, especially in the first part of the book: instructions for sacrifices (Lev.1–7), the investment of the priests (Lev.8–10) and rules on purity and impurity (Lev.11–16).[14]

But holiness does not only affect the religious domain. It also concerns daily life. People are set apart, in order to mirror the Lord's holiness in the way they live. This ethical aspect is found especially in the second half of the book, in the so-called Holiness Code (Lev.17–26).[15] To sum up, in the priestly parts of the biblical tradition, there are

---

Theologische, religionsgeschichtliche, archäologische und ikonographische Aspekte, Forschungen zum Alten Testament 64, eds. Angelika Berlejung and Bernd Janowski (Tübingen: Mohr Siebeck, 2009).

13. Cf. Reinhard G. Kratz, "Heiligkeit," *Handbuch theologischer Grundbegriffe*, Berlejung and Frevel, 242–243. See also Erich Zenger a.o., *Einleitung in das Alte Testament* (Stuttgart: Kohlhammer, 19983), 159–162.

14. For a different view, see Leigh M. Trevaskis, *Holiness, Ethics and Ritual in Leviticus*, Hebrew Bible Monographs 29 (Sheffield: Sheffield Phoenix, 2011). Trevaskis proposes a symbolic interpretation of Leviticus and argues that the ritual instructions in Lev.1–16 in fact are ethical.

15. In 1877 August Klostermann used the term 'Heiligkeitsgesetz' for the first time, to designate Lev.17–26. Ever since, there is an ongoing debate on these chapters as an assumed independent legal corpus and on the literary dependency between the Holiness Code (H) and other priestly writings (P). For a clear overview of the history of research, see Paavo N. Tucker, *The Holiness Composition in the Book of Exodus*, Forschungen zum Alten Testament 2.98 (Tübingen: Mohr Siebeck, 2017), esp. 10–34; Suzanne Boorer, *The Vision of the Priestly Narrative: Its Genre and Hermeneutics of Time*, Ancient Israel and its Literature 27 (Atlanta: SBL Press, 2016), esp. 2–34. See also *Current Issues in Priestly and Related Literature: The Legacy of Jacob Milgrom and Beyond*, eds. Roy E. Gane and Ada Taggar-Cohen, Resources for Biblical Study 82 (Atlanta: SBL Press, 2015); *The Strata of the Priestly Writings: Contemporary Debate and Future Directions*, Abhandlungen zur Theologie des Alten und Neuen Testaments

two ways to experience God's nearness: in the cult and in ethics. With a focus on the narrative progression in the book of Leviticus, Nihan concludes that "the overall sequence suggest[s] a pattern of *growing intimacy* with the divine."[16]

5. HOLINESS OF THE DIVINE

What are the characteristics of the Lord's holiness? Psalm 99 declares, as a repetitive strain: "Holy is he!" (Ps.99:3; 5) and it closes with a hymnal phrase: "Extol the Lord our God, and worship at his holy mountain; for the Lord our God is holy" (Ps.99:9). The psalm illuminates: "Mighty King, lover of justice, you have established equity; you have executed justice and righteousness in Jacob" (Ps.99:4). That is to say: *mishpat* ("justice") and *tsedaka* ("righteousness") are the fundamentals of his holy government.

The psalm is one of the so-called Yhwh-Kingship psalms (Ps.93–100). In this song, the Lord's holiness is intertwined with his kingship. Being king means that he vouches for human rights and that he offers a shelter for those who have no defense. At any rate, the kingship of Yhwh is meaningless when it is not recognized by his people, as Henk Leene underscores in his study on the intertextual relationships between the Yhwh-Kingship psalms and Second Isaiah.[17] The same goes for the Lord's holiness. It can easily be neglected. His holiness only has significance when it is affirmed as such. That is to say, the relational aspect of the notion of holiness cannot be overlooked.

The encounter between Moses and the Divine at the burning bush underscores this relational aspect (Ex.3:1–14). There, the Divine reveals himself to Moses by mentioning his name: "I am who I am" (Ex.3:14). He declares that he is a God of liberation: "I have observed the misery of my people who are in Egypt; I have heard their cry on account of their taskmasters. Indeed, I know their sufferings, and I have come down to deliver them from the Egyptians, and to bring them up out of that land to a good and broad land, a land flowing with milk and honey" (Ex.3:7–8).

95, eds. Sarah Shectman and Joel S. Baden (Zürich: Theologischer Verlag Zürich, 2009). Cf. Christophe Nihan, *From Priestly Torah to Pentateuch: A Study in the Composition of the Book of Leviticus*, Forschungen zum Alten Testament 2.25 (Tübingen: Mohr Siebeck, 2007). The papers collected in *Levitikus als Buch*, Bonner Biblische Beiträge 119, eds. Heinz-Josef Fabry and Hans-Winfried Jüngling (Berlin & Bodenheim: Philo, 1999) focus on the characteristics of Leviticus as a structural unity. See, e.g., Erich Zenger, "Das Buch Levitikus als Teiltext der Tora/des Pentateuch: Eine synchrone Lektüre mit kanonischer Perspektive," *Levitikus als Buch*, Fabry and Jüngling, 47–83. Zenger divides Leviticus into seven parts, with Lev.16–17 as its center.

16. Nihan, *Priestly Torah*, 108 (italics original).

17. Henk Leene, *Newness in Old Testament Prophecy: An Intertextual Study*, Oudtestamentische studiën 64 (Leiden & Boston: Brill, 2014), esp. 83–101.

In relation to holiness, one verse deserves special attention: "'Come no closer!,' the Lord said to Moses. 'Remove the sandals from your feet, for the place on which you are standing is holy ground'" (Ex.3:5). The ground is not holy by nature. It has become so because of the divine presence. In his reaction, Moses affirms the holy character: "And Moses hid his face, for he was afraid to look at God" (Ex.3:6). Attribution is an essential factor in dealing with holiness. Moses' attitude could have been totally different. The strength of the verses from Elizabeth Barrett Browning, that serve as a motto for this article, relates to this. She describes an unexpected alternative reaction of some people, when glancing at the burning bush: "The rest sit round it, and pluck blackberries."

6. Holiness of the People

Leviticus 19 reveals how people's behavior can be set apart, as a way to confirm the holiness of the Divine. Its overture sounds as a program: "You shall be holy, for I the Lord your God am holy" (Lev.19:2) and its closing words are: "I am the Lord" (Lev.19:37).

The chapter touches several domains of daily life. It contains allusions to the Ten Commandments, ritual instructions, guidelines for dignified contact with one another, a careful treatment of the environment and of one's body, and so on. The focus on all kinds of regulations towards the vulnerable is remarkable. To mention a few:

> When you reap the harvest of your land, you shall not reap to the very edges of your field, or gather the gleanings of your harvest. You shall not strip your vineyard bare, or gather the fallen grapes of your vineyard; you shall leave them for the poor and the alien. You shall not revile the deaf or put a stumbling block before the blind. ... you shall love your neighbor as yourself. You shall rise before the aged, and defer to the old. When an alien resides with you in your land, you shall not oppress the alien. The alien who resides with you shall be to you as the citizen among you; you shall love the alien as yourself, for you were aliens in the land of Egypt (verses taken from Lev.19:9–36).

This anthology from Leviticus 19 evokes the following picture: Every single human being is called to look after those who cannot take care of themselves, be it in a material, physical or social sense. Based on the guidelines in this chapter, Aarnoud Jobsen argues that Israel's identity is shaped by holiness: a radical choice for an upright way of life.[18] The

---

18. Aarnoud Jobsen, "Leviticus en Numeri," *De Bijbel theologisch: Hoofdlijnen en thema's*, eds. Klaas Spronk and Archibald van Wieringen (Zoetermeer: Meinema, 2011), 41–50, 44: "... de identiteit van de gemeenschap van Israël [komt] tot uiting als een radicale keuze voor integer leven." See also Thomas Hieke, "Die Heiligkeit Gottes als Beweggrund für ethisches Verhalten. Das ethische Konzept des Heiligkeitsgesetzes nach

continuously repeated utterances of the Divine in this chapter, where he expresses his relationship with his people, stand at the basis of this attitude. Next to the beginning and the end, the phrase "I am the Lord your God," or "I am the Lord," occurs another fourteen times.[19] In their careful treatment of every living creature, people express themselves as holy partners of the Divine (cf. Lev.22:31–33).[20]

7. OLD TESTAMENT ANTHROPOLOGY

What is a human being? What constitutes their identity? What is their position on earth? Nowadays, these are pertinent questions. Not only in relation to self-determination at the end of one's life, but also regarding the exploitation of our planet and its natural resources. Obviously, the search for who people are and for their cultural identity is not new, but at the turn of the millennium these questions have received new emphasis, due to changing circumstances and rapid developments in society.[21]

As far as the interest into a biblical anthropology is concerned, Hans Walter Wolffs *Anthropologie des Alten Testaments* from 1973 stands at the basis.[22] Wolffs point of departure is that, more than being determined by the past, people are open to the future. According to him, scripture offers a view on humankind that is built upon four categories: *nephesh* (throat—vitality); *bashar* (flesh—body); *ruach* (breath—spirit) and *lev* (heart—centre of emotion and intellect). In other words, in biblical texts people are depicted in their needy ("bedürftig"), transient ("hinfällig"), inspired ("ermächtigt") and rational ("vernünftig") condition. "Stereometrie" is characteristic for biblical thinking, that is to say, parts of the body also refer to functions and qualities of the individual.

Levitikus 19," *Mehr als Zehn Worte*?, Frevel, 187–206; Hendrik L. Bosman, "Loving the Neighbour and the Resident Alien in Leviticus 19 as Ethical Redefinition of Holiness," *Old Testament Essays* 31:3 (2018), 571–590.

19. Lev.19:3; 4; 10; 12; 14; 16; 18; 25; 28; 30; 31; 32; 34; 36. Cf. David T. Stewart, "Leviticus 19 as Mini-Torah," *Current Issues*, Gane and Taggar-Cohen, 299–323. Stewart offers a proposal for the structure of Leviticus 19 into fourteen sections, based on these sixteen selfexplanations of the Lord.

20. 1 Pet.1:15–16 cites Lev.19:2 and 1 Thess.4:3–7, with a call to sanctification, alludes to Lev.19. For a description of a way of living which clashes with the Lord's holiness, see, e.g., Am.2:6–7. Cf. the Apostolic Exhortation *Gaudete et exsultate* (Rejoice and be glad) from Pope Francis on the call to holiness in today's world (dated 19 March 2018). See also Rowan Williams, *Holy Living: The Christian Tradition for Today* (London & New York: Bloomsbury, 2017).

21. Cf. Christian Frevel, "Die Frage nach dem Menschen: Biblische Anthropologie als wissenschaftliche Aufgabe—Eine Standortbestimmung," *Biblische Anthropologie: Neue Einsichten aus dem Alten Testament*, Quaestiones Disputatae 237, ed. Christian Frevel (Freiburg: Herder, 2010), 29–63.

22. Hans Walter Wolff, *Anthropologie des Alten Testaments* (München: Chr. Kaiser Verlag, 1974²).

Wolffs research has been criticized for several reasons. To mention two, Wolff suggests that the biblical tradition offers one, coherent view on mankind. Second, his study lacks a reflection on the history of religion. Nevertheless, scholars still regard Wolff's study as a standard work.

As noticed above, the last two decades show a renewed interest in biblical anthropology. In the German language area, Bernd Janowski and Christian Frevel are important representatives.[23] They address several hermeneutical pitfalls in this field of research. First, biblical anthropology is a historical discipline, not only with regard to the growth of these texts over centuries, but also in relation to their origin in the context of the Ancient Near East. Second, actual dilemmas, evoked by insights from evolutionary biology, gene technology and neuroscience, are not reflected upon in the Bible. Despite this, biblical anthropologists maintain that biblical notions can have relevance in moral dilemmas that show up in the first quarter of the twenty-first century.

To explore personhood in biblical writings, Bernd Janowski elaborates on the notion of a "konstellative[r] Personbegriff," a term used by Jan Assmann to describe people in the Egyptian culture.[24] Biblical Hebrew does not know a term for 'person.'[25] According to biblical

---

23. In addition to titles already mentioned, see Bernd Janowski, "Anthropologie des Alten Testaments: Versuch einer Grundlegung," *Anthropologische Aufbrüche: Alttestamentliche und interdisziplinäre Zugänge zur historischen Anthropologie*, Forschungen zur Religion und Literatur des Alten und Neuen Testaments 232, ed. Andreas Wagner (Göttingen: Vandenhoeck & Ruprecht, 2009), 13–41; Christian Frevel, "Gottesbildlichkeit und Menschenwürde: Freiheit, Geschöpflichkeit und Würde des Menschen nach dem Alten Testament," *Anthropologische Aufbrüche*, Wagner, 255–274. See also Dörte Bester and Bernd Janowski, "Anthropologie des Alten Testaments: Ein forschungsgeschichtlicher Überblick," *Der Mensch im alten Israel: Neue Forschungen zur alttestamentlichen Anthropologie*, Herders Biblische Studien 59, eds. Bernd Janowski and Kathrin Liess (Freiburg, Basel & Wien: Herder, 2009), 3–40. For a clear overview and evaluation of some publications on biblical anthropology, see Andreas Schüle, "Anthropologie des Alten Testaments," *Theologische Rundschau* 76 (2011), 399–414.

24. Bernd Janowski, "Der Mensch im alten Israel: Grundfragen alttestamentlicher Anthropologie," *Zeitschrift für Theologie und Kirche* 102 (2005), 143–175; Bernd Janowski, "Anerkennung und Gegenseitigkeit: Zum konstellativen Personbegriff des Alten Testaments," *Der Mensch im alten Israel*, Janowski and Liess, 181–211; Bernd Janowski, "Konstellative Anthropologie: Zum Begriff der Person im Alten Testament," *Biblische Anthropologie*, Frevel, 64–87; Bernd Janowski, "Das Herz— ein Beziehungsorgan: Zum Personverständnis des Alten Testaments," *Dimensionen der Leiblichkeit: Theologische Zugänge*, Theologie Interdisziplinär 16, eds. Bernd Janowski and Christoph Schwöbel (Neukirchen-Vluyn: Neukirchener Verlagsgesellschaft, 2015), 1–45. See also Jan Assmann, "Konstellative Anthropologie: Zum Bild des Menschen im alten Ägypten," *Der Mensch im alten Israel*, Janowski and Liess, 95–120.

25. Cf. Klaus Neumann, "Person," *Handbuch theologischer Grundbegriffe*, Berlejung and Frevel, 339–340.

standards, a person is a compiled unity—a "Kompositum." The body consists of several components— reminiscent of the four categories of Wolff—and as part of the community, every individual plays several roles. Janowski, relying on the work of Robert Di Vito, sums up four identity markers: embeddedness, decenteredness, transparency, and dependency.[26] In other words, individuals in biblical times are embedded in their social environment; the outlines of who they are, are not clearly defined; they do not possess a hidden inner world; their authenticity lies in their obedience towards and dependency from others.[27]

The biblical concept of humanity collides with our current self-understanding. The idea of an independent individual is deconstructed, to put it anachronistically. From a biblical point of view, the web of relations to which a person belongs does not limit their possibilities but, instead, enlarges them. Human identity in biblical times is fluid.

8. Conclusion: A Cautious Commitment

The question of which things exactly are holy, is not the proper one. The proper question is: how can something *become* holy? This question is inextricably linked to the question of how we can recognize holiness in something or someone. Thus, in this essay, I have not employed a material definition of holiness, but a formal one. The clue to holiness is attribution.

Jochen Schmidt's secular interpretation of holiness, is twofold: not being at our disposal, from which an appeal emanates. The stronger the appeal that something unattainable to our interference makes on us, the closer it touches on being holy. I associate this not-being-at-our-disposal to the liturgical aspect of the biblical concept 'holy,' while I associate the appeal it makes to the ethical aspect. In the biblical view, there are two ways to honor that which is holy: by timidly approaching it, and by answering to the plea of those who can not defend themselves.

---

26. In German translation Robert A. Di Vito, "Alttestamentliche Anthropologie und die Konstruktion personaler Identität," *Der Mensch im alten Israel*, Janowski and Liess, 213–241.

27. For a critical evaluation of Di Vito's Old Testament anthropology, see the papers collected in *Individualität und Selbstreflexion in den Literaturen des Alten Testaments*, Veröffentlichungen der Wissenschaftlichen Gesellschaft für Theologie 48, eds. Andreas Wagner and Jürgen van Oorschot (Leipzig: Evangelische Verlagsanstalt, 2017); cf. *Anthropologie(n) des Alten Testaments*, Veröffentlichungen der Wissenschaftlichen Gesellschaft für Theologie 42, eds. Andreas Wagner and Jürgen van Oorschot (Leipzig: Evangelische Verlagsanstalt, 2015). See also Dorothea Erbele-Küster, "Biblische Anthropologie und Ethik," *Was ist theologische Ethik? Grundbestimmungen und Grundvorstellungen*, eds. Michael Roth and Marcus Held (Berlin & Boston: De Gruyter, 2018), 339–351. Erbele-Küster argues that an Old Testament anthropology consists of three components: corporeality, temporality and narrativity.

When applied to the issue of euthanasia, this means the following: the question of human death takes us into a realm over which we as a society do not have control. It is holy ground, which we can only approach with timidity: "Remove the sandals from your feet." It is, moreover, a question which makes an appeal. This I consider the most essential contribution of the Christian tradition to the debate on euthanasia. The biblical concept of holiness invites us, as a society, to consider the request for ending life not as a problem to be solved, but rather as an issue in which we recognize an appeal. This involves a change of perspective. It shifts the attention away from the person making the request, to those around them—the small circle of friends and relatives as well as the larger circle of society. This is in line with the biblical concept of humanity, in which a person's identity is constituted by their web of relations.

By introducing the notion of holiness, biblical language can contribute to overcoming the polarization between two opposing values in the debate on euthanasia: vulnerability versus autonomy. It supports the establishment of a new 'we.' A society which shows a sensitivity for someone's or something's potentially holy character, gains in quality. It will become more modest, because it acknowledges that there are issues and people on which it has no grip. Such a society will be more attentive because it is aware of how easy it is to pass by, and miss, the holy. It will also be more engaged. It will try to answer the call for careful interaction. Every person who longs for the end of life deserves our cautious commitment.

BIBLIOGRAPHY

Assmann, Jan. "Konstellative Anthropologie: Zum Bild des Menschen im alten Ägypten." In *Der Mensch im alten Israel*: *Neue Forschungen zur alttestamentlichen Anthropologie*. Herders Biblische Studien 59, eds. Bernd Janowski and Kathrin Liess, 95–120. Freiburg, Basel & Wien: Herder, 2009.

Belder, J. and A.A. Teeuw. *Mijn leven voltooid?* (My life completed?). Artios-reeks. Heerenveen: Groen, 2018.

Berlejung, Angelika and Bernd Janowski. Eds. *Tod und Jenseits im alten Israel und in seiner Umwelt*: *Theologische, religionsgeschichtliche, archäologische und ikonographische Aspekte*, Forschungen zum Alten Testament 64. Tübingen: Mohr Siebeck, 2009.

Berlis, Angela; Anne-Marie Korte and Kune Biezeveld. *Everyday Life and the Sacred*: *Re/Configuring Gender Studies in Religion*, Studies in Theology and Religion 23. Leiden & Boston: Brill, 2017.

Bester, Dörte and Bernd Janowski. "Anthropologie des Alten Testaments: Ein forschungsgeschichtlicher Überblick." In *Der Mensch im alten Israel*: *Neue Forschungen zur alttestamentlichen Anthropologie*. Herders Biblische Studien 59, eds. Bernd Janowski and Kathrin Liess, 3–40. Freiburg, Basel & Wien: Herder, 2009.

Boer, Theo; Ronald Bolwijn; Maaike Graafland; Wim Graafland and Annemarieke van der Woude. "Pastores in de PKN en hun ervaringen met euthanasie" (Pastors in the Dutch Protestant Church and their experiences with euthanasia). *Kerk en Theologie* 70:2 (2019): 151–172.

Boorer, Suzanne. *The Vision of the Priestly Narrative*: *Its Genre and Hermeneutics of Time*. Ancient Israel and its Literature 27. Atlanta: SBL Press, 2016.

Bormann, Franz-Josef. "Ist die Vorstellung eines '*natürlichen Todes*' noch zeitgemäß? Moraltheologische Überlegungen zu einem umstrittenen Begriff." In *Sterben*: *Dimensionen eines anthropologischen Grundphänomens*, eds. Franz-Josef Bormann and Gian Domenico Borasio, 325–350. Berlin & Boston: De Gruyter, 2012.

Bosman, Hendrik L. "Loving the Neighbour and the Resident Alien in Leviticus 19 as Ethical Redefinition of Holiness." *Old Testament Essays* 31:3 (2018): 571–590.

Brink, Gijsbert van den. "Lijden in de Bijbel: Een verkenning" (Suffering in the Bible: An exploration). In *Lijden en volhouden*, Lindeboomreeks 19, eds. Theo Boer and Dick Mul, 19–35. Amsterdam: Buijten & Schipperheijn *Motief*, 2016.

Browning, Elizabeth Barrett. *Aurora Leigh and Other Poems*. Introduced by Cora Kaplan. London: The Women's Press, 1978.

Di Vito, Robert A. "Alttestamentliche Anthropologie und die Konstruktion personaler Identität." In *Der Mensch im alten Israel*: Neue Forschungen zur alttestamentlichen Anthropologie. Herders Biblische Studien 59, eds. Bernd Janowski and Kathrin Liess, 213–241. Freiburg, Basel & Wien: Herder, 2009.

Erbele-Küster, Dorothea. "Biblische Anthropologie und Ethik." In *Was ist theologische Ethik? Grundbestimmungen und Grundvorstellungen*, eds. Michael Roth and Marcus Held, 339–351. Berlin & Boston: De Gruyter, 2018.

Fabry, Heinz-Josef and Hans-Winfried Jüngling. Eds. *Levitikus als Buch*. Bonner Biblische Beiträge 119. Berlin & Bodenheim: Philo, 1999.

Fortuin, Nienke P.M. *The Search for Meaning in Later Life: An Empirical Exploration of Religion and Death*. Death Studies: Nijmegen Studies in Thanatology 6. Zürich: Lit Verlag, 2020.

Francis, Pope. *Gaudete et exsultate* (Rejoice and be glad). Apostolic Exhortation of the Holy Father on the call to holiness in today's world. Vatican, 2018.

Frevel, Christian. "Anthropologie." In *Handbuch theologischer Grundbegriffe zum Alten und Neuen Testament*, eds. Angelika Berlejung and Christian Frevel, 1–7. Darmstadt: Wissenschaftliche Buchgesellschaft, 2012[3].

Frevel, Christian. "Die Frage nach dem Menschen: Biblische Anthropologie als wissenschaftliche Aufgabe—Eine Standortbestimmung." In *Biblische Anthropologie: Neue Einsichten aus dem Alten Testament*. Quaestiones Disputatae 237, ed. Christian Frevel, 29–63. Freiburg: Herder, 2010.

Frevel, Christian. "Gottesbildlichkeit und Menschenwürde: Freiheit, Geschöpflichkeit und Würde des Menschen nach dem Alten Testament." In *Anthropologische Aufbrüche: Alttestamentliche und interdisziplinäre Zugänge zur historischen Anthropologie*. Forschungen zur Religion und Literatur des Alten und Neuen Testaments 232, ed. Andreas Wagner, 255–274. Göttingen: Vandenhoeck & Ruprecht, 2009.

Frevel, Christian. "Orientierung! Grundfragen einer Ethik des Alten Testaments." In *Mehr als Zehn Worte? Zur Bedeutung des Alten Testaments in ethischen Fragen*, Quaestiones Disputatae 273, ed. Christian Frevel, 9–57. Freiburg: Herder, 2015.

Gane, Roy E. and Ada Taggar-Cohen. Eds. *Current Issues in Priestly and Related Literature: The Legacy of Jacob Milgrom and Beyond*. Resources for Biblical Study 82. Atlanta: SBL Press, 2015.

Groß, Walter. "Zum alttestamentlich-jüdischen Verständnis von Sterben und Tod." In *Sterben*: *Dimensionen eines anthropologischen Grundphänomens*, eds. Franz-Josef Bormann and Gian Domenico Borasio, 465–480. Berlin & Boston: De Gruyter, 2012.

Hieke, Thomas. "Die Heiligkeit Gottes als Beweggrund für ethisches Verhalten: Das ethische Konzept des Heiligkeitsgesetzes nach Levitikus 19." In *Mehr als Zehn Worte? Zur Bedeutung des Alten Testaments in ethischen Fragen*, Quaestiones Disputatae 273, ed. Christian Frevel, 187–206. Freiburg: Herder, 2015.

Janowski, Bernd. "Anerkennung und Gegenseitigkeit: Zum konstellativen Personbegriff des Alten Testaments." In *Der Mensch im alten Israel*: *Neue Forschungen zur alttestamentlichen Anthropologie*. Herders Biblische Studien 59, eds. Bernd Janowski and Kathrin Liess, 181–211. Freiburg, Basel & Wien: Herder, 2009.

Janowski, Bernd. "Anthropologie des Alten Testaments: Versuch einer Grundlegung," *Anthropologische Aufbrüche*: *Alttestamentliche und interdisziplinäre Zugänge zur historischen Anthropologie*. Forschungen zur Religion und Literatur des Alten und Neuen Testaments 232, ed. Andreas Wagner, 13–41. Göttingen: Vandenhoeck & Ruprecht, 2009.

Janowski, Bernd. "Das Herz—ein Beziehungsorgan: Zum Personverständnis des Alten Testaments." In *Dimensionen der Leiblichkeit*: *Theologische Zugänge*. Theologie Interdisziplinär 16, eds. Bernd Janowski and Christoph Schwöbel, 1–45. Neukirchen Vluyn: Neukirchener Verlagsgesellschaft, 2015.

Janowski, Bernd. "Der Mensch im alten Israel: Grundfragen alttestamentlicher Anthropologie." *Zeitschrift für Theologie und Kirche* 102 (2005): 143–175.

Janowski, Bernd. "Konstellative Anthropologie: Zum Begriff der Person im Alten Testament." In *Biblische Anthropologie*: *Neue Einsichten aus dem Alten Testament*. Quaestiones Disputatae 237, ed. Christian Frevel, 64–87. Freiburg: Herder, 2010.

Jansen, Lynn A.; Steven Wall and Franklin G. Miller. "Drawing the Line on Physician-Assisted Death." *Journal of Medical Ethics* 45:1 (2019): 190–197.

Joas, Hans. *Die Macht des Heiligen*: *Eine Alternative zur Geschichte der Entzauberung*. Berlin: Suhrkamp Verlag, 2017.

Jobsen, Aarnoud. "Leviticus en Numeri." In *De Bijbel theologisch: Hoofdlijnen en thema's* (The bible in theological perspective: Headlines and themes), eds. Klaas Spronk and Archibald van Wieringen, 41–50. Zoetermeer: Meinema, 2011.

Kouwenhoven, Pauline S.C.; Ghislaine J.M.W. van Thiel; Agnes van der Heide; Judith A.C. Rietjens and Johannes J.M. van Delden. "Developments in Euthanasia Practice in the Netherlands: Balancing Professional Responsibility and the Patient's Autonomy." *European Journal of General Practice* 25:1 (2019): 44–48.

Kratz, Reinhard G. "Heiligkeit." In *Handbuch theologischer Grundbegriffe zum Alten und Neuen Testament*, eds. Angelika Berlejung and Christian Frevel, 242–243. Darmstadt: Wissenschaftliche Buchgesellschaft, 20123.

Leene, Henk. *Newness in Old Testament Prophecy: An Intertextual Study*. Oudtestamentische studiën 64. Leiden & Boston: Brill, 2014.

Liess, Kathrin. *Der Weg des Lebens: Psalm 16 und das Lebensund Todesverständnis der Individualpsalmen*, Forschungen zum Alten Testament 2.5. Tübingen: Mohr Siebeck, 2004.

Lynch, Gordon. *The Sacred in the Modern World: A Cultural Sociological Approach*. Oxford: Oxford University Press, 2012.

Neumann, Klaus. "Person." In *Handbuch theologischer Grundbegriffe zum Alten und Neuen Testament*, eds. Angelika Berlejung and Christian Frevel, 339–340. Darmstadt: Wissenschaftliche Buchgesellschaft, 20123.

Nihan, Christophe. *From Priestly Torah to Pentateuch: A Study in the Composition of the Book of Leviticus*. Forschungen zum Alten Testament 2.25. Tübingen: Mohr Siebeck, 2007.

Post, Henk and Bert van Veluw. Eds. *12 artikelen over voltooid leven* (Twelve articles on 'completed life'), Geloven op goede gronden. Utrecht: KokBoekencentrum, 2020.

Regionale Toetsingscommissies Euthanasie. *Jaarverslag 2019 Regionale Toetsingscommissies Euthanasie* (Annual report 2019 Regional Euthanasia Review Committees). Den Haag: Xerox/OBT, 2020.

Schmidt, Jochen. "Kultur der Heiligkeit: Über theologische Rede vom Unverfügbaren in einem säkularen Zeitalter." *Zeitschrift für Theologie und Kirche* 113 (2016): 279–290.

Schmidt, Jochen. "Erzählte Heiligkeit: Über Unverfügbarkeit und Menschenwürde." *Zeitschrift für Evangelische Ethik* 61 (2017): 120–124.

Schüle, Andreas. "Anthropologie des Alten Testaments." *Theologische Rundschau* 76 (2011): 399–414.

Sexson, Lynda. *Ordinarily Sacred*. Charlottesville: The University of Virginia Press, 1992.

Shectman, Sarah and Joel S. Baden. Eds. *The Strata of the Priestly Writings*: *Contemporary Debate and Future Directions*. Abhandlungen zur Theologie des Alten und Neuen Testaments 95. Zürich: Theologischer Verlag Zürich, 2009.

Sheldrake, Philip. *Spaces for the Sacred*: *Place, Memory and Identity*, The Hulsean Lectures 2000. London: SCM Press, 2001.

Stewart, David T. "Leviticus 19 as Mini-Torah." In *Current Issues in Priestly and Related Literature*: *The Legacy of Jacob Milgrom and Beyond*. Resources for Biblical Study 82, eds. Gane, Roy E. and Ada Taggar-Cohen, 299–323. Atlanta: SBL Press, 2015.

Trevaskis, Leigh M. *Holiness, Ethics and Ritual in Leviticus*, Hebrew Bible Monographs 29. Sheffield: Sheffield Phoenix, 2011.

Tucker, Paavo N. *The Holiness Composition in the Book of Exodus*. Forschungen zum Alten Testament 2. 98. Tübingen: Mohr Siebeck, 2017.

Wagner, Andreas and Jürgen van Oorschot. Eds. *Anthropologie(n) des Alten Testaments*. Veröffentlichungen der Wissenschaftlichen Gesellschaft für Theologie 42. Leipzig: Evangelische Verlagsanstalt, 2015.

Wagner, Andreas and Jürgen van Oorschot. Eds. *Individualität und Selbstreflexion in den Literaturen des Alten Testaments*. Veröffentlichungen der Wissenschaftlichen Gesellschaft für Theologie 48. Leipzig: Evangelische Verlagsanstalt, 2017.

Wijngaarden, Els van. *Ready to Give up on Life*: *A Study into the Lived Experience of Older People who Consider their Lives to Be Completed and no Longer Worth Living*. Amersfoort: Wilco, 2016.

Williams, Rowan. *Holy Living*: *The Christian Tradition for Today*. London & New York: Bloomsbury, 2017.

Wolff, Hans Walter. *Anthropologie des Alten Testaments*. München: Chr. Kaiser Verlag, 19742.

Zenger, Erich. "Das Buch Levitikus als Teiltext der Tora/des Pentateuch: Eine synchrone Lektüre mit kanonischer Perspektive." In *Levitikus als Buch*. Bonner Biblische Beiträge 119, eds. Heinz-Josef Fabry and Hans-Winfried Jüngling, 47–83. Berlin & Bodenheim: Philo, 1999.

CHAPTER 7
SOWING HOPE IN A POLARIZED AGRICULTURAL DEBATE
Jan Jorrit Hasselaar, Philipp Pattberg and Peter-Ben Smit

1. INTRODUCTION[1]

On October 1, 2019 farmer protests caused the largest traffic jam ever in the Netherlands. Two weeks later, military trucks in the streets of The Hague were preventing farmers from protesting at 'Het Binnenhof,' the political heart of the Netherlands. These protests were a response to recent discussions about reducing the emission of nitrogen. In September 2019, the Remkes commission recommended in the report that 'not everything is possible' and that farms situated close to nature reserves should be bought out or transformed into more environmentally friendly farms in order to reduce these emissions.[2] As indicated, the farmers became furious and caused the traffic jam.

The nitrogen reduction recommendations seem to trigger an underlying feeling of 'us-them' amongst farmers, as expressed by Mark van den Oever, one of the protest organizers, just before the traffic jam: "We feel as if we're being put in the dunces' corner by city types who come and tell us how things should be in the countryside." The 'city type' can appear in many forms: the activist, the politician and the journalist. According to Van den Oever, there is a sentiment among farmers that they get blamed for everything and that the city types try to bully them away. In other words, Van den Over experiences an us-them feeling between farmers on the one hand and 'city types' on the other.[3]

---

1. A special thanks for his constructive remarks to dr. Paul Koster, Department of Spatial Economics, Vrije Universiteit Amsterdam.

2. Adviescollege Stikstofproblematiek, *Niet Alles Kan*: *Aanbevelingen voor de Korte Termijn* (Not everything is possible: Short termrecommendations) (25 September 2019). Available at https://www.rijksoverheid.nl/documenten/rapporten/2019/09/25/eerste-advies-adviescollege-stikstofproblematiek.

3. Emiel Hakkenes, "Den Haag wacht grimmig boerenprotest: 'Stedelingen zetten ons in de verdomhoek'" (The Hague awaits grim farmer's protest: 'City types put us in the dark'), *Trouw*, 28 September 2019, https://www.trouw.nl/nieuws/den-haag-wacht-

Earlier that year, on May 13th, there was a clear physical illustration of 'us-them' when one hundred animal activists from the international organization Meat the Victims occupied a pig farm in the municipality of Boxtel in North Brabant (Netherlands) to draw attention to animal suffering. Farmers gathered to counter-protest and tipped cars that belonged to animal activists into a ditch. As a result of this confrontation, the previously mentioned Van den Oever founded the Farmers Defence Force, an agricultural action group defending the interests of farmers with its own website and a WhatsApp group.[4] "Now, if there is a raid somewhere, all the farmer has to do is send a WhatsApp message and we come to help him."[5] These illustrations seem to indicate a growing 'us-them' thinking in the debate over the future of agriculture.

The debate about the future of agriculture is related to several Sustainable Development Goals (SDG s). In the past few years, the SDG s have become the common language of governments, NGO s and business to address the most pressing development challenges for humanity and the planet, including climate change, biodiversity, poverty, and gender issues. The SDG s prescribe an agenda for sustainable development in the period 2015–2030. However, reaching the SDG s remains a major challenge. As SDG 17 notes, cooperation and partnership are required to achieve the other 16 SDG s; but such cooperation is not always self-evident. One of the main challenges is overcoming polarizing positions between parties when it comes to particular SDG s, as seen in the agricultural sector in the Netherlands.

This article explores a religious-inspired contribution to transition research. It seeks to develop an interdisciplinary contribution to the transition to circular agriculture in the Netherlands by exploring the potential role of the concept of hope. More specifically, we investigate whether the concept of hope might be able to facilitate moving beyond polarization in the transition to circular agriculture in the Netherlands. In doing so and while drawing on theology in Jewish and Christian traditions as a resource, it makes sense to take scripture itself as the point of departure. This takes place in two ways: (a) we focus on the concept of hope, derived from the biblical narrative of the Exodus, set forth by Jonathan Sacks, a British scholar and public intellectual in the tradition of Judaism; (b) we substantiate the dialogical approach to discernment that views diversity and even disagreement and conflict as a resource and catalyst for creativity rather than an obstacle that needs to be overcome or passed over by means of an appeal to canonical hermeneutics as they

---

grimmig-boerenprotest-stedelingen-zetten-ons-in-de-verdomhoek~b2ebabbc/, accessed November 1, 2020.

4. www.farmersdefenceforce.nl.
5. www.farmersdefenceforce.nl.

have been developed in the field of biblical studies and the theological reflection on the canon of the (Christian) Bible.

The remainder of this article is structured as follows. After this introduction, we describe the situation in the agricultural sector in the Netherlands. The following section conceptualizes the problems in the agricultural sector as a wicked problem. The section thereafter highlights subsequent governance challenges when it comes to wicked problems. Next, the notion of hope in the work of Jonathan Sacks is explored. Then, an operationalization of the concept of hope is illustrated in the mining sectors in South Africa. The section thereafter investigates an implementation of the concept of hope in the 'Food Valley' (the Netherlands). Then some questions about ecclesial innovation are made. The last section offers some concluding remarks.

2. DUTCH AGRICULTURE

Having witnessed the Dutch famine at the end of the Second World War, Sicco Mansholt, Dutch Minister of Agriculture (1945–1958) and European Commissioner for Agriculture (1958–1972) was determined to ensure that Europe would be a place without hunger. Mansholt was convinced that Europe needed to become self-sufficient and that a stable supply of affordable food should be guaranteed for all inhabitants of Europe. Therefore, he set in motion a program to modernize agriculture profoundly in order to avoid future shortages and guarantee production efficiency. One of his policy measures was the rationalization and upscaling of farm productivity, which resulted among others in the application of chemical crop protection substances and technological development to save labor. From a production perspective, the Dutch agricultural sector has been highly successful. For example, according to Statistics Netherlands (CBS) and Wageningen Economic Research, the agricultural goods exports from the Netherlands amounted to an estimated 90.3 billion euros in 2018. With this export value, the small country of the Netherlands is the world's largest exporter of agricultural goods after the United States. Agricultural commodities account for nearly one-fifth of Dutch commodity exports: 18.2 percent in 2018. Domestic production accounts for 72.4 percent of these agricultural exports.[6]

In September 2018 Carola Schouten, Minister of Agriculture, Nature and Food Quality, published the vision *Agriculture, Nature and Food: Valuable and Connected*. In this vision she describes the current situation

---

6. Mark Dolman, Gerben Jukema en Pascal Ramaekers, *De Nederlandse landbouwexport in 2018 in breder perspectief* (Dutch agricultural exports in 2018 in a wider perspective) (Wageningen: Wageningen Economic Research en het Centraal Bureau voor de Statistiek, 2019). Available at http://edepot.wur.nl/468099.

of farming, horticulture and fisheries in the Netherlands. Characteristics of these sectors, in line with Mansholt's modernization, are that they produce at low costs and that there is an emphasis on cutting costs and increasing production, resulting in upscaling. In her vision, the Minister highlights the added value and achievement of the sector. However, at the same time she argues that the current production methods are not without cost. In her vision, she states that these methods lead to two substantial imbalances.[7]

First, cost reductions and production increases result in small and sometimes even negative profit margins, which makes the sectors vulnerable in economic terms. This leads to substantial income uncertainty for actors in the sector.

Second, intensive production has come at the expense of biodiversity, the environment, the quality of drinking water and the attractiveness of the landscape.

According to the Minister, these reasons provide an argument to make a transition to circular agriculture. Katrien Termeer, Professor of Public Administration and Policy (Wageningen University), deepens this argument by stating that there are not just two imbalances in the agricultural sector, but that there is a range of problems and challenges, among others strengthening the position of the famer in the chain, synergy between agriculture and biodiversity, adaptation to climate change, reduction of food waste, reduction of CO_2 emissions, animal welfare and limited resources.[8] Termeer uses the term 'wicked problems' to describe these problems and challenges.

3. WICKED PROBLEMS

Wicked problems were originally defined by Churchman,[9] and Rittel and Webber[10] as those incomprehensible and resistant to a solution. Head and Alford argue "that degrees of 'wickedness' can be understood by reference to multiple dimensions and that it is possible to frame partial, provisional courses of action against wicked problems."[11] Wicked

---

7. Carola Schouten, *Landbouw, natuur en voedsel: Waardevol en verbonden. Nederland als koploper in kringlooplandbouw* (Agriculture, nature and food: Valuable and connected. The Netherlands as a frontrunner in circular agriculture) (2018), 11–12. Available at https://www.rijksoverheid.nl/documenten/beleidsnota-s/2018/09/08/visie-landbouw-natuur-en-voedsel-waardevol-en-verbonden.

8. Katrien Termeer, *Het bewerkstelligen van een transitie naar kringlooplandbouw* (Achieving a transition to circular agriculture) (Wageningen: Wageningen University & Research, 2019), 2.

9. C. West Churchman, "Free for all," *Management Science* 14 (1967), B141–B142.

10. Horst W.J. Rittel and Melvin M. Webber, "Dilemmas in a General Theory of Planning," *Policy Sciences* 4 (1973), 155–169.

11. Brian W. Head and John Alford, "Wicked problems: Implications for Public

problems arise in situations wherein "stakeholders may have conflicting interpretations of the problem and the science behind it, as well as different values, goals, and life experiences."[12] Wicked problems are also known to have key characteristics. According to Head and Alford, they are associated with (a) social pluralism (i.e., multiple interests and values of stakeholders); (b) institutional complexity (the context of interorganizational cooperation and multilevel governance); and (c) scientific uncertainty (fragmentation and gaps in reliable knowledge). Wicked problems have been identified and studied in various policy domains, including disasters and crises, climate change responses, natural resource management, health care, urban and regional planning, business planning and cybernetics. Rittel and Webber identified ten primary characteristics of wicked problems:

1. There is no definitive formulation of a wicked problem;
2. Wicked problems have no 'stopping rule' (i.e., no definitive solution);
3. Solutions to wicked problems are not true or false, but good or bad;
4. There is no immediate and no ultimate test of a solution to a wicked problem;
5. Every (attempted) solution to a wicked problem is a 'one-shot operation'; the results cannot be readily undone, and there is no opportunity to learn by trial and error;
6. Wicked problems do not have an enumerable (or an exhaustively describable) set of potential solutions, nor is there a well-described set of permissible operations that may be incorporated into the plan;
7. Every wicked problem is essentially unique;
8. Every wicked problem can be considered to be a symptom of another problem;
9. The existence of a discrepancy representing a wicked problem can be explained in numerous ways;
10. The planner has no 'right to be wrong' (i.e., there is no public tolerance of experiments that fail).

We will argue that these characteristics of wicked problems seem to help us to understand the cause of polarization in the agricultural sector. In the view of Termeer, several of these characteristics of wicked problems

---

Policy and Management," *Administration & Society* 47:6 (2015), 711–739.
    12. Marshall Kreuter, Christopher De Rosa, Elizabeth Howze and Grant Baldwin, "Understanding Wicked Problems: A Key to Advancing Environmental Health Promotion," *Health Education & Behavior* 31 (2004), 441–454.

can be applied to the problems and challenges in the agricultural sector.[13]

First, there are many parties involved in all layers of government (local, regional, national, European, global); an increasing number of policy domains (agriculture, environment, nature, health, energy, aid and trade); public and private domains (farmers, parties in the chain, service providers, governments and civil organizations) and the wider public (citizens, neighbors and consumers). These parties often have different and conflicting values and targets.

Second, and important to understanding the cause of polarization, the parties have different and often conflicting ideas of the problem at hand. This can vary from reduction of the fertility of the soil to presence of too many animals. Due to different points of view and interests, parties have divergent ideas about solutions, ranging from innovative sustainable systems in factory farming to reduction of the consumption of meat.

Third, the impossibility of giving the problem a definitive formulation. The problems change regularly in shape due to interventions and autonomous dynamics (e.g., economic growth); policy intervention (e.g., abolition of the milk quota and agreements regarding climate change); and incidents (Q fever, fipronil, drought and flooding). Most problems have a long history of policy interventions.

Fourth, every problem can be considered to be a symptom of another problem. Many examples can be given of solutions that were useful in the past, but lead to problems in the present situation. The reason for this is that there was only attention to a partial problem, some effects were unforeseen or values in society have changed. For example, measures with regard to animal welfare that caused extra emission of particulates, the consequences of detailed legislation on fertilizers for soil fertility, or undesirable side-effects of several generations of Common Agricultural Policy.

Fifth, today's solutions lead to the problems of tomorrow, including the lack of a stopping rule (to know when a problem has been resolved). Despite the ambitions and efforts of successive governments, the problems appear not to be solved once and for all.

Describing the problems and challenges in the agricultural sector as wicked problems raises at least the corner of the veil of the cause of polarization. The parties involved have often different and conflicting ideas of the problem at hand. Reducing the complexity of the 'wicked problem' to a single cause and a related one-dimensional solution leads to further polarization of the debate about the future of agriculture. Is it possible to tackle this tendency toward polarization?

---

13. Termeer, *Het bewerkstelligen van een transitie*, 8.

4. GOVERNANCE OF WICKED PROBLEMS

Termeer argues that dealing with the interdependent problems and challenges in the agricultural sector demands a transition that is characterized by a shared urgency to deal with the problems and challenges involved.[14] In her vision, the Minister states also that the entire supply chain, the government and consumers have a role to play.[15] Or, to put it in the words of the Council for the Environment and Infrastructure (RLI): "The inescapable need to adapt our food system provides an excellent opportunity to unite farmers, the food processing industry, the retail sector and consumers in a unique coalition for sustainable and healthy food."[16]

Cooperation may be required in order to stimulate a transition toward a circular agriculture, but in the introduction we have seen that there is a current tendency toward polarization. The tendency was also reflected in a large survey in 2018 showing that more than 80% of Dutch farmers want to use more environment-friendly methods. However, the survey also shows that farmers experience a big gap between farmers and consumers/citizens and society, farmers and supermarkets and farmers and their representing organizations. Interests diverge and trust is often lacking. In 2019, an extended version of this survey was done. This survey shows that there seems to be a further polarization of opinions between farmer-citizen and city-agricultural sector. At the same time, although less visible, there is a tendency toward cooperation and connection. What is striking are the more radical and extreme positions of young farmers (under the age of 40) in the debate.[17]

Over the last decennia, several initiatives have been taken to create a transition in the agricultural sector, for example reducing livestock, easing the tension between consumer-citizen perspectives, and strengthening the position of the farmer in the chain.[18] These earlier initiatives all started with high ambitions and a lot of energy and then got stuck in blockades and quietly died due to the presence of taboos, in the sense of strongly held convictions that are hard to change and about which it is hardly possible to speak about. Termeer states that it is necessary for a real

---

14. Termeer, *Het bewerkstelligen van een transitie*, 3.
15. Schouten, *Landbouw, natuur en voedsel*, 20.
16. Raad voor de leefomgeving en infrastructuur, *Duurzaam en gezond: Samen naar een houdbaar voedselsysteem* (Council for the living environment and infrastructure, *Sustainable and healthy: Together towards a sustainable food system*) (Den Haag: Raad voor de leefomgeving en infrastructuur, 2018), available at https://www.rli.nl/sites/default/files/duurzaam_en_gezond_samen_naar_een_houdbaar_voedselsysteem_def_1.pdf.
17. "De Staat van de Boer" (The farmer's state) (2018). Available at https://destaatvandeboer.trouw.nl/.
18. Termeer, *Het bewerkstelligen van een transitie*, 8.

transition to face these taboos and make them a subject of conversation. The best way of approaching such a conversation is a political and societal dialogue.[19] Kim Putters, director of the Netherlands Institute for Social Research (Sociaal en Cultureel Planbureau), also argues for a societal dialogue to deal with wicked problems in Dutch society instead of dealing with them as being relatively 'simple' policy problems.[20]

This chapter investigates a somewhat unexpected—and therefore potentially innovative—approach to support this direction of dealing with wicked problems given by Termeer and Putters. We delve more deeply into the concept of hope of the wisdom traditions of Judaism and Christianity.

5. HOPE

The first sections of this article elaborated on the challenges in the Dutch agricultural sector. The next is about the challenge for the church in these situations. Here we want to highlight 'hope' as a promising concept for overcoming stagnation and conflict in the context of wicked problems. Hope can be considered, together with faith and love, as one of the core values in the Christian tradition (1 Cor. 13: 13). Recently, Volf and Croasmun have reminded us that religious wisdom traditions, and theology as a systematic reflection on them, are about a certain perspective of flourishing life.[21] In the following we argue that, in the context of polarizing positions and resulting paralysis, there is a biblical tradition that identifies 'hope' as a promising concept for overcoming stagnation caused by conflict.

In the twentieth century important contributions on hope were made, such as Ernst Bloch's three-volume compendium *The Principle of Hope* (1954, 1955 and 1959), Jürgen Moltmann's *Theology of Hope* (1964) and Erich Fromm's *The Revolution of Hope* (1968). Although the concept has received much scholarly attention, its potential for addressing 21st century challenges has been left curiously underexplored. For instance, in 2015, literary scholar and cultural critic Terry Eagleton remarked that hope "... has been a curiously neglected notion in an age which, in Raymond Williams's words, confronts us with 'the felt loss of a future.'"[22]

---

19. Termeer, *Het bewerkstelligen van een transitie*, 3, 8.

20. Kim Putters, *Veenbrand: Smeulende kwesties in de welvarende samenleving* (Peat fire: Smoldering issues in the prosperous society) (Amsterdam: Prometheus, 2019), 214.

21. Miroslav Volf and Matthew Croasmun, *For the Life of the World: Theology That Makes a Difference* (Grand Rapids: Brazos Press, 2019).

22. Terry Eagleton, *Hope without Optimism* (Charlottesville: University of Virginia Press, 2015), xi.

To move from the concept of hope to hope as a catalyst for overcoming conflict and contestations in the sector of agriculture, we look in particular at the understanding of hope set forth by Jonathan Sacks, a British scholar and public intellectual in the tradition of Judaism. The reason for this is that Sacks provides a particular view of hope that is promising in relation to the issue of decision making in situations of conflicting positions and uncertainty. Innovatively utilizing the resources of the Jewish tradition, Sacks conceptualizes, based on the narrative of the Exodus, hope as a narrative of individual and societal transformation. In this process of transformation, key stakeholders, individually and collectively, learn to open up their identities, the images—of themselves, others and the world—people live by, and to include the interest of oneself and others into a common identity.[23] Therefore, hope is best expressed as a learning process that seeks to create relations of trust that teach one how to honor both the interest of oneself and others. According to Sacks, this process is supported by two institutions: covenant and public Sabbath. In the covenant, parties with often contrasting interests exchange voluntarily and each on their own terms a promise to take responsibility for a shared future. The public Sabbath has the following characteristics.[24]

First, the public Sabbath as Utopia Now celebrates the liberating perspective, the new 'we,' in the present order not to get lost in the transformation, not to forget that the present situation is no longer one's identity and to remind people of what they are aiming at.

Second, the public Sabbath seeks to orientate people to something larger than their present identity. The Sabbath is a neutral space, as it values the dignity of difference among the participants. The experiences of these differences can make people aware of their own perspective and has the potential to open them up to the possibility of developing a new and common identity.

Third, the public Sabbath seeks to stimulate positive other-regarding behavior, especially relations of kindness and love, that seek to honor oneself and the other, especially those yet excluded. These relations can never be taken for granted and have to be developed, because they are never immune to fear, free-riding, cynicism and power games to gain influence.

---

23. See Jonathan Sacks, *The Politics of Hope* (London: Jonathan Cape, 1997); Jonathan Sacks, *Future Tense: Jews, Judaism, and Israel in the Twenty-First Century* (New York: Schocken Books, 2009); Jonathan Sacks, Covenant & Conversation, Exodus: The Book of Redemption (Jerusalem: Maggid Books, 2010).

24. Jan Jorrit Hasselaar, "Hope in the Context of Climate Change: Jonathan Sacks' Interpretation of the Exodus and Radical Uncertainty," *International Journal of Public Theology* 14 (2020), 224–240.

Fourth, the public Sabbath is an embodied performance that can bring in the power of symbol, music, memory, narrative, poetry, prayer, ritual, art and imagination in order to create and shape a common identity. Music, for example, has the ability to imagine and dream about a different reality than the present one or to express frustration about the current state of affairs, and can thus help to make the first steps to become honest and to put a vision into practice.

Sacks considers a public Sabbath as the key to a politics of hope.[25] The reason for this is that the Sabbath is a regular institution to stimulate individual and societal transformation. Nevertheless, covenant and Sabbath are two sides of the same coin. During the transformation, stimulated by a public Sabbath, the parties involved develop the willingness to exchange promises for a shared future (covenant). Several dimensions of such a public Sabbath can be found in a real-life initiative. The following section discusses an operationalization of Sacks' concept of hope, including a public Sabbath.

6. COURAGEOUS CONVERSATIONS

An example of an operationalization of hope as a transition, including a public Sabbath, can be found in the so-called Safe Space Dialogue (SSD) in South Africa. SSD is a social design approach that has been developed in the context of the transition in the mining sector in South Africa and was expressed in the initiative of 'Courageous Conversations.' This initiative was started by Thabo Makgoba, successor of Desmond Tutu as Archbishop of Cape Town. It consists of a series of courageous conversations between parties involved in the mining chain in order to co-create a vision of the future. The conversations are held in safe spaces. These spaces have several characteristics of the public Sabbaths above. The objective of the SSD is to establish a platform for transformative discussions between representative actors in the mining sector in a way that is not about narrow self-interest, positioning or antagonism, but rather a transparent, honest, and constructive dialogue reflecting on the complex challenges and opportunities that this sector faces. The SSD is supported by a Steering Committee. The composition of the steering committee represents the interests of the various stakeholders involved in the project. The SSD is also supported by several task teams, for example a team on Socio-Economic Development (SED). These teams meet regularly to facilitate, implement and oversee the programs within the mining communities. The diagram below presents the management structure of the Courageous Conversation project in South Africa, including the roles of the Steering committee and its involvement and relationship with the

---

25. Sacks, *Exodus*, 331.

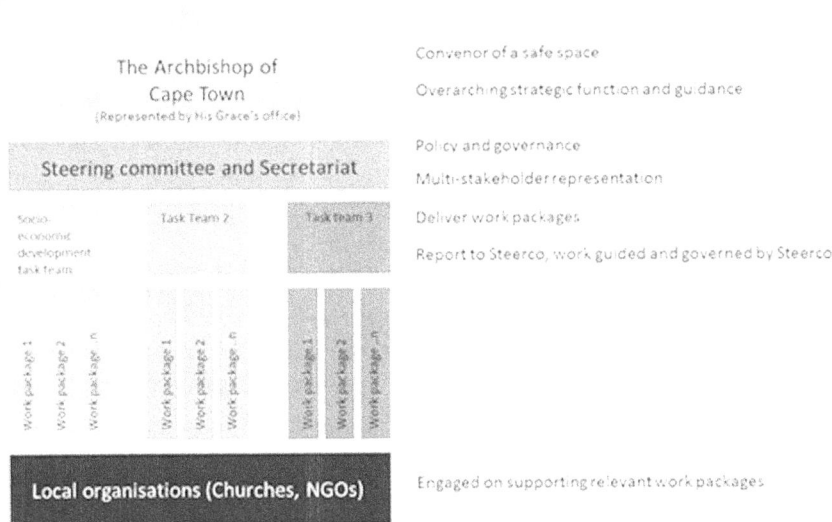

FIGURE 7.1 Management structure of the Courageous Conversations in South Africa.

various task teams.

The next section discusses how such an approach can be applied to the agricultural sector in the Netherlands.

7. FOOD VALLEY CASE STUDY

We have argued that earlier initiatives for a transition in the agricultural sector started with high ambitions and a lot of energy, but got stuck and quietly died. Therefore, Termeer and Putters argue for a political and societal dialogue. Sacks' understanding of hope provides a transition pathway in which dialogue between all relevant parties plays a key role.

During a Round Table, in May 2019, first steps were taken to explore and operationalize Sacks' concept of hope in order to overcome polarized situations in the agricultural sector in the Netherlands, more in particular in the Food Valley.[26] This Round Table was initiated by Rabobank, the municipality of Ede, and an interdisciplinary research group, including economists, theologians and political researchers of the Amsterdam Sustainability Institute of the Vrije Universiteit

26. The Food Valley is an important agro-food centre of Europe and located around municipalities like Ede, Nijkerk and Wageningen, close to the middle of the Netherlands. The reason to choose the Food Valley is twofold. First, in the Food Valley there are intensive relationships between town and country, the presence of farmers involved, global players in the primary sector, the supplying and processing industry and the knowledge and education institutions. These relationships contain the ingredients for a proper case study. Second, Minister Schouten has selected the Food Valley as one of her 'region deals' (Regio Deals) to face challenges as expressed in the transition to circular agriculture (Schouten, *Landbouw, natuur en voedsel*).

Amsterdam. The Round Table brought together farmers, representatives of environmental organizations, bankers, politicians (local, regional and national), clergy, policymakers and scientists. The Round Table was structured by three rounds. The first round started with challenges in the agricultural sector explored from the perspective of a farmer, the perspective of an environmental organization, and from the perspective of an Environmental Assessment Agency. This round made visible that over the years the same kind of problems come back—e.g., manure surplus, biodiversity loss and the number of animals in the sector living under poor conditions— but each time in a different form. Problems related to, e.g., phosphate and fertilizers were addressed technically. As a result, one problem was solved but two new ones emerged. During the discussion, it became clear that in the agricultural sector the problems should be considered in interdependency. But this raises questions like: Where should we start? and Who is responsible?—especially when uncontrollable international dimensions play a role as well. A topic that comes up in the discussion is the difficulty farmers face earning a decent income. Although the farmers state that it is necessary to earn a living, what they really miss is recognition for the work they are doing. The agricultural sector is often blamed for what is wrong, but farmers feel that they rarely receive appreciation for the work they are performing. In the discussion, the importance of good communication was stressed. According to several parties around the table, every topic can be discussed, but it should be done in a respectful way.

In the second round, the perspective of hope as a contribution to overcoming the challenges identified in the first round was explored from a scientific perspective and a perspective from the region. In this round, the daily tragedies with which farmers often have to deal was mentioned, e.g., avian influenza, fipronil and/or the burning down of a stall. Where then is the hope? The question is answered by a reference to two examples in which people worked together toward a shared future. The first example refers to joined participation in courses about the fertility of the soil by farmers, civil servants, ecologists, water authorities, and so on. The second example is about the Manifesto of Salentien in which farmers and politicians explore the future of the agricultural sector. The last round explored the usefulness and necessity of next steps forward of developing hope as a catalyst for furthering responsible and broadly supported decision making in the context of the transition to circular agriculture. The focus of the third and last round is on the question of whether it is appropriate to develop further connections between the discussed concept of hope and a transition toward circular agriculture. In this round, a banker argues that the present perspective toward a circular agriculture is still too abstract to put farmers in motion. The importance is stressed of developing a shared image of the future together as has been done with the Deltaplan for Biodiversity, in line with the above-described concept of hope. In this plan, all stakeholders are involved. Although there are conflicting interests in the present, a shared image and the possibility to create more time for the transition allows stakeholders to explore steps forward in the present. Besides that, it is considered as essential to change the way parties are treating one another. The importance is stressed of creating space for one another, even or especially when there are conflicting interests. A local politician highlights the need for a new covenant between all stakeholders based on taking responsibility for a shared future. Such a covenant allows parties to go beyond a 'we and them' in the present. However, a key question is raised: Who should take the lead in creating such a covenant? A representative of the church states that the churches played such a role in the past, but that it is hard for the church to play this role in the present due to its changed and marginalized role in society. Recommendations are made, for example to organize the next meeting with all relevant stakeholders in order to create a shared perspective for the Food Valley.

8. Ecclesial Innovation

On what basis can the above outline of a communal hermeneutics be built? A number of available—and interrelated—paradigms exist, for instance theologies that proceed from a 'social' understanding of the Trinity, or theologies that use a 'liturgical,' or more emphatically 'eucharistic' paradigm, or theologies that stress the hermeneutical nature of the church *qua* community of interpretation.[27] In the context of discourse that also draws on Christian theology as a resource, it stands to reason to draw on something that is key to most forms of Christian theology: scripture itself, in particular the hermeneutics that can be seen to be implied by the formation of and the subsequent functioning of the biblical canon.[28] As one building block of the argument of this essay, it will be shown here how precisely the Christian tradition's foundational witness can be seen to embody a hermeneutics that undergirds the communal

---

27. Reference to all of these paradigms is made in: Peter-Ben Smit, *Traditie als Missie: 125 Jaar Unie van Utrecht—1275 jaar in de voetsporen van St. Willibrord* (Tradition as mission: 125 Years of the Union of Utrecht—1275 years in the footsteps of St. Willibrord), (Amersfoort/ Sliedrecht: Oud-Katholiek Boekhuis/Merweboek, 2015).

28. What follows has been adapted from: Peter-Ben Smit, "From Divisive Diversity to Catholic Fullness? Canon and Ecclesial Unity Reconsidered," in *Catholicity under Pressure: Proceedings of the 18th Academic Consultation of the Societas Oecumenica*, Beihefte zur Ökumenischen Rundschau 105, eds. Dagmar Heller and Péter Szentpétery (Leipzig: Evangelische Verlagsanstalt, 2016), 391–409.

discernment of hope as discussed above.

Canonical critics, such as James A. Sanders and Francis Watson,[29] have explored in depth the question of whether the way in which a writing or a corpus of writings has come into existence should not be taken into account in its interpretation; both answered this question affirmatively, drawing attention to the hermeneutics implied by the formation and early reception of the biblical canon.[30] Aspects of this include the following, utilizing New Testament examples for the sake of argument (HB/OT examples could also be adduced easily). In the case of the Gospels, as well as, to be sure, in the case of the work of Paul and its reception (in pseudepigraphical Pauline letters, as well as in those of James and Peter), part of the documents pertaining to the prehistory of the canonical writings has been canonized as well. Because Mark and Luke, Matthew, and John have become part of the canon, documents belonging to at least two stages of the process (Mark on the one hand, the rest on the other) of the formation of the authoritative memory of Jesus have been enshrined in its authoritative scriptures. If Matthew, Luke, or even John had been intended to replace Mark, the canon partially reverses this development: now all four are canonical.[31] All of this applies also to the work of Paul and its diverse reception, already in the writings that are now canonical. This has one important implication: The ongoing search for identity 'in Christ' with the appertaining production of ever new authoritative or at least supplementary texts is documented in the canonical writings themselves, which, therefore, are only authoritative in concert with each other, no longer on their own.[32] All

---

29. Cf. James A. Sanders, *Canon and Community*: *A Guide to Canonical Criticism* (Philadelphia: Fortress, 1984) and Francis Watson, *Gospel Writing*: *A Canonical Perspective* (Grand Rapids: Eerdmans, 2013). See also: Peter-Ben Smit, "Authority in the New Testament and the New Testament's Authority," *Ecclesiology* 13 (2017), 83–101.

30. Cf. also, e.g., Theo K. Heckel, *Vom Evangelium zum viergestaltigen Evangelium* (Tübingen: Mohr Siebeck, 1999), as well as the essays in Richard Bauckham (ed.), *The Gospels for All Christians*: *Rethinking the Gospel Audiences* (Grand Rapids: Eerdmans, 1998).

31. See on this, the general argument of Watson, *Gospel*.

32. Michael Wolter, "Die Vielfalt der Schrift und die Einheit des Kanons," in *Die Einheit der Schrift und die Vielfalt des Kanons*, eds. John Barton and Michael Wolter (Berlin: De Gruyter, 2003), 45–68, 65; Judith Gruber, *Theologie nach dem Cultural Turn*: *Interkulturalität als theologische Ressource* (Stuttgart: Kohlhammer, 2013), 20, 25–26; see also: Judith M. Lieu, *Neither Jew nor Greek? Constructing Early Christianity* (London: T&T Clark, 2002), 2–3: "Texts do not simply reflect a 'history' going on independently of them, they are themselves part of the process by which ... Christianity came into being. For it was through literature that ... a self-understanding was shaped and articulated, and then mediated to and appropriated by others, and through literature that people and ideas were included or excluded. What the texts were doing is sometimes as, if not more, important than what they were saying."

of this constitutes, in fact, a prolonged reflection on the hermeneutical consequences of a principle of historical-critical, more specifically tradition-historical research, that is to say: the principle that the genesis of a text is of importance for understanding it. If this is the case, then it becomes particularly inviting to further reflect on the question of what it would mean for the interpretation of the canonical writings whether the fact that historical emergence of the canon had many centripetal aspects does not need to be taken into account when reading its contents. Doing so invites considering the following insights of the New Testament scholar Michael Wolter:

> The intensive search for a linguistically and existentially differentiable and unifying center of Christian identity and the impossibility to determine it unambiguously [was] already an integral part of the historical existence of the Christian communities from the beginning. The tension between unity and diversity would therefore not be a problem given only with the canon, but a fundamental and thus irrevocable fact of the historical existence of Christianity in general.[33]

According to Wolter's line of thought, the conceptualization of a notion such as the 'unity of the church' (as well, to be sure, as that of the 'meaning of the canon') shifts from a fixed or fixable historical or current situation to that of a process. The image that emerges is one in which the canonical writings do not so much constitute a stable and clear form (or source) of Christian identity and unity and communicate this (when read correctly) in an unequivocal way, but are rather the witnesses of (and catalysts for) an ongoing dialogical and even conflictuous search for such unity and identity. This search is evidenced precisely also by the various differences and disagreements between the canonical writings, given that these have been enshrined into one single canon and thus made to be in conversation with each other.[34] While this might sound like a relativization of what one might want to see as 'biblical' view of Christian identity, according to Wolter's line of thought, this is not at all the case; the question is rather how one understands notions such as 'unity' and 'identity' from the perspective of the emergence of the early Christian writings, including the canon itself, which is also a literary

---

33. Wolter, "Vielfalt," 52–53: "Die intensive Suche nach einer sprachlich wie existentiell ausdifferenzierbaren und einheitsstiftenden Mitte der christlichen Identität und die Unmöglichkeit, sie eindeutig ... zu bestimmen, [war] bereits von Anfang an integraler Bestandteil der geschichtlichen Existenz der christlichen Gemeinden. Die Spannung zwischen Einheit und Vielfalt wäre demnach nicht ein erst mit dem Kanon gegebenes Problem, sondern eine fundamentale und damit unaufhebbare Gegebenheit der geschichtlichen Existenz des Christentums überhaupt."

34. The diversity that exists concerning the text of the canonical scriptures of Christianity can be understood along the same lines.

construct. Following this line of thought, one might agree with Wolter again:

> The differentiation of the one confession into different and competing concepts of salvation including their life-world implications [must] not be understood as a loss of an original unity, but [has] been an integral part of the plausibility of the confession itself, without which the reception of the Christian message of salvation would not have been possible. What the testimony to the Christ event means in concrete terms (i.e., with which signs which meaning is ascribed to this testimony) is not fixed from the outset, but is negotiated in context-dependent processes of meaning; this is documented in the canon.[35]

Identity, accordingly, is a continuous process of conversation and even of 'negotiation.' Precisely the differences between the canonical texts provide the necessary conditions for this—without difference, no conversation is possible—and create the space for this.[36] This conversation takes place among different communities and their 'cultures' (e.g., those of Matthew and Mark) and between different political and/or cultural settings (e.g., those of Luke and John, the Seer), in order to discover and narrate again and again what faith is. This conversation can be termed 'intercultural,' as it has been formulated in the work of the Austrian theologian Judith Gruber as follows:

> The differences that a genealogical view reveals in the canon make it appear as a compilation of particular theologies of theologies that bear witness to the Christ event by recourse to the meaning structures of their cultural context. The differences are not faded out, but compiled within the canon. In the differences a space of interculturality is constituted … By making differences visible, the canon creates a space of interculturality in which Christian identity is negotiated; as a normatively set document, it thus standardizes it as a disparate product of intercultural processes of translation and transformation between particular theologies.[37]

---

35. Wolter, "Vielfalt," 55: "Die Ausdifferenzierung des einen Bekenntnisses in unterschiedliche und miteinander konkurrierende Heilskonzepte einschließlich ihrer lebensweltlichen Implikationen [darf] nicht als Verlust einer ursprünglichen Einheit verstanden werden, sondern [ist] ein integraler Bestandteil der Plausibilität des Bekenntnisses selbst gewesen, ohne die die Rezeption der christlichen Heilsbotschaft nicht möglich gewesen wäre. Was das Zeugnis vom Christusereignis konkret bedeutet (d.h. mit welchen Zeichen diesem Zeugnis welche Bedeutung zugeschrieben wird) steht nicht von vornherein fest, sondern wird in kontextabhängigen Bedeutungsprozessen ausverhandelt; das wird im Kanon dokumentiert."

36. See also the notion of the 'epiphanic space' opened up by the (different) 'other,' as underlined by Hans de Wit, *My God*, *She Said*: '*Ships Make Me so Crazy.' Reflections on Empirical Hermeneutics*, Interculturality and Holy Scripture (Amsterdam: VU University, 2008), 65, 87.

37. Gruber, *Theologie nach dem Cultural Turn*, 19: "Die Differenzen, die ein genealogischer Blick im Kanon offenlegt, lassen ihn als eine Kompilation von partikularen

The kind of identity and unity that becomes visible in this way in the writings of the New Testament (or even biblical) canon is one that is less conceptual in character but rather has the shape of an ongoing search for identity and unity, which is fed by the diverse perspectives and witnesses of the canon in conversation with each other and the location of the person and/or community that participates in this search. Conflict and diversity are no longer a threat to unity, but rather necessary for the (ongoing, even eschatologically oriented) search for it.[38]

It is precisely this understanding of the foundational witness of the Christian tradition that undergirds the project outlined in this essay. If identity, emphatically: Christian identity, is both communal and processual, meaning that a polyphony of voices—even dissonant ones!—is needed to propel it forward, then the kinds of communities of discernment as a reinvention of a public Sabbath discussed earlier can well be understood in analogy to what 'church' is, and the 'hermeneutical ecclesiology' implied by the witness of the biblical canon can serve as a source of inspiration to further, precisely for theological reasons, such undertakings in the context of endangered sustainability. On this basis, both the concept of hope, as Sacks has highlighted it and the dialogical approach to the discernment of a potentially common hope, as it has been proposed above, can be seen as continuing lines of thought present in the foremost source of Christian theology, the Bible itself. This also means that churches face the challenge to live up to the dialogical basis that they refer to as a key part of their tradition, i.e., scripture; can churches see this as a form of vocation, i.e., to become and invite others to dialogical communities of discernment, both for the good of the churches and for the common good? The round table referred to above would suggest that this is possible and also point the way. Such tables could well be understood as a further performance of the dialogical identity that is at the heart of the Christian tradition and calls for continuous, faithful and inclusive conversations that do not shun tensions, but balance them out

Theologien erscheinen von Theologien, die vom Christusereignis im Rückgriff auf die Bedeutungsstrukturen ihres kulturellen Kontextes Zeugnis ablegen. Die Differenzen werden nicht ausgeblendet, sondern innerhalb des Kanons zusammengestellt. In den Differenzen konstituiert sich...ein Raum der Interkulturalität. Indem der Kanon Differenzen sichtbar macht, schafft er einen Raum der Interkulturalität, in dem christliche Identität verhandelt wird; Als normativ gesetztes Dokument normiert er sie damit als disparates Produkt interkultureller Übersetzungsund Transformationsvorgänge zwischen partikularen Theologien."

38. See Gruber, *Theologie*, 20: "Christliche Identität geschieht hier performativ im Konflikt— gerade weil über unterschiedliche Interpretationen verhandelt wird, zerfällt christliche Identität nicht. Die im Kanon normative gesetzte konfliktive Interkulturalität weist so einen Weg zwischen einem Verständnis von christlicher Identität, das Differenzen ausblendet, und ihrer Zersplitterung entlang der im Kanon dokumentierten Bruchlinien."

with a desire to walk together, ecclesially and societally.

At the end of this article, it seems to be justified to ask whether the church in general, and the Protestant Church in the Netherlands (PKN) in particular, can play a role in bringing polarized parties together based on hope. To put it more strongly, based on the conference theme, is the church called to contribute to hope in times of polarization? There seems to be only one answer possible.

The PKN presents itself as a place of faith, hope and love, both in a traditional and experimental way.[39] Sacks' understanding of faith, hope and love challenges the church to go beyond its own group of believers and contribute to hope in polarized contexts. What could that contribution be? Several answers are possible. Here we focus on one answer. The Christian community is trained in and devoted to developing places of hopes. Therefore, the Christian community seems to be able to play a facilitating role in bringing different parties and stakeholders together in a workplace of hope. However, such a realization has to start with suitable humility. The church, at least in the Netherlands, no longer seems able to bring them together. Traditional religious leaders do not have this societal role anymore. What is more, their own traditional (church) places of hope show a sharp decline in attendance in recent decades. Most (church) places do not seem able to be of added value with regard to the fears and hopes of most people. One can blame the people for that, but that might be too easy. The church is not only called to hope in a polarized context. The church is also called to reinvent the good news of faith, hope and love in its own context. Therefore, these times of polarization are an opportunity for the church to work with (secular) parties to reinvent and creatively redesign workplaces of hope that are accessible and of added value to all involved.

9. Conclusion

In this article we have explored the potential role of hope, based on the work of Jonathan Sacks, to facilitate moving beyond polarization in the transition to circular agriculture in the Netherlands. This concept seems to provide a new vantage point for enabling cooperation between the stakeholders in the agricultural sector, who hold often strongly conflicting positions. The reason for this is that this concept of hope is considered as a learning process that seeks to create relations of trust in honoring the interests of oneself and others. The institution of a public Sabbath can bring together parties with different, even conflicting, interests because it considers differences as a source of renewal instead of a source of polarization. The question is whether such a concept can also

---

39. https://www.protestantsekerk.nl/over-ons/.

work in practice. Therefore, an operationalization of a similar concept in South Africa was highlighted. The article also presented a case study in which relevant stakeholders in the Food Valley discussed the questions in the sector at hand in relation to Sacks' concept of hope and the operationalization in South Africa. Of course, this raises context-related questions. In South Africa, an Archbishop can lead the conversations, while that is less likely in the Netherlands. But that does not mean that the church in the Netherlands is not also called to contribute to a perspective based on hope in times of polarization. By crossing the divide between theory and practice, by pioneering an interdisciplinary approach, and by focusing on the role of 'hope' in the agricultural sector, the article contributes to bridging the gap between conceptual and practical approaches to 'hope,' several disciplines *and* to overcoming paralyzed situations. Finally, based on the theme, the article states that the church is called to develop places of hope in polarized contexts. These places are also an opportunity for the church to reinvent itself in terms of faith, hope and love in interaction with (secular) parties.

BIBLIOGRAPHY

Adviescollege Stikstofproblematiek. *Niet Alles Kan*: *Aanbevelingen voor de Korte Termijn* (Not everything is possible: Short term recommendations). 25 September 2019. https://www.rijksoverheid.nl/documenten/rapporten/2019/09/25/eerste-advies-adviescollege-stikstofproblematiek.

Bauckham, Richard. Ed. *The Gospels for All Christians*: *Rethinking the Gospel Audiences*. Grand Rapids: Eerdmans, 1998.

Churchman, C. West. "Free for all." *Management Science* 14 (1967): B141-B142.

De Staat van de Boer (The farmer's state) (2018). https://destaatvandeboer.trouw.nl/.

Dolman, Mark; Gerben Jukema and Pascal Ramaekers. *De Nederlandse landbouwexport in 2018 in breder perspectief* (Dutch agricultural exports in 2018 in a wider perspective). Wageningen: Wageningen Economic Research en het Centraal Bureau voor de Statistiek, 2019. http://edepot.wur.nl/468099.

Eagleton, Terry. *Hope without Optimism*. Charlottesville: University of Virginia Press, 2015.

Gruber, Judith. *Theologie nach dem Cultural Turn: Interkulturalität als theologische Ressource*. Stuttgart: Kohlhammer, 2013.

Hakkenes, Emiel. "Den Haag wacht grimmig boerenprotest: 'Stedelingen zetten ons in de verdomhoek'" (The Hague awaits grim farmer's protest: 'City types put us in the dark'), *Trouw* 28 September 2019. Accessed 1 November 2020. https://www.trouw.nl/nieuws/den-haag-wacht-grimmig-boerenprotest-stedelingen-zetten-ons-in-de-verdomhoek~b2ebabbc/.

Hasselaar, Jan Jorrit. "Hope in the Context of Climate Change: Jonathan Sacks' Interpretation of the Exodus and Radical Uncertainty." *International Journal of Public Theology* 14 (2020): 224–240.

Head, Brian W. and John Alford. "Wicked problems: Implications for Public Policy and Management." *Administration & Society* 47:6 (2015): 711–739.

Heckel, Theo K. *Vom Evangelium zum viergestaltigen Evangelium*. Tübingen: Mohr Siebeck, 1999.

Kreuter, Marshall; Christopher De Rosa, Elizabeth Howze and Grant Baldwin. "Understanding Wicked Problems: A Key to Advancing Environmental Health Promotion." *Health Education & Behavior* 31 (2004): 441–454.

Lieu, Judith M. *Neither Jew nor Greek? Constructing Early Christianity*. London: T&T Clark, 2002.

Putters, Kim. *Veenbrand: Smeulende kwesties in de welvarende samenleving* (Peat fire: Smoldering issues in the prosperous society). Amsterdam: Prometheus, 2019.

Raad voor de leefomgeving en infrastructuur. *Duurzaam en gezond: Samen naar een houdbaar voedselsysteem* (Council for the living environment and infrastructure, *Sustainable and healthy: Together towards a sustainable food system*). Den Haag: Raad voor de leefomgeving en infrastructuur, 2018). https://www.rli.nl/sites/default/files/duurzaam_en_gezond_samen_naar_een_houdbaar_voedselsysteem_def_1.pdf.

Rittel, Horst W.J. and Melvin M. Webber. "Dilemmas in a General Theory of Planning." *Policy Sciences* 4 (1973): 155–169.

Sacks, Jonathan. *Covenant & Conversation, Exodus*: *The Book of Redemption*. Jerusalem: Maggid Books, 2010.

Sacks, Jonathan. *Future Tense*: *Jews, Judaism, and Israel in the Twenty-First Century*. New York: Schocken Books, 2009.

Sacks, Jonathan. *The Politics of Hope*. London: Jonathan Cape, 1997.

Sanders, James A. *Canon and Community*: *A Guide to Canonical Criticism*. Philadelphia: Fortress, 1984.

Schouten, Carola. *Landbouw, natuur en voedsel*: *Waardevol en verbonden. Nederland als koploper in kringlooplandbouw* (Agriculture, nature and food: Valuable and connected. The Netherlands as a frontrunner in circular agriculture). 2018. https://www.rijksoverheid.nl/documenten/beleidsnota-s/2018/09/08/visie-landbouw-natuur-en-voedsel-waardevol-en-verbonden.

Smit, Peter-Ben. "Authority in the New Testament and the New Testament's Authority." *Ecclesiology* 13 (2017): 83–101.

Smit, Peter-Ben. "From Divisive Diversity to Catholic Fullness? Canon and Ecclesial Unity Reconsidered." In *Catholicity under Pressure*: *Proceedings of the 18th Academic Consultation of the Societas Oecumenica*. Beihefte zur Ökumenischen Rundschau 105, eds. Dagmar Heller and Péter Szentpétery, 391–409. Leipzig: Evangelische Verlagsanstalt, 2016.

Smit, Peter-Ben. *Traditie als Missie*: *125 Jaar Unie van Utrecht—1275 jaar in de voetsporen van St. Willibrord* (Tradition as mission: 125 Years of the Union of Utrecht—1275 years in the footsteps of St. Willibrord). Amersfoort/Sliedrecht: Oud-Katholiek Boekhuis/Merweboek, 2015.

Termeer, Katrien. *Het bewerkstelligen van een transitie naar kringlooplandbouw* (Achieving a transition to circular agriculture). Wageningen: Wageningen University & Research, 2019.

Volf, Miroslav and Matthew Croasmun. *For the Life of the World*: *Theology That Makes a Difference*. Grand Rapids: Brazos Press, 2019.

Watson, Francis. *Gospel Writing*: *A Canonical Perspective*. Grand Rapids: Eerdmans, 2013.

Wit, Hans de. *My God'*, *She Said*: '*Ships Make Me so Crazy*,' Reflections on Empirical Hermeneutics, Interculturality and Holy Scripture. Amsterdam: VU University, 2008.

Wolter, Michael. "Die Vielfalt der Schrift und die Einheit des Kanons." In *Die Einheit der Schrift und die Vielfalt des Kanons*, eds. John Barton and Michael Wolter, 45–68. Berlin: De Gruyter, 2003.

Part 2: Polarization and the Reformed Tradition

CHAPTER 8
REFORMED SOCIAL THEOLOGY: CONTEXTS AND CONSTANTS
David Fergusson

1. INTRODUCTION

In what follows, I shall sketch in broad outline the social theology of the Reformed churches. My argument is that, while this was shaped in part by the contingent political circumstances that obtained in Europe in the sixteenth century, there are some recognizable theological constants that should be articulated and transposed to other times and places. This adaptation of theological insights to different settings is both a sign of the necessary enculturation of the Christian faith across space and time, and a reminder that our traditions require retrieval and re-articulation.

The goal of social transformation through the establishment of a godly society runs deep in Reformed theology and is shared in multiple ways with other traditions from which we have much to learn. This goal generated several interconnected emphases. These remain relevant in our time of increased fragmentation, populist resurgence, and political uncertainty. Although not an exhaustive list, I shall select seven elements in an effort to demonstrate their interlocking force. Without a renewed commitment to each in our time, the social witness of the Reformed churches will be impaired.[1]

2. ELEMENTS OF A REFORMED POLITICAL THEOLOGY

a. *Politics as a vocation*. In both Lutheran and Reformed theology, political office is ordained by God and necessary for the well-being of the church. For that reason, it was

---

1. In this first section, I have drawn upon a more extended historical treatment in my essay "Politics, Society and Law," in *Oxford Handbook of Reformed Theology*, eds. Michael Allen and Scott Swain (Oxford: Oxford University Press, 2020), 592–608.

entirely proper for Christians to regard the holding of such office as a calling of God. Much of this thinking can already be discerned in medieval accounts of the Christian prince, but it is emphasized in different ways at the time of the Reformation and often against the more exclusionist trends of the radicals. In Lutheranism, the concept of vocation becomes secularized. The service of God is fulfilled in the home, in commerce, and in political life. Vocation is no longer confined to the cloister. Christ is to be served in the world, freely and gladly without the burden of having to perform extraordinary meritorious works. This lent a dignity and seriousness to the responsibilities of the everyday. Exercised within the secular domain, the calling of the Christian was not out of the world but within it, informed by faith and animated by love.

b. *Civil resistance.* A succession of Reformed writers, including John Knox, Peter Martyr Vermigli, and Theodore Beza, developed arguments for civil resistance.[2] These converged upon several convictions. The power of the monarch is neither absolute nor unfettered. Kings and queens are ordained by God to serve the people and they do so in accordance with natural laws that are not of their own making. A second line of argument developed the notion of a local magistracy which had its own responsibility to act lawfully and to promote the common good. Where local rulers find themselves in opposition to national or imperial forces, they have a right, even a duty, of resistance. In doing so, they act not as private citizens but as holders of an office which carries its own responsibilities and rights. Third, Protestant theories of resistance could appeal to classical and medieval traditions of popular consent. These philosophical and theological considerations were conjoined in the seventeenth century by theologians such as Samuel Rutherford.

c. *The coordination of church and state.* In the *Institutes* IV.11.8, Calvin underscores the difference between the offices of pastor and prince. These are to be neither confused

---

2. See, for example, Roger Mason (ed.), Knox: On Rebellion (Cambridge: Cambridge University Press, 1994); Robert M. Kingdon, "Calvinism and Resistance Theory 1550–1580," in *Cambridge History of Political Thought 1450–1700*, ed. J.H. Burns (Cambridge: Cambridge University Press, 2008), 193–218.

nor disjoined. Both offices serve a common end under the divine rule. Together church and state are committed to a sanctified society according to the Word of God, even though pastors and politicians should not conflate their different functions. Ideally, the Church and the state should act together to fulfil the divine will in the ordering of a peaceful, just and harmonious society. This model reflects earlier Christendom notions and assumes that each citizen is to be regarded as baptized into the visible church. In sixteenth-century Geneva, membership of the church and the *polis* are notionally co-extensive. One consequence of this is that excommunication from the former would have entailed exile from the latter. While this has obvious problems for modern pluralist societies, we can at least note that the recommended partnership of church and state was intended to promote social justice and order as well as undergirding ecclesiastical reform.

d. *Democracy*—The Reformation is sometimes interpreted as a democratic movement. This is true only in a restricted and qualified sense. Luther accepted the right of hereditary monarchs to rule. But, as a humanist scholar and lawyer, a French refugee and citizen of Geneva, Calvin was more alert to constitutional issues. He examines these rather tentatively in the closing chapter of the *Institutes* where he expresses a mild preference for an admixture of aristocracy and democracy.

In other settings, however, Reformed theology was keenly alert to the distribution of authority and popular consent. This is apparent, for example, in church government and the public calling of ministers. Each minister is called by God, yet the ecclesiastical rite of ordination must take place always with the consent of the people. Ministerial appointment requires popular legitimation, and should not be imposed top-down by church authority. The government of the church, moreover, involves the rule of elders who function with ministers as a senate-like ruling body. These elders are described by Calvin as senior figures elected by the people. We are someway here from later democratic ideals of universal adult suffrage, but these features of Reformed polity indicate the presence of popular impulses with respect to church government and the empowering of the laity. Inevitably this would have a wider political effect, as already noted in approaches to civil resistance.

e. *Law*—The third use of the law is another distinctive feature of Reformed theology. This is also apparent in Melanchthon's *Loci Communes* where he speaks about a tertiary use of the law in the lives of those who are reborn. This is given for the Christian life so that we can be constantly reminded of our continued sinfulness and the need to do God's works. The *tertius usus legis* reminds us that, even as Christians, our inner self needs to be constrained by the law of God. Since we continue to display the marks of sin, we need the law in both its primary and secondary functions. Reformed theologians, however, went beyond this by stressing the law as exercising a further positive function in relation to individual and social sanctification. For Calvin, the law is a divine gift to enable people to live together in unity with one another and in true worship and obedience of God. This is neither burdensome nor oppressive—the law properly acts for our wellbeing. Hence there is no dialectical opposition of law and gospel in Reformed theology, but an integration of the two under the rubric of the third use.[3]

With respect to its application, however, the third use was to give rise to some tensions. How rigorously are Old Testament injunctions to be applied to the Christian life, the church and civil society? Are there ways in which these can be modified, mediated and interpreted in light of changing social and political circumstances? An overly rigorous application of scriptural precedents could result in some counter-productive measures, while also proving inadequate to growing ideals of toleration, democracy, and equality as these emerged in early modern and Enlightenment Europe. And yet the fundamental impulse of Reformed theology seems right. The laws that govern civil society cannot be construed only in a negative modality as ordinances of restraint. They exist to promote social justice, to advance the common good, and to achieve in some measure the *shalom* proclaimed by scripture.

In several ways, the Reformation contributed to the

---

3. See Edward A. Dowey, "Law in Luther and Calvin," *Theology Today* 41 (1984), 146–153.

development of civil law. For example, one outcome of the Protestant understanding of marriage as a created ordinance, as opposed to a Christian sacrament, was the development of civil marriage law with respect to consent, witness, and grounds of divorce. Education meanwhile came increasingly to fall within the civic realm, while the office of the magistrate, outside the immediate control of the church, was of growing significance.[4]

f. *Nationalism*—Within the Reformed tradition, the different confessions played a role in forming national churches, as in the Belgic and Scots Confessions. Reformed churches were committed to the shaping of societies often modelled on the example of biblical Israel as a covenanted nation. By the seventeenth century, we see the emergence in Europe of powerful and autonomous states that are now related to each other by international law rather than imperial power, even though these states were inclined to engage in empire-building in other parts of the world. Religious forces played a part in this process.

Yet the relationship between theology and nationalism has often been an uneasy one. Some scholars have argued that the romantic nationalism which emerged through the Enlightenment, with its stress on land, language and ethnicity, was a replacement for more traditional forms of religion.[5] Others, echoing criticisms from the political left, see it as lurching towards an aggressive idolatry of kinship and place that divides peoples and threatens a more virtuous commitment to internationalism.[6] For the church, the loyalty commanded by the nation can threaten the allegiance of the baptized to the body of Christ, a polity that transcends language and tribe. And at other times a theory of national exceptionalism, again modelled on the Israel of the Old Testament, has generated attitudes of hostility and superiority to those who belong elsewhere.[7] Nevertheless,

---

4. See John Witte Jr, "Introduction," in *Christianity and Law: An Introduction*, eds. John Witte Jr and Frank S. Alexander (Cambridge: Cambridge University Press, 2008), 1–32.

5. See Adrian Hastings, *The Constructions of Nationhood: Ethnicity, Religion and Nationalism* (Cambridge: Cambridge University Press, 1997).

6. Eric Hobsbawm, *Nations and Nationalism since 1780: Programme, Myth and Reality* (Cambridge: Cambridge University Press, 1992).

7. See the discussion in Karl Barth, "Near and Distant Neighbours," in *Church*

nationalism could also provide a way of promoting the common good of a people, as well as articulating legitimate protest against tyranny, colonialism and globalizing tendencies.[8] There are positive examples of its functioning as a force for liberation and of attracting a commitment to goals wider than those of individual and family. In relation to language, society and territorial boundaries, it is difficult to see how a political philosophy can avoid some acknowledgement of nationhood in comprehending how a *polis* is to be delineated.

A sense of national identity is closely aligned with the Reformed concept of covenant when applied to human associations. This was a feature of political thought in the work of Johannes Althusius and others.[9] Drawing upon scriptural and confessional accounts of covenant, the social order could be conceived according to a succession of covenants to which each of us is bound. In some respects, this parallels Catholic notions of the common good and subsidiarity. A society is structured by covenantal commitments which are a function of our creaturely status. This had at least two important advantages for Reformed political thought. First, it offered an account of society that did not depend upon a sacral concept of kingship that legitimized a top-down authority. Instead, political office is justified by its capacity to facilitate a covenant that binds each member of the state together. Its jurisdiction extends over a territorial region that will tend to be marked by a shared history, customs, languages, laws and faith. Within this territory, the civil authorities, as part of their covenantal function, will enforce the rule of law and seek to protect the citizens of the realm, though this can include a respect for liberty of conscience on matters over which the state should not legislate. The law does not derive from the will of the ruler but has its ground in natural law and divine law which are not of our own making. Moreover, our natural condition is to enter into social bonds each of which has

---

Dogmatics III/4 (Edinburgh: T&T Clark, 1961), 285–323.

8. Jonathan Hearn, *Rethinking Nationalism: An Introduction* (London: Palgrave Macmillan, 2004); Doug Gay, *Honey from the Lion: Christianity and the Ethics of Nationalism* (London: SCM, 2013).

9. See, for example, Thomas O. Hueglin, "Covenant and Federalism in the Politics of Althusius," in *The Covenant Connection: From Federal Theolog to Modern Federalism*, eds. Daniel J. Elazar and John Kincaid (Lanham: Lexington, 2000), 31–54.

its own sphere of operation and rules of conduct. This generates a second advantage of the covenant concept, namely its capacity to perceive a society as comprising not one collective but a variety of interconnected covenantal communities each of which has its own traditions, practices and norms. The capacity of covenantal politics to articulate different consocial spheres was a feature of later Dutch Calvinism, particularly in the work of Abraham Kuyper.

g. *Economics*. Much of the discussion in this field has been dominated by the Weber thesis regarding the causal link between Protestantism and the rise of capitalism. The thesis has been largely discredited on account of the ways in which capitalism similarly flourished in societies less committed to forms of Protestant Christianity.[10] But recent scholarship has also pointed to features of Calvin's writings which display a strong ethical concern for the poor and a commitment to economic justice. First published in 1959, André Biéler's landmark study of Calvin's economic thought drew attention to his extensive deliberations on economic issues, especially in his commentaries and sermons.[11] Though neglected by later Reformed thinkers, this material focusses on biblical concerns for the underprivileged and destitute. Starvation and homelessness are an affront to God, as is the exploitation engendered by lending money at punitive rates of interest.

3. THE VESTIGES OF CHRISTENDOM?

What emerges from this historical sketch is a rich social theology that commits the church to promoting political and civic well-being. Much is attractive in this vision, and anticipates modern developments though under more secular conditions. But the problems of the founding Reformed vision need to be recognized. In particular, the emergence of ideals of tolerance and pluralism generated formidable challenges. The Reformed vision of a godly commonwealth in which the proper worship of God was upheld by the civil magistrate invoked Old Testament ideals of a society united by a common faith—the church or the nation could even be described as a new Israel. This extended to the suppression of other

---

10. See Johan J. Graafland, "Weber Revisited: Critical Perspectives from Calvinism on Capitalism in Economic Crisis," in *Calvinism and the Making of the European Mind*, eds. Gijsbert van den Brink and Harro M. Höpfl (Leiden: Brill, 2014), 177–198.

11. André Biéler, *Calvin's Economic and Social Thought* (Geneva: World Council of Churches, 2005).

forms of worship and religious association that were adjudged blasphemous or idolatrous. In the face of early modern arguments for religious diversity and later claims for freedom of expression, such invocation of a single confessional identity proved impossible to maintain. A range of arguments was advanced that made appeal to the New Testament example of the free and non-coercive expression of faith, the value of peaceful negotiation over violent struggle, the possibility of moral consensus amidst doctrinal difference, the possibility of different faith groups learning from one another in ways that were mutually beneficial, and the need to protect freedom of conscience in matters of religious adherence. Through the eighteenth century, Reformed churches gradually came to deplore compulsory measures in religion and to assign a more limited role to the civil authorities in the regulation of faith communities.

But just as the old model brought dangers of suppression, intolerance and violation of human dignity, newer secular approaches also generate their own difficulties. These have been the focus of recent criticism of political liberalism. Where does the political order find its moral and spiritual basis if not by reference to the religious life of its people? Alternatives have been found to be either too thin, incoherent, or incapable of commanding allegiance. The go-to option has been the language of human rights. But can this be sustained without earlier theological references to human beings as created in the image of God and the frequent injunctions in scripture to attend to the needs of the marginalized, the alien and the dispossessed? And if we are to adopt a substantive secularism in which religious discourse and commitment are confined to a semi-private or voluntary domain does this not prevent citizens and groups from expressing their deepest social commitments in the terms that make sense to them? This can readily develop into a secular intolerance of all public expressions of religion. In response, approaches that favour a procedural (as against programmatic) secularism have been advocated—this invites all exponents of deeply held religious views to express themselves in ways that are accessible to their fellow citizens.[12]

Under these pressures what has happened in Europe is that those churches that have historically had an established or national status have evolved in ways that reflect an accommodation of tolerance and diversity. At the same time, however, elements of their status have been retained and adapted to new circumstances. In an oft-quoted distinction, Wesley Carr, an Anglican writer, has distinguished high and earthed elements of establishment.[13] At ground level, parish churches have continued to view their immediate geographic community as the

---

12. See, for example, Rowan Williams, *Faith in the Public Square* (London: Bloomsbury, 2012), 23–36.

13. Wesley Carr, "A Developing Establishment," *Theology* 102 (1999), 2–10.

locus for service and mission. This takes place through the provision of ordinances for birth, marriage, and death, and also in running a variety of support groups including youth organizations, counseling services, recreational activities, and in generating support for charitable bodies. The involvement of the church in education has also been important in this context, and might be seen as part of a wider process in which a society can continue to be Christianized, though again the limits of this need to be recognized. Meanwhile, the national identity of churches continues to be recognized in national and local ceremonial events, corresponding to Carr's higher level. These involve a fusion of religious and civic functions but suggest a spiritual dimension or setting for the wider community.[14] Here I am thinking of the presence of a religious input to important state occasions such as the opening of a parliament, the coronation of a new monarch, the remembrance of the war dead, the marking of some public tragedy, or the celebration of an important national landmark. Admittedly, there are perennial dangers here of church captivity with the resultant loss of the prophetic function to speak truth to power. Striking a balance between the offer of support and the challenge of criticism is familiar to every pastor. But it is difficult to see how this can be avoided except through a sectarian withdrawal from society which has never been consistent with the foundational vision of the Reformed churches.

A more acute problem surrounds the disconnect between these two dimensions of Christian social engagement that has come about through the rapid process of secularization from the 1960s. The national dimension of religious engagement only makes sense where this is an expression of something that is already embedded at the local level in parish communities. Without this traction, the high-profile ceremonial and civic actions of the church can quickly become quaint, bizarre, or absurdly pompous. Unless it is the expression of the genuinely held faith of a substantial body of people across different sections of society, then these functions of the church become increasingly questionable. Consider some statistics from my own context in Scotland where the national church recognized by an act of parliament in 1921 is Reformed and Presbyterian. This state recognition belongs to an era in which Scotland could reasonably be considered a Protestant society in which the majority of its citizens adhered to the Church of Scotland. But since reaching a peak in 1955, the adult membership of the church has declined by about 80% to just over 300K which today represents only about 6%

---

14. This is explored by Linda Woodhead with reference to the Church of England and the Lutheran Church in Denmark. See "Can We Trust the Church?" in *Schools of Faith: Essays in Honour of Iain R. Torrance*, eds. David Fergusson and Bruce McCormack (London: T&T Clark, 2018), 193–202.

of the population. This decline is continuing at a rate of 4% per annum. While the statistics reveal some implicit commitment to religion, more than one half of the population (58%) identified in 2017 as belonging to no religion.[15] Although this group is not hostile to the church, it undoubtedly displays a large measure of indifference. And given that the church is disproportionately represented by an older generation, these trends are likely to continue for the foreseeable future.

As already suggested, the notion of a 'national church' is fraught with problems which are accompanied by numerous historical illustrations. We might note four difficulties in particular. First, a national church risks becoming the organ of the state through an exchange of privilege for compliance. In providing a spiritual underpinning of state authority, it can too easily deliver a political quietism. This can masquerade as a strategy of 'keeping religion out of politics' while in effect offering tacit support to the regnant powers. A related difficulty arises when the church purports to express the religious identity of a collective such as the Volk or the nation. This can result in a sense of exclusion amongst those who belong to other churches or faiths, or, more dangerously, for migrants whose identity cannot be articulated in similar religious terms. A third problem concerns the extent to which a claim to be exclusively a national church can impede ecumenical cooperation. In this context, it is too tempting for national churches to pretend that they alone have a concern for the society beyond its walls. Other churches have a distinguished, and sometimes better, record of service, charitable giving and social engagement. It is not the sole prerogative of a national church to function in this way. A final problem concerns the incomprehension of churches in the majority world when faced with these older European models. Their different histories do not easily incline towards an adapting of these models. Social engagement and witness can function without any singular recognition on the part of the state. The Christendom model is not a marketable export.[16]

In face of these challenges, so-called national churches might recognize the problems they have faced in the past and thus welcome, in at least one respect, the greater dissociation of church and society that secularization has brought. The loosening of ties with the state that arizes through the sociological phenomenon of 'a differentiation of functions' is to be welcomed. Belonging to a national church no longer confers privileges in terms of holding office, receiving a university education, entering the professions, casting votes, or entering parliament. Equality legislation firmly excludes this. The resultant distancing of the church

---

15. https://www.bbc.co.uk/news/uk-scotland-41294688.
16. See, for example, Kwame Bediako, *Christianity in Africa: The Renewal of a Non-Western Religion* (Edinburgh: Edinburgh University Press, 1995), 249.

from the political state enables a degree of autonomy that facilitates social criticism and independence of action. Instead of presenting itself as a spiritual expression of a single national identity, the church can enhance its breadth by offering an open door to all comers. A focus on its surrounding parish, when suitably inflected, might offer scope for ethnic, spiritual and theological diversity. At this (more important, to my mind) 'earthed' level with an openness to local communities in their particularity and diversity, a national church can adapt to different circumstances.[17] If this arises as an accident of history, so be it. At the same time, these churches, with their particular historical associations with the nation, may find themselves in a position where it can broker relations with other churches and faiths— the Protestant churches of Europe have a decent record in terms of ecumenical commitment and involvement. Admittedly, the risk of patronizing other groups remains ever-present, and in any case maybe this function is for a time only. Nevertheless, the capacity of long-established churches to function in a constructive ecumenical and multi-faith manner is evident in some quarters today. We should recognize that these are the genuine possibilities of what Adrian Hastings calls a 'weak establishment.'[18] If they prove transient, so be it. We should not cling to the vestiges of establishment if it becomes apparent that it is long past its sell-by date. But the position in which we currently find ourselves is ineluctable.

Where then does this leave the notion of a national church that continues to have a presence, albeit reduced, in every parish across the land? Here I suspect some honesty and humility will be required in accepting a diminished social influence, a lower profile, and the need for a greater concentration of energies on tasks such as church planting and evangelism. Those of us who continue to support national churches should beware of inflated arguments that fail to register the applicability of these arrangements to historically particular contexts that are continually evolving.

The socio-political responsibility of a church does not repose upon its size or status. The scriptural commitment to God's justice generates an imperative that is not contingent upon particular historical circumstances, a point recognized by Bonhoeffer in his prison cell reflections on a this-worldly Christianity."

Unlike believers in the redemption myths, Christians do not have an

---

17. See Elaine Graham, "The Establishment, Multiculturalism and Social Cohesion," in *The Established Church: Past, Present, and Future*, eds. Mark Chapman, Judith Maltby and William Whyte (London: Bloomsbury, 2011), 124–140. None of this, I should stress, precludes other churches from doing much the same and at least as well.

18. Adrian Hastings, *Church and State: The English Experience* (Exeter: Exeter University Press, 1991).

ultimate escape route out of their earthly tasks and difficulties into eternity. Like Christ ('My God why have you forsaken me?'), they have to drink the cup of earthly life to the last drop, and only when they do this is the Crucified and Risen One with them, and they are crucified and resurrected with Christ. This-worldliness must not be abolished ahead of its time; on this, NT and OT are united.[19]

No church can avoid facing outwards with a view to enriching the life of its host society. In fields of health and education, this has long been apparent in different contexts. And in relation to the state, the church cannot avoid taking a view on political representation, on war, on the care of children, on rule by law, on the fair distribution of resources and so forth. How and when it acts in an advocacy role is not always clear, but there is no prospect for sealing off the socio-political domain from Christian witness and action.

4. Transpositions of Reformed Social Theology

The aforementioned elements of Reformed social thought need to find expression in different circumstances. At a time of polarization, fragmentation, and prognostications of a crisis for democratic societies, the following suggestions are intended as a Reformed contribution to preserving and improving our politics today.

   a. *Politics as a vocation*. The tendency to treat elected officials with contempt represents a threat to democratic societies. If we construe our politicians as self-serving, cynical, venial or power-hungry this will likely have two effects. The first is that decent and talented people will be disinclined to commit to public service. The second is a self-fulfilling prophecy in which people will tend to live down to our expectations, if they are not held accountable to higher standards or provided with better possibilities. We need to offer support and encouragement to political representatives, as to every holder of public office in our midst. They deserve our prayers, our understanding, and our interest in what they do. This critical support that is owed our political representatives can too easily degenerate into cynicism when a negative register becomes so relentless that it suppresses any degree of sympathy or solidarity with those set apart for political office.

---

19. Dietrich Bonhoeffer, *Works, Vol. 8, Letters and Papers from Prison*, ed. John W. de Gruchy (Minneapolis: Fortress, 2010), 447–448.

In this regard, the churches can exercise political responsibility by the formation of their people for political service whether at local, regional or national level. This can work through providing motivation and a vision of covenanted goods. Much has been written about the importance of social capital generated by faith communities. The capacity of citizens to network, interact and apply their skills in other domains has been documented by Robert Putnam.[20] Moreover, models of living together can be imaginatively transposed from the ecclesial to the civic level, while the rich traditions of Christian political thought can be harnessed for new situations.[21]

b. *Civil resistance*—this strand of our tradition should remind us that support is never uncritical or unqualified. The task of speaking truth to power is a perennial one, as the Hebrew prophets remind us. For this to take place, there needs to be fair scrutiny, accurate reporting, and informed judgement according to our interpretation of the Word of God. This requires education, access to information, and a free press that can function apart from political control or excessive pressure. Politicians did not get a free pass from the Reformers, nor should they today. The two most significant Protestant declarations of the twentieth century were the Barmen Declaration (1934) and the Belhar Confession (1982). While these acknowledged the God-given authority of political rulers, each offered a stark criticism of the circumstances in which they were set. Neither the ideology of the Deutsche Christen nor the policies of apartheid were to be tolerated by a community whose first loyalty was to God of Jesus. Here theological arguments based on scripture were deployed in the cause of resistance. These landmark protests are now part of our international Reformed identity and should be studied afresh by each generation.

c. *Coordination of church and state*. The goal of social

---

20. For example, Robert D. Putnam, *Bowling Alone*: *The Collapse and Revival of American Community*, revised edition (New York: Simon and Schuster, 2020). See also Jeffrey Stout, Blessed are the Organized: Grassroots Democracy in America (Princeton: Princeton University Press, 2012).

21. Emmanuel Katongole argues that African churches need to offer an alternative social vision to avoid either political quietism or a more activist co-option by the civil state. See *The Sacrifice of Africa*: *A Political Theology of Africa* (Grand Rapids: Eerdmans, 2011), 50.

transformation through the coordination of church and state is an aspiration that is again commanded by the gospel. In the past, this was expressed by the ideal of a religiously monolithic society in which church and state were fully integrated. This has now been abandoned by recognition of modern principles of freedom of conscience, the protection of different religious groups under the law, and the accommodation of a diversity of traditions within the public square. Yet this relative distancing of the state from any single expression of faith, does not invalidate the possibility of a constructive partnership or engagement in societal issues. In the late nineteenth century, the partnership was sometimes re-negotiated through a distinction between the church and the kingdom. The church was concerned rightly with the preaching of the Word, the administration of the sacraments, and the pastoral care of its members. But its wider social commitments included a working alongside secular agencies to advance the work of the kingdom of God. This could typically involve a concern with better housing, improved working conditions, fairer remuneration, and universal adult suffrage. In its corporate life, the church was called to be a sign of the coming reign already inaugurated by Christ. Yet other social actors that also contribute towards the divine commonwealth were recognized; these make a vital contribution to civil society, for example in domains such as art, science, education, law, industry and business. This more recent facet of our tradition can also prevent social theology from adopting only a negative posture. If we say 'no' to many things, we should be prepared to give an account of what we are willing to say 'yes' to.[22]

d. *Democracy*. Current political trends suggest that democracy is not the default position of every society through improved education and greater material affluence. This whiggish narrative is now in some doubt with the rise of strong populist leaders commanding significant levels of support amongst younger voters. If we remain persuaded of the value of democracy over against other systems of government, then this will need the tacit support of churches and other

---

22. Isaac Phiri proposed a constructive social role for African churches in increasingly pluralist states. Again, this resembles a model of critical support adapted to a different context. See *Proclaiming Political Pluralism: Churches and Political Transitions in Africa* (Westport: Praeger, 2001).

groups within civil society to maintain the necessary degree of social cohesion and commitment to institutions that buttress it—an independent judiciary, respect for the rule of law, forms of safeguarding that afford minorities protection of their human rights, a welcome recognition of the pluralist and patchwork nature of our societies, the defence of an unfettered press, and the cultivation of habits of civility that enable us to disagree honestly and to find ways of compromising. In this respect, a social theology may sometimes have a conservative caste in preserving and maintaining forms of life that produce cohesion amidst diversity and difference. The institutions of civic life are there to shape us and to contribute to the overall function of a healthy society. But if they are merely occasions for performance or entertainment, they become denigrated.

Recent studies suggest that democracy is more contextual and fragile than we have assumed in previous generations. It cannot be taken for granted as the default setting of our societies. As we face stagnating income levels, identity politics, the power of social media, and suspicion of educated elites, there is an evident risk to democratic institutions.[23] In these circumstances, a theological re-visiting of the case for democracy is needed. The commitment to popular consent, covenant partnership, the rule of law, and balanced reporting needs to be reinvigorated.[24]

e. *Law*. While there has undoubtedly been a growing separation of church from state with respect to the development of positive law, some important connections persist and deserve closer theological attention. Three areas are worthy of consideration. The first concerns the metaphysical links between law and religion. A legal system should reveal both an 'inner morality' and an 'inner sanctity.'[25] In the former, it reposes upon a deep sense in any society of what is fundamentally just and fair. Without this shared sentiment, it will tend to lack tacit support. Closely related to this is

---

23. See, for example, David Runciman, *How Democracy Ends* (London: Profile Books, 2018), and Yascha Mounk, *People vs Democracy: Why our Freedom is in Danger and How to Save It* (Cambridge: Harvard University Press, 2018).

24. The theological case for democracy is examined by Richard Harries, *Faith in Politics? Rediscovering the Christian Roots of our Political Values* (London: Darton, Longman and Todd, 2010), 51–70.

25. See Witte, "Introduction," 28.

the capacity of the law to command respect and obedience on the part of citizens. Without something approaching reverence for the rule of law, its authority is weakened, even when enforced by sheer power. The ways in which legal systems appropriate the symbolism and rituals of religion—dress, processions, court room architecture, and appeal to authoritative texts and interpreters—also provide a powerful visual illustration of this connection. A second domain concerns the development of positive laws. Areas of recent tension are evident here—marriage, divorce, sexuality, abortion, assisted dying, and capital punishment. But these should not prevent us from appreciating the ways in which strong alliances can be constructed, for example in applying principles of equity, ensuring that the criminal justice system can accommodate notions of forgiveness and rehabilitation, and in seeking to establish the truth in possible miscarriages of justice. Finally, in protecting the free expression of religion, theological and secular arguments for liberty of conscience can coalesce, at least in some ways—these need not be in opposition. This area commands widespread attention today, particularly where some forms of free expression generate tensions with other protected characteristics.

f. *Nationalism.* Karl Barth insisted that the divine command meets us as people who are bound to one another by links of history, culture, and language.[26] We can take a justifiable pride in our local identities—our homeland is where we start from and we should remain loyal to it. Yet we are also called to move outwards to meet those more distant and to recognize our solidarity with them. This is a Christian vocation, dramatically manifested on the day of Pentecost and in the eschatological vision of a community transcending tribal and linguistic divisions. While community, land and culture are created goods to be preserved and celebrated, these should be subordinated to wider goals that include hospitality, international cooperation, and a recognition of the dangers that have accompanied forms of ethnic nationalism.

---

26. Karl Barth, *Church Dogmatics* iii/4 (Edinburgh: T&T Clark, 1961), 286–323. See also Nigel Biggar, *Between Kin and Cosmopolis*: *An Ethic of the Nation* (Eugene: Cascade, 2014).

Nationalism has often functioned best as a protest movement in the face of imperialist or totalitarian rule. Religion can be a powerful mobilising force in relation to articulating a shared identity or providing a microculture in which dissent can be fostered. The case of Poland under Soviet rule offers one striking example.[27] At other times, however, the linkage of faith to national identity can become exclusive and threatening to those who belong to a different church or religion. Vituperative verbal attacks on Irish Catholic immigrants by Scottish Presbyterians in the 1920s and 1930s became one of the most shameful episodes in the recent history of my own church.[28] In this context, there is a particular obligation upon 'national' churches to promote ecumenical and inter-faith relations precisely to avoid any false equation of religious identity with citizenship. To this extent, at least, secularization may have done the western churches a favour. With growing numbers now self-identifying as belonging to no religion, the case for a religiously inflected nationalism is greatly weakened. This should caution against exclusive association of a church with any single ethnic group or political faction.

g. *Economics*. The commitment to more egalitarian forms of economic distribution has at least two motives. One is the priority given to poor relief in the tradition. This extends not merely to monetary income but to affordable access to education, housing, and health care. There is a good deal in the Reformed social vision to support this. In addition, there is a growing realization that societies exhibiting the greatest disparities in wealth are also functioning less well. They lose their necessary cohesion, their sense of a common good and collective purpose with a resultant reaction against comfortable elites and those institutions that appear to support them. Here a properly regulated nationalism may have something to offer in generating a sense of a wider corporate identity without lurching into exclusionary sentiments. The social covenant is damaged by excessive levels of economic inequality together with

---

27. For a survey of the diverse links between religion and nationalism see Christophe Jaffrelot, "Religion and Nationalism," in *The Oxford Handbook of the Sociology of Religion*, ed. Peter B. Clarke (Oxford: Oxford University Press, 2011), 406–418.

28. See Stewart J. Brown, "Reform, Reconstruction, Reaction: The Social Vision of Scottish Presbyterianism," *Scottish Journal of Theology* 44 (1991), 489–518.

acquiescence in growing poverty and disadvantage. These may have no simple remedy, but to ignore the problem or to attempt some form of ideological justification is to fly in the face of the Reformed tradition.

In a series of essays, Nicholas Wolterstorff has noted the resistance to poverty found in the writings of Calvin. This, he argues, proceeds not from a sense of sympathy so much as a recognition of the right of the poor to a fairer distribution of resources. It is grounded in the doctrine of the imago Dei and in the command to honour God. Failure to take advantage of readily available measures to alleviate poverty is an offense against God.[29] Bruce Gordon notes the extent of Calvin's preaching from Deuteronomy and the responsibility of Geneva towards refugees. "Landlords should not charge them higher rates, citizens should employ them, and magistrates should judge them as they did others."[30] The relevance of this teaching to predatory loan practices today hardly needs to be underscored.

5. Conclusion

Our churches will no doubt find different ways of interpreting and enacting these theological imperatives. A strategy of retrieval, criticism and adaptation is necessary, whereas withdrawal, renunciation or simple condemnation are all impossible options for social theology today. A positive engagement with our societies needs to be negotiated—this will be shaped in part by the history of our churches, our current social condition, and the possibilities that we can identify in each time and place. Yet, even at a time of increased secularism, these persist in new and promising ways. The above elements of a Reformed social theology are not exhaustive, but these point to ways in which the tradition needs to be rearticulated at a time of increased fragmentation amid the loss of a hopeful political vision. Constructive responses to many of our current ailments are latent within scripture and our traditions. By considering these, the church can continue to demonstrate the political salience of its witness.

Bibliography

Barth, Karl. *Church Dogmatics* III/4. Edinburgh: T&T Clark, 1961.

---

29. Nicholas Wolterstorff, "The Wounds of God: Calvin's Theology of Social Injustice," in Nicholas Wolterstorff, *Hearing the Call: Liturgy, Justice, Church, and World* (Grand Rapids: Eerdmans, 2011), 114–132.
30. Bruce Gordon, *Calvin* (New Haven: Yale University Press, 2009), 298.

Bediako, Kwame. *Christianity in Africa: The Renewal of a Non-Western Religion*. Edinburgh: Edinburgh University Press, 1995.

Biéler, André. *Calvin's Economic and Social Thought*. Geneva: World Council of Churches, 2005.

Biggar, Nigel. *Between Kin and Cosmopolis: An Ethic of the Nation*. Eugene: Cascade, 2014.

Bonhoeffer, Dietrich. *Works, Vol. 8, Letters and Papers from Prison*, ed. John W. de Gruchy. Minneapolis: Fortress, 2010.

Brown, Stewart J. "Reform, Reconstruction, Reaction: The Social Vision of Scottish Presbyterianism." *Scottish Journal of Theology* 44 (1991): 489–518.

Carr, Wesley. "A Developing Establishment." *Theology* 102 (1999): 2–10

Dowey, Edward A. "Law in Luther and Calvin." *Theology Today* 41 (1984): 146–153.

Fergusson, David. "Politics, Society and Law." In *Oxford Handbook of Reformed Theology*, eds. Michael Allen and Scott Swain, 592–608. Oxford: Oxford University Press, 2020.

Gay, Doug. *Honey from the Lion: Christianity and the Ethics of Nationalism*. London: SCM, 2013.

Gordon, Bruce. *Calvin*. New Haven: Yale University Press, 2009.

Graafland, Johan J. "Weber Revisited: Critical Perspectives from Calvinism on Capitalism in Economic Crisis." In *Calvinism and the Making of the European Mind*, eds. Gijsbert van den Brink and Harro M. Höpfl, 177–198. Leiden: Brill, 2014.

Graham, Elaine. "The Establishment, Multiculturalism and Social Cohesion." In *The Established Church: Past, Present, and Future*, eds. Mark Chapman, Judith Maltby and William Whyte, 124–140. London: Bloomsbury, 2011).

Harries, Richard. *Faith in Politics? Rediscovering the Christian Roots of our Political Values*. London: Darton, Longman and Todd, 2010.

Hastings, Adrian. *Church and State: The English Experience*. Exeter: Exeter University Press, 1991.

Hastings, Adrian. *The Constructions of Nationhood: Ethnicity, Religion and Nationalism*. Cambridge: Cambridge University Press, 1997.

Hearn, Jonathan. *Rethinking Nationalism: An Introduction*. London: Palgrave Macmillan, 2004.

Hobsbawm, Eric. *Nations and Nationalism since 1780: Programme, Myth and Reality*. Cambridge: Cambridge University Press, 1992.

Hueglin, Thomas O. "Covenant and Federalism in the Politics of Althusius." In *The Covenant Connection: From Federal Theolog to Modern Federalism*, eds. Daniel J. Elazar and John Kincaid, 31–54. Lanham: Lexington, 2000.

Jaffrelot, Christophe. "Religion and Nationalism." In *The Oxford Handbook of the Sociology of Religion*, ed. Peter B. Clarke, 406–418. Oxford: Oxford University Press, 2011.

Katongole, Emmanuel. *The Sacrifice of Africa: A Political Theology of Africa*. Grand Rapids: Eerdmans, 2011.

Kingdon, Robert M. "Calvinism and Resistance Theory 1550–1580." In *Cambridge History of Political Thought 1450–1700*, ed. J.H. Burns, 193–218. Cambridge: Cambridge University Press, 2008.

Mason, Roger. Ed. *Knox: On Rebellion*. Cambridge: Cambridge University Press, 1994.

Mounk, Yascha. *People vs Democracy: Why our Freedom is in Danger and How to Save It*. Cambridge: Harvard University Press, 2018.

Phiri, Isaac. *Proclaiming Political Pluralism: Churches and Political Transitions in Africa*. Westport: Praeger, 2001.

Putnam, Robert D. *Bowling Alone: The Collapse and Revival of American Community*, revised edition. New York: Simon and Schuster, 2020.

Runciman, David. *How Democracy Ends*. London: Profile Books, 2018.

Stout, Jeffrey. *Blessed are the Organized: Grassroots Democracy in America*. Princeton: Princeton University Press, 2012.

Williams, Rowan. *Faith in the Public Square*. London: Bloomsbury, 2012.

Witte Jr, John. "Introduction." In *Christianity and Law: An Introduction*, eds. John Witte Jr and Frank S. Alexander, 1–32. Cambridge: Cambridge University Press, 2008.

Wolterstorff, Nicholas. *Hearing the Call: Liturgy, Justice, Church, and World*. Grand Rapids: Eerdmans, 2011.

Woodhead, Linda. "Can We Trust the Church?" In *Schools of Faith: Essays in Honour of Iain R. Torrance*, eds. David Fergusson and Bruce McCormack, 193–202. London: T&T Clark, 2018.

CHAPTER 9
PRELUDE TO A "POST-XENOPHOBIC" FUTURE: INTERROGATING THE 1618 BAPTISM DEBATE AT THE SYNOD OF DORT

David Douglas Daniels III

1. INTRODUCTION

The 1618 baptism debate at the Synod of Dort will be interrogated as a topic within the discipline of World Christianity rather than being a topic within the Dutch history, the Long Reformation, the Reformed tradition, or early modern European history. As a topic within World Christianity, the 1618 baptism debate will be questioned with queries such as how did the Global South, specifically Asian religionists, frame and influence the debate at the Synod of Dort?

This chapter will explore how Dort's 1618 debate on baptizing non-Christian Asians provide us with an alternative, non-polarizing way to engage difference. How did this debate offer an alternative discourse to engage the stranger differently and without xenophobia? With rhetoric of fear or xenophobic tropes available to deploy, the baptism debate about these non-Europeans appears to have avoided these options and chose a non-xenophobic approach. The primary sources of the 1618 baptism at Dort include Robert Shell's translation of the essays written by the various delegations expressing their perspective on the baptism question and the account of the debate written by John Hales, an English observer at the Synod of Dort.[1]

This chapter will make three main claims.

1. The 1618 baptism debate at the Synod of Dort transpired

---

1. Robert Shell (ed.), *De Ethnicorum Pueris Baptizandis*: *Reformed Opinions on Baptism of Heathens, The Synod of Dort, 1618–1619* (Cape Town: unpublished, 1991); "Mr. Hales Letters from the Synod of Dort to the Right Honourable Sr. Dudley Carlton, Lord Embassador &c.," in John Hales, *Golden Remains of the Ever Memorable Mr. John Hales of Eton College &c.* (London: Printed for Tim. Garwaithe and the Little North Doore of St. Paul, 1659), 189–190 (renumbered as page 1–2).

prior to the rise of modern racism and orientalism; therefore, its discourse should be "untainted" byxenophobia produced by modern racism and orientalism.
2. The progressive currents within the 1618 baptism debate offer an alternative, non-polarizing, non-xenophobic way to engage difference which could be called xenogenerosity or generosity towards strangers.
3. In the progressive currents within the 1618 baptism debate, there was recognition that the stranger possessed rights, the Christian community possessed responsibilities to the stranger, and that a link existed between baptism and manumission; this perspective might embody what could be called Christian xenogenerosity.

2. Definition Of Xenophobia and Xenogenerosity

Xenophobia is a fear, an irrational fear, of the stranger. It is prejudice, bigotry or hostility toward the stranger as the Other or the outsider. Xenophobia recycles and reproduces the stranger or the Other as a threat, danger, pollutant, contagion, disease, or pathogen. Within xenophobia, the stranger functions as a subversive undermining or overthrowing the social, religious, civic, or national order. Xenophobia employs a rhetoric of protection, security or cleansing to justify its responses to the stranger which range from subordinating or marginalizing the stranger within the community to deporting the stranger from the community. These xenophobic responses produce discriminatory laws as well as regimes of victimization, violence, and violation directed at the stranger.

To describe an alternative discourse to xenophobia, a term utilized by the African-American theorist Fred Moten might be suggestive: xenogenerosity. In this chapter, xenogenerosity will be employed to characterize a practice of communal co-existence. It could be understood as the practicing of generosity toward strangers rather than practicing hostility bred by xenophobia. For Moten, there's a distinction between xenogenerosity and counterxenophobia in which xenogenerosity is "dispossessive availability," an open embrace, and counterxenophobia is "possessive enclosure," or a closed embrace. In dialogue with Afro-British theorist Paul Gilroy, xenogenerosity, like conviviality, registers a "radical openness that brings conviviality alive [and] makes nonsense of closed, fixed, and reified identity and turns attention toward the always-unpredictable mechanism of identification." Like Gilroy's conviviality, xenogenerosity could be set in the context of "cosmopolitanism as a 'network of inter-connectedness and solidarity that could resonate across boundaries, reach across distances, and evade other cultural and economic obstacles.'" In the Christian practice of xenogenerosity or generosity towards strangers, compassion overflows all structures. Generosity towards strangers becomes a new basis for inclusive communities.²

3. BAPTISM DEBATE AT DORT IN 1618

The 1618 baptism debate at the Synod of Dort was prompted by a letter sent in 1612 from Jakarta or Batavia (now modern Indonesia) in South Asia to the Dutch classis of Amsterdam in the province of Holland.

One scholar from the early twentieth century framed the question as *"Whether the children in East India [Indies], who have wholly entered into the families of Christians and who have a Christian protector, who promises to train them in the Christian faith, shall be baptized?"* However, according to the 1618 contemporary English account by John Hales of the debate, the question was framed as *"Can we baptize the children of Ethnicks* (sic)?" Hales located a non-xenophobic term to identify non-monotheist religionists. Rather than pagan or heathen, Hales selected "ethnick."³

Key to the argument of this chapter is that John Hales, a contemporary observer to Dort, translated into English the Latin word ethnicorum as "ethnick." English Protestant authors began translating the term as "ethnicks" rather than heathens or pagans even before the Synod of Dort in 1618. During the sixteenth century, there were references to "An ethnicke and pagan kyng" as well as an "ethnicke philosopher." Robert Fludd (1574–1637) classified ancient Greek philosophy as "ethnick philosophy." According to Colin Kidd in sixteenth and seventeenth century English parlance, ethnic pertained to religious matters. Kidd drew this conclusion from Thomas Blount's *Glossographia* which Blount compiled in 1618–19. However, Blount had more negative connotations than Robert Fludd and others. Blount defined ethnick as "heathenish, ungodly, irreligious: And may be used substantively for a heathen or gentile." Based on the Greek word ethnos, it had been translated in English as "ethnics," "nation," "heathen," or "pagan." As a term of religion, "ethnick" was regularly employed by the British as

---

2. Fred Moten, *The Universal Machine* (Durham: Duke University Press, 2018); Paul Gilroy, *Postcolonial Melancholia* (New York: Columbia University Press, 2005), xv.

3. Henry E. Dosker, Review of doctoral thesis, "De Pro Acta der Dordtsche Synode in 1618. Academisch Proefschrift, ter verkryging van den graad van Doctor in de Heilige Godgeleerdheid" (T. de Vries Dz. Rotterdam: 1914) in *Princeton Theological Review* 12 (1914), 661–662; John Hales, *Golden Remains*, 17 (3 December 1618).

the opposite of monotheists who were Christians, Jews or Muslims. Consequently, ethnic was not used as a derisive term but, in contrast to Christianity as the true, godly monotheistic religion; ethnic referred to the religions beyond monotheism. Ethnics as a term for non-monotheists was a religious rather than racial term; as a term it was even applied to the philosophy of Aristotle and Plato which were ethnic philosophies. In many regards, the term lacked the pejorative tinge of pagan or heathen which were other translations of the term "ethnicorum."[4]

This chapter contends that the Synod of Dort's debate about baptizing children of ethnics offers an inclusive way of framing the incorporation of new peoples outside of Europe who live in the Global South into the Reformed Christian community. Occurring prior to the rise of modern racism and orientalism during the early 1700s, this baptism debate points to a constructive manner in which difference can inform how societies perceive community and peoplehood in terms other than ancestry, land, and language, supplying an alternative to the polarizing currents within today's world.

The conference theme, "The Calling of the Church in Times of Polarization," which frames this chapter is engaged by proposing that in the 1618 debate were references to progressive practices of difference and inclusion that foster xenogenerosity or generosity towards strangers. These practices counter the practices of difference and exclusion or subordination fostered by xenophobia and hostility towards strangers. It should be noted that in the 1618 debate were other practices of differences which ranged from inclusive to exclusive and, possibly, xenophobic.

This chapter's thesis is that the progressive currents within the 1618 Dort debate on baptizing the children of ethnics offers what the author identifies as the Reformed practice of xenogenerosity as an alternative to xenophobia; the Reformed practice of xenogenerosity recognizes that the stranger possesses rights, the Christian community possesses responsibilities to the stranger, and a link exists between baptism and manumission, with these particular rights and responsibilities being based on scripture and framed theologically.

---

4. Oxford English Dictionary, 1545 Udall, Erasm. Par. Pref. 3; 1581: Marbeck, Bk. of Notes 61; Robert Fludd, *Mosaical Philosophy, Grounded upon the Essentiall Truth or Eternal Sapience* (London: Humphrey Moseley Printer, 1659), 30 at https://archive.org/stream/mosaicallphiloso00flud/; Colin Kidd, *British Identity Before Nationalism and Nationhood in the Atlantic World, 1600–1800* (Cambridge: Cambridge University Press, 2004), 34.

4. Periodization: Prior to Modern Racism and Orientalism

A close examination of the 1618 baptism debate at Dort reveals the absence of key tropes related to modern racism and orientalism; these tropes cast the people of the Global South as infantile or inferior peoples. Why are racist and orientalist tropes missing from the accounts and documents of the debate? As an historian, I believe this is because the 1618 baptism debate occurred prior to the rise of modern racism during the late 1600s and of orientalism during the 1700s. Consequently, the 1618 debate at Dort provides texts that were theoretically "untainted" by modern racism and orientalism, possibly, pointing to a constructive manner to engage difference.

Building upon the scholarship of George Frederickson, Cornel West, and Katherine Gerbner, this chapter identifies the rise of modern racism as a late 17th century and 18th century system co-constituted by the Enlightenment, chattel slavery, European colonialism, European imperialism, early capitalism, white supremacy, and legal tactics of the subordination and exclusion of peoples of color. The modern system of racism constructed the differences between Africans, Asians or First Peoples (Native Americans) in contradistinction to Europeans as racial, specifically in terms of the hierarchy of races. While Europeans invented modern racism to organize the way they interpreted and governed people of color, they invented Orientalism to frame the relationship between the West and Asia in terms of the dependency of Asia on the West.[5]

People of the Global South are races with deficits that deem them inferior in comparison to Europeans; they are inferior—ontologically, theologically, legally, politically and scientifically. People of color lack certain cognitive abilities, moral acumen, and spiritual capacity. People of color as racial or deficient appears to be absent from the 1618 baptism debate at the Synod of Dort. Consequently, the questions which will later dominate the era of modern racism were not posed during the 1618 debate on baptism at the Synod of Dort. The delegates at Dort didn't ask: Are ethnics fully human? Do ethnics have souls? Do ethnics possess the intellectual abilities to comprehend the Christian Faith sufficiently to profess the faith according to Reformed Protestant standards? Do ethnics possess the moral ability to live the Christian life

---

5. George M. Frederickson, *Racism: A Short History* (Princeton: Princeton University Press, 2002, 2015), 26–39; Cornel West, *Prophesy Deliverance! An Afro-American Revolutionary Christianity* (Louisville: Westminster John Knox Press, 1982, 2002), 55–57; Katharine Gerbner, *Christian Slavery: Conversion and Race in the Protestant Atlantic World* (Philadelphia: University of Pennsylvania Press, 2018), 74–75; Edward Said, *Orientalism* (New York: Pantheon Books, 1978).

as a gracious response to election by God? Can ethnics be "adopted" into the covenant? These questions were not asked in 1618. The 1618 baptism debate at Dort presupposes that ethnics are fully human, possess souls, have the intellectual and moral capacity to be Christians, and can be "adopted" into the covenant.

How did the delegations at Dort answer *"Can we baptize the children of Ethnicks?*

5. Difference at the 1618 Baptism Debate at Dort

The discourse of difference at this Dort debate utilized various terms and phrases in which the children of ethnic Asians as well as their parents are portrayed. Within the debate, difference is marked in terms of distance and deficit. Distance refers to the space between one religion and another while deficit refers to what is absent in one religion in comparison to another. Difference as distance is deployed in marking mostly as strangers and once as alien:[6]

"strangers to the covenant" (Zelandi; Groningen);
"strangers to the covenant of grace" (Helvetti; Zelandi);
"strangers" to "the knowledge of God and His Christ" (Helvetti);
"strangers to the agreements of the promises" of God (Zelandi);
"strangers to the state of Israel" (N. Holland [Borealis] Synod)
"alien to the state of Israel" (Zelandi).

Difference as distance is also deployed in which they were noted as possessing outsider status over against the Christians' insider status:[7]

"outside the covenant" (Emdan);
"outside the Church" (Drentani);
"born outside the Church" (Hassaic);
without "divine adoption" (N. Holland [Borealis] Synod);
"without hope and living in this world without God" (N. Holland [Borealis] Synod).

Difference as distance marked those "outside the covenant" according to two delegations as including some who even "call on the devil himself" (Geldri) or "worship the devil" (Palatine). These perspectives capture the pejorative sense of heathenism, casting the distance between Chris-

---

6. Jonathan Z. Smith, "Differential Equations: On Constructing the 'Other,'" Thirteenth Annual University Lecture in Religion (Arizona State University, Tempe, 1992); Shell (ed.), *De Ethnicorum*, 56, 64; 16, 15; 16; 54; 51, 54.

7. Shell (ed.), *De Ethnicorum*, 35; 66; 9; 52; 52.

tians and some ethnics in terms of worshippers of God at one end of the spectrum and worshippers of the devil at the other end.[8]

Difference as deficit is deployed in which they were noted for lacking a Christian quality or trait by being:[9]

> "unclean" (Hassaic; Emdan);
> "unsanctified" (Geldri);
> "not sanctified through the sacred covenant" (Transijssulania);
> not "the seeds of the faithful" (S. Holland Synod);
> of unsanctified "origin and root" (Drentani).

While the 1612 question framed difference and othering in religious terms of being non-Christian and non-monotheistic, in the theological responses of the delegations, they framed difference in terms of being "strangers to the covenant of grace" or "born outside the Church." It should be noted that only two delegations added that they were devil worshippers; it could be argued that this was an outlier perspective among the delegations.

For the progressives at Dort, while these ethnics were designated as strangers, these Asians were not identified as a threat to the integrity of the Christian Church, Christian culture, the sacrament of baptism, nor the Reformed Christian identity. The language of fear, prejudice, bigotry or hostility was absent from the discourse of the progressives. Rather than strangers being a phobic object, an object of fear, eliciting fear, strangers were a "counterphobic object;" they were unattached to fear; they operated outside the minefield of fear. The progressives' discourse extended beyond the counter-xenophobic with its possessive enclosure posture to the non-xenophobic, possibly even xenogenerous with its dispossessive availability.[10]

6. Religious Differences

Being characterized as strangers, aliens, outsiders, unclean, even devilworshippers is drawn from the vocabulary of difference as distance and deficit. How the delegates deployed, though, this vocabulary within their various discourses of difference is what determines whether this discourse is embedded within xenophobia or xenogenerosity.

Here are three Reformed Christian frameworks on the non-monotheistic stranger:

1. The Xenophobic Exclusion of the Stranger as Threat.

---

8. Shell (ed.), *De Ethnicorum*, 43; 5.
9. Shell (ed.), *De Ethnicorum*, 9, 35; 43; 61; 47; 67.
10. Moten, *Universal*.

2. The Xenophobic Incorporation of the Stranger as a Subordinate.
3. The Xenogenerous Inclusion of the Stranger as Peer.

Deploying the vocabulary of stranger within the xenophobic exclusion of the stranger as threat emphasizes the stranger in terms of difference as indecipherable or unintelligible. As indecipherable in this logic, they are to be excluded from joining the Reformed Christian community because of the threat that they pose. In this framework, the stranger is irredeemable, permanently outside the covenant, and baptism is to be prohibited for them. While the xenophobic exclusion of the stranger as threat is totally absent from the 1618 debate on baptism at Dort, the other two frameworks are present: stranger as subordinate and stranger as peer. These two frameworks are based on a relationship between the stranger and the Reformed Christian community, recognizing that the stranger possess certain rights and the Reformed Christian community possesses certain responsibilities.[11]

7. Religious Rights of Strangers

What minimizes the xenophobia in the second framework that cast the stranger as a subordinate is the recognition that strangers possess rights. What makes the third framework, the progressive option, non-xenophobic or xenogenerous is the commitment to equality as well as the recognition of the stranger's rights. Both the xenophobic incorporation of the stranger as subordinate and the xenogenerous inclusion of the stranger as peer argue for the rights of non-Christian or Ethnic Asians. The Othering of non-Christian Asians did not lead to the stripping or denial of all rights.

There are four groups of strangers discussed in the 1618 baptism debate at Dort: adults, "adolescents," children around age eight, and infants. Each group of strangers possessed an array of rights, ranging from parental rights, individual rights of conscience and free-will regarding religious faith, the right to Christian instruction to the right to be baptized as any European could. While conservative, moderate, and progressive perspective identified different sets of rights, each perspective listed rights as key.

For every delegation at Dort, Ethnic Asian adults possessed the right to be baptized. For Ethnic Asian adults requesting baptism, baptism could occur after they had been catechized and professed the Christian faith. These adults also possessed the right to reject baptism and Christianity; baptism and Christianity should not be imposed on them. Ethnic Asian

---

11. On types of difference see Smith, "Differential."

adults possessed the right of conscience and free-will regarding religious faith. Moreover, Ethnic Asian parents possess parental rights. According to delegations such as the Hassaic Brethren, non-Christian birth parents possessed particular rights. If the birth parents are living, they should approve of all adoptions; children cannot be involuntary taken from birth parents at the whim of the colonial state. The birth parents can opt for a semi-adoption instead of a full adoption. In the case of retaining full or partial parental rights, Asian Ethnic parents reserve the right to approve or prohibit the baptism of their infant; the birth parent's consent needs to be required, according to the Hassaic delegation. If the birth parents can agree to a full adoption by Christian families, according to the British delegation, they are "renouncing" their parental rights over the infant and transferring to the adopted parents all parental rights.[12]

Non-Christian Asian adolescents possess rights of conscience and free-will in regard to religious faith. Non-Christian adolescents must be granted the right to "oppose the doctrine passed on to them and resist baptism," according to the British delegation. They possess the right to request baptism after they have been catechized and professed. Ethnic Asian adolescents may request baptism "without consultation with their [birth] parents" and they may even go against their birth parents' wishes. This is because "the right and power of parents does not extend to such a degree that they are able to give to their children who have reached years of discretion any order of prescription in the case of religion that goes against the word of God and their own conscience." Additionally, the Hassaic Brethren argue that "neither can the children abide by the judgement and opinion of their parents in the manner of religion, but rather are they bound to look to the wish of God and the judgement of their own conscience." Like adults, Ethnic Asian adolescents may also reject the Christian faith and "resist baptism." They should not to be baptized against their conscience nor their will because the British delegation contended that Ethnic Asian adolescents possess the right of conscience and the right to exercise their will in regard to religion.[13]

While Ethnic Asian children and infants will be discussed in the next section, another category of non-Christian Asians that were discussed at the 1618 debate on baptism was the enslaved. The 1618 debate on baptism addressed the status of enslaved and free candidates for baptism. Baptism cannot be forced on them either. According to the delegation from Great Britain, the enslaved should not "be presented to the Church by their masters" without consenting to be baptized. And if "they should be presented" by their masters, they should not "be baptized by the

---

12. Shell (ed.), *De Ethnicorum*, 8, 10.
13. Shell (ed.), *De Ethnicorum*, 3, 11, 3.

Church" if the enslaved has not requested baptism. Enslaved ethnic Asians who are baptized receive additional rights in baptism. Regarding the enslaved who are baptized, Deodati, the Italian Reformed theologian, stated: "That those baptized should enjoy [the] equal right of liberty with all other Christians...." For Deodati, the "equal right of liberty" includes prohibiting the future sale and transfer of these baptized Asians to others. By virtue of baptism, the enslaved possessed the right to be reclassified from the status of enslaved to the status of "hired servants," possibly this is a form of manumission. If so, then, a link exists between baptism and manumission. According to Robert Shell, baptism enrolled the baptized person into the church and society, bestowing upon them a new status and rights which were both religious and civic. He would categorize the social and political implications of baptism as "civic baptism." For Deodati, this would include the enslaved.[14]

Ethnic Asians possessed religious rights. While they were "strangers to the covenant." Their rights ranged from parental rights, individual rights of conscience and free-will regarding religious faith, the right to Christian instruction to the right to be baptized. Whether as a subordinate or a peer, Ethnic Asians were members of the community to a certain degree. Baptism bestowed more rights, as Robert Shell, as these Asians were enrolled in the church and society.

8. Religious Responsibilities to Strangers

Moderates and progressives both argued for the responsibilities of the Christian heads of household, Christian parents, and Reformed congregations to the non-Christian Asians. The Othering of non-Christian Asians did not lead to European Christians being absolved of responsibilities to non-Christian Asians nor Asian Protestants.

As stated above, according to Deodati, slaveholders had the responsibility of reclassifying baptized enslaved people as "hired servants." For progressives like the delegates from Great Britain, it was "the duty of the father of the family to present" adopted infants of Ethnic Asian parents "to be baptized" and "the duty of the minister" to baptize these infants. There also existed the responsibility to educate all members of the household, including non-Christian Asians, in the

---

14. Shell (ed.), *De Ethnicorum* 4, 17; on a discussion of the Synod of Dort and ethnic baptism see: Robert Carl-Heinz Shell, *Children of Bondage: A Social History of the Slave Society at the Cape of Good Hope, 1652–1838* (Hanover and London: Wesleyan University Press / University Press of New England, 1994), 334–348, 350–356, 362–365.

Christian faith.[15]

With rights and responsibility being vital to the relationship between Reformed Christians and Ethnic Asians, the two Reformed Christian frameworks of the stranger as subordinate and the stranger as peer can be better contextualized and made legible within the scholarly conversation.

9. THE XENOPHOBIC INCORPORATION OF THE STRANGER AS SUBORDINATE

The xenophobic incorporation of the stranger as subordinate captures the conservative and moderate positions. For these positions, the adult and adolescent "strangers" can join the Reformed Christian community but under an additional set of rules than those assigned to Europeans. The catechetical education of Ethnic Asians needs to be longer. They must answer catechetical questions with answers in their own words. It might be best if they also expressed "privately and publicly the rationale of their faith" in Christ, in the words of the Palatine delegation. However, the conservatives unlike the moderates categorically deny baptism to the children of non-Christian Asian parents.[16]

While moderates believed that the infants of non-Christian parents who were adopted into a Christian family could be baptized, baptism, though, should be postponed until adolescence to minimize them deserting Christianity. If baptism was not postponed for these infants adopted by Christian families, two necessary conditions had to be addressed. First, the congregation had to be warned in advance of the upcoming baptism. Second, the heads of households as the sponsors had to guarantee publicly and in writing their commitments to the rearing and protecting of the infant in the Christian faith and community. The Bremen theologians required a record of these sponsors' vows: "let the names of the guarantors with the essential details be entered in a specific register and list."[17]

Fear of the newly baptized deserting the faith later in life led to Ethnic Asians being held in a subordinate position within the Christian community since they were "strangers to the covenant of grace" according to the conservatives and moderates. The xenophobic incorporation of the stranger as subordinate with added requirements for baptism above what was required of Europeans was deemed necessary by conservatives and moderates as a preventive measure to safeguard the Christian faith against these group of Asians recanting the faith.

---

15. Shell (ed.), *De Ethnicorum*, 4, 17.
16. Shell (ed.), *De Ethnicorum*, 6.
17. Shell (ed.), *De Ethnicorum*.

10. THE XENOGENEROUS INCLUSION OF THE STRANGER AS PEER

For the progressives, the xenogenerous inclusion of the stranger as peer best described their framework. They welcomed the baptism of infants, children, adolescents, and adults. All were welcomed!

Regarding infants adopted into Christian families, progressives such as the delegates of Great Britain, adoption by a Christian was equivalent to being born of Christian parents. In this Christian household, the adopted infants became "partakers in the spiritual blessings which was contained in the Church." Consequently, these adopted infants "can be seen to enjoy almost the same right as those in the Church." This is because "to have been so received into the families of Christians and indeed into the Church is a form of profession, just as also to be born in the Church." The Christian adoption of infants of non-Christian Asian parents operates "exactly as if they [these infants] had been born of Christian parents."

The Hassaic Brethren added when parental rights are legitimately transferred from the non-Christian Asian birth parents to the Christian parents these infants "indeed cease, as it were, to be" the children of their birth parents because "through their adoption by Christians, and indeed after their adoption are rightly reckoned as members of the same Church of which those Christians who have adopted them as sons are themselves members." In a sense, then, adoption by a Christian parent "sanctifies" the infant, making them members of the Covenant and eligible candidates for infant baptism.[18]

Hales noted that infants of Ethnic Asian parents:

> ... should be baptized, if they were rightfully adopted into Christian Families, and that their parents had altogether resigned them into the hands of the Christians. They grounded themselves upon the examples of Abraham circumcising all that were of his Family; of Paul baptizing whole households, of the primitive Church recorded in S. Austin, who shews, that anciently children that were *exposititii* were wont to be taken up by the Christians and baptized.[19]

The English delegation crafted an affirmative response to the query from South Asia, framing their argument in terms of Reformed covenantal theology wherein the sign of baptism was analogous to circumcision for Jews. The English delegation interpreted Abraham's act of circumcising everyone in his household, whether they were his biological kin or purchased household servants, as biblical proof that the sign of the covenant

---

18. Shell (ed.), *De Ethnicorum*.
19. Hales, *Golden Remains*, 17 (letter of 3 December 1618).

extended to all persons who were members of a Christian household. Genealogical connections between the Christian head of the household and the members of the household were not a prerequisite to being included in the covenant. Ethnic infants and children, while not born into the covenant because they were not born to Christian parents, could be "adopted" into the covenant and were included by virtue of their membership in the household.

In addition to the Abraham case, this inclusive faction appealed to Augustine who chronicled how Christians rescued abandoned ethnic children, incorporated these ethnic children into their household, and had them baptized. They also took Apostle Paul as a precedent in his baptism of all members of households; they assumed that since infants and underage children were in an average first-century household, they were also baptized. They argued that since such ethnic infants and children lacked the maturity to request baptism, they needed a Christian sponsor to agree to commit to support and encourage them in living the Christian life. The sponsor had to be a Christian married couple who would adopt the underage child or infant through proper channels, becoming the Christian parents of the baptismal candidate. The baptismal candidate would then become a member of a Christian family.

For the delegates at Dort, when non-Christian Asian parents converted to Christianity from their ethnic religions and were baptized, they were no longer ethnics; they now were Christians. Their children of newly baptized parents became part of the Covenant as children born of Christian parents. These children were no longer deemed ethnic. According to the Great Britain delegation, these adopted infants were "called out of paganism by a certain special providence" as indicated by being placed in a Christian family. As noted above, ethnic, then, was a religious term and not a term restricted to ancestry or genealogy.[20]

11. THE TOPIC OF BAPTISM AND THE GLOBAL SOUTH AFTER DORT

After the Synod of Dort, inquiries from the Global South continued to be sent to the classis of Amsterdam, from Brazil in South America in 1637, Curaçao in the Caribbean in 1644, Luanda in Central Africa in 1644, and Asia. A letter from Brazil which was sent by 1637 was addressed by the Classis of Amsterdam on the 16th of November in 1637. On the issue of baptizing "adopted" Native Americans, Africans, and others in Brazil, there were Reformed Christians in Brazil who advocated for, and, possibly, there were clergy who baptized adopted ethnic children. Let-

---

20. Shell (ed.), *De Ethnicorum*.

ters from Curaçao in the Caribbean and from Angola on the central African coast were read before the classis of Amsterdam on the 7th of November in 1644. Reverends John Backerus and Jacobus Beth wrote from Curaçao and Angola, respectively. It appeared that each sought for the authority to baptize the children of Ethnic parents.[21]

The situation of Rev. Beaumont in Curaçao and Rev. Henry Selyns in New Amsterdam involved African parents who had been baptized and were requesting baptism for their infants and young children, and so differed from the issue that prompted the 1618 Synod of Dort discussion in which Dutch adopted parents where making the request. Probably, it was the African parents who were also prompting the issue in Angola. For New Amsterdam, Selyns specifically states: "As to baptisms, the Negroes occasionally request, that we should baptize their children …"[22]

While serving in Batavia, Rev. Adriaan Jacobszoon Hulsebos wrote to the classis regarding baptizing the children of ethnics because different practices were being performed within Reformed Protestant congregations in Asia. In Sri Lanka and the Moluccas, the Reformed Churches adopted an inclusionary baptism policy, opening baptism to all people regardless of their parentage or genealogy. According to Sutarman Soediman Patronadi, "mass baptisms were performed for political reasons under the VOC. No religious instruction was given before baptism" in some cases. Whereas in other places such as Ambon, religious instruction and catechetical examinations were taken seriously during and after Dort.[23]

Regarding the baptized enslaved Reformed Christian, the 1618 debate on baptism at Dort shaped the policy regarding the enslaved in the Statutes of Batavia (1622). Markus P. M. Vink stated:

> The ordinance of 4 May 1622, derived from strict Christian principles rather than Roman law, consisted of nine articles, supplemented with directions for the proper "governance and upbringing of slaves." It decreed that the "alienation of male and female slaves" could only be done "for good and sufficient reasons." Such transactions had to be duly registered before a magistrate or legal authority. Christians could not sell or alienate slaves of any sort to "people outside of Christendom." Unbelievers in

---

21. "Acts of the Classis of Amsterdam" in *Documents of the Senate of the State of New York*, Vol. 14, 112 (16 November 1637); *Ecclesiastical Records, State of New York* (1902), 186 (7 November 1644); Acts of the Classis of Amsterdam" in *Documents of the Senate of the State of New York*, Vol. 14, 112 (16 November 1637); *Ecclesiastical Records, State of New York* (1902), 186 (7 November 1644).

22. *Ecclesiastical Records, State of New York* (1902), 509.

23. Sutarman Soediman Patronadi, *Sadrach's Community and Its Contextual Roots: A Nineteenth Century Javanese Expression of Christianity* (Amsterdam: Brill, 1990), 27; History of Christianity in Indonesia, eds. Jan Sihar Aritonang and Karel Steenbrink (Leiden and Boston: Brill, 2008), 105–107.

Company territories could not buy, receive or hold title to slaves from Christians. …Christian slaveholders were to treat all their slaves with "civility, benevolence, and reasonableness," "to care for them as their own children," and to raise and instruct them in the Christian religion that "they might come to receive baptism." Non-Christian masters could not deny their slaves instruction in the Christian religion and, were they to become Christians, their owners would have to part with them at a "reasonable price" either to a Christian or to the Company itself.[24]

Vink showed that for some Reformed Christians the link between manumission and baptism was re-enforced, including the rejection of Asian slavery by Reformed Christians. Vink noted that "in 1628–1629, both Reformed classes most involved in the overseas world, Amsterdam and Walcheren (Zeeland), wrote to Batavia, that 'it was unchristian to have slaves.' Slavery, they argued, was 'unedifying and not permitted among the Christians in the Indies." In 1662, Cornelius Poudroyen rejected slave trade and slavery as an option within Christianity. He contended manumission should precede baptism:

> It is unbefitting for Christians to engage in this rough, confusing, dangerous, and unreasonable trade, adding to a person's troubles and being an executor of his torments. Instead, if one desires to bring forth good from that evil, one should purchase him [the slave] in order to be manumitted and freed from such great servitude to cruel tyrants, and, if possible, instruct him in the Christian religion.[25]

The Christian practice of xenogenerosity was seemingly present within some Reformed communities of Asia, Africa, and the Americas in the generation following the Synod of Dort. This included in the New Netherlands and Virginia Colony honoring the bond between baptism and manumission in certain cases.

12. Conclusion

While scholars always recognize the Synod of Dort was a pan-European and solely European Reformed confessional council, I would like to argue in light of what was discussed in this chapter that this 1618 debate on baptism could be interpreted as an inter-continental council with European topics as well as pastoral issues of Asians. Could Asians also be "recognized" as "present" as "participants?" The Asian "participants" were present in terms of how their perspectives, concerns, and voice

---

24. Markus P. M. Vink, "A Work of Compassion? Dutch Slavery and Slave Trade in the Indian Ocean in the Seventeenth Century" (2003), http://webdoc.sub.gwdg.de/ebook/p/2005/history_cooperative/www.historycooperative.org/proceedings/seascapes/vink.html (accessed 20 March 2019).

25. Vink, "A Work of Compassion?"

were embedded in the 1612 pastoral case which promoted the baptism debate and how they were also "present" in the baptism debate by being the subject of the deliberations. While I would have preferred them being physically present with the right of voice and vote, I would like to encourage us to recognize the significance of them being "discursively present."

After Dort, the Christian practice of xenogenerosity increased the Reformed Protestants of Color population during the 1600s in the Americas and, especially, in Asia.

1. One can convincingly argue that the 1618 Baptism Debate at the Synod of Dort lacks the xenophobic and racist tropes produced by modern racism and orientalism in discussing Ethnic Asians with ethnic as a religious category. So, it does offer a way to engage difference in a non-xenophobic direction.
2. The progressives during the 1618 baptism debate at Dort with their xenogenerous inclusion of the stranger as peer offered an alternative, non-polarizing, non-xenophobic way to engage difference and the Ethnic Asian as a stranger.
3. Since it could be argued that the progressives within the 1618 Baptism debate with their xenogenerous inclusion of the stranger as peer recognized rights of the stranger, the responsibilities of the Reformed Christian community to the stranger, and a link exist between baptism and manumission, they might be deemed as practicing what could be called Christian xenogenerosity towards the Ethnic Asian.

Does a Christian practice of xenogenerosity offer a way out of our polarizing, xenophobic times? The progressive currents during Dort's 1618 baptism debate supplies content to a Christian practice of xenogenerosity that could be generative for our times. Difference as distinctive rather in terms of deficiencies or distant is promising as a concept. Choice and rights belonging to strangers to decide whether they wanted to seek admission to the Christian community is a positive maneuver. The Christian community being tasked by Reformed Protestants to honor and process the request is an inclusive attitude.

The Christian practice of xenogenerosity redefining the symmetry between ancestry and belonging is a key corrective. Like salvation, life and community are gifts of God. Maybe within the Christian practice of xenogenerosity the host is God and we humans are God's guest; there is just space for divine hospitality. Rather than people, even Christian people, adopting the logic of the host and the guests, the Christian practice of xenogenerosity challenges us to welcome the stranger as a peer with rights, organizing the Christian communities with responsibilities to the stranger and as generous, inclusive spaces where a common humanity unites all as peers and?.

As a prelude to a post-xenophobic future, the progressive currents of Dort possibly offer us a way forward. We can build on Bakhtin to understand that in the xenogenerous church and society is birthed "a second world and second life outside officialdom," a reality outside the reigning logic of xenophobia, the politics of fear, the victimization of the stranger, a reality anticipated by the progressives at the Synod of Dort during the 1618 baptism debate.

Possibly, "The Calling of the Church in Times of Polarization" is to add the practice of Christian xenogenerosity to our other practices. Can we consider choice as belonging to the migrant, the immigrant, the asylum seeker, or the economic refugee to decide whether they want to seek admission to our country or Church? Is the Christian community tasked with honoring, processing, and lobbying their requests? Since the Christian practice of xenogenerosity redefines the symmetry between ancestry and belonging as key to Christian community, does this also apply to national communities, too? As engagers of the Synod of Dort, in practicing Christian xenogenerosity, do we welcome the stranger as peers to our Christian and civic communities as generous, inclusive spaces?

Maybe xenogenerosity can be an alternative to the xenophobia of our times; a Christian xenogenerosity grounded in scripture and theologically by the 1618 baptism debate of the Synod of Dort.

BIBLIOGRAPHY

Aritonang, Jan Sihar and Karel Steenbrink. Eds. *History of Christianity in Indonesia*. Leiden and Boston: Brill, 2008.

Documents of the Senate of the State of New York, Vol. 14 (1637).

Dosker, Henry E. Review of doctoral thesis, "De Pro Acta der Dordtsche Synode in 1618. Academisch Proefschrift, ter verkryging van den graad van Doctor in de Heilige Godgeleerdheid" (T. de Vries Dz. Rotterdam: 1914). In *Princeton Theological Review* 12 (1914): 661–662.

Ecclesiastical Records, State of New York. 1902.

Fludd, Robert. *Mosaical Philosophy, Grounded upon the Essentiall Truth or Eternal Sapience*. London: Humphrey Moseley Printer, 1659. https://archive.org/stream/mosaicallphiloso00flud/.

Frederickson, George M. *Racism: A Short History*. Princeton: Princeton University Press, 2002, 2015.

Gerbner, Katharine. *Christian Slavery: Conversion and Race in the Protestant Atlantic World*. Philadelphia: University of Pennsylvania Press, 2018.

Gilroy, Paul. *Postcolonial Melancholia*. New York: Columbia University Press, 2005.

Hales, John. *Golden Remains*, 17 (3 December 1618).

Kidd, Colin. *British Identity Before Nationalism and Nationhood in the Atlantic World*, 1600–1800. Cambridge: Cambridge University Press, 2004.

Moten, Fred. *The Universal Machine*. Durham: Duke University Press, 2018.

"Mr. Hales Letters from the Synod of Dort to the Right Honourable Sr. Dudley Carlton, Lord Embassador &c." In John Hales, *Golden Remains of the Ever Memorable Mr. John Hales of Eton College &c*. London: Printed for Tim, 189–190. Garwaithe and the Little North Doore of St. Paul, 1659.

Patronadi, Sutarman Soediman. *Sadrach's Community and Its Contextual Roots: A Nineteenth Century Javanese Expression of Christianity* (Amsterdam: Brill, 1990

Said, Edward. *Orientalism*. New York: Pantheon Books, 1978.

Shell, Robert Carl-Heinz. *Children of Bondage: A Social History of the Slave Society at the Cape of Good Hope, 1652–1838*. Hanover and London: Wesleyan University Press / University Press of New England, 1994.

Shell, Robert. Ed. *De Ethnicorum Pueris Baptizandis: Reformed Opinions on Baptism of Heathens, The Synod of Dort, 1618–1619*. Cape Town: unpublished, 1991.

Smith, Jonathan Z. "Differential Equations: On Constructing the 'Other.'" Thirteenth Annual University Lecture in Religion. Arizona State University, Tempe, 1992.

Vink, Markus P. M. "A Work of Compassion? Dutch Slavery and Slave Trade in the Indian Ocean in the Seventeenth Century" (2003). Accessed 20 March 2019. http://webdoc.sub.gwdg.de/ebook/p/2005/history_cooperative/www.historycooperative. org/proceedings/seascapes/vink.html.

West, Cornel. *Prophesy Deliverance*! *An Afro-American Revolutionary Christianity*. Louisville: Westminster John Knox Press, 1982, 2002.

CHAPTER 10
PROTESTANT SCHOOLS AND HOSPITALS IN THE CONTEXT OF RELIGIOUS POLARIZATION IN YOGYAKARTA

Jozef Mepibozef Nelsun Hehanussa

1. INTRODUCTION

The work of missions in Indonesia, especially in Yogyakarta, has come not only in the form of preaching the Gospel and establishing Christian communities, but also through social works that benefit the lives of all the people. The two most prominent kinds of mission works are education and health care. Even after the churches in Indonesia became independent from the colonial mission boards, the work of missionaries in the fields of health care and education continued. The two oldest Protestant churches in Yogyakarta that continue the work of this mission are the Javanese Christian Church and the Indonesian Christian Church. However, the educational and medical work of this mission is no longer centered on efforts to Christianize people who have not received Christ, but rather perceived as an effort by the Church to build a better society. Therefore, schools and hospitals serve people from all religious backgrounds with a tacit promise not to engage in any kind of proselytization. However, the rise of intolerant groups is posing a challenge to the work of Christian hospitals and schools, because these groups are now demanding Muslims not to go to Christian schools or hospitals. This situation has an impact on the development of hospitals as well as Christian schools. One of the obvious impacts is that many Christian schools in Yogyakarta have closed due to a shortage of students.

This chapter aims to examine the presence of mission work through education, health care and development during and after the era of mission institutions. Against the backdrop of an historical overview, it will focus on the challenges to the development of Christian schools and hospitals in Yogyakarta due to the polarization of religion in society in the region, as representative of trends in Indonesia. First, I will describe how Christianity has been present in Yogyakarta through mission work in the field of education and health care. Secondly, I will point out how mission work in education and health care deal with the religious polarization that is occurring in contemporary Indonesian society.

2. Religious Encounters in the Land of Ngayogyakarta Hadiningrat

Ngayogyakarta Hadiningrat, better known as Yogyakarta, is the name of the area under the rule of Hamengku Buwono Sultanate. Before becoming an autonomous sultanate, Ngayogyakarta Hadiningrat was part of the ancient Hindu Mataram Kingdom (bhūmi Mataram or Hindu Mataram) during the 8th to 10th centuries and later part of the Islamic Mataram Kingdom from the 17th century until colonization by the Dutch. The ancient Mataram Kingdom was established by King Sanjaya, who received the title of Rakai Mataram Sang Ratu Sanjaya. Therefore, the name Mataram originally came from this title. Raja Sanjaya was a member of the Syailendra Dynasty (Wangsa) that ruled Medang (Mataram).[1] In the 10th century, Mataram kingdom's power center shifted to East Java. The center shifted to several places, such as Yogyakarta, Kedu, Jombang, and Madiun.[2] According to Indonesian archaeologist Boechari, the rulers of the Syailendra Dynasty, from Dapunta Selendra to Rakai Mataram Ratu Sanjaya, were devotees of Shiva,[3] which is why there are more Hindu temples than Buddhist temples in Yogyakarta.[4] The Syailendra family, starting from Rakai Panangkaran and Rakai Panaraban, later converted to Mahayana Buddhism. However, some royal families retained Hinduism and others became Mahayana Buddhists. Even so, there were power struggles not for religious reasons, but for personal gain.

Despite religious displacement within the royal family or even in

---

1. There was no *Wangsa* Sanjaya. The ruler of the dynasty received the title of *Maharaja*. The territory of maharaja consisted of regions that were autonomously controlled by a *Rakai*. Each *Rakai* had his own genealogy as the ruler of the region. There is no ancient inscription that mentions the name of Wangsa Sanjaya since Sanjaya was not a *Maharaja* but a *Rakai*. Rakai Pangkaran, who constructed the Kalasan temple, was a Maharaja of Wangsa Syailendra. He was given the title Sri Maharaja Tejahpurnapana Panangkaran, Permata Wangsa Syailendra because he was descendant of Dapunta Selendra. See Boechari, *Melacak Sejarah Kuno Indonesia lewat Prasasti* (Tracing ancient Indonesian history through inscriptions) (Jakarta: Kepustakaan Populer Gramedia, 2018), 198–99.

2. There are several reasons for its move. One is the big eruption of the volcano Mt. Merapi in Central Java.

3. Boechari, *Melacak Sejarah Kuno Indonesia lewat Prasasti*, 200–202.

4. Buddha temples much found in Kedu, around Prambanan, Boyolali and Sragen.

ruling dynasties, religious polarization was never as profound a it is today. Boechari mentions in his writings that the two religions coexisted peacefully until the time of Majapahit Kingdom. They did not seek to dispel the beliefs of the ancestors of the local people. Even if a Maharaja ruler adhered to a particular religion, in the royal structure there were always two religious leaders, one in charge of Hinduism and the other in charge of Buddhism. Hindus and Buddhists coexisted peacefully. According to Boechari, this reflected the public's respect for their leader.[5]

Following the Mataram kingdom's shift to East Java, the region was not under any ruler until 1558 when it was handed over to Ki Ageng Pamanahan, a Muslim, who was subject to the Islamic Kingdom of Demak.[6] Islam was then being spread across Java, including Yogyakarta, more under the influence of the Islamic figures called Walisongo or nine saints.[7] Even as an Islamic region, Yogyakarta did not necessarily eliminate the existence of Hinduism and Buddhism which had been the local religions for centuries.

At the time of the Islamic Mataram Kingdom under the government of Sultan Agung (1613–1646), Islam became the religion of the people in the region, including Yogyakarta. The Sultan attempted to consolidate his power using the Islamic tradition, although he continued to practice *Kejawen* (traditional Javanese beliefs) through mystical relations with the Queen of the South Sea.[8] Nevertheless, his Islamic teachings and practices even developed with his mystical relationship with Sunan Bayat or Sunan Tembayat, another Islamic saint who was not one of Walisongo and whose grave is located at Tembayat in what is now Klaten adjacent to Yogyakarta.[9] In 1633, Sultan Agung even made a pilgrimage to Tembayat and afterwards practiced Islamic mysticism and encouraged the influence of Sunan Bayat on the rulers of the Mataram Islamic kingdom. The influence of Islam was also demonstrated by Sultan Agung in a literary work entitled *Usulbiyah* which describes the Prophet Muhammad as a prophet crowned with the Majapahit golden crown. It

---

5. Boechari, *Melacak Sejarah Kuno Indonesia lewat Prasasti*, 202, 234.

6. The influence of Islam over Demak just took place in the middle of the fifteenth century.

7. They are Sunan Gresik, Sunan Ampel, Sunan Bonang, Sunan Drajat, Sunan Kudus, Sunan Giri, Sunan Kalijaga, Sunan Muria, and Sunan Gunung Jati.

8. Merle Calvin Ricklefs, *Islamisation and Its Opponents in Java: A Political, Social, Cultural and Religious History, C. 1930 to the Present* (Singapore: NUS Press, 2012), 4–6.

9. See Nelly Van Doorn-Harder and Kees de Jong, "The Pilgrimage to Tembayat: Tradition and Revival in Islamic Mysticism in Contemporary Indonesia," in *The Blackwell Companion to Contemporary Islamic Thought*, ed. Ibrahim M. Abu-Rabi' (Malden: Blackwell Publishing, 2006), 491–92; Merle Calvin Ricklefs, *Mystic Synthesis in Java: A History of Islamization from the Fourteenth to the Early Nineteenth Centuries* (Norwalk: EastBridge, 2006), 39–40.

became a symbol of the strong unity between Islam and Java, especially the Islamic Mataram Kingdom. Sultan Agung's devotion to Islam was followed by his successors. The royals were urged to live obediently in accordance with Islamic teachings, but the palace continued to preserve the teachings of pre-Islamic literature.

Religious encounters in this era are far from any form of religious polarization. Although Islam became the official religion of the kingdom, other religions or beliefs were tolerated. For example, when Sultan Agung renovated Sunan Bayat's tomb, there was no change in the Hindu influence on the architectural style of the tomb. Therefore, we can find Hindu-style monuments around Sunan Bayat cemetery enshrining devout Muslims. The gates at Tembayat and several other cemeteries were built in the style of Hindu architecture.[10] This resembles the Hindu influence during the previous Mataram Kingdom period. Historian Merle Calvin Ricklefs called this the "Mystic Synthesis," a reconciliation between Javanese and Islamic identity, beliefs, and styles.[11] On the one hand, Javanese people follow Islamic teachings, such as the five pillars and Islamic rituals. Being Javanese as well as Muslim forms their unique identity. On the other hand, Javanese people accept the reality of local Javanese spiritual forces such as Ratu Kidul, the goddess of the Southern Ocean, and the spirit of Mount Lawu (the god of wind). This synthesis is revealed in "The Gift Addressed to the Spirit of the Prophet" (*al-Tuhfa al-mursala ila ruh al-Nabi*), an important Sufi work at the time written in the palace of Yogyakarta, which was originally from Muhammad ibn Fadli'llah al-Burhanpuri (1545–1620). Such synthesis models were used by important Islamic figures, including the Walisongo, to spread Islam throughout Java.[12] Synthesis between Islamic teachings, especially Sufi thought, and Javanese culture and mysticism allowed their teachings to be easily accepted by Javanese people.

This model of religious life encouraged Javanese people at the time to be able to accept and respect differences in religion and belief, i.e., people could respect others without defying their religious beliefs. It has been noted that there was no tension between the Javanese and the Chinese who for centuries lived among the Javanese and maintained their belief as Confucians. Hatred of other faiths and certain ethnic groups, such as the Chinese, did not occur in Javanese society in the early period of the Islamic Mataram Kingdom. It even has been noted that the Chinese fought alongside the Javanese against the Dutch East Indies Company or VOC (*Vereenigde Oost-Indische Compagnie*) in

---

10. Van Doorn-Harder and de Jong, "The Pilgrimage to Tembayat," 492.

11. Ricklefs, *Islamisation and Its Opponents in Java*, 7.

12. Ach Nashichuddin, "Sufism in Java: The Meeting Point between Sufism and Javanese Mysticism," *Harakah* 8:1 (2006), 43–51, 46–48.

the 18th century.[13] Although religion played a role in the formation of community identity, it did not cause religious polarization or stir hatred towards other religions or certain ethnic groups.

3. SPREADING CHRISTIAN FAITH AND POLARIZATION IN THE CHRISTIAN MISSION

When it comes to Christianity, until the middle of the 19th century there was no attempt to spread the gospel to the people in the Ngayogyakarta Hadiningrat area. There were, however, meetings between Christians and adherents of other religions, such as Muslims. The encounter between Christianity and Islam in the Sultan's territory began with the arrival of the VOC in Java. Article 36 of the *Confessio Belgica*, the Dutch Confession of Faith, required not only the establishment of a church but also that the government participate in spreading the gospel, resulting in the first Protestant missions in what is now Indonesia. Fulfilling the obligation of article 36 of the Confession of Faith, the VOC tried to provide appropriate church services for European Christians in its territory during its trade activities in Indonesia. Wherever they set up settlements, a church was established. Therefore, the existence of Christianity under VOC rule could not be separated from the influence of companies in an area.[14]

In the same way, the company's authority could not be separated from the influence of Islam in the area. When the VOC came to Java, Islam had an effective influence in society, especially in the area of the Islamic Mataram Kingdom. The influence of Islam was manifest in the identity of the people who combined Java with Islam: 'being Javanese means being Muslim.' Nevertheless, Javanese people remained open to other beliefs. This is evidenced by encounters and mixes between local beliefs and Hinduism, Buddhism, and Islam. Because Javanese culture and religion were integrated into the soul of Javanese society and because Javanese culture and religion could be appreciated and recognized by Muslims, Islam was also accepted. This resulted in various approaches and understandings of Islamic teachings, as Clifford Geertz explained. Geertz argued that the Javanese with five main occupations, namely farmer, petty trader, independent artisan, manual laborer, and white-collar clerk, teacher or administrator, could also be grouped according

---

13. See Daradjadi, *Geger Pacinan 1740–1743: Persekutuan Tionghoa-Jawa Melawan VOC* (Chinese-Javanese Alliance against VOC) (Jakarta: PT Kompas Media Nusantara, 2013).

14. See Yusak Soleiman, *Pangumbaran Ing Bang Wetan: The Dutch Reformed Church in Late Eighteenth Century Java—an Eastern Adventure* (Jakarta: Sekolah Tinggi Teologi Jakarta & BPK Gunung Mulia, 2012), 59.

to worldview—according to religious beliefs, ethical preferences, and political ideologies. He argued that this produced three main types of cultures that reflect the moral organization of Javanese culture and shape their behavior in all areas of life, namely *abangan*, *santri* and *priyayi*.[15] Compared to Islam, the Christian mission failed to embrace Javanese culture and religion for fear of syncretism. The idea of syncretism showed more of a Western perspective in the missionary era, in so far as the missionaries judged other values contained in the local context, especially in local beliefs, as inferior to those contained in Christian doctrine. They forced people to adhere to 'true doctrine' from a Western perspective.

For the VOC, Java was very important in relation to its economic interests. Therefore, they made Java a province with its own governor that was different from the central government in Batavia. Due to its significant position, the company was very careful in granting permission to Christian pastors to spread the gospel in the region. In the Dutch view, the Christian mission would not fit into Javanese society because Java was synonymous with Islam. Prince Diponegoro's attack on the Dutch in 1825 led them to increasingly believe that the Javanese and their religion, Islam, should not be disturbed.[16] The consequences would affect the stability of the Dutch colonial government. For this reason, evangelism efforts could not be carried out without the permission of the Dutch company or government.

It is clear that although companies officially had responsibility for spreading the gospel, they ignored this responsibility. They were more interested in trading. The authority, influence, and monopoly of VOC business over Java was increased. Therefore, they constantly tried to control two kingdoms, Surakarta and Yogyakarta. The politics of such business created negative Javanese thinking towards the company and people began to identify Christianity with the company. Because of such thinking, Javanese people were not very open to Christianity. It is not surprising that many resisted the VOC and made efforts to expel it from Java.[17] Yet, the company's influence grew dominant and forced the Sultan

---

15. See Clifford Geertz, *The Religion of Java* (Chicago: The University of Chicago, 1976), 4–5. Abangan are a group of Muslims who do not strictly practice the teachings or rules that have been prescribed in Islam. *Santri* are Muslims who adhere to the Islamic religion in *pesantren* (Islamic boarding schools). They have adherence to rituals such as prayer and fasting, and little attention to animism and mysticism. *Priyayi* is often understood to be more related to social status. Some *priyayi* practice Islam like *santri* while others practice religion in a syncretistic way such as *abangan*.

16. J.D. Wolterbeek, *Babad Zending di Pulau Jawa* (Chronicle of the Mission on the Island of Java) (Yogyakarta: Taman Pustaka Kristen (Angotta IKAPI), 1995), 7.

17. See Merle Calvin Ricklefs, *A History of Modern Indonesia Since C. 1300* (Hampshire: The Macmillan Press Ltd, 1993), 81–83.

of Surakarta and Yogyakarta to divide his kingdom into four powers. Even now, Surakarta Palace is divided into the thrones of Pakubuwono and Mangkunegaran, while in Yogyakarta Hamengkubuwono must share its power with Pakualaman.

The companies did, in fact, provide Christian ministry for its own European employees. Therefore, they sent many pastors and supported them financially just to maintain the Christian faith of their employees. The ministers were not allowed to spread the gospel among the Javanese. The company and then the Dutch government worried that the spread of the gospel in Java would stir up hatred among Javanese, especially Muslims, and potentially disrupt the stability of the current government. Wolterbeek says that during the 18th and 19th centuries Dutch Christians made no attempt to preach the gospel to the Javanese. Therefore, the Dutch did not express a deep commitment to article 36 of the Dutch Confession of Faith. Nevertheless, laypeople took more initiative to introduce Christianity and preach the gospel among those around them.[18] In Central Java and Yogyakarta, famous local people such as Christine Petronella Philips-Stevens, Reksodiwongso or Abisai, Tarub, and Kyai Shadrach did attempt to do missionary work. They introduced Christianity initially in the area around Purworejo and from there Christianity spread to Yogyakarta.

Starting from Bagelen in Purworejo, through the efforts of Kyai Sadrach and his students, Protestant Christianity began to spread to Yogyakarta, especially to the Pakualaman areas of Stamps, Temon, and Selong.[19] The people who received the gospel were baptized in Bagelen by Jacob Wilhelm. After Mas Suryahasmara Natataroena from Pakualaman was baptized on May 30, 1887, his house became a gathering place for people in Yogyakarta to listen to the gospel.[20] This continued until Petronella Hospital was established in 1900 and provided a place of worship for them. On August 13, 1889, several people were secretly baptized by Jacob Wilhelm. A little over a year later, on January 21, 1891, the Dutch government allowed Christian ministers to spread the gospel in the sultanate publicly. Until 1919, Christians and churches in Yogyakarta and throughout Java were under the responsibility of the

---

18. See Hadi Purnomo and M. Suprihadi Sastrosupono, *Gereja-Gereja Kristen Jawa* (GKJ): *Benih yang Tumbuh dan Bberkembang di Tanah Jawa* (Javanese Christian Churches (GKJ): Seeds That Grow and Grow in the Land of Java) (Yogyakarta: Taman Pustaka Kristen, 1988), 15–16.

19. Sigit Heru Soekotjo and Agoes Widhartono, *Menjadi Garam dan Terang Kehidupan: 100 Tahun GKJ Gondokusuman* (Becoming Salt and Light of Life: 100 Years of GKJ Gondokusuman) (Yogyakarta: Taman Pustaka Kristen & GKJ Gondokusuman, 2013), 11–15.

20. Jan Sihar Aritonang and Karel Steenbrink (eds.), *A History of Christianity in Indonesia* (Leiden and Boston: Brill, 2008), 674.

church authorities in the classis of Amsterdam.[21] The Yogyakarta Church was responsible for churches in Purworejo, Kebumen, Gombong, and Banyumas through its services. All church-related needs, including church diaconia or service to the poor, were ultimately the responsibility of the classis of Amsterdam.

The Dutch view of the local community and how they understood Javanese people with their identity, culture, religion, and community, had an impact on the spread of Christianity in Java. One important issue until the end of the 19th century related to whether it was necessary to change identity when becoming a Christian: a newly baptized person would be given a new name, usually taken from the bible. Radin Abas after being baptized was named Sadrach, after the character in the Old Testament Book of Daniel. Since then, he has been known as Kyai Sadrach, using the ancient Hindu title preceding the biblical one, now generally used by Islamic teachers in Java. After being baptized, Reksodiwongso was named Abishai, following the name of King David's nephew in 2 Samuel. Natataroena was named Yozef, after Jacob's son in Genesis.

The Dutch also expected anyone who had been baptized to give up his or her own tradition. They could no longer dress like Javanese and were forbidden to watch shadow puppet theater or listen to gamelan. Men could not have long hair. All these things were considered incompatible with Christian teachings and lifestyles, although this was not actually Christian but rather a Western (Dutch) perspective. Missionaries also regarded circumcision as a non-Christian tradition and forbade Christians from being circumcised. Jacob Wilhelm, for example, once protested against Natataroena who circumcised his son despite being baptized as a Christian.[22] A person who practiced circumcision was considered to be in violation of God's law and in danger of being punished by God. The change of identity required from the Christian mission led to polarization in society and made it difficult for Javanese people to be accepted by their own communities after becoming Christians. People tended to think that becoming Christian meant becoming Western. That is why a lay missionary in East Java, Coenrad Laurens Coolen, forbade his disciples from being baptized. Coolen himself was of European descent from his Russian father. However, he did appreciate the Javanese culture he was taught by his Javanese mother who was a noblewoman of the Mataram Kingdom.

The decision of the Synod of Dordrecht (1618) about the baptism of children born to Dutch fathers and indigenous mothers, especially

---

21. A. Algra, *De Gereformeerde Kerken in Nederlands-Indië, Indonesië (1877–1961)* (The Reformed Chrches in Dutch East Indies) (Franeker: Wever, 1967), 101.

22. Aritonang and Steenbrink, *A History of Christianity in Indonesia*, 674.

non-Christians,[23] contributed to polarization in society. It was decided that these children should not be baptized until they themselves learned and accepted Christian teachings and professed their own faith. Some members of the synod meeting actually opposed the decision. They argued that these children should be considered part of a Christian family because their father was Dutch or because they could be adopted and baptized as another Christian child. However, the majority of the synod rejected this position and adopted a view which distinguishes between children born to mixed couples and those with two Dutch parents. In their perspective, only children born from families with two "civilized and humane" Christian parents could be baptized. Yet, in the mission field, some pastors baptized children adopted by Christian families. In their perspective, this was in line with biblical teachings.[24]

Another impact of the 1618 Dordrecht was the separation between the Sacrament of Baptism and the Sacrament of the Eucharist or the Lord's Supper. Dutch missionaries in Indonesia allowed people from other religions to be baptized and participate in Christian services. However, they were not permitted to receive Holy Communion. These (new) Christians were considered not yet fully Christian and were therefore forbidden to take part in the Lord's Supper. Therefore, Christianity itself gave rise to different classes of Christians in society. The decision was in fact contrary to Christian theology. Indonesian Church historian Soleiman has argued that the Dutch Reformed Church sacrificed its own theology.[25] The reason for this was a need to develop a social order that was in line with their Western concept of civilization. This situation caused the number of church members to continue to grow, as being Christian was no longer hampered by doctrines that restricted people from receiving the sacrament. In 1648 and 1736 the separation of the sacraments was discontinued, based on recommendations from the Faculty of Theology of Leiden University. Nevertheless, separation remained. Therefore, the separation of the sacraments in Indonesian churches up to this day must be understood as a legacy of the thinking of the Dutch Reformed Church of the 17th and 18th centuries.

---

23. Soleiman, *Pangumbaran Ing Bang Wetan*, 39–40.
24. Soleiman, *Pangumbaran Ing Bang Wetan*, 40.
25. Soleiman, *Pangumbaran Ing Bang Wetan*, 46.

4. Christian Schools and Hospital in the Context of Religious Polarization

The spread of the gospel through schools and hospitals was a solution to overcome the difficulties of preaching the gospel among Javanese people. Therefore, it is clear that the establishment of schools and hospitals, including in Yogyakarta, was not solely aimed at providing education and better health care to the community. Initially, it was a form of evangelism as well. Bethesda Hospital and the BOPKRI School, now well known, were part of the missionary work in the past. Although Christianity came later to Yogyakarta, compared to Purworejo or Semarang, Yogyakarta became one of the important mission centers, including education and health care. For Catholics, the transfer of the mission center from Muntilan to Yogyakarta contributed to the significance of the city as a cultural capital in Central Java. Meanwhile, Yogyakarta became important to Protestant churches because it was home to Christian schools, hospitals, and theological seminaries (Keuchenius School). Keuchenius was founded in 1906 and became today's Duta Wacana Christian University in 1985. Schools and hospitals will continue to be essential to the missionary work of Protestant churches in the future.

Following the advice of the Reverend Lion Cachet, *Nederlandse Gereformeerde Zendingsvereniging* (NGZV; Dutch Reformed Mission Association) sent Dr. J.G. Scheurer in 1893 to work in the medical field. After moving from Purworejo to Solo and returning to Purworejo for various purposes, Dr. Scheurer moved to Yogyakarta on March 17, 1897. He settled in the Bintaran area near the Sultan's Palace, but lived among ordinary people. Scheurer made one part of his bamboo house into a health clinic.[26] On one part of the clinic wall, he hung an inscription in Javanese script that read: *"Gusti Jesus punika Juru Wilujeng ingkang sedjatos"* (The Lord Jesus is the True Savior). Scheurer read the text to his patients before starting his service. He was known for helping people without expecting a penny from them, and was called *"dokter tulung"* (volunteer doctor). His services even caught the attention of Sultan Hamengku Buwono VII and his court.

In 1899, Sultan Hamengku Buwono VII loaned 28,400 m2 of the Sultan's land to *Zending der Gereformeerde Kerken in Nederland* (ZGKN; Dutch Reformed Churches Mission) to establish a hospital. To express his sincere support to ZGKN to build the hospital, the Sultan sent a letter to Patih Raden Adipati Danoeredjo. In his letter, he explained that hospitals should also provide free services to 100 people. Reverend Van Coeverden Andriani provided financial support for the construction

---

26. Soekotjo and Widhartono, *Menjadi garam dan terang kehidupan*, 21–26.

of the hospital. Therefore, the hospital was named Petronella Hospital, after his wife. The hospital officially opened on March 1, 1900. This health service extended to the areas around Yogyakarta through the establishment of supporting hospitals such as Wates and Candisewu. Petronella Hospital was also able to educate indigenous nurses to support the hospital.

Christian schools, as well as hospitals, make a significant contribution to evangelism. Their important role was confirmed in the 52nd article of *Prataning Pasamuwan* (Church Commandments). Earnest efforts were made to use Christian schools as a means of evangelism. By 1938, more than 100 schools were established and managed by *zending* or Christian missions, with Dutch, local and Chinese teachers.[27] The Javanese Christian Church (GKJ) continued to show its sincere commitment to serving the community through schools and health clinics. The Synod Assemblies I, IV and XI expressly stated that the primary purpose of Christian education was to spread the gospel message. To ensure they were run effectively, Christian school foundations were responsible for managing and organizing the Christian schools. In its function, the school still went hand in hand with the church as a partner in carrying out church services and testifying to the community. Therefore, although the Christian school was managed by the Christian school management, it remained closely related to the church. This inseparable relationship was confirmed in the 1969 Synod XI Session. Thus, institutionally the school was not directly related to the church, but functionally the Christian school was a means of church service and testimony. Therefore, Christian schools remained the responsibility of the church. Later, the Javanese church decided that the church should not be directly responsible for schools. Local relations with Christian schools were managed by the Education Foundation of the Indonesian Christian Education Agency or BOPKRI.

The Christian School and Petronella Hospital (now Bethesda Hospital) were established at a time when education and health care were the primary needs of Indonesians, but very few institutions focused specifically on those needs. This has changed. Nowadays, schools and hospitals serve all citizens regardless of their social or religious status. Many prominent people have been educated in Christian schools or have received medical care from Petronella Hospital. In addition, Christian schools such as BOPKRI High School and Bethesda Hospital provide high-quality services. Muslims in Yogyakarta are the majority and many of their children attend Christian schools. They visit Christian hospitals such as Petronella Hospital to get medical treatment as well.

---

27. Purnomo and Sastrosupono, *Gereja-Gereja Kristen Jawa* (GKj), 110–11.

Sultan Hamengkubuwono's royal family received medical treatment from the hospital as well. It is part of the historical relationship between the sultanate family of Yogyakarta and Petronella Hospital. At the time, the Sultan's family sent some of their children to Christian schools. For example, Gusti Kanjeng Ratu Mangkubumi, the first daughter and possible successor of Sri Sultan Hamengkubuwono X, attended BOPKRI High School 1, which is one of the Christian schools founded by the church's mission.

5. RISE OF INTOLERANCE

Today the situation has become more polarized. There are many schools and hospitals established based on a particular religion. Some schools were established not only for certain religious people but specifically for members of certain sects. Therefore, the challenges experienced by schools and hospitals are increasingly complex, especially when education and health care are associated with religious issues. The supposed threat of Christianization through Christian schools and hospitals has also caused many people to choose not to have their children receive education at these schools or receive medical care from Christian hospitals.

Religious polarization has increased in Indonesian society especially since the emergence of Islamic fundamentalist groups, since the fall of the New Order regime. Such groups, such as Hizbut Tahrir, feel that they must build and strengthen their Islamic identity.[28] The rise of religious radical groups has sparked polarization in society and poses challenges to Christian schools and hospitals to show support and respect for religious differences. For example, the Yogyakarta Islamic Community Forum (FUI), a radical Islamist group, has introduced an anti-Christian school movement.[29] The reason for the establishment of the movement, called G-30-S, is based on the assumption that the faith of many Muslims attending Christian schools has decreased. The influence of anti-Christian groups such as FUI has had a crucial impact on Muslims' views on Christian schools. They have pushed Muslim families not to send their children to Christian schools like BOPKRI because they are supposed to not be open to all religions. They warned that their children would become apostates if they attended Christian schools. The results of a Syarif Hidayatullah State Islamic University (UIN) study in Jakarta on the spread of intolerance in schools demonstrate, for example, that teachers play a leading role in encouraging intolerant attitudes among

---

28. See Institute for Policy Analysis of Conflict, "Mothers to Bombers: The Evolution of Indonesian Women Extremists" (Institute for Policiy Analysis of Conflict, January 31, 2017).

29. See Imam Subkhan, *Hiruk Pikuk Wacana Pluralisme Di Yogya* (The Hustle and Bustle of Pluralism Discourse in Yogyakarta) (Yogyakarta: Kanisius, 2007), 110–13.

students.[30] This shows the urgency of the issue of religious polarization in schools.

The social obligation for Muslim women and girls to wear a headscarf or *hijab* and Muslim-style clothing, even in school, has become a form of political identity creation that also reinforces religious polarization. My colleague told me that his children had trouble playing with their Muslim cousins. The teacher reminded them not to play or connect with people of different religions. This type of polarization even occurs in public schools whose rules should not be based on a particular religion.

Ustad Isa Anshori, a young Muhammadiyah figure, considers any form of Christianization through Christian schools as an activity that Muhammadiyah must oppose.[31] According to him, Muhammadiyah should address this by applying the same method that Christians do. In fact, Muhammadiyah adopted the Christian da'wah model by establishing many schools, hospitals, health centers, and orphanages. They apply this method to draw parents' attention to their children's belief in the Islamic faith. They argue that many Muslim parents tend to ignore their children's faith education by sending them to Christian schools. The chairman of the BOPKRI Purnawan Herdiyanto Foundation said there is a strong Islamist movement that discourages Muslim students from entering Christian schools. The emergence of the movement had a significant impact on the decline in the number of students in Christian schools, especially in BOPKRI schools.[32] Many BOPKRI schools have been closed because there were no more students. The quality of unstandardized schools and low teacher pay standards are another reason for the closure of some BOPKRI schools.

The emergence of the issue of Christianization cannot be discussed without being critical of the model or approach of religious teaching in Christian schools and hospitals. Some Christians, both in schools and in hospitals, still view themselves from the perspective of the old Christian mission. They feel a responsibility to introduce others to Christianity and make them believe in Christ or convert them to Christianity. Therefore, their religious teachings are still focused on Christian teachings. The majority of BOPKRI schools, for example, still adhere to the conventional religious teaching model. In this model, the teachers teach all students about Christianity. They ignore the religious differences of students.

---

30. Rizki Fachriansyah, "Religious Intolerance Thriving among School Teachers: Survey," *The Jakarta Post*, October 2018, https://www.thejakartapost.com/news/2018/10/18/religious-intolerance-thriving-among-school-teachers-survey.html.

31. Isa Anshori, "Respon Muhamdiyah Terhadap Sekolah Kristen" (Muhammadiyah's Response to Christian Schools), (accessed July 3, 2019), http://pkuulilalbab-uika.blogspot.com/2013/04/respon-muhamdiyah-terhadap-sekolah.html.

32. Interview with Purnawan Herdiyanto, Friday, June 28, 2019.

In 1999, the Minister of Education and Minister of Religion issued a decree on the obligation of schools to introduce religious education according to the religion of students. This regulation was affirmed in 2000 through the Decree of the Director General of Education. The decision heightened tensions among private schools other than Islamic schools. The government even prepared sanctions for schools that did not apply the rules. Schools that do not apply the rule will be closed. Under these rules, 150 students of SMK BOPKRI, STM BOPKRI III Kulonprogo decided to leave school. They felt that the school did not want to apply the rule.[33] However, the Department of Education in Yogyakarta took advantage of the situation and did not encourage schools to solve the problem. Instead, they set up a new school to accommodate those students. Since then, banners have often been hung near Christian schools to remind Muslims that they should refrain from attending Christian schools. It is prohibited by Islamic law, according to the intolerant group that hung the banner. Currently, some BOPKRI schools have developed other religious education models that put more emphasis on teaching diverse and universal religious values to all students.

The issue of intolerance is also at stake in the medical world. The emergence and influence of religiously intolerant groups is found among doctors who do not want to serve patients due to religious differences. The emergence of Sharia enforcement efforts in Indonesia sparked discussion in the community about the possibility of the emergence of government regulations that will regulate health treatment according to one's religion. The public is concerned that due to this regulation, among other things, certain religious people will only be willing to be treated by a doctor of the same faith. So far these kinds of conversations have only been rumors. Nevertheless, in Indonesia there is the ability to establish "sharia hospitals." Secretary of the Fatwa Commission of the Indonesian Ulama Council (MUI) Asrorun Niam Sholeh has said that *Sharia* hospitals are needed for the peace of mind of the people in carrying out worship by providing services in accordance with Islamic provisions.[34]

Such issues have arisen since governments, especially the House of Representatives, drafted regulations for governing religious life. In fact, internal affairs of religion should not be regulated by the government. According to Reverend Fendi Susanto, pastor of Bethesda Hospital, the hospital does not discriminate against patients simply because

---

33. Darmaningtyas, *Pendidikan Rusak-Rusakan* (Yogyakarta: LKiS, 2005), 63–64.

34. Rosmha Widiyani, "Viral Rumah Sakit Syariah, Apa Bedanya dengan RS Biasa?" (Sharia Hospital Viral, What's the Difference with Ordinary Hospital?), detikHealth, (accessed October 20, 2020), https://health.detik.com/berita-detikhealth/d-4583924/viral-rumah-sakit-syariah-apa-bedanya-dengan-rs-biasa.

of differences in religious identity. Nevertheless, Bethesda Hospital is suspected of Christianizing through daily pastoral visits. Some Muslims are offended by the fact that the pastor visits and prays for Muslim patients. They regard such visits as part of Christianization even though it is routine and part of the spiritual and pastoral care provided to patients served by the hospital. Reverend Fendi Susanto said that during the visit the pastor will pray for a Muslim or any other religious convert only if the patient asks the pastor to do so. In terms of spiritual and pastoral care, the hospital applies other policies to its employees and medical staff. All staff and medical personnel, regardless of their religion, are required to follow the spiritual care offered by the pastoral section of Bethesda Hospital. Reverend Fendi stressed that it was part of the council's decision to consider Bethesda hospital as a Christian hospital. Nevertheless, Bethesda Hospital consistently allows employees of various religions, especially Islam, to carry out their religious obligations. For example, Bethesda Hospital provides prayer rooms for employees, nurses, and patients' families.[35]

6. Closing Remarks

Churches today are called to respond wisely to religious polarization. They cannot resolve this situation simply by asserting their position or carrying out church services. In predominantly Christian areas, such as Manokwari-Papua, polarization occurred due to a draft regulation that made Manokwari "a Christian city" (March 2007).[36] This would not be possible in Yogyakarta. What is more, strengthening one's own position doesn't solve the problem of religious polarization. The Church needs to be more open to embracing others to show the Church's respect for difference.

Polarization in hospitals may not be as complex as in schools, but religious polarization sometimes occurs in hospitals as well. In Indonesia, religious polarization currently spreads through education and medical work. Schools and hospitals should be exempt from any polarizing motives, especially religious polarization. Therefore, the church's mission through education and health care can no longer be developed in ways or methods that produce uncomfortable feelings of Christianization in others. That is, schools and hospitals should not become media of evangelization for Christians to increase the number of

---

35. Interview with Rev. Fendi Susanto, Tuesday, July 2, 2019.

36. "Perda Injil Manokwari, Antara Sejarah Kekristenan Dan 'Nuansa Intoleransi'" (The Manokwari Gospel Regulation, Between the History of Christianity and 'Natural Intolerance'), January 10, 2019, sec. Indonesia, https://www.bbc.com/indonesia/indonesia-46813787. Melissa Crouch, *Law and Religion in Indonesia: Conflict and the Courts in West Java* (London: Routledge, 2013), 56.

Christians. It would be more meaningful if schools and hospitals focused more on social services than trying to covert people to Christianity. Therefore, Christian ministry through education and health care should show appreciation for differences by promoting humanitarian values that must be upheld by all human beings. Introducing and upholding humanitarian values is not only in line with Christian values and the teachings of Christ, but also a way for Christians to promote and encourage people to live peacefully and appreciate differences. In their schools and hospitals, Christians must commit to combating religious polarization, as it only undermines human relationships and values. This spirit needs to be nurtured and this can be started by Christians in Yogyakarta. Thus, Christians in Yogyakarta must support and strengthen Yogyakarta's reputation as a city of tolerance.

BIBLIOGRAPHY

Algra, A. *De Gereformeerde Kerken in Nederlands-Indië, Indonesië (1877–1961)* (The Reformed Chrches in Dutch East Indies). Franeker: Wever, 1967.

Anshori, Isa. "Respon Muhamdiyah Terhadap Sekolah Kristen" (Muhammadiyah's Response to Christian Schools). Accessed July 3, 2019. http://pkuulilalbab-uika.blogspot.com/2013/04/respon-muhamdiyah-terhadap-sekolah.html.

Aritonang, Jan Sihar and Karel Steenbrink. Eds. *A History of Christianity in Indonesia*. Leiden and Boston: Brill, 2008.

Boechari. *Melacak Sejarah Kuno Indonesia lewat Prasasti* (Tracing ancient Indonesian history through inscriptions). Jakarta: Kepustakaan Populer Gramedia, 2018.

Crouch, Melissa. *Law and Religion in Indonesia: Conflict and the Courts in West Java*. London: Routledge, 2013.

Daradjadi. *Geger Pacinan 1740–1743: Persekutuan Tionghoa-Jawa Melawan VOC* (Chinese-Javanese Alliance against VOC). Jakarta: PT Kompas Media Nusantara, 2013.

Darmaningtyas. *Pendidikan Rusak-Rusakan*. Yogyakarta: LKiS, 2005.

Doorn-Harder, Nelly van, and Kees de Jong. "The Pilgrimage to Tembayat: Tradition and Revival in Islamic Mysticism in Contemporary Indonesia." In *The Blackwell Companion to Contemporary Islamic Thought*, ed. Ibrahim M. Abu-Rabi', 491–92. Malden: Blackwell Publishing, 2006.

Fachriansyah, Rizki. "Religious Intolerance Thriving among School Teachers: Survey." *The Jakarta Post*, October 2018. https://www.thejakartapost.com/news/2018/10/18/religious-intolerance-thriving-among-school-teachers-survey.html.

Geertz, Clifford. *The Religion of Java*. Chicago: The University of Chicago, 1976.

Institute for Policy Analysis of Conflict, "Mothers to Bombers: The Evolution of Indonesian Women Extremists." Institute for Policiy Analysis of Conflict, January 31, 2017.

Nashichuddin, Ach. "Sufism in Java: The Meeting Point between Sufism and Javanese Mysticism." *Harakah* 8:1 (2006): 43–51.

"Perda Injil Manokwari, Antara Sejarah Kekristenan Dan 'Nuansa Intoleransi'" (The Manokwari Gospel Regulation, Between the History of Christianity and 'Natural Intolerance'), January 10, 2019, sec. Indonesia, https://www.bbc.com/indonesia/indonesia-46813787.

Purnomo, Hadi and M. Suprihadi Sastrosupono. *Gereja-Gereja Kristen Jawa (GKJ): Benih yang Tumbuh dan Bberkembang di Tanah Jawa* (Javanese Christian Churches (GKJ): Seeds That Grow and Grow in the Land of Java). Yogyakarta: Taman Pustaka Kristen, 1988.

Ricklefs, Merle Calvin. *A History of Modern Indonesia Since C. 1300*. Hampshire: The Macmillan Press Ltd, 1993.

Ricklefs, Merle Calvin. *Islamisation and Its Opponents in Java: A Political, Social, Cultural and Religious History, C. 1930 to the Present*. Singapore: NUS Press, 2012.

Ricklefs, Merle Calvin. *Mystic Synthesis in Java: A History of Islamization from the Fourteenth to the Early Nineteenth Centuries*. Norwalk: EastBridge, 2006.

Soekotjo, Sigit Heru and Agoes Widhartono. *Menjadi Garam dan Terang Kehidupan: 100 Tahun GKJ Gondokusuman* (Becoming Salt and Light of Life: 100 Years of GKJ Gondokusuman). Yogyakarta: Taman Pustaka Kristen & GKJ Gondokusuman, 2013.

Soleiman, Yusak. *Pangumbaran Ing Bang Wetan: The Dutch Reformed Church in Late Eighteenth Century Java—an Eastern Adventure*. Jakarta: Sekolah Tinggi Teologi Jakarta & BPK Gunung Mulia, 2012.

Subkhan, Imam. *Hiruk Pikuk Wacana Pluralisme Di Yogya* (The Hustle and Bustle of Pluralism Discourse in Yogyakarta). Yogyakarta: Kanisius, 2007.

Widiyani, Rosmha. "Viral Rumah Sakit Syariah, Apa Bedanya dengan RS Biasa?" (Sharia Hospital Viral, What's the Difference with Ordinary Hospital?), detikHealth. Accessed October 20, 2020. https://health.detik.com/berita-detikhealth/d-4583924/viral-rumah-sakit-syariah-apa-bedanya-dengan-rs-biasa.

Wolterbeek, J.D. *Babad Zending di Pulau Jawa* (Chronicle of the Mission on the Island of Java). Yogyakarta: Taman Pustaka Kristen (Angotta IKAPI), 1995.

CHAPTER 11
ELECTION AND HOPE: VAN RULER AND DORT
Allan J. Janssen[†]

1. INTRODUCTION

What can we hope? What hope can the church offer as gospel? What hope in the face of climate change that threatens the very existence of life on our planet? What hope in a world drowning in refugees fleeing the horrors of violence? What hope as authoritarian, nationalistic forces portend the worst of the last centuries terrors? We can, of course, proclaim the great promises of scripture from the pulpit. The biblical narrative has a great deal to say about the future. Much of it is in image and symbol, but there is much as well that points to God's work that touches our current lives that points beyond today to a tomorrow that exceeds our temporal existence. But on what basis? What makes this a 'well-founded hope,' as Hendrikus Berkhof once put it?[1] Is what we say no more than a pipe-dream, a hope against hope? There is something about the human creature that won't let go of hope. But is there, shall we say, an ontological basis for hope, not a hope based in the 'being' of reality, but on a firmer basis, the basis of the one Christians' confess as God?

In this contribution, I intend to explore the ground for hope by examining the first head of doctrine of the Canons of Dort, the doctrine of election. This might seem odd at first glance. Why this old confession?[2] And why this one in particular, steeped as it was (and to the extent it is still under discussion still is) in conflict? Dort may be old, few may refer to it in the course of everyday ministry, but it stands as a monument in the confessional history of the Reformed churches. And it poses a question that cannot be avoided: to what extent if any does the human participate in his or her salvation? Or: to what extent do we participate in the establishment of the foundation of a human hope for the future—

---

1. Hendrikus Berkhof, *Well-founded Hope* (Richmond: John Knox, 1969).

2. Actually, the Canons of Dort are not a confession but an appendix to the Belgic Confession, clarifying particularly Article 16 on election.

or as we must now amend this, of the planetary hope for the future? To say "if it's going to be, it's up to me" is an answer. But does it hold? The Remonstrants gave one answer to that question. Dort another.

In fact, Dort asks whether reliance on human will and action to effect salvation in fact works out. Dort perceives the reality that at base the human will is distorted to the extent that it cannot find its way to salvation. Simple observation should be sufficient evidence that our willing has led the world to war, oppression, racism, and environmental degradation. Dort describes the human at the edge of ruin, no future lest it be with God.

That, however, is not the 'spirit of the age.' We have been socialized, trained from day one, to understand the human as our own project. Yale theologian Kathryn Tanner put it this way:

> Finance-dominated capitalism encourages people to think of themselves in the same way that profit-maximizing businesses think of them: their persons represent capital that must be put to maximally productive use. Simply put: each person must take individual responsibility for making the most out of his or her own life, in a life project that spans the whole of life, both at work and outside it. If one fails at such a project, one has no one but oneself to blame.[3]

Our lives are our own project; if we don't succeed, it's our own fault. Is that where our hope rests, with ourselves? If this might even be the case with the individual human—and for a vast proportion of humanity this is not even a possibility—can we begin to follow this claim with the human community as a whole? At the least, the Canons offer a response in their insistence on election.

There is another reason that Dort might seem to be fallow ground for hope. *Prima facie*, Dort offers not hope but its very opposite. After all, on a superficial reading of the doctrine of election, hope is the last thing that comes to mind. God has decided the number and names of the elect and overlooked the rest. And that's that. What more is there to say? The game is over before it started.

I argue quite the opposite. In the doctrine of election, we are met by a God who transcends our knowing. In fact, because election points to the eternal nature of God and God's good favor, it opens us to a future that is not dependent on the human, but one that emerges from the heart of the God who engages creation from within God's own self. And that is the basis for a well-founded hope, one that finds its substance in the action of God in history.

To assist me in this inquiry, I turn to the twenty-century Dutch

---

3. Kathryn Tanner, "How Finance Capitalism Deforms Us," *Christian Century*, January 16, 2019, 30.

theologian A.A. van Ruler (1908–1970). Van Ruler rather famously held to the doctrine of double predestination. While he left a number of reflections on election in works published in his life-time, the publication of his collected works (now in its sixth volume) includes early extensive studies on election itself. It is these studies that I primarily consult with occasional forays into publications available during his life time. Election describes the action of the Trinitarian God. It is the Father, Son, and Spirit who act as God turns towards God's beloved creation in love.[4]

This essay researches Van Ruler not to offer a comprehensive explication of his doctrine of election, although I need to survey its broader scope. Rather, it is to ask how Van Rulers insights on election give us new insight into how we might read Dort on election as a theological foundation for hope. Can this enable us to confess Dort in the twenty-first century as an "historic and faithful witness" to the word of God?[5]

2. VAN RULER ON ELECTION

Van Ruler did not consider election to be the central doctrine in theology. He called it a *hulpleer*, a "helping doctrine." He compared it to the relation between a potato and salt.[6] The potato is a food that provides the body with sustenance. The salt gives it flavor. By itself, without the salt, the potato will keep the body alive, but there will be little to savor in the eating of it. Conversely, salt without the food makes little sense at all. The 'potato,' the food, is the doctrine of grace. At the heart of election is "[t]he power of God's grace over the human soul in which it is God who decides the matter of eternal salvation and also accomplishes it, so that it does not depend on the human."[7] In discussing the method of approach to the doctrine of election, Van Ruler says that we do not begin with the consideration of the counsel of God, but "with the description of predestination as a *hulpleer* of the doctrine of grace, to accept the definition of

---

4. This is early Van Ruler (1941–1942) who is still quite Barthian in his approach, and at the very time that he is moving from a Christological approach to a pneumatological one; see A.A. van Ruler, *Verzameld Werk*, Deel 4B: *Christus, de Geest en het heil* (Collected Works, Part 4B: Christ, the Spirit and salvation), ed. D. van Keulen (Boekencentrum: Zoetermeer, 2011), 109. Ironically, this is just as Barth is turning to his famous Christological approach to the doctrine of election. See Suzanne McDonald, *Re-Imaging Election: Divine Election as Representing God to Other & Others to God* (Eerdmans: Grand Rapids, 2010), chapter 2.

5. The phrase "historic and faithful witness" is taken from the "Declaration for Ministers of Word and Sacrament" in the Reformed Church in America. The Declaration can be found in the Reformed church's *Book of Church Order*, 130, http://images.rca.org/docs/bco/2019BCO.pdf.

6. Van Ruler, *Verzameld Werk* 4B, 745.

7. Van Ruler, *Verzameld Werk* 4B, 744. All translations are those of the author.

'in Christ,' so to approach the notion of God's decrees and counsel."[8]

But grace gets us only so far. Because grace is not a 'something': "grace is not a thing, not a something, not a power, but *favor Dei*."[9] Grace is a way of talking about how God acts, that is that God's actions are not contingent upon human actions. That God acts in Christ and through the Spirit originates purely from within God, and that God's actions are for the good of God's creation, including humans, is, in shorthand, *grace*. Indeed, in Van Ruler's earliest elaboration of the doctrine of election, he spends a good deal of space on the nature of grace.

Election is the 'salt.' How, then, does the doctrine of election 'spice up' the doctrine of grace? It does so by reminding us of the subject of grace, and the nature of that subject. It is a way of claiming that behind grace is a God who acts. In discussing the meaning of the doctrine of election, Van Ruler says that the doctrine reminds us that we have to do with the living and active God, not the powers of the universe nor idols. However, this is a God who must be revealed to us. This is not the God whom we can access through our own devices. This active God is not a partner of the human but acts transcendentally *vis a vis* the human.[10]

In the last essay that he wrote, Van Ruler reproached those he called the 'ultra-Reformed' with their tendency to what he called the 'predestination idea.' By that he meant that certain Reformed theologians made predestination a principle upon which they built a system. Election is not a principle or idea, Van Ruler argues. It bespeaks the action of God, this particular God, the God of Israel and of Jesus Christ revealed, disclosed to humans.[11]

We can further elaborate by speaking of this as the *eschatological act of the Trinitarian God*.[12] The God who acts, acts in Christ and through the Spirit. The 'intention' behind the act resides deep within God's self. We cannot know the reason or cause. The cause, or the reason, for election is God's self.[13] Election 'protects' this 'unknowing,' if you will. It reminds us that we have to do with the God who is incomprehensible, indeed, whose love is incomprehensible.

It is in this context that Van Ruler states that this is the meaning

---

8. Van Ruler, *Verzameld Werk* 4B, 564.
9. Van Ruler, *Verzameld Werk* 4B, 592.
10. Van Ruler, *Verzameld Werk* 4B, 752.
11. A.A. van Ruler, "Ultra-gereformeerd en vrijzinnig" (Ultra-Reformed and Liberal), in *Theologisch Werk*, Deel III (Nijkerk: Callenbach, 1971), 105–106.
12. Van Ruler compares the *doctrine* of election with the doctrine of the Trinity. The doctrine of the Trinity is not explicitly mentioned in scripture. And while there are scriptural supports for the doctrine of election, the doctrine itself is not explicitly scriptural. However, scripture's story can only be fully understood through the development of the two doctrines.
13. Van Ruler, *Verzameld Werk* 4B, 577, 753.

of "before the foundation of the world" (Eph. 1:4). The 'pre-' in predestination is not temporal but logical. That is, this is not a report of God's decision at a 'time' before God got around to creating the universe. Election is rooted in the eternality of God. Eternality, however, does not mean the infinite extension of time, but stands over and against time. "Eternality is better defined as independence of all time rather than a 'space' before all time."[14] Indeed, election is an historical act of God in that it happens in Christ and through the Spirit. Van Ruler claims that "one cannot remove eternal election to a conciliar decision of God before the reality of the cross and resurrection."[15] "The eternal election comes to lie in the events of cross and resurrection and that this election is eternal lies in the eternal sonship of him who died and arose."[16] Election, then, is *historical*, the eternal God acting in history. Indeed, it happened in what happened with Christ.

However, this is not simply a 'looking back' to what happened at Golgotha and the empty tomb. As historical, election is set within an eschatological horizon. It is not set within the structure of reality itself. In Christ and through the Spirit, we are ushered into a history that is not 'set,' so to speak. The new happens opening us to wonder.[17] In fact, this has a good deal to say about how we understand 'reality.' Reality is in our meeting with God, Van Ruler claims, it is in the "dance of the deeds of God, his electing and rejecting actions. Because God is God in this way, reality has no 'essence': it vibrates (Noordmans) with election."[18] We are elect toward the future, so to speak. Recall, that for Van Ruler, theology is to "think from the end."

However, this is not only to be understood Christologically, but pneumatologically. If only Christologically we remain stuck in a *predestinatio dialetica* (the logic of predestination). To fully grasp the *predestinatio gemina* (double predestination) we need to think pneumatologically.[19] He states that the basic problem in pneumatology is the relation between predestination and eschatology.[20] What might that mean? We now know that election is God's historical action in Christ. It is for the sake of the human. But how does that find its way to the particular person and how does it gather that person within God's greater (good) intentions that extend to the kingdom of God that awaits?

---

14. Van Ruler, *Verzameld Werk* 4B, 667.
15. Van Ruler, *Verzameld Werk* 4B, 665–666.
16. Van Ruler, *Verzameld Werk* 4B, 666.
17. A.A. van Ruler, *De vervulling van de wet: Een dogmatische studie over de verhouding van openbaring en existentie* (The fulfillment of the Law: A dogmatic study on the relationship between revelation and existence) (Nijkerk: Callenbach, 1947), 53.
18. Van Ruler, *De vervulling van de wet*, 353.
19. Van Ruler, *De vervulling van de wet*, 193.
20. Van Ruler, *Verzameld Werk* 4B, 559.

The response to that is to point to the work of the Holy Spirit.

This, too, is historical in that it meets the human within her human history. We are elect in Christ, and now this happens to me, the individual.[21] This, however, must be told to me, addressed to me. Because this is God who is not only the source of my salvation, but the *means*, this happens through preaching, gospel, admonition.[22] This is the call of God on me, on the individual. Van Ruler goes so far in one place as to equate call with election.[23] "The call itself *is* already election."[24] Called, elect, through the work of the Spirit, we believe. And this is our delight: "The deepest ground, the greatest delight, the greatest glory of the life of faith lies in the piece on election. Here faith experiences its real essence in the extreme, for the essence of faith is to be drawn outside oneself."[25]

Talk of the Spirit in the context of election includes but does not end with the individual believer. The work of the Spirit is not limited to the 'internal testimony of the Holy Spirit' for Van Ruler. Indeed. The Spirit has to do with God's presence in the world, ontologically. Van Ruler claims that this is best maintained in the doctrine of predestination.[26] Howso? The eternal God acts historically in Christ and through the Spirit, now present as God's own self. We talk about subjectivity and the Spirit in relation to the subjectivity of the human, my subjective self now regenerated through the work of the Spirit. But it is more, says Van Ruler. This is the subjectivity of God's own self who "posits himself in existence and is present in it."[27] This will be important as we reflect on what we gain from the doctrine of election in our search for hope.

At this point, however, we can note that for Van Ruler this meant that while election was individual and personal—how do I come to salvation in Christ?—, it is not *only* personal. Biblically speaking, there is a certain plasticity to election. There is election of the church, for example: the church is elected in its head, Christ, to bear his image and to display his glory.[28] But there is also election of peoples.[29] Indeed, Israel was elect.

Here we can talk about the counsel or decrees of God, of what kept the old Reformed theologians busy. Recall that I noted above that Van Ruler did not begin with the counsels of God. He says rather, as he came to the end of his long discourse for a course on election, that the notion

---

21. Van Ruler, *Verzameld Werk* 4B, 766.
22. Van Ruler, *Verzameld Werk* 4B, 766.
23. Van Ruler, *Verzameld Werk* 4B, 595.
24. Van Ruler, *Verzameld Werk* 4B, 767. Emphasis in the original.
25. Van Ruler, *Verzameld Werk* 4B, 541.
26. Van Ruler, *De vervulling van de wet*, 229.
27. Van Ruler, *De vervulling van de wet*, 229.
28. Van Ruler, *Verzameld Werk* 4B, 652.
29. Van Ruler, *Verzameld Werk* 4B, 767.

of the eternal decision leads us into the immanent Trinity. Election has to do with God's own self and God's intentions. What happens in history is the realization of Gods thought and will, God's original intentions.[30] This is not arbitrary, not willy-nilly. Here we are at Van Ruler's larger theological project, theocratic thought, and looking to the kingdom of God, God's future drawing us forward.

All this is a way of talking about the God who is the subject of the grace that turns toward the human (and creation) in love. But there is a darker side to election: rejection. Van Ruler accepts double predestination and does so in part because empirical evidence tells him so.[31] But there is something deeper going on. In a difficult paragraph in his 1942 lectures, he claims that God does not simply permit evil, but God does more than that. God even 'intends' evil![32] He wants to insist that God is present in the midst of the horror. The horror is not beyond God's action and control. So that he can claim that "only the doctrine of election gives us the fundamental power that enables us to walk through the dark chasm hurrying to the divine future, waiting on divine action."[33] "That is really the living, active, acting, militant God."[34] He would put it later that we are in the hands of God.[35] In this is hope.

The upshot of this all is comfort, delight, joy even. Van Ruler compares this all with the child who is convinced of the self-evidence and the unshakeable reality of its parents' love. So, too, the believer is convinced that "God is naturally graceful toward him."[36] Van Ruler cites John Calvin in the "certainty of our faith rests solely and completely on the promise of the gospel…it is only substantially strengthened by the doctrine of election."[37] Assured, confident, the child can play; she can delight in a true reality.[38]

3. DORT

How does Van Ruler's doctrine of election further our reflections on the ground of hope as we ask how we can confess in communion with Dort? Let me say, first, that our take-away need not be what the Dort fathers intended, that is, it may move in directions they would not find compatible. But my intention here is not an exegesis of the Canons. It is, rath-

---

30. Van Ruler, *Verzameld Werk* 4B, 671.
31. Van Ruler, "Ultra-gereformeerd en vrijzinnig," 104.
32. Van Ruler, *Verzameld Werk* 4B, 752.
33. Van Ruler, *Verzameld Werk* 4B, 753.
34. Van Ruler, *Verzameld Werk* 4B, 753.
35. Van Ruler, *Verzameld Werk* 4B, 769.
36. Van Ruler, *Verzameld Werk* 4B, 556.
37. Van Ruler, *Verzameld Werk* 4B, 750.
38. Van Ruler, *Verzameld Werk* 4B, 557.

er, to inquire whether the doctrine of election in the Canons is open to a reading that provides a theological foundation to proclaim the hope that scripture's narrative offers. To that end, then, five perspectives gleaned from our foray into Van Ruler.

1. Hope does not rest with a human project. "A king is not saved by his army, nor a warrior preserved by his strength" (Ps. 33:16). There are plans afoot to save the planet from climate disaster through technological fixes. For that matter, history is littered with utopian schemes. And yet we stumble. The Canons begin with the doctrine of election. However, the first paragraph is clear: "Since all people have sinned and come under the sentence of curse and eternal death, God would done no one an injustice if it had been his will to leave the entire race in sin and under curse ...."[39] The Canons characterize sin as rebellion. It is to turn against the offer of grace, to insist on one's own way. The first word is love—whether we start in Genesis 1 with creation or Exodus 3 with liberation. Sin is only a second word, but it infects all of humanity. Nevertheless, within the reality of God, love is prior, it is "from the foundation of the world" (I/8).

   It is a happy theological accident that election is the *first* head of doctrine. The order of the Canons does indeed reflect the order of the Remonstrations. Still, theologically, election comes first in the Canons; the 'fall' doesn't come until the third head of doctrine; it follows not only election, but the means of salvation, the atonement. We begin with the God who *chooses* to turn toward the human in love. The ground of hope is not with us, with neither our projects nor our ability to carry those projects out.

2. Election points us to the eternality of God. "Before the foundation of the world, by sheer grace, according to the free good pleasure of his will, God chose in Christ to salvation a definite number of particular people out of the whole human race ..." (I/8). Eternality not only transcends but encompasses time, so that the God who met us in the past awaits us in the future. Election is not simply something that happened 'back then' before the creation of time. Election

---

39. "The Canons of Dort," I/1, in *Our Faith: Ecumentical Creeds, Reformed Confessions, and Other Resources* (Grand Rapids: Faith Alive, 2013). Hereinafter, reference to the Canons will be by head of doctrine/paragraph.

comes from the heart of the eternal and infinite God. It happened at the cross and happens now in proclamation as the Spirit beckons us and beckons us forward. It is the call to the future, to God's future.

Jürgen Moltmann taught us to understand the biblical story as promise. The fundamental category is not the epiphany of God (or the gods) but promise. By promise we are set on the way to history. Moreover, God is future, before us. God is

> ... a God with "future as his essential nature" as made known in Exodus and in Israelite prophecy, the God whom we therefore cannot really have in us or over us but always before us, who encounters us in his promise for the future, and whom we therefore cannot "have" either, but only await in active hope.[40]

Election, then, speaks of God's call into a future, not a probe into the past. It is not about a predetermination of history's course, nor of the individual's eternal destiny. Nor is it to extrapolate the future from trajectories of the past. It emerges from the eternality of God that encompasses both past and future. But it is drawn eschatologically into the future. The call that beckons me is God calling me into that future and that call is, says Van Ruler, election itself.

This is nicely manifest in YHWH's encounter with Moses in Exodus 3. Israel is elect, called forward out of oppression and slavery. And the one who calls gives Moses the name that is itself set in a future tense, "I will be who I will be." Furthermore, when Moses asks for a sign, YHWH replies that the freed slaves will know that it is YHWH when they get to the mountain. They are called from the eternality/future of God into their own future, a future "on the way."

3. Election entails liberation. The child is confident of the love of her parents and so is freed to play. Election brings about the liberation of the will. Our wills that have been bounded have been set free.[41] "...[T]he will, now renewed, is not only activated and motivated by God, but having been activated by God is also itself active" (III, IV/12). To use

---

40. Jürgen Moltmann, *Theology of Hope* (New York: Harper & Row, 1967), 16.
41. This, of course, is Calvin, particularly as he exegetes Augustine. See John Calvin, *The Bondage and Liberation of the Will*, ed. A.N.S. Lane (Grand Rapids: Baker Books, 1996).

one of Van Ruler's favorite phrases, the human becomes a *mannetje*, something we'd translate into Yiddish, a *mensch*. In salvation we are given back our humanity. We become truly human.

In terms of hope, this means that election does not make us passive, but active. We may not know what the future looks like, not precisely. However, there are some things that we can know. We can "know with God." Van Ruler will go so far as to say that we can "will with God."[42] We have hints and more in scripture of what God intends for God's kingdom. We cannot know precisely what that will look like. My sense is that when we get 'there,' wherever and whenever 'there' is, we will look back and say, "Of course, that's what we've been told all along."[43] But we need not know. The promise is such and the call is such that we are free to work, joyfully and with great energy.

Still, it must be added, that since election is in the call, and since we have heard the call, we are already within a future of hope. That is the work of the Spirit. We do know the work of regeneration. We have heard the declaration of forgiveness. Our past has been made truly past and we are turned toward the future. Hope has been *given* us. And this is 'wellfounded' because it is the work of God, a work that has emerged not from ourselves, but from without, from God's own self.

4. The human is not only freed to act, but is *given to know*, because it has been revealed and proclaimed—the act of the eternal Father in the Son now made known to the believer in the act of the Holy Spirit. And, graced, the believer knows that this is God's good favor. Van Ruler allows us to speak of God's eternal counsel, God's original intention that is projected upon the screen of the eschaton, the intention that is manifest in the kingdom of God, present now in signs, but assured for the future. That original intention is the 'pre-' that while it may not be primarily temporal, includes

---

42. See, e.g., Van Ruler, "Christ Taking Form in the World," in A.A. van Ruler, *Calvinist Trinitarianism and Theocentric Politics*, trans. John Bolt (Edwin Mellon Press: Lewiston, 1989), 138. This is an expression of Van Ruler's well-known doctrine of *theonomous reciprocity*. On this, see also Van Ruler, "Grammar of a Pneumatology," 50–51, in *Calvinist Trinitarianism*.

43. This is the dynamic of the encounter on the road to Emmaus, Luke 24.

the temporal. Hope, then, originates not at the cross, not even in the incarnation, but in the heart of God, originates from an intention that emerges from eternity, but invades and embraces the very human history that we live. In fact, to follow a Van Rulerian trajectory, God's intention is very this-worldly: it includes not only human institutions, societies, governments, and so on, but creation itself.

Admittedly, this sets Dort in an eschatological framework that sits uneasily in early seventeenth century thought. But can election not only be set in that context, but in doing so can it provide a basis of hope?

5. Finally, I move a step beyond Dort when I suggest that Van Ruler offers hints of reading election in such a way that it is not only individual persons who are elect, but a people, a church. Dort is clear that election is of particular persons. And, as we have seen, Van Ruler accepts that reading. But, as we noted, in a few places he suggests that election is also corporate. Dort does give faint hints of this. Many of its biblical references in the first head of doctrine are to passages that have Israel as the object of election. In fact, one of the classic references, Rom. 9:11–13—"Jacob I loved, but Esau I hated"—is perhaps best read as a reference to Israel and not primarily to two ancient individuals.[44]

Nor is this entirely absent from Dort. The call to me as a person comes through the proclamation of the gospel, a ministry (I/3). And, one must say, the ministry of the church. But staying with the individual we can say more. I am called to be a part of a people and God uses this people the incorporate me.[45] This is perhaps most explicitly stated in Answer 54 of the Heidelberg Catechism where the Son of God "gathers, protects, and preserves for himself a community chosen for eternal life and united in true faith. And of this community I am and always will be a living member."

Still, a greater prospect is grounded in the eternity of God. Hope is not only for the collection of individuals we know as the church. This is hope for the earth, hope for the nations, a hope that encompasses all history and all creation. The call of Abraham, the promise, was that

---

44. Van Ruler *Verzameld Werk* 4B, 564.
45. While one may go beyond the text of the Canons here, one hardly goes beyond a theology behind Dort, not if Dort is understood as an appendix to the Belgic (Dutch) Confession, Article 28, where there "is no salvation outside [the church]."

through him "all the families of the earth shall be blessed" (Gen. 12:3).[46]

The ground of hope then is God's self, God who turns toward God's beloved creation. But the ground, the basis, makes for an expansive hope, a hope while the substance of which is revealed, it is never exhausted in its manifestation.

BIBLIOGRAPHY

Berkhof, Hendrikus. *Well-founded Hope*. Richmond: John Knox, 1969.

Book of Church Order, http://images.rca.org/docs/bco/2019BCO.pdf.

Calvin, John. *The Bondage and Liberation of the Will*, ed. A.N.S. Lane. Grand Rapids: Baker Books, 1996.

McDonald, Suzanne. *Re-Imaging Election: Divine Election as Representing God to Other & Others to God*. Eerdmans: Grand Rapids, 2010.

Moltmann, Jürgen. *Theology of Hope*. New York: Harper & Row, 1967.

Our Faith: Ecumentical Creeds, Reformed Confessions, and Other Resources. Grand Rapids: Faith Alive, 2013.

Tanner, Kathryn. "How Finance Capitalism Deforms Us." *Christian Century*, January 16, 2019.

Ruler, A.A. van. *Calvinist Trinitarianism and Theocentric Politics*, trans. John Bolt. Edwin Mellon Press: Lewiston, 1989.

Ruler, A.A. van. *De vervulling van de wet: Een dogmatische studie over de verhouding van openbaring en existentie* (The fulfillment of the Law: A dogmatic study on the relationship between revelation and existence). Nijkerk: Callenbach, 1947.

Ruler, A.A. van. *Reidans: adventsmeditaties* (Round dance: Advent meditations). Nijkerk: Callenbach, 1974.

Ruler, A.A. van. *Theologisch Werk*, Deel III. Nijkerk: Callenbach, 1971.

---

46. One finds this theme throughout Van Ruler's works. In one place, in a volume of meditations, where he explicitly connects this with election, he says: "Israel is elect, it knows the good, there God has revealed the meaning of the world, the social ideal;" *Reidans: adventsmeditaties* (Round dance: Advent meditations) (Nijkerk: Callenbach, 1974), 94.

Ruler, A.A. van. *Verzameld Werk*, Deel 4B: Christus, *de Geest en het heil* (Collected Works, Part 4B: Christ, the Spirit and salvation), ed. D. van Keulen. Boekencentrum: Zoetermeer, 2011.

CHAPTER 12
POLARIZATION AND THE PURSUIT OF UNANIMITY IN THE CHURCH: ECCLESIASTICAL DECISION-MAKING IN THE DUTCH REFORMED TRADITION
Klaas-Willem de Jong and Jan Dirk Th. Wassenaar

When the Reformed Church in the Netherlands came into being and took shape at the end of the sixteenth century, the Netherlands was strongly divided.[1] The Dutch Revolt alienated people from one another, and soon doctrinal disputes started to dominate the churches. In this context, the Reformed Church sought unity. This can be illustrated by the regulations on ecclesiastical decisionmaking at the time, which culminated in the church order established by the national Synod of Dordt in 1619. The synod confirmed a large number of previously introduced provisions, modified some of them and added new ones. No matter how polarization is handled, in the vast majority of cases it ultimately comes down to decision-making. The Church Order of Dort, confirming older regulations for settling disagreements, laid down the basis for decision-making in church assemblies in article 31: "that which is decided by majority vote shall be considered settled and binding unless it is proved to conflict with the Word of God or with the articles adopted in this general synod."[2] In later times, under different circumstances, Reformed churches and theologians have again tried to establish how ecclesiastical decisions should be made.

---

1. This article is a thoroughly edited, modified and elaborated version of two previous publications, K.W. de Jong, "Zo mogelijk met eenparige stemmen" (If possible unanimously), NTKR *Tijdschrift voor Recht en Religie* 10:2 (2016), 107–119, and J.D.Th. Wassenaar, "'… dat God het winnen zal in de kerk …': Een beschouwing over 'meerderheid van stemmen' in de kerk" (… that God will prevail in the church: A reflection on 'majority of votes' in the church), *Ecclesia* 95:4 (2004), 26–29. We want to thank Don and Carla Sinnema for their critical review of a draft of this article, especially regarding the English language.

2. Richard DeRidder, Peter H. Jonker and Leonard Verduin, *The Church Orders of the Sixteenth Century Reformed Churches of the Netherlands: Together with Their Social, Political, and Ecclesiastical Context* (Grand Rapids: Calvin Theological Seminary, 1987), 550.

Thus connecting with one of the sub-themes of this volume, 'Polarization and the Reformed Tradition,' we will first pay attention to the developments in church and theology up to and including 1619. The decision-making by a simple majority of votes was disputed, both in the church and theology of the Dutch Reformation and in the rest of society at the time. We then discuss the second half of the nineteenth century. The church had to deal with polarization then too. Once again, the decision-making process was called into question. Finally, we focus on the process of unifying the three 'Samen op Weg' churches, which was accompanied by great tensions and led to the Protestantse Kerk in Nederland (PKN, Eng.: Protestant Church in the Netherlands) in 2004. In discussing these three moments in church history, we gain an insight into the way in which the Reformed tradition in the Netherlands has dealt with the Church's calling with regard to decision-making procedures in times of polarization. We end with some conclusions.

1. THE INTRODUCTION OF THE MAJORITY PRINCIPLE

It should come as no surprise that, from the beginning of the Reformation period, theologians in Dutch-speaking congregations struggled with the relationship between decision-making and the Word of God. As early as 1550, Johannes a Lasco, minister of the Dutch Strangers' Church in London, reflected on this theme. Though a proposal may acquire the majority of votes, in his opinion, the Word of God should be decisive. Opinions that are not in accordance with the Word of God must be rejected. In any case, when decisions are made, even the appearance of conflict with the Word of God must be avoided.[3]

In the absence of evidence to the contrary, we assume that, from the outset in the sixteenth century, Reformed ecclesiastical assemblies, in principle, decided by majority vote. We could add in line with a Lasco's approach: unless there was a conflict with the Word of God. However, the question as to whether there is a conflict with the Word of God, is ultimately always decided by a majority. If a majority is convinced that the authority of scripture is at stake, it will compel unanimity. Although this special situation has caused heavy battles in Reformed churches, we will confine ourselves to the simple majority principle, because as such it provides sufficient material for reflection.

---

3. F.L. Bos, *De orde der kerk* (The order of the church) ('s-Gravenhage: Guido de Bres, 1950), 116. Cf. for the Latin original, Joh. a Lasco, *Forma ac Ratio* ... [1555], 512.

1.1 Majority Voting and the Pursuit of Unanimity

There are indications that there has sometimes been a practice other than the above-mentioned majority principle. An appendix to the acts of the Synod of Emden (1571) briefly describes how the chairman of a provincial synod is expected to act.[4] He addresses the instructions from the credentials of the attendees one by one. Thereafter, each person is given the opportunity to express his opinion on each point. The chairman makes an inventory of the views that are expressed, "with an explanation of the feelings of most of them and the best of them." The secretary must record this in writing and read it out, "in order that it will be established unanimously." At the end of the meeting the secretary reads everything out again and the attendees express their agreement with their signature. This state of affairs has been interpreted in such a way that there are two votes: the first time by expressing opinions and the second time by agreeing with the decision as formulated by the chairman, confirmed by everyone's signature.[5] Though one would expect a similar procedure regarding the classis, such a regulation is lacking. Seven years later, in the rules established by the Synod of Dordrecht (1578), the procedure for all church meetings is as follows: "In all cases (except those that are explicitly expressed in the Word of God), after having diligently counted the votes, one must follow the advice of the majority in order to subsequently decide. Everyone is obliged to obey this decision."[6] This procedure has been considered to be comparable to the Emden regulation by F.L. Rutgers, who will be discussed in more detail further on; in spite of various opinions, ecclesiastical assemblies are obliged to strive for unanimous decisions.[7] However, that remains to be seen. The first round is referred to here as 'advice,' the second as 'decision.' The 'subsequently'—in Dutch 'daernae'—can also be understood as 'in accordance with.'[8] Although the decision must be followed by everyone in the end, it can be defended that it does not necessarily have to

---

4. F.L. Rutgers (ed.), *Acta van de Nederlandsche synoden der zestiende eeuw* (Acta of the Dutch synods of the sixteenth century), Werken der Marnix-Vereeniging, II/3 ('s-Gravenhage: Nijhoff, 1889), 111. The quotes in the following sentences have been translated from this source. Later quotations in this article are also translated.

5. F.L. Rutgers, "Bespreking der hoofdpunten van het Kerkrecht naar aanleiding van de Dordtsche Kerkenorde" (collegedictaat 1892–1895) (Discussion of the main points of church polity in connection with the Church Order of Dort, Lecture Notes 1892–1895), art. 31 (123), http://kerkrecht.nl/node/1310 (accessed August 8, 2019).

6. Rutgers, *Acta*, 148 (Dordrecht 1578), art. 23.

7. Rutgers, "Bespreking," 123 (art. 31). De Jong followed Rutgers's approach in a publication from 2016 ("Zo mogelijk," 110). However, he came to a different conclusion in the present article.

8. Cf. the digital dictionary http://wnt.inl.nl s.v. 'Daarna', sub 1 and 2.

be made unanimously.⁹ A few years later, the Middelburg Synod (1581) came to the formulation which would be confirmed by both the Synod of The Hague (1586) and the Synod of Dort in 1619, and is quoted above. The difference between this decision-making procedure and that of the provincial synod described in the Emden Church Order (1571) is less pronounced than might appear at first sight. In Emden, explicit consent to the majority decision was required. In the regulations of Dordrecht (1578), the consent was most probably implicit, but from Middelburg (1581) onwards it is clearly implicit.

The practice of decision-making with 'advice' in which each one's opinion is expressed, and the chairman formulates a decision on the basis of the advice received, is in line with what was customary outside the church in the sixteenth century Netherlands.[10] At the local level and in commissions with an advisory character, the majority principle was generally applied. At the regional and national level, as in the Provincial States and the States General, unanimity was required for important decisions, for example, about war and taxes. A delegate to these assemblies was bound by the instructions of his principal. This could complicate negotiations to arrive at a common position. However, in order to avoid an impasse, the States General was allowed to take the decision-making process to a different level and request a binding opinion from the stadholder.[11]

The successive church orders give rise to the presumption that the practice of decision-making evolved in the course of time. But do other sources support this presumption? Their number is very limited. Minutes of meetings held in the early Reformation period are scarce and, almost without exception, they are brief about the decision-making procedure. At the level of the classis, the oldest acts in the source edition *Classicale Acta* are from the Classis Dordrecht and date from 1573. The next to follow originates from the Classis Zuid-Beveland and starts with the year 1579. A single mention in the 1573 acts of Classis Dordrecht shows that in this assembly decision-making by unanimity was not always the case at the time.[12] In the decades that follow, we have found a few indications of the desire to still achieve this. The editors of the acts of the Classis

---

9. Cf. the Classis Dordrecht in 1581 ("ende het advys een yegelicx omvragen ende besluyten," *Classicale Acta* 1573–1620 ('s-Gravenhage 1980–2011), I, 107)). Cf. the sometimes decisive role of the officers ('moderamen') of the Synod of Dort 1618–19, H.H. Kuyper, *De Post-Acta of nahandelingen* ... (The Post-Acta or after-actions) (Amsterdam-Pretoria: Höveker & Wormser, 1899), 104ff.

10. Cf. W. van Vree, *Nederland als vergaderland: Opkomst en verbreiding van een vergaderregime* (The Netherlands as a meeting country: Emergence and spread of a meeting regime) (Groningen: Wolters Noordhoff, 1994), 142–144, 147–150.

11. Van Vree, *Nederland*, 148.

12. *Classicale Acta*, i, 7.

Delft, which date back to 1581, state: "Although the acta sometimes indicate that decisions were made by a majority of votes, they give the impression even more often that very extensive discussions took place first in order to reach an overall consensus."[13] Anyone who goes through the other published acts of classes on this point comes to the same conclusion. Nevertheless, a unanimously supported outcome was not a requirement.[14] This approach became more common in the second decade of the seventeenth century, mainly as a result of the increasingly sharp contradictions between Remonstrants and Counter-Remonstrants. This must have been the reason for a request of the Classis Deventer to the national Synod of Dort that the synod never reached; it wanted to explicitly consider the majority vote binding.[15] There are indications that this was under discussion at this time, especially in the province of Overijssel. For example, a document has been preserved in the city archives of Kampen that suggested that decision-making by majority vote is not the correct method for the complex matters that would be discussed at the national synod. This would lead to bitterness among the minority. The author advocates joint study and decision-making based on consensus.[16]

As far as availability of sources is concerned, the situation for the provincial synods is comparable to that for the classes.[17] In the acts of Noord-Holland, which begin in 1572, a year after the Emden Synod, the word 'united' can be found remarkably often in the decision-making process of the first meetings. Ten years later, however, it is explicitly stated that the majority of votes is decisive.[18] In the decisions of Zuid-

---

13. *Classicale Acta*, vii, xxx.

14. E.g., *Classicale Acta*, v, 279.

15. H.H. Kuyper, *Post-Acta of Nahandelingen van de Nationale Synode van Dordrecht in 1618 en 1619 gehouden naar den authentieken tekst in het Latijn en Nederlandsch uitgegeven en met toelichtingen voorzien. Voorafgegaan door de geschiedenis van de Acta, de Autographa en de Post-Acta dier synode en gevolgd door de geschiedenis van de revisie der belijdenisgeschriften en der Liturgie, benevens de volledige lijst der gravamina op de Dordtsche synode ingediend* (Amsterdam-Pretoria: Höveker & Wormser), 446. Cf. J. Reitsma and S.D. van Veen (eds.), *Acta der provinciale en particuliere synoden, gehouden in de noordelijke Nederlanden gedurende de jaren 1572-1620* (Acta of provincial and particular synods, held in the northern Netherlands during the years 1572-1620) (Groningen: Wolters, 1892-1899), vi, 308; *Classicale Acta*, vi, 47 (Deventer), 123 (Kampen).

16. Erik A. de Boer, *De macht van de minderheid: Het remonstrantisme in Kampen in de spiegel van de nationale synode te Dordrecht* (1618-1619) (The power of the minority: Remonstrantism in Kampen in the mirror of the National Synod in Dordrecht (1618-1619)) (Kampen: Summum Academic Publications, 2019), 113-116.

17. Reitsma and Van Veen (eds.), *Acta*. The oldest acta are from the provincial synod of Noord-Holland (1572), followed by those of Zuid-Holland (1574) and Gelderland (1579).

18. Reitsma and Van Veen (eds.), *Acta*, i, 92 (Noord-Holland, 1582). Cf. i, 318

Holland, known from 1574 onwards, no mention is made of the extent to which they are supported. However, it is clear from a few remarks that this synod strives for unity in many cases, a goal that can also be found later and elsewhere. The acts of the first meeting of Zuid-Holland also show that, in accordance with the Emden regulations and corresponding secular meetings, the acts were signed by all those present.[19]

1.2 THE MAJORITY PRINCIPLE

As indicated, in 1619 the Synod of Dort repeated in its church order (in article 31) the majority principle, which was already widely practiced at that time. However, some relativizing remarks have to be made in this respect. To begin with, the acts of the Synod of Dort itself show a complex decision-making procedure which partly resembles the Emden regulations.[20] Probably reflecting the States General practice voting was by delegation and not by delegate. Each delegation discussed the matter at stake and subsequently submitted its advice to the synod. In case of disagreement within a delegation its members could submit their separate advice. After the opinions of the delegations were read on the floor of the synod, the president would formulate a single synodical decision. This proposal could be altered by those present. If unanimity could not be achieved, final approval occurred by a majority vote of the delegations.

The second relativization is the acceptance of the Church Order of Dort. It was introduced in full only in Utrecht, and with some changes (which, however, do not affect article 31) in Gelderland and Overijssel.[21] But even then, the rules of the church order were not always followed.[22] Other provinces maintained older regulations, which were in the application of the majority principle similar to the Church Order of Dort. This changed when new regulations were introduced for the Netherlands as a whole in 1816. New churches of the Reformed type reestablished the Church Order of Dort from 1834 onwards.

A third relativizing remark concerns the fact that many more provisions in the Church Order of Dort influence the outcome of a

---

(Noord-Holland, 1602).

19. Reitsma and Van Veen (eds.), *Acta*, ii, 155 (Zuid-Holland, 1574; copies the 1571 Emden Synod are also referred to). Cf. Rutgers, *Acta*, 113 (Emden); Van Vree, *Nederland*, 143ff.

20. Hendrik Kaajan, *De Pro-Acta der Dordtsche Synode* (The Pro-Acta of the Synod of Dort) (Rotterdam: De Vries, 1914), 42ff.

21. J.T. van den Berg, "De synode van Dordrecht en de Dordtse Kerkorde" (The Synod of Dort and the Church Order of Dort), in *Handboek gereformeerd kerkrecht* (Manual of Reformed church polity), ed. H.J. Selderhuis (Heerenveen: Groen, 2019), 162–170, 167.

22. Cf. e.g., *Classicale Acta*, ix, 745 (Arnhem), concerning the application of art. 42.

vote. For example, in article 42, the Church Order of Dort opens up the possibility that also ministers who were not delegated to the classis had the right to vote at classis meetings.[23] Despite the fact that this had been explicitly rejected in the past, and despite the ban on hierarchy in the Church Order of Dort, as a consequence of this, the cities in particular gained influence, at the expense of the villages.[24] This development can also be recognized outside the church; the cities, especially in Holland, increased their power in the province by demanding unanimity on more subjects.[25] Other examples of circumstances influencing the achieving of a majority are the prominent voice of the chairman of a meeting, and the necessity of a valid credential to obtain voting rights.[26]

1.3 Interim Conclusion

By adopting the majority principle at all levels and almost everywhere, the Dutch Reformed Church opted for a relatively flexible decision-making process. Church assemblies could give their delegates binding instructions for the meetings of major assemblies.[27] Yet, in the case of a majority, these did not stand in the way of binding decision-making. After all, an appeal was possible against decisions of the church council and classis (and in principle, according to the Church Order of Dort, also of the provincial synod). In this way, the majority of a minor assembly could still be nullified.

2. The Majority Principle Under Pressure

In 1816 the Reformed Church was renamed and called the Nederlandse Hervormde Kerk (NHK, Eng.: Netherlands Reformed Church). A new set of regulations was introduced at the same time.[28] Under this regime,

---

23. Cf. the Church Order of Dort, art. 42. See, e.g., De Ridder, Jonker and Verduin, *The Church Orders*, art. 42.

24. Cf. K.W. de Jong, "Een verkennend onderzoek naar de receptie van een anti-hiërarchisch beginsel in Nederlandse kerkorden van het gereformeerde type" (An exploratory investigation into the reception of an anti-hierarchical principle in Dutch Reformed church orders), *In die Skriflig* 52:2 (2018), 1–9 (https://doi.org/10.4102/ids.v52i2.2350), 3ff.

25. Van Vree, *Nederland*, 148f.

26. Cf. Church Order of Dort, art. 35 (cf. 37, 41).

27. Cf. the more nuanced view of Bos, *De orde*, 134–136.

28. J.C.A. van Loon, *Het Algemeen Reglement van 1816* (The General Regulations of 1816) (Wageningen: Zomer & Keuning, 1942), 223–235. Cf. Fred van Lieburg and Johanna Roelevink (eds.), *Ramp of redding: 200 jaar Algemeen Reglement voor het Bestuur der Hervormde Kerk in het Koninkrijk der Nederlanden 1816–2016* (Disaster or rescue: 200 Years of General Regulations for the governance of the Reformed Church in the kingdom of the Netherlands 1816–2016) (Utrecht: Boekencentrum, 2018).

small boards operated on a classical, provincial and national level, each with their own responsibilities.[29] In this new model of ecclesiastical government, there was no longer any mention of the ancient rule of representation by means of burden or backstabbing. However, this newly gained freedom gave reason to pay less attention to the convictions of lower assemblies, especially to those of minorities with different views. Furthermore, the system of 1816 was in danger of becoming an oligarchy; conflicts of interest could easily arise, which sometimes harmed the church.

In 1852 the General Regulations of 1816 were thoroughly revised.[30] The organization was extensively democratized by the introduction of proportional representation. This revision has to be seen against the background of two developments. On the one hand, there was the constitutional reform of 1848, which gave an enormous impulse to the democratization of the Netherlands. On the other hand, parties with opposing views had emerged within the NHK. Yet, it was not until 1867 that proportional representation was put into practice in the NHK.[31] From then on, male members were allowed to go to the ballot box to express their opinion on the application of a form of equal representation in the board of their congregation. Orthodox parties in particular tried to exert their influence. This development has been described as an 'orthodox Protestant mobilization' which led to great contention in the church.[32] The primary objective was to obtain the majority of votes on the issue,

---

29. Johanna Roelevink, "Het Algemeen Reglement van 1816: een hekgolf in de rivier" (The General Regulations of 1816: A sternwave in the river), in *Ramp of redding*, eds. Van Lieburg and Roelevink, 19–57, 45; Leon van den Broeke, "Regionale (re) organisatie: classicaal bestuur en provinciaal kerkbestuur rond 1816" (Regional (re) organization: Classical administration and provincial church administration around 1816), in *Ramp of redding*, eds. Van Lieburg and Roelevink, 59–75.

30. Johanna Roelevink, "De Hervormde Kerk wankelend op eigen benen: de herziening van het Algemeen Reglement in 1852" (The Reformed Church on shaking footing: The revision of the General Regulations in 1852), in *Ramp of redding*, eds. Van Lieburg and Roelevink, 143–148.

31. Cf. K.W. de Jong, "'Wettiglijk van Gods gemeente, en mitsdien van God zelven geroepen': De voorgeschiedenis van het reglement van 1867 voor de verkiezing en beroeping van een hervormde predikant" ("Lawfully called by God's congregation, and therefore by God himself": The history of the Regulations of 1867 for the election and vocation of a Reformed pastor), *Tijdschrift voor Nederlandse Kerkgeschiedenis* 20:3 (2017), 109–117.

32. Jeroen Koch, "Revolutie, restauratie, reformatie: Koning Willem I, Abraham Kuyper en het Algemeen Reglement van 1816" (Revolution, restoration, reformation: King Willem I, Abraham Kuyper and the General Regulations of 1816), in *Ramp of redding*, eds. Van Lieburg and Roelevink, 162–164; Annemarie Houkes, *Christelijke vaderlanders: Godsdienst, burgerschap en de Nederlandse natie (1850–1900)* (Christian patriots: Religion, citizenship and the Dutch nation (1850–1900)) (Amsterdam: Wereldbibliotheek, 2009), 181.

whether the congregation should influence the composition of its church council or not. As a result, certain groups in this council could obtain the majority and could thus impose their views on the council. These two aspects of majority-composition and decision-making were sometimes confused in the discussion and the reflection we will present hereafter on the basis of four theologians.

2.1 J.H. GUNNING JR.

The first is J.H. Gunning Jr. (1829–1905). Early in his career, in 1860, Gunning considered the majority principle to be the best solution—"as long as prophecy in the congregation had been neglected and despised."[33] He did realize that objections could be raised, because the majority could also make incorrect decisions. He did, however, make a distinction between the area of natural society and "that of the original sanctified, that of the Church" because the testimony of the Holy Spirit is present in the congregation, which will sooner or later punish any recognized insensitivity.[34] In 1867, when proportional representation was finally to be introduced, the discussions about the theme had become heated, and the consequences of the revision had become painfully visible, Gunning published two brochures on universal suffrage.[35] He qualified it as an emergency solution. As the title of one of the writings indicates, the author presented sixteen propositions about the voting rights of the congregation. One of these suggested that

> we should turn to the church council to request that the distribution of the ballot papers be accompanied by an explicit call of the council ... hoping and praying that no one may make use of this right, other than those who in good conscience share the *Faith of the congregation*. This should not give rise to pointless disputes about the nature and content of the Faith of the Congregation, for its determination is left to everyone's conscience in this matter.[36]

---

33. J.H. Gunning Jr., *Openbare brief aan de ouderlingen der Vrije Evangelische Gemeente te Amsterdam* (Public letter to the elders of the Free Evangelical Congregation in Amsterdam) (Utrecht: Van der Post, 1860), 23. Cf. J.H. Semmelink, *Prof. Dr. J.H. Gunning, zijn ontwikkelingsgang en zijne beginselen* (Prof. dr. J.H. Gunning, His development and his principles) (Zeist: Vonk & Co, 1926), 158ff.

34. J.H. Gunning Jr., *De vrijheid der gemeente: Bezwaren tegen de ordeningen der Nederduitsche Hervormde Kerk in onze dagen* (The freedom of the congregation: Objections to the orders of the Dutch Reformed Church in our days) (Utrecht: Van der Post, 1861), 42.

35. J.H. Gunning Jr., *Zestien stellingen betrekkelijk het stemrecht der gemeente, aan de gemeente ter overweging gegeven* (Sixteen propositions regarding the voting rights of the congregation, given to the congregation for consideration) (Amsterdam: Höveker, 1867); *Aan de Hervormde gemeente: Een woord over haar stemrecht* (To the Reformed congregation: A word about her voting rights) ('s-Gravenhage: Gerritsen, 1867).

36. J.H. Gunning J.Hzn., *Prof. dr. J.H. Gunning: Leven en werken*, Ii (Prof. dr. J.H.

In this way Gunning tried "to at least slightly uphold the most important principle, namely *that in the church there is a distinction between the holy and the unholy.*"[37]

Gunning came back to the issue a few years later, in 1869. He reproachfully wrote: "*No majority vote in matters of faith.* Listen, please listen, Reformed congregation, which has warmly welcomed the principle of majority voting, taken over from state institutions and the worldly atmosphere that surrounds you."[38] According to his son, J.H. Gunning J.H.zn. (1858–1940), he wrote this "… with a direct application that left nothing to be desired in terms of clarity for the 'orthodox', happy with their victories obtained by a majority of votes."[39]

Gunning accepted the validity of the majority vote again later on, but he shamefully considered it to be a humiliation of the church.[40] Elsewhere, in state affairs as well as in associations, he was convinced of the principal validity of a majority vote, but in the church he accepted it as a starting point only. "If one wants to climb from a lower state to a higher level, it is necessary to take this state as a starting point, set foot on it and rise higher with the other foot."[41] At this time, Gunning also

---

Gunning: Life and work) (Rotterdam: Bredeé, 1923), 34f.

37. J.H. Gunning Jr., *Aan de Hervormde gemeente*: *Een woord over haar stemrecht* (To the Reformed congregation: A word about her voting rights), in Gunning, J.H.zn., *Prof. dr. J.H. Gunning*, 35. Cf. Jasper Vree, "Gunning en Kuyper: Een bewogen vriendschap rond Schrift en kerk in de jaren 1860–1873" (Gunning and Kuyper: An eventful friendship around scripture and church in the years 1860–1873), in Theo Hettema and Leo Mietus, *Noblesse oblige: Achtergrond en actualiteit van de theologie van J.H. Gunning Jr.* (Noblesse oblige: Background and topicality of the theology of J.H. Gunning Jr.) (Gorinchem: Ekklesia, 2005), 62–86, 66.

38. J.H. Gunning Jr., *Ter nabetrachting van 31 october en ter voorbereiding tot 17 november: Een woord tot de gemeente gesproken* (In review of October 31 and in preparation for November 17: A word to the congregation) ('s-Gravenhage: Van Hoogstraten, 1869), 12.

39. Gunning J.H.zn., 293.

40. O. Noordmans, *Beginselen van kerkorde* (Principles of church polity) (Assen: Van Gorcum & Co., 1932), in *Verzamelde Werken* (Collected Works), 5 (Kampen: Kok, 1984), 184; A. van Ginkel, "Gunnings waardering van de presbyteriale kerkorde" (Gunnings' appreciation of the presbyterial church order), in *Wegen en gestalten in het Gereformeerd Protestantisme: Een bundel studies over de geschiedenis van het Gereformeerd Protestantisme* ... (Shapes of Reformed Protestantism: A volume of studies about the history of Reformed protestantism), eds. W. Balke, C. Graafland and H. Harkema (Amsterdam: Ton Bolland, 1976), 257–268, 267ff; W. Balke, *Gunning en Hoedemaker samen op weg* (The mutual relationship between Gunning and Hoedemaker) ('s-Gravenhage: Boekencentrum, 1985), 177ff. Van Ginkel and Balke may both be dependent on Noordmans' statement.

41. J.H. Gunning Ir., *Verlagen wij onszelve niet! Een woord tot de Hervormde Gemeente* (Let us not demean ourselves! A word to the Reformed congregation) (Nijmegen: Ten Hoet, 1902), 7.

looked beyond the boundaries of his own church, the NHK.[42] The course of the development outlined here, however, shows that the unity of the church was important to him from the very beginning, although for a long time the emphasis was on his own denomination.

2.2 Ph.J. Hoedemaker

The second theologian we want to put into the spotlight is Ph.J. Hoedemaker (1839–1910). He was of the conviction that the church is the body of Christ, not an association, nor a society or an institution.[43] "It is not based on the will of people."[44] Hoedemaker, therefore, had great difficulty with the 1816 organization of the NHK. He found the General Regulations illegal in origin, unbiblical in essence and pernicious in spirit. He also held the church government responsible for the growing dissent, which he abhorred.[45] This was partly prompted and reinforced by a number of personal experiences, in which he was confronted with the consequences of the revision of 1852.[46] The orthodox won, for example in his first congregation of Veenendaal and in the classis to which the congregation belonged, but he realized all too well that for liberals

---

42. M.G.L. den Boer, "J.H. Gunning jr. en de eenheid der kerk" (J.H. Gunning jr. and the unity of the church), in *Heel de kerk: Enkele visies op de kerk binnen de 'Ethische Richting'. Uitgave ter gelegenheid van het vijfentwintigste lustrum van het Theologisch-Litterarisch Studentengezelschap 'Excelsior Deo Iuvante', 18 oktober 1995* (The church as a whole: Some visions within the socalled 'Ethische Richting' on the church. Publication on the occasion of the 25th five-yearly anniversary of the Theological Student Society 'Excelsior Deo Iuvante', October 18, 1995), 97–115, eds. Jaap Vlasblom and Jaap van der Windt (Zoetermeer: Boekencentrum, 1995).

43. Ph.J. Hoedemaker, *De Kerk en het Moderne Staatsrecht* (The church and the modern state law) (Amsterdam-Kaapstad: Hollandsch-Afrikaansche Uitgevers-Maatschappij, 1904), 92–122. Cf. G.Ph. Scheers, *Philippus Jacobus Hoedemaker* (Leiden: Groen, 1939¹, 1989²), 184–197.

44. Hoedemaker, *De Kerk en het Moderne Staatsrecht*, 93.

45. Ph.J. Hoedemaker, *Op het fondament der apostelen en profeten* (On the foundation of apostles and prophets) (Utrecht: Van Bentum, 1885), 57, 60; *De roeping der Gereformeerden in de Hervormde Kerk: Naar aanleiding van de 'Nabetrachting op de kerkelijke crisis, door Dr. Ph.S. van Ronkel'* (The call of Reformed members in the (Netherlands) Reformed Church: In response to 'Review of the ecclesial crisis, by Dr. Ph.S. van Ronkel') (Amsterdam: J.H. Kruyt, 1888), 19. Cf. P.J. Kromsigt, "Kerkrechtelijke beginselen" (Church polity principles), in J. Schokking c.s., *Dr. Ph.J. Hoedemaker 1868–1908: Gedenkboek* (Dr. Ph.J. Hoedemaker 1868–1908: Commemorative book) (Leiden: A.L. De Vlieger, 1908), 39–122, 87.

46. Kromsigt, "Kerkrechtelijke beginselen," 52; *Wijziging der gedragslijn op Kerkelijk gebied: Brief aan Dr. A. Kuyper door G. Doedes, predikant der hervormde gemeente te Velsen* (Modification of the line of conduct in ecclesial matters: Letter to Dr. A. Kuyper by G. Doedes, minister of the Reformed congregation in Velsen) (Utrecht: Kemink, 1875); G. Bos, "Hoedemaker en de reorganisatie van de Nederlandse Hervormde Kerk" (Hoedemaker and the reorganization of the Netherlands Reformed Church)," in *Hoedemaker herdacht* (Hoedemaker commemorated), eds. G. Abma and J. de Bruijn (Baarn: Ten Have, 1989), 33–49, 35.

this could have the ultimate consequence that they would be forced to leave the church.⁴⁷ This was at odds with his conviction.

In this context, it should be emphasized that Hoedemaker's thinking about ecclesiastical conflicts changed somewhat over the years.⁴⁸ In his early days he took struggles for granted, at least vis-à-vis the modernists. In his earliest writings he referred to them as enemies. Later he never did so again. The older he got, the more he considered the battles to be a sin. At that time he found every party formation, including those of a confessional nature, to be pernicious.⁴⁹ Here and there it could work as a corrective, but in his opinion it murdered any healthy concept of church. In 1897 he wrote in the well-known brochure, *The Church as a Whole and the People as a Whole*, with the telling subtitle, *A protest against the actions of the Reformed as a party and a word of farewell to the Confessional Association*: "The law of God is also the law of truth, and is NOT the law of the majority."⁵⁰

In 1904 Hoedemaker, together with a few others, signed an open letter to the synod of the NHK, drawn up by Gunning.⁵¹ They requested an impartial and complete investigation into the possibility and necessity of reorganizing the church administration. In the letter they denounced the party spirit in the church,

> which removes the outstanding issues from a legal settlement by the church itself and leaves them to the endless and fruitless dispute of the parties, and thus raises the lever of the 'orthodox' or 'modern' majority, half plus one. The spirit of little faith, questions the power of the Word where it is useful and orderly, and therefore, by fear of a crooked orthodoxy (as if it could overcome this power), offers itself a humiliating 'proof of poverty.'⁵²

---

47. Hoedemaker, *Op het fondament der apostelen en profeten*, 60f. Cf. for Hoedemaker's first years: Kromsigt, "Kerkrechtelijke beginselen," 58; Ph.J. Hoedemaker, *De Congresbeweging beoordeeld uit het oogpunt der Gereformeerde Belijdenis* (The socalled congress Movement assessed from the point of view of the Reformed confession) (Amsterdam: Wormser, 1887), 65.

48. Scheers, *Philippus Jacobus Hoedemaker*, 187.

49. Hoedemaker, *De Congresbeweging*, 66.

50. Ph.J. Hoedemaker, *Heel de Kerk en heel het Volk: Een protest tegen het optreden der Gereformeerden als partij, en een woord van afscheid aan de Confessioneele Vereeniging* (The church as a whole and the people as a whole: A protest against the actions of the Reformed as a party and a word of farewell to the Confessional Association) (Sneek: J. Campen, 1897), 13.

51. J.H. Gunning Jr., c.s., *Open Brief aan de Synode der Nederlandsche Hervormde Kerk* (Open Letter to the Synod of the Netherlands Reformed Church) (Amsterdam: HollandschAfrikaansche Uitgevers-Maatschappij, 1904). Cf. Balke, *Gunning en Hoedemaker samen op weg*, ('s-Gravenhage: Boekencentrum, 1985), 187–197.

52. J.H. Gunning Jr., c.s., *Open Brief*, 13f.

2.3 A. Kuyper and F.L. Rutgers

The third theologian we would like to discuss is A. Kuyper (1837–1920). In 1867 he took a view similar to Gunning, albeit with a slightly different accent. In the brochure, *Wat moeten wij doen?*, he argues that democracy is not contrary to the nature of the church.[53] However, it should not be accepted because it is foreign to the Reformed Church and its tradition; it comes from outside the church. Still, the deplorable situation of the church makes it necessary for orthodox believers to make use of their right to vote. Kuyper's activist reaction to the increasing struggle following the innovations of 1852/1867 differs fundamentally from that of Gunning and Hoedemaker, although he would be friends with the latter for a long time to come. In 1869 Kuyper analyzed the situation in the brochure *De werking van artikel* 23, and he noted that the goal of an orthodox majority in the synod would not be achieved quickly.[54] In *Tractaat der Reformatie* (1883), he chose a new approach. In his opinion, it is not the majority of votes that are decisive, but "the present royal power of Christ."[55] In the spirit of prayer, office bearers must convince each other "until unity of insight is born."[56] However, when Kuyper was confronted with the fact that majorities in ecclesiastical meetings would certainly not lead to the desired goal and several major assemblies even had chosen an opposite direction, he and his 'Doleantie' movement forced a rift in 1886. Following on from this break, the Gereformeerde Kerken in Nederland (GKN) (Reformed Churches in the Netherlands) came into existence in 1892.

Kuyper's friend and kindred spirit F.L. Rutgers (1836–1917) incorporated Kuyper's ecclesiology into ecclesiastical law. The movement of the 'Doleantie' returned to the Church Order of Dort. Because the majority principle in article 31 of this church order is within the framework of the right of appeal to a major assembly, it concerns the heart of Kuyper's and Rutgers's ecclesiology, in which the local church was in itself a complete church, in principle having an almost full autonomy. Major assemblies consist by the grace of local churches wanting to gather on the basis of the same confession. All principal decisions of those assemblies have to be confirmed by the local churches. Only when a local church considers a decision to be in conflict

---

53. A. Kuyper, *Wat moeten wij doen, het stemrecht aan ons zelven houden of den kerkeraad machtigen?* (What should we do, keep the Right to vote to ourselves or authorize the church council?) (Culemborg: Blom, 1867).

54. A. Kuyper, *De werking van artikel* 23 (The effects of Article 23) (Amsterdam: Höveker, 1869).

55. A. Kuyper, *Tractaat van de Reformatie der kerken* … (Tract on the Reformation of the churches) (Amsterdam: Höveker, 1883), 120.

56. Kuyper, *Tractaat*, 133.

with God's Word, is it allowed to object. Rutgers's interpretation of the synods of Emden (1571) and Dordrecht (1578) as pursuing unanimous decisions in major assemblies must be seen against the background of this strong unity-oriented approach.

2.4 Interim Conclusion

Against the background of democratization trends, theologians started to reconsider the long-standing majority principle from the middle of the 19th century onwards. Gunning and Hoedemaker were of the opinion votes should be avoided in ecclesiastical assemblies anyway. Kuyper, however, initially wanted to make use of votes to realize essential changes in the church of his day. Once having broken with the NHK, other than Gunning and Hoedemaker, he and Rutgers devalued the meaning of ecclesiastical votes by stressing the principle that unity had to be found on a confessional basis. People of the same confession gathered in congregations and congregations of the same confession gathered in major assemblies.

3. The Majority Principle Reworded

On May 1, 2004, the NHK, the GKN and the Evangelisch-Lutherse Kerk (Evangelical Lutheran Church) merged into the PKN.[57] The structure of both the church and its church order have predominantly been derived from the NHK. Elements of the practices in the two other denominations can be found in the elaboration of the structure. In this section we will first discuss the developments within the NHK, then the developments in the GKN, and conclude with the design of the church order of the PKN.

3.1 A New Church Order for the Nederlandse Hervormde Kerk (1951)

After Gunning, many asked for a thorough review of the NHK's organization. It took almost half a century before a new church order was introduced, on May 1, 1951.[58] Many of the requests to the Reformed syn-

---

57. Barend Wallet, *Samen op Weg naar de Protestantse Kerk in Nederland: Het verhaal achter de vereniging* (Together towards the Protestant Church in the Netherlands: The story behind the merge) (Zoetermeer: Boekencentrum, 2005); Hanna Ploeg-Bouwman, *Bewoonde herinnering: Een learning history van het Samen-op-Weg-proces* (Living memory: A learning history of the socalled Samen-op-Weg-process) (Utrecht: Eburon, 2019).

58. H.A.M. Fiolet, *Een kerk in onrust om haar belijdenis: Een phaenomenologische studie over het ontstaan van de richtingenstrijd in de Nederlandse Hervormde Kerk* (A church troubled by her confession: A phenomenological study into the genesis of the battle of convictions within the Netherlands Reformed Church) (Nijkerk: Callenbach, 1953); H. Bartels, *Tien jaren strijd om een belijdende kerk: De Nederlandsche Hervormde Kerk van 1929 tot 1939* (Ten years of battles for a confessing church: The Netherlands

od did not achieve a majority, because they were supported by nine out of nineteen votes. In that light, it is remarkable that in the process of developing a new church order, the need for a two-thirds majority for important matters was considered.[59] Still, no such provision was included in the church order in the end. In its founding articles, the most important guarantee for far-reaching decisions by the synod would be sought in a so-called double synod with twice as many delegates as usual, which had to decide by simple majority.[60] The only other guarantee that applied to all ecclesiastical meetings was that of a quorum of two-thirds of the members.[61] The simple majority became the rule; blank votes were only accepted under very special conditions.[62] Nevertheless, the requirement of a two-thirds majority in certain cases would still be introduced after only five years.[63] Apparently, the previous principal objections were not upheld. In his 1991 commentary, church polity expert P. van den Heuvel (b. 1941) notes:

> The basic rule of every church law (of all confessions and denominations) is that Christ is the only ruler of the church. In a church, democracy is never considered to be the highest good. The truth of God is not established by majority vote. In the church, the Christocracy applies: Christ rules.[64]

And elsewhere in his book: "It is, of course, advisable to strive for unity in the church, or at least for broader agreement."[65]

In working towards what would eventually become the PKN, the NHK synod in 1995 laid down an additional article to the church order for the merger of three denominations.[66] This provision stipulated that

---

Reformed Church 1929 to 1939) ('s-Gravenhage: W.P. van Stockum & Zoon, 1946).

59. W. Balke and H. Oostenbrink-Evers (eds.), *De Commissie voor de Werkorde (1942–1944), oorspronkelijk ingesteld als de Commissie voor Beginselen van Kerkorde* (The Committee for the [Design of a] Workorder, Originally created as the Committee for the [Design of the] Principles of a Church Order) (Zoetermeer: Boekencentrum, 1995), 109, 169–171.

60. *Kerkorde der Nederlandse Hervormde Kerk* (Church order of the Netherlands Reformed Church) ('s-Gravenhage: Boekencentrum, januari 1951) (= HKO 1951), art. XXVIII-4,5 and XIII-2. Cf. P. van den Heuvel, *De hervormde kerkorde: Een praktische toelichting* (Church order of the Netherlands Reformed Church: A practical explanation) (Zoetermeer: Boekencentrum, 1991), 409.

61. HKO 1951, ord. 1-21-10.

62. HKO 1951, ord. 1-24.

63. *Kerkorde der Nederlandse Hervormde Kerk* (Church order of the Netherlands Reformed Church) ('s-Gravenhage: Boekencentrum, mei 1956), ord. 1-21-10. Cf. for similar changes in later editions Van den Heuvel, *De hervormde kerkorde*, resp. 409 en 389.

64. Van den Heuvel, *De hervormde kerkorde*, 24.

65. Van den Heuvel, *De hervormde kerkorde*, 121.

66. Generale Synode van de Nederlandse Hervormde Kerk, 15–17 juni 1995, "Advies van de Commissie voor kerkordelijke aangelegenheden inzake de procedure,

a majority of at least two-thirds of the votes cast was required for the NHK decision to unite into the PKN. The synod arrived at this decision on the basis of the consideration that a large majority should be taken into account, without, however, neglecting a large minority. The synod took the view that the requirement of the said majority was an extension of the usual rules in church and society. Reference was made to the use of organizations to prescribe a special method of decision-making for matters that affect constitution-like regulations. The adoption of both the Charter and the Constitution of the Kingdom of the Netherlands was given as an example. In the NHK itself similar rules had been used in the decision-making process on the church order of 1951: a majority of at least two-thirds was required for the final decision about a double synod. By the way, the other denominations required a qualified majority too when deciding about the merger into the PKN.[67]

3.2 A NEW CHURCH ORDER FOR THE GEREFORMEERDE KERKEN IN NEDERLAND (1959)

In the 1950s, the GKN developed a new church order in which the structure of the Church Order of Dort and the most important articles of that order can be clearly identified. Article 31 was given a completely new wording, in which the decision-making rules were placed in a subparagraph: "The decisions of the assemblies will always be made after joint consultation and, as far as possible, by unanimous vote. If unanimity is not achieved, the minority will comply with the conviction of the majority. The decisions of the assemblies are binding."[68] This change has to be seen against the background of two rifts in the GKN, in 1926 and 1944. The new text calls, as it were, for unity to be maintained. Majority decisions should only be made if unanimity is not feasible. In commenting on the article in his commentary on the GKN Church Order, church historian and church polity expert D. Nauta (1898–1994), following Rutgers and others after Rutgers,[69] refers in general terms to 'old Reformed

---

die kerkordelijk gezien gevolgd dient te worden bij vereniging van de Nederlandse Hervormde Kerk met de Gereformeerde Kerken in Nederland en de Evangelisch-Lutherse Kerk in het Koninkrijk der Nederlanden" (Advice of the Committee for church order matters on the procedure to be followed in case of a merge between the Netherlands Reformed Church, the Reformed Churches in the Netherlands and the Evangelical Lutheran Church in the Kingdom of the Netherlands). Cf. Wallet, *Samen op weg*, 150; Van den Heuvel, *De hervormde kerkorde*, 396.

67. Wallet, *Samen op weg*, 317–322.

68. D. Nauta, *Verklaring van de kerkorde van de Gereformeerde Kerken in Nederland* (Explanation of the church order of the Reformed Churches in the Netherlands) (Kampen: Kok, 1971), 135.

69. E.g., Joh. Jansen, *Korte verklaring van de kerkenordening* (Brief explanation of the church order) (Kampen: Kok, 1923), 144.

synods' where "according to the description given here" decisions were made.[70] However, there is an essential difference between how Rutgers understood the texts of the old synods and the way in which unanimity is given a place in the renewed provision. Whereas, according to Rutgers, unanimity in the sixteenth-century regulations was given a place at the end of the procedure, in the GKN 1959 Church Order the striving for this becomes an integral part of the procedure that precedes the decision as such.[71] Still, the research presented in this article shows the GKN regulation is in line with the Reformed practice at the end of the 16th century.

3.3 THE CHURCH ORDER OF THE PROTESTANTSE KERK IN NEDERLAND (2004)

When the three denominations merged into the PKN, a new church order came into effect. The majority principle in this church order is very similar to that of the GKN, though the line in the Church Order of Dort and the 1959 Church Order about the impossibility of decisions contrary God's Word is lacking: "In all church meetings, decisions should always be made after joint consultation and, if possible, by unanimous vote. If unanimity turns out to be impossible, the decision is made by a majority of the votes cast, in which case blank votes do not count."[72] The fact that the regulation applies to all ecclesiastical meetings and not only to meetings of office bearers is taken from the church order of the NHK. The dependence on the later NHK Church Order also applies to certain provisions according to which a qualified two-thirds majority is required.[73] Still, the GKN church order can be recognized in the basic rule for voting. Only the wording 'as far as possible' has been exchanged for 'if possible.' This seems to be a weakening of the original formula; the significance, however, is that serious efforts should be made to achieve unanimity.[74]

4. CONCLUSIONS

The decision-making in the Reformed Church in the Netherlands initially followed secular practice, although with the general application of

---

70. Nauta, *Verklaring*, 137.
71. De Jong, "Zo mogelijk," 113.
72. *Kerkorde en ordinanties van de Protestantse Kerk in Nederland inclusief de overgangsbepalingen* (Church order of the Protestant Church in the Netherlands) (Zoetermeer: Boekencentrum, 2003), ord. 4-5-1 (cf. ord. 4-4-1).
73. Cf. for a list of these provisions P. van den Heuvel (ed.), *Toelichting op de kerkorde van de Protestantse Kerk in Nederland: Herziene uitgave* (Explanation of the church order of the Protestant Church in the Netherlands: Revised Edition) (Zoetermeer: Boekencentrum, 2013), 172.
74. De Jong, "Zo mogelijk," 117.

the majority principle as it takes shape in the Church Order of Dort, it seems to be ahead of its time, at least in the major assemblies. Nevertheless, the Dutch Reformed Church has realized from the beginning that, due to the special character of the church, decision-making is not a case of a simple majority. Other values are at stake, such as the obedience to (the Word of) God.

The nineteenth century shows a similar pattern. The Reformed Church followed secular practice, albeit that it only embraced this change with delay and restraint. Several theologians criticized the full implementation of the majority principle. They pointed to the church's own spiritual character and thus to the dignity of the church, as well as to the unity of the body of Christ, which in their view is endangered by the majority principle. In this context, historical arguments have been exchanged too. We note that in the sixteenth and seventeenth centuries unity and unanimity were certainly sought in regulations and in practice, but it goes too far to elevate this to a norm, as was done by Rutgers and, following his example, by others in the GKN.

In the church order of the PKN, the two lines come together. Achieving unanimity is an important goal in the decision-making process. On the one hand, this refers to unity in Christ; this unity should be seriously sought. On the other hand, unity in Christ does not depend on the results of a vote.

The Dutch churches in the Reformed tradition have always been strongly influenced by society as a whole in its decision-making regulations. At the same time, in dealing with differences of opinion and even polarization, the Church has given these rules their own color. It has opted for the majority principle on practical grounds, but has always realized that—especially when decisions are contrary to the Word of God—the majority does not in fact have the last word.

Reflecting on these conclusions, we note that they are ambiguous in their handling of polarization. On the one hand, decision makers are challenged to seek unanimity for the sake of the unity in Christ. However, the idea of unity in Christ may entice them to force their own way of expressing this unity in ecclesiastical practice onto others; this will often cause polarization. On the other hand, the alleged unity in Christ may lead to a certain indifference; whatever the decision, the unity remains. There may be no polarization then, but the Church will not fulfil its calling towards polarization. In our view, this calling is in line with the two related theological tasks Pieter Vos describes in the introduction of this volume. Those called upon to make decisions should recalibrate their "view and life attitude in light of scripture and tradition" in order to reach "a new understanding of the common good."[75] Hence, in decision making the Church should keep its distance from both the extremes outlined. As a consequence, it will probably have to go down a narrow path, but it knows from scripture this is the path that leads to life.

BIBLIOGRAPHY

A Lasco, Joh. *Forma ac Ratio* ... [1555].

Balke, W. Gunning en Hoedemaker samen op weg. 's-Gravenhage: Boekencentrum, 1985. Balke, W. and H. Oostenbrink-Evers. Eds. *De Commissie voor de Werkorde (1942–1944), oorspronkelijk ingesteld als de Commissie voor Beginselen van Kerkorde* (The Committee for the [Design of a] Workorder, Originally created as the Committee for the [Design of the] Principles of a Church Order). Zoetermeer: Boekencentrum, 1995.

Berg, J.T. van den. "De synode van Dordrecht en de Dordtse Kerkorde" (The Synod of Dort and the Church Order of Dort). In *Handboek gereformeerd kerkrecht* (Manual of Reformed church polity), ed. H.J. Selderhuis, 162–170. Heerenveen: Groen, 2019.

Bos, F.L. *De orde der kerk* (The order of the church). 's-Gravenhage: Guido de Bres, 1950.

Bos, G. "Hoedemaker en de reorganisatie van de Nederlandse Hervormde Kerk" (Hoedemaker and the reorganization of the Netherlands Reformed Church)." In *Hoedemaker herdacht* (Hoedemaker commemorated), eds. G. Abma and J. de Bruijn, 33–49. Baarn: Ten Have, 1989.

Classicale Acta 1573–1620. 's-Gravenhage: Martinus Nijhoff (I), Instituut voor Nederlandse Geschiedenis (II–IX), 1980-2011.

Boer, Erik A. de. *De macht van de minderheid: Het remonstrantisme in Kampen in de spiegel van de nationale synode te Dordrecht (1618–1619)* (The power of the minority: Remonstrantism in Kampen in the mirror of the National Synod in Dordrecht (1618–1619)). Kampen: Summum Academic Publications, 2019.

---

75. Pieter Vos, "Introduction," 10.

Boer, M.G.L. den. "J.H. Gunning Jr. en de eenheid der kerk" (J.H. Gunning Jr. and the unity of the church), in *Heel de kerk: Enkele visies op de kerk binnen de 'Ethische Richting'. Uitgave ter gelegenheid van het vijfentwintigste lustrum van het TheologischLitterarisch Studentengezelschap 'Excelsior Deo Iuvante'*, 18 oktober 1995 (The church as a whole: Some visions within the socalled 'Ethische Richting' on the church. Publication on the occasion of the 25th five-yearly anniversary of the Theological Student Society 'Excelsior Deo Iuvante', October 18, 1995), eds. Jaap Vlasblom and Jaap van der Windt, 97–115. Zoetermeer: Boekencentrum, 1995.

Broeke, Leon van den. "Regionale (re)organisatie: classicaal bestuur en provinciaal kerkbestuur rond 1816" (Regional (re)organization: Classical administration and provincial church administration around 1816). In *Ramp of redding: 200 jaar Algemeen Reglement voor het Bestuur der Hervormde Kerk in het Koninkrijk der Nederlanden 1816–2016* (Disaster or rescue: 200 Years of General Regulations for the governance of the Reformed Church in the kingdom of the Netherlands 1816–2016), eds. Fred van Lieburg and Johanna Roelevink, 59–75. Utrecht: Boekencentrum, 2018.

DeRidder, Richard; Peter H. Jonker and Leonard Verduin, *The Church Orders of the Sixteenth Century Reformed Churches of the Netherlands: Together with Their Social, Political, and Ecclesiastical Context*. Grand Rapids: Calvin Theological Seminary, 1987.

Fiolet, H.A.M. *Een kerk in onrust om haar belijdenis: Een phaenomenologische studie over het ontstaan van de richtingenstrijd in de Nederlandse Hervormde Kerk* (A church troubled by her confession: A phenomenological study into the genesis of the battle of convictions within the Netherlands Reformed Church). Nijkerk: Callenbach, 1953.

Ginkel, A. van. "Gunnings waardering van de presbyteriale kerkorde" (Gunnings' appreciation of the presbyterial church order), in *Wegen en gestalten in het Gereformeerd Protestantisme: Een bundel studies over de geschiedenis van het Gereformeerd Protestantisme* … (Shapes of Reformed Protestantism: A volume of studies about the history of Reformed protestantism), eds. W. Balke, C. Graafland and H. Harkema, 257–269. Amsterdam: Ton Bolland, 1976.

Gunning Jr., J.H. *Aan de Hervormde gemeente: Een woord over haar stemrecht* (To the Reformed congregation: A word about her voting rights). 's-Gravenhage: Gerritsen, 1867.

Gunning Jr., J.H. *De vrijheid der gemeente*: *Bezwaren tegen de ordeningen der Nederduitsche Hervormde Kerk in onze dagen* (The freedom of the congregation: Objections to the orders of the Dutch Reformed Church in our days). Utrecht: Van der Post, 1861.

Gunning Jr., J.H. *Openbare brief aan de ouderlingen der Vrije Evangelische Gemeente te Amsterdam* (Public letter to the elders of the Free Evangelical Congregation in Amsterdam). Utrecht: Van der Post, 1860.

Gunning Jr., J.H. *Ter nabetrachting van 31 october en ter voorbereiding tot 17 november*: *Een woord tot de gemeente gesproken* (In review of October 31 and in preparation for November 17: A word to the congregation). 's-Gravenhage: Van Hoogstraten, 1869.

Gunning Jr., J.H. *Verlagen wij onszelve niet*! *Een woord tot de Hervormde Gemeente* (Let us not demean ourselves! A word to the Reformed congregation). Nijmegen: Ten Hoet, 1902.

Gunning Jr., J.H. *Zestien stellingen betrekkelijk het stemrecht der gemeente, aan de gemeente ter overweging gegeven* (Sixteen propositions regarding the voting rights of the congregation, given to the congregation for consideration). Amsterdam: Höveker, 1867.

Gunning Jr., J.H. c.s. *Open Brief aan de Synode der Nederlandsche Hervormde Kerk* (Open Letter to the Synod of the Netherlands Reformed Church). Amsterdam: Hollandsch-Afrikaansche Uitgevers-Maatschappij, 1904.

Gunning J.H.zn., J.H. *Prof. dr. J.H. Gunning*: *Leven en werken*, II (Prof. dr. J.H. Gunning: Life and work). Rotterdam: Bredeé, 1923.

Heuvel, P. van den. *De hervormde kerkorde*: *Een praktische toelichting* (Church order of the Netherlands Reformed Church: A practical explanation). Zoetermeer: Boekencentrum, 1991.

Heuvel, P. van den. Ed. T*oelichting op de kerkorde van de Protestantse Kerk in Nederland*: *Herziene uitgave* (Explanation of the church order of the Protestant Church in the Netherlands: Revised Edition). Zoetermeer: Boekencentrum, 2013.

Hoedemaker, Ph.J. *De Congresbeweging beoordeeld uit het oogpunt der Gereformeerde Belijdenis* (The socalled congress Movement assessed from the point of view of the Reformed confession). Amsterdam: Wormser, 1887.

Hoedemaker, Ph.J. *De Kerk en het Moderne Staatsrecht* (The church and the modern state law). Amsterdam-Kaapstad: Hollandsch-Afrikaansche Uitgevers-Maatschappij, 1904.

Hoedemaker, Ph.J. *De roeping der Gereformeerden in de Hervormde Kerk: Naar aanleiding van de 'Nabetrachting op de kerkelijke crisis, door Dr. Ph.S. van Ronkel'* (The call of Reformed members in the (Netherlands) Reformed Church: In response to 'Review of the ecclesial crisis, by Dr. Ph.S. van Ronkel'). Amsterdam: J.H. Kruyt, 1888.

Hoedemaker, Ph.J. *Heel de Kerk en heel het Volk: Een protest tegen het optreden der Gereformeerden als partij, en een woord van afscheid aan de Confessioneele Vereeniging* (The church as a whole and the people as a whole: A protest against the actions of the Reformed as a party and a word of farewell to the Confessional Association). Sneek: J. Campen, 1897.

Hoedemaker, Ph.J. *Op het fondament der apostelen en profeten* (On the foundation of apostles and prophets). Utrecht: Van Bentum, 1885.

Houkes, Annemarie. *Christelijke vaderlanders: Godsdienst, burgerschap en de Nederlandse natie* (1850–1900) (Christian patriots: Religion, citizenship and the Dutch nation (1850–1900)). Amsterdam: Wereldbibliotheek, 2009.

Jansen, Joh. *Korte verklaring van de kerkenordening* (Brief explanation of the church order) (Kampen: Kok, 1923.

Jong, K.W. de. "Een verkennend onderzoek naar de receptie van een anti-hiërarchisch beginsel in Nederlandse kerkorden van het gereformeerde type" (An exploratory investigation into the reception of an anti-hierarchical principle in Dutch Reformed church orders), *In die Skriflig* 52:2 (2018):1–9 (https://doi.org/10.4102/ids.v52i2.2350).

Jong, K.W. de. "'Wettiglijk van Gods gemeente, en mitsdien van God zelven geroepen': De voorgeschiedenis van het reglement van 1867 voor de verkiezing en beroeping van een hervormde predikant" ("Lawfully called by God's congregation, and therefore by God himself": The history of the Regulations of 1867 for the election and vocation of a Reformed pastor). *Tijdschrift voor Nederlandse Kerkgeschiedenis* 20:3 (2017): 109–117.

Jong, K.W. de. "Zo mogelijk met eenparige stemmen" (If possible unanimously). NTKR *Tijdschrift voor Recht en Religie* 10:2 (2016): 107–119.

Kaajan, Hendrik. *De Pro-Acta der Dordtsche Synode* (The Pro-Acta of the Synod of Dort). Rotterdam: De Vries, 1914.

Kerkorde der Nederlandse Hervormde Kerk (Church order of the Netherlands Reformed Church). 's-Gravenhage: Boekencentrum, 1951.

Kerkorde der Nederlandse Hervormde Kerk (Church order of the Netherlands Reformed Church). 's-Gravenhage: Boekencentrum, 1956.

Kerkorde en ordinanties van de Protestantse Kerk in Nederland inclusief de overgangsbepalingen (Church order of the Protestant Church in the Netherlands). Zoetermeer: Boekencentrum, 2003.

Koch, Jeroen. "Revolutie, restauratie, reformatie: Koning Willem I, Abraham Kuyper en het Algemeen Reglement van 1816" (Revolution, restoration, reformation: King Willem I, Abraham Kuyper and the General Regulations of 1816). In *Ramp of redding: 200 jaar Algemeen Reglement voor het Bestuur der Hervormde Kerk in het Koninkrijk der Nederlanden 1816–2016* (Disaster or rescue: 200 Years of General Regulations for the governance of the Reformed Church in the kingdom of the Netherlands 1816–2016), eds. Fred van Lieburg and Johanna Roelevink, 162–164. Utrecht: Boekencentrum, 2018.

Kromsigt, P.J. "Kerkrechtelijke beginselen" (Church polity principles). In: J. Schokking, c.s., *Dr. Ph.J. Hoedemaker 1868–1908: Gedenkboek* (Dr. Ph.J. Hoedemaker 1868–1908: Commemorative book), 39–122. Leiden: A.L. De Vlieger, 1908.

Kuyper, A. *De werking van artikel 23* (The effects of Article 23). Amsterdam: Höveker, 1869.

Kuyper, A. *Tractaat van de Reformatie der kerken ...* (Tract on the Reformation of the churches). Amsterdam: Höveker, 1883.

Kuyper, A. *Wat moeten wij doen, het stemrecht aan ons zelven houden of den kerkeraad machtigen?* (What should we do, keep the Right to vote to ourselves or authorize the church council?). Culemborg: Blom, 1867.

Kuyper, H.H. *De Post-Acta of Nahandelingen van de Nationale Synode van Dordrecht in 1618 en 1619 gehouden naar den authentieken tekst in het Latijn en Nederlandsch uitgegeven en met toelichtingen voorzien. Voorafgegaan door de geschiedenis van de Acta, de Autographa en de Post-Acta dier synode en gevolgd door de geschiedenis van de revisie der belijdenisgeschriften en der Liturgie, benevens de volledige lijst der gravamina op de Dordtsche synode ingediend.* Amsterdam-Pretoria: Höveker & Wormser.

Lieburg, Fred van, and Johanna Roelevink. Eds. *Ramp of redding: 200 jaar Algemeen Reglement voor het Bestuur der Hervormde Kerk in het Koninkrijk der Nederlanden 1816–2016* (Disaster or rescue: 200 Years of General Regulations for the governance of the Reformed Church in the kingdom of the Netherlands 1816–2016). Utrecht: Boekencentrum, 2018.

Loon, J.C.A. van. *Het Algemeen Reglement van 1816* (The General Regulations of 1816). Wageningen: Zomer & Keuning, 1942.

Nauta, D. *Verklaring van de kerkorde van de Gereformeerde Kerken in Nederland* (Explanation of the church order of the Reformed Churches in the Netherlands). Kampen: Kok, 1971.

Noordmans, O. *Verzamelde Werken* (Collected Works), Vol. 5. Kampen: Kok, 1984.

Ploeg-Bouwman, Hanna. *Bewoonde herinnering: Een learning history van het Samenop-Weg-proces* (Living memory: A learning history of the socalled Samen-op-Wegprocess). Utrecht: Eburon, 2019.

Reitsma, J. and S.D. van Veen. Eds. *Acta der provinciale en particuliere synoden, gehouden in de noordelijke Nederlanden gedurende de jaren 1572–1620* (Acta of provincial and particular synods, held in the northern Netherlands during the years 1572–1620). Groningen: Wolters, 1892–1899.

Roelevink, Johanna. "De Hervormde Kerk wankelend op eigen benen: de herziening van het Algemeen Reglement in 1852" (The Reformed Church on shaking footing: The revision of the General Regulations in 1852). In *Ramp of redding: 200 jaar Algemeen Reglement voor het Bestuur der Hervormde Kerk in het Koninkrijk der Nederlanden 1816–2016* (Disaster or rescue: 200 Years of General Regulations for the governance of the Reformed Church in the kingdom of the Netherlands 1816–2016), eds. Fred van Lieburg and Johanna Roelevink, 143–148. Utrecht: Boekencentrum, 2018.

Roelevink, Johanna. "Het Algemeen Reglement van 1816: een hekgolf in de rivier" (The General Regulations of 1816: A sternwave in the river). In *Ramp of redding: 200 jaar Algemeen Reglement voor het Bestuur der Hervormde Kerk in het Koninkrijk der Nederlanden 1816–2016* (Disaster or rescue: 200 Years of General Regulations for the governance of the Reformed Church in the kingdom of the Netherlands 1816–2016), eds. Fred van Lieburg and Johanna Roelevink, 19–57. Utrecht: Boekencentrum, 2018.

Rutgers, F.L. Ed. *Acta van de Nederlandsche synoden der zestiende eeuw* (Acta of the Dutch synods of the sixteenth century), Werken der Marnix-Vereeniging, II/3. 's-Gravenhage: Nijhoff, 1889.

Rutgers, F.L. "Bespreking der hoofdpunten van het Kerkrecht naar aanleiding van de Dordtsche Kerkenorde" (collegedictaat 1892–1895) (Discussion of the main points of church polity in connection with the Church Order of Dort, Lecture Notes 1892– 1895), art. 31 (123). Accessed August 8, 2019. http://kerkrecht.nl/node/1310.

Scheers, G.Ph. *Philippus Jacobus Hoedemaker*. Leiden: Groen, 19391, 19892.

Semmelink, J.H. *Prof. Dr. J.H. Gunning, zijn ontwikkelingsgang en zijne beginselen* (Prof. dr. J.H. Gunning, His development and his principles). Zeist: Vonk & Co, 1926.

Vree, W. van. *Nederland als vergaderland: Opkomst en verbreiding van een vergaderregime* (The Netherlands as a meeting country: Emergence and spread of a meeting regime). Groningen: Wolters Noordhoff, 1994.

Vree, Jasper. "Gunning en Kuyper: Een bewogen vriendschap rond Schrift en kerk in de jaren 1860–1873" (Gunning and Kuyper: An eventful friendship around scripture and church in the years 1860–1873). In *Noblesse oblige: Achtergrond en actualiteit van de theologie van J.H. Gunning Jr.* (Noblesse oblige: Background and topicality of the theology of J.H. Gunning Jr.), eds. Theo Hettema and Leo Mietus, 62–86. Gorinchem: Ekklesia, 2005.

Wallet, Barend. *Samen op Weg naar de Protestantse Kerk in Nederland: Het verhaal achter de vereniging* (Together towards the Protestant Church in the Netherlands: The story behind the merge). Zoetermeer: Boekencentrum, 2005.

Wassenaar, J.D.Th. "'… dat God het winnen zal in de kerk …': Een beschouwing over 'meerderheid van stemmen' in de kerk" (…that God will prevail in the church: A reflection on 'majority of votes' in the church), *Ecclesia* 95:4 (2004): 26–29.

Wijziging der gedragslijn op Kerkelijk gebied: Brief aan Dr. A. Kuyper door G. Doedes, predikant der hervormde gemeente te Velsen (Modification of the line of conduct in ecclesial matters: Letter to Dr. A. Kuyper by G. Doedes, minister of the Reformed congregation in Velsen). Utrecht: Kemink, 1875.

Part 3: The Calling of the Church

CHAPTER 13
FIGHTING AGAINST POLARIZATION: THE INDONESIAN COMMUNION OF CHURCHES, RELIGIOUS PLURALITY AND SEXUAL ORIENTATIONS IN INDONESIA
Emanuel Gerrit Singgih

1. INTRODUCTION

In the years following the Third Millennium in Indonesia, violence against those who were regarded by the majority as deviating from true religious tenets had increased sharply. In the second period of Susilo Bambang Yudhoyono's presidency, the Ahmadiyah people became the target of attacks: their houses were burned, and in 2011 in Cikeusik, West Java, three followers of Ahmadiyah were killed by raging mobs. The outnumbered police could only watch the incident passively. In the town of Sampang on the island of Madura, East Java, followers of Syiah were ousted from their villages, and until today they remain as refugees in Surabaya. In the first period of Jokowi's presidency, the scope of polarization widened to involve people from different religions, and this was caused by politics.

During the Jakarta local election in 2016, the Muslim population reacted strongly against the possibility of having a non-Muslim (i.e., a Christian) as their new governor, and in the end they succeeded in electing a Muslim candidate as the new governor of Jakarta. As their success involved a (false) accusation of blasphemy against the non-Muslim candidate, many Christians resented the outcome of this election. Since then, there have been incidents of attacks against statues of Buddha and Kuan Yin and statues of figures from the traditional wayang stories. In 2019 there were desecrations of symbols of the cross in public cemeteries and even the graves of newly buried non-Muslim people. The public officials bowed to the pressure and the remains were uncovered and moved to other burial places.

Since 2016, LGBT people and those who support them have also become targets of attacks. The police made raids on suspected rendezvous places and workshops on gender issues, transgender people were attacked in public by radical groups wearing white robes, a center for gender studies in the University of Indonesia was closed, following the accusation by the Minister of Research and Technology that it promoted deviant sexual habits, and the Minister of Defence accused LGBT people of being 'proxy agents' of foreign enemies, who were trying to weaken the nation internally. However, a very powerful Minister who was notoriously known for promoting the extension of palm oil plantations defended the LGBT people.

There was also a motion to the Mahkamah Konstitusi (abbr.: MK, Eng: 'The Constitutional Court,' equivalent to the Supreme Court in the U.S.) to treat homosexual acts as criminal offenses, as in Malaysia, which means *criminalization* of the LGBT community. The MK rejected this motion. However, in the discourse concerning the renewal of the Book of Criminal Law by the Executive and the Legislative branches, many were still supporting this move. The move can be contrasted with the Supreme Court of India, which recently repealed the laws concerning homosexual acts.

According to many political analysts, this is a diversion from the real issue of polarization in politics during the general election of 2019 (between Jokowi and his arch-rival Prabowo), which resulted in inter-religious polarization, as both sides were manipulating religious sentiments. This inter-religious polarization caused the shift to the issue of LGBT. The diversionary tactic resulted in scapegoating of LGBT people. However, as it was the result of religious polarization, we can say that the LGBT issue was a side effect of religious polarization.

It is ironic that in the days of Soeharto's totalitarian New Order regime (1966–1998) there was relatively little religious polarization. Obedience to the national ideology of Pancasila as the foundation of the state was strong enough to withstand domination efforts by the religion of the majority. Many of Soeharto's ministers, public servants and army commanders were Christians (Catholic and Protestants). One of his ministers was known as a gay person, and before he was appointed as a minister he was the Head of the Presidential Palace Household.

In the New Order Era, it goes without saying that Christians, the PGI ('Persekutuan Gereja-Gereja di Indonesia'; Eng.: 'The Indonesian Communion of Churches') and the member churches of the PGI, relied on Pancasila in order to be able to face the religion of the majority. That is why at present they often issue a plea to return to Pancasila and why, for them, Pancasila is non-negotiable (Ind: 'harga mati'). Nowadays, however, it seems that Indonesian society is experiencing a paradigm shift, from an 'ideology-based state' to a 'religion-based state.' I have reflected on this change in a separate article and do not want to repeat everything that I have already said in that article.¹ While affirming their loyalty to Pancasila, Christians and Muslims must be ready to accept one another, not just as citizens of the same state, but also as adherents of different religions, who have created new religious precepts (including public theologies) which may enable them to live together in reconciliation and harmony.

Not all are bad stories. In this article, I will also describe efforts to bridge or overcome this polarization, starting with the MK's decision no. 97/2016 (made public on October 18, 2017) which allows adherents of 'spiritual groups' (Ind.: *penganut aliran kepercayaan*) to state their beliefs as such in their electronic national identity cards (Ind.: 'Kartu tanda Penduduk Elektronik,' abbr.: E-KTP). Prior to that, they had to affiliate themselves with one of the six official religions in order to fill the column of religion in the national identity card. I will summarize what the PGI did in response to the MK's decision, and then move to describe how the PGI responded to intimidation of LGBT people, by issuing a pastoral statement on LGBT, how the Christian community reacted to this statement, and how the LGBT community and some Muslims responded to it. I will close with a conclusion, followed by some further reflection on the role of the PGI in overcoming polarization in Indonesia.

2. THE PGI AND RECOGNITION OF SPIRITUAL GROUPS AND ADAT SOCIETY

The MK's decision is crucial for the discourse on religious plurality in Indonesia. Although it is concerned with allowing 'spiritual groups' to disconnect their forced relationship with one of the six official religions and to stand on their own right, the impact of this decision is actually the state recognition of all 'spiritual groups' as legal bodies. For the first time in Indonesian history, these groups, which were formerly categorized as 'spiritual' (meaning lower than 'religious'), are now on par with world religions such as Islam and Christianity. One factor that determined the MK's decision is an argument during the public hearing that the so-called spiritual groups are actually the indigenous or local religions, so why are the imported world religions recognized, but the indigenous or local religions unrecognized?²

---

1. Emanuel Gerrit Singgih, "What has Ahok to do with Santa? Contemporary Christian and Muslim Public Theologies in Indonesia," *International Journal of Public Theology* 13:1 (2019), 25–39.

2. Andi Saputra, "Ketua MK: Kenapa Agama dari Asing Diakui, Kalau dari Leluhur Tidak?" (Chief Judge of Constitutional Court: Why is religion from foreigners recognized, if from ancestors not?), *Detik News*, Sidang Kolom Agama, May 3, 2017,

The problem is that in the Indonesian construction of religion there are two main categories: the first is the religions and the second is the spiritual beliefs. The first has a higher status than the second. Even in the Amended Constitution of 1945 (Ind.: UUD 45) these two categories are found (in chapter 28E, [1] and [2]). However, in the E-KTP, there is only the column on religion and no column on spiritual beliefs. One solution was to create a special E-KTP (electronic national identity card) for followers of the spiritual groups. The Head of The Indonesian Council of Ulemas (Ind.: 'Majelis Ulama Indonesia,' abbr.: MUI), Ma'ruf Amin (who is now the vice president of Indonesia) protested against the MK's decision. He could not accept that the spiritual groups are now equal to the six official religions. He proposed creating a special E-KTP for them.[3] However, in the history of Indonesia, 'special KTP' means discrimination. That was the experience of many former detainees who were accused of being communists during Soeharto's period. In their KTP there was a special sign which indicated them as 'unclean.'

On the other hand, the Minister of Religion, Lukman Hakim Saifudin, welcomed the MK's decision. He reminded the public that spiritual groups were actually under the jurisdiction of the National Education Ministry, and not under the jurisdiction of the Ministry of Religion. That was because formerly they were not regarded as religions.[4] He also proposed a special E-KTP, but for a different reason than MUI; he did not want to place the spiritual groups in an inferior position, but to accommodate their wishes to be recognized fully as spiritual groups, which are not under the umbrella of one of the six official religions. The Minister of Religion also explained that he and the Minister for Internal Affairs will coordinate together, to issue 6 to 8 million new E-KTPs in 2018, to accommodate the MK's decision, according to their estimation on the number of followers of spiritual groups.[5]

---

http://news.detik.com/berita/3491040/ketua-mk-kenapa-agama-dari-asing-diakui-kalau-dari-leluhur-tidak (accessed June 7, 2019).

3. Christie Stefanie, "Ketua MUI tak Setuju Penghayat Kepercayaan Tercantum di KTP" (The head of MUI disagreed with the decision to refer to spiritual belief in national identity cards), *CNN Indonesia*, Nasional, November 15, 2017, https://www.cnnindonesia.com/nasional/20171115155715-20-255829/ketua-mui-tak-setuju-penghayat-kepercayaan-tercantum-di-ktp (accessed June 10, 2019).

4. Ahmad Rafiq and Rina Widiastuti, "Menteri Lukman: Kami Tidak Terdampak Putusan MK Soal Kolom Agama" (Minister Lukman: we are not impacted by MK decision concerning reference to religion in national identity cards), *Tempo.co*, Nasional, November 8, 2017, https://nasional.tempo.co/read/1031909/menteri-lukman-kami-tidak-terdampak-putusan-mk-soal-kolom-agama (accessed June 10, 2019).

5. Fakhrizal Fakhri, "Menag: Mendagri Segera Persiapkan KTP untuk Penghayat Kepercayaan" (Minister of Religious Affairs: Interior Minister will prepare special national identity cards for spiritual groups), *Okenews*, Nasional, April 4, 2018, https://nasional.okezone.com/read/2018/04/04/337/1882044/menag-mendagri-segera-

The Indonesian Communion of Churches (PGI) welcomed the MK's decision. One way of welcoming the decision was the PGI 33rd Seminar on Religions with the theme 'Adat Society'[6] in Parapat, North Sumatra, on March 22–23, 2018, which dealt with the impact of the MK's decision.[7] Concerning the technical problem of E-KTP column/s, the General Secretary of the PGI, Gomar Gultom (Now Chairperson of the PGI), commented that for the PGI, it is not a problem whether the column is marked as 'religion,' or is replaced with a new column, marked as 'spiritual belief.' He also reminded the public that even if there were special E-KTP s for the spiritual groups, it may be rejected by the municipal bureaucracies, as the Marriage Law of Indonesia only considers a marriage as valid if it is performed according to the rites of one of the six official religions.[8] If there is no change in the Marriage Law, then the MK's decision cannot be implemented.

Beside the difficulty of implementing the MK's decision, the picture becomes more complicated by the fact that the spiritual groups are often lumped together with other traditional groups of Adat society, as explained in the book published by the PGI, *Masyarakat Adat*.[9] In the understanding of the PGI, Adat society means a traditional ethnic community, with its own customs and its own living space.[10] The spiritual groups, however, regard themselves as 'modern' groups, but inherited traditional wisdom from the Javanese/ Sundanese mystical tradition. They are groups such as Susila Budi Darma (SUBUD), Pangestu, Sapta Dharma, Sumarah, Suksma Sejati, and many others. They refuse to be categorized as religion, while those who regard themselves as Adat society hold that what they have is religion, not just spiritual belief. They are the Marapu people of Sumba, the Ugama Malim (formerly known as Parmalim) people from the Bataklands, the Kaharingan people from

---

persiapkan-ktp-untuk-penghayat-kepercayaan (accessed June 10, 2019).

6. Ind: *Masyarakat Adat* (Adat Society). The term adat is frequently translated in English as 'social custom', but it is more than that. Many regard adat as the ancestors' legacy and as such can never be abrogated.

7. The proceedings of the Seminar are published shortly after, see below, footnote 9.

8. Kristian Erdianto, "PGI Sepakat dengan MUI soal Pemenuhan Hak Sipil Penghayat Kepercayaan"(PGIagreeswithMUIonfulfillingspiritualgroups'civilrights), Kompas.com, Nasional, https://nasional.kompas.com/read/2018/01/18/09310741/pgi-sepakat-dengan-mui-soal-pemenuhan-hak-sipil-penghayat-kepercayaan?page=all (accessed June 7, 2019).

9. Jimmy M.I. Sormin (ed.), *Masyarakat Adat*: *Pengakuan Kembali, Identitas & Keindonesiaan* (Adat Society: Re-recognition, identity and how to be an Indonesian) (Jakarta: BPK Gunung Mulia-PGI, 2018).

10. Johny N. Simanjuntak, "Mencakapkan Sisi Orientasi dan Intensi Advokasi Masyarakat Adat" (Conversation on orientation and intention of advocating for the Adat Society), in *Masyarakat Adat*, ed. Sormin, 19–29, 20.

Kalimantan and some others. And there are groups, which on the one hand, hold that they are akin to the spiritual groups, but on the other hand, they are not the same as them, such as the religion of Sunda Wiwitan in West Java.

The Kaharingan people are not very enthusiastic about the MK's decision, as they have struggled in the past, to be recognized as religion, and not as a spiritual group. In 1980 the majority of the Kaharingan people in Kalimantan decided to join the official Hindu Dharma religion, which is the majority religion in the island of Bali. As part of an official religion, they enjoyed government privileges such as subsidies to run religious schools. After the MK's decision, most opted to stay within the body of Hindu Dharma, but a minority of them has publicly announced that they have cut their relationship with Hindu Dharma.[11]

Notwithstanding the difficulties, the Adat society has received state recognition concerning their communal property rights. In May 16, 2013, MK made public their decision No. 35/2012, which is popularly known as MK 35: the forests which traditionally belong to the people, and which is known as 'adat forest' cannot be claimed by the state.[12] The impact of this decision is that the Adat society now has territorial rights. If the Adat society and the spiritual groups are now seen as one body *vis-a-vis* the six official religions, then the MK's decision to recognize them as on par with the six official religions makes them strong, so strong, that they can now legally resist efforts by the six religions to convert them into adherents of a religion.

It is this new reality that was in the mind of Gomar Gultom when he reminded the member churches of the PGI that the Adat society had for a long time been placed in the margins and that they were even regarded as invisible. As such, they became mission objects of the six religions.[13] Gultom was referring to the past practice, but I think he was indirectly pointing at what some member churches of the PGI are doing now. The Ugama Malim people are the object of the mission of the Toba Batak church (HKBP) in North Sumatra, the Kaharingan people of the Gereja Kalimantan Evangelis in Kalimantan (GKE), and the Marapu people of the Gereja Kristen Sumba (GKS). It would be interesting to

---

11. Marko Mahin, "Menjadi Subjek: Identitas dan Eksistensi Agama Kaharingan Paska (*sic!*) Putusan Mahkamah Konstitusi Nomor 97/PUU-XIV/2016" (Becoming subjects: Identity and existence of Kaharingan religion post Constitutional Court's decision number 97/PUU-XIV/2016), in *Masyarakat Adat*, ed. Sormin, 129–141, here 130–131, 137–138.

12. Abdob (*sic!*) Nababan, "Reclaiming Identitas: Masyarakat Adat sebagai Subjek (Baru) Kewarganegaraan" (Reclaiming identity: Adat Society as (New) Subjects in Citizenship), in *Masyarakat Adat*, ed. Sormin, 41–63, 59–60.

13. Gomar Gultom, "Kata Sambutan Sekertaris Umum PGI" (Welcoming Address by the General Secretary of PGI), in *Masyarakat Adat*, ed. Sormin, VII–IX, VII–VIII.

see the reaction of these member churches, but no official statements have come out so far. From discussions in my course 'Doing Theology in Context' at the master's program of the Theological Faculty, UKDW, Yogyakarta, there is information that in this period of post-MK's decision, relationships between Christians and Muslims in Sumba are becoming more cordial while relationships between Christians and the Marapu people are becoming more strained.[14] It seems that the Marapu people are now asserting their new identity as a religion and no longer wish to be regarded as followers of paganism.

In Central and East Java, for a long period, the spiritual groups which belong to the Javanese mystical religion (Javanese: Kejawen) became the object of the mission of both Catholic and Protestant missionaries. The teachings of *Kejawen* were regarded as incompatible with Christianity, and there was a strong anti-*Kejawen* sentiment among members of the Javanese churches.[15] However, there was some ambiguity in their attitude. The real antagonist seemed to be Islam, and in order to be strong in facing Islam, the *Kejawen* people also needed to be befriended, in order to attract them to Christianity. It was common in the New Order era to find Christian literature on the situation in Central Java which described the religious-cultural background of Java as *Kejawen* and not as Islam.[16] It is only after the fall of Soeharto in 1998 that they acknowledged the Muslims of Java as followers of Islam, albeit contextual Muslims, meaning they are Muslims but still appreciative of their *Kejawen* heritage.

The PGI's response to the MK's decision has to be welcomed as one way of acknowledging its past mistakes, that is in regarding the world of Adat society and spiritual groups as the world of darkness. Although the churches always deny any accusation that what they brought to these people is *mission civilisatrice*, this is more or less what they were (and are still) doing. Christians in Indonesia are prone to follow outlines of modernization (development programs) which are designed by the state/government without ample study, to see their impact for the future. The modern world of the state/government is identified with the Kingdom of God. During the colonial period, they followed the policies of modernity

---

14. Information from my MTh student Yustiwati Angu Bima (class of 2018–2019). She is Sumbanese.

15. Harun Hadiwijono, *Kebatinan dan Injil* (Spiritual Groups and the Gospel) (Jakarta: BPK, 1970). In his book on dogmatics, *Iman Kristen* (Christian faith) (Jakarta: BPK, 1973), 170–171, he stated that the teachings of the Bible are incompatible with *Kejawen*.

16. Karel A. Steenbrink, *Dutch Colonialism and Indonesian Islam: Contacts and Conflicts (1596–1950)* (Amsterdam-Atlanta: Rodopi, 1993). Steenbrink examined the literature and concluded that the seemingly sympathetic Christian attitude to *Kejawen* was actually anti-Islam.

from the colonial government, and during the period of independence they follow similar policies from the Indonesian government, but the object always remains the same, namely the peoples who live at the margin.[17]

The mission programs of the churches need to be re-examined thoroughly, and here I am using the postcolonial perspective.[18] In the colonial period, the missionaries were moving from the center to the margin ('go!'), which in missiology handbooks is termed as doing mission following a *centrifugal* movement.[19] When the center comes to the margin, the margin is encapsulated by the center. This centrifugal movement is often regarded as the realization of the Great Commission (Matt. 28:18–20), and followed by church-planting (*plantatio ecclesiae*) strategies. During the colonial period, that is in the second half of the 19th century and the first half of the 20th century, these policies succeeded in creating pockets of Christianity in parts of the archipelago. This seemingly successful enterprise has become the norm for mission in the theological minds of the Indonesian churches in the post-independence era. They have continued the colonial way of doing mission.

I have proposed a transformation of this colonial mission into a *postcolonial mission*.[20] The churches still need to do mission work, albeit following a *centripetal* movement. In the Old Testament, the Servant Israel is called to become a model for the world, to live in such a way that attracts the attention of the world. Israel does not go anywhere; the world is coming to Israel (as in Isa. 2:2–5). The PGI also proposed that the church-planting strategies need to be replaced with the concept of *presensia* ('stay!'), which in the understanding of the PGI, does not only mean living together peacefully with people of other faiths, but also living together in solidarity with people at the margin.[21] In this new model, people from spiritual groups and Adat

---

17. Emanuel Gerrit Singgih, "Indonesian Churches and the Problem of Nationality and Ethnicity," in *Faith and Ethnicity*, Studies in Reformed Theology 6, eds. Eddy Van der Borght et al. (Leiden: Brill, 2002), 103–123. In this article I refer to the term *hamajuon* (in the Toba dialect) or *hamajuan* (in the Simalungun dialect), which means progress, and which became a catch-word for the Batak Christians.

18. Elizabeth Mudimbe-Boyi, "Missionary writing and postcolonialism," in *The Cambridge History of Postcolonial Literature*, ed. Ato Quayson (Cambridge: Cambridge University Press, 2016), 81–106.

19. Arie de Kuijper, *Missiologia* (Missiology) (Jakarta: BPK, 1974). It was still reprinted in 2011. De Kuijper summarizes the view of Dutch missiologists such as Verkuijl and Blauw.

20. Emanuel Gerrit Singgih, "Dari Misi Kolonial ke Misi Poskolonial: Misiologi yang Kontekstual bagi Indonesia Masa Kini" (From colonial mission to postcolonial mission), in *Gereja di Era Disrupsi* (The church in the era of disruption), eds. Ebenezer Gaol et al. (Bekasi: Efata, 2019), 141–153.

21. PGI, *Dokumen Keesaan Gereja* (Documents of church unity) (Jakarta: BPK

societies do not necessarily come to the churches because they want to become Christians and church members, but because they appreciate being regarded as equals in this new era of recognition by Indonesian society. *Presensia* means reconciliation, equality, equity, friendship and hospitality, without hidden agendas.

3. THE PGI AND THE PLIGHT OF LGBT COMMUNITIES

As mentioned previously, since 2016 the LGBT community in Indonesia has been facing many verbal attacks from both government officials and public figures, and not infrequently these verbal attacks have been followed by physical attacks by the police and also by unknown groups. As during the post-1965 period, when many people tried to claim that their regions were clean from PKI (followers of the Indonesian Communist Party), this time many people are proclaiming that their regions are free of LGBT people.[22] Surprisingly, on May 28, 2016, the PGI issued a Pastoral Statement in which Christians and member churches are implored to end the burden of negative stigma applied to LGBT people as 'sinners' (Ind.: *orang berdosa*) and/or people with 'psychological disorders/diseases' (Ind.: *berpenyakit jiwa*).[23]

The PGI is not the first to issue a positive statement concerning LGBT people. A year before, the Salemba Reformed-Baptist Church of Grace Community (Ind.: 'Gereja Komunitas Anugerah Reformed-Baptist Salemba') which belongs to the Evangelical wing of Indonesian Christians and is not a member of the PGI, also issued a statement of solidarity with LGBT people. The church called for solidarity on the basis of the sovereign love of Christ, and argued that it is not the homosexuals who have to repent, but the heterosexuals, namely for their

---

Gunung MuliaPGI, 2016), second printing; PGI, "Model-model Bergereja di Indonesia, 2018" (Models of church in Indonesia), abbr. MMBI 2018, unpublished document.

22. Sapto Andika Candra and Andi Nur Aminah, "Kota Padang Komitmen Berantas LGBT" (The city of Padang is committed to evict LGBT people), *Republika.co.id*, Nasional, November 15, 2018, https://nasional.republika.co.id/berita/nasional/daerah/18/11/15/pi7rg1384-kota-padang-komitmen-berantas-lgbt (accessed June 10, 2019); cf. Angga Indrawan, "Komunitas LGBT di Jambi dalam Pengawasan" (LGBT community at Jambi under strict supervision), *Republika.co.id*, Nasional, February 23, 2016, https://www.republika.co.id/berita/nasional/daerah/16/02/23/o2z5y1365-komunitas-lgbt-di-jambi-dalam-pengawasan (accessed June 10, 2019).

23. In the appendix 1 of Emanuel Gerrit Singgih, *Menafsir LGBT dengan Alkitab* (Interpreting LGBT through the Bible) (Jakarta: Pusat Studi Gender dan Seksualitas [Center for the Study of Gender and Sexuality] STFK Jakarta, 2019), 83–87. For an English version, see Stephen Suleeman and Amadeo D. Udampoh (eds.), *Siapakah Sesamaku*? (Who is my neighbor?) (Jakarta: Sekolah Tinggi Filsafat Theologi Jakarta [Jakarta School for Philosophy and Theology], 2019), 311–315.

tendency to enforce their norms on homosexual people.[24] Previously, Stephen Suleeman, a faculty member of Jakarta Theological Seminary had already started organizing workshops on the issue of LGBT, which attracted many participants, who in the end usually produced similar statements.

The response to the PGI Pastoral Statement was mixed. Though many individuals welcomed it, the member churches of the PGI protested, as the draft which had been prepared by the MPH ('Majelis Pekerja Harian'; Eng.: 'The Leadership') was not submitted to the MPL ('Majelis Pekerja Lengkap'; Eng.: 'Representatives of member churches') for consideration. Perhaps that was only a pretext for the real reason, namely a strong anti-LGBT theology. It is ironic that member churches of the PGI, which represent the Ecumenical wing of Indonesian Christians and are known as 'liberals,' have an anti-LGBT attitude. Although many Evangelicals are also anti-LGBT, there are evangelicals who are not against LGBT. As we have seen above, a church which belongs to the Evangelical wing can support the struggle of LGBT people. Yonky Karman, another faculty member of Jakarta Theological Seminary, who wrote a sympathetic introduction to the translation of a book on homosexuality and Christianity, also belongs to the Evangelical wing.[25]

Others protested that the Pastoral Statement will open the way to 'same-sex marriage' (Ind.: 'Pernikahan Sejenis'), which has already been legalized in more than half of European countries, in several states of the U.S. (after the legalization of 'same-sex marriage' by the Supreme Court) and in Taiwan. Vietnam, Thailand and Myanmar also have LGBT-friendly policies, although they have not legalized 'same-sex marriage.' There are also others who protested that the content of the Pastoral Statement is 'unbiblical' or that the argument of the PGI has no in-depth discussion of certain texts which are used to support the condemnation of LGBT people. Gomar Gultom reacted to the charge that the PGI is promoting 'same-sex marriage' by clarifying that the PGI focused on acceptance of LGBT people and did not support or refer to 'same-sex marriage.'[26] Concerning the accusation that the leadership of the PGI

---

24. Guhmanaff, "Kedaulatan Cinta" (The Sovereignty of Love), *Suarakita.org*, Gereja Komunitas Anugerah-Reformed Baptist Salemba, July 1, 2015, http://www.suarakita.org/2015/07/siaran-pers-kedaulatan-cinta/ (accessed June 7, 2019). Also in the appendix 2 of Singgih, *Menafsir LGBT dengan Alkitab*, 89–90.

25. Yonky Karman, "Menyikapi LGBT sebagai sebuah Fenomena Sosio-Teologis" (Consideration of LGBT as a socio-theological phenomenon), in *Homoseksualitas dan Kekristenan* (Christianity and homosexuality), eds. William Loader and Stephen R. Holmes (Jakarta: Bentara, 2018), VII–XIII.

26. Sandro Gatra, "PGI: Gereja Tak Akan Restui Perkawinan Sejenis" (PGI: The church will not bless same-sex marriage), *Kompas.com*, Nasional, July 10, 2015, https://nasional.kompas.com/read/2015/07/10/13020621/PGI.Gereja.Tak.Akan.Restui.

is 'unbiblical,' PGI responded by organizing a Bible symposium on the theme of LGBT on January 9–10, 2017. They asked me to be the resource person for this symposium and I prepared a lengthy paper, which was eventually published as a booklet titled *Menafsir LGBT dengan Alkitab* (To Interpret LGBT from the Perspective of the Bible).[27] I will explain some parts of this booklet and these explanations also function as my evaluation of the Pastoral Statement.

In this booklet, I counter the argument that homosexuality is unbiblical by comparing texts which are hostile to LGBT (such as Lev. 18:22; 20:13; Deut. 22:5; 23:17,18 and Rom. 1:26–27) with texts which are not hostile to LGBT (such as 1 Sam. 18:1–4; 2 Sam. 1:26; Isa. 56:1–8; Dan. 1:1–21; Eccl. 4:9–12; Matt. 19:11–12; Act. 8:26–40).[28] Concerning Gen. 19:1–29 (the story of the destruction of Sodom), I hold that it cannot be used as a biblical base to condemn LGBT people. It is true that in the narrative there is an attempt made to rape two heavenly guests by *all* male inhabitants of Sodom, old and young. From this, however, we may deduce that the perpetrators are both homosexual *and* heterosexual men. This deduction is further supported by the fact that the identity of the perpetrators is strengthened when Lot offers his two virgin daughters to the mob as alternative victims instead of the two heavenly guests. I also added that according to the prophetic tradition (Isa. 1:10–20; 3:9; Jer. 23:10, 14; 49:18; Ezek. 16:46–56), the sin of Sodom is not homosexuality but social injustice and inhospitable attitude.[29]

Before my reading of the texts, I explained my hermeneutical stance, which is still *Sola Scriptura*, but *Sola Scriptura with Pluses*. Even the reformers such as Luther and Calvin never just apply the text as it is to the situation. There is always something more than just 'the plain meaning' of the text. As an example, I traced the history of offices in the churches of the Reformation such as the minister, elder, deacon and superintendent, which on the one hand, are taken from the terms *presbuteros*, *diakonos* and *episkopos* in the New Testament, but on the other hand, are not the same as these three biblical offices. Likewise, I apply *Sola Scriptura with Pluses* concerning the related texts above. The pluses are *Sola Fide*, *Sola Gratia* and *Sola Caritate*. The last one, *Sola Caritate*, is not very common in the Calvinistic tradition, but is becoming more and more influential in Protestant interpretation of the

---

Perkawinan.Sejenis (accessed June 10, 2019).

27. Emanuel Gerrit Singgih, *Menafsir LGBT dengan Alkitab*, Jakarta: Pusat Kajian Gender dan Seksualitas (STFT Jakarta, 2019).

28. Singgih, *Menafsir LGBT*, Ch. III.

29. Singgih, *LGBT*, 43--49. See also David N. Glesne, *Understanding Homosexuality: Perspectives for the Local Church* (Minneapolis, Kirk House Publishers, 2004), 98; NIV Study Bible, eBook, Zondervan, 2011.

Bible.³⁰

I also question the interpretation of texts concerning 'fertility religions' in the Pastoral Statement, which is contrasted with the biblical religion in the Old Testament. Starting from a negative evaluation of fertility religions, the PGI holds that there is no judgement or condemnation of LGBT people in the Bible, especially in the Old Testament, only condemnation of the fertility religions of Canaan. I do not think this is true. There are texts which condemn homosexual acts, but my argument is that texts which do not condemn homosexuality can also be found in the Bible, and that the number of these texts exceeds the number of anti-LGBT texts. If so, then there is no point in holding that LGBT is unbiblical just by citing anti-LGBT texts. The antithesis between the religion of ancient Israel as a historical religion and the religion of Canaan as a fertility religion, which was common one generation ago, cannot be defended any longer. Both have elements of historical and fertility religions.³¹ For example, Yahweh *is* a God of fertility (Hos. 2:7, 20–22).

I also added scientific, cultural and human rights considerations to complement the use of these three considerations in the Pastoral Statement. Contemporary science does not understand homosexuality anymore as a psychological or hormonal disorder, but as a sexual orientation. Therefore, it is important to learn the new vocabulary, such as the importance of differentiating between gender and sexual orientation. I am aware that science alone cannot have the last word. It will depend on the relation between science and religion/faith. In pre-modern days, science was placed under religion. Scientific discoveries can never challenge the worldview of religion. In modernity, religion is placed under science. The worldview of religion cannot undermine the worldview of science. In the postmodern era (which is now), however, science and religion are in an equal position, and the worldview of science is in dialogue with the worldview of religion.³²

In present-day Indonesia, the worldview of religion tends to be dominant, and threatens to dictate the worldview of science and culture. It is as if we are back in the pre-modern days. In the introduction, I mentioned the negative comments about LGBT people and their allies made by the Minister of Research and Technology. When he was reminded by journalists that according to scientific research there is

---

30. Singgih, LGBT, ch. II. When I was in a catechism class long ago, it was more common to refer to *Sola Scriptura, Sola Fide and Sola Gratia.*

31. Singgih, LGBT, 51–53. See also Bertil Albrektson, History and the Gods (Lund: Gleerup, 1967); Niels Peter Lemche, *The Canaanites and their Land: The Tradition of the Canaanites* (Sheffield: Sheffield Academic Press, 1999).

32. Singgih, LGBT, Ch. IV.

no problem with the LGBT people, he retorted that his accusations are not based on the findings of science but on religious truth. It is mind-blowing to hear such comments from a minister of Research and Technology. After the issue of LGBT had become one of the headlines in mass media, the Indonesian Lawyers Club (ILC), which frequently organizes television debates concerning hot issues, invited lawyers and experts in science and religion to a televised evening debate on LGBT.

When it was the turn of the representative of the Indonesian Fellowship of Psychologists to speak, many were dumbfounded to hear him say that homosexuality is a psychological disease.[33] From the audience and from *netizens*, a storm of protests arose, (including a summons by the Jakarta Legal Aid Institute) and after a few days he apologized publicly for his remarks.[34] Although these protests indicated that critical views toward the old biases against LGBT people have become stronger, it does not mean that the tendency to place science under religion has disappeared. After the PGI Pastoral Statement and my booklet had sparked public debate, an Evangelical, Andik Wijaya, a medical doctor who frequently organizes anti-LGBT seminars and 'healing sessions' for LGBT people, posted his reactions on the internet in the form of ridicule and insinuations of criminal intent.[35]

For cultural considerations, the PGI in its Pastoral Statement referred to the traditional culture of the *bissu* in South Sulawesi and the *warok* of Ponorogo, East Java. The *bissu* are a particular group of transgender people, who in the local belief system are regarded as mediators between the human and the divine. The *warok* are a particular group of men, who are believed to have Herculean strength, which can only last if they have sexual intercourse with males. The phenomenon of LGBT is not the product of modern culture, nor is it a product of Western culture. It is part of traditional Indonesian cultural identity, albeit in a form of *counter culture*. The Pastoral Statement also refers to international human rights law, which emphasizes that the freedom to choose one's sexual

---

33. TvOneNews, "[FULL] Indonesian Lawyers Club—"LGBT Marak, Apa Sikap Kita? (16/02/2016)" (LGBT is everywhere, so what shall we do?), *Youtube*, 19 February 2016, https://www.youtube.com/watch?v=ByQG4pPaE7Y (accessed June 20, 2019).

34. Sri Handayani and Achmad Syalaby, "Lengkap, Tujuh Permintaan Maaf Fidiansjah Usai Disomasi LBH Jakarta" (Seven complete apologies by Fidiansyah after threatened with somation by LBH Jakarta), *Republika.co.id*, Nasional, 23 Maret 2016, https://www.republika.co.id/berita/nasional/umum/16/03/23/o4hhk7394-lengkap-tujuh-permintaan-maaf-fidiansjah-usai-disomasi-lbh-jakarta (accessed June 10, 2019).

35. Andik Wijaya, "MPH PGI, *Jangan ada dusta di antara kita!*" (Let there be no lies among us), PGI, June 23, 2016; Gramediapost, "Mewaspadai Gerakan LGBT di Lingkungan Gereja" (On alert for LGBT movement within our congregations), June 18, 2018, https://www.gramediapost.com/2018/06/mewaspadai-gerakan-lgbt-di-dalam-gereja/ (accessed January 22, 2020).

orientation as part of the right to private life is part of human rights.[36] I agree with the reference to traditional *counter culture*, but I also pointed out that in the public space nowadays, where religion is dominant, the traditional *counter culture* is pressurized to become almost invisible. For example, it is now forbidden for male actors to perform as females or transvestites in TV shows.

The discourse on scientific findings, cultural heritage and human rights considerations has uncovered the issue of identity and the right to choose one's identity. The Pastoral Statement acknowledges that it is difficult to separate identity that is the result of *nature* and identity that is the result of *nurture*. They are overlapping. However, in today's context of Indonesia, heterosexuality is the norm, and therefore the discourse on scientific findings, cultural heritage and human rights considerations, which I also consider part of the pluses of *Sola Scriptura*, are mostly ignored. LGBT people are stigmatized as sexual predators who promote sexual permissiveness (Ind.: *kebebasan seksual*). I believe this is the reason why the PGI stopped short of referring to 'same-sex marriage.' I can understand their position and do not want to undermine it by suggesting that I would have a Christian concept of 'same-sex marriage.' However, it cannot be denied that there are gay couples who are very committed to each other, very devout and church-going. Because of this fact, I propose that perhaps member churches could perform a ritual for these committed ones, which in Indonesian is *perestuan* (from the term *restu*). It is not a *pemberkatan* (from the term *berkat*), which means 'blessing,' because 'blessing' has been identified with a church wedding. *Perestuan* is a ritual, but not a ritual for a church wedding. In Indonesia a Christian marriage is valid if it is performed by the clerics and confirmed by the municipality.[37]

After the Bible Symposium on LGBT above, in March 2017, the MPL-PGI met in Salatiga and one of the points on the agenda was evaluation of the Pastoral Statement and reactions to it. There is no press release, but it seems that the Pastoral Statement was rejected by the floor. The MPH will pay dearly for its procedural mistake mentioned above. Since then, the discourse on LGBT has disappeared from within both the MPH and the MPL. The staff of the MPH informed me that they are keeping 'a low profile' position on this issue. Apparently, they continued to do so, until the PGI General Assembly, which was held on the island of Sumba in November 2019. The General Assembly chose a new MPH, with Gomar Gultom in the position of Chairperson and Jacky Manuputty as General

---

36. International Commission of Jurists, *Sexual Orientation, Gender Identity and International Human Rights Law*, Practical Guide 4, https://www.refworld.org/pdfid/4a783aed2.pdf (accessed October 1, 2020).

37. Singgih, *LGBT*, Ch. v.

Secretary.

4. CLOSING REMARKS

I have described the role of the PGI in fighting polarization in contemporary Indonesia. In these two cases of polarization, first, on the status of religion versus 'spiritual groups' and 'Adat society,' and second, on the issue of LGBT, it has become clear that what the PGI is striving for is blunted by the wall of traditional theological stances of member churches of the PGI. We have seen that Gomar Gultom's reminder to re-examine the traditional theology of mission following the government's recognition of the spiritual groups and Adat society went unheeded. The Pastoral Statement on LGBT was rejected by member churches. The positive impact is that the outside world welcomes the PGI initiative on LGBT. Many Muslim figures who advocate acceptance of LGBT people rejoiced at the publication of the Pastoral Statement. For the first time, 'Gaya Nusantara' (an NGO that defends gay rights) dropped its cynical and skeptical attitudes toward religious people and invited experts of religion, both from Islam and Christianity, to meet at the beginning of November 2018.[38] It was agreed to create together a project of interpreting or re-interpreting some scriptural texts in order to build a positive image of LGBT, under the name 'Tafsir Progresif Lintas Agama' (Eng.: 'Inter-Religious Progressive Interpretation').[39]

Because of this positive development, the PGI should not be discouraged by challenges faced internally. The Indonesian Communion of Churches has established signs of hope for all the people of Indonesia, and therefore polarization will not have the last word. I am convinced that the PGI has been advocating for the improvement of society. Therefore, we may conclude that the PGI has been practicing public theology and this may even be the beginning of an inter-religious and inter-cultural public theology. However, if the PGI continues to keep 'a low profile' concerning the issue of LGBT, then it is questionable whether it can successfully advance public theology. I hope that the present MPH-PGI will re-embark on a journey of solidarity with those who are

---

38. Those invited were Stephen Suleeman, Andreas Kristanto, Darwita Purba and Emanuel Gerrit Singgih from the Christian side, and Kyai Hussein Muhammad, Imam Naha'I, Arif Nuh Safri, Amar Afikar and Aan Anshori from the Muslim side. Aan Anshori is the chairperson of 'Jaringan Islam Anti Diskriminasi' (abbr: JIAD; Eng: Islamic Anti-Discrimination Network). Aan Anshori is very active at the grassroots level, promoting reconciliation among religions and reconciliation between non-LGBT and LGBT people. He already receives death threats because of his activities.

39. The project is now completed by the publication of Amar Afikar (ed.), *Tafsir Progresif Islam & Kristen terhadap Keragaman Gender dan Seksualitas* (A progressive Muslim and Christian interpretation concerning gender and sexuality) (Surabaya, Gaya Nusantara, 2020).

marginalized for the sake of the future of Indonesia.

BIBLIOGRAPHY

Afikar, Amar. Ed. *Tafsir Progresif Islam & Kristen terhadap Keragaman Gender dan Seksualitas* (A progressive Muslim and Christian interpretation concerning gender and sexuality). Surabaya, Gaya Nusantara, 2020.

Albrektson, Bertil. *History and the Gods.* Lund: Gleerup, 1967.

Candra, Sapto Andika and Andi Nur Aminah. "Kota Padang Komitmen Berantas LGBT" (The city of Padang is committed to evict LGBT people). *Republika.co.id*, Nasional, November 15, 2018. Accessed June 10, 2019. https://nasional.republika.co.id/berita/nasional/daerah/18/11/15/pi7rg1384-kota-padang-komitmen-berantas-lgbt.

Erdianto, Kristian. "PGI Sepakat dengan MUI soal Pemenuhan Hak Sipil Penghayat Kepercayaan" (PGI agrees with MUI on fulfilling spiritual groups' civil rights). *Kompas.com*, Nasional. accessed June 7, 2019. https://nasional.kompas.com/read/2018/01/18/09310741/pgi-sepakat-dengan-mui-soal-pemenuhan-hak-sipil-penghayat-kepercayaan?page=all.

Fakhri, Fakhrizal. "Menag: Mendagri Segera Persiapkan KTP untuk Penghayat Kepercayaan" (Minister of Religious Affairs: Interior Minister will prepare special national identity cards for spiritual groups). *Okenews*, Nasional, April 4, 2018. Accessed June 10, 2019. https://nasional.okezone.com/read/2018/04/04/337/1882044/menag-mendagri-segera-persiapkan-ktp-untuk-penghayat-kepercayaan.

Gatra, Sandro. "PGI: Gereja Tak Akan Restui Perkawinan Sejenis" (PGI: The church will not bless same-sex marriage). *Kompas.com*, Nasional, July 10, 2015. Accessed June 10, 2019. https://nasional.kompas.com/read/2015/07/10/13020621/PGI.Gereja.Tak.Akan.Restui.Perkawinan.Sejenis.

Glesne, David N. *Understanding Homosexuality: Perspectives for the Local Church.* Minneapolis, Kirk House Publishers, 2004.

Gultom Gomar, "Kata Sambutan Sekertaris Umum PGI" (Welcoming Address by the General Secretary of PGI). In *Masyarakat Adat: Pengakuan Kembali, Identitas & Keindonesiaan* (Adat Society: Re-recognition, identity and how to be an Indonesian), ed. Jimmy M.I Sormin, vii-ix. Jakarta: BPK Gunung Mulia-PGI, 2018.

Guhmanaff. "Kedaulatan Cinta" (The Sovereignty of Love). *Suarakita. org*, Gereja Komunitas Anugerah-Reformed Baptist Salemba, July 1, 2015. Accessed June 7, 2019. http://www.suarakita.org/2015/07/siaran-pers-kedaulatan-cinta/.

Hadiwijono, Harun. *Iman Kristen* (Christian faith). Jakarta: BPK, 1973.

Hadiwijono, Harun. *Kebatinan dan Injil* (Spiritual Groups and the Gospel). Jakarta: BPK, 1970.

Handayani, Sri and Achmad Syalaby, "Lengkap, Tujuh Permintaan Maaf Fidiansjah Usai Disomasi LBH Jakarta" (Seven complete apologies by Fidiansyah after threatened with somation by LBH Jakarta), *Republika.co.id*. Nasional, 23 Maret 2016. Accessed June 10, 2019. https://www.republika.co.id/berita/nasional/umum/16/03/23/o4hhk7394-lengkap-tujuh-permintaan-maaf-fidiansjah-usai-disomasi-lbh-jakarta.

Indrawan, Angga. "Komunitas LGBT di Jambi dalam Pengawasan" (LGBT community at Jambi under strict supervision). *Republika. co.id*, Nasional, February 23, 2016. Accessed June 10, 2019. https://www.republika.co.id/berita/nasional/daerah/16/02/23/o2z5y1365-komunitas-lgbt-di-jambi-dalam-pengawasan.

International Commission of Jurists. *Sexual Orientation, Gender Identity and International Human Rights Law*, Practical Guide 4. Accessed October 1, 2020. https://www.refworld.org/pdfid/4a783aed2.pdf.

Karman, Yonky. "Menyikapi LGBT sebagai sebuah Fenomena Sosio-Teologis" (Consideration of LGBT as a socio-theological phenomenon). In *Homoseksualitas dan Kekristenan* (Christianity and homosexuality), eds. William Loader and Stephen R. Holmes, vii-xiii. Jakarta: Bentara, 2018.

Kuijper, Arie de. Missiologia (Missiology). Jakarta: BPK, 1974.

Lemche, Niels Peter. *The Canaanites and their Land: The Tradition of the Canaanites*. Sheffield: Sheffield Academic Press, 1999.

Mahin, Marko. "Menjadi Subjek: Identitas dan Eksistensi Agama Kaharingan Paska (*sic*!) Putusan Mahkamah Konstitusi Nomor 97/PUU-XIV/2016" (Becoming subjects: Identity and existence of Kaharingan religion post Constitutional Court's decision number 97/PUU-XIV/2016). In *Masyarakat Adat: Pengakuan Kembali, Identitas & Keindonesiaan* (Adat Society: Re-recognition, identity and how to be an Indonesian), ed. Jimmy M.I Sormin, 129–141. Jakarta: BPK Gunung Mulia-PGI, 2018.

Mudimbe-Boyi, Elizabeth. "Missionary writing and postcolonialism." In *The Cambridge History of Postcolonial Literature*, ed. Ato Quayson, 81–106. Cambridge: Cambridge University Press, 2016.

Nababan, Abdob. "Reclaiming Identitas: Masyarakat Adat sebagai Subjek (Baru) Kewarganegaraan" (Reclaiming identity: Adat Society as (New) Subjects in Citizenship). In *Masyarakat Adat: Pengakuan Kembali, Identitas & Keindonesiaan* (Adat Society: Re-recognition, identity and how to be an Indonesian), ed. Jimmy M.I Sormin, 41–63. Jakarta: BPK Gunung Mulia-PGI, 2018.

Rafiq, Ahmad and Rina Widiastuti. "Menteri Lukman: Kami Tidak Terdampak Putusan MK Soal Kolom Agama" (Minister Lukman: we are not impacted by MK decision concerning reference to religion in national identity cards). *Tempo.co*, Nasional, November 8, 2017. Accessed June 10, 2019. https://nasional.tempo.co/read/1031909/menteri-lukman-kami-tidak-terdampak-putusan-mk-soal-kolom-agama.

Saputra, Andi. "Ketua MK: Kenapa Agama dari Asing Diakui, Kalau dari Leluhur Tidak?" (Chief Judge of Constitutional Court: Why is religion from foreigners recognized, if from ancestors not?), *Detik News*. Sidang Kolom Agama, May 3, 2017. Accessed June 7, 2019. http://news.detik.com/berita/3491040/ketua-mk-kenapa-agama-dari-asing-diakui-kalau-dari-leluhur-tidak.

Simanjuntak, Johny N. "Mencakapkan Sisi Orientasi dan Intensi Advokasi Masyarakat Adat" (Conversation on orientation and intention of advocating for the Adat Society). In *Masyarakat Adat: Pengakuan Kembali, Identitas & Keindonesiaan* (Adat Society: Re-recognition, identity and how to be an Indonesian), ed. Jimmy M.I Sormin, 19–29. Jakarta: BPK Gunung Mulia-PGI, 2018.

PGI, *Dokumen Keesaan Gereja* (Documents of church unity). Jakarta: BPK Gunung Mulia-PGI, 2016.

Singgih, Emanuel Gerrit. "Dari Misi Kolonial ke Misi Poskolonial: Misiologi yang Kontekstual bagi Indonesia Masa Kini" (From colonial mission to postcolonial mission). In *Gereja di Era Disrupsi* (The church in the era of disruption), eds. Ebenezer Gaol et al., 141–153. Bekasi: Efata, 2019.

Singgih, Emanuel Gerrit. "Indonesian Churches and the Problem of Nationality and Ethnicity." In *Faith and Ethnicity*, Studies in Reformed Theology 6, eds. Eddy Van der Borght et al., 103–123. Leiden: Brill, 2002.

Singgih, Emanuel Gerrit. *Menafsir LGBT dengan Alkitab* (Interpreting LGBT through the Bible). Jakarta: Pusat Studi Gender dan Seksualitas [Center for the Study of Gender and Sexuality] STFK Jakarta, 2019.

Singgih, Emanuel Gerrit. "What has Ahok to do with Santa? Contemporary Christian and Muslim Public Theologies in Indonesia". *International Journal of Public Theology* 13:1 (2019), 25–39.

Sormin, Jimmy M.I. Ed. *Masyarakat Adat: Pengakuan Kembali, Identitas & Keindonesiaan* (Adat Society: Re-recognition, identity and how to be an Indonesian). Jakarta: BPK Gunung Mulia-PGI, 2018.

Stefanie, Christie. "Ketua MUI tak Setuju Penghayat Kepercayaan Tercantum di KTP" (The head of MUI disagreed with the decision to refer to spiritual belief in national identity cards). *CNN Indonesia*, Nasional, November 15, 2017. Accessed June 10, 2019. https://www.cnnindonesia.com/nasional/20171115155715-20-255829/ketua-mui-tak-setuju-penghayat-kepercayaan-tercantum-di-ktp.

Steenbrink, Karel A. *Dutch Colonialism and Indonesian Islam: Contacts and Conflicts (1596–1950)*. Amsterdam-Atlanta: Rodopi, 1993.

CHAPTER 14
DEVELOPING *KOINONIA* IN AN AGE OF POLARIZATION
The Significance of Ecumenical Dialogue, with Particular Reference to the International Reformed Anglican Dialogue (2015–2020)
Elizabeth Welch

1. INTRODUCTION

Over the twenty-first century there has been a rise of polarization across the world in a number of areas, including: the expression of hatred on social media; divisions over sexual identity; campaigning for climate justice alongside climate change denial; the persecution of refugees; a secularist intolerance of people of faith, leading to divisions between church and world, and increasingly, racism, populism and nationalism. Some of these have taken place not only in society in general, but have also been in evidence in the church. There have been times of fierce internal struggle between different traditions of the church, and within different churches. The divisions and separations of churches from one another that have taken place over many centuries provide examples of polarization, rather than offering an alternative way forward of the reconciliation that is found in God's gift of communion for the world. Separation of one Christian tradition from another can lead into an inward focus of strengthening a separate identity rather than an outward focus of setting an example of reconciliation to a divided world.

This chapter looks at the way in which the understanding, development and rootedness in the church of *koinonia* (communion) offers an essential response to countering polarization, both between churches and in the world. The argument will be made that God's gift of *koinonia* takes God's people deeper into the open, generous relationship with the triune God, leading to a transformed and transforming loving relationship with one another and with God's world. The relationality that shapes the life of the Holy Trinity is poured out as a gift to God's world in order to reverse polarization.

I begin by examining the origins and significance of *koinonia*, then set this understanding within a reference to the historical separation of the churches and the way this can be seen as polarizing, before looking at twentieth century ecumenical initiatives which have taken up and developed the idea of *koinonia*. Next comes the focus on the issues emerging from a contemporary ecumenical dialogue, the International Reformed Anglican Dialogue (IRAD), 2015–2020, for which *koinonia* has been a significant theme. In conclusion, I point to the way in which the relationality which koinonia offers can be seen as both a fruitful and a challenging approach to addressing the deep-rooted issues of polarization, in the church and in the world.

2. THE ORIGINS AND SIGNIFICANCE OF KOINONIA

Koinonia is the Greek word in the New Testament predominantly translated as 'communion.' 'Communion' is often seen as referring specifically to the sacrament of Holy Communion, the body and blood of Jesus Christ, embodied in bread and wine. The use of *koinonia* rather than communion, comes as a reminder of the broader understanding of communion in terms of the relationality within the three persons of the Holy Trinity: Creator, Redeemer and Sustainer, offered as a gift to God's people and opening up human relationality.

Koinonia arises out of the relationship between Father, Son and Holy Spirit and is received in the church as a gift, drawing people into the profound mystery of participation in the life of the triune God. This sharing in God's life leads to a deepening of the significance of relationship, especially in the midst of diversity, within the church, which is offered to a polarized world. *Koinonia* counters the increasing polarization that is seen in church and world, by pointing to the way in which God holds people and creation lovingly together, leading to the difficult path of holding diverse people and views together.

This understanding of the link between Holy Communion, personal relationality and the Trinity has been helpfully developed by a number of writers in recent decades.

Michael Welker looks at the diverse understandings of Holy Communion and concludes with a focus on the Trinity: "In the celebration of holy communion human beings enter into a relationship with the triune God."[1] This understanding of the significance of the relationship with the triune God has been expanded by a number of writers in terms of the nature of persons (both the persons of the Trinity and with regard

---

1. M. Welker, *What Happens in Holy Communion*? (Grand Rapids: Eerdmans, 2000), 167–176. In his appendix he offers a helpful list of books and dialogues that have looked at Holy Communion between 1931 and 1990, 177–181.

to human relationality) and the nature of the church. Awad begins by examining the nature of the self in modernity and takes this thinking further by reflecting on the nature of the 'three persons in one' relational understanding of the triune God as seen in post-modern thinking.[2]

Volf looks at ways in which the Trinity can be seen to be embodied in the church.[3] Fox's work draws together classical and feminist understandings of the Trinity, and focusses on the significance for each of these areas of both personhood and female images in relation to God.[4]

The significance of the use of *koinonia* is both theological and practical as is seen in the outworking of the personal relationality that is a mark of the Trinity. *Koinonia* holds together the theological emphasis on the triune God, with the living reality of God embodied in the church, as in the example of the sacrament of Holy Communion. This embodiment is fulfilled by the sacrificial living out of the church's life in the world.

Understanding God's gift of *koinonia* as already present within each of the churches' separated traditions, raises up the need to re-focus, in each tradition and between traditions, on both the otherness and the presence of God, seeing the way in which God is specifically encountered in any one tradition as both a true reality and yet also pointing to the otherness of the one God who holds all people together. Holding together the sense of encounter with God in one tradition with the awareness of the otherness of God, who holds all the traditions together, points to the need for mutual listening as a key component for addressing polarization. A consequence of this listening is the openness to the mutual examination of the different understandings and interpretations of scripture and tradition, and of the diverse ways in which the one triune God is perceived to be present in the church and the world, to see what can be learnt from one another and how the knowledge of God is not completely contained in any one tradition. Entering more deeply into the nature of *koinonia* offers a way of modelling how the church can address issues of division, (including in such areas as doctrine, sexuality, peace and justice work, or scriptural interpretation) both within churches and between different traditions of the church. The Christian witness in the world is strengthened when churches are seen to speak and act and live together, in places of struggle, injustice and oppression in the world.

Churches, brought into being by Christ and given life by the Holy

---

2. N.G. Awad, *Persons in Relation* (Minneapolis: Fortress Press, 2014).

3. M. Volf, *After Our Likeness: The Church as the Image of the Trinity* (Grand Rapids: Eerdmans, 1998).

4. P.A. Fox, *God as Communion: John Zizioulas, Elizabeth Johnson, and the Retrieval of the Symbol of the Triune God* (Collegeville: The Liturgical Press, 2001). Fox holds together the significant thinking of the Orthodox theologian, John Zizioulas, alongside that of the Roman Catholic feminist thinker, Elizabeth Johnson.

Spirit, have a calling to live relationally, prayerfully, in worship, with the sense of God at the centre, rather than with all too human separatist convictions at the centre. The relationality that arises out of the Trinity, draws humanity and creation, in all its diversity, into an inescapable union with God and with one another. It is this relational union that challenges movements towards polarization.

3. THE SEPARATION OF CHURCHES HISTORICALLY

Particularly during the second Christian millennium, there have been periods of separation and division within and between churches. Some of these have led to polarization, as for example, during periods when people have been excommunicated for their particular understandings and interpretation of the faith or when separated churches have been established that are not recognised by the church from whom they have separated and do not recognise the church from which they have separated. Excommunication carries with it the meaning of putting a person outside the communion of the faith, and runs counter to the inclusive relational *koinonia* revealed in the triune God.

I refer to three periods in the history of the church with regard to times of separation that have taken place in different contexts and centuries and for different reasons, to look at the ways in which each of these times of separation could be seen to be polarizing.

The first example is the major separation between the Eastern church and the Western church arising from the discussion with regard to the role of the Spirit and of the Son during the early centuries of the church. This was one of several factors which contributed to the gradual separation of churches of East and West, symbolized in 1054 by the action of papal legates, led by Cardinal Humbert, placing a Bull of Excommunication on the altar of the Hagia Sophia Church in Constantinople.[5] The debate about "filioque" and whether or not it should be present in the Creed was not simply a debate about a word but involved a theological division over the triune nature of the divine. "The real issue behind the *filioque* concerns the question whether the ultimate ontological category in theology is the person or the substance."[6] Alongside the theological arguments lay cultural and contextual issues. Kalaitzidis points to these as part of the 'great schism' of 1054, referring

---

5. Kallistos Ware gives an account of the event in 1054 and of the history that led up to the separation of East from West, a separation that continued to develop in the centuries after 1054. K. Ware, *Orthodox Church* (London: Penguin Books, 1964), 51–81.

6. J. Zizioulas, *Communion and Otherness* (London: T&T Clark, 2006), 196.

to some of the consequences:

> ... a schism for which today we are aware that despite the existing theological and ecclesiological disputes, a major role should also be attributed to cultural and political reasons. It is of great importance that the separation of the Christian East and Christian West, affected terribly Christian universalism, and helped to increase tendencies towards particularism. If, after this significant politico-religious split, the West became more aggressive, seeking after its dominion, expansion, and supremacy to the detriment of Christian East, the latter became more defensive and suspicious, and at the same time less universalistic, seeking how to be protected from both Latin and Muslim (Arab first, and later Turkish) conquest.[7]

The second example follows from the sixteenth century division within the western church, between what became known the Roman Catholic Church and the various traditions of Reformation Churches. In Europe, reformers such as Luther, Melanchthon, Calvin, and Zwingli, sought to reform the Western Church, in continuity with what they saw as neglected aspects of the Christian faith in the later medieval period. An example of this reforming trend is seen in the seventeenth century in England, when, after the sixteenth century split between the English Church and the Roman Church, there was a further period of separation within English churches. This was symbolised by the 1662 Act of Uniformity, requiring bishops and a common prayer book for weekly use in Sunday worship. This led to clergy being ejected from the Church of England, and the formation of independent, separatist churches. It is ironic to note that an Act which sought unity by imposing uniformity in terms of worship, authority, and organizational structure led in practice to the entrenchment of diverse, separated Christian traditions in England.[8]

The third historical example of separation is of a different nature, looking at the growth of Pentecostalism as a separate tradition of the church. Warrington begins his work *Pentecostal Theology* by writing, "Just over 100 years ago, Pentecostalism was born. Since then, it has grown to be one of the biggest and fastest growing components of Christianity. Its inception in the West is generally identified as being in Azusa Street, Los Angeles, in 1906."[9] Other writers, as for example,

---

7. P. Kalaitzidis, "Theological, Historical, and Cultural Reasons for Anti-Ecumenical Movements in Eastern Orthodoxy," in *Orthodox Handbook on Ecumenism*, eds. P. Kalaitzidis et al. (Oxford: Regnum Books International, 2014), 134–152, 141(19).

8. A. Sell, *The Great Ejectment of 1662: its Antecedents, Aftermath and Ecumenical Significance* (Eugene: Pickwick Publications, 2012) offers a helpful analysis of the causes of the separation and the ecumenical challenges raised.

9. K. Warrington, *Pentecostal Theology* (London: Bloomsbury Publishing, 2008). The many footnotes in the first chapter provide a comprehensive overview of publications on Pentecostalism.

Anderson, Dayton, Hollenweger, and Kay have traced the longer origins of this movement.[10] However, the Azusa Street revival is generally regarded as a key moment in the development of modern Pentecostalism. Since this revival, Pentecostal churches have grown rapidly across the world. While there are a number of significant streams of Pentecostalism, this strand of the church is marked by a range of independent churches, particularly in the Americas, Africa, and Asia.

Vondey describes the growth of Pentecostalism and its complexity: "today's Pentecostalism is a global phenomenon, an ecumenical melting pot, a theological puzzle consisting of a multiplicity of voices and positions, and a major factor in the shaping of late modern Christianity."[11]

While the early days of the rise of Pentecostalism saw an inevitable separation from what might be seen as their parent churches, in view of the emphasis on the experience of the Holy Spirit in the local congregation, it is interesting to note the gradual growth of ecumenical discussions and dialogues in which Pentecostals are involved, particularly in the twenty-first century.[12]

These three periods of the churches' history point to the way in which, when churches are separated from one another, what they offer to the world about unity, koinonia and overcoming polarization is diminished. There are complex reasons for the situations in which the separation of churches occurs. Different Christian traditions each have their own sense of faithfulness to the gospel, leading to the establishment of separate churches, nationally, internationally or locally. However, separated churches diminish the Christian witness to the one God, who holds creation and people in all their diversity together, and reduce the possibility of a positive churches' response to polarization.

This raises the issue of the nature of what the church is modelling in terms of embodying God's way in the world. When self-identity is being affirmed leading to churches living in separation, there are challenges to ensuring that separation does not mean polarization or the support of

---

10. A.H. Anderson and W.J. Hollenweger, *Pentecostals after a Century* (Sheffield, Continuum International Publishing Group, 1999); W.K. Kay, *Pentecostalism: A Very Short Introduction* (Oxford: Oxford University Press, 2011); D. Dayton, *Theological Roots of Pentecostalism* (Ada: Baker Academic, 1987). These writers offer a broader outline of the movement including referring to John Wesley and the development of the Holiness Movement in the USA and the role of revivals in various parts of the church.

11. W. Vondey, "The Unity And Diversity Of Pentecostal Theology: A Brief Survey for the Ecumenical Community in the West," article on www.academia.edu with reference to his book *Pentecostalism: A Guide for the Perplexed* (London and New York: Bloomsbury, 2013).

12. As for example the 2020 international dialogue between the World Communion of Reformed Churches and Pentecostalism, or the dialogue in England between the Church of England and Pentecostal churches.

polarizing views in the world. Separation can lead to the diminishment of the witness to one God, and to the *koinonia* that this one God makes possible.

4. ECUMENISM AS A RESPONSE TO POLARIZATION

In order for the separation which leads to polarization to be addressed, churches need to wrestle and share together with the issues about the faith that are understood differently. These discussions can take place locally, nationally, regionally and internationally, both internally within one particular tradition of the church and externally with Christians of different traditions. Wrestling and sharing together bears fruit when it takes place through engaging together in prayer, reflection and activity. The recent significant work of Receptive Ecumenism has opened the door for Christians from different traditions to engage with a deeper understanding of where each tradition comes from: "The essential principle behind Receptive Ecumenism is that the primary ecumenical responsibility is to ask not 'What do the other traditions first need to learn from us?' but 'What do we need to learn from them?'"[13] The decades across the twentieth century saw positive developments with regard to a growing ecumenical approach. I will describe four areas in which the theme of *koinonia* has emerged: first, the 1910 and 2010 Edinburgh world mission conferences; second, the 2nd Vatican Council; third, the work of the World Council of Churches; and, fourth, bi-lateral ecumenical dialogues.

Firstly, the 1910 World Mission Conference in Edinburgh.[14] This conference followed earlier international missionary conferences in Liverpool (1860), London (1885), and New York (1900). More representative than its predecessors, it served as an important stimulus to the twentieth century ecumenical movement, for where previous conferences had been not had a specific ecumenical approach and had been largely evangelical, participants at the Edinburgh conference represented missionary societies across most of the Protestant spectrum (Roman Catholic and Orthodox societies were still notably absent).[15]

---

13. Receptive Ecumenism started with the initiative of Professor Paul Murray and the Durham University Catholic Studies Centre. It has held international conferences in 2006, 2009, 2014 and 2017 and published a range of books, articles and chapters in books.

14. World Missionary Conference, *Edinburgh 1910, Reports of Commissions* (Edinburgh: Oliphant, Anderson & Ferrier, 1910) gives an indication of the range of issues covered.

15. The majority came from Britain and North America, though 40 societies from other European countries and 12 from South Africa and Australasia were also present.

The 1910 conference was commemorated in 2010 in Edinburgh, with a further look at mission.[16] This conference embraced a much wider spectrum of participants than 1910, including Orthodox, Anglican, Lutheran, Reformed, Methodist, Baptist, Seventh Day Adventist, Roman Catholic, Evangelical, Pentecostal and Independent traditions.

The opening two speakers referred to the challenging issues of unity and diversity. WCC general secretary Rev. Dr Olav Fykse Tveit said: "Mission and unity belong together. To be one in Christ is to witness together to Christ." Rev. Dr Geoff Tunnicliffe, international director of the World Evangelical Alliance said that although it would not be realistic to expect historical differences to be solved in a few days, he hoped that during the conference participants will be able to "listen to one another with love and respect, build bridges rather than create chasms, pray together, learn together, establish new friendships." In saying this, he was pointing to key aspects of the reception and working out of God's gift of koinonia. Secondly, the ground-breaking Second Vatican Council (1962–1965), was the starting point for a gradual opening of a door in order to address the separation of the Roman Catholic Church from the range of other different Christian traditions. Among the many texts considered and approved, *Unitatis Redintegratio*[17] was the key text in terms of ecumenism, focussing on the unity that Christ desired. Neuner, in reflecting back on this Council and its influence, particularly with regard to the understanding of *koinonia*, both within the Roman Catholic Church, and between the Roman Catholic Church and other Christian traditions, writes:

> The idea of the Church as communion, as a reciprocity of churches, is of notable significance ecumenically. It can help us to overcome the divisions we have inherited and forestall threatened schisms. It cannot be the goal of ecumenism to arrive at a uniform church ruled from one centre, in which pluriformity is abolished. The goal of ecumenical efforts is not a universal Church organisation, but for churches to recognise each other as such.[18]

The question remains as to the nature of mutual recognition, and whether there are further steps to be taken to draw churches more closely together, in order for *koinonia* to be more visible.

Thirdly, the task of developing a shared understanding of what

---

For further summary information see https://archiveshub.jisc.ac.uk/data/gb231-ms3291 (accessed October 23, 2020).

16. See conference website, Edinburgh 2010 conference website (accessed October 23, 2020), for further information including list of speakers and texts of conference papers.

17. Second Vatican Council, November 21, 1964.

18. P. Neuner, "The Church as Koinonia, a Central Theme of Vatican 2," *The Way*, March/July 1990, www.theway.org.uk.

koinonia might mean for the life of the church and the life of the world was taken up by the World Council of Churches (WCC).

In 1991, the theme of the WCC Canberra Assembly was 'Come Holy Spirit, Renew the Whole Creation.' In 1993, the WCC Fifth World Conference on Faith and Order in Santiago de Compostela, looked in detail at the *koinonia* aspects of this theme and published the report *On the Way to Fuller Koinonia*.[19] (The report contained insights from the Roman Catholic church, which, while not a member of the WCC, is a full member of the Faith and Order Commission.) This conference included an examination of the scriptural understandings of *koinonia*, and the outworking of *koinonia* in 'Faith, Life and Witness,' as part of a reflection on the background to *koinonia* and the seeking of future ecumenical directions. Wider ecumenical thinking was further developed by the Faith and Order Commission, leading to the 2013 report *Together Towards a Common Vision*.[20] Lorelei Fuchs offers a helpful analysis of the focus on *koinonia* in both WCC meetings and publications, and in international dialogues.[21]

Fourthly, there has been a range of international bilateral dialogues. An example of the way in which communion has been taken up in International Dialogues involving the Roman Catholic Church, is that of the Anglican Roman Catholic International Commission (ARCIC). This Commission reflected in the second and third phases of its meetings "on the church as Communion, local and universal, and how in communion the local and universal Church come to discern right ethical teaching."[22]

In the next section I offer a more detailed example of one specific dialogue, the International Reformed Anglican Dialogue (IRAD), of which I was co-chair. I highlight its emphasis on using the word *koinonia* rather than communion.

In conclusion, after hope-filled starts in the twentieth century with regard to ecumenism, recent decades have seen a debate as to whether ecumenism as a whole has moved forward with any energy. Ivana Noble challenges some of the more recent negativity by pointing to the ongoing awareness of an ecumenical winter. She responds positively, by writing:

> An ecumenical winter, however, is not the death of ecumenism. It is a season when, under the cover of the snow, new life can be prepared, when

---

19. T.F. Best and G. Gassmann (eds.), *On the Way to Fuller Koinonia*, WCC Faith and Order Report (Geneva: WCC publications, 1993). The Roman Catholic Church, while not being a member of the WCC, has been a full member of the WCC Faith and Order Commission since 1968.

20. *Together Towards a Common Vision* (Geneva: WCC publications, 2013).

21. L.F. Fuchs, *Koinonia and the Quest for an Ecumenical Ecclesiology* (Grand Rapids: Eerdmans, 2008).

22. *Unity, Faith and Order*: Report to Anglican Consultative Council 2017.

it is necessary to formulate once again and in different terms what kind of unity we want to move towards and what can strengthen advances in this direction and what prevents them.[23]

There are many different ways of looking at ecumenical issues, from the theological to the cultural, from international and national agreements to local co-operation, from what happens in practice in relation to mission to what is possible in terms of prayer and worship together. These four areas outlined here point to the growing significance of the thinking about *koinonia* in a range of international dialogues within and between different traditions of the church. They are offered as a sign of the new life that is possible when churches come together, despite their differences, to look at their shared gifts and the way in which the gift of God's koinonia embraces diversity. In this way, the separation that too easily leads to polarization can be addressed and offered as a starting point for addressing the deep-seated issues of polarization across the world.

5. AN EXAMPLE OF DIALOGUE: INTERNATIONAL REFORMED ANGLICAN DIALOGUE (IRAD), 2015–2020

I turn now to a recent example of an international dialogue between two different traditions of the church, in order to look at how thinking about *koinonia* has worked out in practice between these traditions; at some of the possibilities and challenges that this understanding opens up; and at the significant interpretation of *koinonia* in terms of 'responsible communion.' This interpretation indicates the way *koinonia* points to the church's engagement with God and the world, making possible open and loving relationships between people and in communities, and thus countering the move towards polarization.

The Anglican Communion, formed in 1867, predates by well over a century the much more recent World Communion of Reformed Churches, formed in 2010 by the significant union between the World Alliance of Reformed Churches and the Reformed Ecumenical Council. (It is interesting to note the deliberate choice of the word 'communion' in the title of this new Reformed body). In 2020, these two communions each have a membership of between 80–100 million people around the world.[24]

---

23. I. Noble (ed.), *Essays in Ecumenical Theology 1* (Studies in Reformed Theology) (Leiden: Brill, 2018), 219–243. The appendix has a helpful analysis of some of the specific issues.

24. Further information about the two communions, their history, their current membership, and their areas of work, may be found on the websites of the Anglican

The Anglican Consultative Council and the World Alliance of Reformed Churches first engaged in formal dialogue from 1981 to 1984, producing the report *God's Reign and Our Unity*.[25] This report covered a wide range of topics, including a renewed missionary perspective; issues with regard to Baptism, Eucharist and ministry in the church; the form of unity, and a range of practical suggestions for developing the shared conversation. For a range of reasons, not least the challenges presented by the priority or otherwise of ecumenical dialogue and areas of disagreement such as ordained ministries, this report and its recommendations were only taken forward in a limited way.

In 2011 a meeting was held in Geneva between representatives of the two communions and a proposal made for a further dialogue, which began in 2015. The first part of the schema for the dialogue identified communion as a key area of conversation.[26] Taking this area forward was felt to provide a way of looking at the underlying commitment of Christian faith and life, rather than looking at issues of organization and structure which might initially prove to be too contentious. The need was identified to step back from the disagreements over these areas in order to develop a shared understanding of God's gift of *koinonia* which provides the basis for moving together beyond the areas of difference and disagreement.

A number of presentations were made in the early meetings of IRAD around the theme of communion, in order to deepen a mutual understanding and awareness of this theme in the two communions.[27]

Communion and of the World Communion of Reformed Churches, http://www.anglicancommunion.org and http://wcrc.ch (both accessed October 23, 2020). A more detailed analysis would indis cate that these two communions are not equally balanced, in terms of size of membership, in different countries around the world. In some countries there are more Anglican churches and members than Reformed, and in other countries it's the other way round. In some countries there are several different national churches that are part of the Reformed tradition, and only one Anglican church nationally.

25. *God's Reign and Our Unity* (London: SPCK, 1984).
26. Schema for Anglican-Reformed Dialogue, part 1, with regard to communion:
1) The Nature of Communion
   a. Reformed and Anglican reflection on their own understanding of communion and identity
   b. Mutual responsibility and accountability of churches within Communions
   c. Mutual recognition and interchangeability of ministries within Communions
   d. Biblical and theological foundations of communion
   e. Degrees of communion (from mutual recognition of baptism through to the full visible unity of the Church)
   f. Communion rooted in justice and justice rooted in communion.
27. The IRAD communiques, giving a brief summary of the meetings in Kerala 2015, Cambridge 2016, Durban 2017, Vancouver 2018 and Hiroshima 2019, may be found on the websites of the Anglican Communion and the World Communion of Reformed Churches (see footnote 23). The presentations were made by the members and staff of

These included looking at scriptural interpretations, from the understanding of covenant in the Hebrew scriptures, to looking at friendship, wisdom, and sacrifice in the New Testament. Theological and historical perspectives on the nature of communion were shared, as well as the undergirding trinitarian origins of communion, as God's gift and calling. The possible unity and diversity of communion was examined, as well as the role of communion in social transformation and the consequences of living in communion. Wider ecumenical thinking was referred to, including the WCC report *Together Towards a Common Vision*.

To avoid discussions being abstract theological debates, at each meeting the theological reflection was rooted in the place in which the meetings were held, and papers were given by people who came from that context. Input to the meetings came also from the wider leadership of the churches represented in each setting.

In Kerala, India, insights were gained from the Church of South India (formed in 1947) and the Church of North India (formed in 1970), united churches which have drawn together Anglicans and a range of other Protestant churches. Input was received about the significant nature of these two churches, and the challenges faced internally and in the India context. These two churches provide helpful models of what is possible when Christians of different traditions commit to working and sharing together across a country.

In Cambridge, UK, a visit was made on the Sunday morning to share in worship in a Local Ecumenical Partnership between the Church of England and the United Reformed Church, where there is one joint congregation. Local Ecumenical Partnerships across the UK have offered a way of sharing together between different Christian traditions, in order to serve and witness more effectively in a local community

Meeting in Durban, South Africa, opened up a conversation about the apartheid era and the way in which some churches colluded with the evils of apartheid, while other churches campaigned against it. Particular attention was given to the nature of 'responsible communion' in terms of the key need for the churches' involvement in social and political areas of life.

The meeting in Vancouver, Canada, focussed on indigenous people and their unjust treatment in different parts of Canadian society, including by the church, with a challenge to listen to the voices of marginalised people, when shaping the life and witness of the church.

The final meeting was in Hiroshima, Japan, where a survivor

---

the IRAD dialogue teams and reflected both the traditions from which the speakers came and the contexts of the various IRAD meeting places around the world.

of the atomic bomb testified to the need for peace and peace-making internationally, and the importance of people of all faiths and none working for a world in which there is an end to war.

The South African appeal for 'responsible communion' formed a significant part of the conversation. The responsible nature of communion is seen as arising out of God's gift of *koinonia* for all the world and the need to embody this communion in each part of the world. This understanding offered a helpful way forward, in terms of seeing communion as engagement with the world, not just as an internal church matter and reinforcing the way in which living in the life of the triune God involves both the community of the church and the participation in God's transforming life in the world.

I turn now to highlight the understanding of koinonia as developed in the Dialogue, followed by a reference to the significance of worship in receiving koinonia, and then pointing to the IRAD conclusions, before drawing out more general conclusions.

5.1 Taking Up the Language of *Koinonia*

The use of the word koinonia rather than communion enabled the commission to look beyond traditional understandings of communion, in order to develop new insights in understanding the Trinity, relationality and the connection between responsible communion and the church's mission in the world. The report highlighted issues such as life-denying forces and marginalised people, and said "It is critical for mission that the Church finds ways to attend to conflict without allowing it continually to divide."[28] This emphasis points to the significance of the way in which koinonia is seen as addressing polarization.

The IRAD commission confirmed the importance of using the language of *koinonia*, rather than communion. "In focusing on *koinonia*, this report offers the Church a fresh opening and renewed language about how to live together, encompassing both unity and diversity within and between churches, and in relationship to the whole creation."[29] The commission felt that *koinonia* thinking can open up new perspectives on the familiar themes offered by 'communion,' with this language opening up wider ways of thinking about areas that are central to the life and faith of the church. This thinking begins by enabling people of different traditions and diverse views to look together at God and the nature of the

---

28. *Koinonia, God's Gift and Calling: The Hiroshima Report of the International Reformed-Anglican Dialogue* (London: Anglican Consultative Council, 2020), paragraph 52 in Section 3, "*Koinonia* in Mission." (In its focus on *koinonia*, the IRAD report has three main sections. The first looks at insights from scripture and church history; the second considers the life of the church; the third turns to mission.).

29. *Koinonia, God's Gift and Calling*, "Introduction."

Trinity and to see the inclusive, loving relationality that flows out of the triune God into the church, the human community and all of creation.

The commission reflected on the way in which *koinonia*

> ... is not always our lived experience, as the gift of koinonia is not fully received. The commission's discussions about koinonia emerged not only from ecumenical concerns, but from the reality that both Anglican and Reformed Christians have been experiencing fierce internal struggles and threats of division within our respective communions, as well as in society at large.

The report emphasises both the undergirding understanding of *koinonia* as it flows out of the life of the triune God as understood in scripture and the tradition of the church, and the development of this *koinonia* in ecclesiological and missional thinking.

In terms of the issue of polarization, the report points to the particular gift of *koinonia* in terms of overcoming division and conflict:

> Even extremely demanding difference and conflict have the potential to teach us more fully about *koinonia* precisely because they demand empathy, deep listening, patience, and humility, which are also necessary for relationships that deepen and grow rather than fracture. Though conflict can be destructive, the gift of *koinonia* turns us away from a posture of defence and persuasion toward one of honest listening and a desire for mutual understanding. In the redemptive work of Christ, *koinonia* disarms destructive conflict. The fullness of *koinonia* amid diversity moves us beyond our fear so as to approach others with curiosity, openness, and compassion.[30]

5.2 BEING DRAWN TO THE ONE GOD IN WORSHIP

Worship and liturgy are primary points in which the people of God together encounter the triune God and receive the gift of *koinonia*, through sharing together as God's people in listening to the Word and receiving the bread and wine. The meetings of IRAD took place in the context of morning and evening prayer, drawing on the riches and insights of the two different traditions. At the beginning and end of each meeting, Holy Communion was celebrated by the co-chair from one tradition, with the Word being shared by the co-chair from the other tradition.

Growing in God's gift of *koinonia* means being drawn more fully to God, and receiving the insights from different traditions of the church. These insights are particularly received through sharing in the varied spirituality and worship that the different traditions have to offer.

Out of this sharing, participation in the divine life is deepened, and the people of God are given the power to live out God's life in relation

---

30. *Koinonia, God's Gift and Calling*, section on "Ecclesiology."

to one another and in God's world. The recognition that each tradition offers worship in response to God's call, gives the starting point from which to engage in discussions about different understandings of the way in which worship is practiced between the different traditions.

Worship develops the sense of God's presence and otherness. Looking at worship not just for what it contains and what the sources of disagreement are with regard to different practices in different traditions, but for what the purpose of worship is and the way it can be shared is valuable in terms of sharing *koinonia* and being renewed in God's gift with one another and for all creation. Being drawn together in worship to the shared source of faith in the triune life, offers the possibility of difference, disagreement and polarization being changed to a renewed appreciation and reception of the transforming power of the loving God.

5.3 IRAD CONCLUSION

The conclusion of the International Reformed Anglican Dialogue points to the way in which *koinonia* is seen as offering a path to addressing polarization, when *koinonia* is described 'a message of hope to a world torn apart by division, conflict, and exploitation.' The reality of polarization and its growing influence across the world is clearly seen. But this is the starting point for change, not the place for succumbing to despair. The greater power of hope is seen in what koinonia still makes possible, for all people, and for the whole of creation:

> Anglicans and Reformed assert strongly that *koinonia* is a gift of God for the whole of creation. It is a participation in the Divine life, through which we encounter the eschatological gift of the New Creation even in a world torn apart by division, conflict and exploitation.

The report spells out the power of hope that *koinonia* offers further:

> Together our communions believe that this abundant, life-giving *koinonia* inspires a sense of gratitude in the life of our churches. Even in situations of conflict, great danger, marginalisation, secularization or persecution, the irrevocable gift of *koinonia* inspires joyful confidence in all the churches as they seek to share the relational abundance of Christ with those around them.[31]

While the IRAD commission represents a small team of people from the Anglican and Reformed traditions, it offers to the wider church the significant insights it has been drawn to during the course of its meetings.

The IRAD report concludes:

> The gift of *koinonia* has strong implications for the Church's life and health.

---

31. *Koinonia, God's Gift and Calling*, "Conclusion."

Despite the real pain of historical separation and manifold disagreement, the nature of *koinonia* as gift was never ours to possess alone nor to deny to one another. Due to the abundance of God's gift, it is inappropriate and inaccurate to speak of having being "in or out" of communion with one another. There are profound implications for how we speak of one another, and of our churches' sharing in the same *koinonia*.

In receiving the divine gift we recognize God's calling to testify to the gift of *koinonia* in the life of the church, to share the gift of *koinonia* in our mission to the world, and to make new disciples. Our two communions also witness to the current incompleteness of the Church's life.[32]

6. CONCLUSION

The historical separation of churches referred to in this chapter diminished with the growth of ecumenical conversations, agreed reports and shared action in the twentieth century. However, this diminishment did not lead to the overcoming of separation. Instead, new issues came to the fore, such as sexual identity, the role of women and the issues with regard to people of different ethnicities, causing division both within and between different traditions of the church.

Moving beyond deep-rooted separated identities to a point of mutual recognition and reconciliation, is challenging. In the twenty-first century there is a need for the church to address her own issues of separation, division and polarization, in order to be more effective in addressing the polarizations in the wider society, so that God's purpose for the church and the whole of creation can be more fully realised.

Deepening the shared understanding of *koinonia*, within and between traditions, offers a way of overcoming polarization, both within the church and in the world. This deeper understanding starts with faith in the one God, who is yet three in one. It emphasises the significance of relationality, starting with the relationality between the Father, Son and Holy Spirit, and then moving to see the ways in which this relationality can be embodied in humanity and creation. Key to this emphasis on relationality is seeing the self in new ways, no longer in a self-centred isolationism and individualism, but as finding wholeness in relation with God and others. Coming closer to the mystery and presence of God invites an attitude of awe, wonder and humility, rather than a self-defensive argument that 'I and I only, have the truth.'

Developing a deeper understanding of koinonia addresses polarization by pointing to the way in which embodying the loving relationality of the one God in the churches' shared life, helps to face up to the challenges of historical differences and divisions. This offers a polarized world a different way forward, of mutuality and the need

---

32. *Koinonia, God's Gift and Calling*, "Conclusion."

to struggle relationally with differences rather than letting them divide. Part of the struggle is about being drawn into relating to those who are different, accepting that, as for example in racism or sexism, differences are second order issues, not a cause for alienation or segregation.

This chapter develops the premise that the church is helped by looking at these areas in her own life, in order to contribute more fruitfully to counter the rise of polarization in the wider community. This is integral to being faithful to God and God's call to the world. *Koinonia* is a gift that arises from both the otherness and mystery of God as well as the incarnation and presence of God, and focusses on being drawn into relationality and inclusiveness. It is this gift that opens up the possibility of countering polarization by building loving, diverse and open communities, within the church and in the world.

BIBLIOGRAPHY

Anderson, A.H. and W.J. Hollenweger. *Pentecostals after a Century*. Sheffield, Continuum International Publishing Group, 1999.

Awad, N.G. *Persons in Relation*. Minneapolis: Fortress Press, 2014.

Best, T.F. and G. Gassmann. Eds. *On the Way to Fuller Koinonia*, WCC Faith and Order Report. Geneva: WCC publications, 1993.

Dayton, D. Theological Roots of Pentecostalism. Ada: Baker Academic, 1987.

Fox, P.A. *God as Communion*: *John Zizioulas, Elizabeth Johnson, and the Retrieval of the Symbol of the Triune God*. Collegeville: The Liturgical Press, 2001.

Fuchs, L.F. *Koinonia and the Quest for an Ecumenical Ecclesiology*. Grand Rapids: Eerdmans, 2008.

God's Reign and Our Unity. London: SPCK, 1984.

Kalaitzidis, P. "Theological, Historical, and Cultural Reasons for Anti-Ecumenical Movements in Eastern Orthodoxy." In *Orthodox Handbook on Ecumenism*, eds. P. Kalaitzidis et al., 134–152. Oxford: Regnum Books International, 2014.

Kay, W.K. *Pentecostalism*: *A Very Short Introduction*. Oxford: Oxford University Press, 2011.

Koinonia, God's Gift and Calling: The Hiroshima Report of the International Reformed-Anglican Dialogue. London: Anglican Consultative Council, 2020.

Neuner, P. "The Church as Koinonia, a Central Theme of Vatican 2," *The Way*, March/July 1990, www.theway.org.uk.

Noble, I. Ed. *Essays in Ecumenical Theology 1*. Studies in Reformed Theology. Leiden: Brill, 2018.

Sell, A. *The Great Ejectment of 1662*: *Its Antecedents, Aftermath and Ecumenical Significance*. Eugene: Pickwick Publications, 2012.

Unity, Faith and Order: Report to Anglican Consultative Council 2017.

Volf, M. *After Our Likeness*: *The Church as the Image of the Trinity*. Grand Rapids: Eerdmans, 1998.

Vondey, W. "The Unity And Diversity Of Pentecostal Theology: A Brief Survey for the Ecumenical Community in the West," article on www.academia.edu.

Vondey, W. *Pentecostalism*: *A Guide for the Perplexed*. London and New York: Bloomsbury, 2013.

Ware, K. *Orthodox Church*. London: Penguin Books, 1964.

Warrington, K. Pentecostal Theology. London: Bloomsbury Publishing, 2008.

Welker, M. *What Happens in Holy Communion*? Grand Rapids: Eerdmans, 2000.

Together Towards a Common Vision. Geneva: WCC publications, 2013.

World Missionary Conference. *Edinburgh 1910, Reports of Commissions*. Edinburgh: Oliphant, Anderson & Ferrier, 1910.

Zizioulas, J. *Communion and Otherness*. London: T & T Clark, 2006.

CHAPTER 15
NO CALLING WITHOUT BEING CALLED: THE *VOCATIO INTERNA* AT THE HEART OF SANCTIFICATION
Henk van den Belt

1. CALLED BY GOD

The Reformed understanding of the gracious and efficacious call to salvation reminds us of the fact that the calling of the church starts with the God who calls and whose creative Word constitutes the church by renewing sinners and uniting them to Jesus Christ. Reflecting on the calling of the church we should not forget to start from the divine beginning, as the Canons of Dort say, what "neither the light of nature nor the law can do, God performs by the power of the Holy Spirit through the Word."[1]

If we discuss the calling of the church to witness in times of polarization, we might forget that the church has been called before she has a calling. The emphasis on her practical calling easily leads to the question of what *we* can do, for instance focusing on the different contexts in which Christians are called to be peacemakers in situations of polarization. What are the most challenging issues of our time? How should the church relate to society? Should the church contribute to the 'common good' or form a 'counter culture'?

Ethical questions deal with what the church should do. That is fine, but before the church acts, she should remember that she is an *ec-clesia*, a "meeting of those whom God in his grace calls out from the state of nature into the supernatural state of children of God, in order to show his glorious mercy."[2] According to this definition from the *Synopsis of Purer Theology* (Leiden, 1625), a handbook of Reformed dogmatics written shortly after the Synod of Dort, the church displays the glorious

---

1. *Canons of Dort* 3/4.6–11.
2. *Synopsis Purioris Theologiae* 40.1–3. For the English translation, see Henk van den Belt (ed.), trans. Riemer Faber, *Synopsis Purioris Theologiae/Synopsis of a Purer Theology: Latin Text and English Translation*, Volume 2, Disputations 24–42 (Leiden/Boston: Brill, 2016), 559.

mercy of God. Only in that consciousness the witness of the church in words and deeds can become effective.

This awareness of being called does not make the church passive, but leads to an active witness in the world. Being aware of the divine call out of the 'state of nature' into the kingdom of God, out of the darkness into the marvellous light of the Gospel, the church also understands her task to proclaim the kingdom and to spread the light. Being called by God does not annul, but sharpens the question how the divine call to be different (*ec-clesia*) takes shape in the world. The calling of the church should not be understood in a moralistic way, because God manifests his mercy in the calling of the church and through the called church to the world.

The church does not have a calling in the first place, but is called by the grace of God. Her call to witness in and to a world full of division and violence is one of the main parts of sanctification. Holiness is not an end in itself but is for the glory of God and the benefit of others. According to the Reformed view the divine call by irresistible grace (the *vocatio interna*) lies at the heart of sanctification. The church is the body of Christ and the family of God. It is only through the efficacious work of the Spirit—who usually works through the Word—that we are united to this body and adopted into this family. God's glory is manifest in his sovereign grace. The most important aspect of becoming, being and remaining a Christian is the mystical union with Christ, into whose body we are called by the Gospel.

Before focusing on two aspects of the church's calling—from whence and to what she is called we will first offer a brief survey of the historical development of the tension between the general call through the gospel and the specific—or efficacious and internal—call though Word and Spirit. This will color the way in which the acknowledgement of being called by God colors the Reformed understanding of the calling of the church especially with regard to polarization.

2. Historical Summary

The theological term calling, or *vocatio*, roots in the New Testament use of the verb καλέω and the noun κλῆσις. The calling of the believer flows from a divine initiative and from sovereign grace. Calling and election are connected in Peter's admonishment to make our calling and election sure (2 Peter 1, 10) and in the so-called golden chain of redemption (Rom. 8:28–30). The link between eternity and time in the chain is the calling: those whom God predestined, He also called. This calling, however, cannot be completely identical with the invitation to repent and believe that extends to all who hear the gospel. Not all who are invited into the kingdom of God actually come. "Many are called, but few chosen," is the sad conclusion to two of Jesus' parables (Matt. 20:16 and 22:14).

To solve this tension between the two meanings of κλῆσις, Augustine developed a concept of effectual calling, a calling which is peculiar for those who indeed come to Christ and to the salvation offered by him.

> By that calling, then, which is according to his plan ... God is at work in the hearts of human beings in order that they may not hear the gospel to no avail, but that, having heard it, they may be converted and believe, receiving it, not as the word of human beings, but as the word of God, as it truly is.[3]

Augustine does not elaborate on the relationship between the gospel and God's operation in the heart, but he does claim that this call of the elect is effective. The distinction between a general calling—which might be ineffective—and the calling of the elect that is always effective, is not a peculiar doctrine of the Reformed tradition. It was well-known in medieval theology; the *Glossa Ordinaria* on Romans 8:30, harmonizing comments from church fathers, says that there is a *duplex vocatio*:

> External calling (*vocatio exterior*) takes place through preachers and is common to the good and the evil, while internal calling (*vocatio interior*) is only of the elect. Concerning the external calling it is said: Many are called but few are chosen. Predestination is fulfilled in calling.[4]

In the Reformation the emphasis shifts to the outward calling through the proclamation of the Word in the Law and the Gospel.

In his early career, Luther was much influenced by the mystical distinction of the outward and the inward word and in his polemics with Erasmus on free will in 1525, he argues that only the inward word conveys grace. God the Father draws and teaches the believers from within by his Spirit.

> There is a different kind of drawing from that which is without: Christ is held forth in the illumination of the Spirit, whereby the man is drawn unto Christ with the sweetest of all drawing: under which he is passive while God speaks, teaches, and draws, rather than seeks or runs of himself.[5]

---

3. Augustine, *De praedestinatione sanctorum* 19.39, PL 44:989. For the English translation, see Augustine, "The Predestination of the Saints," in Augustine, *Answer to the Pelagians IV*, translated by Roland J. Teske, *The Works of Saint Augustine: A Translation for the 21st Century*, I/26 (New York: New City Press, 1998), 149–187, 182.

4. Michael S. Woodward, *The Glossa Ordinaria on Romans*, Teams Commentary Series (Kalamazoo: Medieval Institute Publications, Western Michigan University, 2011), 132. For the Latin text, see the scans of the *Glossa Ordinaria* on www.lollardsociety.org/glor/Glossa_vol6b_EpistPauli_a.pdf.

5. Martin Luther WA 18:782, for the English translation, see Martin Luther, *On the Bondage of the Will*, translated by Henry Cole (London: T. Bensley, 1823), 366.

There is an underlying current in Luther's early works in line with mystical medieval traditions that stresses the necessity of the work of the Holy Spirit for the effectiveness of the Word. In that same year, however, the confrontation with spiritualism, especially that of Andreas Karlstadt led Luther to an opposite emphasis expressed in his *Wider die himmlischen Propheten* (1525). From then on he stressed the primacy of the outward Word and made the gift of the Spirit depend completely on the outward administration of the Word and the sacraments.

At the Marburg Colloquy (1529) Martin Luther and Huldrych Zwingli did not settle their disagreement on Christ's presence in the Lord's Supper, but they did agree 'On the External Word' (*Von dem eusserlichen Wortt*), that "the Holy Spirit, to express it clearly, gives no one this faith or his gift without preceding preaching or oral word or the gospel of Christ. But through and with such oral word He works and he creates faith, where and in whom He pleases."[6] One year later the *Augsburg Confession* (1530), condemns "the Anabaptists and others who think that the Holy Spirit comes to men without the external word."[7] This emphasis is prompted by the polemics against spiritualists.

The main point here is not to demonstrate that the development of the *vocatio interna* in Reformed theology was colored by polemics—and perhaps even polarization with regard to the anabaptists—but that the Reformed emphasis on the necessity of the Spirit's work contains catholic elements that might be lost out of sight because of these polemics.

This emphasis of the mature Luther has become a standard to measure the position of others and to measure later developments, but in fact this position deviated from what was common among the early Reformers in what can be seen as a debate among Augustinian theologians. In the early Reformation Luther's externalism is the exception and not the rule. Franciscus Lambertus, for instance, in his *De Fidelium Vocatione in Regnum Christi* (1525) interprets the calling of believers as "the enlightenment by which God moves someone so by his Word and Spirit that he leaves the kingdom and power of the devil and enters into the realm of the grace and mercy of his Son."[8] Martin Bucer even objects explicitly to the Lutheran emphasis and sympathizes with

---

6. Wilhelm H. Neuser, "Die Marburger Artikel von 1529," in *Reformierte Bekenntnisschriften 1/1, 1523–1534*, eds. Heiner Faulenbach and Eberhard Busch (Neukirchen-Vluyn: Neukirchener Verlag, 2002), 259–267, 264.

7. Augsburg Confession, 5, Die Bekenntnisschriften der evangelisch–lutherischen Kirche (10th ed.) (Göttingen: Vandenhoeck & Ruprecht, 1986), 58. The translation relies on Theodore G. Tappert, *The Book of Concord: The Confessions of the Evangelical Lutheran Church* (Philadelphia: Fortress Press, 1959), 31.

8. Franciscus Lambertus, *De Fidelium Vocatione in Regnum Christi, id est, Ecclesiam* (Strassburg: Herwagen, 1525), 2b.

the spiritualists. He rejects the view—articulated by Johannes Brenz (1499–1570) in his commentary on John—that the Word is a medium and instrument through which the Spirit is conveyed, on the contrary, the Spirit "is not offered together with the Word but is poured out from above that the Word may be understood."[9] Bucer turns against Luther's conviction that "God has determined to give no man what is inward, that is, the Spirit, faith, and other gifts, without what is outward, that is, the preached word and the sacraments."[10] Later, that is after the Marburg Colloquy, Bucer draws closer to Luther, admitting that the Spirit commonly does not work without the Word. Still he maintains the sovereignty of the Spirit to do otherwise.

In the 1539 edition of the *Institutes* John Calvin makes a distinction between the general call and the special call. In the general call God invites all to himself through the outward preaching of the Word. In the special call God causes the preached Word to dwell in the hearts of believers by his Spirit. The special call "consists of the preaching of the Word combined with the illumination of the Spirit." The final edition of the *Institutes* even makes a stronger distinction, saying that the call "consists not only in the preaching of the Word but also in the illumination of the Spirit."[11] The Spirit is essential for the unification of Christ and the believer from the very start of Calvin's theology, but in his later writings, influenced by the polemics regarding predestination, the distinction of the inward call from the outward Word is sharper than at the beginning.

---

9. Martin Bucer, *Enarratio in evangelion Johannis* (Strassburg: Herwagen, 1528). For the critical edition, see Martin Bucer, *Enarratio in Evangelion Iohannis* (1528, 1530, 1536) (Martini Buceri Opera, Series II Opera Latina, 2), Studies in Medieval and Reformation Thought, 40, ed. Irena Backus (Leiden: Brill, 1988), 268. Cf. Johannes Brenz, *In divi Joannis Evangelion Exegesis* (Hagenau: Secerius, 1527), 117. On the debate regarding the Lord's Supper and the exegesis of John 6 see Ian Hazlett, "Zur Auslegung von Johannes 6 bei Bucer während der Abendmahlskontroverse," in *Bucer und seine Zeit: Forschungsbeiträge und Bibliographie*. Festschrift for Robert Stupperich, eds. Marijn de Kroon, Friedhelm Krüger and Robert Stupperich (Wiesbaden: Steiner, 1976), 74–87 and Irena Backus, "Polemic, Exegetical Tradition and Ontology: Bucer's Interpretation of John 6:52, 53 and 64 before and after the Wittenberg Concord," in *The Bible in the Sixteenth Century*, Duke Monographs in Medieval and Renaissance Studies, 11, ed. David C. Steinmetz (Durham: Duke University Press, 1990), 176–180.

10. Bucer, *Enarratio in Evangelion Iohannis*, 268. For the English translation, cf. Stephens, *Holy Spirit*, 202–203 n6. Bucer here cites from Luther's work *Against the heavenly prophets*, WA 18:136. These and other anti-Lutheran passages were deleted in the 1536 revision of the commentary. For the final edition, see Martin Bucer, *In sacra quatuor evangelia enarrationes perpetuae secundum recognitae* (Basil: Johannes Herwagen, 1536), 682.

11. Jean Calvin, *Opera Selecta*, 3rd edition, eds. Peter Barth and Wilhelm Niesel (Munich: Christian Kaiser, 1967) 3:412 (henceforth Calvin, OS). For the final edition see John Calvin, *Institutes* 3.24.2.

In sum, Bucer's and Calvin's emphasis on the necessity of the Spirit to make the Word effective stands over against Luther's later emphasis on the necessity of the Word to let the Spirit work effectively. Both emphases are constitutive for the Lutheran and Reformed traditions.

The distinction between the outward and the inward call is essential for Reformed theology. There also is a tendency, however, to turn the distinction into a dichotomy between Word and Spirit. This tendency has been strengthened in the context of the seventeenth century's turn to the human subject in epistemology.[12] This has made Reformed theology vulnerable for intellectualistic objectivation and pietistic subjectivation in the context of modernity.

Although the later developments show a certain vulnerability, still this Reformed—and originally catholic—notion of the *interior vocatio* that makes the Word of the external calling efficacious in the elect can be helpful in understanding the calling of the church in times of polarization, because the internal work of the Spirit reveals where the conflict really lies and because a Christian life in liberty and holiness is a fruit of the irresistible work of the Spirit through the Word.

3. Called into the Fellowship of Christ

The verb 'to call' implies movement. This is clear from the way in which Christ calls his disciples. They have to take up their cross and follow him unconditionally (Matt. 10:38). He invites all who are weary and burdened to come to him and promises to give them rest (Matt. 11:28).

In the New Testament the verb 'to call' (καλέω) mostly occurs in an authoritative relationship. Those who are invited must come and obey their calling. The shepherd calls his sheep by name and they follow him (John 10: 3). The call usually has the desired effect; it is a *vocatio efficax*. The movement to which we are called is both 'out of' (ἐκ) and 'into' (εἰς). The contrast is formulated most clearly in 1 Peter 2:9 where the suffering saints are to 'declare the praises of him who called them out of darkness into his wonderful light.' The believers in Corinth are called into the fellowship (κοινωνία) of Jesus Christ (1 Cor. 1:9) and the Galatians are called into the grace of Christ (Gal. 1:6).

It is not necessary to explain the term *ec-clesia* etymologically—as the *Synopsis* does above, as being called out of the world—to see that the New Testament calling is related to the contrast between the dominion of darkness and the kingdom of God's beloved Son (Col. 1:13). The

---

12. This is the case, for instance, in John Owen's understanding of the calling as a synonym of regeneration. See Henk van den Belt, "Vocatio as Regeneration: John Owen's Concept of Effectual Calling," in *John Owen between Orthodoxy and Modernity*, eds. Willem van Vlastuin and Kelly M. Kapic (Leiden: Brill, 2019), 148–163.

divine calling takes place in the context of the conflict between the prince of this present evil world and the righteous heir of the kingdom of heaven, and the world to come. To be called means a transformation, or rather a transplantation from one domain into the other, a transition from Babylon into Jerusalem. Living in the world, Christians are not part of the world, but have entered into the kingdom of Christ.

Therefore, conflict cannot be avoided. There is a difference, however, between conflict and polarization. The latter "occurs when a fear born of difference transforms into 'us-versus-them' thinking … polarization entails the belief that rational and productive dialogue and interaction are impossible or fruitless. The result is avoidance, silencing, increased aggression, or violence."[13] Conflict as such does not exclude dialogue and the willingness to listen to the other even if it is with the intention to persuade and convince the other from a strong conviction that he or she is in error.

It is the calling of Christians to avoid polarization, because "reconciliation is the central unifying story of the Christian faith."[14] The kingdom of Christ manifests itself in this world as God's fallen creation, but also stands diametrically opposite to this present evil world as the domain of the prince of darkness. Christians should be peacemakers and therefore often spontaneously object to polarization. That is fine, but this should not be done uncritically. They should be careful with the use of the term, because the essential Christian conflict can also be framed as polarizing by its opponents. Polarization is not a neutral term and can easily become a boomerang.

Some voices link religion to conflict per se and other blame monotheistic religions of being particularly violent. Belief in one God implies that there is only one people of God. Its members think they are called, under god-like leaders, to execute God's justice on earth. Monotheism is a potential harbinger of cultural and political violence.[15]

Polarization is a negative normative term. No-one will be pleased to call himself or the group to which he or she belongs a source of polarization. It is always the 'other' who is blamed for it. In other words, the term itself can have a polarizing effect. It is important to deconstruct

---

13. Lauren Swayne Barthold, *Overcoming Polarization in the Public Square*: *Civic Dialogue* (London: Palgrave Macmillan, 2020), 2.

14. Pieter Vos, "Introduction," 7.

15. For his application of this accusation in particular to the Reformed doctrine of election and for his convincing answer that, on the contrary, predestination accentuates grace, Michael Allen refers to Regina Schwarz, *The Curse of Cain*: *The Violent Legacy of Monotheism* (Chicago: University of Chicago Press, 1997) and Rodney Stark, *One True God*: *Historical Consequences of Monotheism* (Princeton: Princeton University Press, 2001). R. Michael Allen, *Reformed Theology* (London/New York: T&T Clark International, 2010), 112–113.

the use of this term and to remain cautious about it. The accusation that populist movements aim at polarization might be correct, but it can also become an easy reason for the establishment not to listen to the underlying anxieties of the common people; the label of polarization can become a discussion stopper.

Marcus Arvan argues that a model in which moral truths can be discovered, for instance through the Ten Commandments or through Christ, plays a significant role in causing polarization and that a model in which moral truths are created by negotiating compromises is more likely to prevent polarization.[16] Justified Christian opposition against polarization, of course, should not lead to relativizing it moral standards, even if according to others these standards are polarizing per se.

In general, consensus is a blessing, but the church can arrive at a point where the witness to Christ as the Way, the Truth, and the Light simply does not allow for it. Then it is her calling to witness uncompromisingly and that makes her vulnerable for the accusation of polarization. Of course, a main problem is that all Christians agree that there are unnegotiable issues in *statu confessionis*, but that they strongly disagree about which issues these are. In some cases, for instance on the question whether or not homosexual relationships are acceptable, they might agree on the fact that the issue is unnegotiable, but still take opposite positions. Some say that the acceptance of these relationships brings the church in *statu confessionis*, while others say the same about the rejection of these relationships. The fact that the church is often struggling to find her way in dealing with moral issues perhaps is an extra reason to be cautious about the use of polarization. When it is used within the church as a label for groups with whom the majority disagrees it easily becomes a hidden weapon to silence them.

The Reformed and Augustinian emphasis on the inward work of the Spirit can be helpful to discern between forms of harmful polarization and the true conflict between the kingdom of Christ and the present evil age. The emphasis on the inward or effectual calling implies that the borderline between both kingdoms runs right through the visible church. In the words of John Calvin: "as long as Christ remains outside of us, and we are separated from him, all that He has suffered and done for the salvation of the human race remains useless and of no value for us."[17] Thus this emphasis has a critical function for the believers who are called to examine themselves if they are truly called and to 'make every effort to confirm their calling and election' (2 Pet. 1:10). The line of demarcation between good and evil, between light and darkness never

---

16. Marcus Arvan, "The Dark Side of Morality: Group Polarization and Moral Epistemology," in *The Philosophical Forum* 50:1 (2019), 87–115, 88, 89, and 91.

17. Calvin, Institutes 3.1.1.

runs along the sociological lines of a Christian group or sub-group. On the contrary, the line runs right through the lives of the Christians themselves in their struggle to avoid the works of the flesh and cherish the fruit of the Spirit.

Within this fundamental struggle Christians are also called to call others. This is one of the reasons why the terminology of the call is also used for the call to the ministry of the Gospel. In a sense, however, not only apostles, evangelists, teachers and pastors are called to the ministry, but all believers are office bearers and called to be Christ's witnesses, a task for which they need and can expect the help of the Spirit of truth, the Lieutenant-Advocate, who will lead them into all truth and who, through their witness, will convince the world—or prove the world to be in the wrong—about sin and righteousness and judgment and glorify Jesus (John 16:8, 13, 14).

In other words, because those who are called out of darkness into the light of Christ are aware of the fact that there is no essential difference between them and the others, except for the grace of God, they have no reason at all to place themselves as sinners over against, leave alone, above others. We are all the same. The divine calling alone makes a difference and the conflict that flows from the difference made is not a struggle against flesh and blood, but against the powers that often hide themselves in enslaving structures for which we all are vulnerable.

4. CALLED UNTO LIBERTY AND HOLINESS

Exactly because the emphasis on the hidden and efficacious calling highlights the fact that we all need the same irresistible grace, it also sheds light on the character of sanctification or on that to which the church is called. Here again it helps to avoid the confusion of polarization and conflict, because the liberty and holiness to which the church is called are fruits of the same Spirit.

The call to salvation is not an end in itself, but always also a call to a goal or an invitation to move in a certain direction. One of the most important goals is freedom. The Galatians were called to be free, but are also admonished not to use their freedom to indulge the flesh, rather serving one another humbly in love (Gal. 5:13). In 1 Corinthians 7, where Paul writes about the change of status, he advises the believers to remain in the situation 'the Lord has assigned to them, just as God has called them' (1 Cor. 7:17), either circumcised or uncircumcised either in slavery or in freedom. "Each person should remain in the situation— literally 'calling' (κλῆσις)—they were in when God called them" (1 Cor. 7:20).

This verse has led to the misunderstanding that being a slave or being free in itself was a calling, just like being married or unmarried and that consequently any occupation or job is a divine calling. There is nothing wrong with seeing our everyday work as a 'calling,' but that is not what the text says.

The misunderstanding has been strengthened by the very influential interpretation of Luther's translation of the word as 'Beruf' by Max Weber. According to Weber, the modern use of *Beruf* first occurs in Luther's translation of Jesus Sirach 11:20–21 and after that quickly took on its present meaning in the Protestant languages. As a side remark Weber claims that Luther also used the word κλῆσις in the sense of the German *Stand* in 1 Cor. 7. "In verse 20 Luther ... even in 1523 in his exegesis of this chapter, renders κλῆσις with Beruf, and interprets it with Stand."[18] In line with Weber, Luther is more often blamed for misunderstanding and mistranslating 1 Corinthians 7:20.[19] Luther, however, did not translate κλῆσις with *Beruf* but with *Ruf* both in 1522 and in 1546.[20] Moreover, he did apply this text to a secular occupation. On the contrary, in his exposition of 1 Corinthians 7:20–24 (1523) he remarks:

> One should know that the word 'call' (*Ruf*) here does not mean the station (Stand) to which one is called, as when people say being married is your calling or being a priest is your calling, and so forth, everyone has his calling from God. St. Paul is not speaking of such a calling here, but of the Gospel call, that is to say: Stay in the calling in which you are called, that is: just as the Gospel meets you and just like its call finds you, stay there.[21]

Everyone has to stay where God's call has found him or her, except when that is a sinful position, "because this call causes you to be transferred from a sinful station into a pious station."[22] Due to the massive influence of Weber's thesis, the influence of Luther on this issue has been very much exaggerated.

What is worse, however, is that this influential misunderstanding of the Lutheran tradition has led to the idea that the Protestant understanding of calling implies an affirmation of the status quo, even if that is a

---

18. Max Weber, *The Protestant Ethic and the Spirit of Capitalism*, trans. By Talcott Parsons, intr. by Anthony Giddens (London/New York: Routledge Classics, 2001), 160. According to Weber, this translation is the first case in which *Beruf* has a purely secular sense. It did not exist in German nor was it used in previous translations of the Bible, although Luther might lean on Johannes Tauler. Weber *Protestant Ethic*, 159.

19. For instance, by K.L. Schmidt in the article on 'kaleo' in the influential *Theologisches Wörterbuch zum Neuen Testament* (Stuttgart: J.B. Metzler, 1937), 3:493. For the English translation, see *Theological Dictionary of the New Testament* (Grand Rapids: Eerdmans, 1972), Vol. 3, 487–496.

20. Luther, WA Dt Bibel 7:104, 105.

21. Luther, WA 12:132.

22. Luther, WA 12:132–133.

situation of injustice and slavery. On the contrary, the true understanding of the calling by Word and Spirit is the secret of true liberty. Christian liberty is independent of the precise circumstances. If you are called to faith while being a slave, that makes you 'the Lord's freed person' if you are called being free, that transforms you into 'Christ's slave.' "You were bought at a price; do not become slaves of human beings" (1 Cor. 7:23).

According to Luther, by faith in Christ, we become free from all sin and fearless of death, endowed with the eternal righteousness of Christ.[23] Calvin elaborates on this liberty from the very first edition of the *Institutes*. For him it means three things: freedom from the law through faith, freedom of conscience to obey the law without compulsion and freedom in things indifferent.[24]

In Reformed orthodoxy this work of the Spirit was located in the renewal of the will in order to be able to perform good works. According to the Puritan John Owen "faith is in the understanding, in respect of its being and subsistence,—in the will and heart, in respect of its effectual working."[25] The essence of true regeneration lies in the renewal of the will into which God secretly communicates spiritual power. The will is not able to perform any spiritual act unless the Spirit effectuates the act of willing in it.[26] The Spirit uses the Word and the ministry of the church, but both are insufficient without the immediate operation of the Spirit on the will. The Spirit, however, does no violence to the will, because then the will as a will would be destroyed. "In the same instant of time wherein the will is moved it moves, and when it is acted it acts itself, and preserves its own liberty in its exercise."[27] The will by nature is *mobilis* (fit to be moved), in the creating act of faith and obedience by the Spirit the will is *mota* (moved), and with respect to its own act it is *movens* (moving). Thus, in regeneration the *moveable* will is moved so that it starts to become a moving will. Like a girl on a swing who cannot reach the ground: she is movable, but she can't move. Once someone gives

---

23. Luther, *On Christian Liberty*, 18, WA 7, 20–38.
24. John Calvin, *Institutes of the Christian Religion: 1536 Edition* (Grand Rapids: Eerdmans Publishing, 1995), 176. For the final edition, see Calvin *Institutes* 3.19.2–5.
25. John Owen, *The Works of John Owen*, ed. William H. Goold, 16 volumes (London: Johnstone and Hunter, 1850–1853), reprinted (Edinburgh: Banner of Truth, 1965–1968), 1:487. Cf. his remark that faith "doth not consist in, that it is not to be fully expressed by, any one single habit or act of the mind or will distinctly whatever." Owen, *Works* 5:100.
26. Owen, *Works* 3:315 and 356. On Owen's voluntarism and in particular with respect to the effectual call, cf. Gavin John McGrath, "Puritans and the Human Will: Voluntarism within Mid-Seventeenth Century Puritanism as Seen in the Works of Richard Baxter and John Owen" (PhD-thesis at Durham University, 1989), 251–292.
27. Owen, *Works* 3:320.

her a push she starts to swing and can hardly stop moving. The example is mine.

This is in line with the Canons of Dort, that state that the regenerating Spirit penetrates into the innermost recesses of man. He opens the closed and softens the hard heart. He makes the will, which was dead, alive; which was bad, good; which was unwilling, willing; and which was stubborn, obedient. He moves and strengthens it so that, like a good tree, it may be able to produce the fruit of good works.[28] Or in the words of Luther: "Good works do not make a good man, but a good man does good works … the fruits do not make trees either good or bad, but rather as the trees are, so are the fruits they bear; so a man must first be good or wicked before he does a good or wicked work."[29]

In other words, the *vocatio interna* does not make one passive as if the calling of the church or the individual Christian is to accept the status quo without resistance. On the contrary, the divine call empowers the church and individual Christians to strive for a life of liberty and holiness even if the present situation is awful and hardly makes change possible. There is always hope, because the power to change does not lie in human possibilities but in the divine and creative call towards liberty and holiness.

This freedom rooted in justification does not lead to a careless life, exactly because the calling to justifying faith at the same time is a calling to holiness, sanctification, and dedication to God. The believers in Rome "are called to belong to Jesus Christ and to be his holy people" (Rom. 1:6–7, cf. 1 Cor. 1:2). The call is effective, but the effective call is referred to as a motivation. The Ephesians are encouraged to live up to it or "worthy of the calling they have received" (Eph. 4:1). Apparently, realizing that all is of grace this does not lead to a passive attitude, on the contrary, the awareness of the efficacious calling has the potential of activating and empowering the believer.

The *duplex vocatio* always relates the work of the sovereign Spirit to the Word. This implies that it is only from Scripture that the believers know what they are precisely called to, and what the content or the direction of their calling is. At the same time, it is only the Spirit who empowers them to do so and teaches and leads them inwardly how to do it. We can do the wrong things in a right spirit and then need the correction of the Word, but we can also do the right things with the wrong spirit. Hypocrisy is worse than unintended error. In any case, next to the knowledge of the content of our calling, we need the work of the Spirit who recreates those whom God foreknew and predestined to be

---

28. *Canons of Dort*, 3/4.6–11.
29. Luther, *On Christian Liberty*, 23, WA 7, 20–38.

conformed to the image of his Son (Rom. 8:29).

The Reformed understanding of sanctification as a fruit of the inward renewal of the heart implies that the liberty of the one should not diminish the liberty of the other or even hurt him or her, because we are all called out of the darkness into the light of the fellowship of Christ and thus have become members of the same body. Even if Christians strongly disagree, the acknowledgement of their essential unity implies that internal conflicts may not lead to the rejection of the other as a fellow saved sinner if his or her convictions are not mine and even if they are objectionable to me. In other words, the Spiritual character of sanctification teaches the Christian inwardly to distinguish between the person and his or her convictions. This essentially Christian notion of liberty can also be applied to the broader field of living peacefully in society. The liberty to express yourself freely should not turn into the freedom of bashing others.

Applied to the calling to live holily, the emphasis on holiness as a fruit of the inward renewal through the Spirit, conjoined with the awareness of one's own lasting struggle with indwelling sin and the flesh, is the best antidote against spiritual pride. The work of the divine Spirit is characterized by a broken heart. A feeling of moral superiority always leads to polarization. Even blaming others for polarization can be a symptom of hidden feelings of being better than others. The history of Reformed churches illustrates that they have not always lived according to the theological standards. Often fierce battles have been fought on minor issues. Nevertheless, in essence its theological emphases have the potential to discern between essential spiritual conflict and unnecessary unspiritual quarrels. The reason why the Reformed tradition has not always—and perhaps not even often—practiced what it preaches is an issue for further and deeper reflection. In the Protestant principle of Scripture as the highest and sole authority in the church, "next to a church-reforming element, there is indeed a church-dissolving element."[30] The principle, combined with the modern idea that every individual can interpret Scripture according to his own understanding, certainly contains a polarizing element.

5. CONCLUSION

The calling of the church always starts with the acknowledgement that she has been called. God's Word that constitutes the church by renewing sinners and uniting them to Jesus Christ. Being called by the grace of God, the church witnesses in and to a fallen world. The divine call by

---

30. Herman Bavinck, "The Catholicity of Christianity and the Church," translated by John Bolt, *Calvin Theological Journal* 27 (1992), 220–251, 249.

irresistible grace (the *vocatio interna*) lies at the heart of sanctification. The historical development of this concept shows that the Reformed emphasis on the Spirit's work contains catholic elements that easily disappear because of objectivating tendencies in the conflict against spiritualism in the early Reformation. The Reformed emphasis on the inward calling is not a deviation from the Reformation, but rather a correction of a one-sided polemical reaction.

It is important not to label all forms of conflict as polarization. There are genuine and necessary forms of conflict. There is no Christianity without conflict, Christians are called out of the darkness into the light of the kingdom of God. Consensus is a blessing and Christians as peacemakers strive for peaceful coexistence in society. But sometimes the church is called into a 'state of confession' in which the uncompromising witness to Christ as the Truth is her highest calling even if that is framed as polarizing by others. The term polarization is a tar baby, the label itself can be polarizing. Therefore, Christians should be careful in using it. The Christian appeal to God's Commandments or the example of Christ as a moral standard and even monotheism itself can all be framed as forms of polarization.

The notion of the efficacious calling can be helpful to understand the calling of the church in times of polarization. The internal work of the Spirit reveals where the conflict really lies. The border between the two kingdoms does not run along sociological lines, but right through the church itself and even through the heart of the believers who themselves participate in the struggle between the flesh and the Spirit.

The emphasis on the efficacious calling also sheds light on the character of sanctification. Christians are not only called out of the world (*ec-clesia*), they are also called to freedom and holiness. The work of the Spirit empowers them and inspires them to hope for and strive for change even if powerful structures seem to make renewal impossible. Liberty and holiness are fruits of the same Spirit and therefore one cannot use his or her liberty at the expense of the law of God or the wellbeing and liberty of others. Moral superiority always leads to polarization and thus even the accusation of polarization can be a proud form of polarization.

The New Testament relates the call of Christ to the future. It is the eschatological call to a wedding, to the marriage supper of the Lamb. The essential unity of the Church has an eschatological perspective. Due to the renewing work of the Spirit, there is hope. Once we will live in a world without polarization, a world for which the Spirit teaches us to groan with all creation waiting eagerly for the future glory to which we have been called by grace.

BIBLIOGRAPHY

Allen, R. Michael. *Reformed Theology*. London/New York: T&T Clark International, 2010.

Arvan, Marcus. "The Dark Side of Morality: Group Polarization and Moral Epistemology." *The Philosophical Forum* 50:1 (2019): 87–115.

Augustine, *The Works of Saint Augustine*: *A Translation for the 21st Century*, *I/26*, translated by Roland J. Teske. New York: New City Press, 1998.

Backus, Irena. "Polemic, Exegetical Tradition and Ontology: Bucer's Interpretation of John 6:52,53 and 64 before and after the Wittenberg Concord." In *The Bible in the Sixteenth Century*, Duke Monographs in Medieval and Renaissance Studies, 11, ed. David C. Steinmetz, 176–180. Durham: Duke University Press, 1990.

Barthold, Lauren Swayne. *Overcoming Polarization in the Public Square*: *Civic Dialogue*. London: Palgrave Macmillan, 2020.

Bavinck, Herman. "The Catholicity of Christianity and the Church," translated by John Bolt, *Calvin Theological Journal* 27 (1992): 220–251.

Belt, Henk van den. "Vocatio as Regeneration: John Owen's Concept of Effectual Calling." In *John Owen between Orthodoxy and Modernity*, eds. Willem van Vlastuin and Kelly M. Kapic, 148–163. Leiden: Brill, 2019.

Brenz, Johannes. *In divi Joannis Evangelion Exegesis*. Hagenau: Secerius, 1527.

Bucer, Martin. *Enarratio in evangelion Johannis*. Strassburg: Herwagen, 1528.

Bucer, Martin. *In sacra quatuor evangelia enarrationes perpetuae secundum recognitae*. Basil: Johannes Herwagen, 1536.

Bucer, Martin. *Martini Buceri Opera*, *Series II Opera Latina*, 2, Studies in Medieval and Reformation Thought, 40, ed. Irena Backus. Leiden: Brill, 1988.

Calvin, Jean. *Opera Selecta*. 3rd edition, eds. Peter Barth and Wilhelm Niesel. Munich: Christian Kaiser, 1967.

Calvin, John. *Institutes of the Christian Religion*: 1536 Edition. Grand Rapids: Eerdmans Publishing, 1995.

Die Bekenntnisschriften der evangelisch–lutherischen Kirche. 10th ed. Göttingen: Vandenhoeck & Ruprecht, 1986.

Hazlett, Ian. "Zur Auslegung von Johannes 6 bei Bucer während der Abendmahlskontroverse." In *Bucer und seine Zeit: Forschungsbeiträge und Bibliographie*. Festschrift for Robert Stupperich, eds. Marijn de Kroon, Friedhelm Krüger and Robert Stupperich, 74–87. Wiesbaden: Steiner, 1976.

Lambertus, Franciscus. *De Fidelium Vocatione in Regnum Christi, id est, Ecclesiam*. Strassburg: Herwagen, 1525.

Luther, Martin. *Against the heavenly prophets*. WA 18:136.

Luther, Martin. *On Christian Liberty*. WA 7: 20–38.

Luther, Martin. *On the Bondage of the Will*, translated by Henry Cole. London: T. Bensley, 1823.

McGrath, Gavin John. "Puritans and the Human Will: Voluntarism within MidSeventeenth Century Puritanism as Seen in the Works of Richard Baxter and John Owen" (PhD-thesis at Durham University, 1989.

Neuser, Wilhelm H. "Die Marburger Artikel von 1529." In *Reformierte Bekenntnisschriften 1/1, 1523–1534*, eds. Heiner Faulenbach and Eberhard Busch, 259–267. Neukirchen-Vluyn: Neukirchener Verlag, 2002.

Owen, John. *The Works of John Owen*, ed. William H. Goold, 16 volumes. London: Johnstone and Hunter, 1850–1853. Reprinted: Edinburgh: Banner of Truth, 1965–1968.

Schwarz, Regina. *The Curse of Cain: The Violent Legacy of Monotheism*. Chicago: University of Chicago Press, 1997.

Stark, Rodney. *One True God: Historical Consequences of Monotheism*. Princeton: Princeton University Press, 2001.

Synopsis Purioris Theologiae/Synopsis of a Purer Theology: Latin Text and English Translation, Volume 2, Disputations 24–42, ed. Henk van den Belt, trans. Riemer Faber. Leiden/Boston: Brill, 2016.

Tappert, Theodore G. *The Book of Concord: The Confessions of the Evangelical Lutheran Church*. Philadelphia: Fortress Press, 1959.

Theological Dictionary of the New Testament. Grand Rapids: Eerdmans, 1972.

Theologisches Wörterbuch zum Neuen Testament. Stuttgart: J.B. Metzler, 1937.

Weber, Max. *The Protestant Ethic and the Spirit of Capitalism*, trans. By Talcott Parsons, intr. by Anthony Giddens. London/New York: Routledge Classics, 2001.

Woodward, Michael S. *The Glossa Ordinaria on Romans*, Teams Commentary Series. Kalamazoo: Medieval Institute Publications, Western Michigan University, 2011.

CHAPTER 16
'THEY ARE *IN* THE WORLD, BUT NOT *OF* THE WORLD':
BIBLICAL AND CONTEXTUAL REFLECTIONS ON
CHURCH, ALTERITY AND SELF-OTHERIZING
Najib George Awad

1. INTRODUCTION

In one of his church addresses, the former Roman Catholic Archbishop of Chicago, Francis Cardinal George, makes the following thought-provoking comment about Christianity's presence and role in the world today: "I expect to die in bed, my successor will die in prison and his successor will die a martyr in the public square."[1] Such a statement comes from a church figure living in the twenty-first century, in the heart of this era's globally scaled instability, drastic changes and multi-faceted polarization situation. It is an era of polarization in which many Christian intellectuals and authors, from the earth's four corners and from every background imaginable, relate that the Christian church lost ground in the public life of the World. The church was either pushed out of the public square completely or was declared by that square to be the main suspect that should be held accountable for almost all the dark moments and disasters that affected human existence over the past two or three centuries at least. Cardinal George's words do express in their own way the destiny that seems to be waiting for the Christian church in the near future. There seems to be a collective international conviction that the world needs a scapegoat to sacrifice on the altar of human history, and it is religious belief in general, and Christianity and Islam in particular, that is deemed the ideal candidate to be the Lamb to slaughter for such a sacrifice. Within this context, Christianity (in addition to Islam) is not seen as one of the numerable victims of the globally prevailing pluriform

---

1. Cited in D.A. Carson, "The Many Faces of the Current Discussion," in *The Enduring Authority of the Christian Scriptures*, ed. D.A. Carson (Grand Rapids/Cambridge: W.B. Eerdmans Publishing Company, 2016), 3–40, 6. Carson cites this from Robert W. Yarbrough, "'Bye-bye Bible?' Progress Report on the Death of Scripture," in *Them* 39 (2014), 415–427, 427.

of polarization that disturbs our life today. Christianity is seen as one of the active perpetrators of such polarization.

Is this accusation of Christianity fair or unfair; is it realistic or superficial? Christians, like any other religious people dealing with a challenge to their beliefs, tend to respond to charges toward the church not always by defending the church, but rather by leaning toward self-victimization: the church is the victim of the world's unjust persecuting and blame-shifting mentality that makes it often punish Christianity for evil for which it is not responsible. Is this self-victimization tendency what the church needs in today's world? Does the church play any role whatsoever in the polarization condition of today's human life? Is it possible that Christianity is not actually a victim, but more active as a perpetrator in the polarizing context it exists in?

2. ALTERITY IN THE NEW TESTAMENT: WHEN CHRIST'S FOLLOWERS RELATE TO THE WORLD

In their regular reading of the New Testament, Christians tend to sideline the Biblical candid and intriguing tendency not to consider the community of Christ as the victim of the disturbance of the world, but as one of the main potential sources that ought to be held accountable for such situation. We can detect such an orientation in Jesus Christ's farewell prayer to the heavenly Father before the crucifixion in the Gospel of John, Chapter 17. A careful reading of this prayer in the historical background of this gospel's narrative and within the framework of the Johannine author's highly intra-critical voice would seriously challenge the classical reading of Jesus's beseeching of the Father to protect His disciples from the evil one, for they are "*in* the world, but not *of* the world."

This pleading is often understood as Jesus's concern about how the world is going to disturb and threaten the life of his disciples due to their spiritual and religious alterity: They are chosen and blessed, the world is not; they are righteous and saintly, the world is condemned and evil. To the contrary, it is my belief that Jesus might here be seen as transpiring his apprehension for the world *from* his disciples' alterity. The disciples' alterity is not a burden on them before the world. Their alterity might, rather, turn them into a burden on and a threat to the world. Jesus's plea "protect them from evil" in John 17:15 can be Jesus's articulation of his serious fear that his disciples might misuse their alterity to relate to the world not in *caritas* and *koinonia*, but in a selfotherizing and contrariety that will make their alterity a cause of polarization. Had Jesus been confident that his disciples were immune to falling into such a trap, he would have not begged His Father to protect them from evil without also asking the Father to take them out of the world. However, this was not Jesus's request: "I do not ask you to take them out of the world, but to protect them from the evil one" (John 17:15). The disciples were not expected to manifest an alterity that would alienate them from the world, in Jesus's mind. To the contrary, Jesus pleads to His heavenly Father to make them "the visible presence of God *in* the world ... the locus of God's active presence *in* the world after Jesus's departure from the world."[2]

In the light of this possible reading, "they are in the world and not of it" may not actually be a statement of praise and positive recognition of the disciples' righteousness, but rather Jesus's frank expression of his preemptive disappointment regarding his disciples' tendency to make their alterity an excuse for exerting self-otherizing contrariety and a condescending stance toward the world. The key-hermeneutic elements in Jesus's intriguing prayer are the phrases "*in* the world" and "*of* the world." It would be against the core meaning of the incarnation and the eternal *Logos*'s becoming flesh like one of us if 'world' here connoted particular living creatures. Jesus's prayer, then, would discriminately imply that the disciples are ontologically superior above other living beings, thus in an apartheid-like status in relation to them. Against the incarnation logic would also be the term 'world' if Jesus wanted to say by using it that his disciples do not belong to the spatio-temporal reality of the world. This would entail that the followers of Christ exist in a supra-history, or even contra-history, situation, something that contradicts the Johannine teaching that the *Logos* became human *in* the fullness of *time/history*. More problematic still would be the term 'world' if Jesus meant by it a particular living context, for this would make Jesus sound like he was calling the disciples to alienate themselves from their Jewish identity and *Sitz im Leben*, something which the data we have on the historical Jesus contradict and defy. Each one of these potential interpretations of Jesus's term 'the world' depicts him as a preacher of contrariety and otherizing and as a promoter of a twisted and alienating notion of alterity.

The above notwithstanding, Jesus here speaks about 'the world' as a state of being, as something similar to Martin Heidegger's notion of '*Da-Sein*' in its radically and profoundly revised and corrected version in the 'being-with-others' post-Heidegger phenomenological project of Emmanuel Levinas.[3] 'The world' means a state of existence as 'being-

---

2. Rekha M. Chennattu, *Johannine Discipleship as a Covenant Relationship* (Peabody: Hendrickson Publishers, 2006), 132–133. Italics are mine.

3. See on this Martin Heidegger, *Being and Time*, trans. J. Macquarrie and E. Robinson (Oxford: Blackwell Publishers, 1995); Martin Heidegger, *The Phenomenology*

in-relation-with-others-here-and-now.'[4] 'The world' expresses, then, the state of interrelation, of interaction with the others that makes us who we are.

This understanding of 'the world' radically transforms the interpretation of the propositions Jesus uses to distinguish between being '*in* the world' and being '*of* the world.' To be *in* the world means that the Christians, like all other humans, exist in a state of self-perception that makes them be who they are vis-à-vis their relation to others, not only by virtue of their faith convictions. To be '*in* the world' must make relatedness to others revelatory of who the one is, not of what makes the person different in contrariety from others. The disciples' alterity is not supposed to become a barrier that otherizes them divisively from others. It is an alterity, which they become because they are not otherizing themselves in contrariety with others.

On the basis of this meaning of '*in* the world,' the expression 'they are not *of* the world' would not mean that Jesus's followers are not those whose life in the world insists on alienating them, in the name of alterity, from others. It means that Jesus's followers must not be those who think that life can truly be lived for God apart from the different other. It means that, without this state of 'beingin-relation-with-others-here-and-now,' the followers of Christ do not even exist, neither *in* nor *of* any kind of a world. I do not, thus, concur with the reading of Jesus's prayer, in John 17, for God to protect his disciples from evil as his way of indicating that, like him, the disciples are no longer part of their Jewish society but rather represent a "separate anti-society," which is "truly and truthfully set apart, exclusively, without social admixture and contamination—just as Jesus was for their sake."[5]

---

of Religious Life, trans. M. Fritsch and J.A. Gosetti-Ferencei (Bloomington: Indiana University Press, 2010); Emannuel Levinas, *Entre Nous: On Thinking-of-the-Other*, trans. M.B. Smith and B. Harshav (New York: Columbia University Press, 1998); E. Levinas, *Otherwise than Being or Beyond Essence*, trans. A Lingis (Pittsburgh: Duquesne University Press, 1998); E. Levinas, *Totality and Infinity: An Essay on Exteriority*, trans. A Lingis (Pittsburgh: Duquesne University Press, 1969); Glen Morrison, *A Theology of Alterity: Levinas, Vin Balthasar and Trinitarian Praxis* (Pittsburgh: Duquesne University Press, 2013); Najib G. Awad, *Persons in Relation: An Essay on the Trinity and Ontology* (Minneapolis: Fortress Press, 2014), 118–125.

4. Glen Morrison expresses the same idea in different terms when he says "Levinas is not rejecting the category of Being; ultimately he develops a way to transcend the totalizing ways of Being—such as competitive self-interest—to return to Being (existence and reality) with a sense akin to love." Morrison, *A Theology of Alterity*, 34.

5. See this reading in Bruce J. Malina and Richard L. Rohrbauch, *Social-Science Commentary on the Gospel of John* (Minneapolis: Fortress Press, 1998), 244–245. It is my belief that this reading is eisegetically inspired by, if not premeditatedly shaped after, the tendency of some contemporary Johannine scholarship to deem the Gospel of John the most conspicuously anti-Semitic text in the New Testament. On the treatment of

The case is quite the opposite: Jesus is afraid that his disciples' relation to him would create in them a sense of alterity that will turn them eventually into a 'separate anti-society' entity. Jesus is afraid that the world will experience difficulties and face danger from such isolationism and contrasting alterity. Contemporary scholarship on the anti-Judaism traces in the Johannine Gospel is valuable here. It invites us to perceive a manifestation of a radicalized, otherizing form of alterity the disciples started to show in their stance on their surrounding context; an alterity, I am proposing, which alarmed Jesus and drove him to pray for His Father's protection of His disciples from falling into such an evil notion of alterity.[6] It is such fear from his disciples' hard-core self-otherizing that made many scholars who study the Gospel of John detect an anti-Semitic, anti-Jewish accent in this Gospel. It is the belief of scholars that John's Gospel is one of the biblical texts that were used throughout the centuries to otherize the Jews because of the strongly otherizing and sharp self-alterity tendencies one spots in its chapters. There is clearly a hostile language denoting those who are not members in Jesus's group in this Gospel. Yet, it is plausible, I opine, to surmise that otherizing those who were not of Jesus disciples' circle was not necessarily due to their Jewish identity, since Jesus and his disciples were themselves Jews in ethnicity and religious belief (they were not Christians!).[7] The tendency seems to be rather to turn alterity into a form of contrariety and contrast by otherizing those who are not of the elected circle of disciples. These latter do now consider themselves privileged and placed above others by virtue of being the close group around the Messiah, while others are not. It seems to me that Jesus in his prayer to the father is anticipatorily

---

the Gospel of John as an anti-Semitic text, see for example Robert Kysar, *Voyages with John*: *Charting the Fourth Gospel* (Waco: Baylor University Press, 2005), 147–159; Craig A. Evans and Donald A. Hagner (eds.), *Early Christianity*: *Issues of Polemic and Faith* (Minneapolis: Fortress Press, 1993); C. Klein, Anti-Judaism in Christian Theology (Philadelphia: Fortress Press, 1978); R. Bieringer, D. Pollefeyt and F. Vandecasteele-Vanneuville (eds.), *Anti-Judaism and the Fourth Gospel*: *Papers of the Leuven Colloquiuum* (Assen: Royal Van Gorcum, 2001); Cornelis Bennema, *Encountering Jesus*: *Character Studies in the Gospel of John*, 2nd edition (Minneapolis: Fortress Press, 2014), 87–100.

6. Therefore, detachment from the world is the disciples' potential sin, not Jesus's own invitation to them to alienate themselves from the world, nor was this actually his own principle in his own ministry, as some scholars today like to claim. See for example Daniel B. Stevick, *Jesus and His Own*: *A Commentary on John 13–17* (Grand Rapids/Cambridge: W.B. Eerdmans Publishing Company, 2011), 339–341.

7. Richard A. Burridge, "(Re-)Reading the New Testament in the Light of Sibling Rivalry: Some Hermeneutical Implications for Today," in *Confronting Religious Violence*: A Counternarrative, eds. Richard Burridge and Jonathan Sacks (Waco: Baylor University Press, 2018), 39–58, 54–56. See also James D. G. Dunn (ed.), *Jews and Christians*: *The Parting of the Ways AD 70 to 135* (Tübingen: Mohr Siebeck, 1992).

expressing his serious apprehension regarding the consequences of the self-otherizing contrariety of his disciples. He is afraid that in the future their alterity tendency will cause serious damage to the spreading of his message of the Kingdom of God and have dire results for those receivers who are going to be degraded and otherized by his disciples because the latter construe the former as 'foreign others.' The Book of Acts informs us that Jesus's fear manifested in the life of the first Christian communities. In that text, we have stories of gentile Christians led by Stephen, who experience atrocity and otherizing degradation by their Jew-Christian brothers and sisters and their leaders, Jacob and James. The Book of Acts narrates that this tensional contrariety escalated drastically and eventuated the stoning-to-death of Stephen by the members of the other Christian group (Acts 7:54–60).[8] Be this as it may, "protect them from evil" stands here for "protect them from the evil that might stem from their own self-perception." Such self-perception or alterity is evil because it does not only damage one's life with others and in their midst, but, more radically, "destroys the soul."[9]

Reading Christ's prayer in John 17 from a Levinasian perspective of alterity will change radically our perception of Jesus's prayer to his Father. It is a prayer in despair, in fear and trembling, to use Søren Kierkegaard's terms, from the fact that his disciples might succumb to the fact of their existence 'in the world,' but they might cause disturbance by persisting therein as if they are 'not *of* the world'; as if they are detached from it; as if they do not belong to it at all. Being *in* the world but not considering one's self *of* it becomes here Jesus's expression of his unease about his disciples' manifestation of a mistaken perception of alterity. Jesus believes that mirroring his love to the world requires being *of* the world, not just being present *in* it: one must be willing to lay down one's religious alterity for the sake of the world, not to allow this alterity to place the world in polarity with God. After all, has not Jesus himself been the Son of God becoming *of* the world when the *Logos* became human (not just *in* a human manifestation) and dwelt amongst us? Jesus was *of* the world, and not just in it in that sense. Jesus did not turn his alterity into a self-otherizing contrariety. If the disciples would not do that, Jesus fears for the world from them. He manifests in his prayer a radicalized warning of potential dire consequences that might stem from

---

8. See on this dynamic of tension, contrariety and conflict in early Christianity the very interesting studies in Gerd Lüdemann, *Early Christianity According to the Traditions in Acts: A Commentary* (Minneapolis: Fortress Press, 1989); and G. Lüdemann, *The Acts of the Apostles: What Really Happened in the Earliest Days of the Church* (Amherst: Prometheus Books, 2005).

9. John Sanford, *Mystical Christianity: A Psychological Commentary on the Gospel of John* (New York: Crossroad Publishing Company, 1996), 302.

not just considering the world as 'other,' but, more dangerously, treating ourselves as 'others' to the world, as totally exterior to it. Here alterity is not an expression of loyalty to Christ, but a sign of polarizing Christ and the world upon belief in self-righteous, self-protectionist exteriority.

When alterity morphs into exteriorizing contrariety and self-otherizing in the Christians' relation to the world, Christ's community becomes a manifestation of a state of isolation or alienation from God's creation, and a life of faith turns into mere passive and secluding waiting for the second coming of Christ to emancipate his elects from the world. Alterity, again, becomes the core element in a totally wrong interpretation of the meaning of 'waiting for the return of the Lord.'

An insightful lesson on this 'alterity-waiting' dialectic in the New Testament is the story of Jesus's disciples' secluding and otherizing attitude of waiting for the return of the ascended risen Lord, which we read about in the book of the Acts of the Apostles. Acts narrates that, after Jesus Christ's resurrection and ascension to heaven, the disciples lingered in Jerusalem waiting for his immediate return. Acts relates that the disciples stayed put in the city because Jesus asked them to do so (Acts 1:4). And, when the disciples asked Jesus about the time of his return in his royal, kingly glory, he said to them that they merely have to wait for it (Acts 1:6–7). Until that time, the disciples were still thinking of the Messiah and waiting for his return as they learned about its the connotations and meanings in the Hebrew scripture and Jewish religious teaching, especially the apocalyptic literature: the Messiah will come in the full glory of his victorious apocalyptic status to fully liberate his people and emancipate them from the broken, highly polarized world.

What the disciples do is perceive the task of waiting for the return of the Messiah from the perspective of their alterity status as the righteous elect community of Christ. Waiting became their means to maintain and protect this onto-theological alterity: isolating one's self from the evil world, consolidating the community and solely praying and meditating to acquire the purity and holiness needed to welcome the returning Messiah. Waiting is the ultimate manifestation of onto-theological otherizing. Moreover, waiting is the major instrument for protecting this alterity and enjoying its spiritual prerogatives; waiting means becoming not just not *of* the world, but also avoiding being *in* it as well.

Now, it is not a coincidence that the author of the book of Acts makes the story of the Day of the Pentecost the focal theological cornerstone of his understanding of Christ's church's relation to the world. The Day of Pentecost story tells us that something that day, a divine influence from the Holy Spirit (which Jesus promised to send to his disciples in the Gospel of John) changed the disciples' perception of waiting, but also transformed their perception of their alterity. It was God's revelatory agency that day that made clear to the disciples that Jesus does not want them to escape engaging the life of the world. He, rather, wants them to be *in* the world, and he wants them to be in the world as if they are *of* the world as well. He wanted them to wait for him as part of the world, not as exterior to it. Waiting does not mean secluding one's self and lingering remotely and tangentially in fear, trembling and inaction. Waiting means turning alterity into a motif for engagement and symbiotic incarnation of the crucified Christ for the world. Waiting means not to escape from a life loaded with polarizing potentials, but to admit that your otherizing practice of alterity is one of the causes of such a potential polarization. Waiting is an act of engagement, of 'moving-toward' the different other, and spiritual alterity is a state of interaction that heals contrariety and cures self-otherizing.

It is no wonder, as Acts relates, that after the Pentecost experience the disciples left the attic of their hiding and passive protectionism and started to frequent the temple and engage the public worshipers there in theological debates (Acts 2:46). This did not mean, though, that their otherizing perception of alterity was fully healed. Jesus's fear for the world regarding his disciples' alterity and the disturbance it could cause manifests itself frankly in the Book of Acts' narration of the life of the earliest Christians in Jerusalem. Acts tells us that the earliest Christians started to exhibit a sharply polarizing, self-otherizing mentality and behaviors over and against each other. This happened, for instance, when the Jewish-Christians started to alienate and degrade the Greek-Gentile Christians. Such otherizing strategy led to a dispute between the leaders of both groups and eventuated the stoning of Stephen, leading to a public disturbance in the life of the Gentile Christians in Jerusalem. This story is the Acts author's candid relating that the mistaken emphasis on alterity by practicing it as otherizing policy generated a radically drastic polarization that damaged the Christians' life as well as the life of their surrounding social and religious *Sitz im Leben*. The Christians' alterity here is not the victim of worldly polarization. It is, rather, this polarization's perpetrator and cause. The theological lesson the Book of Acts invites us to ponder in relation to the impact of the church's presence in the world is that the question the Christians must ask is not "how can I maintain my difference during my waiting for Jesus's return?" but, instead, be "what should my alterity drive me to do in the world in order to truly be waiting for the return of Christ?"

One can feasibly trace the historical evolution of Christians' dealing with controversies and their attempts at solving clashes and healing polarizations throughout Christianity's, far from angelic, post-Ascension and post-Pentecost history. For instance, one can see how the dialectic the Christians adopted shaped their committing of polarization, not just their attending to it. One can trace how confessions and creeds of faith were used not to heal tension and conflict, but rather to either suppress it or monopolize it—so much so that one cannot but pause at the realization that the church is not always a victim of polarization, but rather this polarization's primary perpetrator.[10] Yet, there is no space to do so here. What one can say is that the biblical attestation of Jesus's concern about the role his people play in the disturbance of his Father's creation finds echoes in post-Ascension Christianity's history and performance. The church could not but present itself at some stages of its history as an entity falling sometimes in creating and perpetrating polarization in human life. This happens when the community of Christ tends to insist on presenting itself as 'foreign' and 'exterior' to the world and on letting its alterity "provoke fear or fascination" rather than prompting "mutual respect."[11]

3. ALTERITY AND SELF-OTHERIZING IN CONTEXT: THE PROTESTANTS IN GREATER SYRIA

There is no life-setting today that is more traumatic, polarized and dangerous for human life in general, and the Christian church's existence in particular, than the context of the Middle East. There is no other location on the globe where one can trace a total reification of the tendencies of polarization that extend from the political to the economic and from the religious to the social sphere. In this part of the world, polarization is often motivated by prejudices about differences in ethnicity, race, religion, culture, gender, sexuality, economic or social background. Driv-

---

10. On such perpetration in Late Antiquity, for instance, see Richard Lim, "Christian Triumph and Controversies," in *Interpreting Late Antiquity: Essays on the Postclassical World*, eds. G. W. Bowersock, Peter Brown and Oleg Grabar (Cambridge/ London: Belknap Press/Harvard University Press, 2001), 196–218; R. Lim, *Public Disputation, Power and Social Order in Late Antiquity* (Berkeley: University of California Press, 1995); Avril Cameron, "Texts as Weapons: Polemic In the Byzantine Dark Age," in *Literacy and Power in the Ancient World*, eds. A. Bouman and G. Woolf (Cambridge: Cambridge University Press, 1994), 198–215.

11. On the understanding of alterity in terms of 'foreignness' and 'exteriority' in theology and biblical interpretation, see for example Pierre Bühler, "Foreignness as Focal Point of Otherness," in *Dynamics of Difference: Christianity and Alterity. A Festschrift for Werner G. Jeanrond*, eds. Ulrich Schmiedel and James M. Matarazzo, Jr. (London/New York: Bloomsbury T&T Clark, 2016), 153–159, 157. A similar approach is also unpacked in Paul Ricoeur's, *Oneself as Another*, trans. K. Blamey (Chicago: University of Chicago Press, 1992).

en by fear about losing what is regarded as valuable, particular groups become prone to demonize other groups as the cause of imagined or real threats. Come to the Middle East, especially the land that is historically known with the name 'Greater Syria' (including present-day Syria, Lebanon, Jordan, Israel and the State of Palestine), and you will see this anatomy conspicuously manifested on the ground. Therefore, nowhere else can one confront face-to-face a down-to-earth depiction of a Christianity struggling with multi-faceted life-or-death forms of polarization as one encounters in this region today. The Protestants of the Middle East are part of that Christianity that is striving to maintain a presence and role in this very disturbed context. And, since I am a child of this Eastern Christianity specifically, I attempt to speak shortly about it and to approach it as a case study of a Christianity that is not merely a victim of a polarized world, but rather one of the perpetrators of such polarization in its *Sitz im Leben*.

In today's Cultural Studies' understanding of identity formation, identities are perceived as the outcome of construction in terms of differentiation: "it is only in relation to the other, the relation to what it is not, to precisely what it lacks" that identity is formed.[12] The Protestants of Greater Syria reflect this understanding of identity in their presence in that part of the world. They also emphasize their otherness and alterity and use them as the foundation of their difference and uniqueness as a Christian community among non-Protestant, larger and more influential, Christians in the region. However, the Protestants of Greater Syria perceive their alterity in such a radical manner that it twists their identity formation in a way which makes them end up far from Jesus's call to his community to be *in* the world, if not *of* it as well. This appears in the nature of their self-perception, which is not exactly formed after *otherness*, but rather formed on the basis of otherizing one's self ontologically and existentially from every other. Self-otherizing, sociologists and anthropologists tell us, does not reflect distinction and particularity, but opposition and discrimination.[13] It is what practically manifests an

---

12. Melanie E. Trexler, *Evangelizing Lebanon: Baptists, Missions and the Question of Cultures* (Waco: Baylor University Press, 2016), 204, citing from Stuart Hall, "Introduction: who Needs Identity?" in *Questions of Cultural Identity*, eds. Stuart Hall and Paul DuGay (London: SAGE Publications, 1996), 1–17, 4. See also Jacques Derrida, *Positions*, trans. Alan Bass (Chicago: University of Chicago Press, 1981); Stuart Hall, "The Question of Cultural Identity," in *Modernity and Its Futures*: *Understanding Modern Societies*, IV, eds. Stuart Hall, David Held and Tony McGrew (Cambridge: Polity Press/The Open University, 1992), 273–326.

13. Richard Rorty, "Human Rights, Rationality and Sentimentality," in *On Human Rights*: *The Oxford Amnesty Lectures 1993*, eds. Stephen Shute and Susan Hurley (New York: Basic Books, 1993), 111–134; André Keet, "Epistemic 'Othering' and the Decolonisation of Knowledge," *African Insight* 44:1 (2014), 23–37; Miranda Fricker,

alterity that is morphed into contrariety, like the one the New Testament reflects genuine fear of. It is this specific form of alterity that makes the Protestants in my birth-land become perpetrators of polarization in their life-setting.[14] Such polarization stems from these Arab-Eastern local *Injīliyyūn's* otherizing of themselves when they insist on ensuring their self-understanding "functions as a [radically alienating and isolating] form of 'Not-Me' dis-identification."[15]

Relevant to this analysis of the Protestants' alterity in Greater Syria is the phenomenon of individualization via spiritual re-identification and re-generation, which asserts a kind of personality "against the morality of a discredited society."[16] This orientation is now one of the constituent, preconditioning conceptions of the evangelistic 'regeneration' gospel of the Protestants during the 19th–20th centuries. It makes these Middle Eastern Protestants believe that to be yourself is to become what the social and cultural others are not, or to *become* what will certainly make you out of that context and alien to it, rather than *in* it or *of* it.

One wonders where these Eastern-Arab Protestants derive such an understanding of alterity from. It is my belief that we need to trace the roots of such a philosophical-theological understanding of alterity in the 'born-to-Christ' principle that the Western Protestant missionaries conveyed to the local inhabitants of the Levant. This philosophical-theological web of meaning provides a framework for the transformation of the word 'evangelical' from an adjective of particular spiritual proclamation of the Gospel into the Arabic '*Injīliy*' description, which designates now a specific nomenclature of a sharply defined and starkly singled-out self-identifying alterity.[17]

Epistemic Injustice: *Power and the Ethics of Knowing* (Oxford & New York: Oxford University Press, 2007); Sune Qvotrup Jensen, "Preliminary Notes on Othering and Agency," in *Sociologisk Arbejdspapir*, 27, 2009, 1–36.

14. On this see Najib G. Awad, After-Mission, beyond Evangelicalism: The Indigenous 'Injīliyyūn' in the Arab-Muslim Context of Syria-Lebanon (Leiden & Boston: Brill, 2020), Part. 3 in particular, where I display at length how the Protestants there got trapped in this polarization responsibility. See also my earlier studies in Najib G. Awad, "Social Harmony in the Middle East: The Christian Contributions," in Christian Citizenship in the Middle East: Divided Allegiance or Dual Belonging?, eds. Mohammed Girma and Cristian Romocea (London/Philadelphia: Jessica Kingsley Publishers, 2017), 63–82; Najib G. Awad, And Freedom Became a Public-Square: Political, Sociological and Religious Overviews on the Arab Christians and the Arabic Spring (Berlin/Zürich: LIT Verlag, 2012), 186–204.

15. Trexler, Evangelizing Lebanon, 204.

16. Michael Polanyi, "Beyond Nihilism," in *Knowing and Being*: *Essays by Michael Polanyi*, ed. Marjorie Grene (London: Routledge & Kegan Paul, 1969), 5–23, 10.

17. David C. Steinmetz, *Taking the Long View*: *Christian Theology in Historical Perspective* (Oxford: Oxford University Press, 2011), VIII. Lest he is deemed one-sided in his approach, Steinmetz clarifies that his diagnosis does not aim at turning the past into something that lacks the church in traditional patterns of thought and action.

In today's socio-cultural and anthropological studies, scholars often speak of the above-mentioned phenomenon of turning a belief-concept into a defining and self-exteriorizing rule. They construe it as a case of "dogmatic transplant of a belief system from a source area to a new destination," or they even call it a case of "colonial evangelism."[18] In the context of Protestantism in Greater Syria, 'evangelism/evangelicalism' is transformed into the '*Injīliyya*' identity. Such identity is shaped after a notion of alterity-exteriority or otherizing that is radical to such an extent that problematizes these local Protestants' presence and role in their homeland and drowns them personally in a serious identity-crisis situation.

My analytical and critical anatomy of the above-mentioned alterity and self-perception case traces it back to the impact of the Protestant missionaries' attempt at the expansion of the European-American Modernist, anthropocentric imagination of alterity and self-perception beyond its historical and geographical territories.[19] In this process, missionaries transmitted particular understanding of selfhood and being-ness that were shaped after Modernist spiritual-evangelistic self-awareness, which lies in a radically divisive and exclusivist otherizing strategy. '*Injīliyyūn*' in the Middle East become the nomenclature of the 'I am not them/they are not us' stance in the mind and life of the Eastern-Arab Protestants on the Middle Eastern indigenous *Sitz im Leben*.

It has been already scholarly acknowledged that American Protestant missions in Syria and Lebanon positively and profoundly "impacted on the emergence of Arabism, Arab Nationalism and the idea of Syria as an Arab national entity."[20] What is yet to be realized is that the local Middle Eastern converts to Protestantism developed yet an alternative identifying alterity to single themselves out from the other communities

---

18. Ruth Kark and Shlomit Lanboin, "Missions and Identity Formation Among the Peoples of Palestine: The Case of the Jewish Population," in *The Social Dimensions of Christian issions in the Middle East: Historical Studies of the 19th and 20th Centuries*, eds. Norbert Friedrich, Uwe Kaminsky and Roland Löffler (Stuttgart: Franz Steiner Verlag, 2010), 101–119; T.O. Beidelman, *Colonial Evangelism: A Socio-Historical Study of An East African Mission at the Grassroots* (Bloomington: Indiana University Press, 1982); Thomas J. Watson, Jr. (ed.), *Identity Formation and the Missionary Enterprise in the Middle East* (Providence: Brown University/Institute for International Studies, 1999).

19. Or the 'expansion of Europe', as this endeavor is described classically by Abdul-Latif Tibawi, *American Interests in Syria 1800–1901: A Study of Educational, Literary and Religious Work* (Oxford: Clarendon Press, 1966); E. Said, *Orientalism* (New York: Vintage Books, 1979).

20. Kark and Langboim, "Missions and Identity Formation Among the Peoples of Palestine: The Case of the Jewish Population," 105. See also F. Zachs, "From the Mission to the Missionary: The Bliss Family and the Syrian Protestant College (1866–1920)," *Die Welt des Islam* 45 (2005), 254–291.

in that region by morphing evangelical/evangelist into a specific form of otherizing identity called '*Injīliyya/Injīliy*.' They understood 'born-to-Christ' to mean now that they are neither in the world, nor certainly of the world they historically and existentially were born into and once belonged in mind, heart and soul to its human setting. This otherizing identification strategy is one of the main causes of the identity-crisis situation of the indigenous Protestants in the Orient that makes them a source of polarization therein.

Scholars of sociology, sociology of religion and cultural studies do seriously draw our attention to the tendencies of superiority, segregating leveling and discriminative hierarchism that underpin some identity-formation processes and zeal toward emphasizing alterity.[21] From the perspective of 'better than others' view, '*Injīliyyūn*' plays in the life of the Protestants of Greater Syria the role of the guardian of that Protestant-evangelical tradition of self-imaging and 'self-exteriorization-in-terms-of-otherizing' culture. This tradition made the Protestant missionaries, and today it makes the Protestant local offspring, not just claim intellectual and religious preeminence, but, more primarily, fosters a mentality of communal, personal and moral *ascendancy* as well.

For so many decades, for example, and from one generation to another, the indigenous Arab-Eastern '*Injīliyyūn*' used to promote news on their moral-ethical perfection in comparison to other Christians or non-Christians in society. They have always claimed that "the '*Injīliy*' never spread lies or relate false information. He or she always relates the truth. When an '*Injīliy*' is summoned to testify in a court of justice, he or she need not (and will not) swear an oath on the Bible that he or she "will say the truth and nothing but the truth, so help me God." The '*Injīliyyūn*,' the reputation tenders, do not need that because their religious faith prevents them from verbalizing anything but the truth. Thus was the conventional folk propaganda, which I grew up hearing Protestants perpetually boasting about in the public domain. This is just a simple, down-to-earth example of using alterity selectively to create a state of othering that impregnates society with a sense of superiority in terms of qualitative 'better-ness.' "Claiming the high moral ground and conflating that with cultural, religious and national identity," as Max Weber taught us long ago, is one of the means that are used sometimes by groups that "seek to create and maintain [a privileged state of] power."[22]

---

21. Abby Day, *Believing in Belonging: Belief and Social Identity in the Modern World* (Oxford/New York: Oxford University Press, 2001), 59. See also M. Nussbaum, *Sex and Social Justice* (Oxford: Oxford University Press, 1999).

22. Day, *Believing in Belonging*, 60; and Max Weber, *The Sociology of Religion* (Boston: Beacon Press, 1922), 56. See also on this tendency in Protestantism in its historical birthplace Max Weber, *The Protestant Ethics and the Spirit of Capitalism*

In this reflection on alterity and polarization in relation to the Arab-Eastern Protestants, I find a manifestation of a polarization-breeding situation, which many Christian communities around the world could be also trapped in and accountable for. This crisis lies not in the fact that the Christians do not have a clear sense and highly sensitive awareness of alterity. It rather lies in the fact that they actually have a radically clear-cut alterity that is closed, divisive and totally otherizing. In the case of Protestantism in my birth-land, this incarnates in a state of a particular alterity called '*Injīliyya*' that is a manifestation of a 'lethal identity,' to use the description of the French-Lebanese novelist, Amīn Ma'louf.[23] The lethal alterity called '*Injīliyya*' makes the Arab-Eastern Protestants exist in the midst of crisis, isolation, alienation and amnesia in their homeland. They live with a-historical, a-contextual self-awareness drowned in individual, self-enclosed selfhood without any memory. The rationale of their alterity causes a crisis in their presence and role in the Middle East because it leads them to otherize themselves, to alienate their being, from the world of the Orient. The crisis is not only their self-otherizing from Eastern culture, but also from Eastern *Christianity*, as they detach themselves from the historical, theological-spiritual *memory* of this region's collective Christianity. Their amnesiac alterity ends up turning them into churches without history; churches without theology; churches without message; and, thus, churches without meaningful and definable Christianity. Eventually, it turns the *Injīliyyūn* not just into a community without memory, but, more dangerously, into a community without purpose and meaning—a community that is always looked at suspiciously as a source of trouble and disturbance.

Julia Kristeva describes the above-displayed attitude with profound eloquence when she speaks about alterity in terms of making one's self 'foreigner' overagainst others. Alterity as an expression of foreignness presents people "not belonging to any place, any time, any love"; humans with "lost origin," clinging to their insistence on "the impossibility to take root" in their surrounding existence, rummaging avidly as far away as possible from any sober or relational remembrance as if present in a perpetually revived state of "abeyance."[24]

Kristeva perceptively asks: is this form of opaque, delusional state of self-certifying alterity an expression of a "deep-seated narcissism? Blank psychosis beneath the swirl of existential conflicts?"[25] If this is

---

(London: Routledge, 1930).

23. Amīn Ma'louf, *al-Houyat al-Qatelah* (Lethal Identities) (Beirut: Dār al-Fārābī, 2004).

24. Julia Kristeva, *Strangers to Ourselves*, trans. Leon S. Roudiez (New York & Oxford: Columbia University Press, 1991), 7.

25. Kristeva, *Strangers to Ourselves*, 8.

the case, maybe it is not unfair, but rather required, to say that by placing themselves in this state of 'foreignness', the *Injīliyyūn* of Greater Syria, or any Christians playing the same otherizing game for that matter, have no real 'self', or that they live as if their true, real self is aloofly concealed and sealed elsewhere. What they relate to other people around them is a fabricated, figurative 'selfhood' shaped after what the surrounding context wants to see, expects to meet and wishes to relate to. To use Kristeva's elegant and precise terms again: "I do what they want me to, but it is not 'me' — 'me' is elsewhere, 'me' belongs to no one, 'me' does not belong to the 'me' they want and expect."[26] Now, if this is the case, does my 'me' truly exist anymore or truly have any definable and perceivable being?

I do fully agree with Stuart Hall's emphasis that identity "is not a fixed essence at all, lying unchanged outside history and culture. It is not some universal and transcendental spirit inside us on which history has made no fundamental mark. It is not once-and-for-all. It is not a fixed origin to which we can make some final and absolute return."[27] Such an identity-perception that lies in contrasting alterity, like the one I touch upon in this chapter, not only causes historical oblivion and traps Christianity in a state of self-forfeiture, more drastically, it robs the Christians of any alterity or tangible self-awareness altogether. For the real problem in such amnesiac alterity, as medicine tells us, "is that not only does the patient forget his loved ones and friends, but he no longer remembers who he [or she] is."[28]

4. CONCLUDING REMARKS

In this reflection on the Church's role in today's world and its application of Jesus's speech on 'being in the world, but not of the world,' I tried to show that today's Church might need to ponder the real nature of its involvement in, and exposition to, the present world's polarization situation. Far from being a victim of such polarization, today's Christianity might be, unintentionally and maybe unconsciously, responsible for perpetrating some polarizations in the world due to how it perceives its own alterity. In such an understanding of alterity, which I exposed biblically and contextually above, there is an emphasis on difference to a radical extent of contrariety that makes our perception of the 'other'

---

26. Kristeva, *Strangers to Ourselves*, 8.

27. Stuart Hall, "Cultural Identity and Diaspora," in *Theorizing Diaspora: A Reader*, eds. Jana Evens Braziel and Anita Mannur (Malden: Blackwell Publishers, 2003), 233–246, 237.

28. Daniel H. Williams, *Retrieving the Tradition and Renewing Evangelicalism: A Primer for Suspicious Protestants* (Grand Rapids/ Cambridge: W.B. Eerdmans Publishing Company, 1999), 9.

shaped after alienating and otherizing preconceptions and prejudices. Christians might still be motivated, by their living in the world, to study the other, to try to understand the other, and to endeavor to accommodate the other into a reasonable and sociable circle of relatedness. Yet, even in this motivation, and despite its arguably genuine sincerity, such an understanding and practicing of alterity like the one I unpacked above prevents the Christians from ending this process of relatedness with allowing the interaction with the others to examine them, to question their taken-for-granted *Weltanschauung*, their own assumptions about the world and the other in it.

Christians today do not hesitate to study their own working strategies and assess their competency and efficiency. However, if the church's perception of alterity is driven by radical contrariety and exteriority, it will not actually allow any interaction with the others, or any existence *in* the world to challenge the Christians' convictions or to make the church scrutinize the private belief, in the service of which it eagerly develops its *modus operandi*. Today's worldly situation might be an invitation for the church to, rather, realize that it does not only exist *in* times of polarization and the church is not just inescapably part of the polarization situation because it is destined to exist *in* the world, though it is not of it. The church is sometimes a partner in committing polarization and its self-perception is a cause of it.

If there is still a calling for the church in today's world, it might be one that invites Christianity to carefully scrutinize its own perception of alterity. Before it launches a prophetic role of critiquing the political and social polarizing injustices of the world, it might need to ponder the impact on the world of its own preconceived alterity, as well as its relation to that world. Maybe Jesus's fear for the world regarding his disciples' alterity is something the Church must also be afraid of when it comes to its own understanding of its existence in relation to that world: is the Church *in* it as if it is *of* it? Or, is it in the world because it insists on proving to this world that it is not *of* it?

BIBLIOGRAPHY

Awad, Najib G. *After-Mission, beyond Evangelicalism: The Indigenous 'Injīliyyūn' in the Arab-Muslim Context of Syria-Lebanon*. Leiden & Boston: Brill, 2020.

Awad, Najib G. *Persons in Relation: An Essay on the Trinity and Ontology*. Minneapolis: Fortress Press, 2014.

Awad, Najib G. "Social Harmony in the Middle East: The Christian Contributions." In *Christian Citizenship in the Middle East: Divided Allegiance or Dual Belonging?*, eds. Mohammed Girma and Cristian Romocea, 63–82. London/Philadelphia: Jessica Kingsley Publishers, 2017.

Awad, Najib G. *And Freedom Became a Public-Square: Political, Sociological and Religious Overviews on the Arab Christians and the Arabic Spring*. Berlin/Zürich: LIT Verlag, 2012.

Beidelman, T.O. *Colonial Evangelism: A Socio-Historical Study of An East African Mission at the Grassroots*. Bloomington: Indiana University Press, 1982.

Bennema, Cornelis. *Encountering Jesus: Character Studies in the Gospel of John*, 2nd edition. Minneapolis: Fortress Press, 2014.

Bieringer, R.; D. Pollefeyt and F. Vandecasteele-Vanneuville. Eds., *Anti-Judaism and the Fourth Gospel: Papers of the Leuven Colloquiuum*. Assen: Royal Van Gorcum, 2001.

Bühler, Pierre. "Foreignness as Focal Point of Otherness." In *Dynamics of Difference: Christianity and Alterity. A Festschrift for Werner G. Jeanrond*, eds. Ulrich Schmiedel and James M. Matarazzo, Jr., 153159. London/New York: Bloomsbury T&T Clark, 2016.

Burridge, Richard A. "(Re-)Reading the New Testament in the Light of Sibling Rivalry: Some Hermeneutical Implications for Today." In *Confronting Religious Violence: A Counternarrative*, eds. Richard Burridge and Jonathan Sacks, 39–58. Waco: Baylor University Press, 2018.

Cameron, Avril. "Texts as Weapons: Polemic In the Byzantine Dark Age." In *Literacy and Power in the Ancient World*, eds. A. Bouman and G. Woolf, 198–215. Cambridge: Cambridge University Press, 1994.

Carson, D.A. Ed. *The Enduring Authority of the Christian Scriptures*. Grand Rapids/Cambridge: W.B. Eerdmans Publishing Company, 2016.

Chennattu, Rekha M. *Johannine Discipleship as a Covenant Relationship*. Peabody: Hendrickson Publishers, 2006.

Day, Abby. *Believing in Belonging*: *Belief and Social Identity in the Modern World*. Oxford/New York: Oxford University Press, 2001.

Derrida, Jacques. *Positions*, trans. Alan Bass. Chicago: University of Chicago Press, 1981.

Dunn, James D. G. Ed. *Jews and Christians*: *The Parting of the Ways AD 70 to 135*. Tübingen: Mohr Siebeck, 1992.

Evans, Craig A. and Donald A. Hagner. Eds. *Early Christianity*: *Issues of Polemic and Faith*. Minneapolis: Fortress Press, 1993.

Fricker, Miranda. *Epistemic Injustice*: *Power and the Ethics of Knowing*. Oxford & New York: Oxford University Press, 2007.

Heidegger, Martin. *Being and Time*, trans. J. Macquarrie and E. Robinson. Oxford: Blackwell Publishers, 1995.

Heidegger, Martin. *The Phenomenology of Religious Life*, trans. M. Fritsch and J.A. Gosetti-Ferencei. Bloomington: Indiana University Press, 2010.

Hall, Stuart. "Cultural Identity and Diaspora." In *Theorizing Diaspora*: *A Reader*, eds. Jana Evens Braziel and Anita Mannur, 233–246. Malden: Blackwell Publishers, 2003.

Hall, Stuart. "Introduction: who Needs Identity?" In *Questions of Cultural Identity*, eds. Stuart Hall and Paul DuGay, 1–17. London: SAGE Publications, 1996.

Hall, Stuart. "The Question of Cultural Identity." In Modernity and Its Futures: *Understanding Modern Societies*, IV, eds. Stuart Hall, David Held and Tony McGrew, 273–326. Cambridge: Polity Press/ The Open University, 1992.

Jensen, Sune Qvotrup. "Preliminary Notes on Othering and Agency." *Sociologisk Arbejdspapir*, 27, 2009: 1–36.

Kark, Ruth and Shlomit Lanboin. "Missions and Identity Formation Among the Peoples of Palestine: The Case of the Jewish Population." In *The Social Dimensions of Christian issions in the Middle East*: *Historical Studies of the 19th and 20th Centuries*, eds. Norbert Friedrich, Uwe Kaminsky and Roland Löffler, 101–119. Stuttgart: Franz Steiner Verlag, 2010.

Keet, André. "Epistemic 'Othering' and the Decolonisation of Knowledge." *African Insight* 44:1 (2014): 2337.

Klein, C. *Anti-Judaism in Christian Theology*. Philadelphia: Fortress Press, 1978.

Kristeva, Julia. *Strangers to Ourselves*, trans. Leon S. Roudiez. New York & Oxford: Columbia University Press, 1991.

Kysar, Robert. *Voyages with John*: *Charting the Fourth Gospel*. Waco: Baylor University Press, 2005.

Levinas, Emannuel. *Entre Nous*: *On Thinking-of-the-Other*, trans. M.B. Smith and B. Harshav. New York: Columbia University Press, 1998.

Levinas, E. *Otherwise than Being or Beyond Essence*, trans. A Lingis. Pittsburgh: Duquesne University Press, 1998.

Levinas, E. *Totality and Infinity*: *An Essay on Exteriority*, trans. A Lingis. Pittsburgh: Duquesne University Press, 1969.

Lim, Richard. "Christian Triumph and Controversies." In *Interpreting Late Antiquity*: *Essays on the Postclassical World*, eds. G. W. Bowersock, Peter Brown and Oleg Grabar, 196–218. Cambridge/London: Belknap Press/Harvard University Press, 2001.

Lim, R. *Public Disputation, Power and Social Order in Late Antiquity*. Berkeley: University of California Press, 1995.

Lüdemann, Gerd. *Early Christianity According to the Traditions in Acts*: *A Commentary*. Minneapolis: Fortress Press, 1989.

Lüdemann, G. *The Acts of the Apostles*: *What Really Happened in the Earliest Days of the Church*. Amherst: Prometheus Books, 2005.

Malina, Bruce J. and Richard L. Rohrbauch. *Social-Science Commentary on the Gospel of John*. Minneapolis: Fortress Press, 1998.

Ma'louf, Amīn. *al-Houyat al-Qatelah* (Lethal Identities). Beirut: Dār al-Fārābī, 2004.

Morrison, Glen. *A Theology of Alterity*: *Levinas, Vin Balthasar and Trinitarian Praxis* (Pittsburgh: Duquesne University Press, 2013.

Nussbaum, M. *Sex and Social Justice*. Oxford: Oxford University Press, 1999.

Polanyi, Michael. "Beyond Nihilism," in *Knowing and Being*: *Essays by Michael Polanyi*, ed. Marjorie Grene. London: Routledge & Kegan Paul, 1969.

Ricoeur, Paul. *Oneself as Another*, trans. K. Blamey. Chicago: University of Chicago Press, 1992.

Rorty, Richard. "Human Rights, Rationality and Sentimentality." In *On Human Rights*: *The Oxford Amnesty Lectures* 1993, eds. Stephen Shute and Susan Hurley, 111–134. New York: Basic Books, 1993.

Said, E. *Orientalism*. New York: Vintage Books, 1979.

Sanford, John. *Mystical Christianity*: *A Psychological Commentary on the Gospel of John*. New York: Crossroad Publishing Company, 1996.

Steinmetz, David C. *Taking the Long View*: *Christian Theology in Historical Perspective*. Oxford: Oxford University Press, 2011.

Stevick, Daniel B. *Jesus and His Own*: *A Commentary on John 13–17*. Grand Rapids/Cambridge: W.B. Eerdmans Publishing Company, 2011.

Tibawi, Abdul-Latif. *American Interests in Syria 1800–1901*: *A Study of Educational, Literary and Religious Work*. Oxford: Clarendon Press, 1966.

Trexler, Melanie E. *Evangelizing Lebanon*: *Baptists, Missions and the Question of Cultures*. Waco: Baylor University Press, 2016.

Watson, Jr., Thomas J. Ed. *Identity Formation and the Missionary Enterprise in the Middle East*. Providence: Brown University/Institute for International Studies, 1999.

Weber, Max. *The Protestant Ethics and the Spirit of Capitalism*. London: Routledge, 1930.

Weber, Max. *The Sociology of Religion*. Boston: Beacon Press, 1922.

Williams, Daniel H. *Retrieving the Tradition and Renewing Evangelicalism*: *A Primer for Suspicious Protestants*. Grand Rapids/Cambridge: W.B. Eerdmans Publishing Company, 1999.

Yarbrough, Robert W. "'Bye-bye Bible?' Progress Report on the Death of Scripture." *Them* 39 (2014): 415–427.

Zachs, F. "From the Mission to the Missionary: The Bliss Family and the Syrian Protestant College (1866–1920)." *Die Welt des Islam* 45 (2005): 254–291.

Chapter 17
Theology of Migration in the Discourse of the World Council of Churches and the Ecumenical Council of Churches in Hungary (2015–2019)
Viktória Kóczián

1. Introduction

The assessment of migration as it is experienced in the 21st century, especially post-2015, has not reached a consensus yet in the ecumenical world. National and international ecumenical bodies have approached one of the most urgent political questions of today: how should we react to the migration of millions intending to move to more stable countries than their own? The political question is being shaped slightly differently in the church: is migration a God-given human right, is it approved by the Bible, do churches need to support the process and its partakers? Moreover, typical issues addressed by the secular world are also considered, such as the future of the Christian religion and culture in a land shared by Christians and Muslims alike and the question of a possible loss of Western and Christian identity.

Although the issue has been dealt with by most international ecumenical organizations, underlining its unquestionable relevance today, I will limit my attention in this study to the analysis of the work of the World Council of Churches (WCC) and the Ecumenical Council of Churches in Hungary (ECCH) in order to illustrate how the discussion on migration is polarized on the global and the local level in the one church and the one ecumenical world. Reflection on the ways the church holds two views on migration that drive people apart is essential in the struggle for the unity of the church.

In this chapter, I will concentrate on addressing the question of how polarization manifests itself around the issue of migration in the ecumenical world. I will focus on analyzing the views and opinions of the above-mentioned two ecumenical organizations as they are expressed in statements, different types of written outcomes of meetings (communiques, messages, greetings), articles and television speeches between 2015 and 2019. The WCC has dedicated a lot of attention in the form of written material to the question of migration compared to the Hungarian national ecumenical body. Although there have been discussions initiated by the ECCH, there is still a lack of published material on the problem of migration. Therefore, the research had to be limited to material produced by individual members of the organization's governing body.

2. The Social and Theological Teachings of the WCC on Migration

Since its beginnings, the World Council of Churches (WCC) has been involved in the protection of people who became migrants and refugees as a consequence of the Second World War.[1] The fourth assembly of Uppsala (1968) adopted the "Statement on the Middle East" in which the WCC expresses its will to "… join with all who search for a solution for the refugee and displaced person problems."[2] Today the work of the WCC on migration is connected to its other work areas on human trafficking, development, conflicts and racism, and a closer cooperation is realized with the United Nations and related agencies. The commitment of the WCC to the support of refugees and migrants is evident from its public communication, and it is clear that as a church organization, it builds its view on a biblical basis. Although the organization's texts about migrants and refugees do not contain many theological elaborations, it is possible to discover underlying theological tenets in its discourse about the issue. A key Christian justification of the protection and support of migrants used by the WCC is the welcoming of the stranger (Matt. 25:35).

The WCC has been following the political and social developments

---

1. "When the World Council of Churches came into existence in 1948, the disastrous humanitarian impacts of the Second World War were still a very present reality. The international community was still struggling to cope with the massive population displacements caused by conflict and crimes against humanity. Churches and their specialized ministries were key actors in the humanitarian response to this unprecedented suffering, and have continued to be in the forefront of assisting refugees and immigrants, from emergency relief to long-term support." From the "Statement on refugees in Europe," September 4, 2015, https://www.oikoumene.org/en/resources/documents/general-secretary/statements/statement-on-refugees-in-europe (accessed March 23, 2019).

2. WCC Central Committee, "Statement on the Middle East," Heraklion, Crete, August 1967, https://www.oikoumene.org/en/resources/documents/central-committee/1967/statement-on-the-middle-east (accessed January 31, 2019).

of the migrant crisis since 2015, has reacted to major events, and voiced its opinion in different statements, news releases and speeches. This research focuses on thirteen documents:[3] five were the outcome of regular meetings of different working groups (Etchmiadzin,[4] Trondheim,[5] Lisbon,[6] Ottmaring,[7] Uppsala[8]), five were produced or presented at conferences with national churches and global ecumenical bodies (Munich,[9] Lunteren,[10] Rome,[11] Tveit Rome,[12] Madrid[13]) and three were statements of the WCC reacting to political and social events

---

3. In this chapter, the documents are referred to by the name of the location of the meeting where they were prepared. As there are more than one document related to the conference "Xenophobia, Racism and Populist Nationalism in the Context of Global Migration," to the reference of one of the documents, the name of the speaker is added as well ('Tveit Rome').

4. "Statement on responses to migrant crises," June 12, 2015, https://www.oikoumene.org/en/resources/documents/executive-committee/etchmiadzin-june-2015/statement-on-responses-to-migrant-crises-doc-no-29-rev (accessed March 12, 2019).

5. "Statement on the Forced Displacement Crisis," June 28, 2016, https://www.oikoumene.org/en/resources/documents/central-committee/2016/statement-on-the-forced-displacement-crisis (accessed March 12, 2019).

6. "Communiqué by the Joint Working Group," September 19, 2017. https://www.oikoumene.org/en/resources/documents/commissions/jwg-rcc-wcc/communique-by-the-joint-working-group-september-2017 (accessed March 22, 2019).

7. "Communiqué by the Joint Working Group between the WCC and the RCC," September 7, 2017, https://www.oikoumene.org/en/resources/documents/commissions/communique-by-the-joint-working-group-between-the-wcc-and-the-rcc-september-2018 (accessed March 22, 2019).

8. "Statement on People on the Move: Migrants and Refugees," November 7, 2018, https://www.oikoumene.org/en/resources/documents/executive-committee/uppsala-november-2018/statement-on-people-on-the-move-migrants-and-refugees (accessed March 23, 2019).

9. "Church Leaders' Consultation on the European Refugee Crisis: Communique," October 29, 2015, https://www.oikoumene.org/en/resources/documents/other-meetings/communique-munich (accessed March 12, 2019).

10. "'Have no Fear': A Statement," June 20, 2016, https://www.oikoumene.org/en/resources/documents/wcc-programmes/umer/mission-from-the-margins/migration/have-no-fear (accessed March 12, 2019).

11. "Message from the conference 'Xenophobia, Racism and Populist Nationalism in the Context of Global Migration,'" September 19, 2018, https://www.oikoumene.org/en/resources/documents/message-from-the-conference-xenophobia-racism-and-populist-nationalism-in-the-context-of-global-migration-19-september-2018 (accessed January 10, 2019).

12. "Greetings of Rev. Dr Olav Fykse Tveit: World Conference on Xenophobia, Racism, and Populist Nationalism In the Context of Global Migration and Refugees," September 18, 2018, (accessed March 12, 2019).

13. "Taizé Greetings WCC general secretary Rev. Dr Olav Fykse Tveit," December 2018, https://www.oikoumene.org/en/resources/documents/taize-greetings-wcc-general-secretary-rev-dr-olav-fykse-tveit-28-december-2018 (accessed January 2, 2019).

(Geneva,[14] US,[15] Myanmar[16]). The majority of documents are the results of cooperation with other organizations (Munich, Lunteren, Lisbon, Ottmaring, Rome, Tveit Rome, Madrid) and only one fourth was an immediate response to actual global events.

The content of the documents demonstrates that, like the UN and related agencies, the WCC focuses on supporting refugees, welcoming them in the destination countries, integrating them in societies, and it argues also for putting an end to the political and social reasons that cause mass migrations. A stressed point in the documents—mostly those of 2016—is the fear societies and churches struggle with, and their rejection of and hostility towards refugees and migrants. Part of this fear is about the loss of identity that plays a very important role in the Hungarian society. Munich recognizes this fear of losing identity in hosting countries. This statement also perceives the renationalization of politics, which indicates an awareness of the role of nationalism within the context of the migration crisis. The US statement alludes to the significance of ethnic and religious identity differences in the processes of international refuge and protection. Lisbon points out the increasing racism churches are concerned about. Uppsala acknowledges the fear of the possible change of Western cultural identities due to the impact of migration.

In its theological reasoning, the WCC uses both Old Testament and New New Testament passages to support its vision on hospitality and welcoming. While migration is viewed as an integral part of human history, migrants and refugees are considered part of the one human family created in the image and likeness of God; therefore, strangers are brothers and sisters and it is a human obligation to welcome and help them. From a New Testament point of view, they embody Christ, who commanded his audience to welcome and support the stranger, the hungry, the thirsty, and the needy.

The theological discussions of migration in 2015 started with the identification of the stranger with the refugees and migrants (Matthew 25) and became extended later with the interpretation of the human

---

14. "Statement on refugees in Europe," September 4, 2015, https://www.oikoumene.org/en/resources/documents/general-secretary/statements/statement-on-refugees-in-europe (accessed March 23, 2019).

15. "Statement on US Presidential Executive Order 'Protecting the Nation from Foreign Terrorist Entry into the United States' and its Impact on Refugees," Januari 31, 2017, https://www.oikoumene.org/en/resources/documents/general-secretary/joint-declarations/statement-on-us-presidential-executive-order-on-refugees (accessed March 22, 2019).

16. "WCC expresses grave concern for Rohingya people in Myanmar," September 14, 2017, https://www.oikoumene.org/en/resources/documents/wcc-expresses-grave-concern-for-rohingya-people-in-myanmar (accessed March 22, 2019).

being as created after the image and likeness of God (Genesis 1). Munich depicts Jesus crossing the border between God and humanity: a parallel between the refugees' border crossing and Jesus' incarnation.

In 2016, the theological argument of Lunteren and Trondheim emphasizes that one should not fear but be hospitable. In 2017, the Joint Working Group between the Roman Catholic Church and the World Council of Churches (JWG) brings a new element into the discussion. Migration, one of the major contemporary social issues that divide churches today, is being turned from a dividing issue into a uniting one, a common service that brings churches closer to each other. The group plans to provide pastoral and practical recommendations regarding this issue that can foster ecumenical cooperation. In 2018, the Rome conference document adds to the discussion that migration is an inherent experience in the Abrahamic traditions. It recognizes that people's fear of migrants suggests that this phenomenon has to be examined as well.

The WCC strongly advocates hospitality, supporting migrants, welcoming them in the destination countries, integrating them in societies, as well as ending the reasons of migration. The decisive theological arguments emphasize, on the one hand, that migrants are part of the one human family created after the image and likeness of God; they are sisters and brothers and therefore there is an obligation to support them. On the other hand, they also embody Christ, who called for helping the stranger, the hungry, and the needy (Matthew 25). Migration is looked at as an integral part of human history, inherent in the Abrahamic traditions.

The WCC's awareness of the challenges of socio-cultural identities in the contemporary migration crisis is indicated in several documents. The organization offers theological views on the problem, mostly providing ethical responses that are based on the narrative of love and hope. However, this answer does not seem to be sufficient, since it does not provide a solution to issues that cause fear, rooted in the differences of socio-cultural identities. To further contribute to the goal of hospitality and ecumenical cooperation as well as supporting member churches encountering fear, silence and division, theological reflection on socio-cultural identities in the contemporary crisis of global migration would be an utmost necessity.

3. THE APPROACH OF THE ECCH TO MIGRATION

The story of the ECCH goes back to 1943 when the Hungarian Reformed and Lutheran churches founded the so-called Hungarian Committee of the Universal Church Council,[17] a special committee whose task was mainly to help the refugees of war. In 1946, the Hungarian Ecumenical Restoration Committee[18] was established for further support of the refugees and works of restoration. This committee included the Serbian Orthodox, the Baptist, the Methodist and the Unitarian churches as well as the Salvation Army. Since 1954, the organization has worked under the name of the Ecumenical Council of Churches in Hungary. Currently, it has eleven member churches[19] and a further twenty churches and church-related organizations cooperate in its work. It considers its main task the strengthening of cooperation among churches and the common witness of Jesus Christ. The ECCH organizes different national and regional activities, e.g., the yearly preparation of the ecumenical week of prayer, the Orthodox Christian Church Days, and the National Protestant Days. The work of the ECCH is done in committees that meet regularly: the committee of social ethics, mission, interreligious dialogue, Christian unity, youth committee, and the women's committee.

As opposed to the WCC, the ECCH has not published any statement on migration, refugees, or the social-political challenges in the period from 2015 to 2019. In the spring of 2015, a conference was organized at the ECCH premises with the theme of migration. The conference produced the material for the 90th anniversary edition of the journal of the ECCH. However, the volume does not represent officially the point of view of the organization. Instead, it is a compilation of papers of various scholars who presented their perspectives at the conference, hence the expressed views cannot be taken as that of the ECCH. A way to grasp the stance of the ECCH in the debate on migration is by assessing the work of the scholars and pastors involved in the work of the organization. For this chapter, the choice is made to examine the work of the two leading figures of the organization, which allows us to take a look at examples of both Reformed and Lutheran theological interpretations of migration in Hungary at the present. Speeches and writings of Vilmos Fischl, Lutheran pastor, general secretary of the ECCH, and of József Steinbach, Reformed bishop, president of the ECCH will be discussed in the following paragraphs.

---

17. Egyetemes Egyháztanács Magyarországi Bizottsága.
18. Magyar Ökumenikus Újjáépítési Bizottság.
19. ECCH member churches are: the Reformed Church in Hungary, the Evangelical Lutheran Church in Hungary, the Baptist Church of Hungary, the Hungarian Pentecostal Church, the United Methodist Church in Hungary, the Eparchy of Buda of the Serbian Orthodox Church, the Hungarian Exarchate of the Ecumenical Patriarchate of Constantinople, the Bulgarian Orthodox Church of Hungary, the Diocese of Gyula of the Romanian Orthodox Church in Hungary, the Diocese of Hungary of the Russian Orthodox Church and the Saint Margaret's Anglican Episcopal Church of Budapest.

3.1 Vilmos Fischl, General Secretary of the ECCH

Vilmos Fischl (1972–) is a Lutheran pastor holding a Ph.D. in military science. Currently he serves both the church and a national institution. He fulfills the role of General Secretary of the ECCH as well as functions as a research associate at the National University of Public Service. Fischl defended his habilitation thesis in 2020 at this university on questions of dialogue between Hungary and North Africa and the Middle East with special emphasis on persecuted Christians. Before, Fischl worked as a Lutheran parish minister and served in the diverse setting of the airport chaplaincy in Budapest. His knowledge on the Islamic religion and culture was enhanced by scholarships in Kuwait and Tunisia. Fischl is often a guest on different programs on religion and politics on the Hungarian television channel M1, owned and operated by the oldest television broadcaster in Hungary (called *Magyar Televízió*) which is run by a public foundation where the Hungarian government represents a decisive majority.

3.2 Differences Between Church and State on Migration and Mission

On the subject of dealing with migration, Fischl calls attention to the differences in practice between church and state in Europe, contrasting the humanitarian Christian approach and the protective policies present in European politics, especially represented by the Hungarian government. It looks as if church and state on a European level are standing in opposition:

> While the leaders of churches in Europe have raised their voice with the aim of providing shelter to refugees and migrants, emphasizing that the principle of humanitarian treatment has to be applied, political leaders often favour other options: their rationale is determined by quotas or protective fences.[20]

Considering the Hungarian scene, the urgent question arises: do church and state represent opposing views and practices regarding the issue of migration? The largest churches (Roman Catholic, Reformed, and Lutheran) have not officially opposed the government's actions on migration since 2015, even though there have been opinions present in them which contradicted the government's views on migration. What is the stand of the general secretary of the ECCH in a country where the governing Fidesz party is strongly against the global migration processes

---

20. Vilmos Fischl, "The Role of Churches in Hungary in Providing Pastoral Care and Humanitarian Help for Migrants," *Academic and Applied Research in Military and Public Management Science* (AARMS) 17:2 (2018), 17–28, 17.

and promotes local humanitarian support in areas of conflict and crisis instead of receiving migrants?

Fischl's discourse echoes the traditional Protestant two kingdoms doctrine when he evaluates the responsibilities of both church and state regarding migration: a separation of the mission of the church and state is recognizable. Fischl argues that the church must respond to human suffering in the current migratory situation in Europe. The church has to "continue to carry out its mission …" which he defines as "the principle of solidarity."[21] However, "the church has no intention of acting as a replacement for the state …" and he pleads that "… the responsibilities of a government are different from those of the church. The former has the additional task of both ensuring and maintaining security."[22] Fischl highlights the necessity of a legal framework in migratory movements that aims at eliminating threats to public order. Since these areas are outside church competency, he seems to emphasize that the state should have the major voice in dealing with the question of migration. In this case, solidarity is subordinated to security, and church is subordinated to the state. Solidarity can be practiced in the limited area that security allows. It is essential to examine here, how the prophetic voice of the church can be articulated in the limited scope that is rendered for it.

3.3 REACTING TO THE PERSECUTION OF CHRISTIANS BASED ON THE CATHOLICITY AND UNITY OF THE CHURCH

Reacting to the global persecution of Christians,[23] Fischl affirms that Hungary is exemplary for having established the 'State Secretariat for the Aid of Persecuted Christians'[24] and acknowledges the excellent functioning of the establishment. He makes a reference to the unity of the

---

21. Fischl, "The Role of Churches in Hungary," 17.
22. Fischl, "The Role of Churches in Hungary," 17.
23. As Péter Szijjártó, Minister of Foreign Affairs and Trade of Hungary, explains, Christianity is the most persecuted religion in the world. Referring to the latest official statistics, the minister asserts that 260 million Christians are persecuted on a world-wide scale and three thousand Christian sisters and brothers were killed in 2020, meaning that eight Christians are killed daily. A further 9500 attacks were performed against Christian buildings and churches. Szijjártó claims that Europeans need to be aware of the fact that this phenomenon is not far away in geographic terms, since the persecution of Christians is present in Europe: attacks against French Christians, the terror acts in Vienna, Austria or the vandalizing of the statue of Pope II John Paul are incidents of Christian persecution. (Recorded speech from the 'Ministerial to Advance Freedom of Religion or Belief,' November 16–17, 2020, posted on Péter Szijjártó's Facebook page: https://fb.watch/1PiykZBnE5/ (accessed November 18, 2020).
24. This institution was established in 2016 with the twofold purpose of raising awareness of Christian persecution worldwide and directly supporting communities of persecuted Christians focusing mainly on the Middle East and the Sub-Saharan territories.

church when he explains that the persecution of Christians affects Hungarians, as the persecuted Christians are brothers and sisters wherever they live in the world. Hungarians must help them and the primary goal is to defend Christians, because Hungary is a Christian country, and Europe is a Christian continent. Helping persecuted Muslims is also a necessity, he continues, but not a primary goal.[25] Fischl concentrates on religious differences when he builds his argument on the catholicity and unity of the church and decides not to focus on ethnic and socio-cultural differences.

3.4 A CHRISTIAN ETHIC OF SELECTIVE ACCEPTANCE?

Fischl argues that acceptance is a basic tenet of the Christian faith; as Jesus received the people, Christians should receive them as well. However, he points out that the command of Jesus is selective, since Jesus' words "receive each other" do not mean the reception of everyone.[26]

Fischl therefore asks the question: who can be received? Do people who claim to be persecuted for religious or political reasons have to identify themselves? He provides one answer quoting the Hungarian imam Miklós Ahmed Kovács: "… we would expect refugees who are useful for the country. We do not need extremist Muslims who do not want to fit in."[27] Fischl indicates that representatives of the Islamic State have no place in Europe or in Hungary, therefore secret services and other professionals are to filter them out. At the same time, Fischl furthers the notion of living together with the Muslims who are already in Europe and who did not come with IS purposes.[28] Fischl makes a link between security concerns and selection for acceptance, but at this point he does not connect reception to categories of national and ethnic identity.

---

25. Television programme 'This Morning' on the topic of the persecution of Christians and the 'false' migration politics of the EU," Ma délelőtt, M1, May 25, 2019, https://www.mediaklikk.hu/video/ma-delelott-2019-05-25-i-adas/?fbclid=IwAR3Bi_Jn4t_rNNppR 5AZNMffmsMaxaR7R9ldghDrxD-Pw_bPY8pCnTpmNqI (accessed July 24, 2019).

26. Television programme 'Face to Face,' Szemtől szembe, December 6, 2018, https://nava.hu/id/3445703/ (accessed August 6, 2019).

27. Vilmos Fischl, "A nemzetközi fellépés tapasztalatai és lehetőségei a civil szervezetek és egyházak szerepe, különös tekintettel a protestáns egyházakra" (Experiences and possibilities of international engagement: The role of civil organisations and churches with special emphasis on the Protestant churches), in *Budapest-jelentés a keresztényüldözésről*, Emberi Erőforrások Minisztériuma (Budapest Report on the persecution of Christians, Ministry of Human Capacities), ed. Balázs Orbán (Budapest, 2017), 185–194, 189.

28. Television programme 'This Morning' on the topic of the persecution of Christians and the "false" migration politics of the EU.

3.5 APPROACHES TO RELIGIOUS AND ETHNIC DIVERSITY

Philip Watt argues that "the language of assimilation is now back in vogue in some EU countries."[29] The approach of integration in the sense of assimilation as opposed to multiculturalism or interculturalism is a common way of thinking in Hungary regarding the present-day Muslim-Christian scene of Europe. In Fischl's works and speeches, integration is also a reflected notion. Referring to the migration into Europe, he argues that Western churches and governments have to deal with the settlement and integration of refugees, while Hungary's role is to provide food and accommodation for them in the transfer period.[30] Clearly, it is important for Fischl that Muslims in Europe are able to practice their faith even though they have to make accommodations due to the culture, the civilization in which they live. They have to integrate in the sense of assimilation. Fischl claims that this type of integration must be sought, and support for this must be given to the newcomers.[31]

The present Hungarian government often talks about the problem of integration. According to Fidesz representatives, the failure of refugee and migrant integration in Western Europe is a sign and lesson that urges Hungary not to accept mass-migration of non-European people.[32]

Fischl insists that countries have the right and the obligation to meet the needs of their community; however, they must also feed the starving people. At the same time, Fischl claims, feeding the hungry is not a sufficient solution, and therefore the reasons behind migration have to be eliminated. He asserts that people should live in peace in their home countries, and states have the right and duty to defend their frontiers. These ideas are also present in the discourse of the Hungarian government. In the public lecture held at the ECCH offices, Balázs Orbán,[33] Minister of State, argued that the plan of Hungary is to offer help in countries where it is necessary. Replying to a request to assess the reactions of the Hungarian churches to the migrant crisis in the period from 2015 to 2019, Orbán emphasized that the government welcomes the cooperation of the churches in Hungary in finding partners in those

---

29. Philip Watt, "An Intercultural Approach to 'Integration'," *Translocations: The Irish Migration, Race and Social Tranformation Review* 1:1 (2006), 151–160, 155.

30. Fischl, "The Role of Churches in Hungary."

31. Television programme 'This Evening,' Ma este, July 2, 2019, https://www.mediaklikk.hu/video/ma-este-2019-07-02-i-adas-3/?fbclid=IwAR3S1CIOXnhcdq-DaVSnbt4ZumnPtk0JjjfsF3qQeC8g5wxUznsHlHXnYig#, acessed July 24, 2019.

32. See, for example, the interview of Zsuzsa Fekete, Director of Communications, RCH, with Prime Minister Viktor Orbán: "Lesz lelki felívelés, ha lesznek keresztények" (There will be a spiritual upswing, if there are Christians), http://www.reformatus.hu/mutat/lesz-lelki-feliveles-ha-lesznek-keresztenyek/ (accessed August 4, 2019).

33. Balázs Orbán, "Migration and the Future of Europe," Public lecture at the ECCH headquarters. April 15, 2019.

countries.

The issue of socio-cultural identities comes to the fore when Fischl argues that culture and civilization in the places where migrants come from are different from the European culture. Although, as mentioned above, Fischl does not connect reception of migrants to the question of socio-cultural identities, he calls attention to the difficulties of the process of integration, specifically due to social and cultural differences between the sending and receiving countries. Tribal societies in Afghanistan, the Middle East, or North-Africa—Fischl argues—represent such a difference in terms of socialization that it is not easy or even impossible to make the transition to the Western type of democratic society and civilization. Fischl indicates that there will be some persons who are successful and many who will fail to integrate.[34] However, when analyzing the refugee mission work of the Reformed Church in Hungary, Fischl takes the point of integration as a measuring tool of the success of the work and indicates a very high integration rate into the Hungarian society: it is mostly 80–90%, but sometimes it is 100%.[35] These data seem to suggest that certain processes of integration can offer a solution to difficulties rooted in sociocultural differences.

Fischl poses the question of how Europe should relate to Muslims, and calls for Europeans to be understanding and humanitarian towards migrants who are lost and perplexed in a totally alien culture. Migrants need help in order to adapt, he argues. On the other hand, he pleads that the receptive and understanding attitude cannot mean renouncing one's own culture and an openness in every single case. There can be no compromises with the Islamic State. He is convinced that it was the total openness of Europe earlier which made it possible for the extremists to plan terrorist attacks in European cities.[36]

3.6 RE-CHRISTIANIZATION OF EUROPE

In an M1 programme with the theme "the persecution of Christians and false migration politics of the EU," Fischl elaborates on the notion of Christian mission, referring to the Great Commission (Matt. 28:16–20), and pleads for the re-Christianization of Europe, suggesting that the primary goal of Hungarian or European Christian responsibility is to spread the faith in the continent where they live: in Europe. He points to behavior in different, perhaps non-Christian contexts, as he argues for

---

34. Vilmos Fischl, *Magyarország párbeszéd lehetőségei Észak-Afrikával és a Közel-Kelettel, különös tekintettel az üldözött keresztényekre* (Dialogue Opportunities of Hungary with North-Africa and the Middle-East with Special Emphasis on Persecuted Christians), Habilitation Thesis, Manuscript, 53.

35. Fischl, *Magyarország párbeszéd lehetőségei*, 58.

36. Fischl, *Magyarország párbeszéd lehetőségei*, 44.

the preservation of Christian identity also when individuals travel and move out of their home environment. He calls for an existential and religious resistance in the context of Muslim-Christian relations, while interpreting the teachings of Jesus as "Christians should not be cozened or be naive and let everything be done to them."[37]

In another television show,[38] Fischl comments on the continuously decreasing number of Christian inhabitants and the growing number of Muslims in Europe. He suggests that this process is reversible, if ministers and priests do their tasks of visiting families, hospitals and provide religious education, and if parents show their children an exemplary Christian life. Fischl acknowledges that the work of the Holy Spirit is also a determining factor in this process.

3.7 Refugees and Migrants, Legal and Illegal

In a public lecture[39] given in Győr, Hungary, Fischl gives account of a WCC visit in Hungary and highlights the significance of the different nature of Western and Hungarian media impacting the work of ecumenical bodies. He points to the differences in the information provided by the Hungarian and the Swiss media, highlighting that the Swiss media does not offer a realistic picture of the migrant situation at the Hungarian borders. He holds the media responsible for the WCC delegates' lack of information. He explains that the WCC's general secretary visited Hungary with a delegation of five as they deemed that there was a crisis situation in the country and the international committee decided to check whether Hungary did everything according to the international regulations. The committee met with representatives of churches and the government: the Reformed Bishop István Szabó, the Lutheran Bishop Tamás Fabiny, the President of the Catholic Bishops' Conference Bishop András Veres, as well as with Bence Rétvári, Minister of State. As Fischl concludes, the delegation left Hungary with a totally different picture from what they had received from the Western media in Geneva. He illustrated this statement with the following example: when they talked about illegal migrants, the delegation did not understand why Hungarians did not use the term 'refugees.' Fischl explained to them that it was because when these people arrived at the Serbian-Hungarian borders they threw away their passports and crossed the green border without the documents. He

---

37. Television programme 'This Morning' on the topic of the persecution of Christians and the "false" migration politics of the EU.
38. Television programme 'Face to Face,' Szemtől szembe, May 22, 2019, https://nava.hu/id/3516839/ (12:28–13:01), (accessed August 11, 2019).
39. "Migráció egyházi és biztonságpolitikai szempontból" (Migration from the point of view of the church and security policy), lecture given by Dr. Vilmos Fischl and Dr. György Nógrádi, published on October 28, 2015, on YouTube, https://www.youtube.com/watch?v=VOnsemR-GT4, (17:25–19:09), (accessed June 30, 2019).

added that the delegation had not known about this phenomenon, as in Western Europe they do not talk about these issues. People there perceive reality through the eyes of the Western press, which states that only innocent refugees come to Hungary.

According to Fischl, illegal migration must be fought, while legal migration is acceptable. He believes that migration can be legal only when migrants hold identification documents and apply for a visa. Fischl holds that it is against international law for a person to travel in Europe without being able to identify himself/herself.[40]

3.8 Hungary Helps

In 2015, when refugees and migrants arrived in large numbers and asked Hungary for permission to enter, the government emphasized the huge pressure migrants would put on the social system. In a questionnaire, the government suggested that it is either the Hungarian families and babies, or the immigration that can be supported financially.[41] According to news releases, Hungary did not want to accept migrants initially because of the financial problem to which the government referred. Later, the issue of the threat of terrorism became the most important argument. This led to the quota denial, fueling the debate on migration between the Western European countries and the Visegrád countries in 2016. The 'Hungary Helps' programme was launched in 2017 with the aim of providing humanitarian support for communities of persecuted Christians and victims of humanitarian catastrophes elsewhere in order to contribute to the eradication of the root causes of migration.[42]

Fischl points out that the main reason why Hungary runs the programme 'Hungary Helps' is that in the migration from 2015 onwards the wealthy Western and Northern European countries were primarily the destination and not Hungary.[43] Fischl argues that the Hungarian government can help through the churches more adequately, as churches already have a built-up network of relations.[44]

---

40. Television programme 'Face to Face,' Szemtől szembe, December 6, 2018, https://nava.hu/id/3445703/ (accessed August 6, 2019).
41. "Nemzeti konzultáció a bevándorlásról és a terrorizmusról" (National consultation about immigration and terrorism), question 12: "Do you agree with the Hungarian government that the need is rather to support Hungarian families and babies to be born than to support immigration?" https://www.kormany.hu/download/7/e2/50000/nemzeti_konzultacio_bevandorlas_2015.pdf?fbclid=IwAR01eqZzka-pDz-P0-rtksePYYSH5ipZ4G5EyucOy-ARJGjpH1oQYDxDegI (accessed August 11, 2019).
42. See https://www.kormany.hu/en/prime-minister-s-office/state-secretariat-for-the-aid-of-persecuted-christians-and-for-the-hungary-helps-program (accessed February 1, 2020).
43. Fischl, *Magyarország párbeszéd lehetőségei*, 6.
44. Fischl, *Magyarország párbeszéd lehetőségei*, 6–7.

3.9 József Steinbach, President of the ECCH

József Steinbach (1964–) is a Reformed theologian, bishop, and leader in the Hungarian ecumenical world. He studied theology in Budapest as well as anthropology, ethics, and social sciences in Veszprém, Hungary. He started serving as a Reformed minister in 1991 and, since 1996, he has fulfilled different leadership roles in the Reformed church. In 2009, he was elected and installed as bishop of the Transdanubian Church District of the Reformed Church of Hungary. Currently, Steinbach teaches practical theology at the Reformed Theological Academy in Pápa, Hungary, and, since 2012, he has served as the president of the ECCH.

3.10 Temporal and Spatial Constraints on Hospitality

Steinbach formulates his opinion on migration in the 2015 anniversary publication[45] of the ECCH. Although, he refrains from either conveying the official position of the church—which can come only from the synod of the church—or claiming that he knows the solution to the problem of migration, he highlights the importance of dealing with this question in an ecumenically concerted way.

Steinbach believes that suffering has to be eased and every suffering person has to be helped, although he restricts this help and support. Providing a biblical foundation to his discourse on migration, he claims that many today quote biblical passages incorrectly about the welcoming of the stranger, as they deprive the text of its context. He explains that

> ... hospitality in antiquity and hospitality according to Christ never meant that the host would have provided the merciful act of hospitality and welcoming endlessly, without limitations; he definitively never gave his house to the person asking for help; it was about a few days and nights and then the person went about his business.[46]

Therefore Steinbach, based on his reading of the biblical practice, suggests that the reception of migrants should be temporally limited as a sufficient Christian response to suffering related to migration.

Even though Steinbach believes that the merciful love of Christ should be practiced in connection with migration, he argues that the responsibility of the individual is limited. He explains that God restricts

---

45. József Steinbach, "Isten színe előtt" (Before God), *Theológiai Szemle* 3 (2015), 132–133.

46. Steinbach, "Isten színe előtt," 133: "... az ókori és a krisztusi vendégszeretet sem jelentette soha azt, hogy a vendéglátó, vég nélkül, és határok nélkül biztosította volna a vendéglátás és a befogadás irgalmas cselekedetét; soha nem adta át a segítséget kérőnek végérvényesen a saját házát. Vagyis csupán néhány napról, éjszakáról volt szó, és az illető ment a dolgára."

the responsibility of the individual to their surroundings. He asserts that "God did not entrust us, everyday people, with all the miseries of the world, but within our own direct environment, our culture and Christianity."[47]

When reflecting on the Christian responsibility of sharing resources, Steinbach examines the connection between justification and helping the needy. While denying that justification depends on helping the physically distanced poor, he identifies the needy as a possible source of danger and calls for protecting the resources in case "the sinful" would want to take them by force:

> We do not have to go to a foreign continent: we also have the poor here. It is a big delusion to think that we become just by helping the poor who live far away.
>
> These people also have the chance to start to fight, with lots of sacrifices and hard work like others have fought as well; creating not a perfect society, but a society more humane and with more welfare …
>
> The sinful … is not busy, does not fight using the opportunities s/he has, does not toil, but repines and expects income, or if s/he does not have it, takes it of the other. …
>
> If people approach us in this way, *we must protect* what we have …[48]

Reflecting on the protection of property, Steinbach envisions the possibility of an attack and invasion against Christians by the foreigner, and he argues that self-defense is a command of Christian ethics: "… we do not harm anyone, we help who we can, but if they want to harm us, we defend ourselves and what belongs to us, we will not let go what God entrusted to us."[49] Interpreting Jesus's command "If anyone slaps you on the right cheek, turn to them the other cheek also" (Matt. 5:39, NIV), Steinbach warns that this command is not for our times, but should be kept only in the eschaton where there is no immanentization of the eschaton: "The Sermon on the Mount is the constitution of the kingdom of God; but until his kingdom comes, it is impossible to turn also the other cheek to the one who hits us, because this is suicide as they for sure will beat us to death."[50] Christian responsibility is further limited, because the burden of decision making is not on the shoulders of the believer but on the leaders of the world. He asserts that world leaders are the on-

---

47. Steinbach, "Isten színe előtt," 133: "Ránk, «mindennapi emberekre», Isten nem a világ összes nyomorúságát bízta, hanem a közvetlen környezetünket, azt a kultúrát, azt az ügyet, ami a miénk."

48. József Steinbach, "Templomtornyok" (Church Towers), *Dunántúli Református Lap* 19:3 (2015), 52–53, 52.

49. József Steinbach, "Az intésről" (About Discipline), *Dunántúli Református Lap* 19:4 (2015), 51–52.

50. József Steinbach, "Az intésről," 51–52.

ly ones able to reflect upon how these people can be helped so that they may have a more dignified life in their homelands where God has placed them, in their own culture.[51]

In an interview for a weekly newspaper in 2017, Steinbach connects the topic of the suffering migrant to the theme of protecting the country, and the Christian heritage and culture, against danger. Steinbach suggests that the Christian answer to suffering related to the issue of migration is to pray, but the nature of further help and support remains undefined:

> I find it unacceptable that we who live in Europe feel unpleasant due to misinterpretations of love and solidarity. We need to protect our Christian heritage and culture, though we are not allowed to define ourselves in contrast to others. When I see people suffering ... I pray and I help as I can. At the same time, I understand that political leaders sometimes have to make determined decisions in order to protect their country. I believe that God requires us to help our direct environment and not to care about all the problems in the world. We are responsible first of all for our families, our smaller and wider environment, and only after this we need to release, as much as possible, the other miseries of the world without putting ourselves at risk.[52]

3.11 "Danger is Palpable": Migration Must be Prevented

Steinbach denies that the Hungarian government and the churches since 2015 have contradicted the love and welcome to which the followers of Christ are called in dealing with migration. Further, he argues that it is impossible to help others if "we endanger our treasures" and he claims that the danger is palpable. He expresses his grave concern about European culture and argues that people who suffer and are persecuted, especially Christians, must be helped, but the solution to migration can only be to handle the problem where it arises. He expresses his ethical evaluation of leaving a homeland and settling in another country, while, at the same time, making a ranking in who needs our support:

> God did not put us accidentally where we were born. I do not understand why the other is more attractive and better than your own. It is like denying my own child in order to help the other. The most important ones are the ones who are entrusted to me, my beloved ones, my belief, my culture, my people.[53]

Using a centuries old image of Hungarian national identity, Steinbach

---

51. József Steinbach, "Az intésről," 51–52.

52. "Ne lökdössük a dominót!" (Let's not push the dominos), interview with Reformed Bishop József Steinbach to the conservative weekly news magazine *Heti Válasz*, April 12, 2017, http://valasz.hu/itthon/ne-lokdossuk-a-dominot-123366.

53. "Ne lökdössük a dominót!"

claims that today Hungary is the last bulwark of Europe.⁵⁴ He is also convinced that the Visegrád Group forms a "safety net" and a counterweight to Western European political thinking. He expresses both his trust that other states will join this alliance and his belief that God will move the future of Europe in this direction of political and cultural thinking.⁵⁵

3.12 THE FINANCIALLY CAPTIVE CHURCH

In a newspaper interview in 2018,⁵⁶ Steinbach is confronted with the accusation of the political opposition, that Christian churches offer support to the government. In his reply, the ECCH president affirms that the churches support the government. He explains that the Reformed Church of Hungary does not have capital to support the congregations, and therefore the congregations must be self-sustaining. For the necessary developments for the church in order to perform its tasks, however, the financial support of the government is necessary.

3.13 TRANSCENDING THE PRESENT

Steinbach warns that present tendencies can have future consequences and suggests that Hungarians face a similar problem to that of migration:

> At the same time, the whole problem should not be approached only from the present. It is unfortunate—and this is our great responsibility or sin, if you like—that we never transcend the present looking into the near or far future, perhaps by modelling what consequences a process can have. We have been warned about these consequences for a long time, while we cannot solve our own similar problems.⁵⁷

---

54. Cf. the idea of *Antemurale Christianitatis* (Bulwark of Christendom), the ones who defend the frontiers of Christian Europe from the Ottoman Empire. The concept of 'bulwark of Christianity' is often applied to Hungary in the discourse of the Fidesz party, see, e.g., in a speech of Miklós Soltész, State Secretary for Religious and Ethnic Relations at the Prime Minister's Office: *Soltész Miklós: Magyarország a kereszténység védőbástyája* (Soltész Miklós: Hungary is the bulwark of Christendom), https://magyarnemzet.hu/belfold/soltesz-miklos-magyarorszag-a-keresztenyseg-vedobastyaja-7306913/ (accessed November 20, 2020).

55. *Soltész Miklós: Magyarország a kereszténység védőbástyája.*

56. "Az Úr nem engedi elveszni Európát," (The Lord won't let Europe to be perished), interview with Reformed Bishop József Steinbach to the *Magyar Idők* (Hungarian Times), a national conservative newspaper associated with the Fidesz government, March 31, 2018.

57. József Steinbach in "Az Úr nem engedi elveszni Európát": "Ugyanakkor az egész problémát nem csupán a jelen felől kellene megközelíteni. Sajnos, és ez nagy felelősségünk, ha úgy tetszik, bűnünk, hogy soha nem lépünk túl a jelenen, a közeli és távolabbi jövőbe tekintve; akár modellezve, hogy egy folyamatnak mi lehet a következménye. Ezekre a következményekre pedig már régóta kapunk figyelmeztetéseket, miközben a saját, ehhez hasonló problémáinkat sem tudjuk megoldani."

Steinbach echoes here the Fidesz government's fear that the reception of migrants in high numbers creates a basis for a future Muslim-dominated society where Christians will lose the rights they have today.

To sum up the views of both theologians, Fischl recognizes two different directions churches and states may take: the way of security and the way of solidarity. In a Lutheran tradition, he distinguishes between the role of the state and the church: he emphasizes the importance of security, therefore the role of the state, while he believes it is important that churches offer humanitarian help. In order to maintain safety in Hungary, he finds the role of security services important, especially, to defend the country against possibly dangerous, destructive people. In terms of reception, he differentiates between peaceful Muslims and Muslims representing an IS ideology; between refugees and migrants; and between legal and illegal migrants. Moreover, he argues that acceptance must be selective. While he accepts the possibility of co-existence with Muslims in European societies and acknowledges the right of Muslims to practice their religion in a dominantly Christian society, he presses the importance of helping in the "locus of the problem" (i.e., zones of conflict, war, etc.), which seems to be connected to the perceived fact that socio-cultural differences make integration into Western societies difficult. Fischl stresses the role of a mission-oriented Christianity that advocates a strong and distinctive identity based on the tenets of the Christian faith with the ultimate purpose of the re-Christianization of Europe.

Steinbach emphasizes easing the suffering of migrants on a temporally limited basis. He denies the biblical background and necessity of welcoming strangers in societies for an unlimited period of time. The concept of the alien, the stranger, and therefore socio-cultural differences, seem to be an obstacle to migrant reception in Steinbach's view. The temporally limited concept of reception is further limited by a spatial constraint: responsibility is first and foremost relevant in direct proximity. Steinbach does not offer a definition of the exact form of helping migrants and rather believes that migration should be stopped, people should stay in their homeland and receive support there.

4. Conclusion

The second half of the 2010s witnessed a growing polarization in the ecumenical movement that centered around the issue of migration. The 2015 influx of migrants to the European continent urged churches and church-related organizations to express their views on the concept of migration, refugee and migrant reception, and the possibilities of socio-cultural co-existence. The process of a theological assessment of the phenomenon started earlier in the WCC than in Hungarian churches, and the global ecumenical body produced more written material in the form of statements, articles and published speeches. Although one would still wish that the ECCH, as the ecumenical body of eleven churches in Hungary, formulates an official opinion on the issue of migration, the issue has been discussed by individual church leaders associated with the organization.

Comparing the concerns of the two organizations, we can see that the theologians connected to the ECCH share certain themes with the WCC: putting an end to the political and social causes of mass migrations, the fear societies and churches struggle with (e.g., loss of identity), differences in ethnic and religious identity, and the social phenomenon of the rejection of and hostility towards refugees and migrants. However, some other concerns of the WCC, such as supporting and welcoming refugees in the destination countries, integrating them in societies, the biblical-theological foundations of hospitality, and the issue of racism are less prominent in the discourse of the two Hungarian theologians. There are, however, several themes that the two Hungarian theologians emphasize and also share with the present Hungarian government: the acute problem of the global persecution of Christians, the doubts about the possibility of a successful integration of migrants into European societies, and the pressing need for the re-Christianization of Europe. The WCC and ECCH theologians' answers to these concerns diverge: while for the WCC these concerns do not mean restrictions on the practice of hospitality, in the discourse of the Hungarian theologians, limitations of migrant reception appear to be both a theologically valid reply and a solution to fears and concerns in society.

The polarized way of thinking of the two ecumenical organizations raises the compelling question of what ecumenical theology has to offer and what the unity of Christians can mean against the backdrop of the migrant crisis in Europe. In order to give voice to the concerns of churches and organizations that share views with the Hungarian theologians, and to reach yet another step towards unity, it is necessary to revisit the following questions in the global ecumenical world.

1. The main emphasis of the WCC is on supporting, welcoming, and integrating refugees and migrants without differentiating between them according to legal status. The Hungarian theologians limit the responsibility of the church, as they divide tasks in the area of migration between church and state, where the unquestionable task of the state is to secure safety, and the task of churches to do humanitarian work based on solidarity within the security frame provided by

the government. In the discourses of Fischl and Steinbach, there is place for a selective reception of migrants, for a temporally restricted way of reception, and for limited responsibilities in terms of geographical location. There is also a call to fight for and protect what is owned by Christian Europeans, including Hungarians. The Hungarian theologians find it more urgent to work on the political and social factors that cause mass migrations, and therefore they support the government-led programme 'Hungary Helps,' which aids needy local communities in war zones, areas of conflict, or natural catastrophes. While the WCC also holds this background of 21st-century migration processes accountable and necessary to deal with, the organization addresses the caring for refugees as a crucial matter. For Fischl and Steinbach, illegal migrants are not perceived as possible subjects of hospitality. Fischl makes it clear that legal migrants should be helped, but migrants without documents are not to be received. Steinbach pushes the responsibility for migrants even further away: to support geographically distant people comes only after helping the needy in the immediate environment. For him, urgency is connected to geographical distance: the closer, the more urgent. Consequently, the concept of human rights in migration needs to be theologically reflected in the global ecumenical discussion and, in this light, ecumenical consensus is needed on what the responsibilities of church and state are in the area of migration especially regarding the practice of hospitality.

2. Fear plays an important role in the discourses of both the WCC and the ECCH theologians. Several WCC documents acknowledge that, as societies and churches accept refugees and migrants, they struggle with fear partly related to the possibility of a cultural change and loss of identity as a consequence of the socio-cultural differences between the European population and the newcomers. The WCC relates it to the problem of racism, but Hungarian theologians do not see racism in the area of migration as a problem to tackle in the Hungarian society. As an answer to fear, Fischl talks about the necessity of the re-Christianization of Europe, while the WCC documents suggest overcoming the fear. The Roman-Catholic-WCC Joint Working Group turns the challenge into a source of blessing and points to

the opportunity that times of migration might bring for the divided Church: through common service it is possible to get closer to each other and take a new step toward unity. Both the issue of socio-cultural identities and the problem of racism connected to migration should be dealt with in further ecumenical dialogue. Migration should be examined in order to discover whether it has the potential to enhance the unity of the Church. Ecumenical agreement is needed on where the place of fear induced by changing social processes is in our theologies, what the theological values of personal safety and property are, and how the safety and well-being of the host and the guest relate to each other.

3. As the WCC argues, based on biblical passages both from the Old and the New Testament, migrants and refugees are part of the one human family created in the image and likeness of God and they embody Christ. Fischl agrees with the WCC that Christian migrants are brothers and sisters of the Christians of the receiving countries; however, for the WCC, all migrants represent brothers and sisters, as everyone belongs to the one human family created after the image and likeness of God. Steinbach interprets biblical hospitality as temporally limited hospitality and this view might also justify the rejection of migrants asking for a new home. Global ecumenical dialogue is required to define the place of refugees and migrants in relation to the one Christian community, to formulate a common consensus about what times of migration teach us regarding the unity and catholicity of the church, as well as who belongs to the one church of God and what responsibilities stem from this belonging.

BIBLIOGRAPHY

"Communiqué by the Joint Working Group," September 19, 2017. Accessed March 22, 2019. https://www.oikoumene.org/en/resources/documents/commissions/jwg-rcc-wcc/communique-by-the-joint-working-group-september-2017.

"Communiqué by the Joint Working Group between the WCC and the RCC," September 7, 2017. Accessed March 22, 2019. https://www.oikoumene.org/en/resources/documents/commissions/communique-by-the-joint-working-group-between-the-wcc-and-the-rcc-september-2018.

Fischl, Vilmos. "A nemzetközi fellépés tapasztalatai és lehetőségei a civil szervezetek és egyházak szerepe, különös tekintettel a protestáns egyházakra" (Experiences and possibilities of international engagement: The role of civil organisations and churches with special emphasis on the Protestant churches), in *Budapest-jelentés a keresztényüldözésről, Emberi Erőforrások Minisztériuma* (Budapest Report on the persecution of Christians, Ministry of Human Capacities), ed. Balázs Orbán, 185–194. Budapest, 2017.

Fischl, Vilmos. *Magyarország párbeszéd lehetőségei Észak-Afrikával és a Közel-Kelettel, különös tekintettel az üldözött keresztényekre* (Dialogue Opportunities of Hungary with North-Africa and the Middle-East with Special Emphasis on Persecuted Christians). Habilitation Thesis.

Fischl, Vilmos. "The Role of Churches in Hungary in Providing Pastoral Care and Humanitarian Help for Migrants." *Academic and Applied Research in Military and Public Management Science* (AARMS) 17:2 (2018): 17–28.

"Greetings of Rev. Dr Olav Fykse Tveit: World Conference on Xenophobia, Racism, and Populist Nationalism In the Context of Global Migration and Refugees," September 18, 2018. Accessed March 12, 2019. https://www.oikoumene.org/resources/documents/greetings-of-rev-dr-olav-fykse-tveit-world-conference-on-xenophobia-racism-and-populist-nationalism-in-the-context-of-global-migration-and-refugees/.

"'Have no Fear': A Statement," June 20, 2016. Accessed March 12, 2019. https://www.oikoumene.org/en/resources/documents/wcc-programmes/umer/mission-from-the-margins/migration/have-no-fear.

"Message from the conference 'Xenophobia, Racism and Populist Nationalism in the Context of Global Migration,'" September 19, 2018. Accessed January 10, 2019. https://www.oikoumene.org/en/resources/documents/message-from-the-conference-xenophobia-racism-and-populist-nationalism-in-the-context-of-global-migration-19-september-2018.

Miklós, Soltész. *Magyarország a kereszténység védőbástyája* (Soltész Miklós: Hungary is the bulwark of Christendom). Accessed November 20, 2020. https://magyarnemzet.hu/belfold/soltesz-miklos-magyarorszag-a-keresztenyseg-vedobastyaja-7306913/.

"Ne lökdössük a dominót!" (Let's not push the dominos), interview with Reformed Bishop József Steinbach to the conservative weekly news magazine *Heti Válasz*, April 12, 2017. http://valasz.hu/itthon/ne-lokdossuk-a-dominot-123366.

"Nemzeti konzultáció a bevándorlásról és a terrorizmusról" (National consultation about immigration and terrorism). Accessed August 11. 2019 https://www.kormany.hu/download/7/e2/50000/nemzeti_konzultacio_bevandorlas_2015.pdf?fbclid=IwAR01eqZzka-pDz-P0-rtksePYYSH5ipZ4G5EyucOy-ARJGjpH1oQYDxDegI.

Orbán, Balázs. "Migration and the Future of Europe." Public lecture at the ECCH headquarters. April 15, 2019.

"Statement on People on the Move: Migrants and Refugees," November 7, 2018. Accessed March 23, 2019. https://www.oikoumene.org/en/resources/documents/executive-committee/uppsala-november-2018/statement-on-people-on-the-move-migrants-and-refugees.

"Statement on refugees in Europe." September 4, 2015. Accessed March 23, 2019. https://www.oikoumene.org/en/resources/documents/general-secretary/statements/statement-on-refugees-in-europe.

"Statement on responses to migrant crises," June 12, 2015. Accessed March 12, 2019. https://www.oikoumene.org/en/resources/documents/executive-committee/etchmiadzin-june-2015/statement-on-responses-to-migrant-crises-doc-no-29-rev.

"Statement on the Forced Displacement Crisis," June 28, 2016. Accessed March 12, 2019. https://www.oikoumene.org/en/resources/documents/central-committee/2016/statement-on-the-forced-displacement-crisis.

"Statement on US Presidential Executive Order 'Protecting the Nation from Foreign Terrorist Entry into the United States' and its Impact on Refugees," Januari 31, 2017. Accessed March 22, 2019. https://www.oikoumene.org/en/resources/documents/general-secretary/joint-declarations/statement-on-us-presidential-executive-order-on-refugees.

Steinbach, József. "Az intésről" (About Discipline). *Dunántúli Református Lap* 19:4 (2015): 51–52.

Steinbach, József. "Isten színe előtt" (Before God). *Theológiai Szemle* 3 (2015): 132–133.

Steinbach, József. "Templomtornyok" (Church Towers). *Dunántúli Református Lap* 19:3 (2015): 52–53

"Taizé Greetings WCC general secretary Rev. Dr Olav Fykse Tveit," December 2018. Accessed January 2, 2019. https://www.oikoumene.org/en/resources/documents/taize-greetings-wcc-general-secretary-rev-dr-olav-fykse-tveit-28-december-2018.

Watt, Philip. "An Intercultural Approach to 'Integration.'" *Translocations: The Irish Migration, Race and Social Tranformation Review* 1:1 (2006): 151–160.

WCC Central Committee, "Statement on the Middle East." Heraklion, Crete, August 1967. Accessed January 31, 2019. https://www.oikoumene.org/en/resources/documents/central-committee/1967/statement-on-the-middle-east.

"WCC expresses grave concern for Rohingya people in Myanmar," September 14, 2017. Accessed March 22, 2019. https://www.oikoumene.org/en/resources/documents/wcc-expresses-grave-concern-for-rohingya-people-in-myanmar.

CHAPTER 18
AGAINST POLARIZATION: FORMING A SENSE OF 'OTHERNESS' FROM A CONVERSATION BETWEEN ANTHROPOLOGY AND NEO-CALVINISM
Louise C. Prideaux

1. INTRODUCTION

On April 22, 2019 the UK marked the first National Stephen Lawrence Day. Stephen Lawrence, a black teenager, was killed in 1993 in an unprovoked racist attack as he waited at a London bus stop. His murder sparked a revolution in the law, in tackling institutional racism within the police force, and in combatting that same racism across communities.[1] Part of the purpose of the instituting of this national day is to inspire British young people to build "an inclusive society for everyone to live their best life regardless of gender, race, sexuality, religion, disability or background."[2] This hopeful vision, established in memory of a black teenager, is for a non-polarized British society where the freedom of those who are considered 'other' is respected and upheld across all kinds of diverse communities, and where young people can thrive and flourish equally, whoever they are.

As Pieter Vos describes in his introduction to this volume, polarization is an increasing challenge within and across diverse societies and communities, but is the Christian church equipped to deal with such a challenge, given that also "the church worldwide and locally is often deeply divided on highly contested issues"?[3] Polarization

---

1. "Independent Report: The Stephen Lawrence Inquiry," Home Office, Gov. UK, https://www.gov.uk/government/publications/the-stephen-lawrence-inquiry#7.46 (accessed December 4, 2019).

2. Doreen Lawrence, "On the first Stephen Lawrence day, let's admit our communities are still unequal," *The Guardian*, UK, https://www.theguardian.com/commentisfree/2019/apr/22/stephen-lawrence-day-british-society-doreen-lawrence (accessed December 4, 2019).

3. As Pieter Vos explains in the Introduction, 2, these divisions appear in issues of sexuality and gender, race and immigration, tradition and theology, amongst many other contested and deeply held beliefs.

penetrates right to the heart of the church itself, raising questions about the character of Christ that is portrayed by his people within the church and in society. From a conversation between cultural anthropology and Neo-Calvinism, I will discuss how forming a sense of 'otherness' can equip the church to offer a different approach to polarization and to offer a Christological hope of restoration which fulfills all the aspirations of a National Stephen Lawrence Day.

For the purposes of this paper, I will draw on anthropological ideas of 'the other' and 'otherness' from the work of anthropologists Louise Lawrence, Mario Aguilar, Joel Robbins, and Will Rollason. I refer to anthropology in a theological discussion in order to highlight themes of self-awareness, the meaning of culture, and language that binds 'the other.' This anthropological theme will extend into the theology of Abraham Kuyper in a discussion of how a sense of 'otherness' might be perceived in Kuyper's sphere sovereignty, albeit with vital caveats, in the form of a respect for 'the other' in their own right. Certainly, a sense of 'otherness' is found in the idea of 'commonness' as discussed by Kuyperian scholar Richard Mouw; I will place this 'commonness' alongside a Kuyperian commitment to freedom of conscience, equality, and justice. Finally, remaining in the neo-Calvinist tradition to consider how a distinctively Christian 'otherness' might be formed in the church, I will turn to a section of Herman Bavinck's confessional spirituality in *The Sacrifice of Praise*. My goal in bringing together anthropological and neo-Calvinist theological insights in this paper is to demonstrate that the church does indeed have a calling in times of polarization, and how in formation and practice the church may exercise this calling to Christian 'otherness' as it engages with all kinds of cultural communities.

1.1 WHY CULTURAL ANTHROPOLOGY?

Historically, theology and anthropology (in general terms) have operated in a relationship which is at best "awkward," and at worst polarized.[4] However, this relationship is currently enjoying a fruitful and transformative development with theologians and anthropologists alike investing in pursuing an open and optimistic dialogue between the two disciplines.[5] An aspect of this developing relationship has been in eth-

---

4. Modern anthropological study has traditionally kept theology at the margins but in 2006 anthropologist Joel Robbins published an influential paper calling for a deeper engagement between the two disciplines, even though the relationship between them remains complex and "awkward." See Joel Robbins, "Anthropology and Theology: An Awkward Relationship?" *Anthropology Quarterly* 79:2, 2006, 285–294 and J. Derrick Lemons, "New Insights from an Old Dialogue Partner," *Theologically Engaged Anthropology*, ed. J. Derrick Lemons (Oxford: Oxford University Press, 2018), Chapter 2.

5. For example, Joel Robbins comments that any thinking about how anthropology

nographic theology where research and fieldwork provide a self-reflection for theologians as they observe theology in practice amongst everyday Christians.[6] This anthropologically informed reflexivity is vital for a theological discussion about how the church responds to polarization internally and externally, but how might this lead to a change in formation and practice? The answer lies, in part, in cultural anthropology being a discipline that studies human cultural activity, cultural processes, cultural changes, and cultural development, although the discipline's understanding of itself has been under scrutiny over the last fifty years: reflexivity has resulted not only in the questioning of how to define 'culture' but also what constitutes anthropology as a discipline.[7] However, for the purposes of this study it may be understood "as an academic discipline that analyses cultures and uses all resources available, including theology, to do more thorough analysis." In this view, anthropology can offer important insights into how to engage culturally with diverse groups of humans. This is because anthropology can unsettle all kinds of cultural and religious beliefs held by an individual or group of individuals which have been deliberately chosen, or inherited and largely un-examined, or even the subtle implications of those beliefs in different cultural settings. This unsettling ultimately reveals the root of what makes anthropology different from theology, and in doing so, leads to a new awareness of self.[8] In fact, it is this *difference* which can aid a theological reflection on

may be informed by theology would benefit by being reciprocated by thinking about how theology may be informed by anthropology. Joel Robbins and Sarah Coakley, "Anthropological and Theological Responses to Theologically Engaged Anthropology," in *Theologically Engaged Anthropology*, ed. Lemons, 355–76, 355.

6. Anthropologist James Bielo traces the development of ethnographic theology back to the early 2000s when "practical theologians and ethicists" began looking "for a more dynamic exchange between the people in the pews and formally trained theological scholars." Bielo is considerate of the points of overlap and difference between ethnography in theology and anthropology and highlights the possibilities inherent in the development of dialogue between the two disciplines. James S. Bielo, "An Anthropologist is Listening: A Reply to Ethnographic Theology," in *Theologically Engaged Anthropology*, ed. J. Derrick Lemons, 140–155, 141.

7. J. Derrick Lemons, "Introduction: Theologically Engaged Anthropology," in *Theologically Engaged Anthropology*, ed. Lemons, 1–7, 5. See also Kim Fortun's description of the transition in cultural anthropology from universalist methods to ethnographic reflexivity: Kim Fortun, "Foreword to the Twenty-Fifth Anniversary Edition," in *Writing Culture: The Poetics and Politics of Ethnography*, eds. James Clifford and George E. Marcus (California: California University Press, 2010), viii.

8. Anthropologist Douglas Davies describes theology and anthropology as having different starting points: while theology presuppose the existence of God, anthropology requires no such presupposition as it is simply the study of human behavior. However, bringing anthropology to bear upon theology creates a new awareness of self which brings about a "philosophical distress" because it requires a critical reflection on our perception of reality. Douglas J. Davies, *Anthropology and Theology* (Oxford: Berg, 2002), 1, 3–4.

polarization. Given this complex relationship, the other part of the answer to bringing in cultural anthropology is that the discipline also provides a lens through which to view 'the other;' in this case, the 'other' is broadly the Reformed theological tradition, and specifically Neo-Calvinist theological developments.

1.2 Why Abraham Kuyper?

In this chapter the distinctive theology in dialogue with anthropology is Neo-Calvinism, with a specific focus on Abraham Kuyper's sphere sovereignty. At first view it may appear that Kuyper's view of society consisting of divinely appointed, organically related spheres which operate in their own right can only exacerbate polarization; for example, where sphere sovereignty has been used as a justification for apartheid.[9] Nevertheless, if sphere sovereignty is intended to operate for the mutual flourishing of all human beings as an outworking of God's common grace, then it may be helpful in considering whether any aspect of 'otherness' can be perceived. Certainly, any response by the church to polarization in society may be considered part of the "redeemed cultural activity" necessary for cultural renewal—a commitment which lies at the heart of Kuyperianism.[10] As I will explore later, just as God has ordained the various spheres in society to live up to their unique callings, so has he ordained individuals to do the same. This is not only the basis for liberty of conscience but also for equal rights, and for an 'otherness' that is similar to that which is found in anthropology. 'Otherness' in anthropology also carries with it a sense of future possibilities, where individuals and cultural groups are not bound by ethnographic interpretations of their past or by colonial ideas of development.[11] The interplay between Kuyperian and anthropological ideas of 'otherness' will provide the foundation for considering how the church might employ 'otherness' in responding to

---

9. South African minister and theologian H. Russel Botman explains that Kuyper's notions of 'difference' and 'separateness' are rightly indicted in the theological underpinnings of apartheid in South Africa. H. Russel Botman, "Is Blood Thicker Than Justice? The Legacy of Abraham Kuyper in Southern Africa," in *Religion, Pluralism, and Public Life*: *Abraham Kuyper's Legacy for the Twenty-First Century*, ed. Luis E. Lugo (Grand Rapids: Wm. B. Eerdmans Publishing Company, 2000), 342–361, 351.

10. Richard J. Mouw, *Abraham Kuyper: A Short and Personal Introduction* (Grand Rapids, Michigan: Wm. B. Eerdmans, 2011), 15.

11. For example, anthropologist Will Rollason locates the problem in the attitude that to be poor is to lack something: "Development takes the liberal, democratic, consumer societies of the North as the norm, and defines 'the poor' as figures of lack... Their future as people who have, or should have 'more' is never in doubt." This attitude colors the ethnographic accounts of Pacific peoples and subsequently puts limits on their futures. Will Rollason, "Introduction: Pacific Futures, Methodological Challenges," in *Pacific Futures*: *Projects, Politics and Interests*, ed. Will Rollason (Berghahn Books, 2014), 1–27, 4.

polarization.

2. Cultural Anthropological Insights Into 'the Other' and 'Otherness'

2.1 Awareness of 'the Other'

Theologian and anthropologist Louise Lawrence writes, "Anthropology helps us straddle the divide between seeing "others" as cultural copies of ourselves and, on the other hand, seeing them as radically "other" from us."[12] This straddling of the divide between two extreme views of 'the other' means that it is not appropriate to project our cultural assumptions onto 'the other.' Neither is it appropriate to dismiss any difference or priority of 'the other' by refusing to engage. It keeps us from both over-emphasizing our preconceived notions of difference and from assimilating 'the other' into ourselves; both approaches result in losing all sense of difference through an attempt to dominate and colonize. Instead, Lawrence writes, "Our dealings with 'others' are to be methodologically sophisticated, wary of any attempt to objectify them and sensitive to their diversity and individuality."[13] In this view, no encounter with those who are culturally 'other' to us should be simplified or avoided. There is no room for imposing either unyielding uniformity or polarization in our social relationships.

2.2 Cultural Complexity: "the Death of Culture"

Anthropology also helps us consider what we mean by 'culture' in our encounters with the cultural 'other.' In anthropological debates surrounding the meaning of culture, the idea that cultures can be decoded and defined absolutely has resulted in what theologian and anthropologist Mario Aguilar refers to as "the death of culture."[14] He explains that although human beings share some similarities "they do not share a culture." To say that someone belongs to the British 'culture' or the American 'culture' is to undermine the complex cultural realities experienced

---

12. Louise J. Lawrence, "Introduction: A Taste for 'the Other,'": Interpreting Biblical Texts Anthropologically," in *Anthropology and Biblical Studies: Avenues of Approach*, eds. Louise J. Lawrence and Mario I. Aguilar (Leiden: Deo Publishing, 2004), 9–25, 22.

13. Lawrence writes that 'the other' is neither a "completely open book" nor "forever foreign to the interpreter," Lawrence, "Introduction," 11.

14. Mario I. Aguilar, "Changing Models and the 'Death' of Culture: A diachronic and positive critique of socio-scientific assumptions," in *Anthropology and Biblical Studies: Avenues of Approach*, eds. Lawrence and Aguilar, 299–313, 307–308.

by that person on a daily basis.¹⁵ 'Culture' as a single, indivisible entity is a myth. Instead, human beings are constantly part of and influenced by fluctuating cultural realities, cultural processes, cultural works, and cultural contexts. Using the term 'culture' to bind people-groups to territories and ethnicities can trigger catastrophic power relationships.¹⁶

For this reason, when engaging with 'the other,' whether they are members of other cultural communities or our own, it is not appropriate to use language that binds them to *our* notions of what we think they are like, which is precisely why theological methodologies in approaching any kind of cultural engagement need to be sophisticated. Both the theologian's and the church's language about 'the other' and the communities to which they belong must be specific, true to their accounts of themselves, and with an awareness that the anthropologist, the theologian, and the everyday church member brings their own partiality to bear on cultural engagement.¹⁷ We always view 'the other' through our own particular set of cultural lenses.

2.3 FROM 'THE OTHER' TO 'OTHERNESS'

A prioritization of 'the other' in our social relationships leads to forming a sense of 'otherness.' Anthropologist Joel Robbins describes an important difference between anthropologists and theologians: on the one hand, anthropologists collect data about how 'the other' lives. On the other hand, theologians focus on *how* 'the other' might live *differently*.¹⁸ Robbins describes this focus as 'otherness.'¹⁹ That is because in anthropology, 'otherness' is associated with allowing 'the other'—whoever they may be—to live differently and innovatively, rather than as a result of repeated cultural traditions. For example, Will Rollason writes in his anthropological collection *Pacific Futures* that in order to explain what is happening among Pacific peoples today "we need to produce an

---

15. Aguilar, "Changing Models," 307.

16. Aguilar associates the danger of using the term 'culture' with genocidal crises such as the Holocaust, the Balkans war, and the Rwandan civil conflict. It happens when "other cultures" are "perceived as foreign, inadequate, dangerous and subject to scrutiny." Aguilar, "Changing Models," 308.

17. James Clifford, "Introduction: Partial Truths," in *Writing Culture: The Poetics and Politics of Ethnography*, eds. James Clifford and George E. Marcus (California: California University Press, 1986), 1–26, 18.

18. Robbins calls this "the critical force of theology" that mocks anthropology by its confidence that an awareness of a different way to live can lead to transformation. Robbins, "Anthropology and Theology," 288.

19. Robbins borrows this term from John Millbank's *Theology and Social Theory* in which Millbank draws a contrast between an "ontology of violence" of social thought and an "ontology of peace" of Christianity. Robbins, "Anthropology and Theology," 291–292.

account of what Pacific people are doing to secure their futures."[20] This is not an account of what anthropologists think the future of Pacific peoples will be based on the traditions of the past, but an account by Pacific people about the way they imagine specific futures for themselves.

2.4 Unbinding of 'the Other'

Rollason describes how, in collecting their data, traditionally anthropologists have imposed their own version of the future upon Pacific people. This version has partly been influenced by colonial discourses of development that are based on what a future 'good life' looks like economically.[21] It has also partly been influenced by the opposite anthropological approach: the pursuit of cultural relativism. In cultural relativism, diversity is celebrated, and the reproduction of indigenous traditions is sacrosanct. The result of both anthropological approaches is the same: anthropologists do not expect Pacific people to produce anything new and different in their futures that sits outside of either cultural reproduction or modern notions of development.[22] What is called for is a more sophisticated methodology, following Lawrence: anthropologists need to cultivate a sense of 'otherness' where the specific desires of 'the other' are prioritized and give accounts of the specific aspirations of Pacific peoples regarding their futures.[23] Rollason summarizes this succinctly: "Just because you can interpret what someone does in terms of the past and a cultural tradition doesn't mean that you must do so."[24]

2.5 Prioritizing 'the Other' in Times of Polarization

Lawrence, Aguilar, Rollason and Robbins demonstrate that a pursuit of 'otherness' in our encounters with different cultural communities requires us to leave behind culturally relativistic perceptions and expectations of 'the other.' Whether anthropologist, theologian, or church member, we cannot impose our versions of reality upon others, either forcing them to be the same as us or defining them by the ways in which they are

---

20. Rollason, "Introduction," 2.
21. Rollason, "Introduction," 4.
22. Rollason explains that because Pacific peoples function not through a system of capitalism and consumerism but on systems of relationships, they do not envision their futures in terms of economic growth and development. Rollason, "Introduction," 3.
23. Rollason describes how normative development discourses define the poor as lacking something: Western development. This is a modern, colonial narrative imposed upon indigenous peoples. Rollason, "Introduction," 4.
24. This is in reference to anthropologist Mark Mosko's account of Melanesians interpreting change and innovation only in reference to their cultural past, which makes it impossible for real transformation to take place in the future. Rollason, "Introduction," 7–8.

different from us. A prioritization of 'the other' leaves no room either for polarization or for a collapsing of distinctions. This prioritization of 'the other' must be active, standing in contrast to the "activity of dividing" that is inherent in polarization.[25] 'Otherness' will enable us to be specific in our cultural encounters and to a resist the fear of 'the other' that leads to hostility, separation, segregation, and polarization. Replacing fear of 'the other' with a sense of 'otherness' will lead to a straddling of the divide between polarization and sameness. Moreover, as anthropologist and theologian Michael Rynkiewich writes, "The ability to see the world through another's eyes has long been linked to the capacity for ethical living."[26] Of course, it is this implicit desire for 'otherness' and for seeing the world through the eyes of 'the other' that lies at the heart of the National Stephen Lawrence Day, because it is meant to encourage communities to imagine different futures for themselves and each other that are not bound to a past history of polarization but where all 'others' can mutually and freely flourish.

3. 'OTHERNESS' IN NEO-CALVINISM

These anthropological insights into 'otherness' are valuable for a critical theological reflection on the church's response to polarization. However, it is the task of theology to locate this 'otherness' in the Christian gospel.[27] Specifically, this paper turns to Neo-Calvinist theology for this task, with a focus on Abraham Kuyper's sphere sovereignty. Sphere sovereignty relies on the premise that God has ordained pluriformity in society with many-varied spheres, sovereign in their own right and ruled by freedom of conscience; at the same time the spheres are related organically to each other under the sovereignty of Christ.[28]

3.1 'THE OTHER' IN SPHERE SOVEREIGNTY

In Kuyperian sphere sovereignty, not only are spheres equal and necessary for the flourishing of society, they also have a divinely given identity that no other sphere has the right to encroach upon.[29] Kuyper saw

---

25. In understanding polarization as an "activity of dividing" it is easier to discern patterns of behavior, attitudes, and language that bind 'the other' to various divisions in society, and in one's own thinking. See Pieter Vos, "Introduction," 4.

26. Michael A. Rynkiewich, "Athens Engaging Jerusalem," in *Theologically Engaged Anthropology*, ed. Lemons, 211–225, 233.

27. Robbins argues that it is possible to recover anthropological 'otherness' without having to convert to Christianity or recognize the existence of God. Robbins, "Anthropology and Theology," 293.

28. James D. Bratt, *Abraham Kuyper: Modern Calvinist, Christian Democrat* (Grand Rapids: Wm. B. Eerdmans, 2013), 130.

29. Abraham Kuyper, "Sphere Sovereignty (1880)," in *Abraham Kuyper: A Centennial Reader*, ed. James D. Bratt (Grand Rapids: Wm. B. Eerdmans Publishing

this sovereignty as having been delegated from God's personal sovereignty.[30] Just as God is free to be God without coercion or manipulation, so he has granted that the different spheres in society should be free—that is, free from manipulation or coercion by a dominating sphere—to create a flourishing organic society where there is cultural development in line with God's original purposes for creation.[31] However, this notion of sovereignty also exists on an individual level. In the final chapter of his book *Rooted and Grounded*, Kuyper says this by way of metaphor: "Each person's calling is not merely to be a human being but to have one's own character."[32] Here is the essence of sphere sovereignty: not only does sphere sovereignty uphold the freedom of other spheres to live up to their God-given calling, it also upholds the freedom of the *individual* 'other' in *their* specific calling. This concern for the individual in their own right is at the heart of sphere sovereignty. When he speaks about the role of the state in upholding "the free movement of life in and for every sphere," Kuyper is not just referring to abstract ideas or institutions; he specifically refers to the individual members of those spheres and the vital importance of preserving their distinctiveness, "not to suppress life nor to shackle freedom but to make possible the free movement of life in and for every sphere."[33] By extension, it is possible to relate this to a sense of 'otherness' similar to that found in the anthropological discussions above.

3.2 THE DANGER OF SEPARATENESS

However, there are vital caveats to put in place with any discussion of Kuyperian sphere sovereignty because of the dangers of the distinctions between spheres stretching to become concrete separations. Instead of upholding civil liberty for all citizens of society through the equality of distinct spheres, a notion of separateness can lead to superiority, coercion and injustice, particularly when undergirded by colonialism and paternalism. Once the separateness of sphere sovereignty

---

Co., 1998), 468.

30. In talking of sovereign authority in his political manifesto, Our Program, Kuyper writes "that the source of sovereign authority does not reside in the law of the will of the people but in God." Abraham Kuyper, *Our Program: Christian Political Manifesto*, ed. and trans. Harry Von Dyke, in Abraham Kuyper Collected Works of Public Theology, Series 1, eds. Jordan J. Ballor and Melvin Flikkema (Bellingham, Washington: Lexham Press), 19.

31. For Kuyper, it was only through the fulfillment of God's purposes for creation that humanity could reach its fullest potential. Abraham Kuyper, *Lectures on Calvinism* (n.p.: CreateSpace, 2012), 53. This sits in tension with Kuyper's advocacy of freedom of conscience and against discrimination in society based on what a person believed or did not believe. Abraham Kuyper, *Our Program: A Christian Political Manifesto*, 69.

32. Kuyper, *Rooted and Grounded*, 32.

33. Kuyper, "Sphere Sovereignty," 468.

becomes institutionalized in the church, and enshrined in law, then what follows includes discrimination on the basis of gender, sexuality, social and economic backgrounds, racial segregation, and ultimately a system of apartheid.[34] This pathogenic seed of separation contained within Kuyper's sphere sovereignty cannot be ignored and calls into question the validity of using this worldview when discussing polarization.

3.3 RECONTEXTUALIZING SPHERE SOVEREIGNTY

However, I suggest that, in view of the caveats issued above, it is still helpful to refer to Kuyper's sphere sovereignty in this discussion because of the view that 'the other' is *both* distinct from *and* equal to us. What is required is a recontextualization of Kuyper's sphere sovereignty.[35] In terms of relating to 'the other,' recontextualization of sphere sovereignty must include an 'otherness' that operates on both an individual and community level, and a prioritization of 'the other' that upholds Kuyper's other commitments to freedom of conscience and equal rights.[36] For example, there is a legitimate and distinctively Christian 'otherness' in Kuyper's exhortation for Christians to alleviate the suffering of the poor, in which he recalls the sacrifice of Christ who suffered for and with human beings. He believed it was the God-given duty of Christians to alleviate conditions of the working classes, not merely through aid, leadership, and whatever else was in their power, but more importantly through a change of heart that viewed "the poorest" as their "own flesh and blood."[37] A recontextualization of sphere sovereignty will involve tempering and reshaping through these other commitments, as well as a return to Kuyper's upholding of societal plural-

---

34. Botman, "Is Blood Thicker Than Justice?" 351.

35. This is not a new idea in the development and application of Kuyperian thought in the 21st century. For example, South Korean pastor Min Kang highlights the growing interest in Kuyper's sphere sovereignty amongst Protestant Christians in South Korea as the church grapples with living out the Christian faith in all spheres of life. Min Kang, "Abraham Kuyper in Korea: hartstochtelijk hervormer, een begrip onder Presbyteriaanse predikanten," *TussenRuimte* 10:3 (2017), 26–31. Translation of the paper "Abraham Kuyper for Korean Protestantism: from the perspective of a Korean Presbyterian Pastor," https://www.academia.edu/35765279/Abraham_Kuyper_for_Korean_Protestantism_from_the_perspective_of_a_Korean_Presbyterian_Pastor. In this case, the recontextualization of sphere sovereignty is being done not by academic theologians but by everyday Christians living out their everyday Christian lives.

36. Botman explains that Kuyper has also been influential on liberative movements because of his commitment to social justice. Botman, "Is Blood Thicker Than Justice?" 347. In addition, a Kuyperian pursuit of freedom of conscience justified 'conscientious disobedience' on behalf of black South African churches. Allan Boesak, *Black and Reformed: Apartheid, Liberation, and the Calvinist Tradition* (New York: Orbis, 1984), 34–35, 49.

37. Kuyper, *The Problem of Poverty*, ed. James Skillen (Iowa: Dordt College Press, 2011), 67.

ism that finds its unity in Christ.³⁸ A contemporary example of this can be found in Neo-Calvinist Matthew Kaemingk's study of Muslim immigration in 21st-century USA: a recontextualized sphere sovereignty is implicit in the way Kaemingk describes how following Christ means to seek not just the good of those who belong to different belief-systems in terms of relief, aid, education and so on, but in seeking the restoration of their human dignity and their ability to be cultivators of creation in their own way and in their own right.³⁹ Kaemingk's work demonstrates how important it is that Kuyper's understanding of Christ as holding nature and grace together as Creator and re-Creator must find an outworking in sphere sovereignty that seeks not to simplify and separate on the grounds of creational difference and diversity, but to provide visible unity *in* pluriformity that has its foundation in Christ as reconciler of both.⁴⁰ In this regard, Kuyper must be 're-Kuypered' through a greater development of his Christology, whereby visible unity through Christ (being in himself the continuity between creation and new creation, nature and grace) is brought to the fore and tempers the idea of distinctions based on creational difference. This is resonant with Vos's description in the introduction to this volume of "rediscovering the continuum" whereby formerly united parties are reunited post-polarization.⁴¹ There is value too in tempering the inclusion of sphere sovereignty in this discussion with a dialogue with cultural anthropology in which the principle of "straddling the divide" can help guard against principles of separation and aid theological self-reflection and critique in the Neo-Calvinist, Reformed tradition.

---

38. For example, James Skillen suggests that Kuyper still has much to contribute to critiquing current dominant ideologies, because of the underlying pursuit of justice inherent in sphere sovereignty. James W. Skillen, "Why Kuyper Now? in *Religion, Pluralism, and Public Life*: *Abraham Kuyper's Legacy for the Twenty-First Century*, ed. Luis E. Lugo (Grand Rapids: Wm. B. Eerdmans Publishing Company, 2000), 365.

39. Moreover, Kaemingk is explicit that Christians who claim to follow Christ should seek the good of their Muslim neighbors regardless of whether or not such encounters result in Christian conversions. Matthew Kaemingk, *Christian Hospitality and Muslim Immigration in an Age of Fear* (Grand Rapids: William B. Eerdmans, 2018), 179.

40. Kuyper's theology demonstrates a bias towards creation and re-creation without explicitly addressing what happens to creational differences—boundaries between spheres, for example—in Christ's redemptive work: "This is why Scripture continually points out to us that the Savior of the world is also the Creator of the world—indeed, that the reason he could become its Savior is only *because* he was its Creator." Kuyper, *Common Grace, Vol. 1*, 271.

41. Vos, "Introduction," 6.

4. Sphere Sovereignty, 'Otherness' and 'Commonness'

In bringing the insights of cultural anthropology into 'otherness' and Kuyper's sphere sovereignty, I have suggested that the upholding of both liberty of conscience and cultural complexity can lead to a prioritization of 'the other' as the church responds to increasing polarization. This prioritization leads to an upholding of the individual 'other' in their specificity equally and in freedom, without coercion or manipulation. It allows 'the other' to flourish in their own right and leads to an attitude of 'otherness' that does not bind 'the other' to preconceived or colonial notions about their past or their future. However, there is a further, related idea which enables a cultivation of 'otherness' in a discussion about polarization, namely the idea of 'commonness.' Commonness comes from the theological idea of the togetherness of a shared humanity—regardless of salvific status—which has its origins in Kuyper's doctrine of common grace.[42]

Commonness relies on shared experiences by a shared humanity, where common ground becomes the place for true relationships and meaningful encounters.[43] Meaningful encounters between members of different cultural communities are especially important, given that from an anthropological perspective no one is ever a member of just one cultural community. In his book *Adventures in Evangelical Civility*, Richard Mouw explains his willingness to "bracket" key evangelical concerns so that genuine dialogue may take place between his community and 'the other.'[44] This puts oneself into the mindset of 'the other' in empathy. Mouw explains that "a spirit of genuine learning" may lead to a meaningful and respectful engagement.[45] However, this must also guard against any notion that one view of the 'common good' is superior

---

42. The idea of the 'togetherness' of humanity is taken from Klaas Schilder's sunousia which may be thought of as a concession to Kuyper's common grace, a doctrine which Schilder heavily criticized. Klaas Schilder, *Christ and Culture*, trans. G. van Rongen and W. Helder (Winnipeg: Premier Printing, 1977), 7, https://spindleworks.com/library/schilder/ChristnCulture.pdf. However, Richard Mouw makes the connection between common grace and the commonness of humanity which creates a basis for social, cultural, and political engagement. See, e.g., Richard J. Mouw, *Adventures in Evangelical Civility: A Lifelong Quest for Common Ground* (Grand Rapids: Brazos Press, 2016), 32.

43. Richard Mouw cites the apostle Paul's encounter with Athenians in Acts Chapter 17 as an example of how an appeal to commonness can help facilitate theological encounters. Richard Mouw, *Adventures in Evangelical Civility: A Lifelong Quest for Common Ground* (Grand Rapids: Brazos Press, 2006), 194.

44. See, e.g., Mouw, *Adventures*, 183.

45. Mouw, *Adventures*, 186.

to another and instead facilitate relationships on an equal footing.⁴⁶

4.1 Commonness Guards Against Separation

In this regard, the pursuit of commonness as part of developing a sense of 'otherness' can guard against polarization in our cultural encounters. In Kuyperian terms it means that we pursue justice for 'the other,' freedom, equality, and mutual flourishing. In anthropological terms there is no wider 'culture' into which other 'cultures' should be assimilated. Instead, commonness and 'otherness' should lead us to step into 'the other's' shoes and learn to live inside their skin.⁴⁷ Commonness and 'otherness' act as lenses upon our understanding of ourselves and our versions of reality. Pursuing the common good enables 'the other' to share the table with us. A sense of 'otherness' asks what kind of table 'the other' imagines sharing. For this purpose, the church not only needs to gather data about other ways to live and reflect critically on how they are distinct from our own perceptions, it also needs to take off its shoes of assumption and step reverently into other cultural worlds to discover better ways of living together. This Kuyperian 'otherness' shields 'the other' from any kind of tyranny; instead, the church pursues on behalf of 'the other' "freedom of expression, freedom of belief, freedom of worship; but above all these freedoms: freedom of conscience."⁴⁸

5. Being Formed into 'Otherness'

'Otherness' challenges the church to take into account diverse and complex cultural realities *as they are actually experienced by* 'the other.' I have argued that a re-imagining of Kuyper's sphere sovereignty can give us the tools to do that. However, Neo-Calvinism is rich in theology which can allow our engagement with 'the other' to be anthropologically post-cultural in character. In other words, in leaving behind bounded notions of 'culture' and expectations of the behavior of 'the other' based on religious or cultural assumptions, the church is able to allow for the possibility of imagining present and future cultural transformation in new ways and resists binding cultural communities to a past history of polarization. From both an anthropological and theological perspective, because of our shared humanity, this post-cultural approach can only lead to mutual flourishing. However, there is a further theological dimension that makes this approach distinctively Christian, and that is its Christological rootedness. Remaining within the Neo-Cal-

---

46. Mouw, *Adventures*, 186.
47. Louise Lawrence writes that "bestowing us with 'A Taste for the Other,' anthropology also teaches that until we seek to know others, we can never have a balanced view of our own identity." Lawrence, "Introduction," 22.
48. Kuyper, *Our Program*, 69.

vinist tradition, it is now Kuyper's younger colleague Herman Bavinck who provides an example of this in his book on confessional spirituality, *Sacrifice of Praise*.

In his chapter on the diversity of confession, Bavinck prioritizes Christ's kingdom. He explains that the Christian gospel is not primarily a philosophy to resolve social problems, neither is Christ a political leader nor the Church a political authority.[49] Instead, the Christian gospel is far greater; as Savior, Christ is able to restore all nature by grace and therefore nothing is rejected.[50] In saying this, Bavinck goes further than Kuyper in demonstrating the implications for visible unity in the restoration and recreation of nature and grace in and through Christ, and helps in the work of 're-Kuypering' mentioned above. If Christ recreates "all natural ordinances" by "the new spirit," then seeking 'otherness' and 'commonness' in our engagement with those who are culturally 'other' to us becomes an expression of Christ's work.[51] It is an intentional, spiritual, confessional, and *participatory* activity. The Christian's response to Christ is to confess him in all areas of life, and towards all peoples: "He who believes, confesses. His life itself becomes a confession, a living, holy, God-pleasing sacrifice in Christ Jesus."[52] 'Otherness' is part of this confession; by confessing we are formed into 'otherness.'

5.1 CHRIST, THE SOURCE OF 'OTHERNESS'

Therefore, it is in the confession of Christ's work in all areas of life that the church may pursue 'otherness' in its response to increasing polarization in society. Kuyper too located the rescue of society in Christ. At the same time as upholding sphere sovereignty, he was deeply moved by the plight of the working classes in the Netherlands. As a statesman, he was committed to establishing just labor policies, as a Christian pastor he was troubled by the souls of the poor, and as a theologian he was concerned with the response of the church in society to inequalities between human beings.[53] These commitments were due to his unshakeable belief in the sovereign rule of Christ, in whom unity and diversity hold

---

49. Christ is Savior first and foremost. Yet, because he is Savior, he is able to restore nature by grace. Herman Bavinck, *The Sacrifice of Praise*, trans. Rev. John Dolfin (Grand Rapids: Louis Kregel, Publisher, 1922), 79–80.

50. Bavinck writes that this does not include the "works of the devil" which have corrupted creation. This is a similar idea to those cultural activities which stem from an orientation away from God's original intention for creation. Bavinck, *The Sacrifice of Praise*, 81.

51. Christ has restored all things; Christians appropriate them biblically and prayerfully. Bavinck, *The Sacrifice of Praise*, 83.

52. Bavinck, *The Sacrifice of Praise*, 58.

53. Kuyper, *The Problem of Poverty*, 67.

together, nature and grace are reconciled, and all things in creation are restored.⁵⁴ This is the Christ of Bavinck's confession, the Christ who stooped down from heaven to step inside our skin and interacted with empathy with 'the other'—his creatures.⁵⁵ In confessing Christ, we confess how he manifested 'otherness,' that he is the source of 'otherness.' In Christ alone lies the power for transformation, for restoration, and for cultural diversity in creational unity, and the answer to polarization. Through this participatory activity of confession, the church may rediscover its purpose, which is, in Pieter Vos's words, "a community gathered around Christ which practices a Christ-like attitude in dealing with conflict and polarization."⁵⁶

6. CONCLUSION

In this paper, I have suggested that forming a sense of 'otherness' in cultural engagement can help the church to respond to polarization in and across diverse communities. Drawing on voices from within cultural anthropology, this 'otherness' is shaped by an awareness of the self's cultural lenses and culturally complex backgrounds, and a resistance to binding 'the other' to preconceived, assumed notions of who they are and who they will be in the future. A recontextualization of Kuyperian sphere sovereignty through Kuyper's other commitments to freedom of conscience and social and economic equality shapes a Christian 'otherness' that is combined with 'commonness.' This approach to those who are culturally 'other'—which includes ourselves and everyone else—respects the unique calling and freedom of 'the other' to be diverse and distinct from us, while at the same time being equal to and sharing common traits with us.⁵⁷ Recontextualization relies on formation into Christian 'otherness' through a confession of Christ that seeks the good of 'the other' through commonness and inclusivity, and guards against separateness and polarization.⁵⁸ Being formed into 'otherness' is Christological, with Christ's incarnation being its fullest expression. The totality of the human experience that encompasses both the unique calling of 'the other' and the unity of all humans, holds together in Christ who is the continuity between creation and re-creation.⁵⁹ Following Bavinck,

---

54. Abraham Kuyper, *Lectures on Calvinism*, 53.
55. Kuyper, *The Problem of Poverty*, 68.
56. Vos, "Introduction," 10.
57. Lawrence, "Introduction," 22.
58. Kuyper describes a united, inclusive church organism in Abraham Kuyper, *The Work of the Holy Spirit*, trans. Henri De Vries (New York: Funk and Wagnalls, 1900), 550–551.
59. Abraham Kuyper, *Common Grace: God's Gift for a Fallen World*, Vol. 1, *The Historical Section*, eds. Jordan J. Ballor and Stephen J. Grabill, trans. Nelson D. Kloosterman and Ed M. van der Maas, in *Abraham Kuyper Collected Works of Public*

a participation in Christ's recreation of natural ordinances and the restoration of nature by grace by virtue of a lived-out confession pursues a distinctly Christian 'otherness.' In this approach, all the aspirations of a National Stephen Lawrence Day are met; Christian 'otherness' facilitates a re-imagining of future communities where the diversity and distinctiveness of 'the other' is upheld, not through separation but through inclusion and visible unity. For the church to exercise Christian 'otherness' against polarization internally and in society, it will take empathy, courage, and deeds which go beyond mere words in order to truly confess Christ's compassion for 'the other' in every area of life:

> Divine compassion, sympathy, a suffering *with* us and *for* us—that was the mystery of Golgotha. You, too, must suffer with your suffering brothers. Only then will the holy music of consolation vibrate in your speech. Then driven by this sympathy of compassion, you will naturally conform your action to your speech. For *deeds* of love are indispensable.[60]

BIBLIOGRAPHY

Aguilar, Mario I. "Changing Models and the 'Death' of Culture: A diachronic and positive critique of socio-scientific assumptions." In *Anthropology and Biblical Studies*: *Avenues of Approach*, eds. Louise J. Lawrence and Mario I. Aguilar, 299–313. Leiden: Deo Publishing, 2004.

Bavinck, Herman. *The Sacrifice of Praise*, trans. Rev. John Dolfin. Grand Rapids: Louis Kregel, Publisher, 1922.

Bielo, James S. "An Anthropologist is Listening: A Reply to Ethnographic Theology." In *Theologically Engaged Anthropology*, ed. J. Derrick Lemons, 140–155. Oxford: Oxford University Press, 2018.

Boesak, Allan. *Black and Reformed*: *Apartheid, Liberation, and the Calvinist Tradition*. New York: Orbis, 1984.

Botman, H. Russel "Is Blood Thicker Than Justice? The Legacy of Abraham Kuyper in Southern Africa." In *Religion, Pluralism, and Public Life*: *Abraham Kuyper's Legacy for the Twenty-First Century*, ed. Luis E. Lugo, 342–361. Grand Rapids: Wm. B. Eerdmans Publishing Company, 2000.

Bratt, James D. *Abraham Kuyper*: *Modern Calvinist, Christian Democrat*. Grand Rapids: Wm. B. Eerdmans, 2013.

Theology, Series 2, eds. Jordan J. Ballor and Melvin Flikkema (Iowa: Acton Institute; Lexham Press, 2016), 172–173.

60. Kuyper, *The Problem of Poverty*, 69.

Clifford, James. "Introduction: Partial Truths." In *Writing Culture: The Poetics and Politics of Ethnography*, eds. James Clifford and George E. Marcus, 1–26. California: California University Press, 1986.

Davies, Douglas J. *Anthropology and Theology*. Oxford: Berg, 2002.

"Independent Report: The Stephen Lawrence Inquiry," Home Office, Gov.UK. Accessed December 4, 2019. https://www.gov.uk/government/publications/the-stephen-lawrence-inquiry#7.46.

Kaemingk, Matthew. *Christian Hospitality and Muslim Immigration in an Age of Fear*. Grand Rapids: William B. Eerdmans, 2018.

Kang, Min. "Abraham Kuyper in Korea: hartstochtelijk hervormer, een begrip onder presbyteriaanse predikanten," *TussenRuimte* 10:3 (2017): 26–31.

Kuyper, Abraham. *A Centennial Reader*, ed. James D. Bratt. Grand Rapids: Wm. B. Eerdmans Publishing Co., 1998.

Kuyper, Abraham. *Collected Works of Public Theology*, Series 1 and 2, eds. Jordan J. Ballor and Melvin Flikkema. Bellingham, Washington: Lexham Press.

Kuyper, Abraham. *Lectures on Calvinism*. n.p.: CreateSpace, 2012.

Kuyper, Abraham. *The Problem of Poverty*, ed. James Skillen. Iowa: Dordt College Press, 2011.

Kuyper, Abraham. *The Work of the Holy Spirit*, trans. Henri De Vries. New York: Funk and Wagnalls, 1900.

Lawrence, Doreen. "On the first Stephen Lawrence day, let's admit our communities are still unequal." *The Guardian*, UK. Accessed December 4, 2019. https://www.theguardian.com/commentisfree/2019/apr/22/stephen-lawrence-day-british-society-doreen-lawrence.

Lawrence, Louise J. "Introduction: A Taste for 'the Other.' Interpreting Biblical Texts Anthropologically." In *Anthropology and Biblical Studies: Avenues of Approach*, eds. Louise J. Lawrence and Mario I. Aguilar, 9–25. Leiden: Deo Publishing, 2004.

Lemons, J. Derrick. Ed. *Theologically Engaged Anthropology*. Oxford: Oxford University Press, 2018.

Lemons, J. Derrick. "Introduction: Theologically Engaged Anthropology." In *Theologically Engaged Anthropology*, ed. J. Derrick Lemons, 1–7. Oxford: Oxford University Press, 2018.

Mouw, Richard J. *Abraham Kuyper: A Short and Personal Introduction*. Grand Rapids, Michigan: Wm. B. Eerdmans, 2011.

Mouw, Richard J. *Adventures in Evangelical Civility: A Lifelong Quest for Common Ground*. Grand Rapids: Brazos Press, 2016.

Robbins, Joel. "Anthropology and Theology: An Awkward Relationship?" *Anthropology Quarterly* 79:2 (2006): 285–294.

Robbins, Joel and Sarah Coakley, "Anthropological and Theological Responses to Theologically Engaged Anthropology." In *Theologically Engaged Anthropology*, ed. J. Derrick Lemons, 355–76. Oxford: Oxford University Press, 2018.

Rollason, Will. "Introduction: Pacific Futures, Methodological Challenges," in *Pacific Futures: Projects, Politics and Interests*, ed. Will Rollason, 1–27. Berghahn Books, 2014.

Rynkiewich, Michael A. "Athens Engaging Jerusalem." In *Theologically Engaged Anthropology*, ed. J. Derrick Lemons, 211–225. Oxford: Oxford University Press, 2018.

Schilder, Klaas. *Christ and Culture*, trans. G. van Rongen and W. Helder. Winnipeg: Premier Printing, 1977.

Skillen, James W. "Why Kuyper Now? in *Religion, Pluralism, and Public Life: Abraham Kuyper's Legacy for the Twenty-First Century*, ed. Luis E. Lugo, 365–372. Grand Rapids: Wm. B. Eerdmans Publishing Company, 2000.

EPILOGUE
Heleen Zorgdrager

Sustained discernment has always been a guiding principle of Reformed theology.[1] Every generation needs to revisit the confessions and declarations of the Reformed tradition and to live them out in response to the challenges of the present. To discern how the church shall bear witness to Christ today, contextual self-explanation and critical self-reflection, as a recalibration of one's basic view and attitude in light of scripture and tradition, are paramount. It is accompanied by the belief, deeply engrained in Reformed identity, that the social, political, and cultural context of every church is acknowledged as an important factor in the way discernment takes place.[2]

In this volume, the authors have undertaken the task of discernment in a faithfully committed and academically inspiring way, giving voice to the questions of their times, their local and regional contexts, and to the faith experiences of people of different continents. The focus on contemporary issues within a theological/ecclesial tradition and in specific geographical contexts is what makes this collection of essays both unique and valuable. There is a shared endeavor to articulate Christian faith and the calling of the church as relevant to conflicts and processes of societal polarization in which the churches and its members are actually involved.[3] The variety of engagements from different

---

1. See *Proceedings of the 26th General Council of the World Communion of Reformed Churches*, Leipzig, Germany, 29 June–7 July, 2017, "Appendix 9a, Concept Paper: Theology. Taking Up the 'Unfinished Agenda' of the Reformation" (Hannover: World Communion of Reformed Churches, 2017), 240.

2. Pieter Vos, "Introduction," 10.

3. We should note here that the essays were written before the COVID-19 pandemic broke out, which increased existing inequalities, and fueled polarizations in local and global contexts. The pandemic stressed the urgency for theology to engage with realities of polarization and to rethink and actualize the church's calling for peace, reconciliation and the integrity of creation in the midst of crisis. Common theological reflection by Reformed scholars was undertaken in the World Communion of Reformed Churches' process "Discerning, Confessing, and Witnessing in the Time of COVID-19 and Beyond," https://wcrc.ch/require (accessed November 13, 2021).

disciplines (political theology, sociology of religion, historical theology, missiology, queer and postcolonial studies, etc.) makes for a rich and varied engagement with a complex subject matter. Authors do not shy away from addressing the inconvenient but unavoidable self-critical question: How do churches and theologies themselves play an active role in processes of polarization? It has turned out, already in the IRTI conference in Amsterdam, 2019, that at the heart of all deliberations the fundamental question arises: how is the 'other' seen and related to in our basic views and life attitudes, and which concepts, notions, or approaches can help to (re)discover the horizon of a new 'we,' a new understanding of common humanity, and the common good?

1. THEOLOGY OF RETRIEVAL AND OF LIBERATION

The chapters contain a wealth of constructive proposals and new imaginations in the ongoing work of Reformed theology. We try to gather the harvest and identify some trends.

About half of the chapters examine a particular contemporary polarizing situation. The other half draw out lines and trajectories from classic Reformed doctrines such as baptism, Christology, sanctification, divine election, covenant, church polity, and vocation. The authors use the resources of Reformed theology to further understand the progressive dynamics of polarization and to interpret it in theological and ethical categories. They acknowledge that the Reformed tradition has often contributed to polarization and its resulting violence and suffering. Interestingly, in many chapters it is felt that more is needed than the classical concepts to theologically counter dynamics of polarization. Concepts and inspirations are also derived from the broader ecumenical tradition, from contemporary philosophy, from Jewish sources, and/or from diverse cultural and religious traditions that continue to serve as sources of wisdom in African or Asian contexts. Authors of this volume show a shared awareness that the 'classical' contents and approaches need continuously to be reconfigured, recontextualized, and creatively actualized in order to speak meaningfully and prophetically to the context.

The volume clearly demonstrates the fact that there is 'unfinished business' of the Reformation.[4] Theologians can engage with this in different ways. On the one hand, there are themes and insights of the Reformation that we have not fully 'made good on' and that deserve renewed attention and study. This is being done in a 'theology of

---

4. *Proceedings of the 26th General Council*, 239.

retrieval.'⁵ J. Todd Bilings has defined the approach of retrieval as "hearing the voices of the past in such a way that they are allowed to exceed and overcome the chatter of the present."⁶ On the other hand, Reformed theology is driven by the urgent need to "read the signs of the times," to focus on the lived experiences of oppressed people and to have theological reflection explicitly governed by the norm of human flourishing, or, as it is increasingly recognized, of planetary flourishing. This 'liberationist approach to theology'⁷ usually includes interdisciplinary conversation with social sciences and humanities, and applying the lens of postcolonial and/or feminist hermeneutics to renew and transform a theological tradition that is still shaped by Western and androcentric paradigms.

2. CLASSICAL REFORMED NOTIONS REREAD AND RETRIEVED

With regard to the first approach, the pathway of retrieving and unpacking the notions of Reformation theology for our times, we can ask: Which notions do the authors attend to and which constructive proposals do they bring to the fore in addressing the issue of polarization?

Well-known and powerful Reformed notions of *covenant*, *justice*, and *vocation* are in the background of David Fergusson's contribution. He proposes transposing impulses of classical Reformed social theology for today, at a time of rising populism. Looking at long-established, 'national' churches in the West-European context, he actualizes notions such as *politics as a vocation*, the *stand for democracy*, and an awareness of the dangers of *nationalism*. They are retrieved in a critical way. The author accounts carefully for the learning process the churches have gone through in their histories. From a different perspective, that of World Christianity, David Daniels also accounts for the learning process of the churches. With Moten's concept of *xenogenerosity*, developed in black studies, Daniels illuminates how in the Dort debates there were already currents who voiced an understanding of the link between baptism and manumission (being released from slavery), as well as an understanding of the commonness of humanity. In today's world, awakened by the Black Lives Matter protests, this sheds light on early Reformation impulses to connect to if the churches want to help overcome the painful divisions and polarizations caused by systemic racism, also in their own midst.

---

5. Martha L. Moore-Keish, *Reformed Theology* (Leiden/Boston: Brill, 2020), 13.

6. J. Todd Billings, *Union with Christ: Reframing Theology and Ministry for the Church* (Grand Rapids: Baker Academics, 2011), 2.

7. Moore-Keish, *Reformed Theology*, 12.

Allan Janssen, whom we honor and commemorate in this volume posthumously, deeply grateful for his committed fellowship in IRTI, shares his thorough knowledge of the Reformed theological tradition by revisiting the doctrine of *election* of the Canons of Dort. His guide is A.A. van Ruler, whose theology was characterized by a deep appreciation of creaturely goodness and an eschatology that connects the future world with our earthly existence. In this light, Janssen reinterprets and revitalizes the doctrine of election. Instead of a doctrine that would feed into a passive attitude, it can be considered as the basis for a well-founded hope. *Hope* is also the key notion in the chapter of Jan Jorrit Hasselaar, Philipp Pattberg and Peter-Ben Smit. They recur to Rabbi Jonathan Sack's concept of hope which allows one to consider conflicting positions as a source of creativity and renewal. The authors apply it to practices of dialogue with various stakeholders and opponents in polarized conflicts between the agricultural sector and sustainability advocates in the Netherlands.

Another topical reinterpretation of Reformed doctrine is found in Emanuel Gerrit Singgih's chapter. Reflecting on the context of the Council of Churches in Indonesia, he proposes mission as presensia instead of a traditional concept of mission, understood as a centrifugal, churchplanting movement. He links this ecclesiology of presence to the call for a renewed understanding of the notion of *sola scriptura*, namely *sola scriptura with pluses*. He asserts that something must be added to the classical notion, in particular *sola caritate*, so that the Bible will no longer be used as a tool for condemning vulnerable groups in the margins, such as LGBT people.

3. UNITY AND HOLINESS

Several authors problematize the divine calling of the church to holiness and truth, in relation to the question of how to build or maintain *unity* in the church and in society. In Reformed history, this dilemma has left its painful mark. Against this backdrop, Klaas-Willem de Jong and Jan Dirk Th. Wassenaar question the 'majority of vote' principle in the Church Order of Dort, article 31. Expressing unity in the church by majority vote can easily lead and has led in the history of Reformed churches to polarization and disunity. Recalibration of ecclesial decisions in light of scripture and tradition remains the task. Henk van den Belt lays out the Reformed understanding of *vocatio interna* for a view on the calling of the church with regard to polarization. According to Van den Belt, it follows from the calling of the church to *holiness* that there are genuine and necessary forms of conflict; however, the acknowledgement of the essential unity of Christians implies that such conflict shall not lead to rejection of the other as a fellow saved sinner. From the context of Protestant churches in the Middle East, Najib George Awad opposes this view. In an intriguing reading of John 17, he diagnoses how churches in Greater Syria, due to a 'self-otherizing' theology, emphasize their being called out of the world instead of their being called to exist in the world. Holiness is falsely understood as 'self-alterity.' It makes them, in the view of Awad, responsible of perpetrating certain polarizations in their societies. He seems to plead, as Singgih, for *mission as presence* in the multireligious context. Also Jozef Hehanussa goes for mission as an actively lived presence and coexistence in society. He stresses that in the multi-religious context of Indonesia, Christians are primarily called to promote and encourage all people to live peacefully and appreciate differences. The churches' mission through schools and hospitals should not contribute to polarization but to harmonious coexistence with people of other faiths, for which he believes the pre-Christian tradition of *religious tolerance* in Yogyakarta can serve as a common resource.

In this way, contemporary Reformed theology has to face the fact of divergent positions when it comes to understanding the relation between the church being called to holiness and the church being called to unity. These positions are not easy to reconcile. The beginning of a constructive dialogue could be found in Elizabeth Welch's presentation of an ecclesiology of *koinonia*, to which the International Reformed and Anglican Communions (IRAD) arrived in their ecumenical dialogues on the nature of communion. *Koinonia* is seen as God's gift and calling. It draws people to the gift of fullness of God's inclusive love, makes people humble, and calls people to live in relationship with one another. This notion seems to be highly suitable as the key to the calling of the church on its way to address polarizations both in the church and in the world. *Koinonia* emphasizes that the unity of the church is always intrinsically related with the unity and peace of the world.

Another promising notion is that of *conviviality*, as the art and practice of living together, which Nadine Bowers Du Toit presents in her chapter on a crossing-boundaries initiative in her home city of Cape Town. The term conviviality, coined in the work of Ivan Illich, was introduced in diaconal ecumenical theology by Tony Addy. The simple sharing of food and drink is at the heart of such practices of living together. For learning to encounter the other in an attitude of hospitality and conviviality, Louise Prideaux, in her innovative reading of neo-Calvinist theology, highlights a Christ-centered approach to deal fruitfully with tensions of *otherness* and *commonness*.

4. OTHER CONSTRUCTIVE PROPOSALS

The proposals of Bowers Du Toit, Singgih, Hehanussa, Awad, and Welch already show a creative adoption and actualization of concepts and inspirations drawn from the broader ecumenical tradition, from contemporary philosophy, from Jewish sources, and from pre-Christian traditions. Other authors join in, addressing the issues of social justice, racism, sexuality and gender, euthanasia, and migration in their contexts.

Jaeseung Cha finds in Daoism a new approach to understand the suffering of Christ as a powerful, sacrificial suffering, without falling into the trap of a glorification of suffering. The Daoist concept of (feminine) *passivity* as an active power of productive and embracing love is explored as a concept that might help to get the conversation started in the polarized debate between traditional atonement theology and feminist critique.

From a postcolonial, Zambian perspective and in sharp criticism of a US fundamentalist separation of Gospel and social justice, Thandi Soko-de Jong presents the *palaver hut model* to include the voices of all members in the Reformed conversation on scripture and social justice. The palaver hut model suggests a postcolonial translation of recognizing the priesthood of all believers. Soko-de Jong also pleads for an ethos of *tcheni pa kalanka*, which is interpreted as applying transformative and liberating hermeneutics in reading and hearing the Word of God in the social context.

For Annemarieke van der Woude, the biblical notion of *holiness* as a relational concept can serve as a meaningful bridging concept between polarized positions in the euthanasia debate in the Netherlands. She describes how a suffering person's request to end their life takes us into a realm over which society does not have control and which grasps believers and non-believers alike with a sensitivity or more precisely timidity. Holiness, Van der Woude concludes, is always attributed in the relationship; not life as such is holy. Every person who longs for the end of life deserves our cautious commitment.

On issues of sexuality and gender, the polarization within and between churches is extremely intense and emotional. For Wim van Vlastuin, apostle Paul's notion of receiving our deepest *identity in union with Christ* is an insight that may help to relativize our sexual identity. Regardless of whether one is heteroor homosexual, the calling is to fight against selfish lust in order to attain holiness in the life with Christ. Heleen Zorgdrager points to risks in recurring to the notion of 'identity in Christ' regarding matters of sexual and gender diversity. In current conservative Reformed discourse, the notion appears to be strongly connected with the view that Christ has sanctioned (heterosexual) marriage as an order of creation, thus undergirding its normativity. Alternatively, she proposes to leave identity discourses and adopt Mark Jordan's queer notion of *sacramental character* and the concept of the *broken middle* of the late Jewish philosopher Gillian Rose.

Viktória Kóczián brings the *unity and catholicity* of the Church to the test of how churches in Hungary and how the World Council of Churches respond to the migration crisis in Europe. The dividing line cuts right through Christianity. Where the Hungarian churches argue from incompatible sociocultural identities and fear of strangers, the WCC stresses a sense of common humanity, responsibility, and solidarity. Kóczián believes that global ecumenical dialogue should continue embracing a Trinitarian economy of grace and hospitality, while addressing more seriously the issues of fear of strangers and sociocultural identity.

5. Conclusion

In sum, this volume shows the strength of both approaches, a 'theology of retrieval' and a 'theology done in a liberationist key,' as well as how much they need one another in the contemporary task of Reformed theology. The new ideas, concepts, terms, imaginations, and visions do not so much replace the familiar Reformed notions, as need to be understood as an attempt to translate the ancient ones in an appealing way for today. They thereby correct the one-sidedness of traditional interpretations, and/or deconstruct the implicit privileged position, and welcome into the conversation the voices of groups from the margins and the wealth of other cultural resources. In this respect it is remarkable that there is little to no reference in the chapters to the pronounced anti-idolatry and Empire criticism of twentieth and twenty-first century confessions of Reformed origins, like the Barmen Declaration, the Belhar Confession and the Accra Confession, which play such an important role in the ecumenical Reformed discourse.[8]

If one takes this volume as a round table conversation of a family called together, the discussion shows a strong mutual commitment, yet also reveals certain strained relations and divergent visions within the Reformed theological communion and within and between churches in the Reformed tradition. There are serious discussions going on. The contributions to this book are part of these ongoing discussions, which are only rudimentary, and therefore flawed, characterized by opposing terms such as 'liberal' versus 'conservative,' or 'mainstream' versus

---

8. See for an overview and interpretation Margit Ernst-Habib, *Reformierte Identität weltweit—Eine Interpretation neuerer Bekenntnistexte aus der reformierten Tradition* (Göttingen: VandenHoeck & Ruprecht, 2017).

'liberationist.' One should be aware that such binaries stigmatize and polarize rather than build bridges in the discussion.

Whether theologians in the Reformed tradition retrieve a classical notion for testing its strength in situations of societal and ecclesial polarization, or whether they creatively look for gifts from other traditions and movements, they are joining in in the common task of witnessing Christ to the world today. As part of such an endeavor, this volume strikes the chord of refreshing and broadening the landscape of global Reformed theology in response to the wounds of the world and in the joyful perspective of Christ's gift of fullness of life for all.

BIBLIOGRAPHY

Billings, J. Todd. *Union with Christ: Reframing Theology and Ministry for the Church*. Grand Rapids: Baker Academics, 2011.

Ernst-Habib, Margit. *Reformierte Identität weltweit—Eine Interpretation neuerer Bekenntnistexte aus der reformierten Tradition*. Göttingen: VandenHoeck & Ruprecht, 2017.

Moore-Keish, Martha L. *Reformed Theology*. Leiden/Boston: Brill, 2020.

World Communion of Reformed Churches. "Discerning, Confessing, and Witnessing in the Time of COVID-19 and Beyond." accessed November 13, 2021. https://wcrc.ch/require.

World Communion of Reformed Churches. *Proceedings of the 26th General Council of the World Communion of Reformed Churches*, Leipzig, Germany, 29 June–7 July, 2017. Hannover: World Communion of Reformed Churches, 2017.

www.ingramcontent.com/pod-product-compliance
Lightning Source LLC
Chambersburg PA
CBHW072144070526
44585CB00015B/998